SOCIAL WORK FIELD EDUCATION: VIEWS AND VISIONS

Edited by
GAYLA ROGERS

Publication has been made possible, in part, by a grant from funds provided by THE ROYAL BANK OF CANADA and assistance from The University of Calgary Endowment Fund.

KENDALL/HUNT PUBLISHING COMPANY
4050 Westmark Drive Dubuque, Iowa 52002

TABLE OF CONTENTS

VIEWS AND VISIONS: A WAY FORWARD

Gayla Rogers

This edited collection of refereed papers is drawn from the juried selections presented at the Conference on Field Education in Social Work held in Calgary, Canada, June 17 and 18, 1994. The book provides a unique contribution to professional education in social work by disseminating up-to-date research and leading edge teaching developments to advance the quality of field education.

The authors include practitioners, academics, administrators and students. They represent perspectives from Canada, the United States, Britain, Australia, Mexico, Brazil and cognate disciplines. Included are the voices of students, field instructors, faculty liaisons, field directors, and other faculty and staff involved in field education.

CONTENTS

This book honors the critical importance of field education. It is divided thematically into seven Parts and, with the exception of the first and last Parts, each one contains a number of chapters. The book opens with Part I featuring a single chapter by Dean Schneck who was the keynote speaker at the Conference on Field Education. He shares his vision of the promise of field education providing a thoughtful and provocative view which sets the spirit and tone for the entire book. The second Part, *Field Education Models,* contains nine chapters describing a range of organizational and developmental models focused on various aspects of school-agency collaboration. The third Part, *Field Education Methods*, presents an impressive twelve chapters filled with ideas, strategies, tools, and techniques to enhance teaching and learning; and, to build and deliver a comprehensive practice curriculum. *Field Education Perspectives*, the fourth Part, includes eight chapters reflecting interesting positions on a variety of issues from the vantage points of students, field instructors, field coordinators, and field educators including views from the United Kingdom and Australia. The seven chapters in the fifth Part, *Field Education and Diversity* each explicitly addresses current concerns regarding preparation of students for ethnically sensitive, anti-discriminatory and culturally competent practice including what we can learn from Mexico and Brazil. The sixth Part, *Views from Other Disciplines*, is an unique contribution to this book providing insights into field education from clinical psychology, education, family medicine and nursing. The views from these cognate disciplines reveal that there is much we can learn from each other. The book ends with a single chapter by Gayla Rogers in Part Seven, *In Pursuit of Quality*. In concluding the book it presents a view and vision of field education to guide us into the 21st century.

BACKGROUND

When I first became acquainted with field educators as a recognizable group, it was 1987 and I was in my first year as Director of Field Education, Faculty of Social Work, The University of Calgary. I attended the inaugural Field Work Symposium at the Council on Social Work Education (CSWE) meeting in St. Louis. I spent two days listening to people who actually talked a language I understood, who articulated dilemmas I had faced but had never discussed with anyone, who cared about and were interested in field education as a substantive area worthy of scholarly attention and debate. I came away stimulated and excited. I knew intuitively that field education was a whole lot more than matching students and making "nice" with agencies but I now found a collection of people who knew it conceptually and empirically as well as practically. I return to that symposium annually, to learn, to share and to connect.

   In Canada, field educators have been gathering during the annual Canadian Association of Schools of Social Work (CASSW) meeting for the last number of years. During these meetings we often spoke about the need for more time on the agenda and more papers on field education. The idea of a conference on field education seemed like wishful thinking. Thanks to the vision of The University of Calgary's organizing committee for the Learned Societies who raised the possibility of hosting "in conjunction" conferences; to the priority given to field education by the Dean of my

Faculty of Social Work, Ray Thomlison; and, to the generosity of The University of Calgary Special Projects Fund, Conference Grants, and the Royal Bank of Canada Teaching Development Fund, I was able to turn the wishful thinking into reality and organize the conference on Field Education in Social Work in conjunction with the Learned Societies. The funds from the Royal Bank of Canada Teaching Development Grant and the Special Projects Fund were earmarked for the publication of this book so that the legacy of the Conference would be the dissemination of the substantive array of information, materials and practices presented and discussed.

ACKNOWLEDGEMENTS

Endeavors such as this do not happen by themselves. There are many people I want to acknowledge who have helped make this book possible. First, I would like to thank Dean Schneck, Urania Glassman and Bart Grossman for inspiring me through their leadership and scholarly work at the CSWE Field Work Symposium and the publication of their book, *Field Education in Social Work: Contemporary Trends and Issues*. I would like to recognize the Canadian contributions to field education and the initiating efforts to gather field educators together made by Marion Bogo, Elaine Vayda, Ellen Sue Mesbur, Barbara Thomlison and Don Collins, and to acknowledge the ongoing involvement of the Field Education Committee of the CASSW.

Credit must be given to the reviewers who diligently juried the submitted abstracts: Helen Szewello Allen from McGill University; Gail Kenyon from Ryerson Polytechnic University; Joan Leeson from Wilfred Laurier University; Bill Marcotte, formerly from the University of Windsor; Helena Summers from the University of British Columbia; and Whalene Whitaker from the University of Victoria. The editorial committee, who wish to remain anonymous, must be acknowledged for reviewing the completed papers for final acceptance into the book.

Finally, I would like to recognize the effort and technical expertise of Doreen Neville and Josephine Hui who worked tirelessly on the book; and, to acknowledge Ken Zielske and Kendall/Hunt Publishers for believing in the book.

VIEWS AND VISIONS: IN PURSUIT OF QUALITY

To achieve greater quality in field education, field educators must have a sound understanding of the complexities of field instruction and professional education, the intricacies involved in developing curriculum and teaching a diverse adult student population, the current realities facing the workplace/field placement, and the future directions of social work as a profession. The views and visions presented herein represent creative, thoughtful and analytic responses to the challenges of delivering quality field education now and in the future.

PART ONE

IN PURSUIT OF QUALITY: A PROMISING VIEW AND VISION

CHAPTER ONE

THE PROMISE OF FIELD EDUCATION IN SOCIAL WORK

Dean Schneck

In bringing together the views and visions of field educators from Britain, Canada, and the USA, this book represents a significant contribution and underscores the value of events that gather field educators. As we take note of our national and regional differences, it is clear that we are not the same; however, we do share many common interests and priorities, the preeminent being the education and inspiration of the next generation of professional social workers. It is well-recognized by all, certainly not the least our students, that field education is a vital and cherished part of the curriculum. No other component commands such attention, energy and resources both in the practice community as well as in the schools.

This common goal makes events such as this invaluable for the discussion and comparison of our models and methods, the definition of educational and practice issues, and in general, the advancement of our mission. *The Promise of Field Education in Social Work* connotes the commitment we all share to move beyond the pious commitments and the recognition of potential, to the business at hand, more pressing than ever, to skilfully prepare competent practitioners and to advance the quality of practice itself. This promise implies a dutiful compact, commitment of resources, and substantial intellectual effort.

This chapter addresses both the instructional mission with our students and the scholarly mission to advance the quality not only of field education *per se*, but of social work practice itself. Efforts to develop the field education component of social work education have waxed and waned over time. Currently we are in a period of ascendancy and organizational strength as witnessed by a Conference in Field Education in Calgary, the Council on Social Work Education Annual Field Symposia and the formation of the North American Network of Educators and Directors founded several years ago by Canadian and American field directors. This organization grew out of the successful field education symposia of CSWE which have occurred annually since 1987. Through this organization, we have "shown the flag" for scholarly and educational development as well as for adequate funding of field programs. Last year, CSWE formed the first standing Commission on Field Education, recognizing the importance of field instruction in meeting the overall curriculum commitment to our students. Indeed, the learning opportunities in field education for the development of practice skills and identity, critical thinking, and the overall integration of learning serve in many ways as the primary vehicle for the professional development of students. Moreover, if well done, field education stands as a constant bulwark against the age-old process/content dichotomy still evident in academia.

In field education, we are uniquely positioned to observe, speculate, and collaborate with our practice colleagues and to shape workable responses to real problems of real people in real time. In a way, our success in field education will presage what's ahead for the rest of society as we strive to promote a cooperative or "communitarian" ethic for our large urban areas and smaller communities and rural areas as well. Whether we see racial conflict or harmony, ethnic strife or co-existence, separatism or pluralism will depend in part upon how well we, in a civil and humane process, define the common good and fashion creative and differential responses to the common needs of all our citizens. We alone, of course, will not determine all of this, but we are important players in the enormous effort ahead to tip the balance away from violence and toward a shared vision of community and collective action to meet human need. Field education, then, holds promise for:

- Our students through their education and entry to the profession.
- The profession through the renewal of its ranks and the contribution of new knowledge and methods.
- The clientele of social work through service, leadership, and advocacy.
- Our communities through the distinct service contributions of students as they are learning.

In examining our instructional mission, I will begin with the area of skills development because this is where most of our students wish to begin. After years in the classroom, course after course of general and theoretical knowledge, they hunger for the opportunity to do something actively and interactively. The appeal of the field practicum for "real world," and "in vivo" learning experiences is best understood by its inherent authenticity and by its actualization of the students' desire to "try themselves out" in a professional role, help someone, and accomplish something. Because the desire to "prove up" or "make the grade" is so powerfully compelling and seductive, it is always a challenge to our teaching to seize the moment with our students to teach the important principles and concepts of practice without detracting from their momentum and enthusiasm.

Teaching practice skills, as we all know, requires substantial amounts of time, resources, and patience. Yet, it is especially important in field education for students not only to know the "what and why," but also the "how to" of practice interventions. The involvement with students as they perform their field duties through supervisory conferences, direct observation, demonstration interviews, case sharing, audio/video tapes, whether by the field instructor or faculty member, has the greatest potential for the transfer of practice judgment and wisdom and for the growth of the student.

Connecting the theoretical with the actual in practice education seems to be best done by an inductive-deductive cycle of inquiry beginning with the immediate practice situation of the student in which they are challenged by the responsibility and the desire to do something meaningful. This presents the opportunity for a guided cognitive process which searches inductively for relevant knowledge, concepts, and the practice wisdom of others. All of this can be fashioned into a construct or application deductively for the specific problem. I have commented earlier:

> If one can envision the student in the field practice situation, the predominant orientation is social work process and problem-solving with an emphasis on action and intervention, as it should be. Methodological questions of where and when to intervene, who or what to target are the presenting dilemmas with all their attendant complexities and anxieties. But process is empty, uninformed, if not reflective of knowledge and value underpinnings--thus, the need in education and practice to move back and forth from conceptual to interactional. (Schneck, 1985)

A teaching environment and an instructional paradigm in which the field teacher (faculty or field instructor) demonstrates and models a facility for moving between the specific and the general has the greatest potential for field instruction. The rhetorical question is:

. . . How does one accomplish mutuality and integration rather than duality and separatism? The answer seems to lie in the ability of students, agency instructors and faculty to build the conceptual and experiential bridges between the students' field experience and learning needs, and the knowledge and skill resources wherever they lie. This can be accomplished through active, spontaneous, and non-possessive teaching/learning skills and activities. (Schneck, 1991a, p. 112)

In "A Teaching-Learning Model for the Integration of Learning in the Field" I have defined a model " . . . which places emphasis upon understanding the nature of the learning sources and knowledge needs within students' experience and the skilful use of teaching-learning methods and processes to facilitate synthesis. This perspective relies upon spontaneity and teaching skill; pre-determined structure provides only a place to begin, not a way to learn" (Schneck, 1991b, p. 71). The work of Marian Bogo and Elaine Vayda (1987), in the development of the integration of theory and practice loop (ITP), strikes a similar chord. Their case examples are among the best I have seen in demonstrating the learning cycle. In adapting the work of Kolb to social work, their ITP loop:

. . . begins with the retrieval of the factual elements of a practice situation. The next step, reflection, focuses on the effectiveness of the retrieved interaction or intervention as well as the identification of personal values, attitudes, and assumptions which modify the retrieved facts. These processes are then linked to professional knowledge that can explain or account for the findings of the preceding steps. This leads directly to the selection of a professional response to the initiating action that began the loop. (Bogo & Vayda, 1987)

This brings us ultimately to the ethical and values development of our students. In field education, we have a compelling obligation to inculcate a strong sense of professional values and ethical practice — some would call it professionalism. Perhaps we can teach, or at least reinforce, important values such as regard for human dignity or self-determination and we should be able to teach ethical principles and rules of conduct for the practice of social work.

Character is another matter. By character, I mean that personal integration of values, attributes and virtues which emanate from the individual, but are formed in a familial and social context. Such character traits as honesty, courage, integrity, and generosity are the soul of our profession, both in the exercise of daily practice and in the ability to persevere throughout one's career. I would argue that the essence and impact of character is so universal that it is equivalent to knowledge and skill in professional practice.

Negatively, deficits in character can be seen occasionally in egregious breaches of trust and conduct (essentially mal-feasance or non-feasance of professional duties) of a few practising social workers or students, or the opportunistic and unethical intellectual practices of a few faculty. Much more common are the daily slights, omissions, and mediocrity which typify some of our colleagues both on campus and in the community. Collectively, these breach our obligations to society and of course, they embarrass us all. Positively, character is the force which drives the search for better answers, more effective and humane methods, and greater competency. For many, character is underpinned by specific religious convictions; while for others, it is based upon a strong set of personal, professional and intellectual values. Either way, it vitalizes all of the unheralded and unrewarded actions of the day-to-day practice lives of social workers.

In this arena, as in many others, actions speak far louder than words. The example we present to our students, the way we treat them, and enact our professional responsibilities, far surpass anything we can say. It is an awesome responsibility, not only to teach how to care for others, but also to exemplify interest and concern for the care-givers. This notion would be anathema to some educators and academics, for whom the professed word or the espoused action is the totality of their statement. As field educators, whether in the integrative seminar, in the social agency, or in the field office, we are expected to do more, to be more. Fulfilling the promise of field education requires nothing less.

In turning our attention to the promise of field education in advancing scholarship for practice, we take note that research and scholarship in field education which has been minimal until recently is beginning to be very evident in the professional journals and conferences. Symposia events, field education conferences, both on a local and national/international level are developing in many venues. Much of this work focuses on the educational and administrative methods and technology necessary for the thoughtful delivery of field education in modern times. Therefore, many field educators have examined issues such as the placement process looking at matters of learning styles, matching variables, student and staff satisfaction surveys, and the use of computer technology to aid all of the above. Others have been concerned with sensitive information which students bring to the field experience from their personal or professional backgrounds. Issues of balance among student confidentiality, fair play, and an obligation to our field agencies and clientele are most evident in this debate. Some have concerned themselves with issues pertaining to field instructors, i.e., the impaired supervisor, abrogation of supervisory commitments, or mistreatment of students including sexual harassment or failure to deliver adequate learning experiences. Still others have done good work in conceptualizing formats for dealing with performance or learning problems of students in the field. Many have written papers concerning access and needs of handicapped students, the older returning or non-traditional students, and those who are only able to attend part time or off-campus programs. Most recently, concerns over the safety and security of field students in the community have preoccupied the concern of many field educators. This occupational hazard is yet another operational or delivery issue requiring our attention and concern.

The discussion and contribution around these issues have yielded a heartfelt sense of camaraderie in the common struggle we all face, and have had practical benefits through the sharing of methods and processes among field educators. It has largely been these kinds of issues and needs which have rallied us and supported our affiliation and organizational development. It is my principled belief, however, that the attention to these issues, alone, will not realize the full promise of field education for social work practice. In a larger sense, our organizational structures, our educational methods and operational procedures, networking and advocacy efforts for field educators derive and have validity only in support of our primary mission — to prepare social work students for the daunting practice challenges of the next century. They represent an absolutely necessary, but not a sufficient condition for progress. In my opinion, field education must also be viewed in the larger context of advancing the quality of social work practice, itself. The skilful development of educational and administrative methods and technology can provide the infrastructure and the affiliations for field educators to develop practice as well as practitioners.

We have often alluded to the special socio-political position of the field enterprise in our home communities. We have referred to it as the nexus of influence, or the intermediary role with one foot in academia and the other in the "real world," where skills of mediation, creative application, and boundary spanning are critical. These are exactly the kinds of skills necessary for practice innovation. I believe an objective analysis of social work's current efficacy would have to state that in many areas, we are falling behind the curve, both in the development and application of effective practice methods. As we make the rounds, we hear from our colleagues in practice that our clients' problems are more severe, more complex, and more intractable. We hear that agencies are saddled with a "more-with-less" philosophy, which has inexorably eroded the quality of service as well as the morale of the social work staff. To be sure, we cannot lay this dilemma entirely at the feet of social work and social work education; but we must accept responsibility at least for rethinking what we are doing to advance practice.

I suggest that our practice development efforts in social work are generally insufficient, far too slow, and sometimes fraught with ideological or political constraints which may trap us in time-worn practices or politically correct platitudes. Sometimes it seems that, instead of reinventing practice, we are renaming the *status quo*. A contradiction seems evident in the observation that:

> . . . While social work knowledge and research is becoming more specific in
> focus, by and large, most practice situations confronted by social workers with

all of their situational dynamics and variables are not informed by a definitive body of knowledge. To be sure, there is a lot of practice wisdom and experience in the "real world", but for the most part, these also have not been defined or validated. It should be recognized, in balance, that this state of affairs does not distress many experienced practitioners who understand the limits of science and empiricism in guiding practice. (Schneck, Grossman, & Glassman, 1991, p. 15)

Whereas it is a cherished academic presumption that theory leads practice, might not the reality be quite different? We know that many social workers' practice is guided more by common sense, personal experience and opinion and agency practices than by a conscious integration of recent theoretical developments or research. This is often seen in the strain between the academic enterprise and the practising professionals. Add to these institutional dichotomies, excessive turnaround time and the preoccupation of some journals with methodological purity at the sacrifice of vigour and relevance, and it is no surprise that few practitioners regularly read the professional literature and fewer still participate in research and development efforts. While we all subscribe to the integrity of the intellectual process and must stand for critical evaluation, it is hard to escape the feeling that we are proceeding glacially "while Rome burns." Yet, as perennial as spring flowers, is the intuitive recognition in both arenas for the interplay between theory and practice. Academic researchers and policy makers yearn for the relevance and credibility provided only in "the real world." And practitioners in a very demanding time seek sources of consultation and value fresh perspectives.

Having assumed the prerogative for making these criticisms, in fairness I must turn the critical eye upon ourselves. We are in such an enviable position in field education to evaluate and provide practice innovation for social work services and methods. We enjoy the trust and credibility of our professional colleagues. We have consistent access to agency services and records; and we have a steady source of talent which could be tapped including both students and field instructors. Clearly, our full potential in this area is unrealized. Though it is unrealized in general, it is not absent in the work and contributions of many of our colleagues.

We have begun to see field educators develop practice models and paradigms to face the contemporary challenges of serving vulnerable populations such as: minority youth, abused and neglected children, the frail elderly, homeless individuals and families, the mentally ill, the AIDS victims and their families, and, of course, the underclass mired in poverty. In these developments, field educators have formed partnerships with agency practitioners to examine and intervene in more creative and responsive ways. Themes include collaboration, interagency teams, resource development, proactivity, and leadership. It is my contention that these kinds of practice innovations which often include new practice protocols originated by field educators and involving students and practitioners comprise the sufficient condition for the full realization of the promise of field education. These projects are not new to social work education. Many pilot or demonstration field units of the 60s and early 70s gave voice to underserved populations and advanced new methods, e.g., community organization, advocacy, generalist or multi-method practice (Schneck, 1991c, p. 233).

As we examine our local communities and reflect upon our own personal interests and commitments and those of our students, opportunities and leadership vacuums abound. Everywhere, we are challenged to formulate new ways to think about and to support human communities. Timeless notions of mutual support and social interdependence have always been operative in human history, long before they were named and studied. Because community forms the matrix for the development of personal identity, value formation, and social participation, it is the venue for our work.

Many communities need one or more of the following: a shelter and advocacy resource for victims of domestic violence or sexual abuse; a day treatment facility for adolescents struggling with substance abuse; an early intervention program with children and families to prevent out-of-home placement; the development of service centres in neighbourhoods or housing complexes to provide social, education, and health services to residents; or the development of group support and educational services to families under stress; or the counselling and educational efforts with Indian youth on the reserves to open up life choices, just to mention a few.

These and similar efforts have been initiated in many communities by field educators and students. All-too-often they are unheralded and recognized only by a grateful local constituency. This is tragic on two counts: first, the lessons deriving from the conceptualization and development of such programs are lost to a larger audience which may well be able to utilize others' experience; and second, it precludes the power and influence which might otherwise accrue to such successes.

Field educators and directors often complain of a lack of status and influence. It is unfortunate and unfair, but many field programs and directors suffer from low status and salary and inadequate resources even though they are managing good programs and making the very best of the resources available to them. Over the past few years, we have learned of arbitrary or capricious treatment by college administrators, or deans and directors; of "restructurings" and cutbacks necessitated by a scarcity or resources; of field directors having to leave their positions in order to make tenure; or of administrative changes which have wreaked havoc on certain programs or forced good people out of field education. We also hear of the long-suffering and tedious defending, rationalizing, and politicking needed to survive — clearly a drain of energy which could be much better spent in pursuit of educational goals and community progress. We are, for the most part, "the nice guys" of social work education. However, the sad reality is that some good people have been put in impossible or compromised positions. Such actions are uninformed at best, and sheer folly at worst. While not epidemic, these and less dramatic examples occur all to frequently.

I contend that these situations would be far more scarce if field directors would enhance their power and influence, not solely through their educational contributions, but also through enterprise. We can do far more to capitalize on the inherent strength and influence realized by our field education endeavors at home. By this I mean accepting leadership roles and highlighting the achievements of our field programs, be they special projects in agencies or the development of new resources. Many of us have such high expectations that we tend to take for granted successful field placements and well-functioning affiliations with agencies. By enterprise, I am suggesting:

> . . . an opportunity through program development of examining a practice imperative and bringing to bear an intervention strategy and service program based on experience and current information. This process of knowledge application also serves to reinforce a crucial ethic of professional practice, i.e., that practitioners as well as educators and researchers share responsibility for the evaluation and development of practice methods and policy. . . . Some of these broader roles will transcend our day-to-day work with field students, but serve to reinforce educational affiliations with field agencies, help develop high quality and innovative field learning opportunities, and may well provide opportunities for practice scholarship and research. (Schneck, 1993)

When field educators and students provide leadership for the development of practice and new resources, they create real influence and power, and it is well-earned and well-deserved. If we are only implementing others' ideas and agenda, others' research and development efforts, we place ourselves in a subservient status no matter how well we fulfil that role. We are seen as skilful educators or managers, but this does not always earn much respect and recognition. It is not unlike the greater status accorded to policy makers than to good administrators. Though competent administrators are valued and often rewarded well, their contributions are not seen as original or as a higher order endeavor as those of policy makers. Quite simply, we, too, have original, valuable and compelling contributions to make. Innovative field projects and roles:

> . . . These projects tend to move the locus of control and autonomy to a better balance point between the school and the community. It can re-orient, in a political economy sense, the supply/demand equation of the school needing field placement agencies to "house" students and the agencies needing field placements to help provide service.
>
> . . . Recognition of these expanded roles should not be construed as diminishing the importance of our educational mission with students. Rather, it incorporates the important and necessary liaison functions of placement, monitoring, linkage,

and advising into the context of a shared initiative for change and development
between the school and community. (Schneck, 1993)

Though some field educators have used the opportunity of the field education
enterprise to develop practice and contribute new resources to their communities, much
of their effort has not seen the light of day in the literature. Certainly, the current
vehicles of dissemination, even with their limitations, are available to us. Perhaps, also,
we need a new medium, conceivably a journal of field education in social work, which
will allow us to publish the creative work of our colleagues. We have discussed such an
endeavor, and it is not at all outside the realm of possibility. The trick, of course, would
be to produce a journal of credible quality while avoiding some of the aforementioned
limitations. In the meantime, in addition to the traditional avenues, consider agency or
governmentally published monographs, presentations at professional meetings, especially
the new distance education technologies, and video presentations. All have particular
utility.

My concern in exhorting such an agenda is that while it may resonate with many
of you, it may be viewed as impractical or too idealistic. We have all attended enough
conferences with high-sounding keynotes of little pragmatic utility. To try to deal with
this concern, I offer the following guidelines and materials (Schneck, 1991b, 1993).

   1) Start small with one or at most two initiatives. Stay focused upon
      them, and see them through to completion even if over several years.
   2) Try to honour the important process principles embodied in collabor-
      ation, teamwork, joint problem-solving, and shared leadership.
   3) Balance innovation and change with mastery. For students in
      particular, but also for practitioners, mastery of basic skill areas and
      task achievement is very important. We cannot be so radical that we,
      by behavior or by attitude denigrate the long-standing contributions
      of current practitioners, nor the need for self-confidence in the
      developing identity of our students.
   4) Try to find an area for development in which community need, your
      interest and experience, and potential university and community
      resources coalesce.
   5) First, do something of value, then promote, promulgate, disseminate.

In summary, I have tried to make the case that, though we begin with an
instructional mission, the necessary condition, many would argue the most important one
in social work education, we do not need to end there, but can expand our role to include
practice innovation and development, the sufficient condition for progress. Positioned
as we are between academia and practice, our role can be frustrating, misunderstood, and
even threatening to some. Nonetheless, most of us cherish it and devote our life's

energies to such endeavors. When we reflect upon such things as I have done during a recent illness, the altruistic and generative nature of our work reveals itself very clearly. It is worth doing, and worth doing well.

> Our primary purpose is to teach the next generation of social work practitioners to comprehend and assist a more complex and problematic world than we would have ever imagined a generation ago when most of us were field students. When well done, field education transcends the art-science, theory-practice, and school-community dichotomies; and not only obtains an open, stimulating and supportive learning environment for students, but also comprises the matrix from which true progress can emerge. (Schneck, Grossman, & Glassman, 1991, p. 16)

I hope my message has been affirming of all that you do for your students and your communities. I wish you success and all good fortune.

REFERENCES

Bogo, M., & Vayda, E. (1987). *The practice of field instruction in social work.* Toronto, ON: The University of Toronto Press.

Schneck, D. (1985). *Models of field education: Examining the common elements.* Paper presented at the CSWE-APM Post Conference Institute.

Schneck, D. (1991a). A dual matrix structure for field education. In D. Schneck, B. Grossman & U. Glassman (Eds.), *Field education in social work: Contemporary issues and trends* (pp. 96-121). Dubuque, IA: Kendall/Hunt.

Schneck, D. (1991b). Integration of learning in field education. In D. Schneck, B. Grossman & U. Glassman (Eds.), *Field education in social work: Contemporary issues and trends* (pp. 66-77). Dubuque, IA: Kendall/Hunt.

Schneck, D. (1991c). Arbiter of change in field education: The critical role for faculty. In D. Schneck, B. Grossman & U. Glassman (Eds.), *Field education in social work: Contemporary issues and trends* (pp. 233-236). Dubuque, IA: Kendall/Hunt.

Schneck, D. (1993). *The enterprising field educator.* Paper presented at the Council on Social Work Education-Annual Program Meetings Field Work Symposium on Diversity, Common Needs, Creative Responses, New York City, New York.

Schneck, D., Grossman, D., & Glassman, U. (1991). *Field education in social work: Contemporary issues and trends*. Dubuque, IA: Kendall/Hunt.

PART TWO

FIELD EDUCATION MODELS: SCHOOL-AGENCY RELATIONS

Part II of this book presents nine chapters examining field education models from a variety of organizational and developmental perspectives. All of the chapters in this section have in common the desire to enhance collaboration and improve or build relationships between social work programs and the communities, agencies, and organizations who participate in field education.

Two organizational models, the teaching centre and field setting models, are described and compared in the first chapter by Marion Bogo and Judith Globerman, while the teaching centre model is featured in the second chapter, written from the perspectives of five field instructors, connected with teaching centres in the Toronto area, Annette Bot, Jan Lackstrom, June McNamee, Sorele Urman, and Marguerite Hutson.

The next three chapters address responses to fiscal restraint and changing management structures reflected in new approaches to school-agency relations and organizational models. The first chapter, by Emeline Homonoff and Pamela Maltz, examines school-agency collaboration in Boston in an environment of scarcity created by a lengthy recession. The other two chapters are related to social work in hospitals. The first of these, by Butch Nutter, Ron Levin, and Margot Herbert, reports the results of an exploratory study of the changes in hospital social work and the impact on field education, while the second, by Judith Globerman and Marion Bogo, presents a model of organizing social work in hospitals and its relationship to field placements.

The last four chapters in this Part address collaboration from a development perspective. The first of these, by Helen Szewello Allen and Eric Shragge, describes the development of community practice through building partnerships and promoting community-based placements in Montreal. The next chapter presents a model of collaboration in establishing school social work services in Newfoundland, by Janet Fitzpatrick and Sue Murray. The third chapter in this series, by Robert McClelland, seeks to develop the social work perspective in correctional settings through field education opportunities. Diana Filiano, Paula Bergman, and Bertha Murphy present the findings of an outcome evaluation of a collaboration project to develop public sector services in Long Island, New York in the final chapter of this Part.

These chapters present an exciting and impressive array of organizational models and development strategies seeking to advance social work services and social work education through collaboration, innovation and education.

CHAPTER TWO

CREATING EFFECTIVE UNIVERSITY-FIELD PARTNERSHIPS: AN ANALYSIS OF TWO INTER-ORGANIZATION MODELS FOR FIELD EDUCATION

Marion Bogo and Judith Globerman

INTRODUCTION

In an effort to address the dynamics between university and field settings this paper presents a conceptual framework that can be used to explore the differences between inter-organization models for field education. The framework includes four key components: ensuring a commitment to education, offering strong organizational supports and resources, building effective collaborative relations, and developing effective communication and reciprocity. Utilizing this framework, the paper examines its usefulness for future research by qualitatively comparing the current and prevalent model, the Field Setting with a new model, the Teaching Centre, to determine whether the differences between models can be illuminated.

Social work field education is a critical component in the preparation of social work practitioners. Students are provided with supervised educational experiences where they have the opportunity to learn to integrate theory and practice and develop necessary practice competencies through service delivery. Field education programs rely on service organizations' willingness to accept students for practicum education, and the voluntary participation of social workers as field instructors. Surprisingly, there is little current literature on the relationships between settings and universities, the variety of existing inter-organization models for practicum education, or conceptual frameworks for analysing current and emerging approaches. In an attempt to address these gaps this paper will present an analytical framework which emerges from the literature. The framework will be utilized to qualitatively describe a current and prevalent model, the Field Setting, and another model, the Teaching Centre, used at one school of social work to determine whether the differences can be clarified. It is hoped that this framework will be used to stimulate a systematic comparison of models used in other schools and result in dialogue and study about a crucial component in social work education. Such knowledge will contribute to the decision-making and planning processes of those faculty and field educators with responsibility for field education.

FRAMEWORK FOR DESCRIBING INTER-ORGANIZATION MODELS

In 1980 Frumkin encouraged the study of school-agency relationships and provided an analytic framework. However, a review of the literature reveals few descriptive, conceptual, or empirical studies on this issue. There has been some analysis of the differences between universities and service settings with respect to environmental, organizational, professional, and educational goals and processes (Bogo & Vayda, 1987; Cohen, 1977; Frumkin, 1980; Tropman, 1977) and some suggestions for responding to the perceived tensions and challenges have been presented. In an attempt to address the dynamics between university and field settings a framework for analysis was developed from a review of the literature (Bogo & Vayda, 1987; Cassidy, 1982; Cohen, 1977; Fellin, 1982; Frumkin, 1980; Rosenblum & Raphael, 1983; Tropman, 1977). Four key components emerged.

First, an organization's commitment to education is a critical factor. Some argue that the education of the student ought to be of primary concern to the organization (Cohen, 1977; Tropman, 1977). Social work educators have been concerned with the prevalence of an apprenticeship approach to field education which is characterized by students learning, often in an imitative fashion, the skills of their particular instructor (Wijnberg & Schwartz, 1977; Cassidy, 1982). In contrast, an educational approach in the practicum includes a broader perspective, for example learning substantive knowledge about relevant populations, social policies and social problems, and contextual knowledge about environments and organizations. It also includes focusing on the linkages between the particular intervention skills and the underlying knowledge and value base. A second component in the analytic framework relates to organizational supports and resources, such as time for field instructor/student conferences and field instructor training. A third factor is how the university and the field collaborate to determine and define what content must be mastered in preparation for successful practice. Effective collaborative relationships are the result of clear definitions of the role and responsibilities of agency and university personnel, effective faculty field liaison, and adequate processes for communication, co-operation, and co-ordination (Fellin, 1982; Gordon, 1982; Rosenblum & Raphael, 1983). A final component emphasizes the importance of effective communication and reciprocity (Fellin, 1982).

Opportunities can be created for personnel in both the university and the practice setting to influence each other in a wide range of joint activities including program and curriculum design, joint research studies and staff development. This four component framework will be used to describe the range of inter-organization models presented in the literature. It will then be utilized to examine in detail two models, the Field Setting and the Teaching Centre, which are currently used in the field practicum at this university.

REVIEW OF MODELS

A review and analysis of the literature on inter-organization models reveals several arrangements. The traditional model of field education is based on an agreement of a service setting to offer a school a "student placement." Usually one student is assigned to or matched with a field instructor at the setting. The student's educational experience is generally organized by the setting's mandate and service delivery programs, and more specifically by the service functions and practice methods of the field instructor. A faculty field liaison from the university is assigned to each student/field instructor pair to monitor the student's learning and progress (Raphael & Rosenblum, 1987; Rosenblum & Raphael, 1983). In this model the commitment to education is dependent primarily on the field instructor. Communication and reciprocity is variable and depends upon the setting's supports to the field instructor and the faculty field liaison's commitment to the setting and field education.

A second model, the student unit headed by a faculty-based field instructor, experienced considerable popularity in the sixties and seventies. Government funding, particularly in under-serviced social service and mental health programs, enabled schools to become more directly involved in field education and experiment with innovative projects. Universities employed faculty-based field instructors to offer field education to units of students in traditional settings, and in settings where social work services were not provided (Singer & Wells, 1981; Marshack & Glassman, 1991), or in emerging areas of practice, for example, to achieve specific competencies for culturally-relevant practice (Benavides III, Lynch, & Velasquez, 1980). Faculty-based field instructors, as members of the university, emphasized the integration of theory and practice. They could provide a conceptual base for practice consistent with that taught in academic courses and draw links to field learning assignments in regular field seminars, individual and group instruction. The student unit provided a supportive learning environment and the opportunity for expanded learning through participating in others' case presentations. As a member of the university faculty the field instructor served as liaison to the university. In this model the key player, the faculty-based instructor, came from the university and the nature of the communication and collaborative relationships between the setting and the university heavily depended upon this individual. The setting was less responsible for the student's program and the setting's commitment to education and the resources and supports it put toward the student program depended upon its working relationship with the faculty-based instructor and their combined efforts at collaboration.

A third model is the Training or Field Instruction Centre which is a structural unit consisting of a group of agencies used for field education for a specific group of students. Tulane University designed a structured and sequenced field experience that was articulated with classroom learning (Cassidy, 1982). To operationalize this design a Training Centre was used which consisted of a range of neighbourhood based agencies from which selected learning opportunities were drawn in a structured manner so as to achieve educational objectives for student learning. Henry (1975) described a similar organizational model used at Adelphi University called the Field Instruction Centre. The Centre consisted of approximately five agencies, within close proximity, which offered a variety of services. Students were assigned to two or more settings each year so that they had a diversified practicum, learned a generic approach to service delivery, and a broad range of practice knowledge and skill. In this model a university based co-ordinator held administrative responsibility for the program, as well as educational roles in training field instructors and offering integrative seminars for students. Mention is not made of the liaison function. In this model the commitment to education is expressed in the development of a learning centre with committed organizational resources and supports. The collaborative relations with the university are lodged in a faculty-based co-ordinator. The emphasis lies in the strength of the diversified educational experience offered by the collaborating agencies.

A fourth design was identified by Showers (1990) who reported on research conducted in twenty-seven hospitals in New York City that offer field practica for a number of schools of social work. While she found variability in programs, many organizations appointed a hospital-based social worker, designated as an educational co-ordinator, who had responsibility for the field education program and used a wide variety of educational activities such as multiple assignments with multiple field instructors, student seminars, and structured learning experiences. Showers contrasted the structural complexity and variation in hospital field program designs with the dominance in the literature of the traditional model of the field liaison-field instructor-student triad as the key structural unit for field instruction program delivery. She concluded that there are many more successful models of field programs than are reflected in the general social work field education literature, and these programs are more effective than traditional field work models. This model lodges responsibility for communication, reciprocity, and collaboration in a setting-based individual who has responsibility for educational development and co-ordination. The settings vary in commitment to education and supports and resources, but the strength of the model is the use of multiple opportunities for learning within single but complex settings.

This brief review of the literature reveals several organization models which universities and service settings use to collaborate in the practicum, with universities often employing several at once. At one end of the continuum is the highly structured field units or faculty led training centres where the university maintains major control over the education of the student. At the other end of the continuum is the individualized model, perhaps the most prevalent form, which is less structured and ultimately relies on the faculty field liaison and field instructor relationship to ensure that the educational goals of the university are being met through appropriate learning and teaching processes. While the literature on the liaison role and responsibilities (Fellin, 1982; Gordon, 1982; Rosenblum & Raphael, 1983), stresses the importance of this function, there is evidence to suggest that, in fact, many teaching faculty are reluctant to take on this assignment, and those who do, do not carry it in a uniform manner. It may be that there is considerable discrepancy between the concept as presented in the literature and actual practice (Raphael & Rosenblum, 1987).

TWO INTER-ORGANIZATION MODELS

At the Faculty of Social Work at this university, two models of field education that are variants of the individualized and the highly structured models are used. In an effort to advance the future development of education models these two models will be qualitatively compared utilizing this analytic framework. The framework includes: 1) an organizations's commitment to education; 2) strong organizational supports and resources; 3) effective collaborative relationships; and 4) effective communication and reciprocity.

The Teaching Centre Model

Commitment to Education

The Teaching Centre is a model that was developed to describe a service organization that identifies social work education as one of its objectives. The organization commits itself to enter into a long-term partnership with the university for the purpose of furthering the quality of social work education and practice, and contributing to the development of knowledge in social work and social welfare. This commitment forms a part of the setting's mission statement and has formal institutional support. University teaching hospitals most typically fall into this category as well as specialized settings in the mental health and addictions fields that are university affiliated and also train students from other health science disciplines. Large government funded agencies in child welfare and municipal welfare, and quasi-private specialized settings in family services and gerontology have also chosen to affiliate as Teaching Centres. The Teaching Centre offers a structured and complex educational program that has some of the features of the hospital field programs described by Showers (1990).

The field educational program in the Teaching Centre reflects its service delivery and social work practice expertise. Social workers in the setting use the generic competency model of the university as a framework and articulate practice knowledge and competencies they deem necessary for effective social work in that service field. The broad range of activities occurring in that organization are reflected in this framework. Each Teaching Centre program is developed by the setting social workers to reflect the integration of theory, research, and practice. The workers articulate their conceptual, theoretical and practice models and utilize these to develop the specifics of their educational programs. The conceptual development of this material stimulates social workers to identify and articulate their expertise. This is an important step in preparing practitioners to become practice educators, for they must be able to communicate to students not only what they do but also why they do it (Bogo & Taylor, 1990). This activity is increasingly important to-day, as social workers must demonstrate the effectiveness of their service intervention in light of fiscal constraints and agency reorganization (Globerman & Bogo, 1993). The conceptually-based practice models that the Teaching Centre develops inform the specifics of their educational program, which is designed so that students engage in a rich and diverse set of learning opportunities to meet their educational goals. A number of social workers in the setting, often in consultation with teaching faculty, participate in this phase of the activity.

Each Teaching Centre develops a statement that presents all aspects of the teaching program, the philosophy, service context, theoretical perspectives, and learning opportunities. Upon review and acceptance of the program by the university, the setting is formally designated a Teaching Centre. In consultation with the university the setting appoints a senior social worker as educational co-ordinator with an adjunct teaching appointment.

The Teaching Centre develops a student manual which is used in a central orientation to the service field, the setting, and its field program. Structured teaching programs usually consist of seminars especially for social work students on substantive, administrative, and support issues relevant to the population, problems, policies, and context affecting that setting. Seminars also use case and project presentations to demonstrate the range of theoretical approaches and interventions of professionals in the organization. From the setting's social workers, those interested who meet certain criteria are appointed as field instructors. Social workers not directly involved as field instructors contribute their practice knowledge to this medium.

Student seminars are effective devices for teaching a broad perspective, reflecting on concepts and practices and hence furthering students' ability to integrate their learning from a specific area with a framework of social work practice, the service field and profession. The development of a student team provides the socio-emotional support social work students request and value. Students are matched with a primary field instructor and multiple student assignments with two or more social workers are also encouraged. Students attend department administrative and educational events and selected interdisciplinary teaching programs. Teaching Centres structure an evaluation process with ongoing and annual review and refinement of the educational program.

Organizational Supports and Resources

The Teaching Centre commits resources to field education through the educational co-ordinator, individual field instructors, and other social workers who participate in teaching students. The role of educational co-ordinator is particularly important as s/he has responsibility for developing and administering the field program. These individuals have practice expertise, are experienced and advanced educators, and have institutional authority to carry out the components of the program. Ideally they are also practice leaders and innovators and participate with the university through teaching sessional courses or conducting practice-based research. The Teaching Centre establishes criteria and procedures for the selection of field instructors. The educational co-ordinator consults with the university in this process, and the university's appointment of new instructors is made upon their recommendation.

The Teaching Centre collaborates with the university in the educational development of field instructors. As is the case in most schools of social work, an intensive training program for new field instructors and regular educational workshops for experienced instructors on emerging issues of importance to a quality field program are offered. In addition, the educational co-ordinator holds regular meetings of all field instructors in the setting to provide additional education and consultation to further the competency of field educators and monitor the progress of the program. These meetings integrate concepts of teaching and learning in professional and practice situations with instructors' current experiences with students. Since these groups consist of both new and experienced instructors, colleagues help problem-solve a variety of common issues related to student learning and progress and offer educational strategies for dealing with difficulties. The opportunity to have first hand knowledge of the way in which other students in a similar setting respond to practice challenges helps instructors, especially those who are new, arrive at objective interpretations of standards and expectations. As Teaching Centres develop a consistent, committed, and expert cohort of field teachers this group contributes to the development and refinement of all aspects of the Teaching Centre's program.

Effective Collaborative Relationships

In the structured Teaching Centre model the roles of the educational co-ordinator are clearly defined within each setting and in relation to the university. The co-ordinator serves as the major link between the setting and the university's faculty field liaison and over time carries the major educational and administrative functions of that role. These functions include the review of all learning contracts, mid-term and final evaluations of student learning, knowledge of the progress of each student and responsibility for intervening in problems in learning and teaching. The educational co-ordinator and field instructors are responsible for the field education. Consultation with the university faculty field liaison is structured on an "as needed" basis. At each setting, in the initial years of developing the Teaching Centre the university faculty field liaison and the educational co-ordinator are in frequent contact as they work together to experiment with aspects of this approach. As programs develop, settings gain more experience in this approach, working relationships are well established over time, and the setting and its personnel develop confidence in their own program and their ability to problem-solve. University teaching faculty are invited to meet with the field instructors about issues of mutual interest such as new curriculum or practice developments. This division of roles and authority empowers the educational co-ordinator and instructors to function as colleagues with teaching faculty in social work education. The major role they play in ensuring the success of the field program is appropriately recognized and institutionalized.

All educational co-ordinators participate in program and policy development in the field program at the university through an active steering committee of educational co-ordinators and teaching faculty with responsibility for the practicum. This committee meets regularly to identify issues of concern for Teaching Centres, and focuses on areas for further development in the field program as well as the academic curriculum. In most instances topics are relevant for field instructors from all settings and have resulted in this group assuming considerable leadership for practicum development. For example, the Teaching Centre Steering Committee was responsible for initiating significant activities to incorporate anti-racist and multi-cultural issues in all aspects of the MSW program.

Collaborative relationships are also encouraged through participation in the Association of Field Practice Educators, a formal organization for field instructors which has representation on all policy making bodies of the Faculty of Social Work. As part of the Teaching Centre programs field instructors from Teaching Centres have been supported by their organizations to play active roles in this association.

Effective Communication and Reciprocity

Reciprocity in inter-organization exchanges is a motivating factor in promoting co-operation. The university introduced a number of innovative activities to forge alliances beyond the practicum. In the interests of promoting stronger links between practice and research, ten health settings and teaching faculty formed a health research consortium. This consortium engaged in a number of joint Teaching Centre-Faculty of Social Work endeavours, such as research on high risk screening (Bogo et al., 1992), joint sponsorship of a conference on practice effectiveness with organizations serving children, and a consultative relationship through a university funded research office. Joint efforts in educational activities include joint sponsorship of visiting lecturers, joint sponsorship of social work study tours from Asia, participation in colloquia at the university and conferences in the setting, sharing audio-visual library collections, and employing experts from the Teaching Centres for sessional teaching.

In summary, the Teaching Centre model provides a unique and multi-dimensional approach for universities and service organizations to use co-operatively in the preparation of social work practitioners. This structured approach recognizes the expertise of the field and institutionalizes what exists, that social work practitioners are the experts in practice and that the modern role of the university educator is to create approaches that facilitate the articulation of that expertise and to develop educational methods so that students can learn to become effective ethical practitioners. A model such as this empowers practitioners as colleagues, shares control of education and uses the scarce resources of the university in an efficient, appropriate, and rational manner.

Field Setting Model

Commitment to Education

Field settings are service organizations or departments that provide specific practicum learning opportunities for one or more students on an annual basis, which may or may not be renewed. The impetus for providing a practicum is initiated by a social worker who wishes to become a field instructor, the university who believes the setting offers valuable learning experiences, or a student who requests that the university develop the practicum since particular learning goals cannot be met in the currently offered field settings. While there must be institutional agreement before a student is matched with an instructor, the negotiations for the practicum are, for the most part, conducted with the designated field instructor and focus on her/his service functions. Annual renewal of the practicum usually depends on that instructor's interest and availability. While these settings usually value having students, they are reluctant to make long term resource commitments to an educational program.

The content of the student's educational experience in the practicum is influenced in large measure by the practice role of the specific field instructor. Most field instructors attempt to involve the student with others and a team where possible, as well as make available other regular educational activities, such as conferences and rounds. The university's competency model is used as a general framework as it is reflected in the activities of the field instructor in the setting. However, it is unlikely that a framework and set of specific objectives with a systematic and structured educational program will be developed by the setting. The university has developed a structured learning contract format to assist the individual field instructor and student dyad to plan the specific practicum with clear expectations of the learning processes and outcomes.

Organizational Supports and Resources

The agency commits itself to support field education through its agreement to have the individual social worker use part of her/his time to provide field instruction to a student. In addition the university expects new instructors to attend an intensive new field instructor training program which involves the worker in bi-monthly seminars during the period the student is in the field. Experienced instructors are invited to attend workshops and meetings with university faculty field liaison. Insofar as others in the setting are contributing their time and expertise to the student, the organization provides considerable resources for education. Many experienced, valued and effective field instructors are in settings where they have been supported in their contributions to education.

Effective Collaborative Relationships

Each field instructor and student dyad is assigned to a university faculty field liaison. As discussed above, new field instructors participate in an intensive structured training program where they learn the necessary educational and administrative theory and process to empower them to become effective field educators (Bogo, 1981). In this first year, field liaison is part of the new field instructor group training experience. Individual liaison with the group leader is available, however this is only used where there are extreme problems with student learning. The effectiveness of the training has led the university to interact with agency employed instructors in their second and subsequent years as equal partners. In this approach the field instructor, like any other course instructor, is the sole teacher with responsibility for the work with the student. Consultation on learning and teaching issues is available from university colleagues, designated as faculty field liaisons, but regular visits are not structured. The university faculty field liaison is responsible for reviewing students' learning contracts, mid-term and final evaluations, and confirming the field instructor's recommended grade.

Educational workshops for experienced instructors on emerging issues are regularly offered and well attended by these instructors.

As discussed above, all field instructors are eligible to become members of an Association of Field Practice Educators, a formal organization for field instructors with representation on all policy making bodies of the Faculty of Social Work. Instructors from field settings have taken on roles in this organization however this is generally a volunteer activity engaged in on their own time.

In summary, for field instructors in settings not designated as Teaching Centres the collaborative relationship with the university is particularly strong in their first year where intensive educational inputs are offered in a structured and organized manner. Thereafter, the field instructor and student work together with input from the university on an "as needed" basis. These settings do not participate in any structured collaboration with the university beyond the initial agreements, essentially leaving the links between the two organizations to the initiative of the field instructor.

Effective Communication and Reciprocity

In the Field Setting model there are few opportunities for organized reciprocity between the setting and the university. The disadvantages of this model are its independence and individualized nature. Even though many social workers provide field instruction every year, the programs of field education they offer vary according to their service, interests, and competing commitments. Students engage in a formal contracting process with all field instructors at both Teaching Centres and Field Settings. However, many aspects of students' learning which are met through the Teaching Centre programs are individually met or compromised in individualized programs at Field Settings.

Although all field instructors are invited to participate in university colloquia and workshops, those in field setting practica rarely participate in the development of new educational models and programs. This is primarily an artifact of the Field Setting model, in that it is dependent on an individual field instructor. Where the field setting has a strong commitment to social work education field instructors supported by their setting more actively engage in reciprocal relationships with the university. In some unique instances, such as new organizations offering programs to under-serviced populations and/or settings with few professionally trained workers, alternate inter-organization models are needed so that students can be involved in learning in emerging areas of practice. It is primarily in these settings that field instructors are actively forging relationships with the university to influence change.

CONCLUSION

The social work literature underscores the importance of studying inter-organization models to understand and develop productive partnerships between schools of social work and settings which offer social service and employ our graduates. While a number of inter-organization education models are described in the literature, a useful framework for analysis and comparison of models is needed. The Teaching Centre Model elaborates on settings' institutionalized commitments to ongoing social work education that is theoretically-based and informed by research. Teaching Centre programs are unique and distinct because they centrally organize and structure the students' field education to reflect the dynamic and changing nature of practice. By confirming field instructors as colleagues of the university-based educators, the Teaching Centre capitalizes on the strengths of practitioners. The second model, the Field Setting Model, relies on well trained ethical social workers to provide quality field instruction based on their knowledge and expertise. Lacking the continuity of established Teaching Centre programs, this model reinforces social workers' own independent commitment to social work field education. The challenge for social work educators is to operationalize the components in this framework so that different models can be examined empirically to determine the effect of the various components in achieving desired outcomes for students, organizations, and ultimately service delivery.

REFERENCES

Benavides, E., Lynch, M., & Velasquez, J. (1980). Toward a culturally relevant field model: The community learning centre project. *Journal of Education for Social Work, 16*(2), 55-62.

Bogo, M. (1981). An educationally focused faculty/field liaison program for first-time field instructors. *Journal of Education for Social Work, 17*(3), 59-65.

Bogo, M., & Taylor, I. (1990). A practicum curriculum in a health specialization: A framework for hospitals. *Journal of Social Work Education, 26*(1), 76-86.

Bogo, M., & Vayda, E. (1987). *The practice of field instruction in social work: Theory and process - with an annotated bibliography*. Toronto: University of Toronto Press.

Bogo, M., Wells, L., & Abbey, S. (1992). Advancing social work practice in the health field: A collaborative research partnership. *Health & Social Work, 17*(3), 223-235.

Cassidy, H. (1982). Structuring field learning experiences. In B. W. Sheafor & L. E. Jenkins (Eds.), *Quality field instruction in social work* (pp. 198-214). New York: Longman.

Cohen, J. (1977). Selected constraints in the relationship between social work education and practice. *Journal of Education for Social Work, 13*(1), 3-7.

Fellin, P. A. (1982). Responsibilities of the school: Administrative support of field instruction. In B. W. Sheafor & L. E. Jenkins (Eds.), *Quality field instruction in social work* (pp. 101-135). New York: Longman.

Frumkin, M. (1980). Social work education and the professional commitment fallacy: A practical guide to field-school relations. *Journal of Education for Social Work, 16*(2), 91-99.

Globerman, J., & Bogo, M. (1993). *Social work and the new integrative hospital.* Unpublished manuscript.

Gordon, M. S. (1982). Responsibilities of the school: Maintenance of the field program. In B.W. Sheafor & L. E. Jenkins (Eds.), *Quality field instruction in social work* (pp. 116-135). New York: Longman.

Henry, C. St. G. (1975). An examination of field work models at Adelphi University School of Social Work. *Journal of Education for Social Work, 11*(3), 62-68.

Marshack, E., & Glassman, U. (1991). Innovative models for field instruction: Departing from traditional methods. In D. Schneck, D. Grossman & U. Glassman (Eds.), *Field education in social work: Contemporary issues and trends* (pp. 84-95). Iowa: Kendall/Hunt.

Raphael, F. B., & Rosenblum, A. F. (1987). An operational guide to the faculty field liaison role. *Social Casework: The Journal of Contemporary Social Work, 68*(3), 156-163.

Rosenblum, A. F., & Raphael, F. B. (1983). The role and function of the faculty-field liaison. *Journal of Education for Social Work, 19*(1), 67-73.

Showers, N. (1990). Hospital graduate social work field programs: A study in New York City. *Health and Social Work, 15*(2), 55-63.

Singer, C. B., & Wells, L. M. (1981). The impact of student units on services and structural change in Homes for the Aged. *Canadian Journal of Social Work Education, 7*(3), 11-27.

Tropman, E. J. (1977). Agency constraints affecting links between practice and education. *Journal of Education for Social Work, 13*(1), 8-14.

Wijnberg, M. H., & Schwartz, M. C. (1977). Models of student supervision: The apprentice, growth, and role systems models. *Journal of Education for Social Work, 13*(3),107-113.

CHAPTER THREE

THE TEACHING CENTRE MODEL OF FIELD EDUCATION

Annette Bot, Jan Lackstrom, June McNamee, Sorele Urman and Marguerite Hutson

Field Education in Social Work has always been an integral component in the preparation of graduates as social work practitioners. The opportunity to integrate theory and practice and develop practice skills and competencies from a practical experiential base are essential to social work education. The field's willingness and readiness to accept students as "learners" and the provision of agency based field instructors allows the practicum to develop as an integral part of formal education. A long-term partnership, based on mutual support and the development of a strong educational practice base can develop between the field and the university.

The University of Toronto and a group of agencies in the area of Metropolitan Toronto came together to develop a unique model of field education called the Teaching Centre Model. This paper will briefly describe: the history of the development of the Teaching Centre Model and it's role; a generic teaching centre and the role of the educational coordinator; and the individualized features of four teaching centres.

HISTORY OF THE DEVELOPMENT OF THE TEACHING CENTRE MODEL

The Association of Field Practice Educators (AFPE) was officially formed in 1973 when a group of Field Practice Instructors and Administrators formed an ad hoc committee to consider ways of participating in the Faculty of Social Work at the University of Toronto to narrow the gap between the field and the faculty. When the AFPE developed into a permanent structure its purpose was defined as two-fold: to maintain an effective working relationship with the Faculty of Social Work and to be involved in the decision making process at the Faculty in order to improve the quality of social work education and to ensure that education remain relevant to the needs of social work practice. Various guidelines were developed during the late 1970's including "The Role of the Field Practicum in Social Work Education" and "Guidelines for Establishing a Contract Between Teaching Centres and the Faculty of Social Work."

In the beginning a variety of educational meetings were sponsored by or held in conjunction with the Faculty of Social Work. The Association worked with the Faculty of Social Work to develop competency based education including the identification of social work practice competency elements. In April 1982 a Task Force on Teaching Centres was instituted by the AFPE. Each Teaching Centre was a social service agency or department within a health care setting which identified social work education as one of its objectives. The Teaching Centre entered into a long-term partnership with the Faculty of Social Work and a formal document was signed outlining the contractual responsibilities of each.

The Teaching Centres agreed to appoint an educational coordinator who would be responsible for the development of a field practice programme congruent with the curriculum of the Faculty of Social Work and in turn they were appointed as Adjunct Social Work Practice Professors and their settings as designated Teaching Centres. The Teaching Centres agreed to provide educational opportunities regularly for a substantial number of students (a minimum of four) based on their own staff compliment, including the provision of educational opportunities for students with special learning needs, such as those with visual, hearing and physical disabilities, and students repeating the practicum.

In February 1983 the first meeting of the AFPE Teaching Centre Committee was held and the Committee began its formal deliberations meeting four times during the academic year. Initially the Academic Coordinator of the Practicum and the Associate Practicum Coordinators at the Faculty were invited as required, but it soon became evident that their full time attendance and participation was vital. The Teaching Centre Committee is a dynamic partnership and working group of Faculty and Teaching Centre representatives and has worked together in an atmosphere of mutual sharing and learning since 1983.

The Teaching Centre Committee offers agencies and hospitals, as a group, an opportunity to influence policy, procedure, and hiring at the university. In addition to speaking directly to the faculty associated with the Practicum Office, the chairman of the Teaching Centre Committee is a member of the AFPE Board of Directors and has a seat on Faculty Council. Through the Teaching Centre Committee the university can also seek consultation from the larger community about issues pertinent to social work education and raise concerns that the faculty and students may have about the field experience. Examples of issues the Teaching Centre Committee has discussed include: the length of time necessary for a field placement; the effect of budgetary restraint on field instructors and the effects of that on students; quality assurance in field instruction; and, the integration of students' thesis with this field work.

The Practicum Office at the Faculty, with the aid of the Teaching Centre Committee, have developed workshops on power differentials, giving feedback to field instructors and multicultural issues and racism for students and field instructors. The Teaching Centre Committee has been a vital body to defend the importance of field education at both the university and in the agencies in the face of increasingly competitive demands. The Teaching Centre Committee has also been used by the agencies to exchange ideas about training and to identify and share problems in an effort to find solutions. Recently a number of geographically close agencies, have decided to present a single seminar series as an attempt to relieve agency staff who are already strained because of budgetary restraint.

THE ROLE OF THE EDUCATIONAL COORDINATOR AND THE TEACHING CENTRE PROGRAMME

The educational coordinator is typically a senior social worker who is an experienced field instructor. The position may or may not be part of the management team of the agency. In some settings there is renumeration associated with the position and in others not. The role is multifaceted and requires well developed skills in the areas of administration, programme evaluation and development, collaboration and consultation. Within the agency the educational coordinator is responsible for the entire education programme. Responsible to both their agency administration and to the university, the educational coordinator manages all of the day to day work of the Teaching Centre, makes recommendations for the development of the programme and implements agreed upon changes. Each agency has taken the tasks of the educational coordinator and shaped them to meet the needs, philosophy and mandate of it's specific setting.

The educational coordinator supervises the field instructors which includes recruiting field instructors and monitoring the quality of their work. Some agencies have well developed criteria for the selection of field instructors, while others simply accept those who volunteer. Similarly, some agencies have developed standards of practice on which the field instructors are evaluated while others do not formally evaluate the instruction. The educational coordinator may simply administer the programme by overseeing the matching process between field instructor and student, ensure the timely completion of learning contracts and evaluations, and keep field instructors and students informed about the ongoing educational events in the setting. The educational coordinator may also provide formal supervision and training for new field instructors and be available for consultation to more experienced instructors who may be having difficulties with their student. Almost all educational coordinators hold group meetings with their field instructors throughout the year to review how the students and instructors are doing, to relay information from the university and other teaching centres, and to facilitate peer support amongst the field instructors.

Some educational coordinators facilitate formal training programmes for the field instructors. The educational coordinator identifies, with the help of the field instructors, areas that are of interest. Some agencies use internal resources to meet the learning needs while others are able to recruit experts based in the community. Some agencies have provided field instructors with extra days of professional development while others ask instructors to include this in their regular professional development activities. Examples of topics that have been of interest to field instructor include the difference between psychotherapy and supervision and models of adult education and training.

The orientation to the agency is a key event as it serves to introduce students to their practicum and the setting. These first impressions can leave long, if not lasting, impressions about how the agency treats and values students. Most educational coordinators minimally set the agenda and recruit others to present the orientation; however, most conduct the bulk of the orientation themselves. This provides one of the few opportunities for the coordinator to spend a concentrated amount of time with the students. Orientations programmes range from a small social gathering introducing staff and students to an intensive two or three day workshop focusing on topics such as the administrative structure and workings of the agency, fire, health and safety issues, presentations about community resources, multidisciplinary collaboration and team functioning, statistics and beginning teaching about site specific assessment and treatment models. Orientation also includes very basic information such as where the washrooms, lunch room and offices are.

Each teaching centre provides individual instruction for the social work students. They contract to provide a minimum of one to two hours per week of instruction. In reality the field instructors often provide more protected time for individual consultation and are readily available for informal talks. The field instructor and student negotiate a learning contract that guides their work for the year and against which the student's performance is evaluated.

All of the educational coordinators help mediate problems that occur between students and field instructors. This is a delicate task as students do not wish to get their field instructor in "trouble" or fear that the educational coordinator will side with the field instructor. Field instructors may hesitate to seek help if they feel they will be blamed or shamed for the problems they are experiencing. An atmosphere of acceptance and fairness is important. Depending on the severity of the problems the educational coordinator may notify the university faculty of specific problems and include them in the mediation process. At times faculty are the first to know of problems and will need to initiate the mediation process by contacting the educational coordinator. Collaboration between the university and agency is essential.

A number of Teaching Centres have begun to offer the students additional didactic teaching. Students are provided an opportunity to learn theory specifically related to issues in their settings and to integrate these new ideas into their practice. This training which compliments theories they are learning in their university courses, is developed and monitored by the educational coordinator and usually falls into two categories: a seminar series which includes a variety of topics relevant to the setting, such as family therapy, adjustment to illness, transference and countertransference, managing the difficult client and issues of death and dying; and, a more intensive training in such models of treatment as brief solution focused therapy or play therapy, thereby allowing students to study a particular modality in more depth. These programmes can include staff who are unable to supervise a student full time but would derive satisfaction from being involved in student education in a more limited way.

Some large Teaching Centres have developed student teams that can be led by the educational coordinator or another staff member. The team is designed to provide an opportunity for peer support and discussion of difficult cases or situations that students often find upsetting. These meetings may also be used to discuss problems students are experiencing with their field instructors, such as being asked to work overtime or being assigned cases which are not considered challenging. Students can use this peer support to assist them in coping in a variety of situations, for example, with the death of a client, dealing with a hostile staff member or making their first child welfare apprehension. One agency uses group supervision for case presentations. The goal of the group supervision is two fold, firstly for the students to have practice presenting cases and seeking help and secondly to learn how to present material for critical review and to accept critical feedback in a professional manner.

In each setting there is some form of programme evaluation which serves as a basis for the next years programme. The evaluations range from simple review by the educational coordinator and the field instructors to more elaborate evaluations using a variety of questionnaires. The review tends to focus on the quality of the content of the practicum and the process of supervision with the expectation that gaps in learning opportunities and problems in supervision will be identified.

EXAMPLES OF FOUR TEACHING CENTRES

The Wellesley Hospital and the Urban Health Initiative

The Wellesley Hospital is a 360 bed hospital serving a large and diverse community in downtown Toronto. In 1991 the hospital began implementing an enhanced mission to become an "university hospital with a commitment to its communities" via the Urban Health Initiative which was designed to be a three way partnership with the University of Toronto and the community. Unique to the Teaching Centre at the Wellesley Hospital is the development of an educational model for social work which incorporated the principles and objectives of the Urban Health Initiative and which will hopefully be an innovative model in North America. Principles of the Urban Health Initiative model include taking a population perspective in the hospital's diverse and complex urban setting, using principles of community development, health promotion and illness prevention in a multidisciplinary matrix. Issues which have always been identified as relevant to health and well being, such as poverty and racism, will hopefully be addressed in creative and effective ways in a hospital, community and university partnership.

The Department of Social Work offers a unique and comprehensive practicum for students. Traditionally, students have specialized in one of four areas: clinical, community development, policy and administration, or research. This model is exploring the integration of these skills and knowledge sets on a dynamic continuum. Activities include intensive community orientation, outreach and networking. Students may work on projects in collaboration with community agencies, advisory panels and coalitions. Opportunities have included projects providing training to frontline workers in family violence, coordinating health care delivery to the underhoused, addressing settlement issues of particular immigrant and refugee groups and reviewing government and community responses to HIV and AIDS. While students continue to work with individuals and their significant contexts, the perspective and repertoire of skills and knowledge have shifted.

Sunnybrook Health Sciences Centre and Programme Management

The move toward programme management structures within many institutions across the country is presenting a major challenge to maintaining a strong social work educational focus. Inherent in this structure is the decentralization of social work and the likely elimination of the Director of Social Work. The restructuring process toward decentralization in 1992 at Sunnybrook Health Science Centre has a tremendous impact on the 45 social workers and students located there. Concern was expressed by various faculties at the University of Toronto as to whether Sunnybrook could remain a suitable institution for the education of students. For a Teaching Centre to function within a programme management structure, at the Hospital must remain committed to excellence in the areas of education and research. The Teaching Centre also requires leadership and a discipline specific infrastructure to carry out the core professional activities associated with a teaching centre. Sunnybrook did respond to the concerns of the University by establishing various mechanisms to support a high calibre of professional practice across the hospital.

A Chief of Service model was adopted with this person having responsibility for the overall leadership of the profession with a focus on education, research and professional standards of practice. Discipline specific councils have been developed to address these areas of professional responsibility. Students continue to be valuable members of the hospital community and this managed hospital has in fact, strengthened the Teaching Centre as a vital part of training and professional identity.

The Children's Aid Society of Metropolitan Toronto, a Geographically Diverse Setting

The Children's Aid Society is an agency with a central administrative office in downtown Toronto with six satellite branch offices geographically dispersed through of the city. The Educational Coordinator, working out of the Human Resources Department, describes herself as a "hands off" coordinator, in that although she is responsible for the recruitment and training of field instructors, the actual supervision of field education is carried out by agency supervisors. Students in this setting do not have student specific orientations and seminars; instead, they have the same orientation as staff and are invited to participate in seminars and workshops that are available to line staff. The role of the educational coordinator is similar to what has already been described earlier.

The Teaching Centre at the Children's Aid Society represents the opposite extreme of adherence to the traditional structure of the Teaching Centre Model because of it's highly decentralized structure. The Educational Coordinator describes many benefits of participating in the Teaching Centre Model including enhancing the commitment of the agency to social work education and elevating the image of child welfare with students and the community in general.

Thistletown Regional Centre/George Hull Centre for Children and Families: Shared Resources

This Centre is a large children's mental health agency in Metropolitan Toronto with a long history of training students of several disciplines. Social Work education has been a significant part of this history. In 1982, a major reorganization at Thistletown Regional Centre moved service delivery from a matrix model to individual clinical programmes serving specific client populations. Discipline departments were abolished and Senior Consultants were appointed to respond to particular professional issues including organizing field placements. In 1985, the Outpatient Community Service was divested from Thistletown and became the George Hull Centre for Children and Families.

This Teaching Centre has a unique administrative arrangement which links the two agencies together for research and staff\student training. There are six distinct service programmes serving specific client populations. In this complex structure, there are two educational coordinators representing the two related agencies. The educational coordinators are linked together by a Teaching Centre Committee which meets three times a year to review and plan a joint programme. Notwithstanding the complexities of this model, it has been both effective and efficient in carrying out a comprehensive social work student programme in a context of shared resources.

CONCLUSION

The Teaching Centre Model is a dynamic model of field education that can be shaped to fit the particular needs of individual agencies. Although there are a core set of requirements to become a Teaching Centre each agency can design and implement the requirements in a way that matches their own needs and philosophy. The collaboration between Teaching Centres and with the Faculty of Social Work contributes to a rich, progressive and evolutionary approach to field practice both in the field and at the University. The Teaching Centre designation enhances the educational image within the agency and community at large. The status accompanying the association with the University has helped social work departments maintain educational programmes and professional identity especially in secondary settings. The Faculty of Social Work has gained the input of the field who are aware of social work issues in a very concrete way. The field has helped the Faculty protect and develop the practicum component of the curriculum and have helped identify gaps in the social work knowledge base. Finally, and most importantly, the Teaching Centre Model encourages the development of high quality, comprehensive and progressive practica for social work students.

We would like to acknowledge the contribution of L. Jackson, Dr. R. Roberts and C. MacDonald without whose help this article would have been incomplete.

CHAPTER FOUR

FAIR EXCHANGE: COLLABORATION BETWEEN SOCIAL WORK SCHOOLS AND FIELD AGENCIES IN AN ENVIRONMENT OF SCARCITY

Emeline Homonoff and Pamela Maltz

Schools of social work depend on the resources of human service settings for a most important part of the curriculum: field education. However, Frumkin (1980) has warned against the "professional commitment fallacy" which assumes that agencies will altruistically subordinate their own needs to their ethical obligation to provide training for future professionals. The relationship between schools of social work and their affiliated training agencies can become particularly strained in times of scarce resources. This paper will utilize and expand Frumkin's suggested framework of exchange theory to analyze school-agency collaboration in an environment of scarcity created by a lengthy recession. Several principles for successful collaboration are proposed: mobilization of concerned and influential participants, respect for the autonomy of systems, appreciation of divergent perspectives and commitment to shared goals (Homonoff & Maltz, 1991). Examples will be presented of efforts to put these principles into action in the relationship between a Boston school of social work and its affiliated agencies.

EXCHANGE THEORY

Exchange theory is based on a view of organizations as systems "composed of many interacting parts that strive to meet certain needs in an attempt to survive within an environment" (Frumkin, 1980, p. 93). Since these needs cannot be met in isolation, organizations rely on other agencies, community groups, legislative bodies, etc. for support. The definition of organizational exchange, then, is "any voluntary activity between two organizations which has consequences, actual or anticipated, for the realization of their respective goals or objectives" (Levine & White in Hasenfeld, 1983, p. 548). The nature of this exchange depends on the characteristics of the environment — such as the availability and predictability of resources — and of the organizations' structure — such as boundaries, hierarchy, and communication channels.

ENVIRONMENTAL CHARACTERISTICS

The current environment in human services is characterized by instability and paucity of resources. In Massachusetts, a lengthy recession has diminished the Commonwealth's resources and fostered conservative limitations on the role of government. In the past year the Human Services budget was slashed; in the Department of Mental Health alone, the budget was $30 million below the previous year's appropriation, three mental hospitals were closed, several psychiatric facilities failed or were merged under "umbrella" agencies, and many state workers were fired or "bumped" into unfamiliar positions. In a recent survey of Massachusetts agencies used as field placements (Bocage, Homonoff, & Riley, 1994), more than half the respondents reported reductions in staff (including supervisors), increased dependence on junior staff for supervision, and low morale. Agencies responded to cutbacks by reducing services that do not produce revenues (including training of interns), by raising fees, and by encouraging staff productivity (Gopelrud, 1983). Clients are another resource for agencies; as private practitioners "creamed" wealthier clients and insurance was increasingly limited to severe emotional disturbances, agencies found fewer clients with manageable problems who could afford treatment (Davis, 1982). Resources also dwindled for social work schools; although numbers of applicants to social work schools were stable or increasing, "host" colleges and universities were feeling the pinch of a demographic slump in college-age youth, and financial aid was sorely lacking.

STRUCTURAL CHARACTERISTICS

The structural characteristics of agencies, and to some extent of social work schools, have also been affected by the current fiscal climate. Retrenchment, privatization, and managed care have reshaped organizations in several areas: domain, autonomy, centralization, and communication channels. First, although some "leaner and meaner" organizations have survived, many agencies whose domains were assured by their tradition of excellence and community services have closed or have been merged into larger human service corporations. Competition for scarce resources pits agencies against one another, and even social work schools may have to fight for dwindling agency placements.

Agencies and social work schools are less autonomous than ever from environmental pressures. Agencies are regulated more and more closely through their contracts with Federal and State funding sources and with numerous insurers; managed care dictates the length and type of treatment for each client (Cagney, 1989). Social work schools are also subject to environmental constraints, such as responsibility to their host educational institution and to educational accrediting bodies.

Fiscal changes have also affected the centralization of agencies, Tischler (1987) and others suggest that future agency structure will be large, diverse but integrated systems of care. The trend will be towards consolidation and centralization of services, as fiscal constraints demand economies of scale and managed care organizations demand linkages with an "umbrella" agency (Gopelrud, 1983; Stoesz, 1988). Within these consolidated agencies there will probably be a wide network of services targeted at specific populations (Tischler, 1987). No longer can social work schools depend on traditional arrangements with their field placements; the current configuration of each agency must be analyzed and more formal contracts must be made, attending to each component of the organization and respecting each level of the hierarchy.

These changes in domain, boundaries, and centralization necessitate changes in communication patterns within agencies and schools of social work. Larger, consolidated agencies with decentralized subsystems require more vertical and lateral communication (Mordock, 1989). Responsibility to outside funding sources and regulatory bodies mandates documentation, quality control, and fiscal accountability for agencies and schools alike. A continuous flow of information is necessary for both agencies and schools to attend to the rapidly changing needs of an unstable environment.

FUNCTIONAL MATCH BETWEEN SCHOOL AND AGENCY

Given these constraints and changes, it is not surprising that the "functional similarity" between schools of social work and field agencies is not constant. As Frumkin defines functional similarity, he asks if agencies provide the necessary range of educational experiences for students, and if the type of education provided by the school meets agency needs (1980, p. 97). The Simmons survey of affiliated field placements (Bocage, Homonoff, & Riley, 1994) revealed several worrisome changes in training of social work interns in Massachusetts. Maintaining an appropriate number of clients for social work interns was increasingly difficult because of cutbacks in Medicaid reimbursement. Those clients available to interns presented with increasingly serious problems and declining resources. At the same time, pressures for productivity and accountability mounted, so that agencies found it difficult to train inexperienced interns who required considerable support and relatively uncomplicated cases (Zakutansy & Sirles, 1993). Staff were often asked to supervise interns at an earlier stage than in past years, and administrators could seldom find the time and energy to oversee the training process.

A NEW DEFINITION OF EXCHANGE

This paper will describe the efforts of one social work school and its affiliated agencies to collaborate in supporting training of social work interns in the current environment of scarcity in Massachusetts. Frumkin (1980) and others (Born, 1982; Ginsberg, 1982; Leader, 1971; Palmera, 1978; Sheafor & Jenkins, 1980) have suggested specific exchanges which social work schools and affiliated agencies might make to acquire additional resources, improve organizational functioning and secure help in attaining organizational goals. In a previous paper (Homonoff & Maltz, 1991), the authors — a field education professor and an agency administrator — extended the idea of exchange to include the exchange of ideas as well as the exchange of goods and services. They outlined several principles for effective interagency collaboration: mobilization of concerned and influential people, respect for the autonomy of systems, appreciation of divergent perspectives, and commitment to shared goals. This paper will illustrate the application of these principles in the relationship between the Simmons College School of Social Work and its affiliated training agencies.

MOBILIZATION OF CONCERNED AND INFLUENTIAL PEOPLE

Leader (1971, p. 54) says of field-school relations: "It is lack of participation that leads to lack of communication and interest." Because of the complexity of organizations involved — with simultaneous consolidation and decentralization of services — multiple levels of communication must be established. The obvious but difficult first step in establishing a constructive relationship between social work schools and field agencies is to convene as many people as possible who are actively concerned about student training.

> Meetings between the School of Social Work and field agencies are frequent and involve several organizational levels. Students' concerns are represented to the agencies by the field advisor, and to faculty committees by faculty and student liaisons. Beginning and advanced supervision seminars at the school encourage field instructors to discuss organizational issues as well as student learning needs. Field advisors meet with agency administrators as well as field instructors, and the school hosts a yearly field education conference, in which agency supervisor and middle managers meet with faculty from all sequences to discuss new developments in theory and practice. Finally, area schools of social work formed the New England Consortium of Graduate Social Work Programs (NECON), which meets every other month to discuss issues that affect field education. In addition to promoting joint political action among social work schools, NECON sponsors a series of conferences and workshops on current developments in the social work field to which field instructors, administrators, faculty, and deans are invited.

In times of fiscal crisis it is not enough to promote communication among concerned people; the social work field needs to mobilize powerful and influential advocates, including agency administrators, deans and department chairs from schools of social work, and officials from the national professional organization.

> The recent conservative administration in the Commonwealth of Massachusetts recently rescinded legislation allowing second year social work interns to be reimbursed for their services through Medicaid. The field directors of area social work schools, supported by their deans, allied with representatives of the National Association of Social Workers to negotiate with the Mental Health Management Association, which had been charged with overseeing part of the Medicaid program. They were successful in restoring some Medicaid reimbursement for second year social work interns.

RESPECT FOR THE AUTONOMY OF SYSTEMS

Although systems depend on each other for survival, they maintain their autonomy as well; they are resilient and resist intrusion and control (Hoffman, 1985). Knitzer (1988) underscores the importance of careful negotiations between systems, saying:

> The need for time cannot be underestimated . . . Changing (organizations) can be as complex a process as trying to change a family's functioning . . . What

it critical is starting the process; providing a context that will nurture and encourage goal oriented cross-system collaborations . . . Let it evolve. (p. 25-7)

Especially in times of scarce resources, social work schools and agencies must beware of taking each other for granted; careful attention must be paid to the needs of each organization, and to the costs of collaboration. Agency staff are often anxious and demoralized about demands for productivity, organizational instability, and the perceived insecurity of the social work profession in times of change and retrenchment. The school of social work can support field agencies' training of interns in several areas. The first is the placement process.

> The many changes attendant to the fiscal crisis have made the field placement process infinitely more complicated. Agencies may contract to take students, then learn that their supervisors have been laid off or transferred. Administrators or training directors may change, interrupting established channels of communication with field advisors. Agencies may have less energy to support anxious, inexperienced students. For these reasons, the school of social work has expended extraordinary time and effort in the placement process. Placement of incoming students begins early; each incoming student is interviewed by a member of the field department, detailed information about his or her experience and learning style is offered to the agency, and potential interns are interviewed by the agency. Field education staff monitor each placement, re-placing students when agencies experience staff layoffs or transfers.

Another area where schools of social work can support field agencies is the advisory process. Although budget crises may tempt social work schools to reduce the number of field faculty, the role of the field advisor (Rosenblum & Raphael, 1983; Urdang, 1993) is particularly crucial in times of scarcity and upheaval (Homonoff, Weintraub, Michelson, & Costikyan, 1994). The following fictional account is a composite of typical interventions required of field liaisons in training sites under stress:

> A relatively inexperienced intern was placed at an agency which had been known for its supportive atmosphere. During the year, the loss of a large grant and the constraints of managed care forced agency staff to increase their caseloads and to shorten the length of client treatment. The social work intern felt that his field instructor was less available than at the beginning of the year, and perceived increased pressure to perform like a member of the staff. An escalating cycle began: the more the anxious intern asked for support from his field instructor, the more the harassed field instructor reacted with frustration and impatience, and the more the intern's anxious pleas for assistance increased. The field instructor, who was supervising for the first time, was reluctant to bother the director of social service, whom she perceived as being overwhelmed

by demands. The field liaison from the school of social work met with the intern, field instructor, and director of social service. The director of social service established weekly meetings with the field instructor, and agreed to allow the field instructor increased credit for supervision in her productivity ratings. The field instructor delineated specific times outside the supervisory hour when the intern could meet with her; at the same time, the field liaison explained to the intern the importance of holding his anxious questions when possible until the appointed hours for supervision. During the year, the field liaison met regularly with the intern and with the field instructor, both individually and jointly, to offer support.

APPRECIATION OF DIVERGENT PERSPECTIVES

Collaboration implies respect for different perspectives. Literature on field education has always reflected an appreciation for the divergence of the social work school's goal of educating students, and the agency's primary responsibility for client service (Born, 1982; David, 1982; Frumkin, 1980; Leader, 1971; Mokuau & Ewalt, 1993; Palmera, 1978; Sheafor & Jenkins, 1981). Increased communication may bring to light the difference in perspectives between faculty and agency staff, and help to clarity their respective roles in educating social work students.

> In a yearly meeting, faculty of the school of social work and field agency staff discussed mutual dilemmas in training social work interns, such as the tension between the School's need to support inexperienced interns and the agencies' need for interns who could "hit the ground running." The subsequent survey of agencies' response to budget cuts elicited helpful suggestions from agencies for change in the school's curriculum, indicating a need for more content on short-term interventions, on group and family therapy, and on advocacy and case management. Another survey will follow up this year on current agency reactions to continued fiscal retrenchment, and will explore in particular the effects of managed care on client service and on training of social work interns.

Since most of the Simmons School of Social Work faculty are involved in clinical work, consultation, research, or policy initiatives with agencies used as field placements, the agencies learn from faculty expertise, and faculty and students from the social work school are kept abreast of important developments in the field. Faculty — and, by extension, their students — also learn from exchange of perspectives with clients. One professor wrote about her mutual conversations with a group of AIDS patients:

> Differences between leaders and group members (being gay or heterosexual, women or men, those who have AIDS or those who don't) create tensions and

important opportunities in the group. Telling one's story to one another, who has not had the experience to understand it, is a particular challenge. It includes inducting each into the other's language and culture and creating a shared language and culture in the group. This occurs through telling and listening to stories. In having the privilege of being accepted as the audience for one another's stories, we have become the listeners the tellers need us to be, and have been changed. At the same time, listening has made the "performance" of stories possible, with group members and leaders being reaffirmed and transformed in a reciprocal process. . . . (Dean, 1994, p. 18)

Certain faculty projects focus specifically on facilitating dialogue among practitioners with differing perspectives. For example, one faculty member has for some time been affiliated with the Jane Doe Safety Fund, a project of the Massachusetts Coalition of Battered Women's Service Groups. She served as the facilitator for a project sponsored by the Fund to bring together workers from several areas of practice — child protective services, the shelter movement, and the courts — to discuss "maintaining the family that can provide safety and support for Its members."

The facilitator structured a series of meetings so that participants were able to hear each others' experience, to develop some common language and common purpose, and to build more collegial and trusting relationships as a base for future work together. In the first meetings, participants "brainstormed" to identify critical elements in a collaborative system to maintain the safety of children and women in families, as well as obstacles to such a system. In particular, each group was asked to identify assumptions they believed members of other systems had about them and their work which interfered with effective collaboration; interestingly, after "checking out" assumptions that they felt were unfair, they were also able to acknowledge some truth to many negative perceptions they felt others held. Finally, after this "process" work the groups were able to move on to concrete goals: refining job descriptions for domestic violence specialists and child advocates, and developing case practice guidelines for DSS workers in situations of spousal abuse and for shelter workers in situations involving children. (Fleck-Henderson, 1993)

COMMITMENT TO SHARED GOALS

MacRae et al. (1984, p. 131) suggest that, for interagency collaboration, "organizations' goals must be convergent enough so that unity of effort is achieved while they are divergent enough so that the organizations retain their unique missions." Once the divergence of goals and perspectives between schools of social work and field agencies is acknowledged and respected, their joint purpose can be underscored: educating competent, up-to-date social workers and improving service to clients. A simple statement of shared goals will hardly suffice to unite disparate organizations; in order to establish real collaboration, schools of social work and their field agencies need collective involvement in joint tasks with tangible outcomes (Homonoff & Maltz, 1991; Skaff, 1988). Fortunately, there are many opportunities for faculty and field agencies to collaborate on project which benefit both parties. For example, the second year research curriculum involves social work students in actual practice-related research projects.

> One agency long utilized as a field placement for Simmons social work interns wished to evaluate its support and education groups for parents of children with severe emotional disturbance. However, the agency did not have the resources to move from an anecdotal to an empirical understanding of the parents' needs. A faculty member from the school of social work arranged for students to conduct a needs assessment, creating and questionnaire and interviewing parents about areas of interest for group focus, and about possible barriers to participation in the program. In addition to procuring invaluable information for the agency, the students achieved a better appreciation of parents' issues in raising children with severe emotional disturbance. The agency, faculty, and students felt that they had collaborated successfully in improving the group program for parents.

In addition to improving service to clients, schools of social work and field agencies can collaborate effectively in joint political action.

> The fiscal crisis in the Commonwealth threatened the demise of one community mental health centre which had for years served as a training site for the school of social work. Interns and faculty joined a community demonstration against the closing of the centre, and wrote letters to their legislators protesting the budget cuts. Funding for the agency was restored, and the training program is alive and well.

BROADENING COLLABORATION

Social work schools are not immune to the changes affecting field agencies. In an environment of scarcity and competition, social work schools will need to share resources with other institutions in order to offer sufficiently diverse, comprehensive and coordinated services to students and training agencies. One area where resources can be shared is among the different undergraduate and graduate programs of each college. The new President of Simmons put forth in her inaugural address a new vision of collaboration within the College: "Being a unified community will mean many things . . . (in particular), we will be able to respond more fully and effectively to emerging opportunities when we can bring the resources of our entire institution to bear upon them, rather than simply the resources of individual segments." One excellent example of this collaboration is the Simmons College collaboration with the Boston Public Schools (which serve as field placements for several social work interns).

> In 1986, the Simmons College School of Social Work and Simmons College Department of Education and Human Services established the Simmons College Institute for Student Support Services, in cooperation with the Boston Public Schools. Initiatives sponsored by the Institute include a two-year program offering academic credit to Boston Public School teachers and psychological services personnel, a series of trainings for psychological and social services personnel, and a partnership with the Yale Child Study Centre for the implementation of Comer's School Development Project in select schools. In addition, the School of Social Work is beginning a pilot project to admit a small number of Boston Public School personnel to an extended master's program.

Just as the individual segments of each college or university, including schools of social work, can find greater strength and resources by collaborating with one another, several schools of social work in one geographical area can increase their strength and resources by joining forces. The Guardian Ad Litem Practicum is one program where two schools of social work collaborated with the court system to develop new training opportunities for social work interns.

> The GAL program trains master's level social work interns as guardians ad litem to three Massachusetts Probate and Family Courts. The project director is a member of the field faculty of a local school of social work, and there is a liaison to the program from another school of social work. The interns receive specialized training both from court personnel and from the project director. The courts benefit by having increased services — both high-quality guardian ad litem reports and mediation — provided by the interns. The schools of social work benefit by the development of new areas of practice for social work interns.

A more ambitious program being planned is a collaboration between many of the social work schools in Massachusetts and the Department of Social Services.

> Representatives of the social work schools have been meeting regularly with the Director of Training for the Department of Social Services to explore joint training programs. Faculty from the schools of social work could offer specialized training to DSS staff, while DSS staff could share their expertise with social work students. Intern placements in area child protection offices

could be expanded. Flexible education programs could be developed by which DSS workers could more easily obtain master's degrees in social work. A viable consortium between area schools of social work and child welfare agencies might also open up eligibility for Federal training funds.

These projects, which have united different departments and schools within the College as well as different schools of social work in the Boston area, represent a promising initiative. As the benefits and costs of the projects become clearer, the definition of fair exchange between university departments, or between schools of social work, will need to be elaborated.

SUMMARY

The relationship between schools of social work and field agencies has been deeply affected by the fiscal constraints and structural changes necessitated in the current environment of scarcity in human services. Schools and agencies can no longer take their exchanges for granted — at a time when collaboration is more imperative than ever. Exchange theory provides an excellent framework for the analysis of environmental and structural changes that affect school-agency relationships. The exchange of ideas and perspectives as well as exchange of goods and services can provide a good foundation for collaboration between schools of social work and their field agencies. Successful collaboration must be built upon the mobilization of concerned and influential participants, respect for the autonomy of systems, appreciation of divergent perspectives, and commitment to shared goals. In order to muster the resources necessary for such collaboration, social work schools will also need to consider establishing a fair exchange with other institutions: with departments and schools from other disciplines, and with other social work schools.

REFERENCES

Bocage, M., Homonoff, E., & Riley, P. (1994). Measuring the impact of the current state and national fiscal crisis on human service agencies and social work training. Accepted for publication in *Social Work.*

Born, C. (1982). Coping with an environment of scarcity: Graduate social work programs and responses to the current crisis. *Journal of Education for Social Work, 18*(3), 5-14.

Cagney, T. (1989). Managed care: A look at the past, a view of the future. *EAP Digest,* Nov/Dec, 47-52.

Davis, M. (1982). Resource scarcity in mental health: Crisis or opportunity in social work education? *Journal of Education for Social Work, 18*(3), 23-30.

Dean, R. G. (1994). Stories of AIDS: The use of narrative as an approach to understanding in an AIDS support group. Unpublished paper.

Dendiger, D., Hill, R., & Butkus, I. (1982). Malpractice insurance for practicum students: An emerging need? *Journal of Education for Social Work, 18*(1), 74-80.

Fleck-Henderson, A. (1993). Maintaining the family that can provide safety and support for its members. Unpublished paper.

Frumkin, M. (1980). Social work education and the professional commitment fallacy: A practical guide to field-school relationships. *Journal of Education for Social Work, 16*(2), 91-99.

Ginsberg, M. (1982). Maintaining quality education in the face of scarcity. *Journal of Education for Social Work, 18*(2), 5-12.

Gopelrud, E., Walfish, S., & Apsey, M. (1983). Surviving cutbacks in mental health: 77 action strategies. *Community Mental Health Journal, 19*(1), 62-76.

Hasenfeld, Y. (1983). *Human Service Organizations.* Englewood Cliffs, NJ: Prentice-Hall.

Hoffman, L. (1985). Beyond power and control: Toward a "second order" family systems therapy. *Family Systems Medicine, 3*(4), 381-393.

Homonoff, E., & Maltz, P. (1991). Developing and maintaining a coordinated system of community-based services to children. *Community Mental Health Journal, 27* (5), 347-357.

Homonoff, E., Weintraub, A., Michelson, S., & Costikyan, N. *Managing the anxiety of change for social work interns and field place.* Unpublished paper.

Knitzer, J. (1988). *Collaboration between child welfare and mental health: Emerging patterns and challenges.* Bank Street College of Education.

Kurz, R. (1989). The fate of clinical training in psychotherapy. *Clinical Supervisor, 2,* 117-121.

Leader, A. (1971). An agency's view toward education for practice. *Journal of Education for Social Work, 7,* 27-34.

MacRae, J., Lawlor, L., & Nelson, B. (1984). Counteracting bureaucratic resistance in welfare and mental health. *Administration in Mental Health, 12*(2), 123-132.

Mokuau, N., & Ewalt, P. (1993). School-agency collaboration: Enriching training, scholarship and service in state hospital placements. *Journal of Social Work Education, 29*(3), 328-337.

Mordock, J. (1989). Organizational adaptation to policy and funding shifts: The road to survival. *Child Welfare, 67,* 589-603.

Palmera, P. (1978). One foot in academia, one in practice. *Social Work,* July, 320-321.

Rosenblum, A., & Raphael, F. (1983). The role of the function of the faculty field liaison. *Journal of Education for Social Work, 19*(1), 67-74.

Shaefor, B., & Jenkins, L. (1981). Issues that affect the development of a field instruction curriculum. *Journal of Education Social Work, 17*(1), 12-20.

Skaff, L. (1988). Child maltreatment coordinating committees for effective service delivery. *Child Welfare, 67*(3), 217-230.

Stoesz, D. (1988). Human service corporations and the welfare state. *Society, 25*(5), 53-58.

Tischler, G. (1987). Meeting patient needs in the 1990's. *Administration in Mental Health, 14*(3-4), 182-190.

Urdang, E. (1991). The discipline of faculty advising. *Journal of Teaching in Social Work, 5*(1), 117-137.

Zakutansky, T., & Sirles, E. (1992). Ethical and legal issues in field education: Shared responsibility and risk. *Journal of Social Work Education, 20*(3), 338-348.

CHAPTER FIVE

THE TREND TO PROGRAM MANAGEMENT IN HOSPITALS: IMPLICATIONS FOR SOCIAL WORK EDUCATION

Butch Nutter, Ron Levin and Margot Herbert

Radical change in the way that health care is delivered, particularly within the traditional hospital setting, will effect the experience of social work students placed in these settings for field education components of their BSW programs. In the recent past, most hospitals have been organized around discipline-based departments responsible for the provision of that particular service throughout the hospital. These departments have also been responsible for supervision of their own staff and for maintaining the quality of professional services. One service provided by discipline based departments have provided is supervised educational practice opportunities for students. Typically, educators have dealt with the department that represented their discipline to secure appropriate learning opportunities for their students. The department administrator would then assign staff to provide discipline-specific instruction and supervision, usually reinforced by staff meetings and case conferences.

The new *experts* in health care, the health care economists and business trained hospital administrators now seem convinced that:

> The traditional hospital operating structure, generally thought of as functional
> in nature, is actually dysfunctional, organized not according to the way patients

are cared for, but rather according to operational specialization. (Lee & Clarke, 1992, p. 30)

The current emphasis is on "focused care" or "program-based care," where patients are categorized according to ". . . clinical care requirements, ancillary utilization needs, support needs, patient care continuums, and the physician customer profile" (Lee & Clarke, 1992, p. 31). In program-based organizations, many functional departments, including social work, have been replaced by multi-discipline and multi-skill teams that focus entirely on a group of patients with similar "customer service requirements" (Henderson & Williams, 1991).

Hospital management and nursing literature is replete with detailed descriptions of these organizational changes and their professional implications (Henderson & Williams, 1991; Monaghan, Alton, & Allen, 1992; Netting, Williams, Jones-McClintic, & Warrick, 1990; Robinson 1991; Stewart & Sherrard, 1987). The social work literature has been less responsive and has focused largely on ways to clarify social work's particular domain rather than finding creative ways to become part of the new design.

As recently as 1985, nearly one third of professional social workers in Canada worked in health care settings. Hospitals have traditionally been a major source of social work field instruction placements. However, issues of field education in the changed hospital context does not seem to have been addressed. Some important questions must be addressed. How will a program based model of service delivery accommodate the needs of faculties of social work and their students for discipline-specific educational opportunities? Who will make decisions about students, and with whom will the faculty liaise? How should social work curricula be altered in order to prepare students and graduates to function better in these radically changed practice environment?

METHOD

Data were collected using a mailed questionnaire designed by the authors. The questionnaire was accompanied by a covering letter that explained the purpose of the study and introduced the three different types of organizational structures the study focused on;

    a)   traditional social work departments;
    b)   self-directed teams; and
    c)   program managed teams.

In Section I of the questionnaire, respondents were asked to define these different organizational structures in terms of *their own* experience. Section II asked respondents to describe their own experience as hospital social workers, and, where applicable, as field instructors for BSW students. Sections III, IV, and V addressed the organizational structures separately, asking questions (a) about respondents' experience; (b) the organization of BSW field instruction; and (c) from whom the respondent received "professional social work supervision." Section VI sought respondents' opinions and advice about what BSW programmes should be doing in order to prepare students to work in health care settings.

Prior to distribution, the questionnaire was circulated to four social workers who are currently working in hospital settings and have supervised BSW students. These social workers were asked to complete the questionnaire, recording the time taken and noting any difficulties with the questionnaire. No major problems were reported and suggested changes were incorporated where appropriate.

The questionnaires were mailed to social workers in hospitals in Alberta where University of Calgary BSW students have had field placements over the past several years. Stamped envelopes were provided and responses were returned (anonymously) directly to the authors. One follow up reminder/thankyou postcard was sent to all potential respondents one week following the due date. Two hundred questionnaires were sent and 70 completed questionnaires were received, representing a return rate of 35%. Although this is not a high return rate, considering the length of the questionnaire, it is about as good as can be expected without any personalized follow-up, procedures that were incompatible with our guarantee of anonymity.

RESULTS

Defining Organizational Structures

We defined *Traditional Social Work Department* (TD), *Self Directed Social Work Team* (SDT), and *Program Managed Teams* (PMT) according to 15 functions. Each function and how we thought each organizational structure performed that function was one row in a table. Respondents were asked to tick "☐yes" if our description matched their experience. If their experience of an organizational structure was different from the description we offered, respondents were to describe their experience of that function in that organizational structure. This was equivalent to asking 45 questions; 15 functions for each of 3 organizational structures. This way of asking about organizational structures seems reasonable straight forward to people familiar with these concepts. While 47 of the 70 respondents completed this section of the questionnaire as anticipated, 23 respondents gave sets of responses that were difficult to interpret. This may indicate that the distinctions made here among organizational structures are not common discourse among hospital social workers.

Table 1 replicates the form used to ask respondents to define the organizational structures as they had experienced them in hospital social work. The first column lists the functions, one in each row. The second, third, and fourth columns, A., B., and C., are the function descriptions for TD, SDT, and PMT organizational structures, respectively. The proportion of respondents who agreed with our description is given for each description along with the number of respondents who supplied information for that cell of the table; e.g., ☑yes=96%, n=50. The fifth column contains descriptions written by respondents whose experience was different than what we described, along with the proportion of respondents who gave each of those descriptions.

Management Structure of Work Group

Nearly all respondents (96%) agreed with "Manager appointed by senior management, may appoint supervisors" as describing a TD. Although most (75%) agreed that "Leader elected by the team for a fixed short term (e.g., six months)" described SDT, some (14%) indicated that there was an "appointed manager" for their self directed team while another 11% indicated that no leader was formally designated. Nearly all of the respondents (92%) who had been in program managed teams agreed that a "Leader appointed by senior management" headed the PMT.

Disciplinary or Vocational Makeup of Work Group

About four-fifths (79%) of TDs were all social workers, but about one-fifth (19%) included other disciplines. Nearly all (96%) SDTs were composed entirely of social workers. All PMTs included more than one discipline.

Scope of Practice of Work Group

About two-thirds (70%) of TDs and nearly all (89%) of SDTs were described as doing "Single discipline — work traditionally done by social workers." Nearly one quarter (23%) of TDs were described as having a multi-discipline scope of practice. This substantially agrees with the proportion of TDs described as multi-disciplined. Nearly all respondents (89%) who had experienced PMTs agreed their work groups' scope of practice was "Multi-discipline—work required to care for patient group."

Recruit and Hire Staff

In nearly all (92%) of the TDs the manager recruits and hires staff. In nearly one half (46%) of the SDTs the team as a whole performed this function while a personnel committee did it in about one fifth (21%) of SDTs. There were many descriptions of how staff were recruited and hired in PMTs. The most popular being "Team as a whole" (36%) and "Program manager" (28%).

Performance Appraisal of Staff

Performance appraisal is nearly always (90%) done by the manager in TDs. In SDTs this function is done in several different ways, the most popular being "Team as a whole" (48%), "Committee of team" (19%), and "Manager" (11%). There appears to be even less agreement about staff appraisal in PMTs: The most popular descriptions being "Team as a whole" (24%), "Program manager" (24%), and "Program manager and social workers" (16%).

Plan and Organize Work to Meet Goals of the Organization

Respondents agreed that this function was usually done by the "Manager" (73%) in TDs and by the "Team as a whole" (74%) in PMTs. There does not appear to be a dominant way of planning work among SDTs: The "Whole team" (41%), the "Team Leader" (30%), and the "Manager and social workers across teams" (22%) were most frequently reported.

Set Standards of Professional Practice

In TDs the "Manager" usually (76%) set standards. This function was usually (82%) performed by the "Team as a whole" in SDTs. The "Discipline Leader" was agreed as setting standards of professional practice by one-third (35%) of the respondents who had been in PMTs; other responses were "Whole team" (23%) and "Social Work Council" (15%).

Set and Monitor Performance Standards; e.g., Productivity

The manager was usually (81%) identified as setting and monitoring performance standards in TDs. The "Team as a whole" did this in two-thirds (69%) of SDTs, while about one in seven (15%) reported "No process in place." This function was performed by the "Team leader" in just over half (61%) of PMTs. In a few (12%) PMTs the "Leader and social work staff" set and monitored performance standards, but "No process in place" was reported in a few (12%) PMTs.

Table 1 Defining Organizational Structures for Hospital Social Work.

Function	A. Traditional Social Work Department	B. Self Directed Social Work Team	C. Program Managed Teams	Performance of function if *not* as defined to left
1. Management structure of work group	A. Manager appointed by senior management, may appoint supervisors ☑yes=96%, n=50	B. Leader elected by the team for a fixed short term (e.g., six months) ☑yes=75%, n=28	C. Leader appointed by senior management ☑yes=92%, n=26	B. *Appointed manager = 14%* B. *None formally designated = 11%*
2. Disciplinary or vocational makeup of work group	A. Homogeneous – all social workers ☑yes=79%, n=48	B. Homogeneous – all social workers ☑yes=96%, n=28	C. Heterogeneous – disciplines as needed to do the work of the team ☑yes=100%, n=29	A. *Heterogeneous = 19%*
3. Scope of practice of work group	A. Single discipline – work traditionally done by social workers ☑yes=70%, n=43	B. Single discipline – work traditionally done by social workers ☑yes=89%, n=28	C. Multi-discipline – work required to care for patient group ☑yes=89%, n=28	A. *Multi-discipline = 23%*
4. Recruit and hire staff	A. Manager ☑yes=92%, n=48	B. Team as a whole ☑yes=46%, n=28	C. Team as a whole ☑yes=36%, n=25	B. *Personnel committee = 21%* C. *Program manager = 28%*
5. Performance appraisal of staff	A. Manager ☑yes=90%, n=48	B. Team as a whole ☑yes=48%, n=27	C. Team as a whole ☑yes=24%, n=25	B. *Committee of team = 19%* B. *Manager = 11%* C. *Program manager = 24%* C. *Program manager & SWs = 16%*
6. Plan and organize work to meet goals of the organization	A. Manager ☑yes=73%, n=48	B. Team Leader ☑yes=30%, n=27	C. Team as a whole ☑yes=74%, n=27	B. *Whole team = 41%* B. *Manager & SWs across teams = 22%*
7. Set standards of professional practice	A. Manager ☑yes=76%, n=49	B. Team as a whole ☑yes=82%, n=27	C. Discipline Leader ☑yes=35%, 26	C. *Whole team = 23%* C. *Social Work Council = 15%*

	A	B	C	Other
8. Set and monitor performance standards; e.g., productivity	A. Manager ☑yes=81%, n=48	B. Team as a whole ☑yes=69%, n=26	C. Team Leader ☑yes=61%, n=26	B. No process in place = 15% C. Leader & SW council = 12% C. No process in place = 12%
9. Ongoing training and education	A. Manager ☑yes=72%, n=46	B. Team as a whole ☑yes=82%, n=27	C. Team as a whole ☑yes=62%, n=26	A. Social Work staff = 11% C. No directions yet = 12%
10. Accountability for controlling job functions	A. Manager & senior management ☑yes=83%, n=47	B. Leader & senior management ☑yes=40%, N=25	C. Team as a whole & senior management ☑yes=70%, n=27	B. Team & management = 20% B. Whole team = 16% C. Team leader & management = 11%
11. Budgeting and expenditure control	A. Manager ☑yes=100%, n=48	B. Leader with approval of team ☑yes=29%, n=24	C. Team as a whole ☑yes=10%, n=28	B. Manager = 29% B. Manager & team = 13% B. Committee & Leader = 13% C. Program Manager = 68% C. Program Manager & team = 14%
12. Represent the work group to management	A. Manager ☑yes=94%, n=46	B. Team Leader ☑yes=76%, n=25	C. Team Leader ☑yes=89%, n=27	B. Manager & team members = 15%
13. Represent the discipline to management	A. Manager ☑yes=94%, n=47	B. Team Leader ☑yes=75%, n=24	C. Discipline Leader ☑yes=62%, n=26	B. Manager & SWs = 13% B. Manager = 13% C. Program Manager = 12%
14. Assigning work and tasks to individual work group members	A. Manager ☑yes=83%, n=48	B. Team as a whole ☑yes=73%, n=26	C. Team as a whole ☑yes=71%, n=28	B. Manager & team = 15% C. Program Manager = 14%
15. Vacation scheduling	A. Manager ☑yes=92%, n=48	B. Team Leader ☑yes=23%, n=26	C. Team Leader ☑yes=48%, n=27	B. Whole team = 38% C. Whole team = 22%

Ongoing Training and Education

"Managers" in most (72%) of TDs and the "Team as a whole" in most (82%) SDTs deal with ongoing training and education. In a few (11%) TDs the Social Work staff are reported as responsible. In PMTs, the "Team as a whole" is reported to handle this function in nearly two-thirds (62%) of cases, and a few (12%) respondents reported "No directions yet."

Accountability for Controlling Job Functions

Job functions are seen as controlled by "Manager and senior management" in most (83%) TDs. The "Leader and senior management" (40%), the "Team and senior management" (20%), and the "Whole team" (16%) were reported as accountable for controlling job functions in SDTs. Two-thirds (70%) of respondents with PMT experience agreed the "Team as a whole and senior management" were accountable for controlling job functions in PMTs.

Budgeting and Expenditure Control

The "Manager and senior management" were agreed as doing budgeting and expenditure control all (100%) TDs. There was no majority agreement about this in SDTs with about one quarter (29%) agreeing "Leader with approval of team" and about one quarter (29%) identifying a "Manager" as accountable for budgeting and expenditure control. Respondents indicated a "Program Manager" did this in about two-thirds (68%) of PMTs. A few (14%) said this function was shared by the "Program Manager and team," and one in ten (10%) agreed the "Team as a whole did budgeting and expenditure control."

Represent the Work Group to Management

The manager does this almost all (94%) the time in TDs. The "Team Leader" usually (76%) represents the work group to management in SDTs, but sometimes (15%) this is done by a "Manager and team members" in SDTs. The "Team Leader" was agreed as representing the work group to management in nearly all (89%) of the PMT responses.

Represent the Discipline to Management

The "Manager" represents the discipline in nearly all (94%) TDs. The "Team Leader" was agreed to perform this function by three quarters (75%) of workers describing SDTs. Others indicated that "Manager and social workers" (13%) or a "Manager" represented social work to management in their SDT settings. A "Discipline Leader" was identified by nearly two-thirds (62%) of respondents describing PMTs while a few (12%) identified "Program Manager" as representing Social Work to management.

Assigning Work and Tasks to Individual Work Group Members

Over four-fifths (83%) of respondents agreed the "Manager" assigned work tasks in TDs. This was usually (73%) done by the "Team as a whole" in SDTs, but sometimes (15%) done by the "Manager and team." In PMTs work assignment was usually done (71%) by the "Team as a whole," but sometimes (14%) done by the "Program Manager."

Vacation Scheduling

Nearly all (92%) respondents agreed that vacations were scheduled by the "Manager" in TDs. For SDTs the respondents identified four main ways vacations were scheduled; "Whole team" (38%), "Team leader" (23%), "Manager and team(s)" (15%), and "Sub-groups" (15%). The "Team Leader" was agreed as scheduling vacations in PMTs by half (48%) of the respondents. Another one-fifth (22%) identified the "Whole team" and a couple said the "Program Manager and discipline staff" (7%) or "Social Work sub-groups" (7%) scheduled vacations in PMTs.

Respondents

The respondents identified themselves as currently working at one of 13 hospitals, 6 in Calgary and 7 in Edmonton. Of the 66 respondents who identified the hospital at which they were employed, 36 were working in Edmonton and 30 in Calgary. Forty-four of the respondents had BSWs, 42 of the respondents had MSWs, 20 respondents had both, and 2 had neither. Of the 37 respondents who had been Field Instructors for BSW students in hospitals, 24 had BSWs, 28 had MSWs, and 16 had both: Only five had not been a Field Instructor at least once in the last five years. These Field Instructors had supervised a total of 172 students, three-quarters of them had been Field Instructors to five or fewer students. When asked "What other roles(s) if any have you played in the education of BSW students in hospitals?", 21 of the respondents who had not been Field Instructors listed a variety of activities. The most frequent were participating in a specific part of student supervision (10), "oriented new students" (7), "lectured or led seminars or in-services" (5), or coordinated field placements (2). Thus, only a dozen of the 70 respondents did not specify one or more roles they had played in hospital field education of BSW students.

Comparisons of Organizational Structures

Directors, Managers, and Supervisors

When the respondents sent in their completed questionnaires in May, 1994, 18 of them claimed to be working in traditional departments (TDs), 24 in self directed teams (SDTs), and 26 in program managed teams (PMTs). All 18 of the respondents in TDs said they had managers or directors, 10 of the 24 in SDTs said they had managers or directors, and 25 of the 26 in PMTs said they had managers or directors. Furthermore, 14 of the TD, 2 of the SDT, and 3 of the PMT respondents said their department or team had "one or more Social Work supervisor positions."

Table 2   Sources of Professional Social Work Supervision

Reported sources of professional social work supervision	Organizational structure			Total* responses
	TD	SDT	PMT	
Director, manager, or supervisor	17	2	8	27
Peer consultation	5	23	8	24
Professional council		4		3
Other	2			2
None - no one - unclear	1	2	11	14
Total respondents	16	22	24	57

*Each respondent could list up to three sources of professional social work supervision.

Professional Social Work Supervision

We asked each respondent "From whom do you receive professional social work supervision?" Up to three responses were coded for each respondent. Table 2 displays the results of this question for social workers who were in TDs, SDTs or PMTs at the time they completed the questionnaire. It is clear that respondents in PMTs indicated the least professional social work supervision, almost half of them indicating that they were receiving none. Respondents in TD and SDTs typically indicated one or two sources of professional social work supervision. However, most of the supervision in TDs came from Directors, Managers, or Supervisors while most of the supervision in SDTs came from peers and is perhaps more properly termed consultation, a term that several respondents in SDTs and PMTs used.

Decisions to Accept Social Work Students

As can be seen in Table 3, decisions about accepting social work students into the hospital are perceived to be more a management prerogative in TD and PMT and more shared in SDT forms of organization. On one hand, it is unlikely that individual social workers are assigned by management to be field instructors without some consultation. On the other hand, it is unlikely that individual social workers decide whether social work students will be accepted into their hospitals. Nonetheless, there appears to be a greater perception of shared decision making among social workers currently in self directed social work teams.

Table 3 Who Decides Whether the Hospital Accepts Social Work Students?

Person or group who decides whether to accept social work students into the hospital	Organizational structure			Total responses
	TD	SDT	PMT	
Management, directors, managers, etc.	6	1	10	17
Management & staff, team, committee	4	15	7	26
Social workers individually	4	4	7	15
Education coordinator	3	3		6
Total respondents	17	23	24	64

Deciding Who Becomes a Field Instructor

Social workers individually are reported as more likely to decide if they will be Field Instructors in TD and PMT settings. At the other extreme, respondents in TD and PMT settings were next most likely to report that who became a Field Instructor was decided by management, including appointed education coordinators. In SDT settings, deciding who will be a Field Instructor is reported to be a shared decision most of the time. Perhaps significantly, one-fifth of the respondents in PMT settings reported not knowing who decided which social workers became Field Instructors. See Table 4 for details.

Table 4   Who In the Hospital Decides If You Can Be a Field Instructor?

Person or group in the hospital who decides whether a social worker can be a field instructor	Organizational structure			Total responses
	TD	SDT	PMT	
Management: directors, managers, etc.	4	1	6	11
Management & staff, team, committee	2	11	5	16
Social work staff individually	9	6	8	23
Education coordinator	3	2	1	6
Not sure/Don't know		1	5	5
Total respondents	18	21	25	64

Work Load Adjustments

Only one-sixth of the respondents reported any formal adjustments of work loads to accommodate the functions of field instruction. Respondents in SDT settings reported sharing decision making, instruction, and work to accommodate students. Over half of the respondents reported no work load accommodation for the added duties of field instruction. About one-sixth gave answers that clearly interpretable into one the these categories. These data indicate that becoming a Field Instructor in most of these hospital settings does not lead to a decrease in other work duties or expectations. Again, sharing was more frequently identified in STD settings. See Table 5 for details.

Table 5   Work Load Adjustments For Field Instructor Functions

Provisions to accommodate field instructor functions into work loads	Organizational structure			Total responses
	TD	SDT	PMT	
Some work load recognition	4	3	3	10
Sharing work & field instruction	0	5	1	6
No workload recognition	11	9	12	32
Other	2	4	5	11
Total respondents	17	21	21	59

Hospital Contacts for Faculty Field Education Coordinators

About two-thirds of the respondents in TD and one-third in SDT and PMT settings indicated there was a particular person in their hospital designated to coordinate arrangements for field placements. Team coordinators were identified as the person to contact by half the SDT respondents. More PMT than TD or SDT social workers indicated that social workers should be contacted individually by faculty education coordinators. About one-sixth of respondents in PMT settings indicated they didn't know who to contact. See Table 6 for details.

Table 6   Hospital Contacts for Faculty Field Education Coordinators

Hospital staff to whom field coordinators should contact to secure placements for students	Organizational structure			Total responses
	TD	SDT	PMT	
Education coordinator	6	5	7	18
Management: director, manager, etc.	5	2	3	10
Team coordinator	1*	11	1	13
Social workers individually	4	4	9	17
Don't know — in transition	1		4	5
Total respondents	17	22	24	63

* "Coordinator" from two social workers in TD settings was coded "Management" in this table.

Changes in Field Instructors' Roles

Respondents currently practising in SDT and PMT settings were asked how changing to that organizational structure had affected the Field Instructor role in their hospital. In SDT three responses indicated that Field Instruction was being encouraged but five responses indicated that pressures of work, etc. were reducing the availability of field instruction or there were fewer students. Five PMT responses indicated organizational change such as changed coordinator or reorganization of field instruction. Two responses indicated that the field instruction role had become more isolated in SDT setting. For example, the Field Instructor doesn't report to anyone and no one is aware if there are problems. On the other hand, three responses in SDT and two in PMT indicated that there was more team work and sharing involved in field instruction than previously. The most popular response (7) for respondents in SDT settings was minimal or no change. As shown in Table 7, eight responses indicated unsureness about changes in PMT settings and eight responses indicated minimal or no change in PMT.

Table 7   How Changed Organizational Structure Affected Field Instructor's Role

Changes in field instructors' roles with change in organizational structure	Organizational structure changed to		Total responses*
	SDT	PMT	
Field instruction encouraged	3		3
Changed contact/organization of field instruction		5	5
Better experience for student	2		2
Less field instruction or fewer students	5	1	6
Field instruction more isolated	2		2
More team work and sharing	3	2	5
Unsure about changes if any	1	8	9
Minimal or no change	7	8	15
Total respondents	19	22	41

* Up to three responses were coded from each respondent.

Changes in Field Education of Social Work Students

About one-third of the respondents in SDT (8 of 21) and PMT (7 of 22) settings indicated that the current organizational structure was providing students with better field education opportunities. However, three SDT respondents indicated fewer field instructors or students and two indicated that field instruction was more isolated. Examples of isolation are that the Field Instructor is totally responsible and students can express their concerns only to the Faculty, there is no one in the hospital to receive student concerns. Nearly half the PMT respondents indicated unsureness about changes in social work field education that may have resulted from the change in organizational structure. About one-fourth of SDT and one-fourth of PMT respondents indicated minimal or no change to field instruction resulted from the change to their present organizational structure.

Table 8   How Organizational Change Affected Students' Field Education

Changes in students' field education after organization structure changed	Organizational structure changed to		Total responses*
	SDT	PMT	
Field instruction encouraged	2		2
Better experience for student	8	7	15
Less field instruction or fewer students	3		3
Field instruction more isolated	2		2
More team work and sharing		2	2
More breadth less depth		2	2
Unsure about changes if any	4	9	13
Minimal or no change	5	5	10
Total respondents	21	22	43

* Up to three responses were coded from each respondent.

BSW Education Curriculum

Section VI of the questionnaire began with, "We are interested in learning your opinion about how BSW education curriculum should be changed to better prepare students to work in current and future hospital and other health or medical care environments." This statement was followed by five questions, four open ended and one closed. We began our analyses by listing all the responses to the four open ended items and consolidating them, with very little reduction, into 91 categories which were then recoded into 9 categories. These categories and their included responses are:

a)   *Individual and family practice skills* — counselling skills; crisis intervention skills; discharge planning; engagement; working with families; family therapy; grief and bereavement counselling; social histories; suicide intervention; therapy (individual, group, and family); transference and counter transference; treatment skills; and clinical skills;

b)   *Community practice* — community liaison and organization and community resources;

c)   *Generic practice skills* — advocacy; assertion skills; assessment skills; case management; computer and keyboard skills; contracting; flexibility in using different methods; intervention planning; interviewing skills; meetings (chairing and agendas); professional presentation; small group processes; termination; trouble shooting; writing and documentation skills; and intervention skills;

d)   *Knowledge base* — abnormal psychology; aging; basic medical terminology (e.g., I.V.); broad theoretical base; client centred focus and empowerment; death and dying; developmental psychology; effects of illness on patients and families; ethics; family dynamics; family life cycle; health care knowledge; medical issues; mental health; over emphasis on specific theoretical frameworks; process recording; psychiatric disorders; rural studies; service ethic; social work role and belief in it; solution oriented perspective; strengths oriented perspective; and systems theory;

e)   *Evaluation and research* — evaluation and research skills; quality assurance; research skills; standards; statistics and evaluation into one course not two;

f) *Administration and organizational effectiveness* — accountability; administration policy; administration knowledge too unstable; administration trends and transitions; administrative skill; conflict resolution/management; government and agency policies; hierarchy administrative model; hiring and performance appraisal; hospital/health care structure, policy, and function; marketing Social Work services; administration important; organizational behaviour/politics; policy and affects on service delivery; present course seems sufficient; supervisory techniques; team work skills and multi-discipline collaboration; and time management;

g) *Self directed practice skills* — self administration within multi-disciplined team; self care skills, safety, change, stress; self evaluation; and self directed practice;

h) *Don't know curriculum* — a variety of ways in which respondents said they didn't know enough about the BSW curriculum to suggest alterations;

i) *Other* — all important; electives; for BSW, direct practice more important than administration; less hypothetical course work taught by researchers; more concentration, perhaps generalist BSW not appropriate; more practical knowledge taught by current practitioners; nothing; self awareness, e.g., own adolescent and parenting issues; and teaching should be evaluated.

Most Important Practice Skills and Knowledge for Health Environments

The first open ended item in Section VI asked, "What are the most important practice skills and knowledge that BSW students should be learning as part of their generalist social work curriculum?" Of the 50 respondents who answered this question, 14 were in TD, 20 in SDT, and 16 in PMT hospital settings. As shown in Table 9, the responses from these three groups were not very different from one another. Generic practice skills were the most frequently mentioned. Individual and family practice skills and knowledge base were next most frequently mentioned followed by administration and organizational effectiveness. See Table 9 for more details.

Table 9   Practice Skills and Knowledge To Include In A Generalist BSW

Practice skills and knowledge to be included in a generalist BSW curriculum	Organizational structure			Total responses*
	TD	SDT	PMT	
Individual and family practice skills	5	5	12	33
Community practice skills	3	3	3	9
Generic practice skills	25	30	28	83
Knowledge base	13	9	9	31
Evaluation and research	1	1	2	2
Administration and organizational effectiveness	5	6	6	17
Self directed practice skills		1	2	3
Other	1	1		2
Total respondents	14	20	16	50

* Up to seven responses were codes from each respondent.

Additional Practice Skills and Knowledge for Your Current Hospital Environment

Respondents were then asked, "What specific additional practice skills and knowledge should BSW students be learning in order to practice in your current hospital environment?" The 136 responses given by 52 respondents to this question are detailed in Table 10. Generic practice skill items do not dominate this list as they did the list for generalist practice in hospital settings, Table 9. In fact, knowledge base topics were more frequently given than generic practice skills, each accounting for 24% and 30% of the responses, respectively. Administration and organizational effectiveness topics were nearly one-fifth (18%) of the responses. A few respondents listed independence and self directed practice skills as important and a few also indicated that research and evaluation skills were important in their current hospital practice setting. Respondents in SDT settings listed fewer additional learning topics than respondents in TD or PMT settings. SDT respondents were much less likely to list additional individual and family practice skills and more likely to list research and evaluation. See Table 10 for details.

Table 10 Additional Learning For Specific Hospital Settings

Additional practice skills and knowledge to be included for hospital settings	Organizational structure			Total responses*
	TD	SDT	PMT	
Individual and family practice skills	6		9	15
Community practice skills	1	1	2	4
Generic practice skills	10	7	15	32
Knowledge base	16	8	15	39
Evaluation and research		5	1	6
Administration and organizational effectiveness	8	9	8	25
Self directed practice skills	3	5	2	10
Don't know curriculum		1		1
Other			1	1
Total respondents	14	19	19	52

* Up to seven responses were codes from each respondent.

Topics to be Dropped from the BSW Curriculum

If BSW curricula are full, then additional material can be added only if existing content is eliminated. Therefore we asked respondents, "What practice skills and knowledge now taught to BSW students should be dropped from the curriculum to accommodate the [additional] learning you suggest . . . ?" As can be seen in Table 11, more than half (59%) of the hospital social workers who responded to this question indicated that they were not familiar with the current BSW curriculum. The next most frequent response category was "Other." There were only 11 suggestions of what should be dropped from the curriculum to accommodate additional learning designed to prepare BSW students for practice in specific hospital settings.

Table 11   Topics To Eliminate From the BSW Curriculum

Practice skills and knowledge to be eliminated in a generalist BSW curriculum	Organizational structure			Total responses*
	TD	SDT	PMT	
Individual and family practice skills			1	1
Generic practice skills		2		2
Knowledge base	1		2	3
Evaluation and research			1	1
Administration and organizational effectiveness	1	3		4
Don't know curriculum	3	9	8	20
Other	3	3	1	7
Total respondents	7	15	12	34

* Up to three responses were codes from each respondent.

Should BSW students be taught more about administration?

Slightly more than half (28) of the 52 respondents who answered this question ticked yes. There were significant differences among respondents from hospitals with different organizational structures. Those currently in SDTs were most likely to agree that BSW students should be taught *more* about administration while those in TDs were least likely indicate that *more* administration should be taught to BSW students. See Table 12 for details.

In addition to asking whether *more* administration should be taught to BSW students, respondents were asked, "If yes, what administration topics are particularly important for BSW students to learn?" Although only 28 respondents indicated they thought more administration should be taught to BSW students, at least 33 offered opinions about specific additional administration topics that should be taught to BSW students. Three-fifths (60%) of the responses to this question were topics that we have categorized as administration and organizational effectiveness.

Table 12   Teach More Administration to BSW Students?

Should BSW students be taught more about administration?	Organizational structure			Total respondents
	TD	SDT	PMT	
Yes	3	16	9	28
No	10	5	9	24
Total respondents	13	18	15	52

$\chi^2(2, N = 52) = 9.278, p < .01$

Respondents suggested five topics that we categorized to be *generic practice skills* as additional *administration* learning. These were advocacy (4); case management (1); meetings, chairing and agenda (3); professional presentation (1); and writing and documentation (1). Self administration (3), self care skills and self directed practice (2) were also suggested by respondents as additional administration learning. It is a bit puzzling that ethics (1), health care knowledge (1), social work role and believing in it (2), and systems theory (1), topics that we classified as knowledge base, were suggested by respondents as additional administration knowledge. Less surprising is that evaluation and research (2), quality assurance (1), and standards (2) were suggested as administration topics. It is clear that respondents who are now experiencing SDT or PMT organizational structures are more supportive of additional learning about administration and organizational effectiveness as part of their BSW curriculum. This is particularly true of social workers currently in SDTs of whom three quarters (76%) indicated that BSW students should learn more about administration and who suggested 34 or the 73 topics summarized in Table 13.

DISCUSSION

We expected to find that different hospitals had implemented the same organizational structures in different ways. This tended to be confirmed by the results from Section I displayed in Table 1. We are surprised that these organizational structures and the fifteen functions we identified do not seem to be common discourse among hospital social workers. Nearly one-third (23 of 70) of the respondents did not complete Section I as we expected and our tentative conclusion is that the distinctions we have made among traditional departments, self directed teams, and program managed teams are not familiar to them. This conclusion is somewhat reinforced by workers in the same hospitals disagreeing about the organizational structure of that hospital. We received responses from social workers in 13 hospitals. Social workers in 4 of those hospitals, 2 in Calgary and 2 in Edmonton, identified themselves as currently working in different organizational structures. For example, five respondents from one hospital indicated that they were working in a traditional department and another five respondents from that same hospital indicated that they were working in a program managed team structure. Similarly, three respondents from one hospital indicated they were working in a traditional department while five of their colleagues in that hospital said they were working in self directed teams. Six respondents from another hospital indicated they were working in a TD setting, while two or their colleagues indicated they were working in an STD setting, and another five of their colleagues chose PMT as the most appropriate description of the organizational structure they were currently working in. However, it is possible, given the rapidly shifting organizational structures in Alberta hospitals, that all of these social workers were relatively accurate about their current work situations.

Table 13 **Administration Topics Particularly Important for BSW Students**

Administration topics to be included in a generalist BSW curriculum	Organizational structure			Total responses*
	TD	SDT	PMT	
Generic practice skills	2	5	3	10
Knowledge base	1	3	1	5
Evaluation and research		3	2	5
Administration and organizational effectiveness	7	19	18	44
Self directed practice	3	3		6
Don't know curriculum		1		1
Other			2	2
Total respondents	6	17	14	37

* Up to four responses were codes from each respondent.

The effects, if any, that different organization structures may have on BSW field education are not well defined by these data. There appears to be as much variability within organizational structures as between organizational structures. The majority perception seems to be that changing organizational structures has disrupted familiar patterns and relationships within colleague groups and between hospitals and the Faculty of Social Work. However, there is not consistent evidence of reduced opportunities for BSW field education in hospitals with SDTs and PMTs. Indeed, there seems to be a perception that learning opportunities for BSW students may have expanded.

On the other hand, the may now be fewer placements in hospitals. This perceived decrease in placement opportunities may be more a function of the specific workers involved than inherent in the organizational structures. However, the availability of field placements in SDT and PMT settings may be much more dependent upon the professional commitment of individual social workers. For example, one hospital in this sample typically accepted only one or two BSW students per year when Social Work operated there as a traditional department. When they moved to a "self directed team" structure, they wanted at least five or six BSW students per session, 10 to 12 per year. During transitions from one organizational structure to another, field placement coordinators may have to relate directly to individual social workers while new institutional arrangements are being developed.

There seems to be substantial agreement that administration and organizational effectiveness should continue to be taught as part of the BSW curriculum. More than half of the respondents who ventured an opinion, indicated that teaching of administration should be *increased*. On the other hand, it is clear that we could be doing a better job of informing social work practitioners about our current curriculum. A substantial proportion of respondents indicated that they were unfamiliar with our current BSW curriculum.

For most social workers practising in these hospitals, becoming a Field Instructor is an act of personal dedication to the profession. Very few indicated that their employers gave any formal recognition of the time and effort involved by reducing their work loads. There is some indication that in SDTs, field instruction is a more shared activity. However, there are also indications that field instruction may be a more isolated activity in SDTs. Respondents mentioned that the field instructor had total responsibility and that if students had difficulties, there was no one in the hospital that they could approach because of the absence of supervisors, managers, and directors. This may be particularly troublesome in PMT settings where a large proportion of the respondents indicated that they were currently receiving no professional social work supervision.

On the other hand, notions of supervision in social work may be undergoing some very useful redefinition. As Marian Bogo (personal communication 1994) pointed out, *consultation* is a much more appropriate description than *supervision* of what professional social workers should be seeking. Consultation with professional colleagues carries with it the information content of *supervision* without the expectation that the consultant(s) can or should control how the social worker uses the information. Thus, seeking consultation would appear to be a much more mature process than being required to submit to and follow supervision. However, it may be very important for hospitals to recognize the importance of this consultation process and to encourage social workers to develop professional councils or professional standards boards as suggested by Globerman and Bogo in the next chapter. At the very least, this will probably require that hospitals recognize participation in these *professional* consultation and affiliation activities, including field instruction, as legitimate parts of their employment duties.

It is clear that changing organizational structures in hospitals are causing considerable distress among social workers who have been employed in those setting for many years. However, the new structures of SDT and PMT with their emphasis upon cooperation and team work are much more compatible with social work values and ethics than the rigid hierarchical organizational structures that have dominated most hospital and other illness care settings in the past. These changes provide exciting opportunities for social workers and the education of social workers. It is clear that these opportunities are not without significant challenges. Partnerships between social work teachers, particularly faculty and field instructors, can significantly advance social work in hospitals and the teaching of social work in hospitals.

REFERENCES

Henderson, J. L., & Williams, B. (1991, July/August). The people side of patient care redesign. *Healthcare Forum Journal.*

Lee, J. G., & Clarke, R. W. (1992, November). Restructuring improves hospital competitiveness. *Healthcare Financial Management.*

Monaghan, B. J., Alton, L., & Allen, D. (1992). Transition to program management. *Leadership in Health Services*, 1(5).

Netting, F. E., Williams, F. G., Jones-McClintic, S., & Warrick, L. (1990, February). Policies to enhance coordination in hospital-based case management programs. *Health and Social Work.*

Robinson, N. C. (1991, September). A patient centred framework for restructuring care. *Journal of Nursing Administration*, 21(9).

Stewart, N., & Sherrard, H. (1987). Managing hospitals from a program perspective. *Health Management Forum*, 8(1).

CHAPTER SIX

SOCIAL WORK AND THE NEW INTEGRATIVE HOSPITAL

Judith Globerman and Marion Bogo

INTRODUCTION

The principles of bureaucratically organized hospitals are counter to the values of social work. In a move to new integrative hospitals, social work can be the champions. The values of the social work profession that emphasize negotiation, change, flexibility, relationships, choice and control, the right to exercise autonomy, and participatory decision-making, are congruent with the principles that form the foundation for the new integrative models for hospitals. A model for the organization of social work practice, continuing education, standard setting, research and the student program, The Professional Standards Group, is proposed for the new hospital age.

Fiscal restraint is leading to more and more hospital restructuring, particularly the movement from bureaucratic to integrative organizations. This has resulted in downsizing and flattening of the administrative structure of hospitals and a concomitant need for professional groups to define and justify themselves to the administration and each other. The issue of maintaining professional boundaries in integrative hospitals has been controversial, with the professions arguing that standards and practice expertise vary, are discipline-specific, and need a home, and some health administrators arguing for cross-trained staff to reduce territorialism as a mechanism to improve patient care and reduce costs (Koch-Schulte, 1991; Henderson & Williams, 1991).

Developing structures to maintain professional disciplines in hospitals has been a challenge for all health science disciplines. Without an organizational model that is congruent with the values of the restructured organization, it has been difficult for the professions to support their arguments for the maintenance of discipline-specific departments. The values of the new integrative hospital and social work do not conflict, and are in fact, quite compatible. This paper examines these values and a model, The Social Work Professional Standards Group (PSG), that depicts the way the discipline can be organized in decentralized integrative hospitals.

THE BUREAUCRATIC MODEL

Most hospitals were organized according to the bureaucratic model (Fogel, 1989). The bureaucratic model, which adopts a pyramidal, hierarchical, centralized structure, assigns responsibility for decision-making, policy formulation, objective setting and control to the upper-levels of management (Weber, 1991). The structure reinforces the maintenance of order by utilizing vertical communication with successive ascending levels responsible for control and accountability.

In the bureaucratic organization, traditionally, rules are set by upper level management, to be carried out by front line workers. However, due to the centralized, hierarchical structure, control by management of the nature of the work and the workers is extremely difficult (Fogel, 1989). With restricted awareness of the nature of workers' experiences and limited ability to control workers, which comes with increased size and a focus on productivity, efficiency, tasks, and outputs exclusively, hospital organizations are beginning to experience value conflicts with workers. The workers, givers of care, receive little emotional and social support from the organization, and patient care, the object of the work, becomes distant from the organizational objectives. With recent financial crises in health care, quality becomes defined by economics not professional standards or patient experience. Although hospitals have attempted to flatten their decision-making and communication structures to address these concerns, they have "perhaps been the slowest to adapt human relations strategies to the workplace" (Porter-O'Grady & Finnigan, 1984; Porter-O'Grady, 1990).

Social work, in bureaucratically-structured hospital organizations traditionally has been organized with a centralized department led by a Director of Social Work. Social workers are hired, assigned to work in units and wards, and fired, by the Director. Consistent with the bureaucratic model, the Director of Social Work was an administrator whose role was to manage workload, budget, policy development, and the development and enforcement of standards. However, what is unique and distinct about the way social workers manage their work on their units in bureaucratic organizations is that they are team players (Donnelly, 1992). Social workers are well equipped through their practice knowledge and skills to work with a variety of professional and staff groups and individuals, focusing as much on the process of the work and on communication, as on outcome (Patti & Ezell, 1988; Brown & Furstenberg, 1992). Although bureaucratic structures give little real power to workers (Fogel, 1989), social workers have used their practice and theoretical knowledge about human behavior and systems to manage their work environments and influence patient care (Berger, 1990).

Systems theory and the ecological perspective are the key theoretical approaches to social work in health care (Germain, 1984; Bogo & Taylor, 1990; Bogo, 1991). Emphasizing the person in environment, these models equip social workers for multidisciplinary practice with individuals, groups, families, and communities. Many social workers in hospitals define their roles with the interdisciplinary staff and patients as facilitators and negotiators (Holosko, 1992; Donnelly, 1992; Holloway & Berger, 1985). Social work has valued these roles and made them a priority, often at the expense of evaluating their clinical practice (Pruet, Shea, Zimmerman, & Parish, 1991). As a result of this focus on process, social workers are very skilled at transforming the nature of their work and the workplace into enclaves of participatory, accountable, and empowering, as opposed to bureaucratic, units (Rehr, 1985; Spano & Lund, 1986).

INTEGRATIVE ORGANIZATIONS

Many hospitals, responding to fiscal constraints, the need to improve productivity and the need to be more accountable to patients, are moving away from bureaucratic toward integrative organizations (Clement, 1988; Charns & Tewksbury, 1993). The literature on hospital reorganization features several organizational models that emphasize a refocussing on the patient (Brider, 1992; Weber, 1991; Lathrop, 1991, 1992; Porter-O'Grady, 1993), reorganizing responsibility and accountability among staff (Porter-O'Grady, 1989; McMahon, 1992; Peterson & Allen, 1986a, 1986b; Porter-O'Grady & Finnigan, 1984), the flattening of the hierarchical structure (Charns & Tewksbury, 1993), and a focus on the rapid and changing nature of knowledge (Drucker, 1991, 1992; Fogel, 1989; Peters, 1992).

The bureaucratic organization of hospitals favours a differentiated model wherein hospitals are organized by function into departments, for example a Department of Social Work. The advantage of this model is that the policies, procedures and goals of professional disciplines such as social work are developed by social work according to the profession's definition of its work. This allows the discipline control over its staff, the knowledge base, standards of practice, relationships with the community and relationships with others in the organization (Charns & Tewksbury, 1993, p. 24).

Hospital organization falls on a continuum from bureaucratic to integrative organizations. In fully integrative organizations discipline-specific departments are eliminated to allow a focus on collaboration, coordination, interconnection, shared resources and integration (Charns & Tewksbury, 1993). However, purely integrative organizations are rarely found in practice (Charns & Tewksbury, 1993, p. 41). Modified integrative models that emphasize integration over differentiation are the current new models for hospital reorganization (Weber, 1991). The key features of these modified integrative hospitals are a patient-focus organized according to programs of service such as "trauma," and/or a population focus, such as "aging." Professional staff are responsible to the programs or units and not to a discipline-specific department. Discipline-specific departments such as a Department of Social Work or a Department of Psychology are disbanded. Integrative organizations that decentralize professional service are not organized according to a matrix model; they are programmatic. The management of integrative organizations is frequently referred to as programme management (Charns & Tewksbury, 1993, p. 41). Although social work would be required to reorganize in these new integrative structures, the basic values of integrative organizations are closer to the values and ethics of the social work profession than those found in bureaucratic organizations.

The Patient-Focused Hospital

Patient-focused hospitals are one of the models for hospital reorganization that encompass the principles of integration over differentiation. This anti-hierarchical, anti-bureaucratic model was developed to enhance service, increase patient and staff satisfaction, improve the quality of care, and reduce expenses (Weber, 1991). Its focus is reorganizing care away from functions to a central focus on the patient. In this model patients are admitted directly to service units, where cross-trained staff who "own the patients" practice shared governance (Lathrop, 1991, 1992; Brider, 1992).

The patient-focused model values the patient and is problem-based. This value and model is congruent with social workers' concern which traditionally has been patient-focused and problem-based (Donnelly, 1992; Cowles & Lefcowitz, 1992).

Accountability and the Hierarchy

A decision-making model utilized in integrative hospitals, that addresses accountability is shared governance. This model flattens the hierarchical accountability structure. It is a model of decision-making utilized in patient-focused hospitals that empowers the worker, shifting ownership of practice decisions to line staff. Under shared governance social work staff are responsible and accountable for all practice, quality and education decisions (McMahon, 1992). A move to shared governance would result in the need for social workers to be trained and to see themselves as autonomous and independent professional practitioners. While these characteristics are currently valued, changes in the organization's structure make these qualities even more necessary. As a result of the elimination of a Department of Social Work, and the development of shared governance, social workers would, like physicians, seek consultation when needed, and would not function under the current social work supervisory model favoured by many social workers (Devereux & Payne, 1991; Ross, 1992).

Currently in bureaucratic hospitals the organization of social work incorporates some of the principles of shared governance. Within a bureaucratic model, social workers have limited power. However, within their units in bureaucratic hospitals, they are frequently more empowered than other professional groups, working collaboratively as key facilitators of interdisciplinary communication (Berger, 1990). Social work's historic involvement in multiple types of practice — clinical care, discharge planning, community care, policy making, and team functioning — has contributed to some autonomy in practice decision-making and some control over their work (Holosko, 1992; Marcus, 1987, 1990; Berger, 1990). Thus the move to integrative hospitals which value collaboration would not be foreign to social workers in hospitals, and would in reality, reinforce and legitimate the work of the profession.

Changing Nature of Knowledge

Drucker (1991, 1992) suggests that the modern organization must recognize knowledge as its primary resource. He emphasizes the need for decentralized, integrative organizations to function as teams to enhance opportunities for knowledge generation: "Because the modern organization consists of knowledge specialists it has to be an organization of equals, of colleagues and associates; each is judged by its contribution to the common task rather than by any inherent superiority or inferiority" (Drucker, 1992, p. 101). Peters (1992, p. 441) reiterates the connection between reorganization and knowledge underscoring how bureaucracies reinforce mediocrity and result in organizations where "experts were transmogrified mostly into policemen, overseeing the manual that defined their function's responsibility. . . ." Against these odds the social work profession in bureaucratically organized hospitals has managed, with much cost and struggle to maintain a focus on the patient and a strong commitment to the right of the patient and family to autonomy and participatory decision-making.

Thus, according to organizational theorists (Drucker, 1991, 1992; Peters, 1992), to maintain its power, its relevance, and its currency, the new integrative hospital must recognize the value of knowledge generation. Drucker (1992) suggests that the modern organization, if it is to survive, must be organized for continuous self improvement, must exploit its knowledge-generating ideas, promote research and education, and must learn to value innovation and change. Organizationally, in integrative hospitals, discipline-specific departments would be replaced with structures that focus on education, research, professional standards and teaching. Within the integrative organization this structure would be responsible for, and final arbiter of all aspects of the work that impact on the profession.

There is no social work literature on the organization and management of education, research and professional standards for practice in integrative hospitals. Porter-O'Grady and Finnigan (1984) recommend, for nursing, a five council system — management, practice, quality assurance, education, and coordination — with functional accountability for practice, governance, quality assurance, professional development, and peer behavior. Structurally this model is cumbersome for hospital social work: there are many fewer social workers than nurses in hospitals; social workers tend to have university degrees; tend to practice more independently and autonomously; roles and responsibilities are more flexible, less structured and less controlled; and social workers have more control over the nature of their work life such as hours and shifts. However, the council model emphasizes the integration of practice with standards and education, and in this way parallels the proposed model for social work.

The main disadvantages of program management relate to the fostering of territorialism by programs and the weakening of a voice for the profession (Charns & Tewksbury, 1993, p. 40). The issue for the social work profession in both the modified and pure integrative model such as program management, relates to power. How does a profession maintain and control standards for professional practice, practitioner education, teaching and research in decentralized, integrative organizations? The challenge for social work is to develop an organizational model that addresses the need to be active knowledge-generating professionals, consumers of research, accountable and autonomous, and focused on practice innovation and change. One such model is "The Professional Standards Group."

THE PROFESSIONAL STANDARDS GROUP

A "Professional Standards Group" is proposed as an organizational framework for the continuing education, research and teaching functions of social work in integrative hospitals where traditional departmental structures have been dissolved. In their mission statements most integrative hospitals commit themselves to further the quality of patient care and contribute to the development of knowledge (Weber, 1991). The challenge for social work is to design a system whose primary goal is the development and support of effective, accountable practitioners, educators, and researchers.

The Professional Standards Group would not be distinct to university teaching hospitals. In community and non-teaching integrative hospitals social work must also see itself as responsive to new knowledge, prepared for innovation and change and willing to manage self governance as autonomous and independent professionals.

The Social Work Professional Standards Group would be the organization's decision-making body, with organizational power for professional issues related to continuing education, standard setting, social work research, and the teaching of students. The Professional Standards Group activities are integrated, and all build on each other. The model in Figure 1 shows the iterative nature of The Professional Standards Group and its position in the integrative hospital. The student programs in university teaching hospitals would be a part of the Professional Standards Group and integrated with many of the activities of the PSG.

All social workers in the hospital would participate in the PSG under the coordination of a Professional Standards Group Coordinator. In keeping with the integrative hospital model, the social workers would be accountable to their units or programs for service, and function within a team context. However, the development, promotion, and maintenance of their professional social work knowledge and social work practice expertise would be in the hands of their professional body - The Social Work Professional Standards Group. The PSG would have definitive responsibility for ensuring standards of professional social work practice.

Standards and Continuing Education

The Professional Standards Group model is cyclical, with no natural point of origin (see Figure 1). Professional social workers join the hospital organization with professional qualifications and expertise. The PSG has responsibility for ensuring that this expertise is further developed and maintained. Thus this discussion of the Professional Standards Group model begins with a discussion of the role of the PSG in developing practice standards.

Standard setting involves incorporation of new knowledge to ensure the most effective professional practice. Drucker (1991, p. 78) identifies education as the key to improving professional practice, which in turn improves service in the organization. New knowledge leads to the development of new standards, innovation and change in professional practice, and mechanisms for evaluating professional practice. Research leads to new knowledge and continuing education, as well as further development of professional practice (see Figure 1) (Pruet et al., 1991). To support this effort and achieve this end, the PSG would be responsible for developing and supporting continuing education of social work staff and standard setting for social work practice in the hospital.

Programs for continuing education would be organized by a Professional Standards Group Coordinator who would utilize several organizational models. One model involves a committee structure wherein social workers would distribute themselves into committees responsible for continuing education programs. In a second model, an allocation model, social workers would be allocated responsibility for programs or aspects of continuing education, by the PSG Coordinator. A third model for the organization of continuing education, a voluntary model, is less structured than the committee or allocation models, and is purely voluntary. In this model workers would decide on the organizational structure necessary to plan continuing education, and volunteer if interested. The success of the continuing education programs, in this, the most autonomous model, depends on the individual worker's strengths, expertise and enthusiasm for new knowledge.

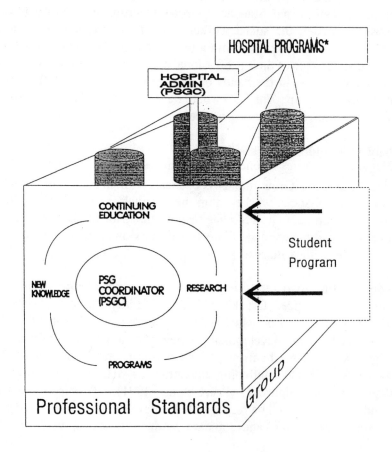

Figure 1   The Professional Standards Group in the Integrative Hospital
* Examples of Hospital Programs: by service — "trauma," by population — "aging."

Most hospital Departments of Social Work have methods for organizing continuing education and standard setting. Without a departmental structure with a key responsible individual, a Director, this function has to be structured in such a way that individual social workers working on disparate programs who have no social work departmental meetings or formal communication mechanisms, are brought together. This structure differs from the traditional departmental structure in that the PSGC functions as a coordinator and the workers, utilizing shared governance, determine the organizational structure. In traditional hospital organizations the Director, while likely to consult with staff, frequently has the authority to make these decisions independently based on her/his expertise, connections with standard-setting bodies, professional organizations, the university, and the hospital administration.

Standard setting is informed by new knowledge which in turn leads to program change, innovation and development (see Figure 1). A number of continuing education programs can be developed that are grounded in social workers' hospital practice. One such program involves workers in journal clubs where relevant social work practice research literature is read, appraised, and discussed by social workers interested in similar issues. The Social Work Professional Standards Group in large hospitals would have several journal clubs where workers would appraise research literature related to their particular practice issues in one journal club, as well as literature that cuts across all units such as articles on social welfare and community health issues or generic social work interventions, in another journal club. These journal clubs usually meet monthly for two hours, with rotating chairs, where one or two social workers take responsibility for leadership.

Social work "rounds" that model medical rounds, are another effective educational program in hospitals. In social work rounds, held monthly or every two months, social workers present case or issue-specific material to their social work colleagues for discussion and consultation. All social workers participate in all rounds, as this forum offers all workers the opportunity to learn about practice and share practice issues across units/wards. Hospital-based continuing education can be organized utilizing external resources as well. Social work "clinic days" are one form of educational program that utilise external experts to present workshops or lectures on clinical subjects or clinical interventions. These "clinic days" are usually organized to attract large numbers of social workers from other centres, for a fee. Besides exposing the hospital workers to a new approach, model, or idea, clinic days serve to bring social workers together, build rapport, increase pride in the profession and institution, and enhance networking across organizations. These programs currently exist in many bureaucratically structured institutions. However, without a departmental structure their maintenance can be lost, resulting in a weakening of the professional discipline. Developing a new organizational model that suits integrative organizations, that involves all the social workers is critical to house, organize, develop and maintain these programs.

In many bureaucratically structured institutions social work supervisors work with individual workers to monitor and evaluate their practice. In an integrative hospital a peer evaluation mechanism would need to be developed through the Social Work Professional Standards Group to assist workers to achieve continuous practice effectiveness. It is through the PSG that standards for social work practice are developed, set, monitored, evaluated, and sanctions applied. All social workers in the hospital are involved in the process of identifying the principles, values, and tasks involved in effective practice. Once standards for social work practice are developed by the social workers, through the PSG they develop mechanisms to evaluate professional practice on the different units. These may vary by unit, or cut across units, such as standards relating to discharge planning. Depending on the way teams or units are organized the PSG Coordinator would utilize social work peer consultation, peer or self-evaluations, or cross-discipline evaluations to monitor and evaluate practice. These data would be used by the PSG Coordinator to make decisions about social workers' progress through the ranks, funding workers to attend external workshops and courses, take leaves of absence to pursue higher education, and provide field instruction for students.

Practice Research

"Every organization must devote itself to creating the new" (Drucker, 1992, p. 97). The development, promotion, monitoring, and maintenance of on-going social work research is paramount for the continuance of the profession in hospitals. Historically, with the need to help patients negotiate their hospital stays in often very dehumanizing environments, social work in hospitals focused on process, not outcome. Social work practice has recently moved dramatically into a knowledge expanding phase as a result of the need for the profession to examine the effectiveness of its work (Rapp & Poertner, 1987; Wells, 1991). Applied research, conducted by hospital social workers, about relevant practice issues is the most valuable model for research and recommended over the appointment of one social work researcher to conduct studies in a hospital (Pruet et al., 1991). However, ongoing research requires training and support of social workers and an on-site researcher who can consult, assist, and supervise social work research is an effective way of ensuring innovation and change.

Research seminars organized for all social workers by The Social Work Professional Standards Group, and held regularly are a useful way of integrating research into the hospital. These seminars are organized to foster peer support and education, teach research, and as a forum for social workers to discuss research issues. The research seminars addressing research methods can be organized in a modular format. In this design, a practice effectiveness module would involve social workers from different units or programs. Each would attend the practice effectiveness module seminars with their own research question about some aspect of their practice, and with a peer group, examine the research process. The workers would be learning by doing, without suspending their practice.

Research seminars are also valuable when utilized to discuss research issues such as the ethics of research with patients, funding and grant writing, issues in research collaboration with other disciplines, or sampling issues. Social workers, both involved and not involved in conducting their own research, are brought together from different units to discuss research issues with colleagues. This is an effective means to familiarize workers with research and demystify research.

The involvement of social workers in hospitals with students' theses is another way to include research in social workers' hospital practice. Traditionally, it is the responsibility of the university course and thesis instructors to teach students research methods. It is not expected that hospital social work field instructors oversee the research education. However, social workers can be involved in assisting students to find relevant research topics, questions, and literature. The social workers are well equipped to discuss issues related to ethics, sampling, and politics of research at the hospital. They can help students negotiate their way with other professional and non-professional staff and gatekeepers, so projects are manageable and less likely to derail. Finally, participating with students in their projects exposes all workers to the process of research, familiarizing them with literature, designs, models, and methods, making research as much a part of their everyday social work lives as their current clinical practice. The sharing of this knowledge and experience can also be a part of the research seminar. Students can regularly present their research questions, designs and dilemmas to social workers in other parts of the hospital for discussion and consultation.

A research consortium model is also an effective way of involving social workers with research. A successful health research consortium in Toronto, Canada involves social workers from 10 hospitals and social work colleagues at a major research university, in collaborative research (Bogo, et al., 1992). They have developed a high risk screening tool which is currently being tested at 5 hospitals. This model fosters inter-hospital collaboration, innovation, and the sharing of knowledge, experience and expertise. Through the consortium other linkages are formed and individual social workers find like-minded colleagues with whom to collaborate. Collaboration with the university also leads to research on teaching and models for consultation and educational practice.

Student Program

"Knowledge workers and service workers learn most when they teach" (Drucker, 1991, p. 78). The Social Work Professional Standards Group is responsible for organizing student teaching in integrative hospitals. The PSG develops an educational program to reflect the integration of theory, research, and practice. The social workers articulate their conceptual, theoretical, and practice models and utilize these to develop the specifics of their educational programs (Bogo & Globerman, 1993). It is the responsibility of The Professional Standards Group to organize and monitor students' educational experiences in the hospital. Involvement of the hospital social workers with students is a key way the social workers can keep current. Whether the hospital has one student or many, active participation in students' educational experiences ensures the survival of the profession.

The student program is integrated with the PSG. Students are involved in the PSG journal clubs, social work rounds, and research rounds. The students' research projects and theses are grounded in their hospital practice and students participate in research seminars and discussions.

Involvement of social workers, who themselves do not offer student practica, in the development of educational programs is also important to the intraprofessional collaboration in integrative institutions. Without the bureaucratic organization that secures a departmental structure, the profession risks disintegration. Within the integrative hospital, involvement in the student educational program is another way social workers can bridge programs/units and meet around professional issues. A number of aspects of the educational program can involve different workers. These include determining criteria for worker entitlement to participate in the student program and organizing support mechanisms for students and field instructors. Social workers can also be involved in developing orientations for students to the hospital, the organization, and the profession. They can be involved in developing educational seminars and programs on generic topics such as ethics, multidisciplinary practice, teamwork, or quality of care in hospitals. Social workers can also develop linkages with educational institutions through students, which serve to promote the development of research, education and practice collaboration.

The Professional Standards Group student program would develop an educational consultative model for social workers who are providing student education. The aim is to develop their competence as social work practice educators through a variety of educational activities such as reviews of student-client tapes and student-field instructor tapes, discussion of common issues and the development of problem-solving strategies, and discussion of theories and alternative practice models.

THE PROFESSIONAL STANDARDS GROUP COORDINATOR

The Professional Standards Group is an organizing framework for professional social work continuing education, standard setting, research and the student program in integrative hospitals where the departmental structure has been disbanded through hospital reorganization. The Coordinator of The Social Work Professional Standards Group must be a senior social worker who demonstrates advanced knowledge of hospital social work. As the key spokesperson for the profession in the hospital, she/he must command respect and as such be an expert in practice, knowledgeable about research, and an experienced advanced educator. The PSG Coordinator is involved in the development of new educational models and research initiatives in the hospital. In the integrative organization these are the key characteristics of a leader, whereas in the bureaucratic organization, the Social Work Director had to be a manager and a comptroller as well. In the integrative hospitals, the PSG Coordinator is the chief of the discipline, comparable to the medical chiefs of service, relinquishing administrative roles. In The Professional Standards Group, the social workers practice shared governance, being responsible for developing, monitoring, and evaluating key professional aspects of their own practice. The PSG Coordinator has to be comfortable with this collaborative model. She/he is the social workers' voice to the hospital administration, a consultant to the social workers, and responsible for ensuring the functioning of The Professional Standards Group.

The Professional Standards Group Coordinator (PSGC) is ultimately responsible for developing, monitoring, and setting standards for social work practice, research, and education. As such the PSGC is responsible for ensuring that systems for education and teaching of both students and social work staff are developed, remain current, are innovative and responsible. The PSG Coordinator is also responsible for social work staff progress through the ranks. The development of criteria for staff movement can be the purview of the PSG Coordinator or a Professional Standards Group committee.

In the integrative hospital organization the PSG Coordinator is a member of the hospital management team. As the profession's champion and advocate the PSGC is responsible to the programs and the hospital management for ensuring professional social work standards and behavior. To bring the professional voice to the decision and policy-making bodies, the PSG Coordinator must be allocated real power in the hospital administration.

Hospital administrative structures vary and a number of new integrative models demonstrate flattened hierarchies with professional advisory committees. The Social Work Professional Standards Group Coordinator can be positioned in a professional advisory committee which usually includes other disciplines' PSG Coordinators plus senior managers responsible for professional services and quality assurance if such positions exist in the hospital administrative structure. This committee would have a direct reporting relationship to the Board, and utilizing a shared governance model, be responsible for policy development, dispute resolution, and decision-making regarding professional issues that cross discipline boundaries and affect all disciplines.

The Professional Standards Group Coordinator would also be expected to have an independent reporting relationship to a senior corporate executive such as Vice-President Professional Affairs, for discipline-specific professional issues. The PSG utilizes a shared governance model and this model ensures that the PSGC represents to the hospital administration the ideas, innovations, challenges, interests, and issues of all of the social work staff. Thus the PSGC does not function independently or autonomously from the PSG.

The Social Work Professional Standards Group Coordinator, through some direct relationship to the hospital administration such as through a professional advisory committee and/or a senior executive officer, would have final authority around disputes with programs regarding professional social work issues. In the spirit of shared governance, ultimate responsibility for professional issues must be situated with the professional discipline.

CONCLUSION

The integrative hospital values patient-focused, accountable and responsible professionals. Collaboration, a flattened hierarchy, and a focus on innovation and the creation of new knowledge are the means to that end. Social work practice is at the forefront in patient-focused teamwork and collaborative management of patient care. However, social workers in hospitals have been slow to evaluate their practice and to practice as autonomous professionals. The movement toward integrative from bureaucratic organizations is a challenge for social work. Therefore, new frameworks are needed so that social work can develop, maintain, and enhance professional knowledge and standards. Interconnections between social workers in various units can be forged around The Social Work Professional Standards Group, which organizes the professional interests of social work in education, research and teaching and serves as a useful model for decentralized departments. "Innovation and change are difficult to achieve" in bureaucratic organizations (Fogel, 1989, p. 17), but The Professional Standards Group model offers an exciting opportunity for integration and change in the integrative organization. The reorganization of hospitals is new and models for the organization of disciplines are all in formation. This paper suggests one model that is currently being developed in several organizations moving from bureaucratic to integrative systems. Comparative research on the efficacy of the various experimental, pilot, and evolving models is critical to the development of effective patient care.

REFERENCES

Berger, C. S. (1990). Enhancing social work influence in the hospital: Identifying sources of power. *Social Work in Health Care, 15*(2), 77-93.

Bogo, M. (1991). Education for social work practice in the health field. In P. Taylor & J. Devereux (Eds.), *Social work administrative practice in health care settings* (pp. 233-245). Toronto: Canadian Scholars' Press.

Bogo, M., & Globerman, J. (1993). Creating effective university-field partnerships: An analysis of two inter-organization models for field education. Unpublished manuscript.

Bogo, M., & Taylor, I. (1990). A practicum curriculum in a health specialization: A framework for hospitals. *Journal of Social Work Education, 26*(1), 76-86.

Bogo, M., Wells, L., Abbey, S., Bergman, A., Chandler, V., Embleton, L., Guirgis, S., Huot, A., McNeill, T., Prentice, L., Stapleton, D., Shekter-Wolfson, L., & Urman, S. (1992). Advancing social work practice in the health field: A collaborative research partnership. *Health and Social Work, 17*(3), 223-235.

Brider, P. (1992). Patient-focused care. *American Journal of Nursing*, Sept, 27-33.

Brown, J. S. T., & Furstenberg, A. (1992). Restoring control: Empowering older patients and their families during health crisis. *Social Work in Health Care, 17*(4), 81-101.

Charns, M. P., & Tewksbury, L. S. (1993). *Collaborative management in health care: Implementing the integrative organization.* San Francisco: Jossey-Bass.

Clement, J. P. (1988). Vertical integration and diversification of acute care hospitals: Conceptual definitions. *Hospital and Health Services, 33*(1), 99-110.

Cowles, L. A., & Lefcowitz, M. J. (1992). Interdisciplinary expectations of the medical social worker in the hospital setting. *Health and Social Work, 17*(1), 57-65.

Devereux, J., & Payne, E. (1991). Social work supervision: A quality function. In P. Taylor & J. Devereux (Eds.), *Social work administrative practice in health care settings* (pp. 133-144). Toronto: Canadian Scholars' Press.

Donnelly, J. P. (1992). A frame for defining social work in a hospital setting. *Social Work in Health Care, 18*(1), 107-119.

Drucker, P. F. (1991). The new productivity challenge. *Harvard Business Review,* Nov/Dec, 69-79.

Drucker, P. F. (1992). The new society of organizations. *Harvard Business Review* Sept/Oct, 95-104.

Fogel, D. S. (1989). The uniqueness of a professionally dominated organization. *Health Care Management Review, 14*(3), 15-24.

Germain, C. (1984). *Social work practice in health care: An ecological perspective.* New York: The Free Press.

Henderson, J. L., & Williams, J. B. (1991). The people side of patient care redesign. *Healthcare Forum Journal,* July/Aug, 44-49.

Holloway, S., & Berger, G. (1985). Implicit negotiations and organizational practice. *Administration in Social Work, 9*(2), 15-24.

Holosko, M. J. (1992). Social work practice roles in health care: Daring to be different. In M. J. Holosko & P. Taylor (Eds.), *Social work practice in health care settings* (2nd ed., pp. 21-31). Toronto: Canadian Scholars' Press.

Koch-Schulte, R. M. (1991). The corporate model: Implications for social work. In P. Taylor & J. Devereux (Eds.), *Social work administrative practice in health care settings* (pp. 9-19). Toronto: Canadian Scholars' Press.

Lathrop, J. P. (1991). The patient-focused hospital. *Healthcare Forum Journal,* July/Aug, 17-20.

Lathrop, J. P. (1992). The patient-focused hospital. *Healthcare Forum Journal,* May/June, 76-78.

Marcus, L. J. (1987). Discharge planning: An organizational perspective. *Health and Social Work, 12,* 39-46.

Marcus, L. J. (1990). Research on organizational issues in health care social work. *Social Work in Health Care, 15*(1), 79-95.

McMahon, J. M. (1992). Shared governance: The leadership challenge. *Nursing Administrative Quarterly, 17*(1), 55-59.

Patti, R. J., & Ezell, M. (1988). Performance priorities and administrative practice in hospital social work departments. *Social Work in Health Care, 13*(3), 73-90.

Peters, T. (1992). *Liberation management.* New York: Alfred A. Knopf.

Peterson, M. E., Allen, D.G. (1986a). Shared governance: A strategy for transforming organizations: Part 1. *Journal of American Nursing Association, 16*(1), 9-12.

Peterson, M. E., & Allen, D.G. (1986b). Shared governance: A strategy for transforming organizations: Part 2. *Journal of American Nursing Association, 16*(2), 11-16.

Porter-O'Grady, T. (1989). Shared governance: Reality or sham. *American Journal of Nursing, 89*(3), 350-351.

Porter-O'Grady, T. (1990). *Reorganization of nursing practice: Creating the corporate venture.* Rockville, MD: Aspen.

Porter-O'Grady, T. (1993). Patient-focused care service models and nursing: Perils and possibilities. *Journal of Nursing Administration, 23*(3), 7-15.

Porter-O'Grady, T., & Finnigan, S. (1984). *Shared governance for nursing: A creative approach to professional accountability.* Rockville, MD: Aspen.

Pruet, R. A., Shea, T. P., Zimmerman, J., & Parish, G. (1991). The beginning development of a model for joint research between a hospital social work department and a school of social work. *Social Work in Health Care, 15*(3), 63-75.

Rapp, C. A., & Poertner, J. (1987). Moving clients centre stage through use of client outcomes. *Administration in Social Work, 11*(3/4), 23-38.

Rehr, H. (1985). Medical care organization and the social service connection. *Health and Social Work, 10*, 245-257.

Ross, J. W. (1992). Clinical supervision: Key to effective social work. *Health and Social Work, 17*(2), 83-85.

Spano, R., & Lund, S. (1986). Productivity and performance: Keys to survival for a hospital-based social work department. *Social Work in Health Care, 11*(3), 25-40.

Weber, D. O. (1991). Six models of patient-focused care. *Healthcare Forum Journal*, July/Aug, 23-31.

Wells, L. M. (1991). Research and social work administration in health care. In P. Taylor & J. Devereux (Eds.), *Social work administrative practice in health care settings* (pp. 177-191). Toronto: Canadian Scholars' Press.

CHAPTER SEVEN

COMMUNITY-BASED FIELD PLACEMENTS: RECENT INNOVATIONS

Helen Szewello Allen and Eric Shragge

INTRODUCTION

Social work has faced an ongoing debate about the role and place of community practice. Community organization has had a long history ranging from protest activity to the development of more traditional social services. Social work has treated community organization as having a place within social work education, either as a speciality or as part of the skills in a generic or generalist curriculum. The dominant image and perspective of social work as direct practice through state or private agencies, has relegated community practice to a marginal status. One attempt has been made at McGill University, School of Social Work to integrate community-based practice into the curriculum through field education.

In this chapter, we describe the development of community-based field work instruction as part of an undergraduate social work curriculum. The development of these placements is situated within a context of the changing structures of social work services and the impact of these changes on social work education. The transition of community organization from a protest movement to a significant part of the social service delivery system has made finding and maintaining community-based field agencies easier. Descriptions of the types of community agencies used is followed by a discussion of a series of issues related to the decision to integrate community practice as a core aspect of the training of social workers.

CONTEXT OF FIELD PLACEMENTS

This section describes the context in which the School of Social Work at McGill University decided to reorganize the field placements for the students in the three year undergraduate program. The BSW program was born in a period in which two interrelated processes were being played out. The first was the fundamental reform of the health and social services linked to the "Quiet Revolution," which built and reformed: social service and health institutions (Lesemann, 1984). The second was the formation of a grassroots social movement in areas of health, social services, housing, day care, and poverty (Favreau, 1989). This movement put in place alternative community-based and self-managed services, and challenged the state through the mobilization of groups that raised demands for social change. Both of these changes had an important impact for social work training.

The social and health services prior to the early 1970s were divided along religious and cultural lines with little direct control by the provincial government. The reform brought with it the development of new institutions in the social and health services. The model used was one based on technocratic centralized planning, with decision-making resting in the hands of the ministry. Another change in this period was the imposition on the child welfare system a legal-bureaucratic structure that both limited the discretion of social workers and reduced their autonomy. This reshaping of practice counter-posed the traditions of a semi-independent profession with the demands of large scale organizations. With this model in place, the hopes of a generic experience for social work students was reduced. Agencies preferred an individual who could fit into their specific bureaucratic mold, one who would follow procedures set out by the Ministry. The traditions of a profession based on a particular set of values and a flexibility in its practice, were severely restricted with these changes.

In the community, the social movements went through periods of expansion and decline, leaving new community-based service organizations as one of their products (Shragge, 1990). The impact of the movement of the late 1960s and early 1970s was to revitalize the teaching of community organization practice. Community organization became associated with grassroots efforts for social change rather than the earlier social planning model. However, despite the dramatic impact of this movement in contesting social policies and social service agencies, the appeal was limited to a small number of "radical" social workers.

The legacy of this period was large bureaucratic social service agencies with little in them that validated the traditions of a self-defined profession. Community practice options existed in a variety of forms, including new feminist practice, but employed relatively few social workers. The School of Social Work remained committed to a professional model, teaching a variety of interpersonal and therapeutic approaches with a generic core in the undergraduate curriculum as though the changes in organizational processes and the resulting practice were incidental. Students, in their placements, faced a dilemma of receiving an education in the classroom that did not prepare them for the realities of the field and their bureaucratic role.

The pattern of centralization of planning and directing the health and social services continued until the government launched another reform in 1991 which brought some administrative decentralization of control of the social and health services to regional authorities, and the incorporation of community organizations as a partner in service provision. The deprofessionalization of practice through the large bureaucracies, and the renewal of the role of community-based practice shaped the context for a change in policy on undergraduate field placements.

REFORMING FIELD OPPORTUNITIES: CHANGING CONTEXT

Prior to the changes in the placement of students, the majority of the students would be placed in two different state social service settings, for example child welfare and a hospital, while a minority would work in some form of community practice. In the state social services both the practice experiences and the supervision was shaped by the bureaucratic context. This often acted to limit the learning because the mandates and the interventions were much more tightly defined than in previous periods. The practice and the field teaching in the community settings had been uneven. A few settings had trained social workers, who were committed to providing regular, structured supervision and teaching. There had been students in a large variety of community-based setting throughout the 1970s and the 1980s, but partly because of the problems discussed below related to supervision, and partly because of a wider ideology within the dominant social work profession and the teaching of social work, many students believed that community organization was not "real" social work, and that training in this area would not lead to future employment. Therefore, these placements remained marginal in the training of social workers.

In part because of the changes in social work practice described earlier — its bureaucratic structures and lack of professional autonomy — and in part because of the appointment of a new director in the School of Social Work, an examination of field education began. A proposal was made in 1989 to re-organize field placements for the undergraduate students in the three year program by shifting the first field placement (second year social work students) to a community-based setting for all students. All third year students (in their second placement) would work in an institutional setting with more traditional forms of social work practice. Thus students in the three year undergraduate graduate program would be exposed to both community and institutional social work.

There were several educational reasons for this change. The community settings offer a range of opportunities for students to work directly with individuals, and small groups, and indirectly through the processes of community development and social action, as well as on the organization of service provision or other community organization projects. The community-based setting allowed students to meet those who used social work services on their own "turf." Thus, students were directly exposed to the problems and needs of clients unsheltered by bureaucracy, facilitating learning about their situation and problems. In addition, a variety of intervention methods, coupled with autonomy to experiment and innovate were characteristic of these settings. The exposure to both types of setting were complimentary, building the generic or generalist practice philosophy articulated from the 1970s.

Those community organizations that were available for placements had survived beyond the period of protest of the late 1960s and early 1970s, diversified their programs and strategies combining both service delivery and social change activities. Despite the low salaries and difficult working conditions, social work graduates had found jobs in these organizations as an alternative to the large bureaucracies of the state, and were prepared to supervise second year students. In other settings, there were good learning opportunities, but social work supervision was lacking. In order to develop the potential of some of these agencies, the School of Social Work had to play an active role. Building a partnership with the community organization in which over time the agency would commit itself to playing a more active role in the supervision and education of the student was part of the development of this relationship. As an interim measure, the School would supply the supervision through the use of its staff or contracting with an independent social worker to do the supervision. For the agencies, students represented a new source of staffing and therefore the potential to enlarge their services, or develop new programs. Students, in many cases were given a high degree of autonomy and responsibility in these new services. In some cases, through the use of grants, students were hired to continue the services during the summer.

With the reform of the social and health services in 1991, that has decentralized certain services, and legitimated community organizations as a partner in the social service delivery, community agencies have taken on greater importance. In addition, the reform transferred and broadened the mandate of *Centre Local e Service Communautaire* (CLSCs). Community-based practice had become linked with the mainstream state agencies, providing both opportunities and contradictions for social work education and practice. The opportunities include at least in theory more resources and status for these services, but with the possibility of greater control over their activities, and a reduction in their social change and/or organizing activities. The demand for students and the variety of placements as well as the availability of supervision have all increased, and the current situation is a surplus of placements in a large variety of settings.

LINKS BETWEEN CLASS AND FIELD

The classroom curriculum, since the beginning of the BSW program, had a required practice course for all second year students taken concurrently with the field placement. The course was based on the generation of generic, generalist practice. The goals were to introduce students to practice theory, and its application to their field placements. One of the recurrent issues was the difficulty that students in community-based setting had integrating the content of their course material with their field work experiences. The case examples and the assignments for the course tended to be drawn from practice with individuals or small groups and from more traditional social work settings. This difficulty became more evident with the shift of all second year students to community-based field placements. The course was reorganized in 1992, in an attempt to integrate the community-based setting with the required practice course.

The course is divided into two parts. The first is a classroom situation in which theory and approaches to practice are discussed. This is complimented by seminars led by two practitioners with experience in community-based settings. The goal of these seminars is to discuss and analyze in very explicit ways the students' experience in the field and link it to the theory of the classroom. The overall objectives of the course as follows:

1)   To develop an understanding of the role of social work in a variety
     of community-based settings.
2)   To analyze the specific context of practice, including the impact of
     the relations of class, race, and gender on the lives of clients, and,
     the influences of organization and social policy on how social services
     are provided.
3)   To examine the processes of social work, and the steps taken in
     implementing social work practice in community-based settings.
4)   In conjunction with field placements, to help students develop their
     practice skills through analysis, critical reflection, and exercises.
5)   The assignments, which are designed to link theory and practice, are
     related to both the lectures, readings, and seminars, and are designed
     to build skills and knowledge in assessment and intervention planning.

Specific topics include: a discussion of the political and social context of the lives of clients; an analysis of the setting itself; perspectives on advocacy and empowerment;

steps in practice; assessment and intervention planning; and, aspects of community practice.

The seminars follow the students process in their field settings. A series of short written assignments directly tied to field experiences are required. The seminars play an integrating role between theory and practice, and students are encouraged to discuss problems and issues from their field practice. One of the benefits of this process is that problems in the field can be confronted early on in the term and appropriate steps can be taken to remedy them. In the seminars experiential learning such as role plays and case studies are introduced. Students analyze their own practice settings, including the power relations faced by both clients and social workers, work on issues such as contracting, and the development of specific goals and plans for their practice. This part of the course has received very positive evaluations and students have derived a great deal of support from these seminars as they enter their first field work experience.

COMMUNITY PLACEMENTS: A DESCRIPTION

Community practice can take on various activities and function. It is the structures of these agencies and groups that often defines the breadth and range of activities in which workers and students are engaged. In larger organizations there is a greater degree of specialization or specificity of projects; whereas, within smaller organizations there is the opportunity to be involved in a greater diversity of tasks, as well as involvement in all levels of the organizational structure, including the Board of Directors, external committees, staff, volunteers and users of the service. The community organizations that McGill uses as field agencies fall into three broad categories:

1)   the CLSCs which are public agencies serving the front-line health and social service needs of a given region;

2)   established community organizations, that often grew out of earlier protest movements, which now employ several staff, have relatively stable funding and have developed a expertise over time with a specific area of service delivery or organizing activity;

3)   developing community organizations that have a shorter history, respond to a very specific social problem, have a few resources and staff, and active voluntary involvement.

Each of these categories of community organizations will be explored in relation to the practice opportunities they present for students.

CLSCs (CENTRE LOCAL E SERVICE COMMUNAUTAIRE)

The mandate of the CLSCs is to provide health and social services to the total population in a given sector located throughout the province of Quebec. The basic services that all CLSCs must provide include short-term counselling and crisis intervention, school social services, children and family services, and services to the elderly. These services are offered by nurses, social workers, home-care workers and doctors. Community organizers in CLSCs research and assess community needs, develop specific programs to meet these needs, and involve specific groups in these processes. Each CLSC, depending on the needs of their particular region, have very different types of services. For example, one CLSC has an elaborate elder abuse program while another provides a range of services to immigrants and refugees.

CLSCs are mini-bureaucracies, with significant size in terms of staff and budget. Because they are public institutions, they gather statistics on all their programs and services. Despite these organizational tendencies, they work with voluntary clients, and allow room for creative and unique service approaches to be developed. Students doing a placement in a CLSC have a choice of teams and diverse modalities of practice. Individual and family counselling, group work, program development and community organizing are possible choices. In some CLSCs several approaches can be part of one student's assignments, i.e., counselling youth, developing a group for youth with specific needs and representing the CLSC on a Board of Directors of a community organization that runs a drop-in centre for youth.

ESTABLISHED COMMUNITY ORGANIZATIONS

As mentioned earlier, a number of community organizations have developed an expertise to meet the needs of a specific populations, have been able to develop a secure funding base and have established a credible tradition as effective advocates. These organizations involve users in their decision making structures, have flexible approaches to service delivery, creative and innovative programs, easy and welcoming access and a strong focus on individual and collective advocacy. The practice in these organizations is action-oriented, motivated by a philosophy of client empowerment. The following are some examples of community organizations that demonstrate the diversity of community issues and problems that are addressed through the involvement of these organizations:

> *Project Genesis* — store front services, outreach, and organizing in a low-income, multi-ethnic neighbourhood.
> *Project Pal* — drop-in centre, life-skills and psychoeducational groups and advocacy with an ex-psychiatric population. Users are actively involved in

program development and participate in the decision-making structures of the organization.

Tyndale — St. George's Community Centre — a comprehensive after-school program in a low-income, multi-ethnic community; with a focus on specific program development for each age group of children and volunteers.

NDG Senior Citizen's Council — individual and collective advocacy, and group services for seniors including social action committees on issues such as housing, income, transportation, etc.

Black Community Council of Quebec — an alternative support and counselling service to black families as a alternative to state youth protection involvement.

AMBCAL — an emergency shelter for youth that provides a residential component and strong family support program, built on a philosophy of family preservation.

Students doing a practicum in these organizations have the opportunity to experience a variety of practice approaches, initiate programs and develop skills in advocacy. To respond to issues as they arise, flexibility is expected of staff and students. Students placed in these settings need to learn to work with limited structure and are offered a considerable amount of autonomy. Some of the organizations have developed specific dossiers for students, Segments of the organizations work that would not get done if students were not part of the organization. This gives students a tremendous sense of responsibility and ownership of a segment of the services provided by an organization. In a number of these organizations students have the opportunity to work collaboratively with users as definers and decision makers in the provision of services. Volunteers are also significant participants in these organizations and students may be involved in recruiting and training volunteers. The professional title of "social worker" is seldom used in many of these organizations; workers are referred to as program coordinators, community organizers, family support workers, or animators. Students therefore, are socialized to the different and diverse roles that individuals trained as social workers take on in these organizations.

DEVELOPING COMMUNITY ORGANIZATIONS

In neighbourhoods or communities, there are often specific needs that are best met through a small organization. A small and developing organization is characterized by significant board involvement in the issue or service being provided, a limited budget, a staff of one or two workers and often a high involvement of volunteers. These organizations are highly focused on a specific issue or social problem. Examples of some small and developing organizations are as follows:

Committee to Aid Refugees — advocacy, education and organizing work with refugees.

L'Abri en Ville — independent-living apartments for people with a history of mental health problems.

St. James United Church Drop-In Centre — a drop-in centre for a predominantly homeless and schizophrenic population.

Montreal City Mission, Project Refuge — a short-term residential program for refugees who fall through the gaps of other services.

Maison Lucien L'Allier — a non-profit housing project offering low-income housing to people with mental health problems.

Youth in Motion — recreational and psycho-educational programs for youth in a low-income, multi-ethnic community.

Students in these organizations are exposed to all aspects of an organization's life. They participate in board meetings, on committees with board members, work closely with the staff, develop projects, run groups or provide advocacy to individuals. Students are an integral part of the functioning of the organization. They are highly valued and are expected to take on a significant segment of the work of the organization. Students participate equally with staff and board in their analysis of the problems being addressed and in the development of creative strategies. These organizations work with limited resources; thus, part of staff, board and student activity becomes that of fundraising. Students in these agencies undertake a wide variety of tasks, all of which are considered part of the social work role.

These three types of agencies have provided a wide variety, and challenging placements for the School of Social Work. Each have advantages and problems. One of the issues that is common is the balance between the needs of the agency or community organization for the development of their services, and the needs of students for their training. Many of the placements because of their lack of resources are under a great deal of pressure and at times their commitment to the education of the students suffer.

FIELD INSTRUCTION ISSUES

Prior to the shift in field policy, there were several problems associated with the limited number of community settings used including the lack of a social work supervisor and/or inadequate time for student learning, and problems with structuring students' work assignments. One of the ways to resolve this problem was to either hire staff who were assigned to these agencies as field teachers, or to assign regular teaching staff of the School of Social Work to these agencies to provide supervision. Although this form of supervision was adequate, it was more desirable to have agency personnel supervise students. The School had to play an active role in developing the settings to meet the learning needs of students. Several issues needed to be addressed to ensure high quality field education.

Agency Culture

Community organizations have a culture that can be relaxed and friendly or busy and hectic and changing from day to day. Students need to adapt to the culture of the organization within which they will be working. The atmosphere can be very confusing to a beginning student who is anxious and wanting to "do" something. It has been important to emphasize to field teachers, that even though they would like the student to "get a feel for the organization" and then decide in what areas they would like to work, students need an orientation and some initial structured assignments to help them ease into the organization.

As well, supervision needs to be clearly structured from the time the placement begins. Misperceptions about supervision can arise in an unstructured environment. As the student engages in practice, they may spend much of their time working along side of their field teacher, organizing activities, running meetings, doing outreach. Through their collegial relationship, and in discussing the work and issues arising out of theses activities, the field teacher sees this as ongoing supervision. The student, however, may critique the field teacher as not providing any supervision as there is no structured time for this activity. In these cases, the field coordinator or another faculty member have worked with field teachers to ask them to structure a supervision time with the student each week and ask the student to do one piece of reflective writing to prepare for this supervisory session.

Field teachers in community organizations have strongly objected to the use of process recording as a teaching tool, sighting its lack of relevance within community practice. Respecting their comments, we have adapted our demand for student work to one item of critical reflective writing per week. We have encouraged the use of the reflective log, which allows a student to summarize their involvement in an assignment and then reflect on their work and pose questions that arise from their experience of the assignment. The reflective log also encourages students to make links between assignments, focusing on important aspects of their learning.

Impact of Organizational Structure

One observation that was made early in this process from feedback both from students and field teachers related to the nature of the experience of a single student in a small and developing organization. Field teachers felt a tremendous responsibility and found supervision quite draining due to the dependence of the student on them for much of their knowledge and skill development, while students felt isolated from other students and had no one other than their field teacher with whom to discuss their unique field experience. We began suggesting to the field teachers that they consider taking two students at the same time. A number agreed and found it easier to supervise two students as opposed to one. This was due in part to the support that the two students could give each other and thus, be less dependent on the field teacher. Students also found this supportive even though they may have only one overlapping day in the field or were involved in only one joint project. The fact that they have each other provides them with the opportunity to compare experiences and to participate in peer supervision.

Articulation of Skill Development

Attention also needs to be given to the articulation of the social work skills that students are expected to learn. While students develop a diversity of skills, they sometimes have difficulty in defining what they are learning because they are not in a structured, traditional milieu. For example, students may spend three hours talking to a refugee claimant while waiting for a hearing without realizing that they are involved in a supportive counselling relationship, learning about another culture, providing information about services, and assisting in the person's adaptation. Naming and defining the skills that are being developed is important in order for the students to be able to articulate their learning experience.

Students in community practice learn a wide range of skills: relationship building with voluntary clients, outreach, working with groups, animation, facilitation, negotiation, advocacy, intervention with a variety of systems, program design and planning. As well, students may develop an awareness of the impact of policy on the lives of the constituency they are working with and gain experience in policy analysis. For example, when working with refugees, students become very aware of the impact refugee and immigration legislation and guidelines have on their work with individuals or groups. When working with seniors, students are exposed to federally and provincially designed income structures and housing regulations that they will need to understand and in order to advocate on behalf of their clients.

For many students arriving in a social work program, their preconceived notions of the profession of social work are practices within a formal worker/client relationship to provide counselling services. Because many community settings do not structure relationships with clients in a formal helping model, students may spend time worrying about whether they are doing "real social work." It is difficult for students to understand that tasks such preparing meals with homeless men who also have mental health problems, playing sports with teenagers, making sure a young person does their homework in a shelter program, or having a discussion about current social issues with seniors are all part of social work process and practice. The importance of these relationship-building activities in informal settings need to be articulated as valid work that are linked to both assessment and direct intervention. Field teachers need to discuss with their students the nature and purposes of their interactions and incorporate these experiences into the philosophy and approach to service delivery in the particular organization. Left without this kind of discussion students can develop some anxiety as to whether they are learning professional skills.

Role of Faculty Liaison

Each agency in which students are placed is assigned a faculty liaison, who is expected to meet with the field instructor and the student several times a year. The purpose of these meetings is to monitor and to review the progress of the student, and if there are problems in the field placement to discuss the situation and try to resolve the issues or recommend that the placement be changed. The liaison will be involved if the student is not meeting the expectations of the agency. At times the faculty liaisons have needed to become actively involved in ensuring that community placements are in fact providing a learning experience for the student and that the student was able to understand and articulate the skills and knowledge they were learning. The faculty liaison, has provided support to the field teacher in structuring the learning experiences and articulating the skills that a student is developing in a particular setting. This has at times meant that the faculty liaison has had to support the field teacher in organizing specific supervision sessions with the student. Sometimes the language used by the School and the community organization can be quite different, and the faculty liaison can assist the student in being able to articulate their practice both in the language of the community and the profession.

The issue of instilling a social work identity can become more difficult if the field teacher is not a social worker. As part of the expansion into community-based field placements, the school of social work invited some community workers, who had many years of practice experience and who offered a unique practice opportunity to become field teachers. As part of their engagement, they were required to take the field instructors course. As a consequence, field placements in diverse settings such as work with refugees and in the black community, became available. In some instances the field teacher was not able to maintain a commitment to the teaching role that was expected and we had to stop using the particular setting. This process has required careful monitoring by the faculty liaison and feedback from students. It has even meant at times, curtailing a placement during the academic year if the placement was not meeting the learning needs of the student or the structure was creating too much anxiety for the student. On the other hand, after the initial problems and screening of placements, several nonsocial workers have become dedicated field teachers, offering a challenging field setting to students.

ISSUES FOR THE SCHOOL OF SOCIAL WORK

Adopting a policy of using community-based placements as a significant component of the placement options has added a number of administrative demands on the School, particularly for the field coordinator. Continual recruitment is required because some of the organizations face instability and high staff turn-over; for example, a small organization may have been supported for three years, through training the field teacher and then the field teacher changes jobs or the organization loses its funding for that position. This means we need to start from the beginning with that organization, seeing who they hire and the person's readiness to work with a student. At other times, however, former students have been hired and a strong connection to the training of social workers is developed. On some occasions faculty have stepped in to provide supervision in situations that were needing support to initiate a new project. Some of the organizations we now use as field placements, began a number of years ago with students initiating a project in the community supervised by a faculty member. This partnership between students and the faculty has resulted in the development of new services and organizational structures within the community.

Many organizations have come to value the role that students can play in service delivery and therefore are seeking out academic institutions requesting students. We are in a unique situation in that we are more likely to have bilingual students and thus our students are attractive to many settings. When these approaches are made, we have an excellent opportunity to present our expectations and philosophy for field placements. Whenever possible visits are made to the organization to meet with the prospective field teacher. The supply of community-based field agencies has rapidly expanded in recent years, and as a result only those that are able to comply with expectations of the School of Social Work are offered to students. The field training component of the school has been strengthened in the process.

CONCLUSIONS

Shifting the focus of field placements to equally represent community and institutional contexts of practice in the three year BSW program came in response to the changing contexts of practice. In addition, it was the product of a debate about the role of social work education in the process of social change and supporting the building of community initiatives. The School of Social Work at McGill plays an active role in a wide variety of community organizations. One consequence has been that some students, who have done their field placements in these agencies, have become employed in these agencies. Thus, the role of social work in a variety of forms of community-based practice has been increasingly legitimated. Social work and social work education will play an important role in the longer term in community practice, and therefore will be drawn into many activities initiated by these organizations. Their involvement in campaigns for social change and their politically and collectively oriented understanding of empowerment will challenge mainstream social work education and practice and lead into a lively debate. A more challenging social work program is the outcome.

REFERENCES

Favreau, L. (1989). *Mouvement populaire et intervention communautaire de 1960 a nos jours, continuités et Ruptures*. Montréal: Centre de Formation Populaire et Les Editions du Fleuve.

Lesemann, F. (1984). *Services Circuses*. Montreal: Black Rose Books.

Shragge, E. (1990). Community based practice: Political alternatives or new state forms? In Linda Davies & Eric Shragge (Eds.), *Bureaucracy and community* (pp. 137-173). Montreal: Black Rose Books.

CHAPTER EIGHT

"NO WE DON'T . . . YES WE DO . . . WANT A FIELD PLACEMENT STUDENT": A PROGRAM DEVELOPMENT INITIATIVE IN FIELD EDUCATION

Janet Fitzpatrick and Sue Murray

Innovative designs for field practica are essential to the survival of field education during these times of economic crisis in our traditional social programs. This paper describes a method for developing quality field practica during a time when cutbacks and restructuring in traditional social work agencies are such that it is increasingly difficult to secure field placements for students. The placement design places high value on collaboration with the professional community, ensures effective teaching and administration of the program, and contributes to advancing the quality of field education.

The major components of the model of collaboration between the university, local school boards and the federal funding agency include: a) a philosophy and rationale for collaboration; b) key features of collaboration; c) an overview of the project's programs; d) program results; and, benefits to the field education program, social work students, service users and the profession of social work.

PHILOSOPHY AND RATIONALE

The collaborative efforts described here stem from a shared vision of high quality intervention for students identified as "at risk" for dropping out of school and from common concerns regarding existing school barriers to working with families. Research indicates that the alleviation of family problems is often a prerequisite to parent involvement in promoting the child's academic success (Hare, 1988). It is recognized that school social workers have much to contribute in enhancing parental participation. In a sense, their quintessential function is to act as a link among home, school and community. School social workers encourage parent-teacher partnerships and parent activism in furthering the cause of school effectiveness (Fruchter, 1984).

There is also a shared recognition of the long term costs to society when students drop out of school. Pallas (1986) reported that the estimated unemployment rate for dropouts shortly after they leave school is more than twice that of high school graduates of the same age. Jones (1977) cited police statistics that show that an unemployed dropout is six to ten times more likely than an employed person to become involved in crime. Levin's (1972) analysis of the social consequences of dropping out also included reduced political participation, reduced intergenerational mobility and poorer levels of health (Dupper, 1993).

As a result of their "person-in-environment" perspective and their extensive knowledge of family and community conditions that contribute to the dropout problem, school social workers are uniquely qualified to assume a greater leadership role in developing more encompassing and effective dropout prevention programs (Dupper, 1993).

BACKGROUND

To date, school based social work services are not available in the province of Newfoundland and Labrador, and school personnel must rely on crisis intervention efforts of the Department of Social Services, particularly the Child Welfare Division, to assist them as needed. In 1990, the Report of the Archdiocesan Commission of Enquiry into the Sexual Abuse of Clergy recommended "that the Roman Catholic School Boards in the Archdiocese establish social worker positions in the schools" (Winter, 1990, p. 149); and "that the Archdiocese work with the professional schools at Memorial University to increase the recognition that child sexual abuse is an area that requires specialized training, and to develop the curricula needed to prepare students to respond more effectively to their clients" (p. 144). In 1992, the Royal Commission of Inquiry into the Response of the Newfoundland Criminal Justice System to Complaints (Hughes, 1992) and the Royal Commission of Inquiry into the Delivery of Programs and Services in Primary, Elementary and Secondary Education (Williams, 1992) also emphasized the need for direct support services to students and their families.

COLLABORATIVE MODEL

In June, 1992, the School of Social Work, Memorial University of Newfoundland, initiated a partnership with two city school boards and sought funding from Canada Employment Centre, "Stay in School Initiative" to establish a "Drop Out Prevention" program in eight schools within the city. The project was given pilot funding and its success resulted in a request to expand the program in the city and to pilot the program in a rural geographic region of the province in partnership with another area school board. The project was given funding of $100,000 for the academic year 1993-1994.

KEY FEATURES OF COLLABORATION

The project is designed around three programs; the social work practicum, service to "at risk" students, and research/evaluation. Each program has specific goals. The immediate goal of the practicum is to teach undergraduate students the practice skills necessary to work with students and families, and thereby create a qualified pool of professionals. The goal of service is to provide immediate individual, family, and group counselling services that would prevent long term personal and family problems. The goal of the research program is to involve social work faculty in research that will contribute to understanding and improving service needs in schools and enhance teaching in the classroom. The long term goal of the project is to define and establish a model of social work services in schools which will be made a permanent part of the education system in Newfoundland. Two key features that underlie the collaboration are evident in each of the programs.

First, there is a shared governance in the design and implementation of the project, which involves key administrators, selected faculty members, special services staff and teachers in the schools, and practicum students. The principal investigator is the field coordinator of the school of social work who works directly with the assistant superintendents of the school boards. The operations of the project are the responsibility of a project coordinator (contractual faculty member, non-tenure track, hired specifically for the project) and three field instructors hired specifically for the project.

Second, service and care for students at risk is characteristically interdisciplinary in nature. Members of the team represent social work, guidance, educational therapy, psychology, and education. Social work interns learn the skills necessary to participate in case conferences and other aspects of multidisciplinary work in which treatment planning is conducted by a variety of professionals.

PRACTICUM

The practicum prepares undergraduate students to work effectively with children, adolescents and their families. The faculty project coordinator (an MSW with 17 years experience) is a field instructor for one third of the social work students which allows for a close integration of the social work curriculum with the practice needs of the education system. There are three other field instructors (an MSW with 21 years experience, who works as a guidance counsellor; a BSW with 15 years experience who also works as a guidance counsellor, and a BSW with 30 years practice experience). Interested students are interviewed by the coordinator and are assigned to a school. In the first year eight students were assigned to eight schools (fourth years students were assigned from September - December, and fifth year students were assigned from January -April). In the second year twenty students were assigned to ten schools in the city and eight students were assigned to four schools in Bay St. George, an impoverished rural area of the province. To date the project has provided field placements for 44 social work students. Field instruction is provided in individual and group format. Through distance education technology (teleconference/video link) rural-based students are linked with city based students for peer consultation and joint field instruction sessions several times during the placement.
The practicum curriculum is built around knowledge, skills and values that are essential to quality care. Practicum competencies that guide the curriculum are organized around three significant areas: essential knowledge and problem solving skills; ethnically sensitive practice; individual, family, group and community directed practice.

SERVICE

Social work practicum students provide individual, family and group counselling services dealing with a variety of issues and social problems. A unique opportunity for learning is provided through a number of prevention initiatives. Social work students involved with this project practice methods of primary prevention in their school settings. For example, two students participated in the establishment of a Family Resource Centre within schools in two rural communities. They were instrumental in developing a toy lending library, which encouraged parental involvement in the school. They also operated a parent support group on a weekly basis to address issues about effective parenting practices and provided a forum for mutual support and information exchange. All students provided teachers and administrative staff with information about child welfare legislation and reporting procedures in situations of suspected child abuse and neglect.

INDIVIDUAL COUNSELLING ACTIVITIES

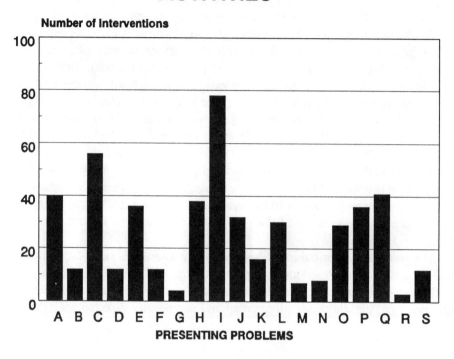

Figure 1A   Individual Counselling Activities

Key: (Presenting Problems)

A	=	Absenteeism	K	=	Trouble with the law
B	=	Attention deficit disorder	L	=	Inability to cope
C	=	Behavioural problems	M	=	Suicide risk
D	=	Sexuality issues	N	=	Family/friend death
E	=	Child abuse	O	=	Socialization problems
F	=	Substance abuse	P	=	Peer relationships
G	=	Pregnancy	Q	=	Emotional/developmental
H	=	Anger management	R	=	Harassment
I	=	Self-esteem	S	=	Other
J	=	Family breakdown			

FAMILY COUNSELLING ACTIVITIES

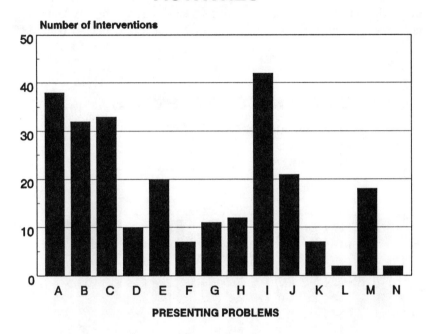

Figure 1B   Family Counselling Activities

A	=	Child management issues	H	=	Family violence
B	=	School attendance issues	I	=	Parent/child
C	=	Behavioural problems communication	J	=	Family transition
D	=	Physical health problems	K	=	Substance abuse
E	=	Mental health problems	L	=	Teen pregnancy
F	=	Attention deficit disorder	M	=	Child abuse
G	=	Family poverty	N	=	Harassment

EVALUATION AND RESEARCH

An extensive evaluation of the project was carried out from January - April 1994. Information was collected from a number of sources, utilizing a variety of methods.

Program activities were analyzed using both qualitative and quantitative measures. Students and family members' comments of their experiences with the program were also recorded. Outcome measures were recorded in terms of determining overall student progress in four categories: (1) attendance, (2) academic performance, (3) behavior and (4) contentment/adjustment at school. A qualitative measure was utilized to determine the helpfulness of the social work service as perceived by the students and family members who received service from the program. Data was collected from 68% of the service users.

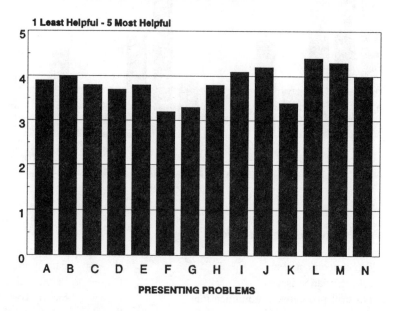

Figure 2   Helpfulness of Services Family Counselling Activities

A	=	Child management issues	H	=	Family violence
B	=	School attendance issues	I	=	Parent/child
C	=	Behavioural problems communication	J	=	Family transition
D	=	Physical health problems	K	=	Substance abuse
E	=	Mental health problems	L	=	Teen pregnancy
F	=	Attention deficit disorder	M	=	Child abuse
G	=	Family poverty	N	=	Harassment

A total of 428 individuals have received social work services from the program. Three hundred and seven families (307) were seen by the practicum students and 365 students and/or family members participated in 73 groups.

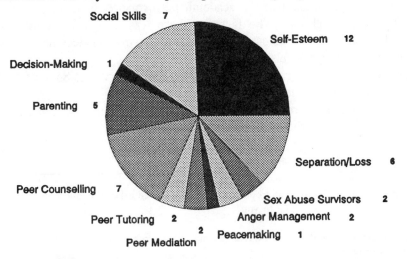

Figure 3A   Types of Groupwork Activities for Students and Parents

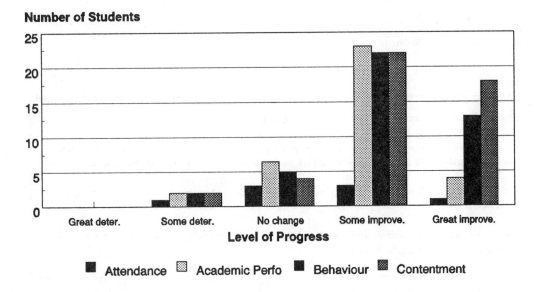

Figure 3B   Student Progress in Four Areas

Outcome measures determined that 79% of students who received service showed "some improvement" or "great improvement" in attendance, academic performance, behavior, and student contentment/adjustment in school. Particularly noteworthy are the significant increases in three areas, namely, academic performance, behavior, and student contentment/adjustment in school. The fact that there was a significant measure of improvement in these areas is an indication that the social work services had a positive impact on student performance levels.

When asked to rate their perceptions of the social work services, 85% of students described the service as being "most helpful."

The following comments from students, family members and school personnel illustrate the overall success of the dropout prevention program:

The following are examples of comments from several students when asked this question: "Did you find the social work services helpful to you?"

"Yes, she was a friend to me and helped me realize I didn't have to be bad to get attention. Now, I don't get in trouble."

"Yes, she helped me with my anger, controlling my temper and understanding that mom still loves me."

"He helped me talk about my problems and to improve my behaviour."

Figure 4A   Students' Comments

Parents' responses about the helpfulness of the social work intern services were:

"the kids trusted here and talked to her about their fears or feelings. She let me know there was someone I could talk to as well. She would let me know how the kids were doing in school."

"She helped me get along better with my son and to understand him better. (I'm) glad to know this person is there for the kids and me if I have any other problems with them."

"It's good to know that there is someone in the school to talk to and (my son) can go see her. It's a lot easier than talking to 'to welfare'."

Figure 4B   Parents' Responses

". . . the Interns are an integral part of our guidance team — guidance counsellor, therapist and interns."

"Many of the parents of these students require assistance with parenting skills. These parents would not have received this assistance from the counsellor or myself to the degree required as was provided by the social work intern."

"The social work intern was able to facilitate communciation and coordination with other helping professionals who were working with the students. . . . better teamwork resulted which benefited the students."

Figure 5A   Examples of Comments from Principals and School Administrators

"A very worthwhile placement; a tremendous learning experience. I would highly recommend that more students be placed with this area. The board and staff are very supportive and recognize the great need for social workers in the school system."

"I feel very strongly that students and families need support — advocacy in dealing with the school system. I tried to provide that whenever possible. As well, I think by supporting pupils and families — teachers too, are supported in their role as educators."

"The school setting is an essential resource that should be utilized. Social workers, from what I have learned and from what other teachers have told me would be a definite asset in th school setting. With students spending so much time in a school setting. With students spending so much time in a school setting, it seems most appropriate that a social worker be on hand to provide intervetnion on an individual and family level. The school setting was an excellent opportunity."

Figure 5B   Social Work Interns' Comments Regarding School Placements

SUMMARY OF RESULTS

The main findings show that:

1)   79% of students who had received social work services showed "some improvement" or "great improvement" in student progress in the four areas of attendance, academic performance, behaviour and student contentment/adjustment.

2)   Individual counselling activities focused primarily (37%) on issues related to student self-esteem, behaviour and emotional/developmental problems.

3)   31% of all family counselling activities centred on issues related to child rearing and management issues, children's behavioural problems and parent/child communication.

4)   235 students were offered counselling in the form of groupwork for a variety of problems/issues. Additionally, the five parenting groups were conducted by social work interns as well.

5)   100% of the parents and students who had received counselling services from the social work interns voiced their approval of social workers in the school system and recommended the continuance of such a program.

BENEFITS OF THE COLLABORATIVE MODEL

Field Program

The project provides a substantial number of quality field placement experiences for undergraduate students, reduces the pressure on the field coordinator to locate placements, and reduces the pressure on traditional agencies to take students every semester. The continuity in field instructors is a welcome relief from the ever-changing assignment of faculty field instructors, and their close liaison with school personnel contributes to mutual goal setting for the program. The budget for the project allowed for travel, and the purchase of supplies and equipment that benefit the entire field program.

Social Work Students

The project provides a unique opportunity for students to practice in the field of preventative social work. While there are cases that require crisis intervention, much of the students work is directed to the prevention of long term individual and family problems. Another benefit for students is the opportunity to be exposed to the education system, and the learning that takes place there. This will benefit them as graduates when they will interact with this system from their position with other social service agencies. Most importantly, this project provides students with an opportunity to experience social work learning in a rural environment where resources are minimal. Students experience rural life first hand and are able to study rural social problems and social policies, community behavior with an emphasis on rural lifestyles and begin to develop skills in rural social work practice.

The Social Work Profession

The long term goal of the project is to define and establish school-based social work services which will provide employment opportunities for social workers at a time when jobs opportunities are being reduced.

CONCLUSION

The primary goal of the collaboration project described in this paper is the implementation of social work services on a full-time basis within the school system in Newfoundland. In using the resources of the school of social work, the education system and federal and provincial funding agencies the project has maintained its focus and simultaneously contributed to the integration and enrichment of teaching, scholarship, and service. Agreement at the executive levels of partner agencies involved in the project clarified the multiple objectives and provided the basis for resolving possible misunderstandings because those at the executive level have authority to address barriers to achieving objectives. All partners involved in the project have a commitment to the improvement of services to children and families and continue to be willing to explore creative change to enhance these services. As a result of this project, increasing numbers of social work students are requesting placement in school settings. The profile of students' contribution to agencies has heightened and the number of requests from other agencies to take students has increased. Joint federal and provincial funding has been approved for the 1994-95 academic year ($175,000.00), and three full-time social work positions will be established by the school boards. Student placements will continue on a regular basis.

REFERENCES

Collins, Lela, B. (1981). School social work as specialized practice. *Social Work, 26*(1), 36-43.

Dupper, David, R. (1993). Preventing school dropouts: Guidelines for school social work practice. *Social Work in Education, 15*(3), 141-149.

Early, Barbara, P. (1992). An ecological-exchange model of social work consultation within the work group of the school. *Social Work in Education, 14*(4), 207-214.

Fruchter, N. (1984). The role of parent participation. *Social Policy, 15*(2), 32-36.

Germain, C. B. (1991). An ecological perspective on social work in the schools. In R. Constable, J.P. Flynn & S. McDonald (Eds.), *Social work: Practice and research perspective* (2nd edition). Chicago: Lyceum Books.

Hare, Isadora. (1988). School social work and effective schools. *Urban Education, 22*(4), 413-428.

Hughes, Samuel, Q. C. (1991). *Royal commission of inquiry into the response of the Newfoundland criminal justice system into complaints.* St. John's, NF: Queen's Printer.

Jones, W. (1977). The impact on society of youths who drop out or are undereducated. *Educational Leadership, 34,* 411-416.

Pallas, A. M. (1986). School dropouts in the United States. In J.D. Stern & M.F. Williams (Eds.), *The condition of education* (pp. 158-174). Washington, DC: National Centre for Educational Statistics.

Williams, Len. (1992). *Our children our future.* Royal Commission of Inquiry into the Delivery of Programs and Services in Primary, Elementary, Secondary Education. Government of Newfoundland and Labrador.

Winter, Gordon et. al (1990). *The report of the archdiocesan commission of enquiry into the sexual abuse of children by members of the clergy.* St. John's, Newfoundland.

CHAPTER NINE

STUDENT PLACEMENTS IN
CORRECTIONAL SETTINGS

Robert W. McClelland

INTRODUCTION

Undergraduate social work practicum students are placed in a wide range of practice settings. They include such diverse fields of practice as mental health, family and children's services, health care, rehabilitation, and corrections. As well, most of these fields attempt to address social problems through micro, mezzo and macro modalities. This diversity is one of the attractive aspects of the profession, but it creates quite a challenge for field faculty charged with assuring that all students receive a generalist educational base.

We frequently encounter practice settings that are not fully attuned to our educational mission. The practicum assignment that I have found most difficult to link to social work education has been *corrections*. Within this field, there are settings that work out better than others. The following discussion will explore the relative merits of corrections settings for student placement opportunities.

This part of the justice system frequently challenges many of the assumptions, values and approaches routinely taught as basic to generalist practice in social work. This is not to suggest that other fields of practice such as child welfare or mental health do not encounter these dilemmas, but rather students encounter more conflicting organizational expectations and practice circumstances in correctional settings than they do in settings where the treatment and rehabilitation mission is attuned to social work practice expectations. I would also suggest that *we* do not do a particularly good job of helping students to respond to these dilemmas. This raises two questions that I would like to explore further. These are:

1)   Are some correctional settings better suited for social work student placements than others?
2)   Can we prepare students better for work with involuntary clients?

Are Some Correctional Settings Better Suited Than Others for Social Work Placements?

This question is best placed in the context of what we intend to teach BSW students about the nature of generalist social work practice. The practicum is a setting in which students are expected to demonstrate: their knowledge of social work practice; and, their skills in working with clients. It also provides the experiential base for many of the assignments in methods classes. A reasonably good match between the requirements of the practice setting and the expectations of methods classes is essential. This question examines the match.

Over the last twenty years, I have been the faculty liaison for many students in a variety of settings. The placements that seemed to demand more accommodation were generally associated with the continuum of justice related settings. These included jails or remand centres, prisons, probation and parole offices, halfway houses and court mandated treatment programs. All these, by definition, involved involuntary clients, but the degree of restrictiveness in particular settings differed dramatically. As well, the attitude toward the client, often labelled inmate, offender, accused, or criminal, varied significantly.

As a setting for learning basic social work values and skills, there are some correctional settings that, I suggest, will provide a better fit for students than others. The most difficult placements, are generally the most restrictive. In other words, jails, remand centres, or prisons are a real challenge. Community-based correctional settings tend to produce a better fit. It is worth noting that there seems to be a growing emphasis on hybrid settings which blend aspects of probation with incarceration (Camp, 1994). Shaping our role in these settings will be important.

THE REMAND CENTRE

To make my point concerning the appropriateness of different correctional settings, I will focus on what I consider the most difficult corrections placement, the remand facility or jail. It exhibits a number of unique characteristics that prove to be a concern for the undergraduate student. The following is a composite description of these characteristics based on my contact with similar settings in both the United States and Canada. To be sure, there are exceptions, but these do not change the overall portrayal.

First, the goals for social worker students are limited by the setting. Interviews tend to be short and are focused on obtaining basic information for the institution. Psychosocial, situational, family, and community issues are not considered particularly relevant. Client self-determination is largely reduced to choices that involve avoiding additional negative consequences. By contrast, most social work students learn in methods class to view the interview as a basic tool for conducting a person-in-environment assessment that will lead to a problem-solving process where the client will exercise substantial control over the goals set (Compton & Galaway, 1989). Students find the conflict in expectations both confusing and frustrating.

Generally, discussion of the alleged crime prior to the court appearance is not allowed and information relating to the offense must be reported. This leaves both parties feeling like they are required to ignore the proverbial elephant in the living room. By contrast, most social work students learn from methods class to focus upon the client's major concern through a process of assessment and prioritizing concerns (Shulman, 1992). Students also learn the power of offering confidentiality when establishing trust and rapport (Cournoyer, 1991). These are clearly limited at the remand facility.

The majority of inmate contacts in a remand centre have limited opportunity for follow-through so developing a treatment plan is not likely. By contrast, most students learn in methods class that social work is a process leading from initial assessment through contracting to problem-solving activities, evaluation and termination. In this process, a working relationship is built between the client and the social worker (Shulman, 1992). This happens infrequently at a remand centre.

Other highly restrictive settings such as prisons share the remand's concern for security. This emphasis is *not* misplaced, but it creates a context in which the client is viewed as dangerous and a threat. The balance of concern given to treatment or rehabilitation versus monitoring and security is decidedly on the side of latter. The inevitable lesson for the student is to be on guard because the client is a potential threat, and rehabilitation as a goal is futile. These correctional settings may promote a revised notion of who is the client and what is the nature of the social work role. Often the student finds it difficult to identify the client, concluding that the institution itself best fits the definition of primary beneficiary. Is this the view of social work practice that we want for the novice social work student?

COMMUNITY-BASED CORRECTIONAL AGENCIES

There are some correctional settings that offer a different balance between security and treatment, and where the social work responsibilities are more compatible with the practice needs of BSW students. These can be roughly categorized as community-based correctional agencies (Fields, 1994). Probation and parole, intensive supervision programs (ISP), targeted treatment services, and diversion centers are becoming the primary rehabilitation focused programs for low-risk court mandated clients. This is where, I believe, social work practice can find the most receptive environment. Inevitably, the "get-tough" attitude toward offenders leads to greater reliance on community-based correctional programs because high-risk offenders get mandatory or extended incarceration while prison space remains limited (Beyer, 1994). Community-based correctional programs are, like it or not, a growth industry.

Damon Camp (1994), offers a useful analysis of staff responsibilities in community-based diversion programs. The activities associated with the counselling staff are of particular interest for social workers. These centers are a cross between traditional probation and incarceration. It is the "get-tough" community-based alternative, if you will. Probationers work in the community and reside in the centre. Camp's research showed that there were a surprising number of shared responsibilities within the centre. As an example, counselling (particularly crisis-intervention assistance which was classified as a counsellor's responsibility), appeared to be something that was provided by a wide range of staff members (Camp, 1994, p. 262). Likewise, monitoring resident movement and activity, which was viewed as a correctional officer's responsibility was a frequently reported task by most of the staff (p. 269). Camp concluded that cross-training of skills for all staff was sorely needed.

Of particular interest, are the findings that relate to the Senior Counsellor position. Although tasks associated with this classification generally garnered low frequency rates by staff as a whole, they were rated highly in overall importance and need for training. This indicated that staff valued these tasks even though they did not directly engage in the activities. No other position received such high rankings for its primary responsibilities (Camp, 1994, p. 269). Tasks associated with our role carried a very high status in these setting. When placing a student in a host environment such a corrections, where social work is not a dominant role, this recognition of value can be very important.

Even in settings where counselling *is* a valued activity, special attention needs to be paid to structuring the experience so students have the skill building activities that we demand of them. At a minimum, this includes the basic steps in problem-solving, including assessment, planning, intervention, evaluation, termination, and follow-up (Kirst-Ashman & Hull, 1993). Community-based corrections appears to be the place where we should concentrate our attention.

Can We Prepare Students Better for Work with Involuntary Clients?

In methods classes, we acknowledge that involuntary clients may be a real challenge, but we do little to turn this recognition into practice concepts of use to students. As well, we grossly understate the influence of organizational norms on the ability of students to practice what we teach. We make assignments based on the assumption that the student will be assigned clients amenable to the helping process, but the activities assigned to social work students in many correctional settings can place severe limitations on the student's ability to fulfil these requirements. There are, to be sure, some experienced students who can learn from the inconsistencies between what we teach and the realities of the practice setting, but can we count on correctly selecting these students? For that matter, is it fair to the student?

James Barber (1991) in his book, *Beyond Casework*, asserts that we do an inadequate job of acknowledging the unique aspects of social work practice with involuntary clients. The concern for client self-determination frequently is translated into practices that stress empathy and non-directiveness (Barber, 1991, p. 43). Hepworth and Larsen (1986, p. 26), as an example, stress that rapport building is the first task of the social worker. Social workers must have a non-judgmental attitude, show acceptance, honour the client's right of self-determination, respect the client (worth, dignity, uniqueness and individuality) and promote problem-solving capacities. This is great stuff! I teach it myself, but we must elaborate upon the helping relationship when involuntary clients are involved. Fortunately, there are a few authors who have struggled with these distinctions.

Barber (1991) suggests that the novice social worker may bury the political dimensions of the work, avoiding conflict and assuming an apologetic stance to reduce client hostility. This may evolve into what he calls "casework by concession" where the worker defers to the client whenever possible. The antithetical style could be called "casework by oppression." Here the worker forgoes developing a working relationship and demands compliance by threatening the revocation of freedom. This drift to either extreme is, to my mind, indicative of an inadequately developed knowledge base.

Ron Rooney (1992) speaks to this concern in his book, *Strategies for Work With Involuntary Clients*. He identifies a number of consequences of this missing knowledge base. One dilemma that is particularly important in the education of students is that "practitioners may be held responsible for influencing client changes that are infeasible, illegal, or unethical" (p. 13). Students who are still forming their professional identity need help in sorting out these important issues. Rooney confronts the "nothing works" lament in a review of the research on effective interventions with involuntary clients. He notes that positive outcomes appear to be based on interactions characterized by motivational congruence. This congruence relies on distinguishing between negotiable and non-negotiable items for intervention. In particular, the terms of the legal arrangement should be distinguished from the areas open to client control. As well, the limits of social worker discretion need to be clear.

The literature suggests that legally mandated clients *do* have more successful results than had earlier been thought to be the case, but coerced intervention often produces only time limited benefits. The benefits do *not* last beyond the use of external pressure (Rooney, 1992, pp. 87-89). Enhancing the appearance *and* reality of choice is very important, even if partially constrained. Rooney (1992, pp. 322-324) also offers a useful guide for evaluating the overall climate for practice within an agency. The answers to these questions would be particularly valuable in screening the appropriateness of various correctional settings. There are five (5) questions to be explored:

1) To what extent do involuntary clients have significant input into the development of semi-voluntary contracts as opposed to passive involvement in involuntary case plans or "notices of agency intent"?
2) To what extent are goals legal, ethical, clear, specific and feasible?
3) To what extent is pejorative labelling of client behavior avoided?
4) How is power used and understood?
5) To what extent is there parallel process in the use of power in the setting? [Are staff passing on the treatment they receive ?] (pp. 322-324)

This kind of assessment would also be a useful assignment for a student as part of an organizational analysis of his or her placement.

CONCLUSION

To conclude, I suggest that the answer to both of the questions posed originally is YES. First, I believe we need to be careful in selecting correctional placements for beginning social work students. Some correctional settings may be inappropriate for social workers in training. The growing number of community-based settings appear to offer the best match between agency mandate and school expectations. These practicum settings need to be evaluated as well to be sure the value base of social work is being acknowledged and reinforced. Rooney's agency assessment questions provide a good beginning for this evaluation. Second, we can do a better job of teaching an approach to working with correctional clients that is built on basic social work principles but recognizes the unique dynamics involved in fulfilling court mandated requirements. Further development of Rooney's motivational congruence concept would be useful. Finally, corrections is, like it or not, a growing job market. We need to pay more attention to the development of the knowledge base that informs social work practice in this area. Of particular importance will be the demonstration of practice effectiveness to combat the pervasive belief that rehabilitation efforts are futile. Schools of social work have an opportunity to influence corrections, but we must do a better job of preparing students for entry into this field of practice. By paying more attention to the development of appropriate field opportunities for BSW students.

REFERENCES

Barber, J. G. (1991). *Beyond Casework*. London: MacMillan Press.

Beyer, J. A. (1994). Assignment to intensive supervision: An assessment of offender classification and subjective override in the state of Idaho. In C. B. Fields (Ed.), *Innovative trends and specialized strategies in community-based corrections* (pp. 19-39). New York, NY: Garland.

Camp, D. D. (1994). Diversion centre operations: An assessment of staffing needs. In C. B. Fields (Ed.), *Innovative trends and specialized strategies in community-based corrections* (pp. 255-276). New York, NY: Garland.

Compton, B., & Galaway, B. (1989). *Social work processes* (4th ed.). Belmont, CA: Wadsworth.

Cournoyer, B. (1991). *The social work skills workbook*. Belmonth, CA: Wadsworth.

Fields, C. B. (Ed.). (1994). *Innovative trends and specialized strategies in community-based corrections*. New York, NY: Garland.

Hepworth, D., & Larsen, J. (1993). *Direct social work practice: Theory and skills* (4th ed.). Belmont, CA: Wadsworth.

Kirst-Ashman, K. K., & Hull, G. H., Jr., (1993). *Understanding generalist practice*. Chicago, IL: Nelson-Hall.

Rooney, R. H. (1992). *Strategies for work with involuntary clients*. New York, NY: Columbia Press.

Shulman, L. (1992). *The skills of helping individuals and groups* (3rd ed.). Chicago, IL: F. E. Peacock.

CHAPTER TEN

A MSW TRAINING PROGRAM:
AN UNIQUE COLLABORATION

Diana M. Filiano, Paula K. Bergman and Bertha F. Murphy

INTRODUCTION

Professional education for Department of Social Service (DSS) casework staff is a strategically sound way to improve services to clients and to prepare workers to deal more effectively with complex situations. This chapter presents a description of the findings of an outcome evaluation of a special training project which is a joint effort between the Suffolk County Department of Social Services (DSS) and the School of Social Welfare at SUNY Stony Brook (both in Long Island, New York). This project was developed in response to an identified need in DSS for professional social work staff with more advanced skills to deal with the multitude of problems addressed by public sector services. These data indicate that there are a number of areas in which the graduates perceive they have enhanced their knowledge and skills. In general, they have indicated that this training directly improved their ability to serve the DSS population.

As local departments of social services move forward to face the challenges of the 1990's and to implement welfare reform, there is a need to respond to the complexity of client issues. Continued professional development is essential in today's environment of rapid change (Taylor, 1993). Offering professional social work training to staff is one way to address these needs. In addition, there is a need for institutes of higher education to develop innovative approaches to social work education (Lieberman, Hornby, & Russell, 1988). Professional education for department of social services casework staff is a strategically sound way to improve services to clients and to prepare workers to learn new attitudes and approaches to deal more efficiently and effectively with complex situations (Lieberman & Hornby, 1987). The DSS/MSW Project was developed to address these issues and demonstrates one approach to improving public sector services. The objectives of the project focus directly on professional social work training of staff since improving caseworker knowledge, skill and job performance will positively impact service delivery to clients. Thus, the project was evaluated based on the respondents' assessment of the extent to which they agreed that the project contributed to improved ability to perform their job responsibilities.

IDENTIFICATION OF NEED

Suffolk County, with over 1.3 million inhabitants, constitutes approximately two-thirds of the eastern section of Long Island, New York (911 square miles). It is unique with regard to population, political climate, and the needs of the individuals who access public social services. There are currently 13,000 AFDC cases encompassing 25,000 minor dependent children. Additionally, there are 200 home relief cases and 1,100 active cases served by the Adult Protective Services Unit.

The Suffolk County Department of Social Services (DSS) recognized the increased complexity of problems faced by its clients and the diminishing number of resources available to deal with them (Suffolk County Department of Social Services Request for Proposals, 1990). There was a need to expand the knowledge and skills of department staff to prepare them for the challenges ahead. At the time of the request, Suffolk County's Department of Social Services had 1,380 occupied staff positions of which only 49 were held by individuals with a Master of Social Work (MSW) degree (3.55%). This is the lowest number in any county of New York State.

Since many staff had life and work experience (35% were over the age of 50 and most staff had been employed for 5+ years), most in-service training was no longer adequate or appropriate to meet their needs. However, a degree program would help employees refine their skills, continue their professional growth, and improve services to clients (Booz, Allen, & Hamilton, 1987). As there was a low staff separation rate, this type of program would benefit the Department because many staff would continue to utilize their newly acquired knowledge and skills to improve service delivery. In order to develop the knowledge and skills necessary to select among various intervention strategies, understand diverse treatment modalities, and assess the impact of environmental influences, an MSW training program was chosen.

BACKGROUND

The School of Social Welfare at the State University of New York at Stony Brook has formed a partnership with Suffolk County to provide eligible Department of Social Services casework staff with the opportunity to obtain a Master of Social Work degree. The DSS/MSW Project is the result of this collaboration. The purpose of this project is to provide professional education and training to Department staff members in order to enhance the ability of the Department to implement its mission of assisting people to become financially, socially, and emotionally independent. The major objectives of the project are:

1) To increase the knowledge and skills of staff in the assessment of client problems and situations.

2) To enhance the ability of staff to develop and implement strategies and interventions to deal effectively with client problems and situations.

3) To improve the capacity of staff to understand the strengths and weaknesses that are present in the client situations and to marshal resources that can contribute to changing client situations and strengthening and empowering clients to cope more independently with their situations.

4) To extend staff understanding of cultural differences among client groups and to provide services in ways that are consistent with cultural and ethnic patterns.

5) To improve the capability of staff to undertake increased supervisory, administrative and service delivery and policy planning functions within the Department of Social Services.

6) To increase the Department's credibility in dealing with other service systems in the community.

The project is designed to enable completion of all requirements for the MSW degree within a three year time period, and, although on a modified program, project participants are integrated into the School's graduate social work program. The project's curriculum is organized to provide training as an advanced generalist and to specialize in areas focusing primarily upon: the development of advanced practice skills with individuals and families, the development of skills to assess service delivery systems, and the development of programmatic and management interventions at the case, organizational, and policy levels. The model for the field component of the project involves placing students in agencies serving disadvantaged and at risk populations in Suffolk County. The students are exposed to different models of service delivery as they learn how to provide culturally appropriate interventions and strategies for attainment of goals.

Full-time field instructors who are part of the project staff are assigned to work with the agencies and the students placed there. A formal relationship is maintained with the Department and the School of Social Welfare through the Department's Director of Staff Development and Training who, along with the Project Coordinator, is involved in the recruitment of project participants and facilitating resolution of school and work related issues.

METHOD

This study used a survey design and, as a first step in an outcome evaluation, it focused on the experiences of graduates of the DSS/MSW Project. The instrument was developed in a committee of project staff and School faculty and was divided into two sections. In section A, each scale item came under one of four categories (skills, knowledge, values and communication) and served to operationalize the project's objectives (detailed earlier in this paper). All items were rated using a 5-point Likert type scale ranging from *strongly disagree* to *strongly agree* (some of the findings are presented as generalized collapsed categories of agree or disagree). *Not applicable* was also a choice for those items which did not pertain to the respondent's job role. Respondents identified the extent to which they agreed that the project contributed to their improved abilities in the four categories identified above.

Section B consisted of open-ended questions to explore additional outcomes which may not have been anticipated in the project objectives. These findings will be presented in the Summary portion of the paper. There have been two graduating classes (1993 and 1994) and all received a mailed survey ($N=24$). Seventeen (67%) were anonymously returned. The software package SPSS PC+ was used in the data analysis. Frequency distributions and cross-tabulations for correlation were utilized. With this type of evaluation, no significance tests were used as no hypotheses were being tested.

DISCUSSION OF DEPARTMENT SUPERVISOR EVALUATIONS

As was noted, the student evaluation was a first step in the overall project evaluation. Ongoing student *and* DSS supervisor evaluations are recommended using a pre/post test design. In this study, an effort was made to survey the respondents' Department supervisors in order to evaluate their assessment of the student/workers' job performance since participation in the project. However, although data were collected on 10 respondents, the return rate was lower than that of the participants. This low return has been demonstrated in recent findings of supervisors in the nursing profession (Howard & Hubelbank, 1989). Also, it was recognized that several factors (frequent supervisory transfers, unit transfers, restructuring) mitigated against this being a reliable and valid tool. As per the comments and the frequency of *undecided* responses, most of the supervisors were unable to adequately assess student improvement as a result of the student/worker's participation in the project as they did not know the student/worker's performance prior. However, several comments are worth noting.

An impact of having employees who are students of the project appeared most in the area of disruption to the unit. Now, with the project soon to enter its fifth year, the DSS staff supervisors have made efforts to minimize this and may now begin to see benefits to the unit. One supervisor, who commented at length about this issue, stated:

> This unit's functioning has been impacted by two workers enrolled in the program. . . . However, with the benefit of trained and better comprehending workers as the goal, the short term disruptions are balanced by the long term benefits, especially to the agency and the clients.

While many supervisors could not accurately assess the impact of the project on their employees, informally, some have reported that they can see professional development via more effective, less emotional client interactions. Others have also informally stated that the workers appear to have greater insight into the factors impacting their clients. Efforts will be made in future evaluations to address this limitation as the contributions of the supervisors are very valuable to the project's evaluation as a whole.

FINDINGS

Demographics

This sample consisted of full-time Department of Social Services (DSS) employees who were graduates of the DSS/MSW Project. While three respondents chose not to provide this information, the number of YEARS this sample was employed by DSS ranged from 5-27 years, with a mean of 13 years with the Department. The AGE of the respondents ranged from 36 to 61, with a mean of 45 years. Over 35% of the respondents were in their forties. Two respondents chose not to provide information with regard to their SEX. Of the remaining, there were 12 women and 3 men. This closely resembles the ratio of women to men in non-administrative positions at DSS.

Skills

Sixteen out of 17 respondents report that the DSS/MSW Project has contributed to their ability to assist clients with problem identification, make more comprehensive assessments of client problems, and assess other forces impacting client systems. A more diverse response was found concerning the ability to make comprehensive assessments of service needs in collaboration with the client *(N = 17)*: *Agree = 11*; *Undecided = 2*; *Disagree = 3*. Fewer (*9*) stated that the project assisted them in helping clients achieve agency related goals. Seventy-one percent of the sample indicated their ability to facilitate client empowerment was improved as a result of the project. Fewer, (*59%*) agreed that this also helped them better able to facilitate service delivery; five were undecided.

With regard to administrative skills, the respondents also indicated an improved preparedness as a result of the project. Twelve respondents felt better able to undertake both supervisory and administrative responsibilities. Eleven indicated the project helped to prepare them to assume policy planning functions. With four undecided and three not applicable, seven respondents indicated a better ability to work with the private sector.

Knowledge

In terms of acquiring an understanding of human development in general, 82% stated that the program contributed to this. While many of the respondents may not have an opportunity to conduct research within their professional roles, 76% of them indicated that the project contributed to an understanding at least, of research literature. Nearly 65% of respondents agree that they have a better understanding of how social policies affect client populations. In addition, almost 71% agree that they now better understand what is entailed in program development. Of those (*11*) who agree that their awareness of how policies affect clients has increased, all agree that they can also assess other forces impacting their clients. This may suggest that the project had influence in terms of assisting the respondents in recognizing external factors on client systems.

Aside from representing political and social forces, some of these external factors have to do with the lack of available resources. Only 29% of the graduates indicate that the project assisted them in locating resources for clients. Almost 53% of the respondents indicate that the project helped them to identify gaps in services within the community as well as on a broader level. Although education and training can help workers more accurately assess client problems and effectively utilize scarce resources, the presence of service gaps affects worker's ability to locate appropriate resources.

These constraints can negatively impact the facilitation of service delivery; while 53% of the sample agreed that the project was of assistance in increasing their ability to facilitate service delivery, nearly 30% were undecided. Four out of the five respondents who were undecided, disagreed that the project improved their ability to locate resources. This reflects the ongoing frustration and difficulty many workers have with finding services for their clients. The frequency distributions on these items may indicate that while the project can be very helpful in terms of understanding social work theory, the extent to which it can assist with the identification and acquisition of resources will depend on availability within the community. This reflects a community problem rather than lack of education and/or training.

Half of the respondents have been working for the public sector for over 10 years and many, as a result of their field placements, for the first time, experienced the private sector from within. The responses for this following question varied. Two respondents strongly disagree and three respondents disagree that the project made a contribution to their understanding of the difference between the sectors. The largest group (*6*) was undecided and an additional six either agreed (*3*) or strongly agreed (*3*).

Values

Fifteen of the 17 respondents indicated that as a result of the project, they have a broader understanding of cultural diversity. Such understanding directly relates to a sensitivity toward providing culturally appropriate services. Sixty percent indicated that they now are better able to provide services that are culturally appropriate. Both of the participants who reported that they strongly disagree that the project increased their awareness of cultural diversity, also strongly disagree that the project assisted them in their ability to provide culturally appropriate services.

Eighty-two percent of respondents are better prepared to focus on client strengths as a result of the project. Similarly, 82% agree that their understanding of the effects of oppression on different client populations has been enhanced by participation in the project.

Communication

With regard to the skills of communication, over 76% of the sample agreed that their awareness of the use of self has been increased since participation in the project. For instance, when viewing the skill of active listening, increased self awareness correlates with an improved ability to listen to clients. Most (*83%*) agree that their ability to use this skill with clients has improved since participation in the project. This correlates with the 11 out of 12 who felt better able to use this skill with colleagues as well.

While five respondents disagree that the project enhanced their ability to articulate their thoughts in writing, 11 agree that this area has been improved. Twelve respondents agree that formal and informal verbal exchanges have been enhanced. Fifty-nine percent agree that their ability to collaborate with colleagues around identifying service needs has improved since participation in the project.

DISCUSSION FROM AN EMPOWERMENT AND STRENGTHS PERSPECTIVE

The issue of empowerment and the incorporation of a strengths perspective (Saleebey, 1992) is strongly emphasized by the School in both the classroom and the field. These concepts are integrally linked and are part of the values and skills of social work. According to this study, the students have begun to integrate these into their practice, and a correlation was identified between some of the variables. For instance, the development of good listening skills provides a foundation for learning the interview skills used to make an assessment of the client's situation. Without this, the worker cannot identify service needs jointly with the client.

Client empowerment can best be facilitated if the client, as well as the worker, is actively involved in the service plan. Of the 14 who agree that they are better able to use listening skills with clients, 72% felt more equipped to facilitate client empowerment while the others were undecided. Likewise, of the 16 respondents who agree that they are better prepared to assist clients with problem identification, 75% agree that they can better facilitate client empowerment; the others were undecided. This may suggest that improved ability to include the client in the assessment and service delivery plan will encourage the facilitation of client empowerment.

Additionally, the perspective of focusing on client strengths is correlated with facilitating empowerment. Of the 14 respondents who agree that they have a better ability to focus on client strengths, 86% agree that they can better facilitate client empowerment; the others were undecided. Thus, there appears to be an improved capacity to understand the strengths and weaknesses that are present in the client situations. With this, workers can marshal resources that can contribute to changing client situations and strengthening clients to cope more independently with their situations.

SUMMARY

An holistic perspective in assessment and intervention has been a persistent quest and responsibility for social work practitioners and educators (Skolnik & Papell, 1994). This approach fits closely with the generalist model of the School of Social Welfare. The formulation of a partnership between the Department of Social Services and the School of Social Welfare has made it more possible to actualize this in field instruction as well as in the curriculum. Project staff, in conjunction with School faculty, tailored the class and field components to best address the project's objectives. Exposure to varied practice models, applicable to both the public and private sectors, is expected to help DSS staff expand their role and adopt new attitudes and approaches. This has been initially demonstrated in this study, as this evaluation focused on the students' assessments of their preparedness for different roles and the attainment of social work skills and values.

Throughout this project's tenure, staff and faculty have directly participated in and maintained control of its implementation in facilitating these objectives. For instance, public welfare issues are presented and integrated in the classroom, so DSS students can directly and immediately apply acquired knowledge to their Department work. Their non-DSS field placements worked to enhance student understanding of the private sector. And, according to this study, students found this experience to be one which in turn helped them to connect and contract with private sector agencies when working within their Department positions. Some indicated that they felt this was helpful in providing a broader view of social work. This design differed from similar programs in that other projects of this sort placed Department students in other Department positions for their field placements.

There have been a number of desirable outcomes which were reflected in the open-ended questions. Many respondents reported increased confidence in performing their job responsibilities. Their ability to integrate knowledge was helpful in its application to their work with clients. Students must learn how to use knowledge and make decisions in unpredictable situations (Rogers & McDonald, 1992). One third of the respondents reported having an heightened awareness of social issues such as poverty, homelessness, oppression, domestic violence and cultural diversity. Their self perceptions as *professional* social workers appeared to benefit them not only in their work, but in an enhanced sense of credibility and respect when working in the community. Although all were not in agreement, some indicated that the interaction of the DSS students with staff and students at placement agencies and the classroom appeared to informally provide mutual understanding of the Department and its functions as well as the private sector.

As indicated by these findings, there are a number of areas in which DSS/MSW Project graduates perceive they have enhanced their knowledge and skills and therefore, have directly improved their ability to serve the DSS population. The respondents were generally in agreement that the project contributed to their ability to work with clients within the parameters of their Department of Social Services positions. The perception of their experience with the project was that it contributed most to growth in the categories surveyed of social work knowledge, skills and values. In turn, their understanding of the internal and external factors and dynamics affecting their clients appeared to be enhanced. The study also found that the respondents acquired a more comprehensive understanding of the complexities of the systems in which they work. In addition, there was an indication that communication skills were enhanced. Having the opportunity to enhance such skills was recognized as an asset as these skills are essential for social work practice.

This unique collaboration between the School of Social Welfare at the State University of New York at Stony Brook and the Suffolk County Department of Social Services is one approach to improving the provision of services in the public sector. By expanding the knowledge and skills of Department staff, service delivery will be improved because staff will be better prepared to meet the demands of complex of client needs. The School of Social Welfare is able to accomplish its goal of providing a learning environment for those who wish to deepen and extend knowledge and experience in the development of social change. In addition, it can meet its commitment to emphasize service to groups who have been historically oppressed and devalued. While the findings suggest that the major objectives of the project have been met, there is a need for continued evaluative research and development of programs encouraging such partnerships.

REFERENCES

Booz, Allen, & Hamilton. (1987). *Department of Human Resource job analysis and personnel qualifications study.* Unpublished report. Washington, DC.

Howard, E., & Hubelbank, J. (1989). Employer education of graduates: Use of the focus group. *Nurse Educator, 14*(5), 38.

Lieberman, A., & Hornby, H. (Eds.). (1987). *Professional social work in public child welfare: An agenda for action.* Portland, ME: University of Southern Maine, National Child Welfare Resource Centre for Management and Administration.

Lieberman, A., Hornby, H., & Russell, M. (1988). Analysing the educational backgrounds and work experiences of child welfare personnel: A national study. *Social Work, 33*, 485-489.

Rogers, G., & McDonald, L. (1992). Thinking critically: An approach to field instructor training. *Journal of Social Work Education, 28*, 166-176.

Saleebey, D. (Ed.). (1992). *The strengths perspective in social work practice.* New York: Longman Publishing.

Skolnik, L., & Papell, C. (1994). Holistic designs for field instruction in the contemporary social work curriculum. *Journal of Social Work Education, 30*, 90-95.

Suffolk County Department of Social Services. (1990). *Request for proposal, educational degree program, Suffolk County Department of Social Services for a Masters degree in Social Work.* New York: Author.

Taylor, I. (1993). A case for social work evaluation of social work education. *British Journal of Social Work, 23,* 123-138.

PART THREE

FIELD EDUCATION METHODS: LEARNING TOOLS, TEACHING STRATEGIES AND TRAINING ISSUES

The twelve chapters included in this section all deal with field education methods and teaching and learning concepts, issues and practices. They provide a valuable contribution to the field education literature. These chapters offer practical suggestions, a variety of useful tools and a selection of effective teaching strategies for facilitating learning and improving teaching. Some are directed specifically at training field instructors. Others outline the essential ingredients of a practice curriculum. And still others address issues and processes involved in the instruction, supervision and evaluation of students.

To begin this Part, Nick Coady argues for a reflective inductive model for integrating theory and practice, followed by Sheena Findlay's discussion of the teaching of ethics in field education. The critical aspect of writing as an important part of practice and a skill to be learned in the practicum is addressed by Anthony Paré and Helen Szewello Allen.

Learning tools and teaching techniques for field instructors and students are the main topics in the next five chapters. Gail Kenyon describes the use of live simulation for training field instructors, followed by Urania Glassman's articulation of a curriculum for the education of field instructors. Next is a description of work done in the United Kingdom to train practice teachers (field instructors) and ensure consistency for students through structured activities. Sherrill Hershberg and Joanne Moffatt present a number of learning tools that can be used in the field instruction process, while Barbara Thomlison and Don Collins describe the use of structured consultation and role play to address different types of student learning situations challenging field instructors.

The last group of four chapters in this Part discusses supervision and evaluation. Jan Koopmans describes the use of a multidisciplinary reflecting team in the practicum, while the view of students' experience of a reflecting team approach to field instruction is presented by Barbara Thomlison. An alternative model of student evaluation which builds on strengths and focuses on learning is described by Kate McGoey-Smith. The last chapter in this Part discusses the difficulties of the student-at-risk in the practicum, written by Heather Coleman, Don Collins and Debbie Aikins.

These chapters fill a gap in the literature by providing a much needed contribution of topics, tools and techniques that address salient training issues. They can be utilized by field instructors and students in the teaching-learning exchange in the field practicum to enhance the supervision, instruction and evaluation processes.

CHAPTER ELEVEN

A REFLECTIVE/INDUCTIVE MODEL OF PRACTICE:
EMPHASIZING THEORY-BUILDING FOR UNIQUE CASES VERSUS APPLYING THEORY TO PRACTICE

Nick Coady

The thorny issue of how to integrate classroom theory with field practice is longstanding and continues to be problematic not only for social work students, but also for faculty and practitioners, including field instructors. Social work students commonly are hard-pressed to find a comfortable fit between the theories that they learn in the classroom and the work that they perform in the field placement. On one extreme, students fail to see any connection between theory and practice. They may be able to articulate an impressive theoretical practice model in a class paper, but when asked to describe their actual practice they admit sheepishly to "flying by the seat of their pants" and feeling "unprofessional" in doing so. On the other extreme, students latch onto some theoretical model that they have learned in the classroom or field placement (usually one which is narrow and fashionable) and they use it in a rigid, formula-like fashion that is comfortable neither for them nor the clients that they work with. Although many would be loath to admit it, faculty and practitioners often struggle with these same issues.

This paper examines common problems and contentious issues concerning the integration of theory and direct social work practice. In particular, the extent to which the deductive use of theory occurs in practice and the assumed importance of this process is questioned. It is argued that a positivistic, technical-rational philosophy in social work has obscured the fact that practice is primarily a reflective/inductive process.

A HISTORICAL PERSPECTIVE ON THE POSITIVISTIC, TECHNICAL-RATIONAL OUTLOOK IN SOCIAL WORK

The common assumption that good professional practice involves primarily the deductive application of scientific theory and technique is derived from the positivistic, technical-rational outlook that has gradually infiltrated social work, as well as other professions, since professions became ensconced in the universities early in the twentieth century (Schön, 1983).   Since the 1920s, when social casework began to adopt positivistic Freudian theory and to move away from its idealistic, pragmatic, and humanistic roots in an effort to achieve professional status, the "party line" in social work education has been that "effective or 'good' practice must be rooted in a sound and established theoretical foundation and that, without this foundation, the quality of practice suffers" (Goldstein, 1986, p. 352).

In the 1930s and 1940s, proponents of the Functional school of casework reasserted the importance of humanistic and artistic elements in practice. Papell and Skolnik (1992) have noted that Bertha Reynolds and Virginia Robinson, among others, stand out as social work educators who stressed the artistic and creative elements of practice, as opposed to the rational-technical elements. Referring to casework, Reynolds stressed that "learning an art . . . cannot be carried on solely as an intellectual process" (cited in Papell & Skolnik, 1992, p. 21). Similarly, Robinson observed that "wisdom that goes beyond knowledge must eventually be achieved" (cited in Papell & Skolnik, 1992, p. 21).

Following the rapprochement of the Diagnostic and Functional schools in the 1950s, Perlman (1979) noted how the increasing pressure on social services for accountability and scientific proof led to renewed denigration of the humanistic elements of practice, particularly of the importance of the worker-client relationship. It should also be noted, however, that social work's positivistic leanings continued to be fuelled by the desire for professional status. For example, although Greenwood (1957) saw some drawbacks to the move toward professionalization, he noted that "continued employment of the scientific method" (p. 45) would help social work to "rise within the professional hierarchy so that it, too, might enjoy maximum prestige, authority, and monopoly which presently belong to a few top professions" (p. 54).

"The increasing demand for empirical testing and validation of our knowledge and practice" (Hartman, 1990a, p. 3) that surfaced again in the 1970s heightened the emphasis on a positivistic, technical-rational outlook. Pronouncements such as "If you cannot measure the client's problem, you cannot treat it" (Hudson, 1978, p. 65) and "Science makes knowledge, practice uses it" (Rein & White, 1981, p. 36) reflected the prominent positivistic belief that quantitative research is needed to generate empirically-based theory, which can then be deductively applied in the form of techniques (Scott, 1990). Hartman (1990b) has described how the acceleration of the shift in power from the profession to the university in the 1970s was another factor that reinforced the emphasis on research and theory over practice. This view fits with Schön's (1983) contention that universities adhere "for the most part, to a particular epistemology, a view of knowledge that fosters selective inattention to practical competence and professional artistry" (p. vii).

TO WHAT EXTENT IS THEORY APPLIED IN PRACTICE?

Although the positivistic, technical-rational outlook has continued to dominate social work, an increasing number of authors have expressed opinion and cited evidence that questions the assumption that most practitioners deductively apply theoretical knowledge to the specific circumstances of clients.

Siporin (1988) has lamented that "the art of social work is neglected in academic pronouncements and the literature" (p. 177); however, he has contended that "among practitioners, social work is understood as a creative art form rather than as a science" (p. 177).

Goldstein (1986, 1990) has reviewed a number of social work studies (Carew, 1979; DeMartini & Whitbeck, 1987; Harrison, 1987; Kolevzon & Maykranz, 1982; Sainsbury, 1980; Sheldon, 1978) that explore the extent to which social workers make use of theory in practice in the traditional sense. On the basis of such studies, he has suggested that "what many social workers do often has little connection with what they know in theoretical terms" (Goldstein, 1986, p. 352). Furthermore, he has concluded that "despite the insistent pursuit of a scientific image for social work, the experiential and subjective characteristics of direct practice continue to call for a humanistic identity" (Goldstein, 1990, p. 38).

From his study of five professions (engineering, architecture, management, town planning, and psychotherapy), Schön (1983) concluded that much of professional practice does not involve the application of established theory and technique. Rather, he suggested that most professional practice involves what he calls "knowing-in-action" and "reflection-in-action." DeRoos (1990) has noted how these two related concepts equate, in social work, to practice wisdom.

"Knowing-in-action" connotes the "spontaneous behaviour of skilful practice . . . which does not stem from a prior intellectual operation" (Schön, 1983, p. 51). Schön acknowledges that some knowing-in-action may reflect prior learning that has become internalized; however, he maintains that much of this develops naturally as "knowing how" and was never dependent on "knowing that."

"Reflection-in-action," which Schön sees as the key to good professional practice of any kind, involves "thinking on your feet" when faced with an uncertain or unique situation. He contends that this happens commonly and involves improvising and reasoning inductively to "construct a new theory of the unique case" (Schön, 1983, p. 68).

Importantly, Schön (1983) notes that "because professionalism is still mainly identified with technical expertise, reflection-in-action is not generally accepted — even by those who do it — as a legitimate form of professional knowing" (p. 69). This might explain why most social workers continue to "tow the party line" that practice is based on the deductive application of theory. Given the prevailing positivistic, technical-rational outlook, "uncertainty is a threat; its admission is a sign of weakness" (Schön, 1983, p. 69).

Harrison's (1987) exploratory study of 25 exemplary British social workers lends specific support to Schön's conceptualization of professional practice. Harrison found that three types of reflection, "consistent with the basic reflective process Schon identified" (p. 409), were characteristic of the practice of the social workers in his study. He concluded that "much practice is not based on the deliberate, deductive application of preconceived guides or models" (p. 395).

Thus, there is a growing body of evidence and opinion that social work practitioners (and other professionals) may not apply theory in their practice to the extent that is commonly assumed. Instead, it would seem that many social workers are "reflective practitioners" (Schön, 1987) whose working styles are characterized more by spontaneity, intuition, and inductive reasoning than by the conscious, deductive application of theory and techniques.

CHARACTERISTICS OF EFFECTIVE PRACTICE

In acknowledging studies that raise questions about the extent to which social workers use theory in practice, many social work authors have lamented this fact and have assumed that effectiveness is compromised by such practice (Goldstein, 1986). Research in the field of individual psychotherapy, much of which includes social work practice, suggests, however, that practice effectiveness is not associated primarily with the use of theory and technique.

The last two decades of research on individual psychotherapy have yielded two major striking and consistent empirical findings. First, "there is little evidence of clinically meaningful superiority of one form of psychotherapy over another" (Lambert & Bergin, 1994, p. 181). This fact calls into question the assumed importance of "specific factors" such as theory and technique.

Second, there is overwhelming evidence to support the strong association between client outcome and a therapeutic relationship that is characterized by warmth, empathy, trust, and acceptance (Horvath & Symonds, 1991; Lambert & Bergin, 1994; Orlinsky, Grawe, & Parks, 1994). These findings support Jerome Frank's (1961) long-held view that "common factors" (i.e., interpersonal, affective, and social factors that are common across therapies) are the main therapeutic ingredients of counselling (Lambert & Bergin, 1994).

The conclusions about the importance of common versus specific factors are reinforced by two other sets of research findings. First, many studies have demonstrated that "paraprofessionals . . . are sometimes able to be as helpful as practicing clinicians" (Lambert & Bergin, 1994, p. 182). Second, results from a wide range of studies on the concept of social support suggest that having a close, emotionally supportive relationship is associated with physical and psychological health across many different life-stress situations (Wills, 1985). These findings lend support to the belief that a warm and caring human relationship has substantial therapeutic value.

Thus, there is a large body of empirical evidence which suggests that practitioners' effectiveness is dependent to a large degree on "relationship skills, facilitative attitudes, wisdom based on experience, and related nontechnical skills" (Lambert & Bergin, 1994, p. 181). This research suggests that practitioners' interpersonal style and personal qualities are more important than their theoretical knowledge or technical proficiency. It is ironic, yet quite encouraging, that this empirical knowledge, which has been generated largely from within the positivistic, technical-rational perspective, lends credence to the belief that "effective practice is less a technical enterprise than it is a creative, reflective, and, to a considerable extent, an artistic and dramatic event" (Goldstein, 1990, p. 38).

NEGATIVE IMPACT OF TECHNICAL-RATIONAL OUTLOOK ON PRACTICE

One of the major consequences of emphasizing theoretical knowing and technical doing is the tendency to overlook and sometimes denigrate the importance of the artistic/humanistic elements of practice. In contrast to the warmth, empathy, collaboration, and egalitarianism that characterizes effective helping relationships, the technical-rational outlook seems more apt to foster an expert-centred approach that is cool, calm, and dispassionate.

As Gitterman (1988) has lamented, professional education often "formalizes our work and stiffens our approach" (p. 36) and can result in hiding "behind professional masks" (p. 37). In a similar vein, Mahoney (1986) has commented that the emphasis on conceptual knowledge in educating and training counsellors leads to "the unconscious search for a 'secret handbook'. . . of practical 'how-to-do-it' knowledge and explicit techniques for achieving specified ends" (p. 169-170). Unfortunately, there are a good number of "secret handbooks" (i.e., fashionable, bandwagon models of practice) on the market, and practitioners with a technical-rational mindset are apt to force-fit clients and their problems into narrow, prescriptive theoretical frameworks. Alternatively, if practitioners do not adopt a secret handbook, they are apt to suffer in silent embarrassment with feelings of inadequacy.

A REFLECTIVE/INDUCTIVE MODEL OF PRACTICE

The view that is being proposed is not that theory and technique are unimportant. Although there is little empirical evidence to support the importance of "specific factors," commonsense and clinical wisdom suggests that theoretical frameworks and therapeutic techniques, if approached critically and used tentatively, can add to practitioners' effectiveness. The important point is that, counter to the positivistic, technical-rational outlook that prevails in social work, at least in academic settings, effective practice does not consist solely, or even primarily, of a deductive application of theory and technique.

PARALLELS TO QUALITATIVE RESEARCH

Effective practice has more similarity with the reflective/inductive, theory-building paradigm of qualitative research than with the positivistic, technical-rational outlook that stresses the deductive application of theory. The qualitative research paradigm fits with the view that the practitioner "is more of a theory-developer than a theory-consumer" (Goldstein, 1986, p. 355). It is beyond the scope of this article to provide a thorough overview of qualitative research methodology; however, a review of some basic qualitative principles and strategies helps to illustrate the parallels to a reflective type of practice.

The parallels between qualitative research principles and basic, longstanding humanistic social work principles are quite striking, as illustrated by the following quotes from a book on qualitative research by Patton (1990):

> . . . each case . . . is treated as a unique entity (p. 50);
> This holistic approach assumes that . . . a description and understanding of a person's social environment . . . is essential for overall understanding (p. 49);
> Understanding comes from trying to put oneself in the other person's shoes, from trying to discern how others think, act, and feel (p. 47);
> . . . getting to know . . . participants on a personal level . . . is in sharp contrast to the professional comportment of many evaluators who purposely project an image of being cool, calm, external, and detached. (p. 47)

It is clear that these descriptions of the qualitative research approach parallel descriptions of good clinical practice principles.

As opposed to deductive analysis that uses a priori theory to search for data that will confirm (or disconfirm) the theory, a qualitative approach uses inductive analysis. In inductive analysis, one "attempts to make sense of the situation without imposing preexisting expectations on the phenomenon or setting under study" (Patton, 1990, p. 44). Theories about clients' problem-situations are developed gradually from a felt understanding of their direct experience rather than imposed a priori through theoretical frameworks. "The neutral investigator enters the research arena with no axe to grind, no theory to prove, and no predetermined results to support" (Patton, 1990, p. 44). A reflective/inductive consideration of the wide range of data that is gathered leads to the identification of patterns and themes, which culminates in a holistic understanding. It should be stressed that great care is taken to check with the people under study to ensure that the emergent theory fits for them (Patton, 1990).

The reflective/inductive, theory-building approach of qualitative research requires the social work practitioner "to develop the skills for finding courage in the face of the uncertain" (Papell & Skolnik, 1992, p. 22). This type of practice is based on the recognition that each client's problem-situation is unique and that the practitioner needs to work collaboratively with the client to build a new theory of the unique case that is grounded in the client's experience. This type of reflective/inductive practice involves the "elevation of art, intuition, creativity and practice wisdom to essential places in professional functioning" (Papell & Skolnik, 1992, p. 20).

The qualitative research tradition does have some limitations as a paradigm for direct practice. First, although many experienced practitioners have gained comfort and skill in working in this reflective/inductive, common-sense fashion, students and recent graduates are less likely to have the confidence to rely on such a process. Second, although qualitative research strategies provide some guidelines for developing understanding of clients and their problem-situations, they do not offer guidance in intervening to promote change.

PROBLEM-SOLVING PROCESS

One way of providing some structure and guidelines to the type of intuitive process that is being recommended is to use the problem-solving process that has become one of the major generic components of social work practice (Compton & Galaway, 1994). The problem-solving process, which was first suggested as a process for social work practice by Perlman (1957), represents a reflective/inductive process whereby practitioner and client work together to develop understanding of the problem-situation and to intervene toward enabling better social functioning. Unfortunately, the technical-rational outlook has led to a devaluing of the problem-solving model.

Although there are many conceptualizations of the stages in the problem-solving process, the general thrust is that the practitioner needs to (a) develop tentative, preparatory empathy for the client as much as possible before they meet; (b) engage with the client through the provision of warmth, support, and empathy; (c) elicit a wide range of information from the client about the problem-situation; (d) collaboratively make sense of the information to come to an understanding of the major problems and resources; (e) collaboratively come to a decision about how to tackle the problem by weighing the pros and cons of different plans of action; (f) support the client in carrying through with the plans; (g) monitor the effectiveness of the plans; and (h) review the process and outcome of working together with the client so as to maximize learning and to work through emotional issues in terminating.

The problem-solving process described above has many parallels to the qualitative research process of developing understanding. It involves a lack of a priori assumptions; the gathering of a wide range of information; and building, through an empathic/inductive and collaborative process, a theory of the unique case. Furthermore, the problem-solving process provides guidelines for intervening that are consistent with a humanistic, creative, reflective process. It should be stressed that problem-solving in social work practice is not a rigid, linear, process. It is a complex, cyclical process in which stages may overlap, occur simultaneously, and recur. Problem-solving needs to be approached flexibly and managed creatively. It should also be stressed that problem-solving in social work practice is not a cold, intellectual, dispassionate process. Perlman (1979) has elucidated how good problem-solving is necessarily a deeply human encounter that is intertwined with relationship development: "Relationship is the continuous context within which problem-solving takes place. It is at the same time, the emerging product of mutual problem-solving efforts; and simultaneously it is the catalytic agent" (p. 151).

INTEGRATING A DEDUCTIVE USE OF THEORY

As mentioned earlier, the argument that practice is primarily a reflective/inductive process does not preclude the value of using theory in a traditional sense. Theories can be helpful as adjuncts to the reflective/inductive model of practice. A tentative consideration of how a wide range of theories may apply to the particular circumstances of a particular client can help in both the assessment and intervention phases of problem-solving.

As is commonly taught, higher level theories such as ecological systems and human development theories can prove particularly helpful as frameworks for data collection and assessment. The entire range of low-level practice theories may also prove helpful in alerting the practitioner to potential themes in the early phases of problem-solving, and they can certainly provide ideas for intervention — if they fit with the theory of the unique case that emerges from a reflective assessment.

The idea of using a broad range of theoretical frameworks eclectically and tentatively as adjuncts to an inductive, problem-solving process is as difficult as it sounds. The most common problem is the difficulty in balancing the inductive and the deductive approaches in an interview. It is difficult to remain in tune with the client and at the same time to entertain how a range of theories and techniques may enhance understanding and intervention. It seems that what most commonly happens is that tendencies to intellectualize, theorize, and second-guess our instincts cause us to "lose the feel" of a good interview. In an instructional video (Shulman & Gitterman, 1988), Shulman has described how workers' natural helping abilities, or "gut instincts," are often stifled by too much thinking and analysing.

Another problem that prohibits supplementing an inductive theory-building approach with the deductive application of theory is the confusion and mystification that continues to surround theories of helping. One issue is that the sheer number of apparently diverse therapeutic models to choose from is overwhelming and confusing. Also, the mystification of the language that is used in much of the professional literature is a major stumbling block. This is as true for the more recent family systems theories (Coady, 1993a) as it is for the more traditional theories such as psychoanalysis. Efforts need to be made to demystify theoretical frameworks and make them more user-friendly. Academic instructors could help in this regard by grouping like theories into classes (e.g., psychodynamic, cognitive-behavioral, humanistic, family systems, etc.) and then summarizing in plain language what each class of theory has to say about the etiology and treatment of human problems. Such a process can help to make theories less mystified and intimidating for students. Demystification also takes away the power and allure of theories so that students are more apt to see them as resources to supplement their natural, reflective/inductive, problem-solving practice.

TEACHING THE REFLECTIVE/INDUCTIVE MODEL OF PRACTICE

The problem of teaching skills necessary for the reflective/inductive model of practice is a challenging one for classroom and field instructors. Although didactic teaching is not conducive to such skill development, it is important to teach theory and research, such as that reviewed in this article, that lends credibility to this model of practice. Also, in addition to qualitative research and problem-solving frameworks, there a number of postpositivistic theories (e.g., narrative, feminist, cognitive theories) that could be taught as support for reflective/inductive practice.

Schön (1987) has contended that "Professional education should be redesigned to combine the teaching of applied science with coaching in the artistry of reflection-in-action" (p. xii). He has argued that "reflective practicums" that emphasize "learning by doing" should become the core of professional curricula. Schön's model of the reflective practicum involves a radical restructuring of "the usual figure/ground relationship between academic course work and practicum" (Schön, 1987, p. 310). Although it is beyond the scope of this article to analyze the implications of Schön's model for social work education, there are a number of ways that the development of skills conducive to reflective/inductive practice can be facilitated within the current structures of classrooms and practicums.

Papell and Skolnik (1992) have suggested how process recordings that foster reflection can be used in the classroom and the field. For instance, the author has employed a type of process recording to have students analyze, reflectively and intuitively, the effective and ineffective aspects of an interview and what they could do to make the next interview better. Subsequent to this, they are asked to link their own analyses, retrospectively, to theoretical frameworks and concepts so that they can see how their thoughts and behaviours parallel existing theory. Schön (1987) has noted that "case teaching" of this type helps students "to think differently about the theories offered by researchers when they realize that they hold comparable tacit theories of their own" (p. 324).

Papell and Skolnik (1992) have also noted how the use of role plays can be helpful in developing reflective talents. More specifically, there is a need for "greater emphasis on small, hands-on, interviewing skills courses that focus on the development of empathic/collaborative mindsets, relationship skills, and flexible use of self" (Coady, 1993b, p. 296). In coaching students to utilize natural interpersonal and reflective skills in role play and actual interviews, the author has found that Shulman's advice, to hold off on theorizing and analysing until after the interview, is helpful (Shulman & Gitterman, 1988). Thus, students are coached not to think about the correct communication skill or the perfect intervention during an interview. Instead, students are coached to tune-in, listen closely, build a fund of empathy and support, ask the simple questions, use their spontaneity, and trust their instincts (Shulman & Gitterman, 1988). Schön's (1983) analogies of the baseball pitcher getting a "feel for the ball" and the musician developing a "feel for the music" can be helpful in this regard. Theorizing and analysing are important after the fact and can be achieved through in-depth debriefing/feedback and analysis of videotapes.

Another skill/personal development suggestion is to maximize opportunities for students to view experienced practitioners' interviews in their practicums and to debrief with these practitioners about the interviewing process. Such opportunities would enable students to demystify and gain insight into the process of "professional artistry" (Schön, 1987). A related ideal is for both field and classroom instructors to "assume more of a collegial rather than an expert role with their students as they work together in a reflective, learning, and problem-solving venture" (Goldstein, 1986, p. 356).

A final point to be stressed is that in order to facilitate the type of learning that is being advocated, schools of social work need faculty who are skilled practitioners. With the academizing of schools of social work, it is increasingly rare to find practice teachers who have "authentic knowledge about practice grounded not only in research and theory but in experience as well" (Hartman, 1990, p. 48). In order to remedy this trend, "Admission criteria for social work doctoral programs, the hiring policies of schools of social work, and the reward system within social work academia need to be adjusted" (Coady, 1993b, p. 296).

CONCLUSION

Many of the struggles that students, instructors, and practitioners have with integrating theory with practice are based on an erroneous perception that the basis for good practice is the deductive application of theory. In contrast to the positivistic, technical-rational outlook that perpetuates this myth, a reflective/inductive model of practice suggests that effective practice is largely a function of natural, intuitive, interpersonal and problem-solving abilities. Classroom and field instructors need to promote awareness and understanding of the reflective/inductive model of practice to balance the prevailing emphasis on the deductive application of theory to practice. As Papell and Skolnik (1992) and Scott (1990) have noted, the reflective/inductive model of practice is linked to social work's historical emphasis on practice wisdom, clinical judgment, and experiential knowledge.

REFERENCES

Carew, R. (1979). The place of knowledge in social work activity. *British Journal of Social Work, 9,* 349-363.

Coady, N. (1993a). An argument for generalist social work practice with families versus family systems therapy. *Canadian Social Work Review, 10,* 27-42.

Coady, N. (1993b). The worker-client relationship revisited. *Families in Society, 74,* 291-298.

Compton, B. R., & Galaway, B. (1994). *Social work processes* (4th ed.). Belmont, CA: Wadsworth.

DeMartini, J. R., & Whitbeck, L. B. (1987). Sources of knowledge for practice. *Journal of Applied Behavioural Science, 23,* 219-231.

DeRoos, Y. S. (1990). The development of practice wisdom through human problem-solving processes. *Social Service Review, 64*, 276-287.

Frank, J. (1961). *Persuasion and healing: A comparative study of psychotherapy*. Baltimore, MD: Johns Hopkins University Press.

Gitterman, A. (1988). Teaching students to connect theory and practice. *Social Work with Groups, 11*, 33-41.

Goldstein, H. (1986). Toward the integration of theory and practice: A humanistic approach. *Social Work, 31*, 352-357.

Goldstein, H. (1990). The knowledge base of social work practice: Theory, wisdom, analogue, or art? *Families in Society, 71*, 32-43.

Greenwood, E. (1957). Attributes of a profession. *Social Work, 2*, 44-55.

Harrison, W. D. (1987). Reflective practice in social care. *Social Service Review, 61*, 393-404.

Hartman, A. (1990a). Many ways of knowing. *Families in Society, 71*, 3-4.

Hartman, A. (1990b). Education for direct practice. *Families in Society, 71*, 44-50.

Horvath, A. O., & Symonds, B. D. (1991). Relation between working alliance and outcome in psychotherapy: A meta-analysis. *Journal of Counseling Pychology, 38*, 139-149.

Hudson, W. W. (1978). First axioms of treatment. *Social Work, 23*, 65-66.

Kolevzon, M. S., & Maykranz, J. (1982). Theoretical orientation and clinical practice: Uniformity versus eclecticism? *Social Service Review, 56*, 120-129.

Lambert, M. J., & Bergin, A. E. (1994). The effectiveness of psychotherapy. In A. E. Bergin & S. L. Garfield (Eds.), *Handbook of psychotherapy and behavior change* (4th ed., pp. 143-189). New York: Wiley.

Mahoney, M. J. (1986). The tyranny of technique. *Counseling and Values, 30*, 169-174.

Orlinsky, D. E., Grawe, K., & Parks, B. K. (1994). Process and outcome in psychotherapy-- Noch Einmal. In A. E. Bergin & S. L. Garfield (Eds.), *Handbook of psychotherapy and behavior change* (4th ed., pp. 270-378). New York: Wiley.

Papell, C. P., & Skolnik, L. (1992). The reflective practitioner: A contemporary paradigm's relevance for social work education. *Journal of Social Work Education, 28*, 18-26.

Patton, M. Q. (1990). *Qualitative evaluation and research methods* (2nd ed.). Newbury Park, CA: Sage.

Perlman, H. H. (1957). *Social casework: A problem-solving process*. Chicago: University of Chicago Press.

Perlman, H. H. (1979). *Relationship: The heart of helping people*. Chicago: University of Chicago Press.

Rein, M., & White, S. (1981). Knowledge for practice. *Social Service Review, 55*, 1-41.

Sainsbury, E. (1980). Research and reflection on the social work task. *Social Work Service, 23*, 13.

Schön, D. A. (1983). *The reflective practitioner: How professionals think in action*. New York: Basic Books.

Schön, D. A. (1987). *Educating the reflective practitioner*. San Francisco: Jossey-Bass.

Scott, D. (1990). Practice wisdom: The neglected source of practice research. *Social Work, 35*, 564-568.

Sheldon, B. (1978). Theory and practice in social work: A re-examination of a tenuous relationship. *British Journal of Social Work, 8*, 1-25.

Shulman, L., & Gitterman, A. (1988). *Integrating the personal with the professional self* (Videotape). Montreal, QB: McGill University, Instructional Communications Centre.

Siporin, M. (1988). Clinical social work as an art form. *Social Casework, 69*, 177-183.

Wills, T. A. (1985). Supportive functions of interpersonal relationships. In S. Cohen & S. L. Syme (Eds.), *Social support and health* (pp. 61-82). Orlando, FL: Academic Press.

CHAPTER TWELVE

TEACHING THE UNTEACHABLE? THE TEACHING OF ETHICS IN FIELD EDUCATION

Sheena B. Findlay

Traditionally, social work values, and the ethics which derive from these, have been seen as foundational to the profession, a presumed unifying force among contending ideologies and practice modalities. However, in the years between the 1983 and the 1994 revision of the Canadian Code of Ethics, faced with the rapid acceleration of complex multidimensional problems both in society and in the profession, practitioners have been challenged to make ethical decisions for which their undergraduate education has often not prepared them. The question for social work educators including field educators, is how best can we prepare students for the competent ethical decision making which will be essential in dealing with professional dilemmas in the rest of this decade. Increased concern in the profession about ethical issues and the teaching of these has been reflected to some extent in the literature. Compared to professional writing on practice modalities or research, the material on ethics in general is fairly small, but there has been a steady development of a substantive body of literature within the last ten years on the teaching of ethics (see for example texts by Abbott, 1988; Rhodes, 1986; Reamer, 1990; Loewenberg & Dolgoff, 1992; monographs/research studies by Gross, Rosa, & Steiner 1980; Reamer & Abramson, 1982; Lewis, 1987; Joseph, 1988, 1991; Joseph & Conrad, 1983; Black, Hartley, Kirk-Sharp, & Whelley, 1989).

The emergence of these texts is certainly an indicator of the resurgence of interest in the teaching of ethics, but this should probably be taken in the context of the research studies (Joseph & Conrad, 1983; Black et al., 1989) as well as the Hastings Centre recommendation (Reamer & Abramson, 1982) which indicate and express concern that, in US schools, ethics are taught mainly by the "pervasive" method, i.e., ethics content diffused throughout the curriculum, rather than taught by discrete courses. A recent survey (Findlay, 1993) showed that Canadian schools are mainly using a pervasive method of teaching ethics in a somewhat random fashion, which in the view of this writer, raises the expectations in field practicum. Most Canadian schools anticipated that there would be considerable integration of professional and ethical practice in field; what was not specified was how they intended to structure the learning for such integration.

Three other themes from the literature of significance to field education, are the issue of social work educators as role models to students (Reamer & Abramson, 1982; Lewis, 1987), the general impact of social work education on students' values and their socialisation into the profession (Abbott, 1988), and one research study (Conrad, 1988b) on the role of field instructors in the transmission of social justice values.

In sum, there has been an increase in interest in the teaching of ethics judged by the growth of professional writing and research yet what has been done serves to highlight how much there is that we do not know about the teaching-learning endeavour in the area of ethics. We do not know, for example, much about the ethical profile of our admissions groups in a Canadian or regional context although some of our screening procedures do address in a general way, an applicant's suitability for the profession. Nor is there much written about the human side of ethical teaching and learning; we may recognise social learning as an important part of social work theory, but we appear to make limited planned use of the ethical learning which undoubtedly takes place between students and their peers, their faculty, or their field instructors — at least as far as the professional literature would indicate.

I believe that we have no research on how effectively the ethical aspects of our respective curricula do actually prepare students for social work practice. We assume that there is a connection between our means of teaching ethical content and the manner in which graduates under the later pressures of practice in organisational systems, their own life stage demands, and a radically altering societal context, make their ethical decisions. In fact, I think we know little about this area of social workers' lives. John Cossom (1992), reviewing a number of doctoral dissertation research studies since 1980, points up many inconsistencies in the ethical positions of practitioners, a dearth of empirical knowledge on the subject, and considerable dissatisfaction with the ethical preparation of workers by schools of social work.

Finally, it is clear that with only one research study (Conrad, 1988b) directly on the topic over perhaps fifteen years, we do not know much about the manner in which ethics are communicated in field education. In the Canadian survey (Findlay, 1993) of ethics teaching in undergraduate programs, respondents were quite assertive that social work practice courses taken together with field learning are the major place in the curriculum for the integration of social work values. The ethical content covered in practice courses, however, showed considerable variation both in topics and time allotment; there was some limited commonality on teaching about personal/professional values, Code of Ethics, and confidentiality. On the teaching of ethics specifically in field practicum, most schools responded with a general statement that content deals with ethical issues as these arise in particular agencies. Two French schools specified the teaching of confidentiality, professional secrets, and issues with colleagues/other disciplines; one school raised the issues of the ethics of learning, field instruction, and learning contract. Overall, however, few schools were able to describe clearly planned educational objectives for the teaching and integration of ethics in field education.

It seems probable that in Canadian schools of social work we assume that students will take in by osmosis from classes, peers, faculty, field instructors, the ethical underpinnings necessary for a well functioning professional person. A related assumption is that students will all be exposed to ethical issues and provided with opportunities to practice ethical decision-making in their field agencies, without the necessity for schools to plan and monitor for this aspect of professional learning. Contrary to such assumptions, it is the view of this writer that ethics can and must be taught as any other area of a school's curriculum, that educators must plan for the teaching of ethics preferably in a combination of pervasive and discrete classroom courses, and that particular attention must be given to the inclusion of ethics teaching in field education.

Conventional wisdom would probably agree that field practicum — being the place where students begin to translate theoretical knowledge from many sources into practice skills — is also the place where students do their major work on the process of translating terminal value positions into ethical professional behaviour. One way of facilitating this process is to sensitise field instructors to the importance of teaching ethics in practicum and to provide them with some principles and methods for doing so. Some of the content of this paper, along with a workshop, was originally given in 1992, 1993 to instructors at the School of Social Work, Memorial University, as part of the field instructors' course in three different locations in the province. In 1993, the workshop was expanded to include a session with field instructors along with their students, subsequent to a session with instructors alone. The workshop format makes use of several sets of group exercises designed to facilitate ethical consciousness-raising and decision-making among participants.

In planning to teach ethics in field, instructors will, as for any course in the curriculum, begin by identifying learning objectives, which might be as follows:

1)   to increase students' intellectual understanding of the common ethical
       issues as these are seen in the particular field placement setting;

2) to facilitate growth in students' self awareness on their own personal/professional values and on selected ethical positions specific to the field agency;

3) to provide opportunity for practice in ethical decision-making including the skills of analysing the sources of ethical significance, identifying personal values raised by issues, weighing ethical factors, making conscious ethical choices and defending one's ethical positions.

There are also some underlying principles which seem to this writer to be particularly relevant to the teaching of ethics. Firstly, since the Code of Ethics itself, and some classroom teaching of ethics, tend to be terminal and abstract, it is important that practicum teaching attempt to maximise integration by responding to different learning styles, i.e., experiential, conceptual and social learning. Secondly, ethical awareness can be particularly threatening to students in a profession where there are strong messages to be "value-free" as well as politically correct. Instructors therefore need to work at developing a genuinely safe context for exploration, discussion and making choices.

So if instructors are going to teach ethics to students in the agency, what do they need to know to be effective? I would suggest four areas of knowledge: ethical self knowledge; knowledge of the main areas of ethical choices in practice, as these are seen in the field setting; knowledge of students' current ethical understanding and awareness; knowledge of some ways of teaching ethics in the agency setting.

ETHICAL SELF KNOWLEDGE

If we intend to try to make students aware of ethical issues in our own agencies, and if we allow for students to learn in part from our own modelling, it seems to me that we must ask ourselves where we are now in relation to our own consciousness of ethical issues.

I think most practitioners take for granted that they practice according to the Code of Ethics in much the same fashion as they assumed they did at graduation. However, the evidence is that not only do peoples' values change overtime (Rokeach, 1975), but also societal values, the profession's and those of professional practitioners (Conrad, 1988b; Abbott, 1988). Conrad, for instance, found that a high percentage of instructors saw the importance of ethical transmission in field and were transmitting predominantly egalitarian views, though those longer in professional employment and/or field instruction were likely to transmit more utilitarian views. As well, those in management after about five years out of school showed a much stronger adherence to a libertarian orientation. Many of us, it seems to me, would be hard put to express exactly what our own value priorities are after some years of practice. We might give a general terminal position on values of social work, but possibly not recognise changes at the instrumental level until forced to do so when a particular ethical issue comes up to challenge our comfortable assumptions. It may be that in professional midlife some of the additional factors which consciously or otherwise influence our decisions are such issues as "I have a spouse/children," or "I want a promotion" or "I need my work support group/job."

I am not suggesting that any of us need to be (or even can be) ethical paragons to teach others but we need to be ethically aware of where we are, at this stage in our professional lives. At the least we need to be able to identify how we deal with the ethical demands of our own agencies, our own administration, and how we respond to the professional challenges of burnout, coasting, being coopted by the system. Our most effective model to students is not of someone who, ethically speaking, has all the answers, but of someone who is alert to the issues in their own work, still struggling with the process and confident enough to be able to share that process.

MAIN AREAS OF ETHICAL CHOICES IN PRACTICE

Reamer (1990), Loewenberg and Dolgoff (1992) identify some characteristic ethical decision-making areas in practice; instructors need to reflect on how they are manifested in the particular field agency, so that students can be sensitized to them.

Resolving One's Personal and Professional Values and Ethics

Students often arrive at the field setting assuming that their personal values pose no problem in relation to the values and ethics of the profession. If they keep these in terminal form, then the possible incongruences may not show. When they encounter real people, whether clients or co-workers, there can be a shock as circumstances force them to activate in practice their assumed beliefs. They find that some clients are resistant to all their good suggestions, some lie, some cheat, some manipulate. As well they discover that social workers in practice are human, not perfectly aligned with social work values at the level of ethical decisions. First time field students struggle with the reality of their own biases, and with the unfortunate illusion of social work as value free or value neutral. Field instructors need to lookout for signs of this struggle and "give permission" to engage in it, particularly as students may be afraid to admit this.

Recognition of the Inherently Conflicting Rights/duties of the Profession

As the field placement progresses and students begin to look somewhat beyond their own concerns, they are likely to begin to see, for example, the conflict between the worker's duty to help and serve and the limits to personal freedom of clients, as in self determination issues; right to treatment, consent to treatment; and, confidentiality. They may begin also to appreciate conflicts between the rights of more than one client, as in parent/child, husband/wife; rights of clients vs. rights of society, and institutionalization/community integration. Essentially, here students are struggling with the contradictoriness of the expectations placed on social work practitioners and need help in *recognising* the situations in which the Code of Ethics does not give more than general guidelines. They also need help and practice in *actually making ethical decisions* where utilitarian and egalitarian outcomes are ranked against each other.

Relationships Within the Agency and/or Between the Agency and Other Community Resources, Learning to Become an Ethical Social Work Employee/Colleague

Looking at the research (Conrad, 1988a, 1988b; Abbott, 1988; Lewis, 1987; Joseph & Conrad, 1983) and at my own experience, this seems to be the most contentious one for students and agency practitioners alike. For seasoned professionals this gets at one's loyalty to the employing organisation and peer support group, versus one's loyalty to the profession's ethics concerning service. Some characteristic questions arise concerning agency policy and practice on confidentiality, on fully informed consent to treatment, public loyalty to policies/service delivery methods which demean clients, or appropriate service in times of financial restraint. Also in this category would be supervisory and collegial relationships including issues such as professional behaviour at the office, field instruction ethics, dealing with alcoholism, sexual harassment, whistle-blowing etc. Helping students with this area, which is often problematic for field instructors themselves, requires a willingness to self disclose rather than conceal one's own struggles, and an effective modelling of the process of ethical problem-solving.

Social Justice and Macro Change

The 1994 Code of Ethics gives rather cursory attention to the broader professional mandate to work for a more humane and just society particularly in the community immediate to one's own agency. Some students will initially give a great deal of attention to social justice concerns in placement in part because they have probably had recent academic input on this topic, and discussion in a fairly broad ranging philosophical mode harnesses their sense of distributive justice. Opportunities for practice will vary according to the agency's functions and the idiosyncrasies of individual instructors. I think it is the instructor's role to raise consciousness about justice issues as these are exemplified in the field practice setting, helping the student to engage with the "practice of the possible" rather than the ideal. In any of the foregoing areas of ethical decision making instructors need to ask themselves "how does this show in my own workplace?", "how have I resolved the typical dilemmas here?", "how can I set up a learning — and appropriate level of decision making experience — for the student in these areas?"

STUDENTS' CURRENT ETHICAL UNDERSTANDING AND AWARENESS

We, as partners in social work education, need to have an understanding of where our students in general can be expected to be in relation to the process of translating their terminal values into ethical positions and behaviours. Students, like everybody else in the profession, derive their current beliefs, both personal and professional, from similar sources i.e., North American values, mediated through family, community, churches, schools, peer groups, to produce a unique mix in adult life; professional values, which also ultimately derive from North American values and the history of social work as a culture; the Code of Ethics as a general guideline to expected professional behaviour; a limited amount of classroom teaching on ethics, depending on the teaching policy and practices of their school; and, socialisation into the profession from faculty and peers. The extent to which students have *integrated and internalised* these sources will vary considerably according to age, life stage and experience.

Two early writers (Rokeach, 1973; Perlman, 1976) emphasized an ongoing values clarification process in all of us of moving what we believe into what we *do*. Writing from a feminist perspective and building on Gilligan's work, Blythe, McVicar Clinchy (1989) reminds us that the college years are, or can be, a prime time for work on this process. Potentially, field students will be struggling to sort out questions of who they are, what they really believe, what social work will do for them, what being a professional means though we have to also remember that realistically, students are dealing with many *other* life and career related issues, while they are in field practice; some at this stage of their lives are only open to learning on carefully selected topics! As well we have to recognise that they will be dealing with input on ethics from other sources, such as peer socialization, faculty socialization, and classroom content on values and ethics, which may not be mutually congruent. The research suggests that while students come to social work education with some predisposition towards social work values in general the impact of social work education on socialisation into the profession is unclear (Varley, 1963, 1968; Judah, 1979; Abbott, 1988). We can anticipate that students will come to field education with a reasonable general identification with social work values, but not necessarily any clearly thought out positions on day-to-day ethics.

TEACHING ETHICS IN THE AGENCY SETTING

In teaching ethics in the agency it is necessary to consider students' different learning styles. Some students, as social learners, learn much from observation of peers or role models; others, conceptual learners, learn primarily from concepts, analysing ideas from classroom content, books, library sources and from trying to apply theory; and, still others, as experiential learners, learn mainly from experimenting and doing, making mistakes and then correcting or adjusting. Field curriculum on ethics therefore should attempt to respond to different learning styles with different teaching modes and use an approach which incorporates elements of all three. I have suggested ways of teaching ethics which I have found useful.

Assist Student with Initial Values and Ethics Self Assessment

Facilitation of ethical self assessment can be a useful part of orientation to field practice setting, and preparation for learning contract. Part of an instructor's efforts to get to know students — who they are, where they are in their life journeys, what kind of learners they are etc. — is to assess together with the them, their beginning positions concerning social work values and the ethics which derive from these. Doing this not only gives both a baseline from which to work, as with any other field objective, but also highlights to the student the instructor's sense of the importance of this aspect of professional formation.

One device for assessment is to use Levy's classification (1976a, 1976b, 1982, 1993): preferred conceptions of man-in-society; preferred outcomes for people; preferred instrumentalities for dealing with people. Another is to modify Corey, Corey and Callanan's (1989) more clinically oriented values and ethics inventory. Both of these can be adapted to fit the particular setting, in fact it can be an enlightening exercise for instructors and colleagues to work together on an ethical assessment questionnaire for their own agency. Ethical self assessment includes some conceptual as well as experiential learning, and, if the instructor or fellow students self-disclose, some social learning.

Articles on Social Work Ethics and on Ethical Issues Specific to the Agency

Relating to the needs of the more conceptual learners, it is helpful to have prepared for distribution to field students some theoretical sources, preferably directly related to the agency context. It is important that instructors set up situations where students must *make use* of the literature, either by assigning an article to be prepared for discussion at field instruction sessions, or by having people present the article and the ethical issue at a student discussion group/staff meeting. This responds to conceptual learners but also stresses experiential and social aspects if peer/colleague presentation is involved.

Log Entry — Weekly Ethics Check In

Another useful idea is to put a heading in the outline for weekly field recording asking "what ethical issues came up for you this week, either involving you or others in your agency?", and discuss in supervision. The field instructor has opportunities to turn critical incidents of daily practice into "teachable moments" by putting these through a "values screening" process. Again, the main emphasis is experiential but there's potential for conceptual, if the instructor can reference the theory, and for modelling, if he/she self discloses.

Group Process in Ethical Learning

If the instructor has a group of students in similar placements s/he can run sessions on ethics specific to the field of practice, and can also try role played situations to bring ethics into very pragmatic real life focus. This can be helpful for dealing with the situation where either an ethical issue does not naturally occur in a particular week, or where there are one/several students who seem ethically unaware. While the research on this topic is limited, it does suggest that social learning — from peers, faculty, and field instructors, is an important influence on students' socialization into the profession. In a field group format, one can incorporate conceptual learning through journal articles and didactic material from the instructor; one can make use of experiential learning through group critique of ethical incidents or role played vignettes; and one can consciously plan to facilitate social learning through group discussion, structured debate, interviewing colleagues in the group on ethical issues, and through the instructor's intentional use of self-disclosure. Essential to the effective use of this learning device would be the instructor's skills in leading group process so as to provide a safe, nonjudgemental but yet challenging, learning climate.

CONCLUSION

Underlying all of these suggested methods for teaching ethics in field is the concern of this writer for providing as many opportunities as possible for students to practice ethical decision making, so that they will be able to make effective ethical choices in their future professional lives. The research indicates that we do not know much about how we actually make ethical decisions in situations of conflict between two or more competing goods and most models favour an ethical version of problem-solving (Litke in Yelaja,

1982; Reamer, 1990; Joseph, 1991; Cossom, 1992). I believe that in both class and field, we should teach the skills of analysing and evaluating ethically significant factors, identifying personal values, defending one's positions, and making informed decisions. The area of ethical education for practice is a crucial and somewhat under emphasized part of socialization into the profession. Field instructors have an essential role in facilitating in students the development of an ethical identity so central to professional practice.

REFERENCES

Abbott, A. A. (1988). *Professional choices; values at work.* Silver Springs, MD: National Association of Social Workers, N.Y.

Black, P., Hartley, E. K., Kirk-Sharp, C., & Whelley, J. (1989). Ethics curricula; a national survey of graduate schools of social work. *Social Thought, 19,* 141-148.

Canadian Association of Social Workers (1994). Social Work Code of Ethics.

Clinchy, B. McVicar. (1989). The development of thoughtfulness in college women. *American Behavioral Scientist, 32*(6).

Conrad, A. P. (1988a). Ethical considerations in the psychosocial process. *Social Casework, 69,* 603-610.

Conrad, A. P. (1988b). The role of the field instructor in the transmission of social justice values. *Journal of Teaching in Social Work, 2*(2), 63-64.

Corey, G., Corey, M., & Callanan, P. (1993). *Issues and ethics in the helping professions.* Pacific Grove, CA: Brooks Cole.

Cossom, J. (1992). What do we know about social workers' ethics? *The Social Worker, 60* (3), 165-171.

Findlay, S. B. (1993). Teaching ethics for practice in the 'real' world of the nineties. Unpublished presentation, May 1993 Canadian Association of Schools of Social Work Conference/Learned Societies, Ottawa.

Gilligan, C. (1982). *In a different voice; Psychological theory and women's development.* Cambridge, MA: Harvard University Press.

Gross, G. M., Rosa, L., & Steiner, J. R. (1980). Educational doctrines and social work values; match or mismatch? *Journal of Education for Social Work, 16*(3), 21-28.

Hastings Center Institute of Society, Ethics, and the Life Sciences. (1980). *The teaching of ethics in Higher Education.* The teaching of ethics Institute, Hastings-on-Hudson, N.Y.

Hokenstad, T. (1987). Teaching practitioners ethical judgement. *National Association of Social Workers' News, 4.*

Joseph, M. V. (1988). *Developing and teaching models of ethical decision making* (Monograph). Chicago: School of Social Work, Loyola University of Chicago.

Joseph, M. V. (1991). Standing for values and ethical action; teaching social work ethics. *Journal of Teaching in Social Work, 5*(2), 95-109.

Joseph, M. V., & Conrad, A. P. (1983). Teaching social work ethics for contemporary practice; an effectiveness evaluation. *Journal of Education for Social Work, 19*(3), 59- 68.

Judah, E. H. (1979). Values; the uncertain component of social work education. *Journal of Education for Social Work, 15*(2), 79-86.

Levy, C. S. (1976a). The value base of social work. *Journal for Education in Social Work, 9,* 34-42.

Levy, C. S. (1976b). Personal versus professional values; the practitioner's dilemma. *Clinical Social Work Journal, 4,* 110-20.

Levy, C. S. (1982). *Guide to ethical decisions and actions for social service administrators.* New York: Howarth Press.

Levy, C. S. (1993). *Social work ethics on the line.* Binghampton, NY: The Haworth Press.

Lewis, H. (1987). Teaching ethics through ethical teaching. *Journal of Teaching in Social Work, 1*(1), 3-14.

Loewenberg, F. M., & Dolgoff, R. (1992). *Ethical decisions for social work practice* (4th ed.). Itasca, IL: F.E. Peacock.

Perlman, H. H. (1976). Believing and doing: Values in social work education. *Social Casework, 57,* 381-390.

Reamer, F. G. (1990). *Ethical dilemmas in social service* (2nd ed.). New York: Columbia University.

Reamer, F. G., & Abramson, M. (1982). *The teaching of social work ethics*. The Hastings Center, Institute of Society, Ethics, and the Life Sciences.

Rhodes, M. (1986). *Ethical dilemmas in social work practice*. Boston: Routledge, Kegan, Paul.

Rokeach, M. (1973). *The nature of human values*. New York: MacMillan Free Press.

Siporin, M. (1982). Moral philosophy in social work today. *Social Service Review, 56*, 516-538.

Varley, B. K. (1963). Socialization in social work education. *Social Work, 8*(4), 102-9.

Varley, B. K. (1968, Fall). Social work values; changes in value commitments of students from admission to MSW graduation. *Journal of Education for Social Work, 4*, 67-76.

Wells, C. C., & Masch, M. K. (1986). *Social Work Ethics, Day to Day*. Illinois: Waveland Press, Inc.

Yelaja, S. (Ed.). (1982). *Ethical issues in social work*. Chicago, IL: Charles C. Thomas.

CHAPTER THIRTEEN

SOCIAL WORK WRITING: LEARNING BY DOING

Anthony Paré and Helen Szewello Allen

Writing is a critical aspect of social work practice, especially in agencies and institutions, where recordkeeping occupies a considerable amount of time and fills clients' files. The documents in those files describe, monitor, assess, and proscribe behaviour and have far-reaching consequences for individuals, families, even whole communities. This profound influence, and a number of other factors — including client access to files and increasing concern about legal accountability — make writing a difficult and important part of professional life. For social work students, the field placement experience can be greatly affected by the extent of their participation in organizational writing practices; the nature of that participation is the focus of this chapter.

The centrality of writing in social work is particularly important in the light of current composition theory, which views writing as a complex social activity with a critical role in the creation and perpetuation of organizational knowledge, beliefs, values, and procedures. Studies of workplace writing (e.g., Spilka, 1993) have demonstrated how texts are part of repeated institutional practices that include procedures, other (past and future) texts, and relationships. So, for example, a psychosocial assessment evolves out of a relatively stable repertoire of non-writing procedures: interviews, telephone calls, meetings, reviews of previous documentation, testing, reflection, and so on; the completed text (itself a regularized pattern of sections, terminology, and rhetorical intentions) sets in motion another series of habitual practices: treatment plans, meetings, further records; the text sustains and sits at the centre of a web of relationships among the worker, client, family, and other professionals (nurses, psychiatrists, lawyers, teachers, etc.).

In current composition theory, these repeated, intertwined patterns of text and context are defined as "genres" (see Miller, 1984; Devitt, 1993). This definition goes beyond the traditional notion of genre as the repetition of textual features to encompass regular patterns in the social activity surrounding and supporting repeated texts. Learning to write the documents that are the textual centre of genres can be a difficult task. Newcomers to the field of social work — either students in placement or recent graduates — must learn more than the form and content of a given record; they must also grasp the place and function of the record in the ongoing work and culture of the organization.

The highly setting-specific nature of workplace genres makes school-based instruction in professional writing somewhat ineffective; it is simply not possible to replicate in the classroom the intricacies of workplace contexts. As a result, field-based educators must bear the brunt of responsibility for introducing newcomers to social work records. Unfortunately, this important task is rarely discussed in the literature or by supervisors in the field. Instead, a wide variety of informal teaching methods have evolved, some more successful than others. In this chapter, we examine some of those methods, evaluate their effectiveness, and suggest alterations to school- and field-based instruction that will ease the passage from academic to professional social work writing.

Social work records have always played an important role in practice. They have been used to document pertinent data as well as to record service encounters. Initially, records were lengthy, providing verbatim accounts or chronological narratives of all transactions. Early on in the history of the profession, the efficiency of narrative records was debated, with suggestions being made for the use of check lists and forms. In response, Mary Richmond (1925) offered nine reasons for detailed narrative records:

1) records help workers be more effective by providing the full complications of a case;
2) records allow someone else to continue treatment when workers get sick, go on holiday, or move to new points of service;
3) records can be used as a starting point when people return for service years after their case has been closed;
4) records help in the supervision of staff;
5) records help train new workers;
6) records offer data for the study and improvement of treatment;
7) records can be grouped around presenting problems to provide the opportunity to assess effective treatment;

8)   records contain the full and detailed descriptions that allow for
      problem-solving in difficult cases; and finally
9)   records provide public evidence of the activities of social work.

Richmond made a plea for "full, day-by-day recording of what is happening" (p. 216). This early debate has set the scene for an ongoing discussion within the profession about the use of social records and their appropriate form and content. What has not been much debated is the teaching of recording skills. Social work students receive virtually no school-based training in the writing of social work records. In our review of 15 Canadian university calendars, we found not a single undergraduate or graduate social work course devoted to writing in social work; indeed, we found scant reference to professional writing in the hundreds of course descriptions we read. Following an extensive review of social work literature, Simon and Soven (1989) argued that "the teaching of writing in social work education remains an underdeveloped domain that merits educators' full attention in the 1990s" (p. 49). Our own, more recent, review of that literature suggests that Simon and Soven's call has been ignored: we found no articles on the teaching of social work writing.

As mentioned above, part of this neglect has to do with the difficulty of designing classroom conditions that simulate the diversity of expectations in organizational writing. However, even when they are in the field, students often receive little or no direct instruction in recording. Our impression, based on observation and interviews with students and field instructors, is that students learn to write records by examining old records on file, sometimes at the suggestion of their field instructors, but often out of desperation when no support is offered and a record is due. Apparently, this practice has a history: in 1949, Sytz observed that "students are inclined to model their recording after that which they see in the agency records. For these are the records of real people the student will see today or tomorrow" (p. 400).

Using existing records as models presents a number of problems. The writing can be clear or confused, effective or ineffective, but judgments about its quality cannot be made on the basis of the decontextualized texts themselves. All of the personalities, politics, interpersonal relations, and dynamics in play at the time of writing are lost. Moreover, old records do not reflect new approaches to assessment and treatment or new directions in service delivery. Using old models means looking back, rather than critically reflecting on the writing needs of the current situation.

Records not only document social "facts" in descriptive terms, but also provide diagnoses and problem definitions that are judgments formed by the social worker. These judgments are subjective and limited to a particular moment in time. Social science researchers are taking a social constructionist view of reality as "an ever-changing pattern of meanings that people construct daily from their past experience or cultural heritage, present knowledge and experience, and future possibilities" (Holbrook, 1983,

p. 651). Thus, the social record reflects the reality that has been negotiated between the worker and the client with the information and assessment that both have been willing and able to share. Records on file, therefore, give students a partial and distorted view of the cases they describe.

Records are also part of a larger systems of benefits and controls. For example, they determine who gets welfare, whether a child is placed in foster care, if a refugee claimant gets refugee status, whether a person with a mental health problem is a voluntary or involuntary patient. Records are powerful documents that support and enhance treatment or deny services. On file, however, they are removed from their dynamic involvement in this larger system. For a newcomer, the story told by an individual record may seem unrelated to social power relations, organizational policies, historical trends, or other larger frameworks.

In other words, language is political, but newcomers may not discern the politics that are played out in and through social work records. Professional language has been criticized as creating distance between the social worker and the client. "Language, like our official institutions, is never neutral and reflects not only the personality of the writer but also carries the official weight of the agency supported by professional jargon in the record" (Holbrook, 1983, p. 655). Language reflects the writer's values, class, racial understanding, and gender perspective and influences the record that a particular writer will produce. Records, however, are almost always couched in a neutral or "objective" style, and do not acknowledge the writer's participation in the written record. Recognizing and adopting this formal, detached stance is extremely difficult for social work students (and we might well ask whether we want students to be successful at imitating this style).

Given that social work records are so important and that learning to write them is fraught with difficulties and problems, we were curious to discover the ways in which students went about the task. Our findings — based on years of informal observation by one author, and research interviews conducted by the other author — suggest a continuum of approaches ranging from passive observation to full participation. At the less engaged end of that spectrum, students read other people's reports, sit as spectators at meetings and client interviews, and occasionally write "practice" texts that do not go into files. Full participation means involvement in the genre networks described above; that is, students become immersed in the full range of activities that lead up to and follow from social work records. Although the degree of engagement does seem to increase with level of education and time spent in the field, we found undergraduates who were working much like frontline social workers and graduate students who watched passively from the sidelines.

The following interview excerpts provide examples of some of the ways that social work students learn to write on the job. Although it is unlikely that a student would experience only one of these approaches, and some students experience all of them, certain approaches do predominate in any given field placement. In the first series of excerpts, the students have apparently been left to their own devices.

> Q: And for these assessments, are you following a format?
> A: Evidently, there are two formats. There's a format you are kind of supposed to follow . . . and there's a format that they actually use. . . . but yeah, there's definitely a format which apparently changes from department to department, like in Child Psychiatry it's different from the Rehab units.
>
> *****
>
> An incident did come up last week with the woman I work with who's not my supervisor. . . . she was told by the supervisor to write a referral note about a kid who was being transferred to [a psychiatric hospital], and she didn't know where to begin to write this letter. . . . So I helped her write the letter, but it was very frustrating because we had no guidance or help whatsoever.
>
> *****
>
> Q: Are you expected to keep documentation on clients for the clinic?
> A: We are, but so far that's been pretty vague. . . . We are supposed to keep weekly progress notes and I gather there's a format and I sort of found out what the format was by going through some old case notes and finding the format that was used in the past.

These accounts suggest uncertainty, frustration, confusion. There may be some merit to a sink-or-swim instructional approach, but it is difficult to imagine what advantage is gained by leaving students in this kind of quandary. These beginners are working with clients and collaborating with colleagues. However, they have been left to discover the writing demands of their particular setting, apparently without assistance from their field instructors. The assessment format change from psychiatry to rehab may reflect complex differences in policies, procedures, worker-client relations, readership, and use of the record; a referral note to a psychiatric hospital is no simple rhetorical task; and learning to write progress notes by studying old records, as mentioned above, prevents critical reflection on the act of writing in the current situation.

This reliance on old records is most obvious in the next series of comments, which describe what is probably the most common method of initiating students into the world of social work records: sending them to the files.

> Q: How did you learn how to write psycho-socials?
> A: Um, I think I made copies of [agency] formats, and my supervisor gave me a big file of things she had. . . . And then you learn by reading, and really you sort of crib material from other assessments.
>
> *****
>
> Q: How is the format provided to you?

A: There are headings and then some of the sections have, you know, for example, 'include data about home, community, neighbourhood, religion,' and so forth. And then, you know, you plough through somebody else's file, somebody else's assessment, to see what kind of information they included. . . . I was told, "this person writes wonderful assessments, go read them."

*****

Q: Are you writing documents that go into client files?

A: Yes. I'm actually, right now, trying to write up an assessment. . . . I looked at some old assessments to see how I'm supposed to write it up. . . . [My supervisor] found three that she thought were really good that would give me a good idea how to write them.

In these cases, the reliance on old records was recommended, and possibly monitored, by field instructors. But again the question arises: can students appreciate the complex and dynamic interactions that precede and follow from these texts? Is it enough to adopt the tone, terminology, structure, and rhetorical strategy of old documents, no matter how "good" they may have been in the situations that spawned them? Of real concern is the extent to which this approach perpetuates the structure, style, and content of old records and, more importantly, leads to the uncritical adoption of underlying attitudes and values.

In the next series of excerpts, students describe what have been called "dummy runs" (Britton et al., 1975); that is, writing that simulates real recordkeeping but never actually gets used.

I watch my supervisor's interviews and then write an assessment which she reads and comments on, but they don't go into the file. . . . She said maybe later.

*****

Well, it's kind of silly, because there's one of my patients who's been in there for 30 years, and I really don't see the point of my writing an assessment, given that there's not anything new I could possibly have to say about him. But it's from the point of view of practice, of how to write it, an unbiased assessment.

Field instructors who use simulations are clearly conscious of the students' need to learn to write agency records. And such simulations, done on the job, surely have more value than similar approximations performed in the classroom. However, the student who cannot "see the point of [her] writing" needs help in situating that writing in the larger organizational context. Why should the assessment be "unbiased"? What constitutes bias in this situation, and what are its consequences?

The next series of comments may also describe dummy runs, but there is one important difference: these students are in an apprentice relationship with field instructors, who offer criticism and suggestions on draft versions of records. This approach allows field instructors to draw students' attention to features of form and content. Furthermore, they can fill in the contextual gaps around a particular record, explain the rationale for regular formats, and offer tips on writing. This moves the student further along the continuum toward full participation. However, even this method may not be totally satisfactory, as the first student's closing "I guess" and the third student's frustration suggest.

Q: How have you learned to write?

A: I learned mostly by. . . . I wrote it, and I showed it to my supervisor and, I mean, all the information was right but it was all under the wrong headings and so I had to end up shifting things around and then I redid it and it was fine, I guess.

*****

Q: Has your supervisor helped you to write?

A: My supervisor was very good about correcting everything, giving it back to me. I often wrote reports 8 times over because she wanted me to understand what I was doing. She was really wonderful about . . . explaining if I was in a different setting how my writing style would change.

*****

Q: Did you do any writing?

A: [Yes, but] it was very confusing because it wasn't clear as to what exactly they wanted. So I would get back, you know, I would submit [the report] to my supervisor and my supervisor would look at it and most of the parts were okay. There were some parts that just needed total revision. Why I couldn't know this beforehand is beyond me. . . . the expectations of my field work, my written work, was I would say, generally unclear. So I think the demand is left up to trial and error, I suppose. . . . But it never really clicks in until the time comes when you're actually writing it yourself and you know the family or you have a good impression of where the family is at.

This student's final comment captures what we believe is the key element in effective placement writing instruction: actually writing. Initial placement experiences may not allow for the writing of working records, and some of the approaches to instruction we have described above — such as dummy runs and the apprenticeship method — are of value, but for students to learn the place and function of records in the day-to-day life of social work nothing can replace the full integration described in these final interview excerpts:

Q: How are you learning to do [Initial Assessment Reports]?

A: We would have assessment team meetings, and there were various aspects within the assessment process that needed some clarification. Besides, I did the first couple of them with [fellow student]. . . . We basically shared a lot of ideas and — that was a very interesting process, that was. And we would pull our supervisor aside, too, and bounce off ideas, and other colleagues. So we had resources. We could access our team. We could access our supervisor. . . . I was put, and [fellow student] was put, in a situation where we have to respond . . . not only to the family but . . . to the Director of Assessment — what the requirements, policies, and things of that nature need to reflect. We have to respond to the Director of Professional Services. . . . I think it's very important to respond to what the social worker needs to know and what the child care worker needs to know. So, we're writing basically to a family of professionals that need to know where to go with this case.

As a full, cooperating member of a team, this student experienced writing as an integrated aspect of social work practice. The record he produced was not a disembodied text but a connecting component in a dynamic process that included meetings, consultation, policy considerations, clients, administrators, child care workers, and social work colleagues. Most important, perhaps, he has grasped the function of the record — its place within the agency's work and its influence on the "family of professionals" he hopes to join.

We believe there is an enormous, qualitative difference between this learning by doing and the learning by looking or modelling described in the previous excerpts. The student who engages in writing as part of a collaborative enterprise with real-world consequences learns about writing, and about social work, in a way that classroom study or file searches can not provide. Consider the subtle knowledge a final-year undergraduate displays in this interview excerpt:

A: There's one instance where, guys like 20, 21 or so and his first admission was when he was thirteen and a half, so he's had, you know, this big change between a 13 year old and a 20 year old and my supervisor wanted me to write a sympathetic assessment, and so I kind of skewed it to make it sympathetic.

Q: Interesting, why did she ask for a sympathetic assessment.

A: We are going to try to place this individual and the way things work is that you have to present to a committee, who decides whether he should be placed . . . placement in a foster home. She wanted it really just to be sympathetic. And I then sort of . . . report the facts and then let the reader interpret for themselves. In this particular case, it was a fire setter, and she wanted his fire setting behaviour

> cast in a certain light, and so that's what I did. I write much better than she does. So she had me writing. And I wrote a wonderful assessment but it was you know, an integration of the last seven or eight years of medical, educational, and psycho-social assessments, and then it was sort of showing how we wanted to show it.
>
> Q: In every case, or in that particular case?
>
> A: No, it's that particular case. Other cases, you know, in social work you want to show the strengths not the weaknesses so, the kinds of things that you know you wouldn't say, you know, this client is stupid and limited. You would say this client had x amount of possibilities or whatever.
>
> Q: You say that in social work you stress the strengths but not the weaknesses; is that professional or disciplinary?
>
> A: It's me, and it's really a sharp contrast with the medical profession that finds the weaknesses and fixes them. We're not really supposed to do that. You're supposed to say, okay, this person has this, this person is smart, this person has a strong social support network, what can we do? Not say, this person has no money, this person lives in a dump, it's hopeless you know. The end is just to say the opposite.

Again, the student was immersed in the context and saw how the record was enacted, how it came to life, in the organization. She is sensitive to the politics and power of writing, its ability to determine the provision or denial of services, and she is able to explain how the text operates within an intricate web of relationships, a sequence of procedures, the influence of other texts, and the rhetorical conventions of the profession. As her frequent use of "we" suggests, she has entered the field of social work through participation in the full activity of the genre.

By way of conclusion, we would like to consider some of the implications of our work. Although there is much left to learn about social work writing in general, and the teaching of social work writing in particular, we believe our study points to some necessary changes in the schools and in the field. First, and most importantly and ambitiously, we believe that social work educators and practitioners need to take a long, critical look at the place and purpose of their professional writing. In short, they need to problematize it: they need to recognize the complexity of social work records, the integral role they play in all aspects of practice, and the difficulty students face when they first encounter these influential texts. Second, in order to alert students to the critical nature of social work writing, schools must find ways to introduce them to professional recordkeeping. We do not think that simulations of workplace writing are worthwhile. However, examining documents that form the textual centre of organizational genres, and listening to practitioners explain the activities that lead up to, and the consequences that follow from, those documents, would go some way toward preparing students for their field writing. Third, once in the workplace, students should be fully immersed in professional genres. Dummy runs and examination of texts certainly have some value for students in the initial stage of placement; however, these activities should be accompanied by discussions of the role and implications of those texts in the larger context. For full understanding of records and their place in practice, students must eventually participate as members of a "family of professionals." Fourth, and finally, field educators need to initiate a discussion of social work records among themselves and in their places of work. Writing should be put on the profession's agenda. When students arrive in the field, they should be exposed to the procedures, politics, and power of the written record in social work practice.

REFERENCES

Devitt, Amy. (1993, December). Generalizing about genre: New conceptions of an old concept. *College Composition and Communication, 44*, 573-586.

Holbrook, T. (1983, December). Case records: Fact or fiction? *Social Service Review*, 645-658.

Miller, Carolyn. (1984). Genre as social action. *Quarterly Journal of Speech, 70*, 151-167.

Richmond, Mary. (1925, November). Why case records? *The Family*, 214-216.

Simon, B. L., & Soven, M. (1989). The teaching of writing in social work education: A pressing priority for the 1990s. *Journal of Teaching in Social Work, 3*(2), 47-63.

Spilka, R. (Ed.). (1993). *Writing in the workplace: New research perspectives.* Carbondale, IL: Southern Illinois University Press.

Sytz, F. (1949, December). Teaching recording. *Journal of social casework*, 399-404.

The authors wish to thank the Social Sciences and Humanities Research Council for research funds that helped support their work.

CHAPTER FOURTEEN

LIVE SIMULATION IN FIELD INSTRUCTOR TRAINING

Gail Kenyon

INTRODUCTION

Some readers may be familiar with the 1970's television satire of talk shows called "Fernwood Tonight." Those of you who were followers of this program may remember the character William W. D. "Bud" Prize, the self-appointed ambassador-at-large for Fernwood, Ohio. Let me quote Mr. Prize in introducing the topic of this paper: "This is not the real thing, it is only a stimulation." While this example is one of the malapropisms that this character was known for, it is also a clever play on words, for what is a simulation if not a "stimulation." This provocative method of teaching is now widely used in many fields of study. The author will expand that realm, by looking at the use of simulation in training social work field instructors to carry out the responsibilities of field education.

BACKGROUND

While some authors see simulation and gaming as synonymous (Faherty, 1983), there is good reason to differentiate between the two teaching methods. Games generally have a competitive quality while simulation usually does not. Lauffer (1973), as cited in Faherty (1983), defines social simulations as:

> . . . models in which the essential components of a social system, the rules by which it operates, can be separated and manipulated through play; models through which people may be helped to manage the complexities of their social environment. (p. 112)

Faherty (1983) artfully describes simulation when he says:

> It freezes a time, a place or an action and allows the viewer or participant the luxury of entering into the picture, as it were, and sensing its complexities and inter-relationships. It is analogous to stopping the life process, as one would stop a videotape playback, and walking around between and among the players to attempt to understand what they are doing and why. (p. 112)

A useful distinction coined by Faherty (1972) and rephrased by Wodarski and Kelly (1987) is to separate simulations into three types: person models, person-machine models, and pure machine models. While many concepts may apply to all three, we will be focusing on the first of these, the person model.

We must remember that a simulation is a representation of reality, not a duplication of reality. As an experiment each experiment will be somewhat different (Pfeiffer & Ballew, 1988a). The simulator in a live-person model simulation is a trained, healthy person, but not a professional actor. Simulators are trained on one or more roles derived from real case examples. Those roles are modified to suit the training needs and to ensure confidentiality. We have several variations on a particular role. The simulator may custom-mould the role for a particular training purpose, such as, adding or deleting complicating variables, or increasing the severity of a particular problem. Also, simulators are trained to focus on a given stage of intervention or specific mode of intervention. For example, they can portray the beginning stage of treatment or termination issues.

The most well-developed area of use and research of the live-person model is in medical school training and assessment. Since the 1960's medical schools under the guidance of Dr. Howard S. Barrows and others have been developing and expanding the use of what were first called "programmed patients" (Barrows, 1993, p. 443). Medicine uses a wide range of simulators including "subjects" who demonstrate anatomy, "practical instructors" who are lay instructors who submit to examination by students, "patient instructors" who are real patients trained in portraying their illness or disease to students, and many more (Barrows, 1993, pp. 443-4).

Barrows's contribution began with training an artist's model to portray neurological signs for the assessment of clinical clerks at the University of Southern

California School of Medicine. The terminology changed to "simulated patient" and then to "standardized patient" (Barrows, 1993, p. 444). Standardized patients were usually healthy individuals who had been trained to simulate a patient or any aspect of a patient's illness, including psychological, emotional, historical, and physical factors.

As Barrows moved to McMaster University and then to Southern Illinois University School of Medicine, the method of training developed and spread. Now standardized patients are used in the training of medical students and physicians and in research all over the world. At a Consensus Conference of the Association of American Medical Colleges in June of 1993, Barrows reported that six consortia of 23 medical schools are developing a variety of ways of assessing clinical competence using standardized patients (Barrows, 1993). The Medical Council of Canada has brought together a number of Canadian investigators to develop clinical practice examinations that will become part of Canada's certifying examinations (Barrows, 1993).

McMaster University Faculty of Health Sciences established its own Standardized Patient Program in 1970 and is now one of the largest in the world. Early in that decade McMaster University began using this technique in the training of both nurses and social workers. While the assessment component is far less developed in these disciplines, nursing uses standardized patients in various assessment roles, and social work uses them in practice teaching.

At Ryerson Polytechnic University School of Social Work, the Interpersonal Skills Teaching Center started using simulated clients from the McMaster program in 1991. Since 1992 Ryerson has been training its own simulators for use in the Faculty of Community Services. Simulators are used in all years of social work and practice teaching, and in the evaluation of students who wish to challenge the Field Practicum for course credit.

SIMULATION IN SOCIAL WORK TRAINING

This method of teaching is useful for teaching skills, research, and evaluation, for testing out theories, and for learning about how a system works. It is found in medicine, nursing, business, human resources training, political science, armed forces, law, administration, teacher training, and other areas. The use of simulation in social work training is recommended for teaching and evaluating reasoning skills, assessment skills, and challenging the learners knowledge base.

One or more simulators can be brought into the classroom to portray individual clients, couples, families, therapeutic groups or community groups. Students have the opportunity to engage in the simulation while others observe and give helpful suggestions. The instructor can stop the simulation for discussion or to relate theory to practice. At the end the simulator gives constructive feedback to the students about their interventions.

Simulators are trained in one or more roles or characters. Once simulators know their character well, they can adapt that character for many uses. Simulators also must be trained in the appropriate process so that they can portray the process being simulated, for example: they may be simulating a client in therapy, a member of a task-focused group, or a student in supervision. They need only be trained, however, to the extent that the character they are simulating might be familiar with the process. Also, the simulator is trained in giving feedback to the trainee, the student or participant engaging in the simulation. This process involves the simulators leaving their character at the end of the simulation to explain and describe their responses to the interventions of the trainees. Such feedback is an crucial part of the learning.

During simulations either the participating trainee or the facilitator of the simulation can stop the process at any time. This is called "taking time-out." Using time-out allows the trainee to ask for help from the non-participating trainees or from the facilitator. It also gives others a chance to give suggestions and lets the facilitator make comments.

One property of simulation discussed by Hays and Singer (1989) is "fidelity." A term first used in reference to computer programs like flight simulators, fidelity refers to the relationship between the simulation and real life: the higher the fidelity, the more life like the simulation. Another characteristic of simulation is participant control. In a simulation of any kind, the participant or trainee must be able to control the situation to elicit a response. The participant is not a passive recipient of the experience. A third property of simulation is the opportunity for direct feedback to the participant or trainee from the simulator. Criteria for evaluating the trainee's performance can be added here. Finally, simulation takes place in real time: in other words, the events that happen must take the same time they would in real life. For example, a simulation of a group will take the same amount of time that a real group would take to accomplish the same tasks. The difference with a simulation is that phases can be left out, so that the overall effect becomes one of compressing the duration of the group.

While simulation and role playing are similar in their goals, they have several important differences. Pfeiffer and Ballew define role playing as "a spontaneous human interaction that involves realistic behavior under artificial or 'imagined' conditions" (1988b, p. 7). This interaction is similar to person model simulations but there are critical differences. During a simulation, the trainees retain their own characters and are encouraged to respond naturally. The simulator plays a predetermined role familiar only to the simulator and the facilitator. She never leaves that role during the course of the simulation. The true character of the simulator is unknown to the trainee. These factors increase the fidelity or realism of the experience.

Simulation also provides a more controlled experience for the trainee than role playing. The role of the simulator is predetermined, often rehearsed, and various responses prearranged according to a real case example. Unlike role playing, the simulator is not concerned with how well they are seen by their peers as playing the role. The simulator is confident in their role and ability, often having played the role many times before.

Is this then only acting? Again there is a clear difference between the performance of an actor and a simulation. An actor's primary role is to entertain, to portray a person and situation that provokes and engages the audience. Simulators are not interested in the response of the audience to their role. Their primary responsibility is to the trainee in the simulation. Their goal is to respond in a manner as true to their character as possible. Their second responsibility is to reflect honestly to the trainees what they felt during the simulation and how the interventions of the trainee affected their character. This distinction in purpose and relationship to the audience differentiates simulation from acting.

The simulation retains all the benefits of role playing, such as safety for both clients and trainees, realistic representation of real life experiences, motivational stimulation, trainee control of pace and involvement, and time for processing. At the same time, simulation eliminates some of the pitfalls. They are more consistent than role playing; preplanning is easier and more effective. Feedback comes from a trained simulator, and is not influenced by peer relationships or power issues with the instructor or other participants.

EFFECTIVENESS

Some controversy surrounds the efficacy of simulation. Cherryholmes (1966), Boocock and Coleman (1966) and Robertson et al. (1967) as reported by Faherty (1983) state that there is no evidence to suggest that simulations teach cognitive data or problem-solving skills any better than lectures, group discussions, or media. But studies by Abt (1968) as cited in Faherty (1983) in favor of simulation say it clearly teaches facts, processes of the system under study, and the costs and benefits of alternative strategies. Faherty (1983) concludes that if its greatest strength is simply motivational, then simulation serves a valuable purpose for teaching and learning. Whatling and Wodak (1979) present Scheffler's (1977) contention that:

> The authenticity of the simulated client brought reality to the theoretic background and no lecture or reading material, however well-presented, could have made the same impact. (p. 37)

Others contend that some learners benefit from the simulation itself, while others gain from the discussions that follow each simulation (Fennessey as cited in Horejsi, 1977).

Much research has been done on the use of standardized patients for assessment purposes in medical training. Results show that using simulation for assessment is both reliable and realistic (Colliver & Williams, 1993). Colliver and Williams (1993) in an exhaustive review of the research on the use of standardized patients made the following conclusion:

> . . . the collective evidence suggests that medical education can move ahead to realize the benefits of standardized-patient examinations, with confidence that this approach gives as good or better assessment of clinical performance than do conventional methods. (p. 458)

There is a distinct lack of information on the use of this technique in social work education, however. Little writing has been done on the application of simulation in teaching or in assessment. No research is available on the effectiveness of simulation in social work education or training.

BENEFITS OF SIMULATION

1) Simulation provides cognitive, interactive, and affective learning in a safe and controlled environment.

2) Simulations allow the trainee to practice skills in a situation that is life-like but without imposing on a real person in crisis or someone with service needs.

3) As a teaching method, simulation provides a transition between theory and practice.

4) Simulation is flexible, allowing trainees to try out hypotheses regarding interventions.

5) A simulation is portable. Rather than requiring the trainees to travel to a distant location to meet with a client, the simulator can be brought to the trainees.

6) Time is not a restriction. The simulation can go on as long as the training allows. Points can be repeated, different techniques tried. The

simulation can be stopped for discussion or clarification at any time by the simulator, the trainee, or the facilitator. As well, the trainee can experience the situation at several different points in time. For example, a first, third, and final interview could be simulated in one training session.

7)   There is a reduced risk of harming, offending, or tiring the client. Emergency or highly sensitive situations can be safely portrayed. Trainee anxiety about the client's well-being is eliminated. Embarrassment about the novice status of the trainee is also reduced.

8)   Simulations provide a controlled environment for learning. Extraneous variables can be kept to a minimum for the benefit of the trainees. Conversely, additional variables may be added to challenge the trainee or to explore another aspect of the situation.

9)   Finally, the simulator's training in providing feedback is a benefit to the trainees. Discussion about the comments of the simulator is also possible and further clarification can be provided.

DRAWBACKS

Simulation has a cost. Simulators must be paid for training time and for actual time spent with the trainees. These costs may be absent with role playing. This method requires time for the simulation, the feedback and the discussion. As it is not spontaneous, simulation requires preplanning.

Unplanned learning, a problem in role playing, also poses a risk in simulations (Glandon, 1978 as cited in van Ments, 1983). Role stereotyping and biases are by far the greatest danger. Poor planning of roles can reinforce unintentionally the stereotypes and biases of the trainees. For example, the simplification of a case, or even the choice of a particular case, may overemphasize a racial group or stereotype a gender. As well, users of simulation need to be cautious about the over-simplification of issues. The implication that problems can be solved simply with the correct intervention is a hazard in the use of this kind of teaching method. Careful debriefing to identify assumptions and challenge stereotypes, is necessary.

SIMULATION AND ADULT LEARNERS

The experiential learning cycle can be described as a sequence of events starting with experiencing or doing. Learners then talk about this experience, which in turn allows for processing the information and looking for patterns. These patterns may be generalized and principles inferred. The result can be the application of new learning. New experiences are generated; the cycle repeats itself (Pfeiffer & Ballew, 1988c).

Teaching methods that incorporate experiences offer a structured way to stimulate this cycle of learning. Simulations are an excellent example of a structured approach to experiential learning. The participant is provided with new and challenging experiences, but is protected from some of the risks and anxieties associated with experiential learning in real life. The environment of the simulation gives an opportunity to the trainee to process and generalize this learning at the time of the experience. In every day life processing of new learning must wait until other obligations, such as service to clients, paper work, or staff meetings.

Inductive learning, proceeding from observation or experience rather than from *a priori* truth, is the method most associated with adult learners. The use of live simulation is particularly suited for use in adult learning. Simulation is active, problem-focused and experiential. Participants can involve themselves in planning and implementation. This method is easily adapted to groups. All these properties have been identified as conducive to adult learning (Waldron & Moore, 1991).

THE RYERSON EXPERIENCE

As part of our annual Field Instructor Workshop series designed to provide training to new field practice instructors across three years of undergraduate practicum, a workshop on the Educational Role of the Field Instructor was designed. Prior to the workshop a large group of field instructors had been polled regarding issues that are problematic to them in field instruction. From their responses two common themes emerged: difficulties with confrontation, and the distinction between personal issues and professional issues. As the experiential component of the workshop, two simulators were employed to portray students in a field instruction meeting at their field placement. Each student demonstrated a difficulty that highlighted one of the identified issues.

After the introduction of the topic at the beginning of the workshop, a brief didactic segment followed. At this time participants were given a framework within which to view their role as educators in the practicum process. Handouts and an article to read later were distributed. After questions, the first simulation was introduced. Participants were given a brief description of the student and when this field instruction session was to have occurred, that is, the early, middle, or termination phase of the practicum.

The first simulation was of a young student with low motivation for social work. This student was somewhat manipulative and seductive. The participants were asked to step into the role of field instructor and proceed as they saw fit. Several participants began the simulated field instruction session and after a few minutes stopped to ask for help from the other participants. Other participants were stopped by the facilitator to allow as many people as possible an opportunity to try out the role. During this time the simulator did not leave his role. During breaks in the simulation, referred to as time-out, he looked down and avoided eye contact with participants. After several participants had engaged in the simulation and some discussion had ensued, the simulation was ended. The simulator gave general feedback about his character and specific feedback to those participants who had tried the role of field instructor. All participants were encouraged to ask questions of the simulator.

This process was then repeated with the second simulation. This simulation was of a mature, high-achieving student, suffering from several stresses in her life including child care problems and financial worries. Again, participants were asked to engage in the simulated field instruction meeting as they would if this were their own student.

PARTICIPANTS' RESPONSES

Overall the Field Instructors enjoyed the workshop and felt they benefitted from it. They commented on the usefulness of the feedback given by the simulator and the opportunity to ask questions about the simulators' responses. Even those who did not participate directly in the simulation commented that they recognized themselves and their student in the simulation and found this valuable. Several field instructors also commented that they appreciated the discussion with their peers, adding to the learning gained from the simulation. Many of the field instructors regretted that there was not more time to continue the simulation. One suggested a similar workshop for Field Instructors and their students.

One of the drawbacks in using this method are highlighted by the comment of a field instructor. She felt that field instructors who actually participated in the simulation were brave. This method asks field instructors to take risks. While this request may be appropriate, given that we ask students to take risks in their practicum, such expectations may inhibit some participants. Clearly, many Field Instructors struggled with the lack of a right answer for these simulations. They found it challenging to accept that there were not preplanned, clear solutions for each simulated situation. The simulations presented complex problems for workshop participants to struggle with and learn from, like real student and field instructor situations.

FUTURE PLANS

The introduction of live simulation to the Field Instructor Workshop Series proved to be successful. At the least, the method added variety and stimulation to the learning experience. Comments from the workshop participants indicate that there was even more benefit. Future applications in this context might include the teaching of specific skills in using different methods of field instruction; joint workshops with student and field instructor simulators; and the opportunity for both field instructors and students to participate in a simulated field instruction session. This teaching method could be further developed by the addition of identified favorable outcomes such as suggested by the "Best-Solution Approach," proposed by Gaines Robinson and Robinson (1989). This approach involves establishing several possible responses and rating the ones that have the best outcome and highest efficacy. Trainees and trainers could evaluate a trainees performance, thereby increasing the knowledge and skill that could be reapplied. Regardless of whether you are like Fernwood's self-appointed ambassador-at-large and are "consumptive of the literature," or whether this is your first introduction to the use of simulation in social work training, this is a teaching method you are bound to be reading more about in years to come.

REFERENCES

Barer-Stein, T., & Draper, J. A. (Eds.). (1993). *The craft of teaching adults.* Toronto: Culture Concepts Publishers.

Barrows, H. S. (1993, June). An overview of the uses of standardized patients for teaching and evaluating clinical skills. *Academic Medicine, 68*(6), 443-51.

Boocock, S. S., & Schild, E. O. (1968). *Simulation games in learning.* Beverly Hills: SAGE Publications, Ltd.

Colliver, J., & Williams, R. G. (1993, June). Technical issues: Test application. *Academic Medicine, 68*(6), 454-60.

Errek, H. K., & Randolph, D. L. (1982). Effects of discussion and role-play activities in the acquisition of consultant interview skills. *Journal of Counselling Psychology, 29*(3), 304-308.

Faherty, V. E. (1983, Spring). Simulation and gaming in social work education: A projection. *Journal of Education for Social Work, 19*(2), 111-118.

Gaines Robinson, D., & Robinson, J. C. (1989). *Training for impact*. London: Jossey-Bass Publishers.

Hays, R. T., & Singer, M. J. (1989). *Simulation fidelity and training system design; Bridging the gap between reality and training*. New York: Springer-Verlog.

Horejsi, C. R. (1977, Winter). 'Homemade' simulations: Two examples from the social work classroom. *Journal of Education for Social Work, 13*(1), 76-82.

Horn, R. E., & Cleaves, A. (Eds.). (1980). *The guide to simulations/games for education and training* (4th ed.). Beverly Hills: SAGE Publications, Inc.

Pfeiffer, W. J., & Ballew, A. C. (1988a). *UA training technologies 1: Using structured experiences in human resource development*. San Diego: University Associates, Inc.

Pfeiffer, W. J., & Ballew, A. C. (1988b). *UA training technologies 4: Using role plays in human resource development*. San Diego: University Associates, Inc.

Pfeiffer, W. J., & Ballew, A. C. (1988c). *UA training technologies 5: Using case studies, simulations, and games in human resource development*. San Diego: University Associates, Inc.

Tansy, P. J., & Unwin, D. (1969). *Simulation and gaming in education*. London: Methuen Educational Ltd.

Taylor, J., & Walford, R. (1978). *Learning and the simulation game*. Beverly Hills: SAGE Publications, Inc.

van Ments, M. (1983). *The effective use of role-playing: A handbook for teachers and trainers*. New York: Nichols Publishing.

Waldron, M. W., & Moore, G. A. B. (1991). *Helping adults learn*. Toronto: Thompson Educational Publishing, Inc.

Warren, M. W. (1969). *Training for results: A system approach to the development of human resources in industry*. Don Mills: Addison-Wesley Publishing Co.

Whatling, T., & Wodak, E. (1979). The simulated client in social work training. *International-Social-Work, 22*(2), 34-37.

Wodarski, J. S., & Kelly, T. (1987, Winter). Simulation technology in social work education. *Arete, 12*(2), 12-20.

CHAPTER FIFTEEN

SPECIAL ISSUES IN THE EDUCATION OF FIELD INSTRUCTORS

Urania Glassman

INTRODUCTION

There is a need to provide formal structures for the education of field instructors that not only focus on the roles and skills of field instruction, but offer those conceptualizations about learning which are germane to social work education itself. Therefore, teaching the teachers cannot become merely the supervision of their endeavors with students. To further their teaching of students, it is necessary to disseminate to field instructors the body of knowledge which underpins social work field education. This knowledge joins concepts about experiential education with the practice theories and skills our professional mission mandates us to teach.

This chapter describes prototypic educational designs for teaching concepts about field education and enhancing field instructors' skills with students, and presents several key conceptualizations that should be required learning for every field educator.

EDUCATIONAL DESIGNS FOR TEACHING FIELD INSTRUCTORS

Common Principles

While the structures for educating field instructors are varied among the schools, there are several principles common to all types of programs. *First*, the educational experience of field instructors should be conducted within the collective structure of a class or seminar, not on a tutorial basis, to familiarize participants with the scope of educational issues in field instruction. *Second*, a chance to focus on theories of education and to relate these to their own experience with their students should be provided within the class or seminar. *Third*, those conducting classes and seminars for the education of field instructors should utilize the parallel process by employing case materials and process recordings, thereby modelling their usage as educational tools for student learning. *Fourth*, the substantial portion of any educational program for field instructors should be designed to coincide with their actual work with a student in order to maximize the chance to use live material and provide support in a timely manner.

Structures

One educational structure is the required course for all new field instructors. For instance the New York area schools of social work over fifteen years ago, developed a joint curriculum that is the equivalent of a 30 hour course, usually run over two semesters in all area schools. Written assignments are required, and participation is mandatory for all first time field instructors. Another structure is the series of one day seminars usually on some educational theme relevant to field instruction. Provision of educational clinics for field instructors who bring their current problems and issues with students to these clinics is also useful. Field education experts teach the courses and seminars. The live materials of field instructors' interactions with students should be utilized in all educational programs, and combined with theoretical presentations. This should include process recordings of supervisory meetings with students.

EXPERIENTIAL LEARNING: A NECESSARY THEORETICAL BASE

The theories of John Dewey (1938) in American education focused educators on the centrality of experience in the learning process. Theories about experiential learning have been used to teach children and to develop alternative educational programs for all educational levels — including colleges and universities. Often relegated "alternative" status in traditional education, experiential learning comprises up to one half of the curriculum in many professions, including social work.

Social work education of necessity places a heavy emphasis on doing. The student's ability to practice social work is central, and the development of a conscious use of self is the vehicle. The practice of social work is to be conducted in a proactive and purposeful way, not reactively. Students are expected to develop a conscious use of self through the differential application of knowledge and values to the unique practice situation.

The adult education theorists have developed a range of models to help educators understand the educational experience and transaction between student and educator, and the student's struggle to become an effective practitioner with a client system. Along with the centrality of experience, many constructs relevant to field education are built upon the premise that learning in the field is sequential (Siporin, 1982; Reynolds, 1942).

Brown (1980) describes the experiential learning occurring in professional education in a three stage model. The first level involves HOW TO LEARNING. Through the process of imitation and replication of a distinct set of tasks the learner accumulates enough experiences to help guide him or her to the next level of role socialization. ROLE SOCIALIZATION involves understanding the unique aspects of the professional role and beginning to see how these integrate with theories and values. The final level in this educational process is the LEARNER MANAGED EDUCATIONAL AGENDA wherein the learner is able to become increasingly adept at taking initiative in planning for his or her own learning. This is harder to do at the first level because the student, not having had enough experiences in trying out the many aspects of the professional role, is unable to know what the role truly entails.

This principle of sequential learning is reflected in Bertha Reynolds (1942) consideration of the unique aspects of social work field education, and her subsequent presentation of a five stage model of education particularly relevant to the field experience: *first*, is the ACUTE SELF CONSCIOUSNESS STAGE; *second* is the SINK OR SWIM STAGE; *third* is the STAGE OF KNOWING WHAT IS REQUIRED BUT NOT BEING ABLE TO DO IT; *fourth* is the STAGE OF RELATIVE MASTERY; and *fifth* is the STAGE OF TEACHING WHAT IS MASTERED. Understanding these stages helps the field instructor appropriately direct teaching strategies.

Another hallmark of experiential education is presented in Kolb's (1984) discussion of Lewin's dictum, "Feelings as well as thoughts, are facts" (Kolb, 1984, p.11). Kolb notes that in an experientially oriented educational framework, "Learning is the process whereby knowledge is created through the transformation of experience" (Kolb, 1984, p. 38). This conceptualization is consonant with the epistemological theories of Berger and Luckmann (1966) who focus on the social construction of reality through the intersubjective process of consensual validation.

For social work field education these conceptualizations are utilized in a particular way to help the student catalyze the learning and to improve practice proficiency. Bogo and Vayda (1991) describe the FEEDBACK LOOP as particularly representative of the processes of social work field education. The FEEDBACK LOOP begins with the occurrence of a particular practice experience. This experience is then to be retrieved and presented to a field instructor. Together the student and field instructor reflect upon the experience, bringing to bear upon it a variety of theory for their collective consideration of future actions. Through the feedback process a formulation of future action representing the professional response is developed, and the student embarks on a yet another practice experience to enact newer practices and uses of self, thereby propelling the feedback loop once again. RETRIEVAL, REFLECTION, LINKAGE, and PROFESSIONAL RESPONSE create the continuum in the feedback loop (Bogo & Vayda, 1991).

Knowles (1972) attested to the centrality of problem solving for the adult learner. He described the necessary ingredients of a positive learning environment for social work field education, discarding the nomenclature of *pedagogy* and instead using the term *andragogy* (from the Greek work andras for man). A more contemporary term would be *anthrogogy*. Necessary conditions in his schema include: a) a recognition by educators that adult learning is primarily problem centred; b) the creation of a non-judgmental atmosphere for learning which involves and presupposes the establishment of mutuality between the student and field instructor; c) opportunity for students to create learning agendas.

It is critical for field educators to familiarize themselves with these theories and educational models, and to have opportunities to participate in educational situations where they can discuss with one another the relevance of these concepts to their own student situation.

PROCESS RECORDING - A VITAL INTEGRATIVE LEARNING TOOL

Process recording is used as a tool for catalyzing the student's expanding conscious use of self by creating a systematized arena for deepening the integration of action with theory, knowledge and values. Process recording is recommended as the learning tool of choice for field education. Use of process recording affords the student opportunity for reconstruction and retrieval of a prior practice experience. Utilizing an outline for process recording which is designed to guide the student through a formal sequence in the retrieval (Bogo & Vayda, 1991) of the practice situation, further catalyses the learning. Through the actual construction of a process recording the student is able to bring cognition to bear on an otherwise affectively centred experience. The practice experience, with its focus on the student's current abilities in using the self purposefully, is presented, reviewed and reflected upon. Through this reconstruction of the interactions and affects, the student cognitively reviews the experience, thereby beginning the process of transforming the experience into knowledge (Kolb, 1984). Further feedback within the field instruction conference enables the development of a range of interventions and future action plans which comprise the professional response (Bogo & Vayda, 1991)

Outline for Process Recording

Recommended here, is an outline for process recording (Papell, 1984) that begins with a PRE-ENGAGEMENT section which helps the student learn and habituate the importance of preparing for every single encounter with clients. In this section, in order to develop the skills of preparatory empathy (Shulman, 1992), the student is required to consider how the client might be feeling and thinking at this time, and how the student might feel in the clients shoes. The NARRATIVE, the longest section, follows, which combines observation, interaction and worker's feelings in a form that holds the story together. In this way the student learns that the process is not fragmented, and that listening, thinking, intervening, observing, and feeling, are part of the totality of the intersubjective experience.

It must be noted that there is no such thing as verbatim recall. Events are always being reconstructed, and, in the process, these events are absorbed and integrated by a professional ego whose purpose is to "transform experience into knowledge." Asking students to write a script as if a play dialogue, or using a three column process recording which separates intervention from thinking, feeling, and observing, tends to fragment the intersubjective process.

A brief IMPRESSIONS section follows the narrative, in which the student can state how he or she felt about the meeting. In this section one can see what the student's major concerns were and how they were manifest. The next section asks the student to identify FUTURE ACTION PLANS which is a beginning training towards furthering the development of the conscious use of self. In addition, it may highlight the need for between session work by the student on the client's behalf. Finally, the student is asked to identify QUESTIONS for the field instruction conference which begin to facilitate the student's ability to develop an agenda for the field instruction conference and to eventually learn to develop and manage broader learning agendas in keeping with the various theories of experiential learning.

Process recordings of groups are similar, except names of members present and absent are included, and the meeting number is noted. Family process records follow a similar venue to group recordings with names and ages of family members included. Utilized in community organization field education are the combination process recording/log in which the student focuses on the conscious use of self in meetings and as a planner.

Using a Process Recording

The process recording is read line by line with the field instructor during the field instruction conference. Either can stop at any point to consider the student's use of self, feelings, intents of interventions, and impact on client system. Theory is appropriately retrieved but the discussion focuses on the process, and entertains future uses of self.

In preparation for the review of the process recording, the field instructor reads the recording *without writing on it*. He or she decides which practice issues should be considered at this time according to immediacy, priority, and the stage of learning the student is in. If the student is a beginning first year student who is just forming a group and worrying about survival, a focus on technique or a discussion of various stage theories of group development is too advanced for the worried student to consider or learn from.

Once selecting the germane practice issues for that process recording, the field instructor returns to the record, writes numbers in portions of the process which he or she would like to review, and prepares a sheet with corresponding numbers and relevant questions to guide the field instruction conference. The field instructor uses the student's questions and agenda, helps guide the conference, and at the end, returns the process with the question sheet to the student so that he or she retains feedback from the field instructor in written form. Writing "good" in red ink on the process recording often results in an attempt by the student to please the field instructor rather than to focus on examining his or her own key practice issues and concerns during the field instruction conference (Schwartz, 1982).

Process Recording for the Education of Field Instructors

Asking field instructors to prepare process recordings of their conference with a student where the student's process recording was used as a teaching tool, helps the field instructor consider his or her own uses of self and interventions with students, and enables an integration of educational practice with educational theory. Preparation of a process recording also helps the field instructors to experience first hand the use of process recording as an educational tool. Thus, in considering the use of process recording with students, field instructors do not have to rely on their own prior experiences as students, but can relate more immediately to the present situation. Asking a field instructor to present his or her process recording for review in an educational seminar, class, or clinic, not only helps the participants to focus on their own teaching, but provides a model for the field instructors that helps them further consider how to use student process recordings.

EDUCATIONAL ASSESSMENT

Field instructors are required to formulate an educational assessment of the student using a variety of educational constructs to enable this formulation. Two distinct types of formulations are required in the development of an educational assessment: 1) how the student learns; and 2) what the student needs to learn. The first is governed by understanding if the student is primarily an intellectual learner, experiential learner, or task oriented learner (Berengarten, 1957; Papell, 1978), and requires the utilization of stage theory of education and professional role development to assess the learning pattern and style. The second is to identify what the student has learned and what the student still needs to learn, using the school's field education curriculum to provide the framework.

Misconceptions and pitfalls, especially for beginning field instructors, in developing educational assessments, include the application of stringent practice standards which may be used to label the student as deficient or blocked, rather than suitable educational standards which focus on identifying the skills and roles to be learned, and ascertaining the assignments, experiences and types of cognition which will facilitate the learning.

A set of typologies of student learners have been identified elsewhere (Fishbein & Glassman, 1991) and roles of the field instructor described in an effort to help field instructors use a process model to be more effective teachers. These typologies are: 1) the NON-AFFECTIVE THINKER, which requires the field instructor to maintain a focus on content rather than to oppose the student by becoming too deeply affective; 2) THE FEELER is usually the student who may over-identify with clients, especially in the beginning phase. This student requires a supportive rather than oppositional approach from the field instructor, with a patient effort to help the student eventually experience his or her differences with the clients; 3) THE DOER is frequently the student who has been previously employed at a social agency and has learned to be task oriented rather than process or theoretically oriented. This student requires affirmation for being unafraid to tackle a task along with encouragement and permission to be reflective; 4) THE FRAIDY CAT tends to avoid tasks that produce anxiety. The goal of the field instructor is to help the student perform the role. He or she should remain patient while partializing and prioritizing the tasks in order to ease the student's anxiety; 5) I-AM-NOT-A-STUDENT is usually someone who was competent elsewhere, may be currently employed at an agency, and who is experiencing difficulty taking on the student role. The field instructor has to hold the student to the task, maintain educational focus and requirements, while also affirming the student's prior competency; 6) ME, I-AM-ONLY-A-STUDENT tends to hide behind the role asking for absolution from the serious responsibility of working with clients for fear of harming them. The field instructor has to maintain educational focus, requiring the student to function in a mature responsible manner; 7) The STARKLY DIFFERENT student is the person who is different with regard to the rest of the people in the setting, and as a result is inadvertently left out of the informal structure, which makes it almost impossible to learn. For instance, it may be a young male student in an all female staff unit, or a reserved older student among young workers, or a lone African American student. Field instructors have a responsibility for facilitating their student's entry into the informal as well as the formal system. This includes taking responsibility for facilitating social connections such as lunch and informal chit-chat with others. If there are no other students at the agency, the student is most at risk, placing more burden on the field instructor for insuring the student's connectedness; 8) The KNOW-IT-ALL is the student who is trying to prove competency to the field instructor by bringing to bear on each situation every theory he or she ever heard of. As a result the student is not able to hear the field instructor. The field instructor has to stop the student's behavior, pointing out when he or she is trying to prove competency as an impediment to learning; 9) The I DON'T TRUST AUTHORITY student does not accept the field instructor's authority and as a result is usually impossible for the field instructor to deal with. An intervention from a faculty advisor or even the Field Work Director is required which points out the negative behavior to the student, and uses the school's authority to stop the student from the constant need to one-up or disqualify the field instructor.

It has been helpful to use these typologies in the training of field instructors by asking them how their own students reflect these characteristics, what specific behaviors the students have presented, the difficulties the field instructors have had with certain students, and to consider together a range of strategies that could be useful in dealing with particular students. It is also valuable for field instructors to consider which learning styles of students are difficult or easy for them to work with. Asking field instructors to identify which qualities are most characteristic of themselves as learners is also useful to their work with students.

HELPING FIELD INSTRUCTORS TEACH SPECIFIC SKILLS TO STUDENTS

Foundation Practice Skills

Field instructors are required to develop the ability to teach students specific uses of self that focus on professional roles and skills, to utilize conceptualizations about the use of practice skill over time — from engagement, to assessment, to problem solving, and termination — and to use themselves in unique ways to help the student develop these skills. Utilization of the school's field curriculum provides guidelines. Field instructors can improve their abilities and enhance their collective understanding through a seminar format, wherein they are asked to identify those skills their students need to learn next, to consider the student's obstacles to learning, and to describe strategies and tools they can use to teach these skills.

For instance, field instructors repeatedly struggle with teaching students how to identify and stay with latent issues presented by clients, or how to use silence in a group or with individuals. Field instructors express concern about helping students learn to maintain focus in the work with clients, but without making agendas which violate the process. They wonder about what is the most effective strategy to use in helping their students to take risks. Field instructors have consistently revealed great concern about how to help students deepen self awareness when it appears the student's own unexplored issues are the obstacle to understanding and helping the client. In addition, field instructors need help in identifying their own issues regarding their students and determining how their issues help or hinder their student's learning. Some issues might include the expectation that the student will follow a learning pattern similar to that of the field instructor, or will see life's issues similarly.

Teaching Skills of Method

Another problematic area in the education of field instructors centres around the teaching of method when the field instructor is not an expert in one or two practice methods. A field instructor in a family agency may not feel able to teach group work or community organization. A field instructor in a community centre may feel inadequate when faced with the prospect of teaching casework claiming he or she doesn't work with individuals and failing to comprehend that all crisis interventions and individual interactions utilize casework principles.

Several principles are involved in helping field instructors to teach method. For first year students, the field instructor needs knowledge along with the ability to universalize and apply generic concepts to method (Schwartz, 1982). Field instructors have to be encouraged to translate what they already know well about social work practice into group work, case work, or community organization terms, and to struggle with the formulation of suitable assignments and appropriate applications of concepts. Asking them to read relevant concepts is usually helpful (i.e., Hartman & Laird, 1983; Glassman & Kates, 1990; Cox et al., 1987; Shulman, 1992; Bernstein, 1984). They must be reminded that they are social workers who do know how to practice in at least one method. Expecting them to make the leap into another method is realistic for work with a beginning student.

However, to preserve the "minority methods" and to prevent a sweep by casework as the central method, every school of social work should require all agencies to describe how they will address teaching of method for field instructors in the form of seminars, workshops, and outside consultations. Clarity should be developed about what the school will provide and what the agency will provide.

    More problematic in a different vein is the teaching of method at the advanced second year level. Ideally, someone who does not know a method well should not teach it at the advanced level. However, what we are now finding is that as a result of the generic curriculum of the last two decades, fewer people know about group work and community organization. While striving for the ideal is desired, we must support agencies who are deficient in one or two methods to help their staff gain proficiency through the use of expert consultants and training programs. Agencies require help from the schools in the domain of method, especially in group work and community organization (and some require help in family practice). Without this help there will be even less suitable placements available in group work and community organization than those few we have now.

    Several agencies have attempted to teach their staff about group work and community organization by hiring expert consultants to conduct training and to facilitate in the development of groups and programs in the agency. For instance, one health care agency developed what is now a formidable group work program through a policy change which required every social worker on staff to run a group. This policy was formulated and supported when the agency engaged the on-going services of a group work consultant for the staff. As a result, every field instructor in that agency is able to teach group work.

CONCLUSION

In this era of shrinking resources, it is essential that schools of social work allocate resources for the education of field instructors, by assigning full time faculty who teach practice and field education experts to the development of curricula and institutionalized structures for the education of field instructors. These important endeavors cannot be relegated to the part time faculty, nor to the agency alone. Therefore, it is up to field work faculty under the direction of a visionary and proactive field work director, to maintain standards for field education which of necessity require allocation of resources, and the stalwart assertion of need in this critical arena.

REFERENCES

Berengarten, S. (1957). Identifying learning patterns of individual students: An exploratory study. *Social Service Review,* 31(4), 407-417.

Berger, P., & Luckmann, T. (1966). *The social construction of reality.* Garden City, NY: Doubleday.

Bernstein, S. (Ed.). (1984). *Explorations in group work*. Hebron, CT: Practitioners Press.

Bogo, M., & Vayda, E. (1991). Developing a process model for field instruction. In D. Schneck, B. Grossman & U. Glassman (Eds.), *Field education in social work: Contemporary issues and trends* (pp. 59-66). Dubuque, IA: Kendall Hunt.

Brown, G. (1980). Three types of experiential learning: A non trivial distinction. *New Directions for Experiential Learning, 8*, 47-58.

Cox, F., Erlich, J., Rothman, J., Tropman, J. (1987). *Strategies of community organization* (4th Ed.). Itasca, IL: F.E. Peacock.

Dewey, J. (1938). *Experience and education*. New York: MacMillan.

Fishbein, H., & Glassman, U. (1991). The advanced seminar for field instructors. In D. Schneck, B. Grossman & U. Glassman (Eds.), *Field education in social work: Contemporary issues and trends* (pp. 226-232). Dubuque, IA: Kendall Hunt.

Glassman, U., & Kates, L. (1990). *Group work: A humanistic approach*. Newbury Park, CA: Sage Publications.

Grossman, B. (1991). Themes and variations: The political economy of field instruction. In D. Schneck, B. Grossman & U. Glassman (Eds.), *Field education in social work: Contemporary issues and trends* (pp. 36-46). Dubuque, IA: Kendall Hunt.

Hartman, A., & Laird, J. (1983). *Family centred social work practice*. New York: Free Press.

Knowles, M. (Spring, 1972). Innovations in teaching styles and approaches based upon adult learning. *Journal of Education for Social Work*, 32-39.

Kolb, D. A. (1984). Experiential learning. *Experience as the Source of Learning and Development*. Englewood Cliffs, NJ: Prentice Hall

Lemberger, J., & Marshack, E. Educational assessment in the field: An opportunity for teacher learner mutuality. In D. Schneck, B. Grossman & U. Glassman (Eds.), *Field education in social work: Contemporary issues and trends* (pp. 187-197). Dubuque, IA: Kendall Hunt.

Mesbur, E., & Glassman, U. (1991). Humanistic foundations for field instruction. In D. Schneck, B. Grossman & U. Glassman (Eds.), *Field education in social work: Contemporary issues and trends* (pp. 47-58). Dubuque, IA: Kendall Hunt.

Papell, C. (1978). *A study of styles of learning for direct social work practice*. Unpublished doctoral dissertation. Wurzweiler School of Social Work, Yeshiva University.

Reynolds, B. (1942). *Learning and teaching in the practice of social work.* New York: Farrar and Rinehart.

Rogers, C. (1969). *Freedom to learn.* Columbus, OH: C.E. Merrill.

Schneck, D., Grossman, B., & Glassman, U. (Eds.). (1991). *Field education in social work: Contemporary issues and trends.* Dubuque, IA: Kendall Hunt.

Schneck, D. (1991). Integration of learning in field education: Elusive goal and educational imperative. In D. Schneck, B. Grossman & U. Glassman (Eds.), *Field education in social work: Contemporary issues and trends* (pp. 67-77). Dubuque, IA: Kendall Hunt.

Schon, D. A. (1987). *Educating the reflective practitioner.* San Francisco: Jossey-Bass Publishers.

Schwartz, W. (1982). *Seminar for faculty advisors.* Six week program held for faculty at Adelphi University School of Social Work.

Shulman, L. (1992). *The skills of helping individuals, families, and groups.* Itasca, IL: F.E. Peacock.

Siporin, M. (1982). The process of field instruction. In B. Sheaffer & L. Jenkins (Eds.), *Quality field instruction in social work.* New York: Longman.

CHAPTER SIXTEEN

USING OPEN LEARNING MATERIALS IN FIELD EDUCATION

Mark Doel and Steven Shardlow

INTRODUCTION

This chapter provides an overview of a three-hour workshop presented on June 17, 1994 at the Conference on Field Education, held at the University of Calgary. The aims of the workshop were as follows:

- to introduce the model of practice teaching[1] developed at the University of Sheffield;
- to experience aspects of this model through small group exercises;
- to relate the Sheffield model to flexible (open and distance) learning.

---

1   The language and concepts used to describe field education are very different in the UK and Canada. In the UK *practice teaching* refers to the work done by the person in an agency *practice teacher/field instructor* who is responsible for promoting a student's learning whilst the student is on *placement* (completing the *practicum*). The term *practice teacher* does not mean the faculty member who teaches social work practice. For the most part this paper uses the terminology current in the UK.

During the workshop, participants were given the opportunity to test out some of the open learning materials[2] currently in use through the University of Sheffield.

The UK Award in Practice Teaching and Open Learning

Before describing the use of open learning materials in practice teaching (field education) it is necessary to describe some of the current arrangements for social work education and practice teaching in the United Kingdom (UK). There are approximately 5,000 places per year for students to obtain the basic professional qualification in social work the Diploma in Social Work (Dip SW) — usually a two year qualification (CCETSW, 1991). A unique feature of social work education in the UK is that each programme must be provided by a partnership between at least one University and one Social Work Agency. There is a national body, the Central Council for Education and Training in Social Work (CCETSW) charged with the responsibility, laid down by statute, to regulate the quality of social work education. A very considerable emphasis is placed upon field education: students spend on average 50% of their course on placement in an agency (the practicum) which is a very high proportion in relation to other European States (Lorenz, 1986). The quality of social work education is then highly dependent upon the quality of practice teaching in agencies. The work of practice teachers (field instructors) is central to the development of students' competence in social work practice.

Since 1989 there has been a national award for practice teachers (CCETSW, 1989). This award may either be obtained by competing a course of study — lasting at least 150 hours or by submitting a portfolio of work that demonstrates the competence of the practice teacher (the latter option is only available to experienced practice teachers, new practice teachers must obtain the award by attending a course). There are some forty programmes across the country offering the practice teaching award.

At the University of Sheffield there has been considerable interest in developing a range of open learning materials for field education. These have been used in two distinct ways. First, materials have been developed for practice teachers (field instructors) to use with their students during a placement (for example, see *Social Work Practice*, Doel & Shardlow, 1993). Second, materials to be used on programmes leading to the practice teaching award, such as the Practice Teaching Video Series (edited and scripted by Doel & Shardlow, 1990); and most recently, a learning package (Doel,

---

2   Open learning — this is used to refer to materials that a student may use at any time where access to the materials is not determined by the need to attend a programme of learning at a given time or place; students who are geographically distant from the educational centre organizing the learning may also use the materials — often referred to as distance learning.

1993). This is currently being used to provide materials for a pilot project of open learning routes to the practice teaching award in two different regions of the UK. Before describing some examples of these learning materials, some features of the University of Sheffield's approach to field education are described.

KEY ELEMENTS OF THE UNIVERSITY OF SHEFFIELD APPROACH

At the University of Sheffield over recent years a distinct approach to practice learning (field instruction) has evolved. This heuristic approach results from the work of practice teachers, empirical research, development of training materials; courses for practice teachers and theory construction. It has been termed the *Structured Learning Model* and is based upon the following key elements:

- the recognition that social work is practised within societies riven by various stratified forms of socially structured difference;
- that practice learning must be firmly grounded on principles derived from educational and psychological theories about how people learn;
- the need for a defined practice curriculum to guide the process of learning;
- the employment of a rich variety of methods of learning during a placement (practicum);
- clear pre-defined standards for the examination of practice competence.

It is beyond the scope of this paper to elaborate upon all these elements, or how they interact to reveal a model of practice learning in any detail. A full account of this model is due for publication in 1995. One of these elements, the idea of a curriculum for practice is the starting point to understanding how the structured learning approach to practice teaching (field instruction) has been used with open learning materials.

THE PRACTICE CURRICULUM

Notions of curriculum have been commonplace in college-based learning but have only recently gained general currency in agency-based learning. "Curriculum" is not a particularly friendly word in Britain, with the political controversy of the national curriculum in schools. In these circumstances, it is important to make the idea of curriculum a friendly concept which aids, rather than hinders, learning (Doel, 1988).

Elements of a Curriculum

At the centre of a curriculum is the syllabus, which consists of four elements:

- the content of the learning;
- the methods used to promote the learning;
- the sequence and position of learning opportunities;
- the assessment of the learning.

These are the what, how, when, where, and whether. The core value of a curriculum is that it provides a map for the student's learning. It is an explicit statement of expectations, some of which are negotiable and some of which are not. In the field of practice learning, some aspects of a curriculum may be difficult to control, such as the timing of learning opportunities. The careful mix of learning from planned, timed simulations and learning from live activities is part of the art, science and technology of practice teaching. The question of sequence should not be abandoned because of the challenges of the practice learning environment. However, the term "sequence" is linear, and it needs supplementing with the notion of "position" — like pieces in a jigsaw puzzle.

A curriculum is not effective if it feels like a straitjacket. It should provide form and framework to the work with a student not a rigid set of directions. The student will be expected to demonstrate specific results, but the routes to those outcomes will be varied. Translating the general curriculum into specific content for your setting and with particular meaning for each individual student is a practice teaching skill.

Different Routes to a Practice Curriculum

There are a number of different routes which can be used to begin to construct a curriculum for practice learning. Doel (1988) has identified three different routes: the paradigm, the broad framework and the empirical.

The Empirical Approach

This approach re-constructs a curriculum based on what is considered to be the best of existing practice. The task of the curriculum-builder is to inspect the implicit and unsystematic curriculum and reframe it so that it is explicit and systematic; take the parts that "work" and make them work better. The curriculum below illustrates a modular approach applied to the first placement of the Diploma in Social Work in South Yorkshire, England (South Yorkshire Dip SW, 1993), a development of Doel's practice curriculum (1987). It outlines three main areas or units of practice learning, each of which is divided into smaller clusters of learning or modules.

Unit 1		Values in Action
Module	1.1	Orientation
	1.2	Practice philosophy
	1.3	Power and oppression
	1.4	Anti-racist practice
	1.5	Professional boundaries
	1.6	Self-presentation

Unit 2		Direct Work with People
Module	2.1	Communication skills
	2.2	Preparation for direct work
	2.3	Beginnings(exploring problems)
	2.4	Middles (work on problems)
	2.5	Endings(reviewing work)
	2.6	Selecting a practice method

Unit 3		Managing the Work
Module	3.1	Time management
	3.2	Workload management
	3.3	Managing the resources
	3.4	Skills in recording
	3.5	Working in a team
	3.6	Working with other agencies

The first Unit starts with the student and looks out at the work through her or his eyes. It helps students and practice teachers (field instructors) to articulate their beliefs and values, alongside each other. The second Unit is concerned with the student's skills in direct work with people who use the agency's services. Students develop their interpersonal skills and planning abilities to bring purpose into their direct contacts, and to work systematically with people over time. There are beginning, middles and ends to planned pieces of work with clients. In the third Unit the student is expected to look through the agency's eyes, learning to cultivate good professional practice in the daily reality of a social work agency. The emphasis is not just on individual professionalism, but how to be a team member and how to make links with other agencies and work in an inter-disciplinary way.

This first placement gives the student a grounding in social work practice, ready for further class-based learning and a second placement in a focused area of practice, where learning is associated with a particular client group or practice setting.

METHODS OF LEARNING WHICH PROMOTE ACCELERATED LEARNING

The Structured Learning Model focuses on the *how*, methods of learning, as much as the *what*, the content of learning while in a placement. The methods used by practice teacher (field instructor) and student can significantly help or hinder learning. Learning should be promoted in a variety of different ways, whilst a student is on placement, if the experience is to be satisfying for the student. Historically, practice teachers have placed considerable emphasis upon learning through direct practice with clients, in conjunction with the practice tutorial.[3] Open learning materials, to be used according to the students' learning needs, greatly enhance the flexibility of learning.

Often learning about social work is very unpredictable learning — the range of learning opportunities presented to the student is so diverse that introducing the idea of sequence is problematic. Students may be faced with complex tasks before they have achieved competence in basic skills. Similarly there may be little opportunity for students to demonstrate their ability in some areas of practice if there is a complete reliance upon "live practice" i.e., the arrival on the agency's doorstep of the type of clients with the type of problems that the student needs to learn about. Learning by simulation, using open learning materials, offers the opportunity for controlling the learning environment to meet the students' needs. It therefore offers the opportunity to promote learning in

---

[3]   Practice tutorials or tutorials — used to describe the face to face teaching session between practice teacher and student — tutorials avoid the connotations of supervision, and the inelegant "practice teaching session."

areas that would not otherwise be possible. Another aspect of simulated learning is that it offers a possibility to accelerate students' learning. Where a student is grappling with issues and ideas a simulated exercise in this aspect of practice can often speed and enhance the student's learning in a way that might not be possible with other forms of learning.

Appendix 1 contains one example, the *boundaries exercise*, of a simulated exercise used by practice teachers (field instructors) and students, it is taken from a collection of open learning materials, *Social Work Practice* (Doel & Shardlow, 1993).

The Boundaries Exercise: An Overview

Students often find it difficult to know what a professional relationship means in practice and how it differs from a personal relationship. This activity is designed to highlight the differences between friendships and what we might call workshops. It helps the student become more skilled at deciding where the boundary between personal and professional should be drawn.

This exercise consists of a number of questions designed to expose practice dilemmas. It may be used in a variety of different ways: a student and a practice teacher can discuss their responses to these questions; or a group of students can consider the similarities and differences in their responses to these questions. Such dilemmas focus on the "distance" social workers place between themselves and the people who use their services. Through using an exercise such as this the student has the opportunity to rehearse possible responses and to understand some of the principles that underpin ethical practice.

Video Triggers

Another form of simulation is to use video, which has the capacity to make a situation feel very immediate. It draws viewers into common experience in a powerful, graphic way. Pre-recorded video is a useful tool for direct, open, or distance learning. Its value for learning at distance is obvious, in offering a three-dimensional "page" for the learner to use. However, there are drawbacks:

Entertainment Mode. We often experience television as a passive pass time, so it is easy to "switch off" from video, or to become critical if it is not sufficiently entertaining.
"Clutter". Video can be too graphic — unexpected details like a bright red shirt, can achieve prominence over the message the video was intended to convey.
Expense. Professionally produced videos are costly, and home grown varieties

are often of poor visual and audio quality, which rather defeats the purpose of the video. Equipment for inter active video (CD-TV) is still prohibitively expensive.

Pre-recorded videos are more likely to find their mark if they are relatively short (to guard against entertainment mode) and the viewer is clear about their purpose. It is important that the viewer interacts with the video, not in the technological sense but with the content of the video. For example, the very opposite of this process is a video lecture. This might be a quick way of giving information to geographically distant learners, but it feels "distant" as there is no inter-active opportunity.

At the University of Sheffield a range of video tapes, about practice teaching, have been produced (Doel & Shardlow, 1990; Shardlow, 1988; Shardlow & Doel, 1988; Shardlow & Doel, 1990). Taking one of these as an example, *Placement Triggers*, consists of thirty brief vignettes. In each vignette one a student speaks directly to the viewer and poses a problem, a "sticky moment," from the student's practice. Each scene ends with a visual "...........?" and viewers are invited to consider how they might respond to the student, as in the following example:

> I'm going to see that family this afternoon. The ones who've been leaving their children on their own. They go out to the pub every night, and the neighbour said they don't have any toys to play with . . . the children are left on their own without any toys. So, what I thought was, I don't know if you think it is a good idea, but I could go along to talk to the family and see if the parents would like some toys — tell them how we get the toys given to us at Christmas — and they would get to know me a bit. Then perhaps we could talk about them going out and leaving the kids on their own. Do you think that's a good way to do it ?

This example is suggestive of a student who does not understand his/her role in child protection. These tapes have been used in a variety of ways, for example, to trigger discussion about how to respond and to provide a stimulus for role simulation exercises.

THE EXAMINATION OF PRACTICE

There are a variety of different problems associated with the evaluation of social work students' practice competence, some of the major problems being:

- the difficulty of establishing evidence of such a complex skill;
- that social work is a set a diverse activities — definitions of the constituents of social work are inevitably contested;
- a lack of theorizing about how to examine practice.

We have sought to develop a "macro" model for the examination of practice competence "Examination by Triangulation" (Shardlow & Doel, 1993). However, there is also a need to develop "micro" level models to inform our approach to the examination of individual pieces of practice. We would like to draw attention to three important principles to be used when examining a particular piece of practice.

Specific Areas of Practice

Before you can make a judgement about whether the student is ready to practise, you need to make a judgement about what *is* good practice. What will the student's practice be judged against?

If you were evaluating a student who was learning to cook, you would look at different skills in cooking — from an ability to boil an egg (not that easy, actually) to competence with soufflés. In each dish you would look for presentation and colour as well as taste and texture. You might inspect a collection of dishes, to see how the student balances a meal over-all. You would also want to assess other aspects of these skills, such as kitchen hygiene, economical cooking, knowledge of nutrition and ability to work as part of a culinary team. "Readiness to cook" is a composite ability which needs breaking into its smaller parts, while not losing sight of how they relate to each other. It is the same in social work.

Prior to the Evaluation Event

It feels unfair if we are judged against standards which we did not know about. A student cook who understands a "good" boiled egg to be one with a firm white and a softish yolk will feel cheated if the egg is judged by different criteria. Aesthetics is a notoriously difficult area to find agreement (check your criteria for a "good" cup of tea against the criteria of your student and your colleagues). However, if you know your colleague's criteria *before* you make it, you will know whether you have been successful. In other words, a minimum expectation is that you know what the criteria are, even if you are not in full agreement with them.

Collaboration with Others

If you are the sole judge of good practice, there will be factors which you do not think about, and the ones you do include will be influenced by your own cultural biography. As we saw with the simple case of a boiled egg or a cup of tea, criteria are not written in tablets of stone. It is important to check your notions of good practice with others, so that you can get a "triangulation" of opinions. If there is serious disagreement between you and the student about criteria for good practice in a particular area it is crucial this emerges before the evaluation event, not after it.

In particular, it is important that the student takes part in developing the criteria. The consideration of what is "good" practice is where the twin features of learning and evaluation meet, and students are more likely to be successful if they are in a position to *know* whether they have succeeded or not! The very act of discussing criteria for good practice aids the student's learning, because they are learning *why* they do, as well as *what* they do. This process helps to make evaluation and learning congruent with each other. The three principles are designed to provide a balance between objectivity and subjectivity in the evaluation of the student. This approach provides an opportunity to develop relatively objective criteria from a subjective base. It helps to ensure that criteria are sensitive to the context of this particular student in this particular setting.

In appendix two an simulation exercise, *Yardsticks,* is presented that helps frame the examination of student's competence in small measurable events. It is designed to be used by practice teachers to help them explore an approach to measuring a student's competence. This exercise *Yardsticks* is taken from Teaching Social Work Practice (Doel et al., 1993). Once the practice teacher has practised this model in simulation, it can be used directly with students. This exercise has been used as part of two open learning programmes on as a pilot. This the simulation exercise has been thoroughly evaluated on conventionally taught programmes.

CONCLUSION

The development of open learning materials for field education remains at an early stage of development in the UK. There is considerable interest in developing these approaches to learning, both among students and practice teachers. There is a need to identify, both at the national and international level the range of open learning materials available. However, knowing what is available in itself is insufficient, there is also a need to evaluate the materials and to learn how to improve them.

REFERENCES

CCETSW. (1989). *Regulations and guidance for the approval of agencies and the accreditation and training of practice teachers* (Paper 26.3). London: Central Council for Education and Training in Social Work.

CCETSW. (1991). *Rules and requirements for the diploma in social work* (Paper 30) (2nd ed.). London: Central Council for Education and Training in Social Work.

Doel, M. (1987). The practice curriculum. *Social Work Education,* 6(3), 6-12.

Doel, M. (1988). A practice curriculum to promote accelerated learning. In J. Phillipson, M. Richards & D. Sawdon (Eds.), *Towards a practice led curriculum* (pp. 45-60). London: National Institute for Social Work.

Doel, M. (1990). Putting the heart into the curriculum. *Community Care,* 797, 20-2.

Doel, M., (1993). *Teaching social work practice (Pilot Version).* Sheffield: University of Sheffield.

Doel, M., & Shardlow, S. M. (1990). *Initial interviewing skills.* Sheffield: Practice Teaching Video, The University of Sheffield.

Doel, M., & Shardlow, S. M. (1993). *Social work practice.* Aldershot: Gower.

JUSSR. (1986). *Social skills in social work.* Sheffield: University of Sheffield.

Lorenz, W. (1986). Social work education in Western Europe: Themes and opportunities. *Issues in Social Work Education,* 6(2), 89-100.

Shardlow, S. M. (1988). *Basic skills for practice teachers.* Sheffield: Practice Teaching Video, The University of Sheffield.

Shardlow, S. M., & Doel, M. (1988). *Placement triggers.* Sheffield: Practice Teaching Video, The University of Sheffield.

Shardlow, S. M., & Doel, M. (1990). *Working together.* Sheffield: Practice Teaching Video, The University of Sheffield.

Shardlow, S. M., & Doel, M. (1993). Examination by triangulation: A model for practice teaching. *Social Work Education,* 12(3), 67-79.

Shardlow, S. M., & Doel, M. (1995). *Enabling practice learning.* Houndmills, Basingstoke: Macmillan.

South Yorkshire Dip SW. (1993). *Practice one handbook.* Sheffield: South Yorkshire Diploma in Social Work.

We wish to acknowledge the assistance of the British Council in supporting our visit to Canada to present at the Conference on Field Education held in conjunction with the Learned Society meetings, Calgary, June 1994.
Parts of this paper are taken from Teaching Social Work Practice, (piloted 1993-4) by Doel, M. with acknowledgement to Sawdon, C., Sawdon, D., & Shardlow, S.M.

Appendix 1 Boundaries Exercise

> BOUNDARIES consists of a number of questions designed to expose practice dilemmas. These dilemmas focus on the "distance" social workers place between themselves and the people who use their services.

Purpose

Students often find it difficult to know what a professional relationship means in practice and how it differs from a personal relationship. This activity is designed to highlight the differences between *friendships* and what we might call *workshops*. It helps the student become more skilled at deciding where the boundary between personal and professional should be drawn.

Method

1)   This activity often gets best results with several participants, but it can be done by a single practice teacher and student. Arrange a time to meet and outline the purposes of the activity, but not the details — you want spontaneous responses.

2)   Give each person a copy of BOUNDARIES and take each of the six sections in turn to trigger discussion (about five to ten minutes for each section). Kick off the first item yourself with a Never, Always or It Depends and invite others to join in with their responses.

   Relate the discussion to actual experiences in order to avoid idealized replies. Encourage dissent and try to tease out any general principles which have come out of the discussion.

3)   Sum up the main areas of consent and dissent and write down any general principles which have come out of the discussion. Ask for feedback from everyone about the usefulness of the exercise. (About one hour total).

Variations

This activity has been used successfully in many different settings, usually in the early stages of the placement (and even as part of a pre-placement meeting).

You may wish to tailor the details of BOUNDARIES to your particular work base. For example, if you are a social worker based in a hospital it may be the boundaries between the health care staff and the social work staff that you wish to highlight. There are dilemmas, too, in the patient-doctor relationship which you could compare with client-worker activities.

You can use BOUNDARIES to highlight a particular dimension of practice, for example an anti-oppressive framework. How would issues of race and gender change the answers to these questions?

BOUNDARIES

Where do we draw the boundary between personal and professional relationships? Can you answer Always or Never to any of the questions below?
If your answer to a question is It Depends, what does it depend on?

The term client is used to include resident and user, too

RECIPROCATION
1 Do your clients call you by your first name?
    Do you call them by their first name?
2 Would you accept a service from a client
    - let them knit you a jumper?
    - advise you what is wrong with your car?
    - mend an electrical fault in your home?

INTERVIEW CULTURE
3 On a home visit would you accept
    - a cup of tea?
    - an alcoholic drink?
    - a meal?
4 In the unit, ward or group room would you
    - talk about personal matters with other people present?
    - make a cup of tea for the client?

SELF-DISCLOSURE

5   Do you compare life experiences with clients
     - let them know how you feel about their circumstances?
     - let them know what sort of day you've had?
     - talk about your work with other clients?
6   Do you share personal information with your clients
     - good news, such as your partner has been promoted?
     - bad news, like your father suffers from Alzheimer's?
7   Would you give your home address or phone number?

SOCIAL CONTACT

8   Would you accept from a client
     - a wedding invitation?
     - an invitation to a party?
9   Would you avoid frequenting a place where a client worked?
10   Do you lend money to your clients?

TOUCH

11   Do you shake hands with a client when you meet for the first time?
12   Would you touch a client who is upset
     - on the arm? round the shoulders? on the knee?
13   Would you cuddle or romp with the children of clients?

LOOKING THE OTHER WAY

14   Do you ignore your client's illegal activities
     - claiming benefit when they are working?
     - the presence of a cannabis plant in their home?
     - electricity that has been reconnected by the client?
     - an absconder who is being harboured?

with acknowledgements to Kate Langford

This exercise is taken from Doel, M., & Shardlow, S. M. (1993). *Social Work Practice*, Aldershot: Gower.

Appendix 2 Yardsticks Exercise

Yardsticks provides a model to help you to develop criteria for competence in specific areas of practice and in collaboration with the student. This provides both a model of evaluation and a means by which students can learn how to evaluate their own practice. To this extent it is a method of evaluation which is "congruent" with the student's learning needs.

Purpose

This module focuses on the separation of learning and assessment, exploring the distinction between learning *processes* and assessment *events*.

Method

- For this exercise you will be working in small groups to devise criteria of good practice which will be used to assess a particular piece of a student's practice.

- The groups will return after twenty minutes to observe the student's practice (via a segment of videotape or a role play).

- Each group will use the criteria of one of the other groups in order to assess the student's practice.

Variations

It is possible to complete this Activity as a practice teacher-student pair. In this case, you use your own criteria to assess the practice on the video, rather than swapping with somebody else.

The particular example uses a trigger from a video-tape produced by the Joint Unit for Social Services Research at Sheffield University (JUSSR, 1986). Any other similar five to ten minute videotape of social work practice can be used (or you can make your own) to illustrate other areas of practice. Alternatively, you can use a role play as an example of practice.

The *Yardsticks* model can be used with any identified piece of social work practice, and once you have rehearsed it as an exercise, you should try using it directly with a student. You should involve the student in the process of developing the criteria.

Yardsticks One

Included in your student's learning objectives for the placement is:

> *to develop helping skills with people in distress, and especially the skill of expressing empathy*

As the practice teacher, you have said that you will provide an opportunity for this during the placement.

Developing Criteria

You are going to develop criteria to assess the student's work in this area. In practice, you would include the student in the process of developing criteria, but for this exercise you are doing it in groups with other practice teachers. It has been agreed that the student's practice will be assessed using only the agreed criteria.

> *what are the criteria of good practice for helping people in distress and expressing empathy?*

You may find it helpful to brainstorm a list of factors and then prioritize them into four or five main points. Make your final list as *specific* as possible, so that it can be understood by other practice teachers who have not been involved in your discussions. Write down your criteria as clearly as possible (use a sheet of flip-paper if you are doing this as a large group exercise).

Yardsticks Two

Sampling Practice

The criteria which have been developed now need to be used with a sample of the student's practice. For the purposes of a training exercise, a short piece of video is the most effective way of doing this (or video-taping a short role play, and playing this back). For example, there is a ten minute scene of practice which illustrates a student expressing empathy with a distressed client in the video, *Social Skills and Social Work,*

(JUSSR, 1984, fifth scene). If you are using another group's criteria rather than your own, familiarize yourself with their criteria and watch the video extract with these criteria in mind.

Yardsticks Three

The Evaluation

After watching the sample of practice, it is time to make your evaluation of the student's work in the light of the criteria you have agreed to use (these might be your own, or criteria devised by another group, if you are doing this as a large group exercise).

Give a "first impression" rating for <u>each</u> of the criteria, using these categories:

- very good
- good
- average
- poor
- very poor
- not possible to rate

In addition, if you are in a group: Share your ratings to see what similarities and differences there are. If there are criteria which it was not possible to rate, discuss why.

Discuss these two questions:

- were the criteria useful to help assess the student's practice and would you modify them in any way?
- with hindsight, are there other criteria which you would like to include?

This exercise is taken from Doel, M. (1993). *Teaching Social Work Practice (Pilot Version)*, Sheffield: University of Sheffield.

CHAPTER SEVENTEEN

LEARNING TOOLS:
A VALUABLE COMPONENT OF THE
FIELD INSTRUCTION PROCESS

Sherrill Hershberg and Joanne Moffatt

INTRODUCTION

This paper focuses on several learning tools used in field instruction. It begins with a description of three approaches to field instruction: the articulated approach, the competency-based approach and the role systems approach, which provide the framework for the learning tools. Reference is also be made to adult education principles, which underlie the field instruction process. Various roles and expectations of field instructors, as identified in some of the literature, are presented. Each learning tool is described and discussed within the context of four categories: Foundation Tools, Continuous Tools, Preparation for Practice Tools, and Beginning Practice Tools. Reference is made to a few central elements of the University of Manitoba Field Program, including the Key Roles and Responsibilities Document and the Evaluation Document.

APPROACHES TO FIELD INSTRUCTION

The principles of adult learning provide the foundation of our work with students. The following three approaches to field instruction (Bogo & Vayda, 1986) relate most closely to the learning tools presented in this paper. These are:

1) The Articulated Approach;
2) The Competency Based Approach;
3) The Role Systems Approach;

The Articulated Approach

This model prepares the student to become fully aware of what is involved in a practice intervention, why that intervention has been selected according to a theoretical foundation, and how the necessary helping techniques should be used. Learning begins with introduction to a professional knowledge base, followed by practice (Bogo & Vayda, 1986). Sheafer and Jenkins present a strong case for planned linkages between academic and field content wherein curriculum is carefully sequenced. In our faculty, the Field Instruction Course and the Practices Course are co-requisite requirements and students have opportunities to use their field intervention experiences in Practices assignments, and correspondingly to apply the theory they have learned in Practices class to their field situations.

The Competency Based Approach

The Competency Based Approach defines learning objectives in specific, observable behavioral terms, designs learning activities and teaching approaches that assist in the development of those skills, and creates evaluation measures to use in assessing learning in relation to the original objective. The Outcomes/Evaluation document of our university's field program designates 13 areas in which students must develop and demonstrate competence according to their level in the program. Some examples of the required competencies are:

- application of theory to practice;
- self awareness;
- communication;
- contracting skills;
- the ability to evaluate one's own performance;

The Role Systems Approach

The Role Systems Approach as identified by Wijnberg and Schwartz focuses on the transactional nature of the relationship between student and field instructor. This relationship is egalitarian in nature, and is based on (Bogo & Vayda, 1986, p. 23):

> shared recognition of expertise and competence of both learner and teacher. The ideal learning climate is characterized by respect, openness, collaboration, and an expectation of active involvement in planning, implementing, and evaluating learning and progress in the field. Role expectations of student and field instructor are arrived at through ongoing negotiation.

The roles and responsibilities of students, instructors, and others related to the educational process in field are clearly articulated in several documents in our Field Program. These documents are shared with students at the beginning of the academic term, provide the basis for individual goal setting in the program, and for ongoing discussion with students as goals are monitored, modified, and achieved.

ROLES AND RESPONSIBILITIES OF FIELD INSTRUCTORS

Nisivoccia (1990, p. 8) refers to "the metamorphosis of the professional self" and the struggles students encounter, particularly in the early weeks of the field placement. She points out that field instructors need to be aware of knowing the time phases in the process. She further states that student learning is both time and content structured. In addition, Nisivoccia (1990, p. 14) underscores the fact that "field instructors must link structure, form, limits and distinction of roles to the learning process." She also refers to Robinson, who has identified five limits which define the supervisory process.

1) professional character of the relationship between the supervisor and student in which the supervisor sets the tone;
2) limits of time;
3) limits of case material;
4) limits of other factors such as classroom influences on the student;
5) limits determined by the supervisor's equipment and the student's ability and readiness to learn.

Nisivoccia cites Shulman (1983), who has articulated several skills required by field instructors. During the initial phase of the field instruction process, Shulman states that important tasks include "preliminary empathy, developing an educational contract, and mediating between the student and the learning process as well as the student and the learning environment."

Dea, Grist, and Myli (1982) discuss learning tasks in considerable detail as related to four major stages of learning based on a problem-solving process: Engagement, Assessment and Planning, Intervention, and Evaluation & Termination. They state that instructors need to be aware that the integration of each faculty's educational objectives, the learning and teaching availabilities in the agency, and each student's ability do not happen easily or automatically. They argue for a planned approach to student learning tasks and outline the practise tasks, educational content, and typical student learning tasks related to the four stages of learning.

Price (1976) discusses issues of balance between required learning and what the learner considers to be important. She states that adult education principles fit well with social work practice. She identifies six elements of teachers of adults: provision of a positive environment with genuine respect for the student, ability to convey the mission of the adult educator, using students' life experiences, creating a non-threatening environment, planning and structuring the curriculum, and guiding or tutoring each student in how to evaluate their own performance.

LEARNING TOOLS: RATIONALE AND CONTEXT

Written learning tools are meant to assist with the goals and tasks of field instruction as identified above. We have found the tools helpful in operationalizing our roles and responsibilities as instructors, and believe they can be modified to suit a broad range of social work programs, instructors and students. Essentially, the tools are student-oriented exercises and tasks with a series of questions which the student is asked to reflect upon and complete. These are reviewed and discussed during individual instructional sessions. Most of the tools are familiar and have been used by many instructors in a variety of ways. We have adapted, redesigned and ordered them for our own use. It is important to emphasize that we believe the tools are valuable only when linked with theoretical approaches, adult education principles and roles, some of which have been outlined. In addition, the specific field requirements and curriculum objectives of each faculty provide an important context for the tools.

Some considerations in using the tools flexibly include sensitivity to cultural issues as well as individual student learning goals and styles. In addition to helping formulate student goals and contracts, we believe the tools provide students with a sense of grounding, direction and clarity, especially during the initial phase of the field placement. The tools also facilitate self-directed learning, reflection, self-awareness and assist in monitoring progress and identifying areas for further student growth. In particular, we believe it is important for instructors to be clear as to whether and to what extent the tools will be part of the formal student evaluation.

GROUPING AND DISCUSSION OF TOOLS

We believe learning experiences in field need to be assigned selectively. To develop an educationally oriented field experience, it is also important to sequence and time student learning experiences carefully, to determine options available in the field placement setting, and to identify clearly what needs to be learned and how goals will be achieved. Conceptually, we have chosen to group the tools with particular reference to time and sequence issues. Although the tools can be used at any time and on an ongoing basis throughout the field placement, they will be introduced and presented sequentially, as we believe this generally reflects the student learning process.

Foundation Tools

Foundation tools are defined as those learning tools which help to form the basis of the field experience. Development of learning tasks requires both student and instructor to have an understanding of the student's individual learning patterns and accomplishments. It is also important that students have a sense of their own strengths and are able to recognize their abilities and expertise in order to negotiate their field learning experiences. Two tools which assist in addressing these issues are introduced at the outset of the field placement.

Student Self-assessment and Learning Goals

This tool provides an entry point for both student and instructor to begin an educational assessment as well as to develop a working relationship. The tool is useful in empowering students to identify their competencies, validate their previous experiences, and begin to think about how they best learn, so that field experiences will be suited to their unique learning style. It is also a preparatory step to developing the learning contract.

The Learning Contract

The learning contract helps students to clearly formulate both their learning goals, and how these will be achieved. The process invites discussion with the field instructor, and can be an important building block in the ongoing student instructor relationship. The contract is intended to be formulated early in the term in order that the student and instructor have clarity about the specific goals and tasks, their educational relevance, and the student's or instructor's roles as they relate to these. The objectives of all tasks are related to the overall goals of the specific field program. The students' own learning goals may be adapted to fit within this context. As students become more involved in formulating their own goals, they are in a better position to monitor and self evaluate their performance.

Continuous Tools

These are tools which are used on an ongoing basis throughout the field placement experience. They reflect the developmental nature of student learning and provide opportunities for professional self-awareness and accountability.

The Log

The log is a valuable tool for both students and instructors. It provides an opportunity for students to monitor their own learning experiences from both broad and specific perspectives, and it provides an ongoing summary of a student's performance in field for both student and instructor. The framework of the log assists students with setting goals clearly, and monitoring progress towards them, in focusing on self awareness both as it relates to educational experiences and professional growth, and focusing on theoretical linkages to practice situations. Monitoring of professional self development is enhanced when logs are dated and completed at regular intervals. The field instructor can easily monitor a student's weekly progress through the log and use the information provided as a focus for supervisory meetings. It is also an excellent means of reviewing the student's progress in several areas if the logs are re-read at the end of the term.

Time Sheets

The time sheet is a tool specifically designed for accountability in the field program. It helps students account for their time and the balance of direct service and other tasks in the field program. By providing students with a clear illustration of how they are spending their time in field, students can negotiate the use of time in different ways which may better fit their own individual learning styles. It is useful for instructors in their co-joint planning with students as this relates to attainment of goals and expectations.

Preparation for Practice Tools

Three tools are included in this category, all of which are intended to provide specific experiences for students to relate to context and agency setting, professional roles and purpose as well as process and content issues. These tools can also be viewed as part of the information-gathering phase of social work practice. The tools are introduced during the first month of the field placement, providing students with direct opportunities, choices and responsibilities to engage in activities related to direct practice, but without responsibility for direct client contact during this initial stage of the field placement. These tools are a precursor to the engagement phase.

Taped Interview

This tool has several purposes; some of these include: an opportunity to initiate contact and arrange an interview with agency workers, to conduct an interview, to engage directly with staff, and to learn more about the agency setting. These experiences help to begin using skills such as contracting, interviewing, building working relationships, and gathering information purposefully.

Shadowing/Observation

This tool provides direct observation of social workers in a variety of situations and roles, as well as micro and mezzo aspects of practise. The tool can also be helpful in reflecting upon worker styles, interviewing skills, and generic concepts.

Closed File

This tool assists in preparing students for interaction with their first client system. It helps to focus student learning on process and content issues and phases of practice. It is intended to facilitate student reflection in terms of how they will approach their first client system, what information will be needed, who will be involved in the process, how issues and goals will be identified, and what intervention models will be appropriate.

Beginning Practice Tools

These tools are introduced once students are directly involved with client systems. They are intended to provide students with opportunities for self-reflection, self-awareness and the conscious use of self. Three tools are included in this group:

Intervention Record and Summary of Client/collateral Contact

This tool was developed in response to students' questions and concerns about how to plan for and evaluate interviews, and how to approach an interview in a more methodical way. The tool emphasizes a concept which some students find difficult to integrate at the beginning of the term: every contact related to a client is an intervention. The Intervention Record and Summary of Client/ Collateral Contact breaks down the steps for intervention, and helps students to see how interventions are planned, occur, and then are evaluated. It also provides an opportunity for students to identify the nature of the student/client or collateral relationship. Additionally, it clearly differentiates between process and content issues in a given intervention, and provides students with opportunities to develop their skills in making these distinctions. In the beginning phase of practice it may be more useful for students to use this tool in all interventions. As students become more comfortable with the planned approach to practice interventions, they may choose to use the tool more selectively.

Process Recording

This is an excellent tool for helping students identify both their own feelings in an interview, and their communication skills. The section on issues is one used by some Schools of Social Work. It is designed to help students move beyond their gut level response to reflections, and ultimately to an objective analysis of the issues involved for the student and the client in an interview situation.

Tape and Self Critique

There are two central purposes to this exercise:

1) It helps the student to set clear goals for an interview, and then evaluate her/his own performance. When educational goals are clearly set out, students can monitor their own progress, and can become real participants in the feedback process, independent of the field instructor (Suanna Wilson, 1981).

2) This exercise assists the instructor to evaluate the student's ability to reach goals, and to offer constructive comments if needed. It also helps the instructor to reinforce the student's strengths in the interview situation, and provides an opportunity to assess how students self evaluate.

CONCLUSION

In summary, this chapter has provided a brief review of three approaches to field instruction, an overview of some of the roles of field instructors, and a discussion of a number of learning tools selected to assist in the delivery of effective field instruction. We hope that it will stimulate further thinking and development of meaningful ways in which to facilitate student learning in the field.

REFERENCES

Bogo, M., & Vayda, E. (1986). *The practice of field instruction in social work: Theory and practice*. Toronto: University of Toronto Press.

Dea, K. L., Grist, M., & Myli, R. (1982). Learning tasks for practice competence. In Shaefor and Jenkins (Eds.), *Quality field education in social work* (pp. 237-261). New York and London: Longman.

Hagen Hartung, B. J. (1982). Practicum instructor: A study of role expectations. *Journal of Sociology and Social Welfare, 9*(4), 662-670.

Hersh, A. (1984). Teaching the theory and practice of student supervision: A short-term model based on principles of adult education. *The Clinical Supervisor, 2*(1), 29-44.

Larsen, J. (1980). Competency based and task centred practicum instruction. *Journal of Education for Social Work, 16*(1), 87-94.

Nisivoccia, D. (1990). Teaching and learning tasks in the beginning phase of field instruction. *The Clinical Supervisor, 8*(1), 7-22.

Price, H. G. (1986). Achieving balance between self-directed and required learning. *Journal of Education for Social Work, 12*(1), 105-112.

Shulman, L. (1983). *Teaching the helping skills: A field instructor's guide*. Illinois: Peacock Publishers.

Wijnberg, M. H., & Schwartz, M. C. (1977). Models of student supervision. The apprenticeship, growth and role systems model. *Journal of Education for Social Work, 13*(3), 107-113.

Wilson, S. J. (1981). Field instruction techniques for supervisors. *The Free Press*. New York.

CHAPTER EIGHTEEN

USE OF STRUCTURED CONSULTATION FOR LEARNING ISSUES IN FIELD EDUCATION

Barbara Thomlison and Don Collins

Managing a field education learning environment is like setting the stage for a play. The stage is the agency and the community is in the wings. As a field educator, you have roles as writer, director, and major actor. You are free to set up the props as you wish, guide the action, and establish the script. Others will have a say and opinion, but the play itself requires direction, and a planned systematic approach to be ready for opening night. Social work field education is not dissimilar to a dramatic production. The field educator plays an instrumental role in planning, organizing, rehearsing, promoting and managing a quality practicum experience. While most students rehearse and prepare for their debut on opening night as scheduled, a few students present larger challenges and dilemmas to field educators, and may not be ready to fulfil their role and go on stage. This paper presents the use of structured consultation as one method to assist students with their achievements.

The ideas in this chapter are derived from two sources: a student focused book intended to guide social work students through the peaks and pitfalls of the social work practicum (Thomlison, Rogers, Collins, & Grinnell, *The Social Work Practicum: A Student Guide*, 2nd edition); and, a workshop presented at the Conference on Field Education in Social Work, The University of Calgary. To begin we describe the practicum as a learning experience, then a summary is provided of role play exercises which illustrate the use of structured consultation for learning concerns.

PRACTICUM AS A LEARNING EXPERIENCE

Field instructors need to reinforce the idea to students that the social work practicum is a form of learning that has been carefully designed to incorporate all the advantages of the apprenticeship system while minimizing the disadvantages. *It is a learning experience and not a work experience.* It is a core social work course where the planned integration between practice and theory can occur. As a field educator, a primary function is to focus on teaching conceptualization skills for students which link learning in the classroom to learning in the field. At the commencement of the practicum, students need to be engaged as active participants in their learning (Collins, Thomlison, & Grinnell, 1992).

The social work practicum is an opportunity to apply theoretical knowledge and personal wisdom to practice situations in a purposeful and effective way. At one level, applying knowledge may involve assisting students in remembering theory behind engaging a client in treatment, preparing for a community needs assessment, planning to discharge a patient to community, or determining consumer service satisfaction. At a different level, applying knowledge means helping students in utilizing the total knowledge and understanding acquired throughout a lifetime in order to evaluate and reflect on what they are doing, and what the individual and societal consequences are likely to be if certain decisions are taken.

As soon as possible students need to perceive the practicum as linking learning in the classroom to learning in the field. An initial learning exercise is important to ensure students know what the field agency is doing and how these services fit into the broader framework of social work. Students need to be assisted to first examine their role within the agency and the agency's role within the social service delivery system and community in general. When students have done this, they will have a better understanding of what role they will serve in the agency system and what kind of social service they will be practising. From this beginning, students start to see a direct relationship between the functional experience gained in the practicum and the theoretical knowledge learned in the classroom. Setting the practical experience at a level that students find challenging but not overwhelming can be exacting and even precarious if planning is not taken (Collins et al., 1992). The workshop (June 1994) provided an illustration for field educators of three learning issues addressed through role play as a structured consultation.

THE USE OF STRUCTURED CONSULTATION

The field instructor provides knowledge, instruction and support to the student through structured consultation during educational supervision. Supervision is designed to provide high rates of consultation which evolve and taper off over the course of the practicum. The field instructor measures the student's progress through the use of the practicum educational plan and other feedback methods such as process recordings, tapings, observations and live supervision. The primary responsibility of the field instructor is to facilitate the student's practicum educational plan through the service delivery system of the agency.

Student success is greatly dependent upon the skills, abilities, knowledge and behaviours accomplished in the particular field placement. Structured consultations can provide students with the necessary support and environment for such learning to occur. Role play during the consultation is a method to facilitate learning. Although the use of a single role play with students does not necessarily resolve the issue of concern. Competency in the area determines the frequency and use of structured consultation. Undoubtedly, role play issues are challenging to implement sensitively and to creatively adjust to the individual situation. Although numerous structured learning activities may be used during field education, this paper is restricted to the use of student — field instructor role play. The use of structured consultation activities is also one method to improve field instructor effectiveness as well as to manage and monitor student progress and performance (Collins et al., 1992).

The workshop illustrated three types of student learning situations resulting in performance and progress dilemmas which challenge field educators: 1) students who are marginal in performance or even failing; 2) students who are bright but unquestioning and compliant; and 3) students who do not challenge themselves, avoid change and progress. Each scenario utilized a student and field instructor role. The basis of the structured consultation was one of the above issues. To initiate the role play with a student, it is suggested that field instructors focus on the goals of the student's educational practicum plan to articulate the area(s) of student progress or lack thereof.

Role Play: The Marginal or Failing Student

Objective: To support and recognize lack of progress and learning with a student who does not recognize this.

Response: Students who do not recognize their lack of achievement may be the most difficult. In this dilemma it is very important to use every supervision session and opportunity to provide direct feedback on performance. Feedback needs to be both verbal and in written form.

At first, these students will be overwhelmed with information. They may despair of ever being able to change all that is necessary, in fact they may even have difficulty remembering all the names, rules, and procedural details that everyone else takes for granted. In fact these students may not ask you the field instructor or other staff for help. As the field educator you need to help the student view the practicum as a mutual learning experience and not a competition. Teach the student to ask for help articulating their concerns and questions.

Although the individual supervisory consultation is still considered primary, group supervision and consultation can enrich and complement the experiences for these students in a variety of ways. Group consultations allow a wider range of learning activities to be undertaken, provide experience in group interaction, give students an awareness of professional identity, and provide a sense of support which may be necessary in these situations. Prior to the structured consultation ask students to review their learning contract and decide how well they have achieved on the basis of documented evidence — that is, on the basis of written reports, process recordings, videotapes, and so forth. The student will then go into their consultation more prepared to absorb whatever feedback they receive. Students will also be in a position to confirm that their omissions and mistakes have been properly balanced with their triumphs.

The primary purpose of structured consultation is to assess the student's achievements to date in order to properly focus and direct their future growth. One of the major tasks after the consultation will be to revise the educational plan by paring down or supplementing some learning objectives and adding or eliminating others.

Field instructors act as one of the gatekeepers for the social work program. In this capacity, they are responsible for upholding social work standards and ensuring that students who are not yet competent do not pass the practicum until they have achieved the minimum standards (stated as learning goals) required by the social work program. Nevertheless, it may at times be difficult for you to assess a student as "unsatisfactory" because of the student's reaction, as well as the reactions of the field liaison and field coordinator.

Role Play: The Bright but Compliant Student

Objective: To assist students in recognizing potential and to clarify values to address learning objectives.

Response: These students are also difficult. Their enthusiasm and eagerness never seems to get translated into potential action. Always compliant, these students fail to challenge and question their learning by accepting and agreeing with each opportunity or situation. These students may find that there is both too much and too little to do during the practicum. Small decisions they need to make may cause them unnecessary worry because they may be anxious to make a good impression and do the right thing. These students need to feel confident in using their common sense and prior knowledge. They need to know they are allowed to make a few mistakes before they are able to put their worries into perspective.

For these students learning has elements of anxiety, frustrations, and painful self searching. Feelings of discomfort are not necessarily equated with positive learning for them. Learning may not be seen as a pleasant experience. The student suffers from a lack of confidence in what is to be learned — both with the content, subject and skill — and this interferes with the development of self-direction. Questioning and challenging is not viewed as acceptable from their belief system. There are two useful techniques for coping with compliant students. First, have the student keep a journal of their thoughts and questions, new input and alternate views of a situation. Empowerment of the student occurs through participation, expression of opinions, ideas, and criticism; and opportunities to make choices. Second, role play many situations with the student to reduce their sense of confusion and to develop self-confidence in their own abilities. Guidance and regular practice opportunities foster self-determination.

Role Play: The Student Who Avoids Change and Progress

Objective: To develop and refine appropriate and challenging social work competencies.
Response: The student with this difficulty must be kept focused on the learning issue.

The role play has to find a "hook" to challenge the student. Providing support is the first step, and then focusing on and recognizing student strengths moves the student to the awareness phase. This encourages the student to recognize the possibilities of what they do that is effective. Problem solving is focused on mistakes and does not usually assist students to begin to think in a new way. Rather it often produces confusion, and may mislead students into thinking and believing they are effective when they are not. Generating solutions is more likely to increase students' awareness of their learning issue. Thus, knowing what is going okay is more likely to assist students in finding new solutions for areas where they are receiving little recognition. It is important not to let students' satisfaction with learning become equated with progressive learning.

DISCUSSION AND SUMMARY

To accomplish learning in the field, students must be able to generalize from the particular field placement so they can transfer their learning from one context or situation to another. Students need to be able to use ideas to inform their practice and to generate theories about what works from a practice experience. Students also need to be able to step back from their work and critically reflect on it; and perhaps most importantly they need to learn how they learn. In this way, you are enabling students to create and structure a learning environment conducive to lifelong learning. This requires more than learning what to do in a particular setting in order to accomplish a job or task (Thomlison et al., in press). The student needs to see themselves as a learner rather than as a worker or as a colleague or a new staff member in the practicum setting. As well, it is critical that you, the field educator see the student as a learner (Thomlison et al., in press). Student learning occurs in many different ways. It can be intentional, planned and sequenced. Learning can also come about by trial and error and even through mistakes or other chance occurrences. Learning occurs in several ways for everyone and so it will be for the student during the field education experience. Thus the potential for learning from multiple sources and in various ways needs to be valued. Learning in the practicum is about assisting students to develop appropriate qualities and attributes to function as professional social workers.

The environment in which learning is to occur should promote friendliness, a balance between formality and informality, and interaction. Learning will be obstructed if the student sustains feelings of being a stranger. Activities that reflect rigidity and ceremonial structure also impede learning progress. Active exchange and sharing encourage personal involvement and enriches the experiences of both student and field instructor.

Structured consultation and the processing of the consultation activities both provide learning for the student. Through the verbal discussions, a field instructor can bring into awareness various points that the student had not realized through the role play alone. In this sense, the role play becomes a tool or a medium for the learning that comes out through the discussion process. The role play may have value even without processing. Consultation should focus on strengths versus mistakes. Some students need a considerable amount of discussion to integrate their experience into knowledge; others do not. Positive teaching approaches are characterized by clear descriptions of what needs to be accomplished, opportunities to practice and active involvement of and understanding by the student.

REFERENCES

Collins, D., Thomlison, B., & Grinnell, R. (1992). *The social work practicum: A student guide* (2nd ed.). Itasca, IL: F.E. Peacock.

Thomlison, B., Rogers, G., Collins, D., & Grinnell, R. (in press). *The social work practicum: A student guide* (2nd ed.). Itasca, IL: F.E. Peacock.

CHAPTER NINETEEN

THE USE OF THE REFLECTING TEAM TO ENHANCE STUDENT LEARNING

Jan Koopmans

INTRODUCTION

Social work students have the need to learn a great deal about a variety of clients and psychological problems as well as about types and styles of therapy. In many settings, however, students have only the time to carry a small supervised caseload. Involving students in a weekly reflecting team gives them the opportunity to work with many different types of clients and observe a number of therapists while being involved themselves in the process of therapy.

In the last decade various descriptions of reflecting teams appeared in the family therapy and supervision literature (Anderson, 1987, 1991; Prest, Darder, & Keller, 1990; Young et al., 1989). The reflecting team method has been defined as "the process in which observing trainees and supervisor discuss their hypotheses and constructions about family members/therapist interactions, beliefs, etc., in front of family members and the therapist" (Young et al., 1989).

We developed a model of a reflecting team at the Tom Baker Cancer Centre six years ago in response to the educational needs of our students and the psychological needs of our more challenging clients. We felt that a reflecting team would be useful not only to families but to other client systems (individuals, couples and groups) as well.

Because of the very favourable response to the experience of the reflecting team from our students and clients over the years, I feel it is worth sharing the model. I believe it is very adaptable to any social work setting provided that one has access to a room with a one-way mirror.

DESCRIPTION AND STRUCTURE OF THE TEAM

The reflecting team is scheduled for one half day once a week during the student's practicum. Our team consists of two instructors and four students. Usually, the presence of two to five people behind the mirror is considered optimal. Each member of the team takes a turn inviting the clients to the team and leading the interview. The rest of the team stays behind the one-way mirror during the interview.

The session is divided into a fifteen minute pre-session to inform the team about the clients; a one and one half hour interview of the clients by one of the team members while the rest of the team observes and may phone in questions or comments; a ten minute break; a fifteen minute reflection by the team with the clients and interviewer observing from behind the one-way mirror; a five minute debrief in which the clients and interviewer return to the room to briefly discuss the thoughts and observations of the reflecting team and a half hour debrief by the team after the clients leave. This last session helps the students to understand the therapeutic techniques used and the progress that has been made.

At the beginning of the practicum the instructors invite clients to the team and are in charge of the phone. The students role at this time is to observe and participate in the reflection. As the students feel more comfortable they take turns inviting clients and doing the interview as well as take their turns on the phone. We have found it useful to designate the person on the phone as the leader of the session for the day. That person is also the chairperson when the team gives their reflections to the clients. The team can become confused and be less effective if one person is not put in charge. Students are given a lot of support when they first assume this position.

Clients are invited to the team and their participation is voluntary. Clients are informed that they have the opportunity to attend a session where they will be able to receive feedback from a variety of counsellors. In our experience most clients are willing and even eager to engage in this therapy. At the beginning of the interview clients are asked what they hope to gain from the experience and this information guides the interview. The person who has invited the clients leads the pre-session, chooses someone to be on the telephone and outlines what their objectives are for the session. One may invite a new or interesting client or a client with whom one feels "stuck" and would appreciate feedback.

At the time of the reflection, the team and clients switch places and the clients and interviewer observe the team from behind the one-way mirror. Teams are expected to be non-judgemental. Feedback is always given to the clients in a respectful, discreet and as positive a manner as possible. The team tries to understand each client's perspective and reflect this back but often reframes in a way that allows them to see their problems in a new light. As a general rule, as many sides of a psychological conflict as can be seen are discussed. Comments are presented tentatively or speculatively not as final pronouncements. We have found it helpful to audiotape the team's comments for the clients to take home as it is difficult to take in all the information at one time.

Following the reflection the interviewer and client return to the interview room briefly to discuss the feedback. They are asked what stood out for them from the comments of the team that they found useful or with which they disagreed. There is a tendency for the clients to want to discuss the reflection at length but this should be discouraged. This takes away from the impact of the reflection and it is important to leave time for the students and instructors to debrief. The clients will be able to debrief at length at their next scheduled interview with the therapist.

EVALUATION

Feedback from clients has been consistently favourable. In the six years that the team has been offered there have been only two clients who have not found the comments of the reflecting team to be useful. Clients have felt affirmed by having the full attention of a therapy team. Numerous clients have made the remark that they have never felt so understood. Clients consistently appreciate all the ideas expressed during the reflection and feel this has greatly enhanced their ability to move ahead. The instructors and students often find the sessions helpful in setting the therapy off in new directions and often evaluate the session as being worth several therapy sessions in terms of what has been accomplished.

Students have over the past six years consistently evaluated the team as the training experience that allowed them to learn most about a variety of clients and therapeutic techniques. They find it very helpful to process with a team and see that there are many ways to be helpful to clients. Beginning students are immediately able to participate on the team as observers and in the reflecting team which gets them involved and challenges their skills. Later they are able to take on all the tasks and the debriefing session becomes a peer supervision. Students are able to determine for themselves how fast they prefer to proceed. Students feel supported in trying new interventions knowing that they have the team as back up. The students gain confidence in working in front of others. All sessions are videotaped so that the work can be reviewed and evaluated.

PROBLEMS

The major limitation of the use of reflecting teams is the fact that they require considerable time. In settings with major time constraints the team approach could be offered less often. We have found, however, that the time is justified when the benefits to clients and students are taken into account.

There could be a problem at the beginning of the practicum in terms of performance anxiety for the students. The anxiety diminishes as the students see that the responsibility for the session is shared by the team. The interviewer is not expected to develop insights and interventions. Their role is to engage the clients. The team has the time to sit back and analyze the client situation. Hence the student interviewer comes to see the team as supportive rather than evaluative. It helps if the supervisor models one way of working with clients rather than insisting on the "right" way. It also helps if student's reflections are seen as equally valid along with the instructor's comments. We have certainly found that even the reflections of new students are valued by clients.

Occasionally, there are clients who for some reason would find it difficult to hear the comments of the team. We always give clients the choice of hearing the reflection directly or sending the interviewer back to retrieve the feedback. Almost all clients choose to hear the reflection directly. If it is felt that the client system has not been understood in the time allotted or that the team does not feel in a position to give a constructive reflection, the interviewer is called back to receive feedback and the choice of listening to the team is not given. This has only happened two or three times in the six years.

VARIATIONS AND INNOVATIONS

In reading the literature on reflecting teams one sees that there are many variations to this model. We have found that in the beginning of the practicum it is helpful to conduct the session in as straight forward a manner as possible until the team has become comfortable with each other and is functioning at a high level. At this point innovations may be made.

At times, our team has studied a particular model of therapy and tried to use this model for several sessions. Sometimes the team has sent letters to the client following the session to further the therapy. When students have felt they have a lot to learn from certain clients, the clients have been invited back for an additional session. At times guests are invited to be part of the team. A social worker may be invited who has specific expertise with the problem that the clients are presenting that day. The students' faculty liaison may visit as well. The guest is less intrusive if prepared to function as part of the team for that session and takes part in the reflection.

It is not necessary to have the use of a telephone to use the reflecting method. Notes can be put under the door or the interviewer can be called out of the room briefly. Some teams observe the interview without interruption and then give a reflection.

CONCLUSION

One of the dilemmas facing a field instructor is how to give a student the breadth and depth of experience necessary to develop competency in the field. The reflecting team gives the student the opportunity to work with a wide variety of clients while leaving time for in depth work with their own caseload.

It should also be mentioned that participation in the team benefits the field instructors as well. Working together with our students in this interactive and open team allows our students to impact our practice and our lives with their unique insights and experience. Each meeting of the team offers surprises and opportunities for all participants.

REFERENCES

Anderson, Tom. (1987). The reflecting team: Dialogue and meta-dialogue in clinical work. *Family Process, 26*(4), 415-428.

Anderson, Tom. (1991). *The reflecting team: Dialogues and dialogues about the dialogues.* New York, NY: W. W. Norton and Co., Inc.

Prest, L. A., Darder, E. C., & Keller, J. F. (1990). "The fly on the wall" reflecting team supervision. *Journal of Marital and Family Therapy, 16*(3), 265-273.

Young, J., Perlesz, A., Paterson, A., O'Hanlon, B., Newbold, A., Chaplin, R., & Bridge, S. (1989). The reflecting team process in training. *Australian and New Zealand Journal of Family Therapy, 10*(2), 69-74.

CHAPTER TWENTY

STUDENT PERCEPTIONS OF REFLECTIVE TEAM SUPERVISION

Barbara Thomlison

Educational supervision is one of the key ingredients in the transfer from learning in the classroom to learning in the field. Professional concerns, skills, and self awareness are developed and refined in the process of educational supervision. The most frequently used type of supervision during the social work practicum is one student and one field instructor (individual supervision) who meet regularly for planned, formal educational conferences. Other types of supervision include group or peer-interaction supervision, and team supervision. Although group and team supervision is less often available, this approach to field education exposes students to a wider selection of learning experiences. As agency resources decrease and programs restructure, field coordinators and field instructors need to re-examine the merits of group and team educational supervision. This paper illustrates one attempt at confronting the aforementioned challenges facing field coordinators to meet the needs of students in field practicums where insufficient qualified social work field instructors are available.

The purpose of this paper is to report students' perceptions of a specific type of group supervision — a reflective student team supervision. A brief review of educational supervision is first presented, followed by the field research approach used to study the issue, the data summary and then, implications for social work educational supervision are discussed.

EDUCATIONAL SUPERVISION

Educational supervision can take many different formats, but this paper is concerned with group or team educational supervision. Group or team educational supervision enables students to see a wider range of individual problem-solving techniques and the opportunity to compare different experiences among the participants in the group (Collins, Thomlison, & Grinnell, 1992). For example, a case is more useful when team members observe the student's practice and provide feedback on performance or, if students discuss the case with other peers who have a range of different individual perspectives regarding the assessment and intervention plans. Presentations and even role plays can be more effective if there are a number of participants, each watching and giving feedback and trying to improve on the performance of others.

Group Educational Supervision

Group supervision is also an effective medium for students to develop professional skills, obtain moral support, self confidence and awareness. Participants may also address sensitive or challenging practice and personal issues. Some students may even learn more effectively in a group environment while others may need both group and individual supervision. Learning styles and sources of learning will differ but, students want and need input from alternate viewpoints. The best student practicum practices provide for teaching and learning processes to be balanced in individual and group structures, with the added dimension of live supervision for maximum educational opportunities.

Live Educational Supervision

Educational supervision in this paper also refers to the use of a student peer team for educational supervision, training and reflective intervention or treatment for clients. Interdisciplinary and family therapy team settings often use this form of group supervision (Berger & Dammann, 1982). In general, the essence of live supervision involves performing family practice in front of a one-way mirror. The supervisor and other team members watch and listen from behind the screen and are able to give direct feedback to the student or practitioner in the consulting room through a variety of communication devices, such as telephone, bug-in-the-ear, notes or other means. The benefits of live group educational supervision to the learning process are great yet few social work students have the opportunity to experience live supervision in the field. The dynamics inherent in this style of educational supervision characteristically and routinely provide three key components to learning in the field: 1) immediate feedback on performance; 2) multiperspective case/project analysis; and 3) enhanced professional competence and personal development (Collins et al., 1992).

Feedback on Performance

In order for feedback to be useful for students it needs to be timely. That is, feedback needs to occur as soon as possible after the event for the greatest likelihood of change, and it needs to be stated clearly in a language easily understood to be meaningful. Feedback also requires receiving information that is balanced — focused on both the positives and negatives, strengths or limitations, *but* providing suggestions or alternatives to a specific event, incident or action. Feedback needs to also be reciprocal, providing opportunities for the learner to comment and contribute varying perspectives (Collins et al., 1992).

Given the structure and function of reflective team supervision, feedback opportunities are ideally suited to this approach, and in fact are essentially integral to the method. Students not only receive the most immediate feedback during practice, they learn to present feedback in their role as team member.

Multiperspective Case or Project Analysis

Student cases or projects need to involve analysis from multiple perspectives. This requires more than careful scrutiny of procedures or review of activities undertaken by the student. Critical thinking and analysis of assignments from multiple perspectives extends students' knowledge of theories and concepts from the classroom. This process also includes drawing on other personal and professional experiences so that students transform the current practice into meaningful learning (Bogo & Vayda, 1987). Participants of the reflective team bring diverse variables to the implications of any context. Exposure to differing discipline-specific concerns and issues can assist other students to understand a practice situation more critically (Collins et al., 1992). This form of practice analysis may potentially be more powerful and intense for significant learning than many one to one student supervision forums.

Professional Competence and Personal Development

Practice situations typically elicit a range of feelings, emotions and value conflicts. Students need to discuss and understand how their practice impacts client systems and organizational responses, as well as how practice affects learning. The impact of differences such as discipline socialization, age, gender, ethnicity, race and ability is not only more evident on a team, it is also easier to discuss within the group. Team members not only observe the student member in practice but are immediately available to generate strategies and skills for understanding diversity issues. Reflective team members bring rich and purposive experiences toward assisting team members to know personal and professional boundaries (Collins, et al., 1992). Essentially the practical and supervisory factors of reflective team interactions and exchanges may largely be concerned with what, when, and how students are challenged by practice. Team members are both learners and teachers as well as members of the service team. These multiple roles contribute to powerful professional and personal learning experiences.

The study presented in this paper was based on the aforementioned framework. The next section addresses the field education issue of shortage of qualified agency-based field instructors and the use of a reflective team supervision approach to the problem.

THE FIELD EDUCATION ISSUE

In most social work programs, every effort is made to provide MSW students with a quality setting and a qualified field instructor. This is increasingly a problem as community and agency programs and resources vanish or restructure. A field education issue emerged for the field coordinator in one graduate social work program when an MSW field instructor in a specific interdisciplinary child and family treatment setting was unavailable. A strategy to the use and provision of educational field instruction in this setting was to allow the social work students to participate via a reflective student team with an agency supervisor and to ask the faculty liaison to join the reflective team during the field practicum period. At the end of the practicum, the Faculty sought to involve the students in an exploration of the accounts of their learning experiences as team members. This paper presents findings of the students' response to this learning experience.

THE REFLECTIVE TEAM AND THE STUDENTS

The Reflective Team

A total of six students comprised the reflective interdisciplinary team in the setting. Of the practicum students in the setting, three were MSW social work students, with one student from each of the following disciplines; a master's level nursing student and an educational psychology student; and a doctoral level psychology student. The student team was assigned to a family intervention program in the agency. However agency workload demands made it necessary for three different agency staff to assume responsibility for the day to day management of the students. Only the social work students were without a qualified professional social worker in the agency to provide their educational supervision.

Due to time and workload constraints of the agency staff, it was decided with the students and the social work faculty liaison that, rotational supervision on the reflective team would be the best use of individual agency staff. In other words, the team structure at any one time consisted of all the students (six), the faculty liaison social worker and one of the three agency program staff. Each agency staff person served in a four or five week block of time, in a management-consultative role, on the team before rotating out of the role. At any time however, any of the agency staff were available to all of the students for consultation and could also participate on the team. The social work faculty liaison met twice weekly at the agency with the social work students; during family sessions as a member of the reflective team and for team debriefings and group supervision. Telephone contacts also occurred.

The Social Work Students

The three social work students varied in terms of their prior social work experiences and their academic standing. Of the two male social work students, one had experience from a therapeutic program and one had child welfare experiences. The female student had lengthy child welfare experiences also. All of the practicum students were from early middle age to late middle age. All were positive in their choice of practicum. One of the students was marginal in academic performance. The non social work students were also early to middle age and all were female.

APPROACH TO THE STUDY

The study employed an exploratory approach using an open-ended mailed questionnaire and a focus group in an effort to better understand what the supervision experience was like for student members of the reflective team. This approach lent itself to an exploration of student perceptions, ideas and thoughts of the reflective team as an educational experience.

DATA COLLECTION, REDUCTION AND ANALYSIS

A two step data collection strategy was utilized. After the practicum was complete, the six graduate students were contacted by telephone by the social work faculty liaison. All students agreed to voluntarily participate in the exploratory follow-up study. The first step involved a mailed questionnaire consisting of two open-ended questions. Question one asked students to describe how the student reflective team contributed to their learning experience and their process of professional development. Second, they were asked to describe any critical incidents during the reflective team experience which were central to their learning. Students were asked to comment anonymously.

Students mailed the questionnaires back to researcher. The extensive comments on the six questionnaires were reviewed by a social worker, independent of the setting, and the social work faculty liaison. The descriptions produced from the questionnaires were used to generate a picture of the supervision experience. In this study the data are the words, phrases and comments from the students. Data analysis of the content followed typical data reduction procedures (Williams, Tutty, & Grinnell, 1994).

Unitizing

Data processing was analyzed at two levels. One was identifying information about supervision behaviors and functions. Another was identifying information pertaining to individual and professional development as students proceeded through the practicum. Any general trends or references about student learning processes were noted as the questionnaires were analyzed.

Initially data reduction was handled by breaking information down into the smallest meaningful units such as phrases, words and concepts that could stand alone. Typical examples were: "The team gave me a positive image of social work." or "The team showed a more positive image of other professions." or "The team changed the way I view others and the way I work with others." Each questionnaire was read numerous times with units or phrases being highlighted and marginal notes made about the responses without regard for patterns or themes. Marginal notes were the thoughts, impressions or ideas of the researcher for the particular reading of the questionnaire.

Analytical Notes and Resorting

The highlighted units of information were then organized into categories or themes onto separate sheets of paper. Often phrases fit into more than one category or unit. Data were reviewed several times, independently by each researcher, until no further information emerged from the content analysis. Comments or analytical marginal notes made the researcher included: "This student talked about the energy developed by team supervision," or "This student expressed positive comments about supervision styles."

Identification of Themes

The resulting 89 phrases were then organized into themes. Units were combined wherever possible without losing information or the essential meaning from the units. Eventually four themes were identified with each theme having from four to 12 phrases represented in the category. The four general themes were: supervision, reflecting team leadership, student relationships, and miscellaneous comments.

The second step involved the focus group meeting with the six students at the practicum setting. The purpose of the focus group was to ensure comments and contents were accurately interpreted from the questionnaires. Agreement, clarification, and feedback on the aggregated comments of the student team experience lasted for three hours.

STUDY LIMITATIONS

Several limitations of this study are apparent: the small number of students, the short study period, and the lack of information about students' initial learning goals and styles of learning. Additional triangulation methods and measures of learning would have be valuable contributions to understanding students' educational supervision in this context.

THE FINDINGS

The findings are presented according to the four themes that emerged from the data analysis: supervision, reflecting team, student relationships, and other comments.

Supervision

The variety of supervisors (agency staff and faculty liaison) presented much more feedback to the students than their prior supervisory experiences. Feedback centred on student practice skills, professional styles, as well as personal relationship attributes. Students received information about how other students experienced them and how they came across to others. Rotational supervision reinforced the idea that there is more than one right way to practice, through the first hand exposure to multiple treatment perspectives of the various agency staff.

Exposure to rotational supervision allowed students to experience a variety of teaching and learning opportunities. For the most part students reported being challenged by the changing supervision, however, the shifting styles created difficulties for students where therapeutic orientation or perspective changed. As students became accustomed to one style of management-consultation supervision it was soon to be replaced with another. For about half of the students constant adaptation to these tensions of supervision was a minor issue of concern.

Closely related to the interdisciplinary theoretical and conceptual exposure, students spoke about the importance of a sense of increased confidence and validation of their skills that emerged. Prior learning was valued and validated, and the use of new skills was constantly encouraged for the various practice situations encountered.

All students commented on the anxiety of being observed particularly during the first quarter of the practicum and development of the team. Anxiety and stress was highest for those students experiencing first time live supervision and group supervision. Only two students had been exposed to prior intense supervision and therefore anxiety was compounded by the multiple new roles for the students: being a observed in a family session; being an proactive team member; learning live intervention techniques; learning critical analytical responses and presentations; and actively planning and participating in group educational supervision. These tensions in learning tended to decrease over time as confidence increased and students learned their peers also provided supportive feedback to them. It would appear that trust must be developed by the individual in the management - consultant role in order that students overcome anxieties.

Respect from supervisors and students played an important role in maintaining trust. Early in the practicum respect was demonstrated by supervisors by asking students for their opinions and receiving enthusiastic non-judgmental responses in their work with families. The autonomy given to the team by the supervisors also fostered respect and allowed for rapid skill development and learning. Students played an active role in fostering a climate of trust through "peer supervision" roles. In summary, the various styles of supervision and supervisors among students and staff, gave students more feedback regarding how they came across to others and their clients that was established rapidly in the practicum and maintained throughout.

Reflecting Team

Students' evaluation of the reflecting team indicates that it was a very helpful and valuable learning approach, offering many opportunities for immediate feedback on the student's skill and style of work, as well as ongoing theoretical and interventive guidance. The reflecting team was viewed as most valuable for acquiring a system's perspective of family interaction and of the student and agency system perspective. Students had the opportunity to see all students and supervisors practice and consequently apply the aspects of various theoretical perspectives to the practice situation.

All students felt accepted as members of the team and once comfortable with the one-way mirror became highly comfortable with the team format. Individual confidence seemed related to the increasing skill, caring, commitment, and support of the team for one another. However, some students thought their professional boundaries and identity became less clear as the team developed.

Students also remarked that their sense of professionalism appeared heightened during team supervision. The reflective team taught them to question their practice and redefine themselves in light of feedback. Through consultation, support and teamwork that characterized this practicum, all students were induced to conceptualize more frequently as a result of the diverse functions of the team. Team members constantly probed and questioned each other. In summary all students valued the opportunity to learn and teach through the reflective team and group supervision.

Student Relationships

Friendships developed beyond the practicum with all students considering their relationships among each other to be close and special. Students felt they could share confidences with others. Rituals developed in the form of regular luncheons at particular cafes as supervisors changed, and planning sessions outside of practicum by telephone. Readings were shared and discussions of student papers and presentations were all part of the process that emerged on this student team. Through the peer consultation process and support, students tapped into the personal support and teamwork that characterizes professional practice teams. The student team took on a life and personality of its own. Those who were not part of the team were like outsiders of a family.

One of the limiting factors due to the friendships, was the timidity students felt toward being overly critical of the work of their peers. One student remarked that she wished she had received more intensive critique of her work. She thought the closeness of the team protected one another from facing negative aspects of their learning.

Other Comments

In general students viewed the opportunity to follow more than their own cases through to completion in an active way to be highly beneficial. As well, being a member of an all student team was less intimidating and allowed for increased mutual learning and teaching. On the down side, students had differing views of the supervisors, but most thought having one senior supervisor from beginning to end is best.

IMPLICATIONS FOR FIELD EDUCATIONAL SUPERVISION

Reflective team supervision activated learning at a high level and at varying levels. Tensions created at the beginning of practicum dissipated as students learned to adapt to the intensive scrutiny of live supervision. Students adapted quickly to the method of supervision, and learning appeared to develop rapidly. Learning and teaching processes seemed balanced by the challenge of live supervision vs. support of the team; risk-taking vs safety of the student group; demand for work vs self-directness; and education vs. training.

Challenge appears central to reflective team supervision yet leads to integration of new ideas and skills. Students take on more responsibility in this forum as they watch others and are encouraged to try new approaches. Marginal students may also thrive in this environment as they receive more stimulation from more sources. However, student success appears dependent upon the skills, abilities, and experiences of the other students. Conversely, success of the student team may be dependent upon the quality of the educational supervision provided. In this study the success of the student team appears centred on four factors: 1) giving students the autonomy to develop a peer team; 2) support and recognition of student contributions from both students and supervisors; 3) establishing varied and structured supervision approaches or opportunities; and 4) maintaining professional accountability through continuous assessment and evaluation of student learning goals focused on professional and personal competencies.

SUMMARY

This exploratory follow-up study of student reflective team experiences appears to have many benefits for students, agencies, and faculties. Direct and indirect work with many families over the practicum strengthened student skills of assessment and analysis of systems. Team supervision taught particular skills that may not have been taught in an individual supervision model. For the weak or marginal student there appeared to be great benefits, as the student was exposed to more approaches than usual by providing extensive opportunities for learning. Members of the team grew increasingly comfortable with each others style and above all, learned that communication is a principal method of teaching and learning provided that trust is established within the student supervisory team.

As the faculty liaison to the student reflective team I can emphasize that learning and satisfaction was high. It is important that the faculty liaison see herself as a learner as well. The cost of this learning experience however was high in terms of the amount of time consumed, particularly during the first time the model was implemented. While this is a highly intrusive form of learning, it was perceived by the participants as an effective form of field education.

Group supervision can be changed and improved to meet the needs of a variety of students. It may be that the rotating supervision at this setting provided a very healthy balance of teaching styles that would be beneficial to students who have specific learning styles or those students who present learning challenges for field instructors. In this study, students did not specify under which conditions group supervision was most helpful. It may be the case that students who are flexible in the way they learn, cope better and are perceived by field instructors as having a greater ability. It may be the case that rotational supervision is very helpful to students with inflexible learning styles because it increases the chance for learning styles to be matched between student and supervisor. One of the limitations of this research project which makes the conclusions speculative is that learning styles were not studied. If learning styles can make the difference between passing or failing, attention needs to be directed to this either through teaching students to broaden the way they learn hopefully before their practicum experience or through identifying and recognizing the importance of the learning styles of supervisors and students. Students who may be at risk of failing may actually flourish in the kind of practicum setting that offers rotational supervision.

REFERENCES

Berger, M., & Dammann, C. (1982). Live supervision as context, treatment and training. *Family Process, 21*, 337 - 344.

Bogo, M., & Vayda, E. (1987). *The Practice of field instruction in social work.* Toronto: The University of Toronto Press.

Collins, D., Thomlison, B., & Grinnell, R. (1992). *The social work practicum: A student guide.* Itasca, IL: F. E. Peacock.

Williams, M., Tutty, L., & Grinnell, R. (1994). *Research in social work* (2nd ed.). Itasca, IL: F.E. Peacock.

CHAPTER TWENTY-ONE

BUILDING ON STRENGTHS: RECONCEPTUALIZING EVALUATING STUDENT PERFORMANCE IN THE FIELD PRACTICUM

Kate McGoey-Smith

INTRODUCTION

Social work students, when facing entry into field practice, will often express their fears and concerns about "saying the wrong thing" to clients. So much so, that many students will admit to retreating to total and utter silence as a preference to possibly "harming" the client. This would certainly seem a prudent strategy. However, it only serves to reinforce the perspective that choosing an appropriate response from an overwhelming, knowledge-induced array of options is a hit-and-miss proposition. Consequently, this leaves many students anxiously voicing the need for "a book with all the right responses" in it. The demand for such a book of wisdom rises dramatically when students enter field. It is in field, observing the practice of experienced, competent social workers/field instructors, that students often become totally mystified by how practice competency is developed and achieved. And field instructors, themselves, may inadvertently reinforce this mystical perspective because of their own difficulty in articulating what has become intuitive, "gut" responses to the practice situations they face on a daily basis (Bogo & Vayda, 1986).

Subsequently, it becomes the students' challenge to understand and the field instructors' challenge to explain how practice competencies are developed and achieved.

These most immediate challenges become all the more pressing in the light of the time-limited, work relationship which exists between the student and the field instructor. Their work relationship is dual-purposed. It serves the double function of teaching and evaluating student performance (Sheafor & Jenkins, 1982). Of these two functions, Sheafor and Jenkins (1982) suggest that the field instructor appears to be more comfortable in his or her role as a teacher than evaluator. For it is in field instruction, that this teacher-student relationship most closely approximates the social worker-client relationship. For example, the field instructor willingly helps the student "transform knowledge into understanding and understanding into doing" (p. 79). Furthermore, the field instructor offers whatever encouragement and assistance is needed for the student to achieve his or her desired goals including (it would seem) entrance into the profession. These tasks of teaching speak directly to the social work practice of helping rather than harming (Sheafor & Jenkins, 1982).

However, difficulties often arise even when a close, friendly, working relationship has been established between the field instructor and student. These difficulties are most often related to the field instructor's responsibility for providing an objective evaluation of the student's professional capacity and performance (Thompson, Osada, & Anderson, 1990). Wilson (1981) reports that field instructors and students alike "rate performance evaluation as one of the least enjoyable and most dreaded aspects of field instruction" (p. 164). Yet the performance evaluation is a vital part of the learning process (Butler & Elliot, 1985). The performance evaluation involves an analytic appraisal of a student's progress toward practice competency. It informs the student of his or her progress toward achieving a particular learning objective and what more is needed to achieve full practice competency. It serves to benefit not only the student who is learning but the practicum agency and its clients (Sheafor & Jenkins, 1982). Therefore, "without performance evaluation, the entire field instruction process would be meaningless" (Wilson, 1981, p. 164).

It is as a result of recognizing both the resistance to and vital need for performance evaluation, that this author proposes the Practice Development Indicator (PDI). The PDI is an alternative evaluation tool which pinpoints and describes the student's progress toward practice competency. It is believed to be a more meaningful and effective alternative to conventional grading systems which rely on numerical rankings or singular positive/negative adjectives to evaluate performance.

By contrast, in its application, the PDI teaches students to utilize an analytic process by which practice competency is examined and understood. This analytic process is both cumulative and cyclical in nature. And it is through this process, that individual, analytic learning strengths are inherently achieved and built upon each other. Subsequently, this alternative evaluation tool services the needs of field instructors to more accurately and objectively assess student performance and also provides students, themselves, with a tool for understanding their own practice competencies. Because the

PDI illuminates the process of practice competency, this provides field instructors with a tool for demystifying and articulating their own intuitive, "gut" responses, that is, a demonstration of fully integrated theory and practice, to practice situations they face on a daily basis.

The conceptualization of the PDI was the result of listening to and working closely with a dedicated group of field instructors, students and faculty members serving together on an advisory committee. The purpose of this advisory committee involved examining current field practices and offering suggestions which would serve to improve or enhance these practices. In order to fully grasp how the PDI works, it is be helpful to view it within the context it is proposed to be utilized:

1) recognizing the homogeneity and heterogeneity of social work training;
2) combining the learning contract and evaluation form into one document;
3) identifying essential performance outcomes for practice competency;
4) viewing the PDI within the adapted framework of Bogo and Vayda's (1986), Integration of Theory and Practice (ITP) Loop; and
5) specifying the benefits of utilizing the PDI as an alternate evaluation tool.

RECOGNIZING THE HOMOGENEITY AND HETEROGENEITY OF SOCIAL WORK TRAINING

Field educators, either in their role as a faculty field liaison or field instructor, need to recognize and accommodate the numerous complexities inherent in social work training. Firstly, all students in the social work program have subscribed to the same basic courses and acquired the same knowledge foundation resulting in a *homogeneous* learning situation. Secondly, these students, male and female, vary considerably in age, economic, social, cultural, ethnic, educational and work backgrounds resulting in a *heterogenous* learning situation. Thirdly, practicum settings in the community vary considerably in their focus of service. For example, services may be more or less directed toward clinical, community and/or research and policy work. As well, the range of issues or concerns addressed may involve prevention issues through to acute distress situations. In addition, the population of consumers served may include males and females; children to seniors; individuals to groups, all resulting in a *heterogenous* learning situation. Finally, the overall outcome goal of social work programs is to graduate competent, beginning social workers which results in a *homogeneous* learning situation.

It is by recognizing the complexities of this learning situation and thereby balancing the homogeneity of the practice knowledge with the heterogeneity of the field experience, that greater quality assurance in graduating competent, beginning social workers is possible. The PDI incorporates this balance and reflects the understanding and demonstration of practice knowledge in the field: the thinking, knowing, doing and being of professional practice (Rogers, 1993).

ONE DOCUMENT: COMBINING THE LEARNING CONTRACT AND EVALUATION FORM

Anecdotal information from field educators and students suggests that while learning contracts are diligently addressed early in the practicum, less importance is given to these learning contracts later, during formal, performance evaluation periods. Consequently, the existence of two separate documents tends to exacerbate a disjointed review of the student's performance. Therefore, one document that contains the learning contract within the evaluation form assures a greater continuity of reviewing and evaluating the student's performance. The PDI is utilized within the context of this single document. This document is comprised of several components listed in the following order (see Appendix A):

- Performance Outcome
- Individualized Outcome
- Rationale for Outcome
- Activities
- Practice Development Indicator
- Mid-term Comments
- Final Comments

IDENTIFYING ESSENTIAL PERFORMANCE OUTCOMES FOR PRACTICE COMPETENCY

Sheafor and Jenkins (1982) suggest that the "adequacy of any professional program in social work is based on the practice competence of its graduates" (p. 67). Therefore, a "vision of practice that can be described in terms of what social workers should do" is needed (Armitage & Clark, 1975, p. 22). Consequently, in the learning contract and evaluation form, a total of nine performance outcomes are identified. The articulation of these outcomes reflects the basic homogenous elements of social work practice. These basic elements include understanding and demonstrating practice knowledge (the thinking, knowing, doing and being) of developing: a Professional Self; Engaging; Contracting; Assessing; Planning; Implementing; Documenting; Evaluating; and Terminating.

These homogenous performance outcomes need to be individualized to reflect the heterogeneous learning situations involving both the student and the practicum setting. Therefore, to accommodate this learning situation, a section heading entitled, "Individualized Outcome"; directly follows each of the nine performance outcomes. For full articulation of each of the nine performance outcomes, refer to Appendix B.

THE PDI IN RELATION TO THE ITP LOOP

The PDI was conceived as a result of frustration with the inadequacies of conventional, value-laden grading systems which rely on numerical rankings or singular, positive/negative adjectives to evaluate and label student practice performance. The practicum student has "the right to clear criteria for performance evaluation" (Munson, 1978, p. 105). Yet, these conventional grading systems are often viewed as subjective (Royse, Dhooper, & Rompt, 1993).

Other potential inadequacies of these grading systems include: error of central tendency — a tendency to rate specific aspects of student performance at the midpoint, or average; halo effect — a tendency to make global judgements and rate all aspects of student performance in the same way; contrast error — a tendency to judge the student by one's own standard of performance which fails to consider student variation or level of learning; and leniency bias — a tendency to rate students at a high level (Joseph & Conrad, 1983). Field instructors, already squeamish about assessing student performance, often pose even greater resistance when these conventional grading systems are utilized (Sheafor & Jenkins, 1982).

Field Instructors are more comfortable in their role as teachers than evaluators. Therefore, the PDI addresses this preference by being an analytic, learning process and performance evaluation tool. The PDI is based on an adapted version of Bogo and Vayda's (1986) Integration of Theory and Practice Loop (ITP Loop). This Loop, made applicable for social work education, was itself adapted from adult learning theory principles and Kolb's four-stage learning cycle, entails a four stage process:

1) the *retrieval* of factual elements of the practice situation;
2) *reflection* which focuses on the effectiveness of the intervention and identification of the student's values, attitudes and assumptions;
3) *linkage* to professional knowledge that can explain these findings; and,
4) selection of a *professional response* to the situation that began the loop.

It may be used to teach social work practice at any level of intervention, with a variety of populations, purpose, and setting. It can be micro or macroscopic depending on the facts retrieved.

The PDI is composed of seven levels of practice which progressively build one analytic learning strength upon another to reflect the thinking, knowing, doing and being of competent practice. These seven levels of practice are as follows: 1) discerns practice knowledge needed to perform; 2) reflects on practice knowledge need to perform; 3) formulates a knowledge-based plan for practice; 4) initiates practice with support; 5) performs adequately with support; 6) performs competently with minimal support; and 7) performs competently. Of these seven levels of practice, the first three levels correspond cumulatively to the first three stages of the ITP Loop. The latter three practice levels which are cyclical in nature correspond to the fourth stage of the ITP Loop. Each level of the PDI is accompanied by learning responsibilities of the student and monitoring responsibilities of the field instructor. Guidelines for these responsibilities would be contained within an accompanying field manual. For an itemized description of the PDI and associated responsibilities, refer to Appendix C.

THE BENEFITS OF THE PDI

As an analytic learning and evaluation tool, the PDI contains several beneficial features. Firstly, it monitors the progress of the student toward achieving each of the nine performance outcomes of practice competency. This monitoring is of a non-value laden, descriptive nature. Secondly, the determination of the student's progress necessitates the development of an interactive, consultative process between the student and field instructor. Consequently, this increases the objectivity of the evaluator. Thirdly, individual checkmarks are used to indicate the student's attainment of each practice item on the PDI. This presents the student with a visual impact of his or her progress and success. Which is important because "students frequently report that they do not know what they are doing right because they never are told by their field instructors" (Bogo & Vayda, 1986, p. 58). Fourthly, this analytic measure not only pinpoints and describes the progress of the student but also encourages the recognition of and building upon individual, analytic learning strengths. These learning strengths are necessary for meeting professional development responsibilities in the student's future role as a professional social worker. Finally, the PDI is accompanied by an invitation for field instructors to offer narrative comments of a constructive nature. These include recognizing particular performance strengths and when necessary, realistic ways progress can be made.

Since the PDI monitors and measures a progression from beginning competency to the experience of competency, it may be applied to evaluate students progressing from a beginning course to a more advanced course in field instruction. It is at the discretion of the teaching faculty and its community partners to determine at what point along the PDI that a student is considered to have passed or failed the field instruction course, as well, the PDI requires training sessions to develop a set of performance outcomes (educational objectives) for their entire program of field instruction. Subsequently, this reduces orientation time for both the field instructor and student as well as ensures greater proficiency in the use of the PDI. For an operationalized example of the PDI, refer to Appendix A.

In conclusion, the PDI challenges field educators to consider an alternative to conventional grading systems. This new alternative invites field educators and students to share in the responsibility for learning and evaluating practice competency in a manner that builds on strengths.

REFERENCES

Armitage, A., & Clark, F. (1975, winter). Design issues in the performance - Based curriculum. *Journal of Education for Social Work, 11*(1), 22-29.

Bogo, M., & Vayda, E. (1986). *The practice of field instruction in social work. Theory and process.* Toronto, ON: University of Toronto Press.

Butler, B., & Elliot, D. (1985). *Teaching and learning for practice.* England: Gower.

Joseph, M., & Conrad, P. (1983). *Practice theory and skill development for supervision in the helping professions.* Maryland: Pen Press.

Munson, C. E. (1987). Field instruction in social work education. *Journal of Teaching in Social Work, 1(*1).

Rogers, G. (1993). *Materials and notes from field instructor training workshops.* Calgary, AB: Faculty of Social Work, University of Calgary.

Royse, D., Dhooper, S., & Rompt, E. (1993). *Field instruction: A guide for social work students.* New York: Longman.

Sheafor, B., & Jenkins, L. (Ed). (1982). *Quality field instruction in social work.* New York: Longman.

Thompson, N., Osada, M., & Anderson, B. (1990). *Practice teaching in social work.* Birmingham: Pepar.

Wilson, S. (1981). *Field instruction: Techniques for supervisors.* New York: Collier McMillan.

APPENDIX A: OPERATIONALIZED EXAMPLE

Social Work Field Instruction I/II

Performance Outcome 1: Developing a Professional Self

Demonstrates a commitment to recognize, understand and practice values consistent with the Social Work Code of Ethics and Standards of Practice. This includes: demonstrating sensitivity and acceptance of human diversity on both a personal and professional level; addressing individual and systemic barriers related to racism, sexism, classism, anti-semitism, ageism, ableism, and homophobia; recognizing, through critical self-reflection, the impact personal values and behaviors have on others; and meeting supervisory and placement policy and practice requirements.

Individualized Outcome: (Reflects student and placement) — Student/Field Instructor complete

To recognize the access barriers and specific needs of clients who experience physical challenges, and work through own issues of discomfort with disabled persons.

Rationale for Outcome: *Lack of exposure and opportunity to work with this population.*

Activities: *Barrier Analysis Inventory (completion November 2, 1994). Take on small caseload (3): forming effective working relationships.*

Please use (✓) checkmarks to indicate student's attainment of each practice item on the PDI:

Practice Development Indicator (PDI)	Discerns practice knowledge needed to perform	Reflects on practice knowledge needed to perform	Formulates a knowledge-based plan for practice	Initiates practice with support	Performs adequately with support	Performs competently with minimal support	Performs competently
Mid-term:	✓	✓	✓	✓			
Final:	✓	✓	✓	✓	✓		

Comments: Please provide constructive feedback for this performance outcome, in terms of describing the student's performance, its effectiveness and realistic ways progress can be made.

Mid-term: *Robin, openly identifying feelings of anxiety regarding engaging the disabled client, prepared for this initial contact through supplemental readings and role plays with me. Robin diligently analyzed these role plays to determine the most effective way to sensitively engage.*

Final: *Robin produced a comprehensive and coherent Barrier Analysis Inventory on schedule. As well, Robin has demonstrated through analysis of audiotaped sessions, a more relaxed, comfortable rapport with clients. Robin is aware that it is more difficult to work with clients of similar age and is committed to ongoing reflection about this. Discussing this in methods class and with peers would be of help, since Robin is the only student here.*

APPENDIX B: PERFORMANCE OUTCOMES

Performance Outcome 1: Developing a Professional Self
Demonstrates a commitment to recognize, understand and practice values consistent with the Social Work Code of Ethics and Standards of Practice. This includes: demonstrating sensitivity and acceptance of human diversity on both a personal and professional level; addressing individual and systemic barriers related to racism, sexism, classism, anti-semitism, ageism, ableism, and homophobia; recognizing, through critical self-reflection, the impact personal values and behaviors have on others; and meeting supervisory and placement policy and practice requirements.

Performance Outcome 2: Engaging
Demonstrates the ability to consistently and effectively engage others: supervisor(s), team members, staff, peers, resources and consumer/client groups.

Performance Outcome 3: Contracting
Utilizes effective communication and interview skills to clarify purpose, roles and explore expectations in the process of establishing and maintaining a mutual contract with others: supervisor(s), team members, staff, peers, resources, and consumer/client groups.

Performance Outcome 4: Assessing
Demonstrates an understanding of person-in-environment perspective when collecting information from a variety of sources; identifying existing needs, strengths and priorities; organizing the information descriptively; and, inviting collaborative analysis of issues/concerns with all those involved.

Performance Outcome 5: Planning
Designs collaborative intervention plans incorporating the assessment; develops realistic goals which link interventions to the available services/resources; and, articulates a rationale supporting these choices.

Performance Outcome 6: Implementing
Demonstrates an ability to understand; articulate the theoretical rationale; and, implement the interventions while monitoring both its process and progress.

Performance Outcome 7: Documenting
Documents in descriptive, measurable terms the process, progress, and outcomes in accordance with agency and social work practices.

Performance Outcome 8: Evaluating
Demonstrates the ability to evaluate the effectiveness of the process, progress, outcomes and services; and in so doing to invite, receive and incorporate constructive feedback from supervisor(s), team members, staff, peers, resources, and consumer/client groups.

Performance Outcome 9: Terminating
Consolidates and identifies the transferability of learning while recognizing, describing and dealing effectively with issues of termination with supervisor(s), team members, staff, peers, resources and consumer/client groups.

APPENDIX C: ASSESSMENT OF LEARNING STRENGTHS AND PRACTICE

Related to the Performance Outcomes

Learning and Monitoring Responsibilities

Practice Development Indicator (PDI) Levels of Practice	Student's learning responsibilities	Field Instructor's monitoring responsibilities	Integrating Theory and Practice Loop (ITP) Stages*
1) Discerns practice knowledge needed to perform	• recalls the <u>content</u> of the practice experience as a participant and observer. • describes what happened, the setting and circumstances, person-in-environment perspective. • includes the beginning, middle and ending of the practice experience.	• monitors student's performance using a variety of methods: observation, co-working, live supervision, audio- or videotape, process recording, summary record, or verbal report.	1) Retrieval
2) Reflects on practice knowledge needed to perform	• reflects on the <u>process and outcomes</u> of the practice experience. • identifies the feelings and reactions of all the participants (including own) in the practice experience. • considers how and in what way the practice was effective/ineffective.	• explores the student's feelings, thoughts, assumptions, and relevant personal history regarding the practice experience. • examines the student's practice behavior and its effect. • provides feedback regarding the student's performance. • feedback should be: timely; clear and direct; systematic; empathetic; reciprocal; based on criteria expressed in the performance outcomes; and, stated in behavioral terms.	2) Reflection
3) Formulates a knowledge-based plan for practice	• explores and explains the process and outcomes of the practice experience in relation to theory, such as: generalist framework, human development theory, public policy issues, research and evaluation content, cultural-sensitive framework, systems theory, role theory, social change theory. • thinks about why the participants might have felt/reacted in the ways they did in relation to theory. • creates a plan of action: theory-in-action.	• begins with the student's cognitive associations. • elicits the student's rationale and understanding. • offers own cognitive associations. • identifies the theoretical concepts used to explain, examine and analyze the client practice phenomena. • encourages the student to look for relationship between the theory and the specific practice experience. • helps student to use relevant theories to form a new professional response.	3) Linkage

Practice Development Indicator (PDI) Levels of Practice	Student's learning responsibilities	Field Instructor's monitoring responsibilities	Integrating Theory and Practice Loop (ITP) Stages
4) Initiates practice with support	• makes an informed response to the practice situation. • recognizes the need to retrieve, reflect and link practice experience.	• explores alternative responses to the practice experience. • uses a variety of teaching activities to describe and demonstrate responses: modelling, roleplaying, co-working and live supervision.	**4) Transition to professional responses**
5) Performs adequately with support	• provides evidence of performance through: observation, co-working, live supervision, audio- or videotape, process recording, summary record or verbal report. • demonstrates the ability to process and practice the first 4 PDI items with support from the Field Instructor. • recognizes and seeks constructive feedback.	• fulfils monitoring responsibilities as outlined in the first 4 PDI items. • offers constructive feedback and support. • sets the agenda for supervision.	**5) Professional response**
6) Performs competently with minimal support	• provides evidence of performance. • demonstrates the ability to effectively process and practice the first 4 PDI items with minimal support from the Field Instructor. • recognizes and seeks constructive feedback. • contributes to the agenda for supervision.	• continues to monitor student's performance. • recognizes student requires only minimal support. • sets some of the agenda for supervision.	**6) Professional response**
7) Performs competently	• provides evidence of performance. • demonstrates the ability to effectively process and practice the first 4 PDI items with independence from Field Instructor. • recognizes and seeks consultation as needed. • sets most of the agenda for supervision.	• continues to monitor student's performance. • recognizes and supports student's independence. • makes self available for consultation. • contributes to the agenda for supervision.	**7) Professional response**

*Bogo, M., & Vayda, E. (1986). The practice of field instruction in social work, Toronto, ON, University of Toronto Press.

CHAPTER TWENTY-TWO

THE STUDENT-AT-RISK IN THE PRACTICUM

Heather Coleman, Don Collins and Debbie Aikins

INTRODUCTION

Social work educators are anxious to address issues related to the student-at-risk of failing in the practicum. Unfortunately, both research and dissemination of information about the problem are sparse. This has led field instructors, field liaisons and field directors to conclude that they are working in isolation without the benefit of shared experience or research. The paucity of information on student difficulty in the field spawns a false impression that problem students in the practicum are rare. Clearly this is not so. In fact, there is a strong possibility that serious problems occur regularly in social work practica (Rosenblum & Raphael, 1987). Though field-related problems occur regularly, the professional literature suggests that termination from the field or a program is almost nonexistent (Cole & Lewis, 1993).

Few would argue that gatekeeping in social work education is crucial to screen out students unsuitable to the profession. The integrity of the profession and the well being of social work clients depend upon competent gatekeeping activities performed in educational programs. While throughout the educational process, several opportunities are available with which to screen out unsuitable students, programs often fail to do so.

Instead educators may anticipate that another mechanism in the process may tag students and that "someone else" will deal with them.

"Gatekeeping at the door" is the first option. But, available data suggest that few social work programs exercise gatekeeping at admissions (Cunningham, 1982; Cole & Lewis, 1993; Hepler & Noble, 1990). Usually admission standards are based primarily upon concrete criteria for grading and evaluation. Expecting to locate problems at admission is complicated by the fact that detecting the potential for professional practice is a difficult, if not impossible task (Cunningham, 1982; Peterman & Blake, 1986). Once students enter a social work program, deciding suitability for the profession becomes more difficult as it loses its concreteness.

Other opportunities for gatekeeping occur in course work, the field, or in licensing and hiring practices after graduation. Apparently these opportunities are not being capitalized upon since few students are being tagged anywhere in the system. Peterman and Blake (1986) comment that "our entrants are our exits." In a survey of nine programs by the same authors, only 30 students were dismissed out of 1075 enrolled. Problems justifying dismissal for these students included behavioral problems, communication difficulties, and a failure to integrate theory and practice. Clearly, terminating a student already admitted to a program is a quandary few programs have addressed since no standard mechanism of dismissing inappropriate students has been effective thus far. However, most involved in the educational process agree that the field is the most productive place to identify and deal with students who display personal difficulties but are performing adequately in their academic work.

While failing a student in the field is neither straightforward nor easy, few would negate its necessity. Gatekeeping and professional monitoring of competence is a fundamental professional function to ensure the quality of education and maintain the credibility of the profession by (Hepler & Noble, 1990; Pease, 1988). There are many reasons for the reticence of a program to fail a student, including legal concerns, decreased enrolment affecting budgets, and the movement toward licensor (Hepler & Noble, 1990; Moore & Urwin, 1990; Peterman & Blake, 1986). Obviously professional gatekeeping supersedes practical issues involved in maintaining a program's survival.

Judging from the infrequency of occurrence, failing a student in a practicum is a complicated task.

> There is inevitable turmoil and cost in time and effort on the part of students, faculty and agency personnel when students become enmeshed in serious field difficulties. However few, such difficulties command a disproportionate amount of energy and resources without concomitant assurance of satisfactory resolution. (Rosenblum & Raphael, 1987, p. 54)

Without careful monitoring and accurate evaluation of student field performance, the "field is an accident waiting to happen." The time is overdue for educators, field instructors and professional regulating bodies to confront the issues in collaboration.

DILEMMAS

There is a constellation of issues concerning the student-at-risk most of which converge in the practicum. When problems arise, according to the literature, they are usually considered in isolation without notice of how they interconnect. They include: due process, liability, how to articulate and institute normative standards of practice regarding students in general, and the gatekeeping role of the practicum. These concerns underscore the weak links in the professional education of social workers. Other matters include idiosyncratic issues of how to best match the student with an appropriate practicum and how the individual roles of instructor, liaison, and field director are coordinated. Some issues are treated individually in the literature, but seldom in concert. The decision to fail a student is thus based upon a conglomeration of interrelated factors that cannot be addressed in isolation.

Many students at risk in the field perform satisfactorily in the academic component of the program. Even so, unsatisfactory performance in a classroom differs from unsatisfactory performance in a practicum. Course achievement is based primarily on academic ability, while in the field, skills are tested and professional competence is established. In other words, the classroom taps into intellectual achievement; the practicum evaluates the "total person." Thus, classroom achievement should not be expected to consistently parallel achievement in the field. "The practicum is regarded as integral to the educational program and is often proving ground for social work students to test what has been learned" (Rosenblum & Raphael, 1987, p. 53). For students-at-risk, the field instructor must confront such nebulous issues of personal unsuitability for the profession and issues such as standards of practice and relationship skills.

Timing

Rapid identification of a student-at-risk is important so that corrective measures can be implemented. Frequently, problems that appear in early course work are rationalized as difficulties of adjustment or an expected reaction to change (Moore & Urwin, 1990). At the same time, this rationalization can block early intervention with a student experiencing difficulty in the practicum. Field instructors should observe a student long enough to identify maladaptive and repetitive behaviors and to decide if the students can make changes to these patterns, but simultaneously not risk making hasty or premature decisions about students capable of responding to the feedback. Unfortunately, determining the point where indicators become failures that justify dismissal, rather than problems that can be corrected, is a "line drawing exercise." While students are expected to be students and even make mistakes as they are learning, when the problems are intractable, it is necessary to make a decision and initiate procedures to fail a student.

Deciding when to fail a student is fraught with many pitfalls. Only when there is sufficient evidence about the student's performance can the instructor place the student "at-risk" or even fail the student. At the minimum, problems should be identified, discussed and recorded by midterm evaluation. These patterns should be discussed with the student and the school should be advised of the emerging problems. "Early attention to difficulties that arise in the field, including careful assessment and appropriate action, would help to reduce the drain on all the parties involved and might prevent destructive outcomes" (Gelman & Wardell, 1988).

Normative Standards

When students have problems in their practicum, termination is confounded by the lack of standardized criteria with which to evaluate students' performance. There is little agreement about the specific skills and knowledge needed in the field, and in what sequence this content is best learned (Koroloff & Rhyne, 1989). No agreement has been reached within the social work profession as to precisely what having a BSW or MSW degree means; that is, the body of knowledge that students must possess upon graduation is not clearly delineated. Because the body of knowledge has not been outlined, the phases on the road to acquiring the degree are equally hard to define. Consequently, competency is elusive to demarcate, and measure (Ginsberg, 1982). To a certain extent, defining quality is subjective and depends on the goals and objectives set by the program, its philosophy and ideology, and the trends of the times (Ginsberg, 1982). The difficulty in agreeing on the core skills competent social workers should possess is a necessary obstacle for the profession to overcome if student evaluation is to be meaningful (Koroloff & Rhyne, 1989). Because of the lack of agreement within the profession about what the foundation competencies are, defense of decisions challenged by those outside the profession often lacks the substance and clarity needed for action.

Given the current vagueness of standards, increasingly the profession needs to concentrate on the evaluation of performance and effectiveness of our graduates (Ginsberg, 1982). Frequently, students who fulfil the academic requirements of a program, but lacking basic competency skills are still permitted to graduate. While the performance of social work students should be an important component in measuring quality, at the present it is not at all clear how to measure this. Educational leadership is needed so that performance goals can be clearly articulated into specific, evaluable competencies.

Red Flags

Without a set of standardized expectations framing practice competency, it is difficult to generate a list of behavioral indicators to "flag" a failing student. While witnessing a student performing at an unsatisfactory level in the field is unpleasant, no educator wants an incompetent student to graduate from a social work program.

While there are many recommendations in the literature about what constitutes failing performance, operational definitions are nonexistent. There are a variety of reasons why students are placed at-risk in the practicum. For instance, students may be unclear of their expected role in a practicum, and be abrupt, awkward, or defensive in interacting with others. Feedback offered by the field instructor to correct dysfunctional behaviors may be received defensively. Some authors argue that a student should be flagged when there is a failure to internalize the value system of the profession or understand the complexities of the knowledge base. There may also be a problem if the student demonstrates skills or displays affect incongruently with the circumstances, and has poor communication skills, or poor performance in the field (Peterman & Blake, 1986). Others suggest that problem students are identified by their resistance to change, inflexibility, moodiness, complacency, intolerance, blamelessness, defensiveness or lack of imagination (Pease, 1988). Often students at-risk may also be the subject of complaints by clients and agency personnel. All complaints require documentation and the information given to the student.

With few exceptions, one incident of a problem behavior will not be sufficient to identify failing performance. Rather, a *pattern* in the student's attitude, behavior or performance marks failing performance in the field (Peterman & Blake, 1986). A concern for field instructors and social work faculty alike is that even when problems are evident, knowledge on how to proceed with failing a student may be unavailable. For example, it is difficult to terminate a student because of overt psychiatric problems (Peterman & Blake, 1986). If termination is hard to accomplish because of obvious problems, "social work educators are on shaky legal ground when they dismiss students who are deemed inappropriate due to reasons such as failure to form meaningful professional relationships, or judgemental behavior . . . " (Peterman & Blake, 1986). Thus dismissal from a program because of personality or behavioral problems incompatible with social work practice is a challenge.

Considering these problems, research describing problematic behaviors of students at risk of failing in the practicum in various programs would enrich social work field education. Qualitative research to develop the list of red flag behaviors of problematic field performance is a good starting point that would lead into an investigation of how various programs successfully deal with problems in the field. Still, it is important to keep in mind the consequences of the development of a list of red flags identifying student failure. Perhaps the biggest danger of creating a list of problem behaviors would be to inappropriately label a student as a failure or to prematurely tag a student for failure without allowing time to rectify the problem.

Evaluation

Evaluation of student performance in the field can be a stressful experience for students and instructors alike. "Students and field instructors alike rate performance evaluation as one of the least enjoyable and most dreaded aspects of field instruction" (Wilson, 1981, p. 164). The primary purpose of evaluation, particularly a midterm evaluation, is to evaluate the student's performance and to facilitate the student's learning for the remainder of the practicum experience. The task is to summarize student achievements for the benefit of the agency, the social work program, and the student so that it is clear what remains to be achieved. An inaccurate evaluation has a lasting impact on the profession, the field instructor, and the social work program. Field instructors, on one hand, who do not perform the evaluative role objectively and conscientiously, fail in their responsibility to clients, communities, the profession, and the student.

There have been several explanations offered for the difficulty embedded in evaluations. Over-identification with the student, rather than with the educator role, insecurity about one's ability to evaluate, hesitancy to judge performance out of commitment to a nonjudgemental attitude, and fear that students' deficits reflect on the instructors' competence are among the reasons forwarded (Kerrigan, 1978). Additionally, field instructors may be anxious about their competency as supervisors (Matorin, 1979) or be troubled by the authoritative role inherent in supervision. Usually, field instructors are keenly attuned to the impact of a negative evaluation upon students. Finally negative feedback may be a problem for instructors who want to be liked by students.

The social work profession takes pride in its provision of more support during supervision than other disciplines. Large amounts of support, however, may interfere with giving students direct and particularly negative feedback. Social worker professionals have been socialized to be non-judgemental and bring to their career a mission to fight for the underdog and the oppressed (Peterman & Blake, 1986). Professional socialization may encourage field instructors to be constructive and positive and help people overcome problematic behaviors whenever possible. Professional training has also taught them to accept people unconditionally and to avoid imposing personal values on others. Yet, *there is a difference between clients and students*. While clients do not "pass" counselling, students are in the position of passing or failing. These distinctions may generate anxiety and self-doubt in field instructors (Matorin, 1979).

Field instructors must be assisted to shift their role from that of a helper to that of an educator. The shift can only be achieved by clear communication links between field instructors and the respective programs. Ongoing and direct communication is also necessary because management of issues surrounding the student-at-risk is complicated by several layers of communication in the field instruction structure. Issues are intensified when it is realized that failing a student in the practicum typically means termination from the program (Rosenblum & Raphael, 1987, p. 54).

There is also a concern that inaccuracies and subjective impressions may creep into evaluations, some of which stem from the biases of field instructors. A major drawback in the evaluation system is that *subjectivity* is an unavoidable component of the process. Records, written and taped, and documented examples supporting the field instructor's opinion of student performance in various areas are necessary, but the decision is still an opinion. Practica also widely vary in the stringency of the learning experience. Some field instructors' standards are higher than others; some practicum requirements are more stringent than others. The same student turning in the same performance may be assessed as poor in one practicum setting and satisfactory in another, or as poor and outstanding respectively by different field instructors even in the same practicum setting. Thus, articulating normative standards of practice is like "climbing a slippery slope" but it is a slope that has to be tackled. As mentioned previously, Supreme Court decisions in the United States suggest that vague and subjective measures alone cannot be used for evaluation purposes (Pease, 1988), underscoring the need to create clear and concrete standards of practice.

It is extremely rare that a student is rated "unsatisfactory" without a preliminary warning and a great deal of input by the field instructor. An unsatisfactory rating should only follow from an identified major problem that has persisted despite efforts of the field instructor, the faculty liaison, and the student to solve it. That is, evaluations should occur without surprises.

ROLES

Field Instructor

The onus is usually placed on the field instructor to function as primary gate keepers for the social work profession. For students-at-risk, the field instructor is a central figure in students' learning experience and is often the only person to possess concrete evidence of a student's performance (Koroloff & Rhyne, 1989, p. 4). They can monitor students' daily progress by observing skills, values, attitudes, and the integration of knowledge. Since the practicum is the primary arena for the assessment of professional potential, the field is where gatekeeping assumes its most concrete function. The practicum is where learning translates into practice (Collins, Thomlison, & Grinnell, 1992), but unfortunately, it is also where difficulties of gatekeeping are most cogent (Moore & Urwin, 1990, p. 117).

Experienced field instructors have previous experience with practicum students as well as professional workers and are cognizant that inadequate social work practice can harm clients, generate damaging impressions of the agency in the community, and produce a negative impact on other professionals. Even experienced field instructors may have problems with evaluation. Support is particularly important for field instructors who, as agency based professionals, are not faculty members and may not have had any prior experience with an unsatisfactory student. Indeed, new faculty members and "seasoned faculty" alike often struggle with the task of failing a student or confronting the unsatisfactory performance of a student. Further, failing a student in the field demands skills and personal qualities that may be unfamiliar to even the most experienced field instructor. This new territory requires that social work programs take initiative to support and direct field instructors throughout the process.

Evaluation of students is an onerous responsibility faced by field instructors. Accepting the responsibility of teaching in the field is a tribute to the dedication of field instructors since few are paid by a social work program. Further, for many, their efforts are essentially a volunteer activity performed out of a sense of professional obligation. The field instructor is charged with the difficult role of making a distinction between students who will evolve into competent social workers from those who will not.

When encountering the issue of unsatisfactory student performance, it is incumbent on field instructors to make the transition from clients to students and evaluate student performance. During student evaluation, judgement and evaluation become interchangeable. As gatekeepers, field instructors are compelled to impose professional standards and values upon students and even decide that a student fails to meet professional standards of practice. Just as students seldom greet evaluation eagerly, it is not surprising that many field instructors shrink from evaluating students, particularly when the evaluation involves negative feedback and consequences. The decision to fail a student, can therefore generate turmoil and indecision for field instructors. Field instructors who are considering failing a student in the field require support from both the field liaison and the social work program. Insecurities about making a decision are overshadowed by concerns about future clients who will inevitably be affected if the student were allowed to continue.

The issue of the field instructor's responsibility as a teacher plays a role in evaluations. Teachers of adults feel some responsible for ensuring that students learn. Therefore, when students fail to learn, there may be nagging doubts in field instructors' minds about their personal effectiveness as a teacher and a supervisor, worrying that perhaps the material could have been presented differently or there could have been more or different feedback, a different client, a different project. Even when field instructors realize they have done all they could for the student, there may be a lingering inclination to assume personal responsibility and to allow the student to pass the first practicum in anticipation that in the next practicum the students' performance will improve. An honest, direct evaluation takes courage.

Field Liaison

Usually the field instructor only recommends the grade; it is contingent upon the program, funnelled through the field liaison, to assign the final grade and make the failure official. Therefore, the field instructor must receive full support of the social work program if the negative evaluation is to have an impact.

It is important for administrators of social work programs that competent social work students are graduating from their program. If a student failing in the field is academically talented, has an engaging personality, or has otherwise won favor with the faculty, the field liaison must transmit the recommendation of the field instructor to the social work program. The role of the field liaison is crucial to safeguard the integrity of the gatekeeping function and provide appropriate linkage so that the field experience has an educational focus rather than an apprenticeship approach (Smith, Faria, & Brownstein, 1986). First line support for the instructor's decision must therefore be provided by the liaison. The liaison can facilitate field instruction by helping field instructors accomplish the transformation from client service delivery to student education. As a representative of the program and the profession, the field liaison is charged with facilitating, monitoring and evaluating the practicum, and can take leadership and support in focusing attention early and repeatedly on progress and problems in learning (Rosenblum & Raphael, 1983).

To further complicate the process, a negative evaluation may create friction with the affiliated social work program. The field liaison may not concur that the student should be given an unsatisfactory evaluation. Programs may transfer the student to another practicum setting or pressure the field instructor to revise the evaluation, perhaps through the field instructor's supervisor or someone senior in the agency's hierarchical structure. However, working at cross purposes is both unusual and undesirable, particularly if solid communication links between the field instructor and the field liaison have been established. Rarely do social work programs fail to support the recommendation of a field instructor, especially if field instructors document their teaching methods, the learning opportunities afforded to the student, and the student's performance in specific learning objectives and back them up by concrete examples.

Field Director

The field director carries the responsibility for orchestrating the practicum experience. This involves ensuring as much consistency as possible among practicum settings, and making certain that field instructors and field liaisons have the knowledge and support to fulfil their professional responsibilities. Because we live in a litigious environment, certain concrete steps need to be taken regarding student supervision and evaluation to avoid legal battles and appeals. The field director should set the tone under which all correspondence and reports regarding the student should be recorded. Field instructors and liaisons must be impressed with the importance of documenting all contacts with the student. It should be noted that contact notes on every student should be recorded, despite how well the student is performing. Appeals have been lost when field instructors have recorded only on the behavior of the student-at-risk. It is also the role of the field director to develop open communication patterns between an agency and the social work program, including documenting reasons undergirding decisions made in the field and backed up by concrete examples of the student's problematic behaviors. Decisions lacking documentation will seldom stand up in an appeal. It should be noted that feelings and general impressions are not sound reasons for any decision. Concrete evidence may also help students recognize the reality of problems and accept decisions more readily (Moore & Urwin, 1990, p. 121).

THE REVIEW PROCESS

Roles of field director, field liaison and field instructor must be laid out clearly and agreed upon (Rogers, 1990). Further, the mechanism for appeals in every particular program should be available in a policy and procedure manual on the field and provided to all parties involved in the practicum experience. Certainly, appeals are not a pleasant experience for field instructors and students but a carefully managed practicum may avert many stressful appeals. Clearly, the field instructor will be on more solid ground if contact notes concerning students were recorded throughout the practicum experience.

Mindful of due process, the evaluation of a student whose performance and aptitude have been judged unsatisfactory should ideally be a natural outcome of a *mutual* evaluation by the student, the field instructor and the field liaison. However, it is unrealistic to expect that many students would agree with the assessment that they are performing unsatisfactorily in the field, and the procedure that follows this determination may be used as the basis of an appeal.

When a concern about the student's progress arises, the field instructor should follow several steps. First, the lack of progress by the student requires documentation on each contact with the student during the practicum. It is good practice to keep contact notes on every meeting with the student in addition to any feedback about the student from clients or the agency. If this is done, many obstacles can be eliminated later, especially if the decision encounters an appeal. Secondly, when concerns surface about the student, the field instructor needs to share the concerns with the student immediately. Thirdly, the field liaison needs to be alerted to the concerns and should request a consultation between the field instructor and student. It is important for the student to be actively involved throughout the process. The student may request clarification about the concerns in writing. Students should also contact the field liaison. With tri-partite meetings, written documentation and open discussion of concerns at the first sign of trouble, a formal appeal process may be averted.

Circumstances where the professional development of the student is questioned should be reviewed in its total context. When a problematic situation develops, either the field instructor or the student may request a formal review of the situation. The review should include a written statement regarding the specific requirement for what the student needs to successfully accomplish to complete the practicum. The student-at-risk should be notified in writing of the decision. The midterm evaluation is an excellent vehicle for the notification. If the field instructor decides to terminate the student from the practicum, the field director must also be informed. The written notice should contain a statement of concrete examples of behaviors that place the student-at-risk (Cole & Lewis, 1993). At this point, the field director must be accessible to the concerned parties for consultation and problem-solving. There are several possible outcomes of the review including: the student is required to leave the field placement, but continues in an alternative practicum; the student is asked to withdraw for that semester with the opportunity of returning later; and, the student is required to withdraw from the practicum completely with the recommendation that the student also withdraw from the program.

A hearing will provide the opportunity for both sides to present their view, with the rights of all involved protected (Cole & Lewis, 1993). Students should have the opportunity to present a defense and produce testimony on their own behalf. The results of the hearing should be presented in written form and accessible to the student (Cole & Lewis, 1993).

CONCLUSION

Social work educators are the first-line gatekeepers of the profession and have a professional obligation for graduating professionals who are academically, behaviorally, and ethically suited to practice as social workers. Occasionally, field instructors in conjunction with the field liaison must face the option of student failing in the practicum. Yet, failing a student in a social work program remains a troublesome issue for the profession. Accurate identification of a student-at-risk should evolve as a cooperative endeavor between the educational program and the practicum. Withdrawing a student in a practicum requires integrity and courage and is frequented by stress and frustration on the part of the student, field instructor, field liaison and field director. Ongoing communication and liaison activities are to be a part of that process (Gelman & Wardell, 1988, p. 71).

A review of professional literature revealed that limited research on the termination of students has been published, and the few studies available demonstrate that termination is almost nonexistent. Predicting potential for professional competence cannot be adequately assessed by academic standing alone. While the focus in the literature has been on admission practices, or "gatekeeping at the door," the more difficult aspect of decision making is that of terminating the "unsuitable" student who has been already admitted. While clearly defined admission policies and procedures uniformly and conscientiously applied may reduce the number of subsequent problematic situations that may require attention and action, not all students deemed unsuitable to the profession are denied admission.

The failure to terminate students may be due, in part, to fear of possible legal ramifications (Cole & Lewis, 1993, p. 150), lack of standardized criteria for competence and lack of knowledge on how best to proceed. Litigation and appeals currently focus on the retention in a program of students deemed inappropriate to the profession. One wonders what would happen if, instead of litigation pressuring programs to retain inappropriate students, programs were held liable for graduating inappropriate students. Legal ramifications are intimidating to field instructors and would be avoided in part by expanding the knowledge base on students-at-risk in the practicum. This can be accomplished by continuing to work on standardized practice competencies and by sharing information about problem situations encountered regularly in the field.

It is not fair to expect that field instructors accomplish the gatekeeping function alone. An evaluation conference would provide a structured opportunity for key figures in the practicum experience to remove students rather than having field instructors to make individual decisions that may be viewed by students as arbitrary. Often, concerns about students have been evident before the midterm evaluation. Direct disclosure to student about the concerns as early as possible means they can focus on a remedial plan to improve. It is imperative that the field instructor, field liaison and student all work together, communicating clearly what is expected in the field placement for satisfactory performance. Equally important is the clear communication between the field instructor, field liaison and student of what constitutes unsatisfactory performance. A student who is asked to withdraw from the field should not be surprised that they are not performing at a satisfactory level. Clearly we need to expend our knowledge about standards of professional practice and what behaviors constitute failure in the field.

REFERENCES

Alperin, D. (1989). Confidentiality and the BSW field work placement process. *Journal of Social Work Education, 25*(2), 98-108.

Cole, B., & Lewis, R. (1993). Gatekeeping through termination of unsuitable social work students: Legal issues and guidelines. *Journal of Social Work Education, 29*(2), 150-159.

Collins, D., Thomlison, B., & Grinnell, R. (1992). *The social work practicum: A student guide.* Itasca, IL: F.E. Peacock.

Cunningham, M. (1982). Admissions variables and the prediction of success in an undergraduate fieldwork program. *Journal of Education for Social Work, 18*(2), 27-34.

Gelman, S., & Wardell, P. (1988). Who's responsible?: The field liability dilemma. *Journal of Social Work Education, 24*(1), 70-77.

Ginsberg, M. (1982). Maintaining quality education in the face of scarcity. *Journal of Education for Social Work, 18*(2), 5-11.

Helper, J., & Noble, J. (1990). Improving social work education: Taking responsibility at the door. *Social Work,* 126-133.

Kerrigan, I. (1978). The field teacher as social work educator. *University Microfilms International.* New York: Columbia.

Koroloff, N., & Rhyne, C. (1989). Assessing student performance in field instruction. *Journal of Teaching in Social Work, 3*(2), 3-16.

Large, D. (1963). Four processes of field instruction in casework: The field instructor's contribution to instructor-student interaction in second-year field work. *Social Service Review,* 263-273.

Matorin, S. (1979). Dimensions of student supervision: A point of view. *Social Casework, 60*(3), 150-156.

Moore, L., & Urwin, C. (1990). Quality control in social work: The gatekeeping role in social work education. *Journal of Teaching in Social Work, 4*(1), 113-128.

Moore, L., & Urwin, C. (1991). Gatekeeping: A model for screening baccalaureate students for field education. *Journal of Social Work Education, 27*(1), 8-17.

Pease, B. (1988). The ABCs of social work student evaluation. *Journal of Teaching in Social Work, 2*(2), 35-50.

Peterman, R., & Blake, R. (1986). The inappropriate BSW student. *Arete, 11*(1), 27-34.

Rogers, G.(1990). *BSW Field Education Manual.* Faculty of Social Work, The University of Calgary.

Rosenblum, A., & Raphael, F. (1983). The role and function of the faculty field liaison. *Journal of Education for Social Work, 19*(1), 67-73.

Rosenblum, A., & Raphael, F. (1987). Students at risk in the field practicum and implications for field teaching. *The Clinical Supervisor, 5*(3), 53-63.

Smith, H., Faria, G., & Brownstein, C. (1986). Social work faculty in the role of liaison: A field study. *Journal of Social Work Education, 22*(3), 68-78.

Wilson, S. (1981). *Field instruction techniques for supervisors.* New York: Free Press.

PART FOUR

FIELD EDUCATION PERSPECTIVES: VIEWS FROM VARIOUS VANTAGE POINTS

The eight chapters in this section of the book each contribute a dynamic perspective on field education from a different vantage point.

We begin with a view of the liaison role from the vantage point of field instructors experiencing two different models of liaison which presents the results of a study by Anne Fortune, Jaclyn Miller, Amy Rosenblum, Bonita Sanchez, Carolyn Smith and William Reid. Continuing with the perspective of field instructors, Ina Freeman and Bud Hansen describe the results of a study of field instructor perceptions of the field education process, and Barry Hall and Gayla Rogers compare the views of rural and urban field instructors regarding social work education and practice.

From the point of view of students, Emeline Homonoff, Arlene Weintraub, Sonia Michelson and Nancy Costikyan describe what happens to students' education when placed in an agency that is experiencing major change. Joan Feyrer and Whalene Whitaker present the views of students regarding four different models of matching students with placements. From the perspectives of American and Canadian students, Bart Grossman and Robin Perry examine and compare students' commitment to serving the poor and present a model of social work education that prepares social workers for public social services.

The final two chapters in this part present perspectives from other countries. Luke Fusco has developed principles of practicum education based on his study of Australian social work programs, while a view from the United Kingdom is presented by Stephen Nixon, Steven Shardlow, Mark Doel, Sheila McGrath and Rose Gordon whose study defined quality components in field education.

These perspectives all strengthen and augment the knowledge base and encourage field educators to expand their understanding. The various vantage points described, discussed and developed in these chapters enhance comprehension of the complexity of field education.

CHAPTER TWENTY-THREE

FURTHER EXPLORATIONS OF THE LIAISON ROLE: A VIEW FROM THE FIELD

Anne E. Fortune, Jaclyn Miller, Amy F. Rosenblum, Bonita M. Sanchez, Carolyn Smith and William J. Reid

The role of faculty field liaison has traditionally been an important part of the field instruction component of the curriculum in social work education. Though it has been explicated in the literature, and its functions identified (Rosenblum & Raphael, 1983; Smith, Faria, & Brownstein, 1986; Raphael & Rosenblum, 1987), there are no empirical data describing and comparing participants' experience (field instructor, liaison, or student) with the liaison role as carried out under different liaison models. This paper reports a study that compares field instructors' perception of the liaison role under two very different models. It builds upon research by Smith, Faria, and Brownstein (1986) by using the faculty field liaison functions identified in their national study.

REVIEW OF LITERATURE

The linkage between the academic institution and the agency in which students complete field practicum is a central concern in social work education. In 1987 Raphael and Rosenblum reviewed the evolution of the liaison role in social work literature and highlighted the following developmental themes: the liaison "linkage" function appeared early (1900s) in the British literature; several authors in the late 1940s and early 1950s wrote about the "faculty advisor," "faculty representative," or "faculty consultant" who performed advisory, educational and administrative tasks with agencies and field instructors; in the 1960s British social work expanded on the role of faculty "tutor" to include educational integration; and, in the late 1970s and 1980s, elements of the liaison role, (e.g., evaluating student progress, educating field instructors, communication, integration, coordination, and continuous linkage) were elaborated in the United States and Canada. Overall, they found that use of the liaison as a central figure in the field practicum was widespread and, although different titles were used, it was seen as an important and complex role in social work education (p 157).

In an earlier paper, Rosenblum and Raphael (1983) explicated liaison roles as facilitator, monitor, and evaluator. Using this conceptualization they designed an operational guide to liaison duties that is specific to each of four liaison visits during an academic year (Raphael & Rosenblum, 1987). The guide includes a description of the liaison activity, the instructional relationship, expected student performance, and student learning goals at each point. It focuses on maintaining high practice standards in education and facilitating both field instructor and student learning; it emphasizes educational/monitoring as opposed to administrative/monitoring.

Sheafor and Jenkins (1982) were also clear that the liaison role is an active one: "the liaison can not responsibly stand back and serve merely on call or as a consultant" (p 118). The liaison is the most continuous link between the school and the agency and must monitor sufficiently to assure that the school's requirements are being met. "It is also essential to visit before problems arise so the liaison is not viewed merely as a troubleshooter, though she or he clearly carries that role in addition to others" (p 121).

This insistence on the active role of the liaison in managing problems in the field is echoed by Rosenblum and Raphael (1987) who note the many obstacles that exist to early identification of a problem. For example, difficulty field instructors have evaluating performance; concern about damaging the field instructor/student relationship; desire to be accepting and nonjudgmental of the student. They propose that regular liaison visits help to remind the field instructor of the school's standards . . . "[I]n this way the seeds of an evaluative component are sown, serving as a counterpoint to the natural emphasis on nurturance and support which characterizes the beginning instructional relationship" (p 59). Regular visits also assist field instructors in recognizing obstacles that may be keeping them from surfacing a problem in its early stage. While this speaks to the difficulties field instructors have reaching out to the liaison, Rosenblatt and Mayer (1975) found that most students did not use the liaison in the way the role was intended. This was particularly so around difficulties in the placement, when a vast majority of students said they did not call on their liaison.

The reluctance of participants to use the liaison when problems develop was also identified in later research on student satisfaction with field instruction (Fortune, et al., 1985). This study found that the quality of supervision and the relevance of learning experiences contributed the most to student satisfaction with field. School-agency linkages contributed the least; this scale was composed of five items about the faculty field liaison and school-agency communication. In addition, complaints about the field liaison made up the largest group of negative comments on an open-ended question (p 103). This finding can be interpreted either as a repudiation of the liaison role by students or as poor implementation of that role by individual liaison faculty. The authors conclude, "[H]owever, even if such linkages are irrelevant for students, they remain important to the agency and to integrating the curriculum . . . " (p 103).

A later study of student satisfaction with field instruction also concluded that, "students do not value the liaison" (Fortune & Abramson, 1991, p 108). By itself, the liaison scale was associated with satisfaction in this study, (i.e., the more involved with the liaison, the more satisfied), however, the association was low and all scales demonstrated some relationship to satisfaction. Using a stepwise multiple regression to identify the most important elements of field to students it was found that the quality of the field instruction was most important and the liaison scale was not significantly related to satisfaction (p. 104-5). This led Fortune and Abramson to recommend that liaisons can, "offer greater input as consultants to the field instructor . . . [L]ess emphasis on monitoring the student and more emphasis on helping the instructor . . ." (p 108).

Smith, Faria, and Brownstein (1986) addressed the issue of the importance of specific activities in the liaison role directly. They carried out a three phase study which collected data from practicum directors, field instructors and liaisons. The first phase focused on the schools and addressed assignment of faculty to the liaison role, education and title of liaisons, evaluation of liaisons, and a listing of liaison functions and responsibilities. Content analysis of the list resulted in ten categories of liaison activities: linkage, mediator, monitor, evaluation, consultant, teacher, advisor, advocate, practicum placement, administration. The second phase (Faria, et al., 1988) focused on field instructors' perception of the liaison role and found that linkage and practicum placement activities were most important to them, while administrative functions were the least. Field instructors were also asked the functions their liaison actually does perform and linkage, mediator, and monitor were the most frequently cited. The teacher and consultant functions described as so important in the social work education literature were rated very low in importance by these field instructors.

The third phase (Brownstein, et al., 1991) asked faculty liaisons from 12 schools to describe and rank the liaison functions they perform. The functions of monitor, linkage and advisor were ranked as the top three in importance. In addition, potential liaison role conflict was evident in that liaisons often reported not being able to function in roles they valued, (e.g., teacher, advisor, consultant) while spending much of their time in activities they consider less important (e.g., mediator, administration).

In sum, the conceptualization of the liaison role emphasizes the importance of continuous close contact among liaison, field instructor, and student in order to facilitate student learning and to prevent or identify student learning problems. The research on the implementation of the liaison role describes a different situation: a reluctance by students or instructors to turn to the liaison when problems occur. And while it is clear that liaisons do a great deal of monitoring, linkage, and mediation, field instructors and liaisons do not agree on their overall value to the field instructor.

Recently, several authors have expressed deep concern about the decline in the educational rigor of field advising and the low status of the liaison role in the current academic environment (Urdang, 1991; Hanna, 1992). They attribute this state of affairs to lack of appreciation by the university for unique faculty roles in professional education such as teaching and consulting. Hanna points to a "cycle of the deprofessionalization of social work education, leading to the selection and the continuous reinforcement of faculty who have little practice experience, expertise or interest . . ." (p 157) as the root cause, and says that, "[I]f the role of field advising is retained at all, it is viewed as an administrative function, i.e., defining the faculty's requirements, carrying out carefully documented student-in-difficulty procedures, etc. . . . (with a) de-emphasis of the *academic* component . . . " (p 157). Hanna and Urdang describe essential liaison skills for the academic component to include: advanced practice, ability as a clinical consultant, teaching, and a solid, well integrated knowledge base.

Thus, there is an interesting paradox regarding the faculty field liaison role and its importance in social work education. While Raphael and Rosenblum (1987) concluded, that "liaison practice is widespread and has a long tradition in social work education . . . [and] reflects an appreciation of the importance and complexity of the liaison role . . ." (p. 157), Raskin's most recent (1994) Delphi study of field instruction priorities found that field experts can not reach consensus about the state of development or definition of the faculty liaison role. A more pressing concern was that, "role development exceeds role implementation" (p. 87). Questions that need addressing include how the role is carried-out and "which (if any) of the . . . roles and functions make a difference? . . ."

All the studies reviewed found many configurations and emphases on different liaison functions at different schools of social work. This study begins to examine the effect of such differences by looking at the differential impact of liaison functions as carried out in two distinctly different models of faculty field liaisoning. Field instructors from two schools of social work, each with a different definition and operationalization of the liaison role, participated in the study. One school, Virginia Commonwealth University, employs the more traditional intensive model with an emphasis on continuous monitoring and consultation, while the other, State University of New York at Albany, emphasizes mediation. The two also differ in the type of routine contact, the purpose of the contact, and the role of the liaison.

TWO LIAISON MODELS

The Intensive Model

In the Intensive Model, at Virginia Commonwealth University, the liaison is an active participant in the educational experience in the field and is central in the management of the field practicum. This model uses both full and part-time faculty. Some faculty in each category function solely as faculty field liaisons while others also teach in the classroom. As a result, liaisons loads can vary from a one course equivalent (approximately 10 students) to a full load (approximately 45 students). All liaisons meet with their students in a group at the beginning of the academic year at a field orientation planned by the Field Office. The liaison is required to make two agency visits a semester with each of the student/field instructors pairs on their liaison load. In preparation for these regular visits, which have an educational focus, the liaison reviews student learning contracts, process recordings, conference agendas, and other written materials submitted by the student. The purpose is to assess the learning and teaching issues unique to each student/field instructor dyad so as to facilitate the educational process, to monitor the appropriateness of assignments, and to share relevant information about the curriculum. Difficulties surfaced by any party, e.g., student, liaison, field instructor, or agency personnel, is attended to first by the faculty field liaison. Meetings with all parties involved (including the Director or Assistant Director of Field Instruction) often occur in the process of resolving these difficult situations. Any of the parties involved may request such a meeting at any time. Other educational events are also offered by the school for all field instructors: an opening field meeting is held at the beginning of the academic year; a seminar series for new field instructor; a spring institute; and attendance at selected continuing education events.

The Trouble-Shooting Model

The Trouble-Shooting Model, at the University at Albany, SUNY, assumes that carefully selected and well-trained agency practitioners can carry out the field instructor role with minimal routine oversight by the university. However, when difficulties occur, intensive supports are mobilized to resolve the problem rapidly. In this model, full-time faculty members rotate onto the Field Committee where their duties include acting as faculty field liaisons. Each liaison is assigned a number of agencies and is responsible for contact with that agency, the field instructors, and the students assigned there. Routine liaison responsibilities include a formal meeting with students in a group at the beginning of the year, an individual student meeting toward the end of the year, calling each field instructor once a semester to monitor the placement, reading students' learning contracts, and reading the field instructors' evaluations of students three times a year. Grades

(Satisfactory-Unsatisfactory) are assigned by the Field Office based on the field instructor's evaluation, after liaison approval. Liaisons also meet with students to assist in the matching of placements. If all goes well, the liaison's only direct contact with the field instructor is through the telephone call. Other supports are routinely provided. New instructors are expected to complete a structured, year-long seminar in field instruction. The Field Office sends letters and newsletters two or three times a semester in addition to student-related material. Most importantly, if problems are identified, the liaison or Field Office mobilizes a team to deal with the problem immediately. Problems are most often identified by the field instructor, who may call the liaison or Field Office or request a meeting. The liaison may also identify problems based on the Evaluation or telephone calls, as may the student, and/or the classroom teacher (especially practice instructors). Once identified, the liaison mobilizes a team comprised of the faculty liaison, the field instructor, the student, a staff member of the field office, and the student's advisor. The team meets with the purpose of finding a mutually-agreeable and educationally sound solution. In short, once a problem is raised, the response is rapid and intense.

In sum, the two models differ in the type of routine contact between agency and school, in the purpose of the contact, and in the role of the liaison. In one model routine contact is in-person, with both field instructor and student, and focused on educational issues. In the other model, routine contact is over the telephone, with the field instructor, to monitor satisfactory progress. The role of the liaison in teaching and monitoring the learning activities and the way resources are brought to bear when difficulties are encountered in the field instruction relationship are distinguishing features. This study queried the field instructors at each school to get some insight into how the differences between the two models affect their perceptions of the liaison role, school-agency communication mechanisms, and potential resources when problems occurred. Do they see differences in the importance of liaison functions or in the resources they would use? What are their preferences for communication between the agency and school?

METHODOLOGY

Questionnaire and Sampling

The eight page questionnaire included sections on the importance of liaison activities, communication between school and agency, resources when the instructor encounters a problem, and characteristics of the field instructor, agency, and recent student. The letters inviting field instructors to participate were identical at each school except for the letterhead and the order of names: at each school, the school and its staff were listed before the other school and its staff. Questionnaires were mailed in early summer 1993 at Albany, in mid summer 1993 at Virginia Commonwealth University. They were sent to all field instructors who had supervised a student during the 1992-93 academic year. There were two follow-ups: a reminder letter at 10 days and a second questionnaire to those who had not responded 3 weeks later. Response rates were 149 of 215 at Albany (69%) and 189 of 450 at Virginia Commonwealth (42%).

The Respondents

Nearly three-quarters of the 338 field instructors were female (73%). Most were trained as clinicians (80%) and had experience both as practitioners (50% received their MSW at least ten years earlier) and as field instructors (only 13% were field instructing their first student and three-quarters had supervised at least two other students). Two-thirds of the agencies were host settings; most offered individual services (90%) and/or family (79%) and group (73%) services. The most common practice areas were family services (76%), children (70%), mental health (66%), and substance abuse (48%). Most field instructors currently supervised only one student (83%), while 3% had three or more students. The students were women (86%). Thirty-eight percent were in their first-year practicum, 46% in their second, and 16% were in a single advanced standing placement. Most placements were concurrent with coursework (82%), while only 5% were placements arranged in the student's employing agency. Asked to rate the quality of the student compared to other social work students at the same level of education, the majority lived in Lake Wobegon: half the students were above average, either slightly (30%) or considerably (33%). Only 15% rated their student as below average.

The field instructors under the two models differed on some characteristics (probability ≤ .05). More of the Intensive Model (Virginia Commonwealth University) instructors were female (80% to 64%). Formal training in field instruction was reported by fewer instructors under the Trouble-Shooting Model (SUNY-Albany) (59% compared to 73%) where a seminar in field instruction is required of new field instructors. Intensive Model (VCU) field instructors had more second-year students (51% to 45%) and fewer (10% vs. 21%) students in advanced standing (students with a BSW who began their placement in the summer and continued through the school year). The Intensive Model (VCU) settings were more likely to be in mental health (49% to 31%) and to offer individual (94% vs. 85%) or family services (85% vs. 72%). They were less likely to include administration (21% versus 32%), policy (15% vs. 25%), research (12% vs. 23%) or other services (5% to 12%). These differences are consistent with differences in the two programs: the advanced standing program under the Trouble-Shooting Model (Albany) is proportionately larger and students in both advanced standing and first year practica engage in a broad variety of generic social work tasks. The micro practice track under the Intensive Model (VCU) is more focused on clinical tasks. At the time of this study, the Intensive Model's second year specialization in micro-mental health was the largest specialization and presumably best represented among the students and field instructors. Because of the differences in instructor and agency characteristics between schools, key characteristics were used as controls if the characteristic was also related to the dependent variable.

RESULTS

Importance of Liaison Activities

The first section of the questionnaire addressed the broad categories of liaison functions such as placement, linkage, mediation, and evaluation. The functions are those roles that Smith, Faria, and Brownstein identified in their national studies of field directors, field instructors, and faculty field liaisons (Smith, et al., 1986; Faria, et al., 1988; Brownstein, et al., 1991). For this study, we asked field instructors: "Educating social work students in the field requires many activities to coordinate between school and agency and requires the cooperation of many people at the agency and the school. Below is a set of functions. How important is each of these activities to your functioning as a field instructor?" The 17 functions, were drawn, with permission, from the study by Brownstein et al. (1991). Each item represented an aspect of the 10 roles discussed earlier (linkage, mediator, etc.). The scale was anchored: 5=very important and 1=not at all important. Table 1 gives the items and responses of field instructors under the two models, in the order they appeared on the questionnaire.

The two liaison functions most important to field instructors related to teaching and evaluating students: serving as a role model for students, and evaluating student progress throughout the placement and reading student written material. Least important were placement development functions such as developing field placements and assisting the instructor in making the transition from practitioner to teacher, and the administrative function of ensuring completion of forms. In the middle, with ratings around 4.0, were activities related to linkage, mediation, evaluation, advocate, and consultant to the field instructor. There were some differences in importance of functions under the two models. In these analyses, if the two models also differed on a relevant characteristic, such as the gender of the field instructor, the characteristic was controlled statistically by including it in the analysis of variance.

Table 1 **Importance of Liaison Activities to Functioning as a Field Instructor: Perceptions of Field Instructors Under Two Liaison Models**

Liaison Activities: 5=very important 1=not at all important	Intensive Model (VCU) mean	Trouble shooting Model (Albany) mean
Develop field placements[2]	2.77	3.05
Match students and agencies[1]	3.57	4.16
Inform agency of and interpret school policies[1]	3.75	4.00
Assess fit between curriculum and agency educational opportunities	4.03	4.10
Assist in resolving problems	4.16	4.21
Assist student in planning practicum	4.05	4.03
Monitor agency, field instructor and learning opportunities for quality	4.24	4.12
Evaluate student progress throughout; read student's written material	4.53	4.39
Assign student grades[2]	3.85	4.05
Evaluate field instructor and agency for continued use	3.80	3.77
Assist field instructor in transition to teacher	3.60	3.60
Assist in developing learning objectives[1]	4.08	3.86
Assist student to integrate coursework and practicum[2]	4.38	4.21
Role model for students	4.62	4.49
Provide information when student is under academic review	4.18	4.07
Ensure completion of forms	3.60	3.77
Write final summary of student performance	4.24	4.22

[1] Difference between models statistically significant when controlled for related variables (ANOVA, $p < .05$).

[2] Probability of difference between models between .05 and .10 (ANOVA).

Under the Trouble-Shooting model (Albany), field instructors placed much more importance on matching students and agencies (with agency service to individuals and "other" services controlled, analysis of variance, $p < .05$). They also placed more emphasis on informing agency personnel of school policies and interpreting expectations (field instructor gender was controlled). On the other hand, they thought assistance with development of specific learning objectives was less important than did the Intensive Model instructors (gender was controlled). Several differences were tendencies, with a probability between .05 and .10. Instructors in the Trouble-Shooting model placed more importance on developing field placements (no variables controlled), although in both models this was unequivocally the least important function. They said assigning grades was more important (no controls) but assisting students to integrate coursework and practicum was less important (gender controlled).

In sum, field instructors under the Trouble-Shooting Model accorded greater importance to functions related to practicum placement (development and matching), linkage, and student evaluation. Intensive Model instructors felt teaching functions such as developing objectives and integrating field and class were more important. These differences are consistent with the emphases in the two models. In the Intensive Model, the liaison is more engaged in the teaching process, visiting the agency and meeting with instructor and student at least twice a semester, reading process recordings before a visit, and providing direct feedback to students and field instructors. In the Trouble-Shooting Model, these teaching and oversight functions are delegated to the field instructor; the liaison's visible functions relate to placement, communication, and issuing of grades. Clearly, the instructors valued those elements of the liaison functions they were most familiar with, and placed less importance on those that were not as visible.

School-Agency Communication Mechanisms

The two models differ dramatically in means of communication between the agency and school. In the Intensive Model, there is a large meeting of all liaisons, field instructors, and classroom instructors at the beginning of the year, and new field instructors receive a 12 hour training seminar. The liaison visits the agency twice a semester, meeting with field instructor, student, and often with the agency director or coordinator of training. Many liaisons stay with the same agency for years and become the first line of contact for agency personnel. In the Trouble-Shooting Model, field instructors are expected to attend a year-long seminar in field instruction their first year. Each semester, the Field Office sends two or three informational mailings. Liaisons telephone once a semester but do not have in-person contact with the agency unless problems are identified (by any party). When there are problems, the field instructor may contact either the liaison or Field Office, or the liaison may initiate contact if difficulties are identified through student evaluations.

How do field instructors perceive these differences? One section of the questionnaire included two items designed to address this concern. First, field instructors were asked to rank order means of access to the school in terms of importance to them in providing field instruction. The most important was ranked 1, second most important as 2, etc. By forcing them to rank order, we hoped they would discriminate among means of communication that are all important. The items and the average range for each model are given in Table 2. Under both models, field instructors ranked as most important ready access to the liaison should problems arise. They also agreed that least important were the formal seminars in field instruction and other means of communication. They disagreed strongly on two items (p < .05): Intensive Model field instructors ranked routine visits or calls by the liaison as second most important, an average rank of 2.33, while Trouble-Shooting Model instructors ranked their regular telephone calls fourth (3.39, just ahead of the seminars). Conversely, Trouble-Shooting Model instructors ranked ready access to the field office should problems arise as second most important (2.75 average rank), while Intensive Model instructors ranked it fourth (3.61). Within each group, there was considerable consensus on the rank order of items (Kendall's W, a measure of concordance, was .54 for the Intensive Model and .48 for the Trouble-shooting Model, p=.00 for each). In short, both groups felt the most important communication mechanism was access to the liaison in an emergency. For each, however, the second-most important mechanism was one they were accustomed to: routine liaison visits under the Intensive Model, or access to field office staff in the Trouble-Shooting Model.

A second way of evaluating communication was an item which focused explicitly on liaison visits as a way to maintain regular contact between the school and individual instructors in non-emergency situations. Instructors rank-ordered their preferences among the following possibilities: regularly-scheduled in-person visits, regularly-scheduled telephone calls, and no regularly-scheduled contact but school personnel "on-call" for consultation. The results are given in Table 2.

The field instructors under the two models differed in preference for all items. The Intensive Model instructors unequivocally preferred regular in-person visits by a liaison (average rank 1.31) and rejected the consultation-only model (2.60). The Trouble-Shooting instructors preferred regular telephone calls by a slight margin (1.87) but their rankings did not indicate an overwhelming preference. The Kendall's W confirmed their lack of consensus: it was .01 (p=.24) among Trouble-Shooting instructors, indicating no agreement. By comparison, the Intensive Model instructors agreed among themselves (Kendall's W = .42, p =.00). Thus, the Intensive Model instructors strongly preferred the regular visits, while Trouble-Shooting instructors did not agree among themselves that the contact they receive, or any other, was clearly best.

Predicted Consultants When the Field Instructor Encounters Problems

A major difference between the Intensive and Trouble-Shooting Models is the regular in-person presence of the faculty liaison (Intensive) and the rapid mobilization of a team to deal with problems (Trouble-Shooting). However, even the most conscientious liaisons are not available all the time, and field instructors may be reluctant to "call out" a trouble-shooting team (Rosenblum & Raphael, 1987). When field instructors encounter problems with their students, who do they really turn to for consultation? Is the school or liaison the resource of choice, or do instructors try to handle it themselves or within the agency? And, does the utilization of given resources vary with different types of problems?

Table 2   Importance of School-Agency Communication Mechanisms: Rank Orders of Field Instructors Under Two Liaison Models

	Intensive Model (VCU)	Trouble-shooting Model (Albany)
Ranking One: Items ranked in terms of importance to you in providing field instruction 1=most important, 6=least important	Mean Rank	Mean Rank
Seminars in field instruction given by school	3.91	3.66
Routine visits or calls by liaison[1]	2.33	3.39
Ready access to liaison should problems arise	1.97	1.95
Written material from school explaining activities, policies, etc.	2.87	2.85
Ready access to field office should problems arise[1]	3.61	2.75
Other	5.86	5.82
Ranking Two: Rank ways to maintain regular (non-emergency) contact 1=preferred contact, 3=least preferred contact	Mean Rank	Mean Rank
Regular in-person visits by school representative[1]	1.31	2.03
Regular telephone calls from a school representative[1]	2.06	1.87
No regularly-scheduled contact but school personnel on-call for consultation and troubleshooting[1]	2.60	2.06

[1]   Difference between models statistically significant (t-test, $p < .05$).

Because the rate of actual problems is relatively low, we posed hypothetical situations an instructor might encounter. One section of the questionnaire offered ten common problems with students and asked "if you ran into such a situation, who would you turn to for advice, support or help in handling the situation?" Seven possible categories of people were listed, from the field instructor's supervisor in the agency to teaching faculty at the school. Instructors were asked to list all to whom they would turn. For the data analysis, only the first three consultants mentioned were included (less than 1 percent of items included more than three consultants). Table 4 includes a condensed version of each scenario and the consultants the field instructor would turn to, while Table 3 summarizes the number of times each type of consultant was mentioned in the 10 scenarios.

Table 3 **Predicted Consultants When Field Instructor Encounters Problems with Student: Comparison of Field Instructors Under Two Liaison Models**

Total Mentions in 10 Problem Scenarios

Consultant:	Intensive Model (VCU) Mean	Trouble-shooting Model Mean
Liaison[1]	5.08	4.37
Other university staff (total):[1]	1.19	2.34
Field office personnel[1]	.90	1.56
Teacher of seminar for field instructors[1]	.22	.72
Classroom faculty	.06	.06
Agency staff (total):	3.55	3.85
Agency supervisor	2.52	2.81
Colleague	.46	.48
Other field instructors in agency	.57	.56
Student	.24	.33
Handle it by self without help	3.48	3.71

[1] Difference between models statistically significant when controlled for related variables (ANOVA, $p < .05$).

Field instructors were most likely to turn to the liaison (Table 3). They were also likely to try to handle a problem themselves or turn to resources in the agency:

overall, handling it oneself or using an agency consultant was mentioned about as often as a school-based resource. However, there were distinct differences in use of the liaison and other school personnel between the two models. Intensive Model instructors turned more to the liaison than the Trouble-Shooting instructors, an average of 5.08 mentions to 4.37 (analysis of variance, $p < .05$, controlling for individual and family services). Conversely, the Trouble-Shooting instructors were more likely to turn to all non-liaison university staff (2.34 to 1.19) and especially to field office personnel (1.56 mentions to .90) (both analyses control for formal training in field instruction). There were no significant differences in consulting agency personnel or handling it by one's-self. In short, school personnel are important resources for problems with students, but field instructors go directly to Field Office staff more when the liaison is not a regular visitor to the agency. Under both models, non-school personnel were seen as significant sources of assistance.

Different problems elicited different consultants (Table 4). Field instructors were most likely to handle it themselves when process recordings were overdue and when the student was not ready to take a case: in both these scenarios, they were unlikely to turn to others at all. Apparently, these situations were seen as a manageable part of the teacher-learner relationship (or else, something one did not admit to others). Agency-based personnel were consulted most often when the student refused an agency policy; when the instructor didn't get along well with the student; when the student was a former client of the agency; and, when menial tasks were assigned the student. In three of these four scenarios, the field instructors were also likely to consult the liaison or other university personnel; only one, assignment of menial tasks, was kept "in house."

The liaison or university staff were consulted often, and exclusively, when the agency did not have appropriate learning opportunities; the student protested an evaluation; the student claimed school policies had changed; or, the student's skills were not as advanced as the instructor thought they should be. Comparing the scenarios to the liaison activities reported earlier, most of the scenarios where school personnel were seen as the primary resources fell into the functions of student evaluation and mediation or problem resolution. These were the functions field instructors rated as important in helping them do their jobs. However, two scenarios included functions the instructors rated as relatively unimportant: assessing the fit between curriculum and agency learning opportunities (agency lacks appropriate learning experiences) and interpreting school policy (student says policy about extra time off has changed). In both cases, instructors appropriately turn first to school personnel, even though they do not see the overall function as important to their day-to-day teaching.

**Table 4 Who to Turn to When Facing Different Student Problems:
Scenarios and Consultants Under Two Liaison Models**

	Intensive Model (VCU)	Trouble-shooting Model (Albany)
Likely consultant for advice in situation:	Percent	Percent
Agency does not have the learning opportunities the school expects		
Liaison[2]	74	63
Other university staff[2]	25	53
Agency personnel	31	30
Handle by self	01	01
Student refuses to follow a policy, believing it inconsistent with social work values		
Liaison	66	68
Other university staff[1]	13	28
Agency personnel	61	70
Handle by self	15	11
Overdue process recordings, FI believes case not go well and student afraid of poor evaluation		
Liaison	30	24
Other university staff[1]	03	11
Agency personnel	19	22
Handle by self	67	72
Student protests evaluation as "satisfactory" rather than "superior"		
Liaison	69	57
Other university staff	08	18
Agency personnel	27	32
Handle by self	36	48
FI and student don't hit it off		
Liaison	51	47
Other university staff[1]	06	17
Agency personnel	57	56

Handle by self	39	44

Student was a client of the agency in the past
Liaison	46	41
Other university staff[1]	16	20
Agency personnel	52	53
Handle by self	22	28

**Menial tasks assigned to student, supervisor says it is to
pay back time for supervision**
Liaison$_2$	37	29
Other university staff[1]	09	16
Agency personnel	74	81
Handle by self	20	23

Student says not ready to take family case
Liaison	22	21
Other university staff[1]	02	06
Agency personnel	15	20
Handle by self	78	79

Student asks for extra time off, says school policy changed
Liaison[2]	61	49
Other university staff[1]	29	45
Agency personnel	03	03
Handle by self	30	26

Student's skills not as advanced as they should be
Liaison[1]	58	44
Other university staff[1]	10	23
Agency personnel	22	27
Handle by self	44	46

[1]   Difference between models statistically significant (chi-squared, p, .05).
[2]   Probability of difference between models between .05 and .10 (chi-squared).

In terms of differences between models, the differences in individual scenarios follow those reported for overall resources: Intensive Model instructors turn to the liaison more and other university staff less than do Trouble-Shooting instructors. They are equally likely to handle a difficulty by themselves or consult agency personnel.

SUMMARY AND CONCLUSION

Field instructors operating under these two liaison models experienced some liaison activities in the same way and others very differently. There was agreement by field instructors in the Intensive and the Trouble-Shooting Models that the two activities most important to their functioning as a field instructor were, "serve as a role model for students" and "evaluate student progress throughout placement, reads student written material (e.g., process recordings, case summaries)," and the least important was, "recruit, evaluate, and develop field placements." This is in contrast to field instructors in the Faria, et al. (1988) study who ranked linkage (interpreting policies, expectations, etc.), practicum placement, and consultant as the most important liaison responsibilities, and administration, advocate and teacher as the least important.

Most of the differences between instructors under the two models were in the items with mid-level importance. Field instructors in the Trouble-Shooting Model placed more importance on matching students and agencies, conveying information about school policies, developing field placements, and assigning grades. Intensive Model instructors placed significantly more importance on assistance in developing learning objectives, and assisting the student to integrate coursework and practicum. These differences reflect the defining characteristics of each model, with the Trouble-Shooting Model instructors focusing on placement, linkage, and student evaluation (administrative tasks) and Intensive Model instructors on teaching and integrating (educational tasks). However, the differences must be considered in the context that both groups consider teaching-related activities to be the most important and placement development least important.

This finding may contribute support for the observation that it is the implementation of the liaison role that needs to be better understood (Raskin, 1994). If under two liaison models, which define these functions quite differently, both sets of field instructors experience role modelling and review of written materials as contributing the most to their functioning, then one explanation is that the implementation of these functions can be handled in a wide-range of ways. If this is so, further exploration of field instructors perceptions in this regard would contribute to a richer understanding of implementation of the liaison role. However, since the review of written materials was rated as important by field instructors in the Trouble-Shooting Model (a task the liaisons do not perform), it is possible the question was misinterpreted: i.e., it is important to them as field instructors, but not necessarily as an activity of the liaison. In both models the field instructors role includes role-modelling and reading written materials. These two critical elements are emphasized in field instruction training seminars.

When asked to rank order the resources made available by the school, both sets of field instructors ranked, "ready access to the liaison when problems arise" the most important and, "seminars in field instruction" the least important. As would be predicted from the differential emphases in each Model, Intensive Model field instructors, rated "routine visits by the liaison" second while the Trouble-Shooting field instructors rated "ready access to the field office should problems arise" second.

The low valuation of field instruction seminars is in direct contrast to the importance placed on field instructor training in both models and in the literature (Abramson & Fortune, 1990; Bogo, 1981). This is especially puzzling because the field instructors placed a high value on their teaching role and the seminars were intended to help them learn to teach. It may be that seminars did not focus sufficiently on the teaching role or that they inadvertently conveyed a condescending attitude toward the instructor's skills, thus reinforcing the low status deplored by Urdang (1991) and Hanna (1992). Or the instructors may have underestimated the difficulty of learning to supervise (Akin & Weil, 1981) and consequently devalued the seminar. More likely, we think, is that field instructors were responding to what helps them do their jobs in the immediate situation. Like students who believe that theoretical classroom material is less relevant than suggestions about the case they have now, the field instructors valued access and support for resolving immediate issues. And they valued concrete, immediate assistance more than the conceptual base that, in the long-run, is designed to enable them to deal effectively with many different problems and situations.

Despite the importance of immediate assistance from the school, when given a problem situation, field instructors turned to other resources as well. Under both models, instructors were likely to handle the situation themselves when it involved student learning behavior that might reflect badly on their teaching capacity. They were likely to turn to agency personnel for assistance if the problem involved agency policy and procedures, including assignment of duties and in solving the situation of the student having been a client at the agency. They turned to the school for similar problems, for mediation, and for difficulties related to student evaluation.

The breadth of resources instructors would use under both models suggests that we may need to rethink how schools offer support. Full support for field instructors may be an unnecessary ideal . . . they use other resources even under the continuous support of the Intensive Model. On the other hand, other agency personnel are involved in field instruction and might find support or training helpful as well. In addition, the selective use of resources based on the type of problem suggests that education for field instructors might be better targeted to areas of need. For example, instructors' independent problem-solving skills could be bolstered in the relationship areas they seem reluctant to take to outsiders, while their policy interpretation and collegial negotiation skills might be the focus for discussion of the agency context of field instruction.

The field instructors under the two models differed in resources used only after they turned to the university. While both turn to the faculty liaison for assistance, the Intensive Model instructors use the liaison significantly more often and the Trouble-Shooting instructors who turn to other university staff. This again reflects preferences for that to which the instructors are accustomed. That pattern is also evident in their choices of preferred contact with the school: the Intensive Model field instructors expressed a clear preference for "regular in-person visits by a school representative" while Trouble-Shooting field instructors ranked "regular telephone calls from a school representative" as first. However, field instructors in the Trouble-Shooting Model did not express a strong preference for telephone calls over other means of contact, while the Intensive Model instructors clearly ranked in-person, telephone, and no regularly scheduled contact in descending order of preference. This is the only evidence that the Trouble-Shooting instructors might have reservations about the lack of regularly-scheduled in-person contact with a school representative.

In summary, field instructors operating under distinctly different field liaison models agreed on many essential elements of the liaison function, on school-agency communication and on persons who would be helpful to them problems were encountered. When they differed, each group of field instructors expressed preference for elements of their school's Model: what they receive is what they prefer and what they consider important. One might have expected that if field instructors in either of these Models were not getting what they needed, or considered important in accomplishing their goals with students, they would have indicated a preference for a resource, contact, or activity they were not getting: instructors in neither model did.

Based on this study one could propose that the less intensive Trouble-Shooting Model is a better use of scarce resources. And, since there is no evidence that the Model is less preferred or deemed less important by the field instructors who are experiencing it, this is something to be considered. On the other hand, the concerns expressed throughout the literature for schools to take a strong conceptual and educational role in monitoring and guiding the field practicum, through the liaison role, remains a consistent thread. Although field instructors in previous studies did not rate the liaison teaching activities highly (Faria, et al., 1988), and student satisfaction studies have demonstrated a low value placed on the liaison role (Fortune, et al., 1985; Fortune & Abramson, 1993), field instructors in this study rated two teaching functions as most important.

Further research into the differential use of supportive resources, as well as analyses of the effect(s) on the quality of student outcomes, will contribute to our ability to recommend one model over another. There are different motivations for asking and answering these questions, ranging from the conceptualizations of the ideal educational model to the practicalities of budget restrictions. The lack of support for field instruction in the university, and the realities of cutbacks and financial exigencies will be important to consider in determining which variables will be included in future efforts. The results of our study strongly indicate there are many ways of providing support that are satisfactory to field instructors. Rather than searching to define the single best model, we think that many models are acceptable. The essential element, in our opinion is a coherent model which is supported by field faculty and administration.

REFERENCES

Abramson, J. S., & Fortune, A. E. (1990). Improving field instruction: An evaluation of a seminar for new field instructors. *Journal of Social Work Education, 26*(3), Fall, 273-286.

Akin, G., & Weil, M. (1981). The prior question: How do supervisors learn to supervise? *Social Casework, 62,* 472-479.

Bogo, M. (1981). An educationally focused faculty/field liaison program for first-time field instructors. *Journal of Education for Social Work, 17,* 59-65.

Brownstein, C., Smith, H. Y., & Faria, G. (1991). The liaison role: A three phase study of the schools, the field, the faculty. In D. Schneck, B. Grossman & U. Glassman (Eds.), *Field education in social work: Contemporary issues and trends* (pp. 237-248). Dubuque, IA: Kendall/Hunt.

Fortune, A. E., & Abramson, J. S. (1993). Predictors of satisfaction with field practicum among social work students. *The Clinical Supervisor, 11*(1), 95-110.

Fortune, A. E., Feathers, C., Rook, S. R., Scrimenti, R. M., Smollen, P., Stemerman, B., & Tucker, E. L. (1985). Student satisfaction with field placement. *Journal of Social Work Education, (21*(3), Fall, 92-104.

Faria, G., Brownstein, C., & Smith, H. Y. (1988). A survey of field instructors' perceptions of the liaison role. *Journal of Social Work Education, 24*(2), Spring/Summer, 135-144.

Hanna, E. A. (1992). The demise of the field advising role in social work education. *The Clinical Supervisor, 10*(2), 149-164.

Raphael, F. B., & Rosenblum, A. F. (1987). An operational guide to the faculty field liaison role. *Social Casework, 68*(3), March, 156-163.

Raskin, M. S. (1994). The delphi study in field instruction revisited: expert consensus on issues and research priorities. *Journal of Social Work Education, 30*(1), Winter, 75-89.

Rosenblatt, A., & Mayer, J. (1975). Objectionable supervisory styles: Students' views. *Social Work, 2.*

Rosenblum, A. F., & Raphael, F. B. (1983). The role and function of the faculty field liaison. *Journal of Education for Social Work, 19*(1), Winter, 67-73.

Rosenblum, A. F., & Raphael, F. B. (1987). Students at risk in the field practicum and implications for field teaching. *The Clinical Supervisor, 5*(3), Fall, 53-63.

Sheafor, B. W., & Jenkins, L. E. (1982). *Quality field instruction in social work.* N.Y.: Longman.

Smith, H. Y., Faria, G., & Brownstein, C. (1986). *Social work faculty in the role of liaison: A field study,* 22(3), Fall, 68-78.

Urdang, E. (1991). The discipline of faculty advising. *Journal of Teaching in Social Work* 5(1), 117-137.

CHAPTER TWENTY-FOUR

FIELD INSTRUCTORS' PERCEPTIONS OF THE SOCIAL WORK FIELD EDUCATION PROCESS

Ina Freeman and Forrest C. (Bud) Hansen

Professional social workers have all experienced practicums during their training. Some selected practitioners are now offering field instruction to students. What are the field instructors' perceptions of: a) their expectations of students in the field; b) their primary roles as field instructors; and c) their preparation for field instruction? To ensure the quality of professional social workers, these and other questions need to be answered.

Most professions require practitioners to successfully complete some type of supervised and monitored internship. The largest single component of BSW and MSW curriculum is the practicum (Hamilton & Else, 1983). The 1984 Curriculum Policy Statement of the Council on Social Work Education has defined field education as a "professional foundation area" (Mesbur, 1991, p. 155). Unfortunately, the academic world continues to undervalue field education (Hamilton, 1981) or remains ambivalent about it (Gerrard, 1981). The field instructor is a bridge between the worlds of academia and practice. The field instructor must, to be effective for both the students and the profession, understand and be effective in both worlds. Unfortunately, field instructors are rarely valued for their unique qualities by either world. The survival of both the profession of social work and university social work programs rely upon the credibility of practitioners that is partially hinged upon the quality of the field educational experience and the knowledge base imparted (Grinnell, 1988). Both worlds build and rely upon the other, not only for training and human resources, but also for professional identity.

Agencies who employ the professionals and the universities who are the gatekeepers of the profession must work together. It is, however, the field instructor who educates the student to meet the demands of practice while attaining their personal goals. The creativity (Katz, 1975) and solidarity of purpose that are melded into a practicum by a field instructor should be conjointly advocated by the School and its field instructors.

LITERATURE REVIEW

Writings showing concern for the welfare of others and a code of ethical concepts can be found in the Hebrew, Assyrian, Mesopotamian and Chinese societies (Morris, 1986). In North America, the growth of capitalism changed the concern and ethics into a paternalistic charity administered by government.

In 1898, the New York School of Philanthropy was founded (George, 1982) in response to the need expressed by various charity organizations for education for volunteers who carried caseloads (Kadushin, 1985). This school formalized the apprenticeship training used in the field by charitable societies (George 1982). Within this school, field work was initially augmented by informal group education, and later by formalized lectures. With the growth of social work as a profession, these schools joined universities and the focus shifted from apprenticeship to theory based education and field education was discontinued by some universities.

The discontinuance of the practice component of social work education was addressed in 1932 by the American Association of Schools of Social Work (George, 1982). The curriculum standards established at that time included both academic or theoretical study and field practice. This milestone equalized the focus of training of new social workers between academic and practice. Some schools accepted this challenge by formulating specialized courses for field instructors and teachers, others hired field instructors (George, 1982).

In 1952, the National Association of Schools of Social Administration amalgamated with the American Association of Schools of Social Work to form the Council on Social Work Education (George, 1982). Within the curriculum study of 1959 published by this council, a serious study of undergraduate education was recommended (George, 1982). By 1961 the Council on Social Work Education issued a guiding statement including field instruction in undergraduate education (George, 1982). As social work Education progressed, the academic standards were formulated and structured for the student, but little attention was paid to those who perform the most valuable service to the profession, the field instructor.

In Canada, the Canadian Association of Social Workers approved a Code of Ethics on June 3, 1983. Section 9, Subsection 9.1 deals with the provision of and responsibilities for field instruction, and Section 8 deals with the professional social worker as a teacher. This is asserted by Coughlin (1970) who states that the social work practitioner is a contributor and a consumer of the ever increasing amount of information dealing with the human condition. The field instructor has the primary responsibility for the integration of research and practice, for it is the practitioner who has the client base, and upon whom the research will directly impact (Hamilton & Else, 1983).

Prepared field instructors offer the student the potential to formulate a field experience that is rich and rewarding. The experience is enriched with full cooperation between the field instructors and the educational setting. Many authors call for an open channel for communication to flow to and from both educators and practitioners to enhance the job readiness of the graduating student (Austin, 1978; Bogo & Vayda, 1987; Hamilton & Else, 1983; Maier, 1981; Meinert, 1979; Quaranta & Stanton, 1973). It is recognized that this integration effectively facilitates the growth of a social work student into a professional social work practitioner.

In a survey of field instructors across Canada by Thomlison, Watt, and Kimberley (1980) the desire for training for field instruction was indicated. Bogo and Vayda (1987) write that one of the field instructors' concerns was for comprehensive and ongoing training to adequately fulfill the role of field instructor. Lacerte and Ray (1989) indicate that American field instructors want recognition, reward and training. Some training is occurring (Rogers & McDonald, 1990; Rogers & Rodway, 1990), but the training is rarely ongoing. Similarly, the literature abounds with authors who recognize the necessity of coordination between the agency, field instructor and university for planning of the field placement (Sheafor & Jenkins, 1982; Bogo & Vayda, 1987; Rogers & Rodway, 1990; Marshack & Glassman, 1991). The reality is that this coordination is difficult to implement.

The literature abounds with articles stipulating the needs of a student within the practicum, how these needs might best be met and how the experience affects their practice. The literature does not elaborate on what the field instructor learns from the student, or how the field instruction experience affects the field instructor's practice. This abyss in knowledge must be filled to encourage the development of quality education of future practitioners.

METHODOLOGY

This study was completed at the University of Windsor in 1991. It was designed to adhere to the professional role of a social worker to be "the creator and disseminator of knowledge, and . . . the contributing partner" (Grinnell & Siegel, 1988, p. 18). The study is based upon the analysis of the perceptions of professional social workers who provide field instruction. The instrument contained requests for information that was both quantitative and qualitative due to the relative unfamiliarity of the subject (Epstein, 1988) within social work literature. The questionnaire was designed to collect data that would describe the population of field instructors and their perceptions.

All questions following the demographics were measured using a five point Likert scale, with one meaning no, never or not important, and five meaning yes, always or extremely important. The returned questionnaires were then analyzed using SPSS/PC+.

The five major areas of this study were:

1) The socio-demographic characteristics of the field instructors;
2) Factors that influence participation in Field Instruction;
3) Preparation for the role of field instructor;
4) The field instructors' evaluation of the role of the School of Social Work regarding field instruction;
5) The field instructors' perceptions of the experience of field instruction.

The questionnaire was mailed to all the field instructors affiliated with the University of Windsor, School of Social Work during the five year span from September 1985 to April 1991. These field instructors were obtained from both Southern Ontario and Southern Michigan. The return rate of field instructors in Canada was 43%, and from Michigan was 79%. In total there were 41 field instructors who indicated involvement in third year field instruction; 47 in fourth year; and 34 in Masters level. Some of these respondents were no longer involved in field instruction. Specifically, eight at third year; eleven at fourth year; and nine at the Masters level.

The Socio-Demographic Characteristics of the Field Instructors

The percentage of males involved in field instruction increased with the student level (37.6% at third year, 49.0% at fourth year, and 54.5% at Masters level). Overall, this study found that 53.1% of the responding field instructors were female and 46.9% were male. A study by Thomlison et al. (1980) noted that in Ontario, 61.7% of the interviewed field instructors were female, and 38.3% were male (p.57).

Behling, Curtis, and Foster (1982) indicate that field instructors do not view age as a determinant of success of field instruction. However, field instructors who are older may have more life experiences to draw from, and may command more respect both in the field and from students. The study found that the mean age of third year field instructors was 39 years and fourth and Masters level was 40 years. This finding was different, that is, field instructors were older than would be expected from either the

McDonnell (1987) study or the Thomlison et al. (1980) study. It was also interesting to note that female field instructors were clustered in the younger age groups.

The degree that should be held by field instructors has sparked debate (Wilson, 1981; The Council on Social Work Education, 1984; Rogers & McDonald, 1989; Smith & Baker, 1989; Thyer, Williams, Sowers-Hoag & Love, 1989). The University of Windsor has 66.6% of the field instructors with a MSW and with all field instructors for Masters level students (100%) having an MSW.

The University of Windsor lies on the river separating Canada and the United States. Because the University of Windsor places students in American placements, the field instructors were asked their citizenship. The majority were Canadian. It is interesting that there are more American field instructors at the Masters level than at the undergraduate level. It is similarly interesting that the American field instructors at the undergraduate level have been field instructors for approximately twice the length of time (7.6 years) as have the Canadian field instructors (4.6 years). However, at the Masters level, the American field instructors have been field instructors for approximately one half the length of time (3.5 years) as have the Canadian field instructors (6.5 years).

The length of supervisory experience of a field instructor was determined. It was found that the mean number of years of supervisory experience was similar (approximately 4 years) for all levels of student.

The experience with the position of Field Instructor was also asked. Wayne, Skolnik, and Raskin (1989) found 47% were first time field instructors in a cross Canada study. In contrast, this study found that only 17% of the sample were first time field instructors for third and fourth year, and 23.5% for the Masters level. This is a major difference and suggests a maturing of the profession in the south western region of Ontario.

Granger and Starnes (1982) indicate that field instructors lack the formal teaching experience that is instrumental in being a field instructor. Silvester (1987) writes that the only training many field instructors receive for field instruction is their supervisory or field instruction experience. This leaves the profession at risk of becoming incestuous with poor attitudes and dated practices being passed to new practitioners by untrained supervisors. The University of Windsor does not offer training in field instruction. Therefore, it is not surprising that field instructors generally (average of 84%) had not taken field instruction courses. The 16% that had taken field instruction courses included half day seminars and on the job training, not necessarily a structured, formalized course.

Social work is a profession that touches most fields of practice, from micro to macro, and from institutional to community. Also, it is important that social work students be exposed to the holistic field in which they will eventually practice. Therefore, it is important that social work students have the opportunity to learn from the area in which they anticipate practicing. Field instructors were asked their field of practice to determine the breadth of opportunity for students. Most field instructors were in micro practice, eliminating opportunities for education in macro practice. The largest single field employing field instructors in all levels was mental health institutions (32.2%). Approximately half the number in mental health were employed in physical and general health (16.5%). The percentage of those who practiced in the area of disabilities was slightly less at 12.1%. Overall, 60.9% of the practitioners were in health related fields. Many of the remaining field instructors practiced in institutional settings, such as Children's Aid Societies (Child Welfare), Boards of Education and Human Justice and Corrections (23.2%). This may reflect the availability of field instructors, but may restrict the practicum experience for the students. The question that remains is why is there not a broader base of practice settings? The Thomlison et al. (1980) study indicated that only 30% of the population of responding field instructors in Ontario were based in Health Agencies (p. 54). On the other hand, possibly this indicates that the health related fields were the main growth areas at the time of the study.

Similarly, the method of practice of the field instructors was elicited. It was found that 43.3% of the field instructors were involved in administration, with the second highest being individual counselling (23.3%). Family practice placed a poor third (10.0%), and community organization placed fourth (9.5%).

Table 1 **The Importance of the Reasons for the Decision to Become a Field Instructor by Level of Instruction (N=122)**

Reasons for Decision	3rd	4th	MSW	Total	$\underline{F}$	$\underline{P}$
Professional responsibility	4.1	4.1	4.1	4.1	.03	.97
Professional development	4.0	3.8	3.6	3.8	1.4	.24
Intellectual challenge	3.8	3.9	3.7	3.8	0.2	.81
University affiliation	3.6	3.4	3.3	3.5	0.7	.51
Stay/Keep current with literature	3.1	3.0	3.1	3.1	.05	.95

Note: In the following tables, Mean ranks on a 1-5 scale are shown with higher scores being more important or favorable.

Factors that Influence Participation in Field Instruction

Factors that influenced the practitioner's decision to become a field instructor may be similar to the reasons the field instructors decided to continue in that role. Table 1 shows that all levels of field instructors ranked the reasons for involvement in field instruction in the following decreasing order: a) a professional responsibility (4.1); b) recognition of field instruction as an opportunity for professional development (3.8); c) an intellectual challenge (3.8); d) affiliation with the University (3.5); and e) the potential opportunity to remain current with the literature (3.1). There were some differences among the answers according to the level of student the field instructor was teaching. But there were no statistically significant differences among the levels, thus indicating that the field instructors have similar reasons for accepting this position.

The field instructors were asked to rate the importance of field instruction to them personally, and the personal satisfaction derived from the experience. It was found that personal importance and personal satisfaction was very high across all levels of students (4.1 and 4.6 respectively). This was a finding that is more significant because both participating and non-participating field instructors recognized the personal importance and satisfaction as high. This may be reflected in the positive commitment level of the field instructors of the University of Windsor.

The ideal model of field instruction is one of mutuality between the field instructor and the student (Lemberger & Marshack, 1991). This model intimates that both parties are honest, mature and open to learning. The reality of field instruction involves other components, such as a differential in power base, a personal need to be liked, differences in philosophical outlooks, establishing a therapeutic relationship and others. A field instruction experience that is not based upon an educational model may subvert the educational value of the experience. The survey indicated that most field instructors placed a moderate value (3.6) on being liked by the student, placed no value on establishing or maintaining a personal friendship (1.7) and did not encourage discussion of personal problems outside the field instruction sessions (1.7). All of these results were in keeping with an educational model of field instruction.

Preparation for the Role of Field Instructor

Munson's (1981) article suggests that many field instructors do not have formalized training for supervision, instead modelling their supervisory style upon their field supervisors. As indicated in Table 2, the field instructors at all three levels of students indicated that they had no identifiable mentor (2.6) for their supervisory style or they slightly based their supervisory style on their field instructor (2.6).

The open-ended comments given to this question indicated that field instructors based their style of supervision on multiple inputs: their years of practice; personal reflection; readings; individualized philosophy of the practice of social work; a background in experiential teaching techniques; their field experience; the field instructors' own needs for supervision "translated to student supervision"; and, workshops on leadership and supervisory styles. This would coincide with the suggestion by Walden and Brown (1985) that students be offered ongoing integration seminars throughout the field placements. Raskin's 1989 survey suggested that the willingness of the field instructor to take courses pertaining to field instruction was significantly correlated to the degree obtained, the personality, the post MSW experience, and the previous teaching and supervisory experience of the field instructor. That is, those professionals who had the most to offer a student through field instruction were most willing to take courses to improve. This suggestion may be enlarged to include field instructors who indicated they saw instruction on "how to" as moderately beneficial. The University of Windsor does not offer specialized courses to prepare field instructors for their responsibilities. The absence of these courses may impact upon the finding of no identifiable model for their supervisory style. Silvester (1987) postulates that a good experience for both the field instructor and the student may be achieved when the School of social work takes the time and energy to match the field instructor's personality, work philosophy and value system with those of the student. The field instructors surveyed indicated that they regarded having a compatible student was of moderate to high importance (3.9) to them.

Table 2   Model for Supervisory Style by Level of Instruction (N=122)

Supervisory Style	3rd	4th	MSW	Total	F	P
Former field instructor	2.5	2.6	2.5	2.6	.00	.99
None identified	2.6	2.8	2.6	2.6	.14	.87
Former supervisor	2.4	2.5	2.3	2.4	.28	.85
Colleague	2.4	2.4	2.3	2.4	.02	.98
Present supervisor	2.4	2.1	2.1	2.2	.99	.43
University instructor	2.0	1.8	1.8	1.9	.45	.64
University Methods prof.	1.7	1.8	1.7	1.8	.23	.79

The Field Instructors' Evaluation of the Role of the School of Social Work Regarding Field Instruction

Wayne, Skolnik, and Raskin (1989) suggest that many Canadian practitioners see limited or nonexistent relevance between the current university curriculum and direct practice. This suggests that these Canadian practitioners find students often lack the necessary information regarding the realities of practice within an agency. As shown in Table 3, the participating field instructors felt that the School of Social Work and classroom instruction prepared students only moderately for Field Instruction (3.2) or for practice (3.2).

On the other hand, field instructors felt that field instruction prepared the student for practice well (4.0). field instructors were generally satisfied with: the level and degree of communication with the school (3.6); the supportiveness of the School of Social Work to field instructors in their role (3.6); the receptiveness of the School of Social Work to their input (3.6); and, the effectiveness of the School of Social Work in meeting field instructors' needs for successful field instruction (3.3). As observed from the table, this satisfaction decreased slightly from a mean of 3.5 for third year field instructors to a mean of 3.4 for fourth year, and was substantially lower for field instructors of Masters level students (2.9), although the differences were not statistically significant.

Table 3   **Field Instructors' Evaluation of the School's Role of Social Work Regarding Field Instruction (N=122)**

School's Role	3rd	4th	MSW	Total	F	P
Effectiveness of field instruction for student to practice	3.9	4.1	4.1	4.0	1.1	.35
Satisfaction with communication with school's field instruction personnel	3.8	3.6	3.5	3.6	.43	.65
Supportiveness of school to field instructors in their role	3.8	3.7	3.4	3.6	.77	.46
Receptiveness of the school to their input	3.8	3.6	3.3	3.6	1.2	.31
Effectiveness of the school in meeting field instructors' needs for successful field instruction	3.5	3.4	2.9	3.3	2.1	.13
Effectiveness of school in preparing student for field instruction	2.9	3.2	3.5	3.2	4.3	.02
Effectiveness of classroom preparation of student for practice	3.1	3.2	3.5	3.2	1.4	.26

It is interesting to note that there was a significant difference in perception of the effectiveness of the School in preparing students for Field Instruction. The degree of effectiveness increased from a mean of 2.9 for third year to 3.2 for fourth year and to 3.5 for Masters level instruction. This finding suggests that students get better prepared as their level of education increases. This finding would be expected if the School was fulfilling the mandate to educate.

The results also indicate moderate satisfaction with the School of Social Work for preparation of tomorrow's social worker for the role in the professional community. Rosenfeld (1989) discussed the finding that as communication increased and improved, the level of personal satisfaction, satisfaction with the School of Social Work and the perception of support by the School to the field instructor improved. He also found that this communication was most effective when it was personal contact via either telephone or personal visitation. The School of Social Work may wish to examine ways to improve the communication between the School and the field instructors to improve the quality of field education for the student and the profession.

Hoffer (1991) finds that Schools of Social Work were not receptive to field instructors' input concerning the educational process. This study indicates moderate satisfaction (3.6). The educational institutions are preparing the students for practice in the field and should consult with professionals in the field to determine course content.

Field Instructors' Perceptions of the Experience of Field Instruction

The field instruction program of educational institutions allows students a "hands on" experience, and provides an opportunity to gain competence in the profession. Unfortunately, Schools of Social Work historically do not instruct field instructors how to best utilize the field instruction experience for both their benefit and the benefit of the student (Martin & Alper, 1989).

As stated in Table 4, all field instructors ranked their generalized expectations for the student as high.

The field instructors' expectation for the student to adhere to the Social Work Code of Ethics as the highest (4.9) was important considering the growing desire to have social work recognized as a profession. The next highest expectation, that the student would engage in personal growth during field instruction (4.7), may call for examination by the School of the field instructors' delineation of this expectation. The students' personal growth is neither measurable nor the realm of an educationally based field instructor. Students are not clients, and this must be clearly defined. The student's ability to: identify professional practice capabilities; identify professional needs; improve writing skills; integrate criticism positively into practice; and, improve verbal expression all show statistically significant differences between the expectations of field instructors for third year, fourth year and Masters level. This indicates an increase in the expectations of the student consistent with expected professional development.

Table 4　　Generalized expectations for the student during placement (N=122)

Expectations	3rd	4th	MSW	Total	F	P
Code of Ethics	4.8	4.9	4.9	4.9	.49	.61
Personal growth	4.6	4.8	4.7	4.7	1.5	.23
Verbal expression	4.2	4.5	4.6	4.4	4.1	.02
Integrate criticism	4.1	4.6	4.7	4.4	8.9	.00
Written expression	4.1	4.4	4.6	4.3	4.7	.01
Appearance	4.2	4.2	4.2	4.2	.11	.90
Identify needs	3.6	4.2	4.5	4.0	11.4	.00
Identify capabilities	3.6	4.0	4.5	4.0	11.4	.00

The role of a field instructor as found in the literature (Sheafor & Jenkins, 1982) is that of a teacher. The roles that are actually used differ. Webb (1988) links Field Instruction to apprenticeship. Hagen (1989) delineates the role of field instructor to orientation, supervision and evaluation. Table 5 contains the field instructors' perception of their primary role within field instruction. As noted in the table, the role of Role Model was viewed as the most important (4.4). Although only approaching statistical significance ($p=.07$), the role of supervisor and teacher decreased with the increasing level of the student. This suggests that field instructors perceive a change in orientation is needed as the student progresses through the levels of education, as would be expected. It suggests a move from a beginner to a more autonomous practitioner. The roles of co-worker (2.8), researcher (2.4) and control agent (2.3) were ranked very low. Although this is expected for the role of co-worker and control agent, it is distressing to see the field instructors' indicated unwillingness to accept the necessary link between practice and research.

The field instructors were asked to rate their perception of their responsibility for the student. Field instructors for undergraduates rated their answers as: the development of practice knowledge (4.3); and, a sense of contractual responsibility (4.0). Field instructors for graduate students perceived their responsibility to be primarily contractual (4.3), followed by the development of practice knowledge (3.9). This might be explained by the assumptions that many Masters level students have more practice experience, and are able to work more autonomously.

Table 5   Primary Role of the Field Instructor (N=122)

Primary Role	3rd	4th	MSW	Total	F	P
Role model	4.6	4.3	4.3	4.4	1.2	.30
Facilitator	4.2	4.3	4.3	4.3	.13	.88
Supervisor	4.6	4.2	4.0	4.3	2.7	.07
Teacher	4.4	4.2	3.9	4.2	2.8	.07
Agency resource	4.4	4.2	4.1	4.1	.70	.50
Evaluator	4.2	4.0	4.0	4.1	1.1	.33
Co-worker	2.7	2.7	3.0	2.8	.46	.63
Researcher	2.5	2.4	2.3	2.4	.28	.76
Control agent	2.3	2.2	2.3	2.3	.03	.97

Richmond (1897), Anderson (1985), and Smith and Baker (1989) indicate that the educational goals for students of social work BSW programs are generalist, while the educational goals for students of social work MSW programs are more specific. The field instructors goals for the student to understand the concepts and theories concerning client functioning (4.4) is seen as the most important. Field instructors for third year viewed the concepts and theories of the dynamics of functioning as second most important (4.3), whereas the field instructors for fourth year and Masters level students ranked the understanding of intervention strategies as second most important (4.4). These were reversed for the third most important concept. The other concepts and theories, in ranked order of importance, were the operation of the social worker in a professional context (3.9), ego functioning (3.6), policy context (3.6) and research methods (2.7). Due to the holistic nature of social work practice, this is an area the School may wish to examine, for without an understanding of social policy, social workers may not choose the best intervention for their clients. It is distressing that the understanding of research methods ranked last, and was seen as generally not important. The profession of social work relies upon the existence of social work oriented research. Without this, the profession would not exist as a separate entity from the fields that do publish research.

Generally, field instructors established as a goal for students the development of a commitment to all the goals established by the University of Windsor. The primary goal was the development of a commitment to respecting an individual (4.7). The other goals of adherence to professional ethics (4.5), development of a sense of professional responsibility (4.5), recognition of the importance of knowledge (4.4), the development of professional practice skills (4.4), the belief in the abilities of the client (4.4), and the students' development of a compatible philosophy with professional social workers (4.3), were ranked very closely, with little appreciable difference between their perceived importance.

Field instructors ranked the development of practice skills while the student was engaged in the practicum as important. This development can only be accomplished in a placement setting as the social work literature clearly differentiates between learning how to practice a skill and actually doing it. Field instructors were asked to rate the importance of the goals for the student in developing their practice skills in assessment (4.4), helping relationship (4.4), intervention (4.3), evaluation or feedback (4.2), planning (4.1) and termination (4.1). The only statistically significant difference was between the field instructors for third year students and field instructors for Masters level in the area of intervention. Field instructors for Masters students had statistically significant higher expectations (4.5) for intervention skills than third year students (4.1).

Table 6 shows that field instructors perceived maturity and an interest in the agency as of primary importance in the selection of the student across all levels of field instruction. Other factors which may impact on the selection process include prior knowledge of the agency (F (2,119) = 3.5, p=.03), prior experience in the field of social work (F (2,119) = 4.5, p=.01), and relevant experience to the agency (F (2,119) = 5.0, p=.01). Not surprisingly, these last three factors show a statistical significance in the increase in importance with the MSW level of education. These statistically significant differences would be expected between a novice in the first practicum and an experienced student at the Masters level.

Table 6   Field Instructors' Perception of Important Qualities for a Student (N-122)

Student Qualities	3rd	4th	MSW	Total	F	P
Maturity	4.4	4.5	4.7	4.5	1.6	.21
Interest in agency	4.1	4.3	4.4	4.3	1.2	.31
Prior knowledge	3.1	3.4	3.8	3.4	3.5	.03
Prior experience	3.1	3.1	3.8	3.3	4.5	.01
Relevant experience	3.1	2.9	3.6	3.2	5.0	.01

The ultimate goal of the educational experience is to graduate professionals who are capable of practicing autonomously. Obviously during the beginning phase of placement, a student does not have the competence to work autonomously. At what point do field instructors expect students to be autonomous? It would be expected that the time frame would be greater for third year students and shorter for Masters students. As expected, field instructors indicated an increasing expectation for students to practice autonomously at increasing educational levels. It is interesting that field instructors for third year and graduate level students expected the student to practice autonomously by mid placement, and the field instructors for fourth year expected the students to practice autonomously before termination. There is no expectation for students to practice autonomously at the beginning of placement, and all field instructors have some expectation that all students will practice autonomously at some point during their placement. However, the large standard deviations indicated that the field instructors' expectations were not uniform, which should encourage the University to examine and define these expectations more carefully.

CONCLUSION

Field instruction programs are a part of social work education at the university level. These programs and the field instructors who participate in them share in the gatekeeping function of the educational process. The Council on Social Work Education and the Canadian Association of Schools of Social Work have recognized the value of field instruction to the point that they require every School of Social Work to have field instruction.

This study has examined the demographics and perceptions of field instructors associated with the University of Windsor School of Social Work with respect to their experience within the field instruction process. The responding field instructors represented both present and past field instructors of third year, fourth year and Masters level students. The demographics clearly indicated a different perspective from that presented in the literature. Field instructors were older, had more practical experience, and only 17% were first time instructors. These findings suggest a maturing of the profession and of field instruction. This maturing may be more apparent in this instance because the University of Windsor was the first in North America to enrol students in a four year Honors BSW program.

This study indicates that field instructors are affected by the process of field instruction. It is the field instructors' sense of professional responsibility that gives them personal satisfaction with the process of field instruction. It is the professional responsibility that mandates social workers participate in research and use the results of this research in practice. This should form a link between the School of Social Work and the practitioners who are selected as field instructors. This linkage is not highly rated by the field instructors, and the profession as a whole should examine and correct this fault. Field instructors do not have a specific model for supervisory style, but the highest ranking model is the former field instructor. This indicates the power that field instruction experience has upon students when they enter the profession, and for many years while they are practicing. Schools of Social Work must attend to the fact that field instruction is vital to the profession. The field instructors ranked their satisfaction with the School of Social Work as only average to moderate (3.3, 3.6). Field instructors bridge academia and practice. Thus, they are the optimal partners in ensuring that the School of Social Work produces competent, professional social workers. This partnership should be strengthened for optimal preparation of tomorrow's social worker and for relevance to today's professional.

The generalized expectations for the student during placement including adherence to the Code of Ethics, continued personal growth, good verbal expression, ability to integrate criticism, good written expression, neat appearance, and the ability to identify client needs and capabilities must be incorporated into the students' curriculum. The field is sending a clear message to the Schools of Social Work that these are the areas that the field considers important for the student and the profession. Schools of Social Work should build in mechanisms to continually consult with those who provide field instruction to determine what to teach the students in preparation for field work. It is unfortunate that the field instructors do not recognize the importance of research, and the integral link via field instruction to opportunities to review and do research. Perhaps if the Schools of Social Work were to make research a more integral component of practice, this failure could be rectified. Field instructors are also sending a clear message to the Schools of Social Work that an important quality for a student to have is maturity. Perhaps maturity needs to be examined, defined and required as a pre-requisite for entry to Schools of Social Work. However, maturity is an elusive term that first requires an operational definition for which there is consensus.

Further research is indicated from this beginning study, and from the conclusions drawn from this study. To better understand the perceptions of field instructors, and to better integrate academia and practice all Schools of Social Work need to encourage their field instructors to participate fully in the education of tomorrow's practitioners.

REFERENCES

Anderson, J. (1985, Fall). BSW programs and the continuum in social work. *Journal of Social Work Education, 3*, 63-72.

Austin, M. J. (1978). Statewide academic planning for social work education: A case study. *Journal of Sociology and Social Welfare, 5*(2), 230-249.

Behling, J. C., Curtis, C., & Foster, S. A. (1982). Impact of sex-role combinations in student performance in instruction. *Clinical-Supervisor, 6*(3-4), 161-168.

Bogo, M., & Vayda, E. (1987). *The practice of field instruction in social work, theory and process.* Toronto, Buffalo, London: University of Toronto Press.

Coughlin, B. J. (1970). Reconceptualizing the theoretical base of social work practice. In L. Ripple (Ed.), *Innovations in teaching social work practice.* New York: Council on Social Work Education.

Epstein, I. (1988). Quantitative and qualitative methods. In R. M. Grinnell, Jr. (Ed.), *Social work research and evaluation* (3rd ed.). Itasca, IL: F.E. Peacock Publishers, Inc.

George, A. (1982). A history of social work field instruction: Apprenticeship to instruction. In B. W. Sheafor & L. E. Jenkins (Eds.), *Quality field instruction in social work: Program development and maintenance.* New York: London.

Germain, C., & Gitterman, A. (1980). *The life model of social work practice.* New York: Columbia University Press.

Gerrard, V. (Ed.). (1981). *Contemporary Social Work Education, 4*(1), i-ii.

Granger, J. M., & Starnes, S. (1982). *Field instruction model for baccalaureate social work.* Syracuse, NY: Syracuse University School of Social Work.

Grinnell, R. M. Jr., (Ed.). (1988). *Social work research and evaluation* (3rd ed.). Itasca, IL: F. E. Peacock Publishers, Inc.

Grinnell, R. M. Jr., & Siegel, D. H. (1988). The place of research in social work. In R. M. Grinnell Jr. (Ed.), *Social work research and evaluation* (3rd ed.). Itasca, IL: F. E. Peacock Publishers, Inc.

Hagen, B. J. H. (1989). The practicum instructor: A study of role expectations. In M. S. Raskin (Ed.), *Empirical studies in field instruction.* New York: Haworth Press.

Hamblin, G., & Lewis, S. (1988, Winter). Some factors affecting the quality of social work placements. *Social Work Education, 8*(1), 10-16.

Hamilton, N., & Else, J. F. (1983). *Designing field education philosophy, structure and process.* Springfield, IL: Charles C. Thomas, Publisher.

Hoffer, A. (1991). *Education for social work responsibilities and challenges in the world of work.* Report on a North American Delphi Study, University of Calgary.

Kadushin, A. (1985). *Supervision in social work* (2nd ed.). New York: Columbia University Press.

Katz, S. N. (Ed.). (1975). *Creativity in social work: Selected writings of Lydia Rapoport.* Philadelphia: Temple University Press.

Lacerte, J., & Ray, J. (1989). Recognizing the educational contributions of field instructors. In D. Schneck, B. Grossman & V. Glassman (Eds.), *Field education in social work: Contemporary issues and trends.* Dubuque, IA: Kendall/Hunt Publishing Company.

Lemberger, J., & Marshack, R. (1991). Educational assessment in the field: An opportunity for teacher-learner mutuality. In D. Schneck, B. Grossman & V. Glassman (Eds.), *Field education in social work, contemporary issues and trends.* Dubuque, IA: Kendall/Hunt Publishing Company.

Maier, H. W. (1981). Chance favours the prepared mind. *Contemporary Social Work Education, 4*(1), 14-20.

Marshack, E., & Glassman, V. (1991). Innovative models for field instruction and departing from traditional methods. In D. Schneck, B. Grossman & V. Glassman (Eds.), *Field education in social work, contemporary issues and trends.* Dubuque, IA: Kendall/Hunt Publishing Company.

Martin M. L., & Alper, S. (1989, Summer). Mutual responsibility in supervision: A student workshop. *Arete, 14*(q), 52-56.

McDonnell, J. L. (1987). *A survey of manpower in the social service field of Windsor and Essex county and attitudes about the professional association (OAPSW).* A Thesis for the University of Windsor.

Meinert, R. C. (1979). Concentrations: Empirical patterns and future prospects. *Journal of Education for Social Work, 14*(2), 51-58.

Mesber, E. S. (1991). Overview of baccalaureate field education: Objectives and outcomes. In D. Schneck, B. Grossman & V. Glassman (Eds.), *Field education in social work.* Dubuque, IA: Kendall/Hunt Publishing Company.

Morris, R. (1986). *Rethinking social welfare: Why care for the stranger?* New York: Longman.

Munson, C. E. (1981). Style and structure in supervision. *Journal of Education for Social Work, 17*(q), 65-72.

Raskin, M. S. (1989). Field placement decisions: Art, science or guesswork? In M. S. Raskin (Ed.), *Empirical studies in field instruction*. New York: The Haworth Press.

Richmond, M. (1897). The need of a training school in applied philanthropy. In C. Barrows (Ed.), *Proceedings of the national conference of charities and corrections*. Boston, George H. Ellis.

Rogers, G., & McDonald, L. (1989). Field supervisors: Is a social work degree necessary? *Canadian Social Work Review, 6*(2), 203-221.

Rogers, G., & McDonald, L. (1990, June). *Evaluation of field instruction certificate course.* Presented at the Canadian Association of Schools of Social Work/Learned Societies Conference, Victoria, B.C.

Rogers, G., & Rodway, M. R. (1990, June). *Comparing the academic and articulated approaches to the practicum.* Presented to the annual meeting of the Canadian Association of Schools of Social Work/Learned Societies, Victoria, B.C.

Rosenfeld, D. (1989). Field instructor turnover. In M. S. Raskin (Ed.), *Empirical studies in field instruction*. New York: The Haworth Press.

Quaranta, M. A., & Stanton, G. (1973). Planning curriculum change in a large traditional field instruction program. *Journal of Education for Social Work, 9*(1), 55-78.

Sheafor, B. W., & Jenkins, L. E. (1982). *Quality field instruction in social work, program development and maintenance*. New York, London: Longman, Inc.

Silvester, D. (1987). *Communication issues between field and faculty: Are we achieving our educational objectives.* In Selected Presentation from the First Provincial Conference on the Professional Practice of Field Instruction in Social Work Education. Toronto: University of Toronto.

Smith, S. L., & Baker, D. R. (1989). The relationship between educational background of field instructors and the quality of supervision. In M. S. Raskin (Ed.), *Empirical studies in field instruction*. New York: Haworth Press.

Thomlison, B., Watt, S., & Kimberly, D. (October, 1980). *Trends and issues in the field preparation of social work manpower*. Canadian Association of Schools of Social Work.

Thyer, B.A., Williams, M., Sowers-Hoag, K., & Love, J.P. (1989). The MSW supervisory requirement in field instruction: Does it make a difference? In M. Raskin (Ed.), *Empirical studies in field instruction* (p. 249-256). New York: Howarth Press.

Walden, T., & Brown, L. N. (1985, Winter). The integration seminar: A vehicle for joining theory and practice. *Journal of Social Work Education, 21*(1), 13-19.

Wayne, J., Skolnik, L., & Raskin, M. S. (1989). Field instruction in the United States and Canada: A comparison of studies. In M. S. Raskin (Ed.), *Empirical studies in field instruction.* New York: Haworth Press.

Webb, N. B. (1988). The role of the field instructor in the socialization of students. *Social Casework: The Journal of Contemporary Social Work, 69,* 35-40.

Wilson, S. J. (1981). *Field instruction, techniques for supervisors.* New York/London: The Free Press, A Division of MacMillan Publishing Co. Inc./Collier MacMillan Publishers.

CHAPTER TWENTY-FIVE

A VIEW FROM URBAN AND RURAL FIELD INSTRUCTORS: PERSPECTIVES ON SOCIAL WORK PRACTICE AND EDUCATION

Barry L. Hall and Gayla Rogers

Over the years much has been written about the differences in social work practice between rural and urban settings. The major categories examined by researchers have focused on direct practice, classroom education and the role of the social worker. What is generally lacking in the literature is an analysis of whether or not there are any differences in how rural and urban field instructors teach social work practicum students.

Historically, social work theories and the field instruction component have been taught in large urban centers. Those students wishing an experience in smaller rural communities would seek out such opportunities with the expectation that the field instructors would be able to integrate the academic requirements set by the faculty. Past empirical research has examined the utility and transferability of generalist social work practice methods to rural and urban social work practitioners. Hoffman and Sallee (1987) surveyed 246 alumni from 8 different university undergraduate programs in the United States with the purpose of identifying any differences in the application of generalist social work skills between rural and urban settings. Their findings were for the most part inconclusive. Other empirical studies have resulted in similar conclusions and it was often commented that there were probably far more similarities between rural and urban practice methods than what was previously known (Fitzpatrick, Edwards, & Olszewski, 1980; Hardcastle, 1985; Whitaker, 1985; York, Denton, & Moran, 1989).

Nevertheless, research continued but with a different approach whereby the focus was on specific populations of clients being served by social workers in rural and urban contexts. In one study, a survey analysis was carried out on 250 income eligibility workers and 300 clients. Once again, the results indicated no significant differences in methods of social work practice but the researchers suggested that clients in rural settings presented different issues than their urban counterparts (Kropf, Lindsey, & Carse-McLocklin, 1993). In the practice area of spousal abuse the major finding was that at times the rural practitioners were offering more services to the clients (Bogal-Allbritten & Daughaday, 1990). Empirical studies in the field of child welfare generated results that ranged from: not expecting urban child welfare service programs to automatically meld into a rural environment; the general skills of the social workers were appreciably the same; and, the identification of child neglect was not significantly different when comparing the diagnostic ability of rural and urban social workers (Craft & Staudt, 1991; Horner & O'Neill, 1981; Jankovic, 1981; Tarleau, 1981). As was the case for generalist practice methods, the results of the clinical practice studies were for the most part inconclusive. Generally, the studies seem to suggest that more research emphasis should be placed on examining the contextual differences of social work practice and field instruction as opposed to primarily focusing on micro-counselling skills.

Emphasis has also been placed on whether or not the professional faculties of social work within the university systems were appropriately preparing students for practice in rural and small communities. The research is descriptive and ranges from: comments on an antirural bias of curricula; observations that schools are dropping the number of courses that prepare students for rural practice; a call for more systematic teaching of knowledge regarding rural communities; if the faculty members were aware of the nuances in rural practice; poor training or rural social welfare workers; and, whether or not the faculty liaison had a sufficient knowledge base to effectively supervise students training in rural settings (Cole, 1981; DeWeaver, 1988; McKay, 1987; Martinez-Brawley, 1986, 1988). Collier (1984), for example, contends social work fails its rural clients by applying inappropriate methods developed for use in urban settings. Overall, the literature arrives at the general conclusion of a perceived paucity of professional preparation for rural social work practice.

Other writers have commented on their view of the uniqueness of the social work role in a rural environment. It has been suggested that there is a blurring between the professional and the citizen when working and living in a rural community (Twente, 1980). Whittington (1985) spoke of social workers needing to be more conscious of their professional profiles due to their high visibility in the community. It was suggested that the lack of anonymity in a rural setting is a unique factor which can create additional stress for the social worker. Studies have focused on the perceived critical relationship that must exist between a rural social worker and their community, sighting that such connections are not as crucial within large urban settings; and, others have noted that rural as compared to urban practitioners tended to be more self-directed and autonomous resulting in more creativity in developing resources for their clients (Jones, 1981; Waltman, 1986).

An area in which there is a dearth of research is an examination of whether or not practicum instruction methods used by the field educators are any different between an urban and a rural setting. The field practicum is an extremely intrical part of professional social work education since it is at this apex where the theory learned in the classroom becomes tested in the actual field. Patchner and Sattazahn (1991) have commented that both rural and urban field instructors have similar views of the need for their students to be able to apply theory, knowledge and practice in a credible manner. Field instruction has been described as a dynamic learning process that effects both the field instructor and the student as well as the necessity for looking beyond the teaching of skills to including an analysis of individual field instructors' style and creativity (Gitterman, 1989; Nisivoccia, 1990). The purpose of the present research was to address the gaps in the rural/urban literature by analyzing field instruction methods. Specifically, the study set out to determine if rural field instructors viewed field education training needs, field teaching methods and the prepared practitioner differently than urban field instructors.

METHODOLOGY

In this study, field instructors, who were also social work practitioners, provided the perspective on social work practice and education within the field settings. Two groups of field instructors (n=19) participated in the study. Both groups of social work field instructors were affiliated with the same large university faculty of social work which operated on three sites: two urban and one rural. One group was comprised of rural field instructors connected to the rural division (n=9), while the other group involved field instructors associated with the larger of the two urban sites (n=10). Both groups of field instructors had previous supervisory experience with BSW students and operated under the same field education guidelines using the same criteria and objectives as laid out by the Faculty of Social Work. A structured interview schedule that consisted of 37 questions which had been formatted on a 4-point Likert scale was used to collect the data. The interview schedule was pretested, resulting in some minor adjustments in wording in order to ensure clarity. The questionnaire was designed specifically to study and obtain quantitative data on socio-demographic profiles, attitudinal measures regarding social work education and practice, as well as field teaching methods.

Constructs emerging from the literature were used to develop the questionnaire. The constructs were as follows:

a) Training needs — the field instructor's perception of what students need to learn and the kinds of experiences and opportunities they need to have to prepare them for professional practice. Eleven of the 37 questions related to training needs. Examples of some these questions are: *Students need to understand the role of nonprofessionals in the delivery of social services; Students need to be self-directed in this setting; students need opportunities to work with volunteers; Students need opportunities to work with clients from different cultures and ethnic backgrounds; It is important for students to complete a community project in the practicum.*

b) Prepared practitioner — the field instructor's view of the core elements, roles and practices of competent social workers. Eight questions pertained to this construct and included such questions as: *Social work students who have a generalist field experience are better prepared for the profession than students who have specialized in a specific area; The use of natural helpers are important components of practice in this setting; The agency where I work has demands and stressors not found in other practice settings; The problems clients bring to this agency are typical of most social service settings.*

c) Content and methods — the field instructor's opinions about the content addressed in field teaching and the methods used to teach this content. This construct also had to do with the application and integration of theory taught in the classroom with the field practica. Eight questions focused on this area. For example: *The generalist approach to practice is the most useful for field teaching; Social work research is an important aspect of the field education experience; Students receive enough classroom content relevant to the my setting; There is a definite connection between what is being taught in the methods class and what I teach in the field.*

d) Field education — the field instructor's perspective on the relationships between agency and university, field instructors and faculty liaisons, as well as administrative issues regarding field placements. There were 10 questions related to this construct, such as: *The faculty liaison is knowledgeable about and sensitive to the type of social work practices in my setting; I receive sufficient administrative support from my agency to carry out my field education responsibilities; The student has enough time in the practicum; The time and cost for student travel to carry out practicum activities is an issue in field education at my agency.*

Using a purposive sample, 30 field instructors were contacted and given information about the study, its purpose, methodology and ethical considerations, and to invite them to participate in the research. The researchers mailed an informed consent to be signed and questionnaires to be completed to 24 field instructors who consented to participate. In total 19 questionnaires were returned: 10 from urban field instructors and 9 from rural field instructors, giving a total response rate of 79%.

Frequency distributions were used on the demographic information collected and on certain of the demographic variables multiple response analysis was performed. Cross tabulations on the 37 Likert-type scale questions were computed by using SPSS for

Windows. For ease of analysis and because of the limited number of cases it became necessary to combine the 4-Likert scale response categories into two categories: "strongly agree" and "agree" were collapsed into a single "agree" category, while "strongly disagree" and "disagree" became a distinct "disagree" category.

FINDINGS

Demographic information is first presented to provide a picture of the respondents: who they are and what they do; and whether or not there were differences between urban and rural field instructors on the demographic variables. Field instructors' perceptions and opinions of the *training needs* of students including outcomes of social work education; the knowledge, skills and roles of a *prepared practitioner*; the *content and methods* used in field teaching including integration of theory and practice; and, administrative and relationship issues in *field education* are discussed. Differences between rural and urban field instructors on any of those dimensions is also described.

DEMOGRAPHIC INFORMATION ABOUT THE FIELD INSTRUCTORS

Who Are They?

Of the 19 respondents, 10 (53%) were urban field instructors and 9 (47%) were rural field instructors. There was little difference in the mean age of the field instructors and a slightly smaller age range in the rural group. The mean age for both groups was 37 years with a range of 26 to 59 years. The mean age for the urban group was 39.3 years with an age range of 26 to 59 while the mean age of the rural group was 38 with a range of 28 to 52.

Interestingly, there was a marked difference between the two groups by gender. The urban field instructors are female by a ratio of 9 to 1. The rural field instructors are much more balanced with 5 out of 9 field instructors being male (55%). Given the small sample size, it is difficult to draw any conclusions on the basis of gender differences of these two groups but it is an intriguing difference which might entice further investigation.

In terms of educational background of the field instructors there was only a slight difference between the two groups. In the urban group 90% of the field instructors had an MSW or BSW degree with one urban field instructor indicating "other" regarding educational qualifications. In the rural group two-thirds (67%) held an MSW or BSW degree with one-third (33%) indicating "other" regarding educational background. One explanation which may account for this difference is the difficulty rural areas have in attracting professionals with degrees and another explanation may have to do with the fact that there are fewer positions available for degree holders in rural areas.

Table 1   Gender and Educational Background

	Urban (n=10)		Rural (n=9)	
	n	%	n	%
Gender (n=19)				
Female	9	90.0	4	44.4
Male	1	10.0	5	55.6
Education				
MSW	2	20.0	2	22.3
BSW	7	70.0	4	44.4
Other	1	10.0	3	33.3

All of the respondents, except one urban field instructor, worked full time. Only 26% belonged to their professional association and were registered social workers, which is not surprising since both are voluntary in the province of Alberta, Canada. The rates of membership and registration between urban and rural groups were similar with 3 of 10 urban field instructors and 2 of 9 rural field instructors indicating they belonged to the professional association and were registered.

It seems that this group of rural field instructors were seasoned practitioners as no one had less than one year of practice experience with a mean of 7.88 years of experience as compared to their urban counterparts where 4 of 10 field instructors had less than one year post-degree practice experience. Both groups were fairly similar in the years of being a field instructor. Minimally, each group had one respondent who had only been a field instructor for one year. The maximum number of years as a field instructor in the rural group was 9 years as compared to 6 years for the urban group.

Even though rural field instructors may not as often hold social work degrees, they have all worked in social work practice for more than one year and have been field instructors slightly longer on average than their urban counterparts. Generally, both groups of field instructors were quite similar.

Table 2   Age, Years of Social Work Experience, and Years as Field Instructor

| | Urban (n=10) | | | | Rural (n=9) | | | |
	Mean	SD	Min.	Max.	Mean	SD	Min.	Max.
Age	39.3	9.0	26	59	38	7.45	28	52
Social Work Practice Experience	9.11	5.95	4	20	7.89	3.79	0	12
Field Instructor with this Faculty	2.44	1.67	1	6	3.22	2.86	1	9

Table 3   Member of Alberta Association of Social Workers (AASW), Registered Social Worker (RSW)

| | Urban (n=10) | | Rural (n=9) | |
	n	%	n	%
AASW				
Yes	3	30.0	2	22.2
No	7	70.0	7	77.8
RSW				
Yes	3	33.3	2	22.2
No	6	66.7	7	77.8

What Do They Do?

Field instructors were asked to indicate on a check list the roles or functions that were applicable to what they did in their agencies, resulting in multiple responses. The most frequently indicated role by both rural and urban field instructors was *direct service with clients* (83% of all cases, 89% urban and 78% rural). The next most frequently indicated roles by rural field instructors were *community work* and *supervisor (not student)* (each at 56% of the rural cases). *Supervisor (not student)* was also the third most frequently indicated role by urban field instructors (50%) but *community work* according to this group of urban field instructors was listed as their least indicated role (22%). Slightly more rural field instructors indicated they did *research* (33%) than the urban field instructors (22%), while more urban field instructors saw themselves as *agency administrator/management* (56%) than rural field instructors (33%). Thus, there was a marked difference between urban and rural field instructors in their perception of doing community work and fewer rural field instructors viewed themselves in the role of agency administrator.

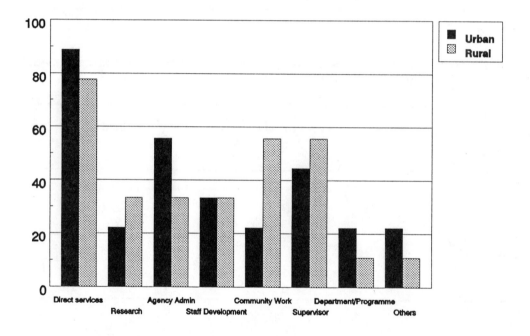

Figure 1   Role or Functions of Field Instructor by Area*

*   Percentage is based on the number of responses. The total number of responses is 56. Urban: 28 responses; Rural: 28 responses.

Data was also collected on the type of services provided by the agencies where the field instructors were employed. The field instructors indicated on a check list as many types of services as applicable, resulting in multiple responses. Most services provided by both groups of field instructors fell into the category of *personal social services* (63% overall, 60% urban and 67% rural). *Community development* was the next most frequently indicated service provided by the agencies employing rural field instructors (44%) but it was amongst the least offered of the services in the agencies where the urban social workers worked (10%). The other types of services provided by the rural group were slightly different according to the respondents as 44% were involved in *health* compared to 20% in the urban group and 33% were involved in *education* compared to 10% in the urban group. Least offered in both groups was *social planning and policy* and *justice/corrections*. No conclusions can be drawn regarding this information because the sample size is so small but it does describe differences in the types of services, particularly in community development, provided by this group of rural and urban field instructors.

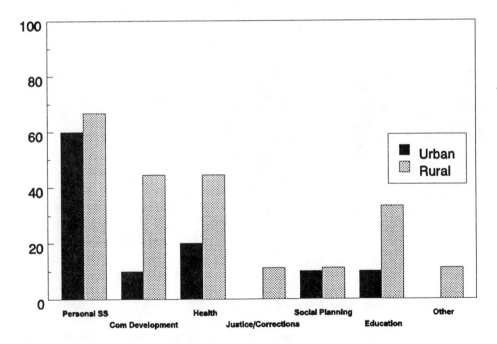

Figure 2 Services Provided by Agency by Area*

*   Percentage is based on the number of responses. The total number of responses is 31. Urban: 11 responses; Rural: 20 responses.

An indepth examination of the category of personal social services was done to see who the clients being served were and whether there were any differences in the client groups being served by urban or rural workers. Interestingly, none of the urban field instructors indicated they served the elderly with services to children/adolescents, adults, and families equally represented. The rural field instructors delivered most of their services to both adults and families, next most often they served children/adolescents, and least, but still represented, they served the elderly.

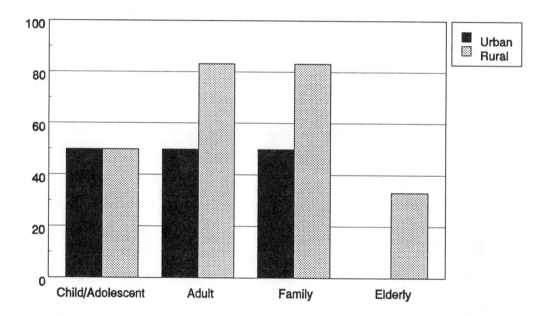

Figure 3   Client Group Served by Agency by Area*

*   Percentage is based on the number of responses. The total number of responses is 24. Urban: 9 responses; Rural: 15 responses.

The demographic information collected showed few differences between rural and urban field instructors overall. The differences that did emerge were noteworthy: the difference in the gender balance between the two groups of field instructors; the difference in the time spent in the role of community worker; and, in the amount of community development.

SIMILARITIES AND DIFFERENCES OF OPINION

Training Needs

Questions were developed to examine field instructors' perceptions and opinions about what students needed to learn in the practicum. They were asked about the types of learning opportunities they believed were important for students to experience as part of the field placement. None of the questions showed any considerable differences between the urban and rural groups of field instructors. In most cases there was a high degree of consensus particularly around students understanding the norms of the community, the role of the nonprofessional, having knowledge of community resources, students being aware of their image in the community, and that there were sufficient opportunities in the agency for students to learn social work practice.

Some slight differences showed up on specific questions such as, *I find that students need to be more self-directed when working in my agency* where 100% of the rural field instructors and 80% of the urban field instructors agreed with this statement. In a similar vein rural field instructors were unanimous in their agreement with the statement, *Students need to be aware of the impact of local organizations such as churches and service clubs,* while 70% of urban field instructors agreed. In both of these instances the trend on the urban side was to agree with the statement but not to the same extent as the rural field instructors. One other example of a slight difference had to do with home visits where close to 80% of rural field instructors viewed it as integral to the students field experience versus 60% of the urban field instructors seeing it that way.

Urban and rural field instructors were equally split on their opinion regarding the need for students to work with volunteers (53% agree and 47% disagree). They were also similar in their opinions about the importance of students completing a community project as part of the practicum in that the same number of field instructors from both groups (74% in total) agreed it was important.

The most interesting finding under the heading of training needs and one that begs for further enquiry was the consensus from both groups of field instructors regarding the importance for students to have opportunities to work with clients from different cultures and ethnic backgrounds. Almost all field instructors (95%) *disagreed* with the statement indicating they did not believe it was important that students have opportunities to work with those from different cultural or ethnic groups. This finding is surprising in light of the recent attention to multicultural issues but may be understood in the context of the populations served by the agencies involved in this research. It may be that those participating in the study simply did not serve diverse cultural groups by virtue of geography or the nature of services provided and therefore did not see it as an important part of the students' practicum experience in that setting.

Prepared Practitioner

Field instructors' views of the prepared practitioner reflected less consistency than their opinions about training needs but overall there appeared to be a fair amount of agreement between urban and rural field instructors. For example, they both agreed that a generalist field experience better prepared students for professional practice (89% rural, 70% urban) and that social workers needed to be more creative to work in their setting (100% rural, 80% urban) with slightly more agreement by rural field instructors. They also both disagreed that rural practitioners were disadvantaged with slightly more rural field instructors agreeing with the statement (22% rural, 10% urban).

All of the urban field instructors and two-thirds of the rural field instructors agreed that it was important for social workers to practice autonomously. All of the rural field instructors and 60% of the urban field instructors agreed that the problems clients bring were typical of most social service settings. It could be that urban settings tended to deal with specific problems and were more specialized possibly requiring more autonomy whereas in rural areas the agencies had to deal with a broad range of problems that were more typical and leave less room for autonomous practice.

Urban and rural field instructors were evenly split in their opinion that their clients were knowledgeable about how a social worker could assist them (47% agree, 53% disagree) and they were similar in their views of their agency as a practice setting with demands and stressors not found elsewhere (74% agree, 26% disagree).

Contents and Methods

With regard to the content of field teaching, the methods used by field instructors to deliver that content and field instructors perception of the courses students take at the university, there was a considerable degree of agreement between the urban and rural field instructors. There was 100% agreement that value issues were important in teaching in the field setting and almost 95% of all field instructors agreed that students have opportunities to test a range of practice theories. Both rural and urban field instructors agreed that the generalist approach was the most useful for teaching in the field setting and that the community development aspect of practice was important but not to the same extent, in that all rural field instructors agreed with these two items, while only 70% of urban field instructors agreed. This difference was not surprising given the nature of rural practice.

Several items highlight very useful findings that the Faculty needs to pay attention to and investigate further. Only 30% of the urban field instructors and 11% of the rural field instructors agreed that research was an important aspect of the field education experience. It could be that field instructors viewed "research" in a narrow way that might not include such activities as program or practice evaluation or effectiveness and outcome studies that might be considered appropriate types of research to be included in the practicum. It was also not surprising that fewer rural than urban field instructors regarded research in field education as important. Another item of concern had to do with the finding that all the rural field instructors and 70% of the urban field instructors *disagreed* with the statement that there was a connection between what is taught in methods class and what is taught in the field. In this case fewer rural than urban field instructors saw the connection. Related to this was the finding that almost 90% of all the field instructors *disagreed* that students were able to apply the content of their social work courses to practice situations. Both groups of field instructors were evenly split in their opinion about students receiving enough classroom content relevant to their setting (58% agree, 42% disagree). The researchers would have expected that this finding would be consistent with the above two findings and are not sure how to account for the difference in opinion: field instructors did not agree there was a connection between what was taught in the classroom and the field, they did not think students were able to apply the content of courses to practice situations but they were ambiguous about the relevance of the classroom content to their setting.

Field Education

In considering some of the administrative and procedural issues regarding field education there were two items where there was a clear and distinct difference between the views of urban and rural field instructors. Seventy-eight percent of rural field instructors compared to 30% of urban field instructors reported that they believed the time and cost for student travel to carry out practicum activities was a major concern. Given the nature of rural practice and the distances involved in delivering services this stance was not surprising. Of more curiosity perhaps was the finding that 60% of the urban field instructors in contrast to 11% of the rural field instructors agreed that at times they questioned whether the faculty have sufficient knowledge of what was happening in the context where they worked. This response could be interpreted in one of two ways: either that rural field instructors did not question whether faculty had sufficient knowledge because they knew they didn't or because it was simply not something they questioned. What is important is that this is one of the few items where there was this degree of disagreement between rural and urban field instructors.

This sample of field instructors were similar in their views that the faculty liaisons were *not* seen as knowledgeable about and sensitive to practice in their settings and were *not* considered competent to assist field instructors in the field education process. Field instructors also agreed that they did *not* receive sufficient support from their agencies to carry out field education responsibilities. Findings like these are important for the Faculty to take note of and investigate further.

Other areas of agreement between the two groups of field instructors included their opinion that there was enough time in the practicum for students to appreciate the unique characteristics and structure of the setting (95% agree), and that there were unique and distinct challenges to providing quality field education in their setting (100%). They were also unanimous in their opinion that it was *not* important that adequate office resources be available for the student to ensure quality field education.

SUMMARY AND CONCLUSIONS

The results of this research support previous findings in the rural/urban debate. Even though both groups primarily provided personal social services to their client base it is very evident that the roles of the rural field instructors were far more weighted in the area of community development than was the case for the urban professionals. This finding provides the basis for the rural instructors to be very concerned about the cost of travel for their students which was not the case for the urban group; therefore, reinforcing data from past studies that rural social work involves covering large geographic catchment areas. The results also support Patchner and Sattazahn's (1991) work whereby both groups of instructors agreed on the general learning needs of the social work students in their field training. Despite a small difference, the rural social workers supported the importance of the generalist model of training more than did their urban counterparts. In general, the study results lend further support to the more recent research findings that there is not a large difference between rural and urban social workers.

Perhaps, as a different approach, it is more important to consider areas of agreement and the significance for the urban based universities. This study demonstrated far more agreement than disagreement and as a result it may be more useful to be supporting and building upon likeness as opposed to difference. Despite agreement on general generalist goals for the training of the students a disturbing component emerged. Both groups of respondents did not place much emphasis on the need for students to be exposed to peoples from other cultures. This result is surprising due to the large coverage of this subject area receives in the popular press and the general acknowledgement for students to have this knowledge in the academic settings. The problem may be that students are not receiving sufficient classroom instruction on multi-culturalism and thereby do not request of the field instructor that their training caseload include people from different cultures.

Another area of agreement between rural and urban field instructors is the general lack of support for the importance of research in the training of social workers. Given the increasing importance for social workers to be critical consumers of the vast amount of clinical research in the public domain it is imperative they be able to utilize the knowledge gleaned from outcome studies. Further, research methods in program evaluation regarding the efficacy of one's own practice as well as agency goals and objectives is, given the current socio-economic conditions, fast becoming a primary skill for social work. It may be that the field instructors' definitions of research are vastly different from those of the academic faculty; therefore, suggesting a serious sharing of information gap that has yet to be addressed.

The results of this study have raised some concerns about the relationship between the field and what is taught in the classroom. The identified gap is not unique to professional faculties, and remains to be an issue that needs constant attention and evaluation. The fact that urban and rural field instructors have consensus provides an excellent opportunity for the urban based program to bring all the constituencies together with the purpose of seeking solutions. Further, it may be helpful if more effort is placed on ensuring that senior agency personnel completely understand the time requirements and roles of their staff when they become field instructors. Only after being satisfied that the agency will support the field instructors should faculty begin the process of working with the instructors.

The results of the study have pointed out more similarities than differences between urban and rural field instructors. Generally, the field instructors have the goal of providing opportunities for learning that will contribute to the graduation of competent entry-level social workers. It is incumbent upon faculties of social work to move away from only considering difference but to analyze those areas where field instructors from urban and rural contexts have agreement. It is important to recognize that the small number of respondents in this study limit the generalizability of the results to other training centers. The intent of this exploratory study was to begin to analyze a different set of roles of professional social workers which had not been previously presented in the urban and rural literature.

REFERENCES

Bogal-Allbritten, R., & Daughaday, L. (1990). Spouse abuse program services: A rural urban comparison. *Human Services in the Rural Environment, 14*(2), 6-10.

Cole, W. (1981). Training social workers for rural areas. In E. Martinez-Brawley (Ed.), *Seven decades of rural social work: From country life commission to rural caucus* (pp. 170-176). New York: Praeger.

Collier, K. (1984). *Social work with rural peoples: Theory and practice.* Vancouver: New Star Books.

Craft, J., & Staudt, M. (1991). Reporting and finding of child neglect in urban and rural communities. *Child Welfare, 70*(3), 359-370.

DeWeaver, K. (1988). Has social work education abandoned preparation for a rural practice? *Human Services in the Rural Environment, 11*(4), 28-32.

Fitzpatrick, J., Edwards, R., & Olszewski, C. (1980). Job priorities of rural services workers: Implications for training and practice. *Arete, 6*(4), 35-44.

Gitterman, A. (1989). Field instruction in social work education: Issues, tasks and skills. *Clinical Supervisor, 7*(4), 77-91.

Hardcastle, D. (1985). Rural stereotypes and professional caregivers. *Arete, 10*(2), 26-33.

Hoffman, K., & Sallee, A. (1987). *Linking practice skills for the rural and urban poor.* Unpublished manuscript.

Horner, B., & O'Neill, J. (1981). Child welfare practice in small communities. *Human Services in the Rural Environment, 6*(3-4), 16-23.

Jankovic, J. (1981). Issues in rural child welfare. *Human Services in the Rural Environment, 6*(3-4), 4-7.

Jones, L. (1981). *Distinctive features of mid-west rural poverty: Implications for social work practice.* Unpublished manuscript.

Kropf, N., Lindsey, E., & Carse-McLocklin, S. (1993). The eligibility worker role in public welfare: Worker and client perceptions. *Arete, 18*(1), 34-42.

Martinez-Brawley, E. (1986). Issues in alternative social work education: Observations from a Canadian program with a rural mandate. *Arete, 11*(1), 54-64.

McKay, S. (1987). Social work and Canada's north: Survival and development issues affecting aboriginal and industry-based communities. *International Social Work, 30*(3), 259-278.

Nisivoccia, D. (1990). Teaching and learning tasks in the beginning phase of field education. *The Clinical Supervisor*, *8*(1), 7-22.

Patchner, M., & Sattazahn, D. (1991). Social work field instructors: A rural and urban comparison. *Human Services in the Rural Environment*, *15*(2), 16-20.

Tarleau, A. (1981). Rural child welfare: Education and practice issues. *Human Services in the Rural Environment*, *6*(3-4), 9-15.

Twente, E. (1980). Social casework in rural communities. In E. Martinez-Brawley (Ed.), *Pioneer efforts in rural social welfare: First hand news since 1908* (pp. 289-297). Pennsylvania: Pennsylvania State University.

Waltman, G. (1986). Mainstreet revisited: Social work practice in rural areas. *Social Casework*, *67*(8), 466-474.

Whitaker, W. (1985). A survey of perception of social work practice in rural and urban areas. *Human Services in the Rural Environment*, *9*(3), 12-19.

Whittington, B. (1985). The challenge of family work in a rural community. *The Social Worker*, *53*(3), 104-111.

York, R., Denton, R., & Moran, J. (1989). Rural and urban social work practice: Is there a difference? *Social Case Work: The Journal of Contemporary Social Work*, *7*(4), 201-209.

CHAPTER TWENTY-SIX

THE ANXIETY OF CHANGE: NARCISSISTIC DEVELOPMENT OF SOCIAL WORK INTERNS AT A FIELD PLACEMENT IN DISTRESS

Emeline Homonoff, Arlene Weintraub, Sonia Michelson and Nancy Costikyan

The anxiety of change is central to the experience of social work trainees. Appropriate levels of anxiety can challenge interns to progress from an initial grandiose conception of themselves as all-knowing and all-loving to a more realistic professional ego ideal. This progress depends on a supervisory relationship which offers the intern both encouragement and opportunity to idealize the field instructor (Brightman, 1984). If the agency used as a field placement is itself experiencing the anxiety of change, this kind of supervisory relationship is very difficult to sustain. This chapter describes the efforts of a training director, field instructors and a field liaison from a school of social work to maintain an optimal environment for social work interns' learning in an agency in the throes of organizational upheaval.

OPTIMAL NARCISSISTIC DEVELOPMENT OF THE TRAINEE

Brightman (1984) describes the manner in which anxiety fuels the trainee's progression from an archaic grandiose professional self to a more realistic professional ego ideal. Interns begin their training with a grandiose wish to become omniscient, benevolent and omnipotent. As the intern confronts the shattering realities of clinical practice, a secure supervisory relationship is crucial to support the process of mourning, modification and eventual reintegration of the intern's ego ideal. Field instructors provide mirroring by showing pride in interns' accomplishments and empathy with their stress and confusion. In addition, field instructors, through their competence and enthusiasm, become idealized figures for their interns; through gradual non-traumatic disappointments this idealized parental image becomes transformed into a more modest and flexible professional ego ideal.

THE CHALLENGE OF A FIELD PLACEMENT IN CRISIS

Field agencies may have difficulty maintaining a holding environment which manages interns' anxiety when the agencies' staff are experiencing their own anxiety over change. Federal and State cutbacks in funding for mental health and social services have recently forced many agencies to take a number of measures for survival. One common strategy is for a smaller agency to ally with a larger organization, "trading some autonomy for increased financial stability" (Gopelrud, p. 74). In these "capture-surrender" mergers, considerable friction may be generated between the two agencies because of differences in history, values, service practices, fiscal management and personnel policies, governance structures and/or community relations approaches (O'Brien & Collier, 1991). The merger of one community mental health center which had long been used as a field placement for Boston area schools of social work was fraught with such tension. The smaller agency, which we will call the Jonah Clinic, had an excellent reputation as a treatment and training center; in addition to its other programs, it took special pride in its commitment to psychotherapy. In contrast, the larger agency, which we will call Whole Health and Life Experience (or WHALE), focused on community program development, outreach and case management. The staff of the Jonah Clinic was united by a strong sense of personal commitment and responsibility, whereas WHALE required more formal and impersonal internal and external accountability to unite its myriad loosely-connected units. As O'Brien & Collier (1991, p.23) state:

> Overcoming historical differences can be a major obstacle to a successful merger. When people are confronted abruptly by a new perspective, they often become even more steadfast in their determination to hold on to the old ways.

Without adequate time, money or incentive to implement the merger successfully, integration was felt by the Jonah Clinic to be forced. Experiencing considerable anxiety, uncertainty and disenfranchisement, the staff began to question their future at the agency. The crisis of the clinic posed a serious threat to the training program. The commitment of the agency to training, and the ability of interns to withstand organizational stress, could not be taken for granted. The morale of field instructors needed to be bolstered in order for them to foster optimal narcissistic development in their interns. Disruption of agency procedures, as well as pressures for increased service to increasingly difficult clients, made choice of appropriate cases for interns difficult. Although group process can neutralize interns' anxiety about agency changes and modulate the interns' idealization of their field instructors, treatment teams required extra support to meet this need. Finally, the school of social work sought to address these issues of organizational change in its curriculum. In each of these areas, the training director, field instructors and field liaison from the school of social work expanded their traditional roles to support the training program.

AVOIDING THE "PROFESSIONAL COMMITMENT FALLACY"

Most social work schools hope that the relationships they establish with agencies as placements for interns will endure indefinitely. However, Frumkin (1980) questions the assumption — which he calls the "professional commitment fallacy" — that social service agencies will altruistically subordinate their own fiscal needs to their ethical obligation to provide training for future professionals. Especially in times of resources scarcity, the expense to agencies of training interns may seem overwhelming. Although the Jonah Clinic had trained social workers for over twenty years, the field liaison did not take it for granted that it would be able to continue indefinitely. She met with the training director to assess the ability of the agency's field instructors to give "one last try" for the interns. In addition to procuring the basic necessities — like office space and telephones — for the interns, the training director also reinstituted the teams that had been disbanded in the merger, and made arrangements for a training seminar at a nearby hospital.

MATCH OF INTERNS AND AGENCY

In times of fiscal cutbacks, managed care and increased accountability, many agencies are now requiring experienced, mature social work interns (Bocage, Homonoff, & Riley, 1994). For this reason, the field education department of the School of Social Work instituted an earlier and more intensive placement process to ensure a proper match between interns and field placements. Both first- and second-year interns are individually interviewed by staff of the field education department to assess their abilities as well as their wishes for placement. The team of field liaisons responsible for matching interns and placements is given complete information on the current status of each agency as well as on each intern. The placement process is begun early enough to leave time for interns to be interviewed by prospective placements. In the case of the Jonah Clinic, the field education department made sure to send prospective interns with considerable experience, whom the training director and potential field instructors interviewed in depth.

BOOSTING MORALE

The crisis in the Jonah Clinic caused constant frustration for field instructors in their efforts to support interns and to present themselves as figures for idealization. Traditional procedures were overridden and new directives issued daily, and staff were leaving in droves. The experience of rapid changes in the agency's physical plant exemplified the sense that the agency was falling part.

> Because one of the buildings which had housed the Jonah Clinic was being converted to space for a residential program, workers never knew what chaos to expect. Large puddles would appear in the halls; two-by-fours would be hauled outside windows of therapy offices. The kitchen, which for years had served as a "family space" for staff, was demolished. One day staff arrived to find that, since the locks had been changed, they could not gain entrance to their offices.

The ensuing demoralization could have seriously threatened the supervisory process. As Brightman (1984, p. 309) notes:

> It was particularly important to . . . trainees that their supervisors should be enthusiastic about their work as therapists, should see it as valuable and take it seriously, and should have faith in its effectiveness. Evidence of apathy, cynicism or pessimism in the supervisor tends to interfere with an identification by the trainee; if an identification had begun, the appearance of such sentiments could provoke strong disappointment and doubt.

To maintain morale, the training director carefully polled staff to ascertain their willingness to supervise one more year, and held regular support meetings with field instructors.

SELECTION OF INTERN CASES

Normal developmental disillusionment in the grandiose professional self depends on optimal challenge in the therapeutic work — just enough to stretch the trainee's ability and not so much as to mobilize defenses. However, selection of proper training cases for interns is more and more difficult as clients present with increasingly severe problems and increasingly fewer resources (Bocage et al., 1994). In addition, procedural changes can wreak havoc with case assignment. For example, before the merger a special intake department had carefully chosen appropriate intern cases; when this department was abolished, problems in assignment were more frequent.

> An intern complained to her field instructor that she had been assigned a new client who was the brother of a client she was seeing in treatment. The training director intervened to protect the interests of both the client and the intern by sharing with the new intake worker her grave concerns about the ethical conflicts involved in the assignment.

THE SUPERVISORY PROCESS

For the most part, field instructors were able to help interns manage the narcissistic vulnerability of the novice role. The interns became used to riding the "narcissistic roller coaster"; as one, Nancy C., wrote in her log for her clinical practice course:

> For a while I have been wondering if my comfort level and sense of competence derive entirely from my work with my clients — i.e., when I have a "good" session I feel good about myself, and when I have a "not good" session I feel worse about myself. I keep feeling this inner anguish about not having enough to give my clients.

This intern was supported throughout the vicissitudes of her training as her field instructor, Nancy W., demonstrated understanding of an intern's anxiety and offered constant encouragement.

> Nancy W. left a note in Nancy C.'s mailbox saying, "I was moved by your account of your interview. Your client can be very difficult, and you have done a wonderful job with her. She is fortunate to have you." Nancy C. carried the note in her appointment book all year.

Nancy C. experienced perhaps more disillusionment than was optimal; Nancy W. was absent not only for her vacation but also with an extended bout of pneumonia. Nevertheless, Nancy C. was able to maintain the connection by identifying with her field instructor; as she wrote in her log:

> Nancy is on vacation this week. She is presenting a paper in California on the use of ritual in psychotherapy. She is the "big Nancy" and I am the "little Nancy" left behind to manage on my own . . . I found myself expressing the internalized Nancy W. by talking with a client about using ritual to mark the imminent death of a loved one.

THE ROLE OF THE FIELD LIAISON

The combination of low agency morale and excessive clinical challenge occasionally put a strain on the supervisory relationship. Lynch (1987, pp. 100, 103, 106) describes the "parallel process" that can occur in the supervision of a trainee treating a suicidal client:

> The trainee searches for ongoing validation from both patients and supervisors that he or she is indeed caring and compassionate and can indeed heal all, know all, and love all. When confronted with evidence to the contrary, the trainee may respond in a range of ways: feeling depressed, worthless, rageful, etc. . . . The trainee is in a form of crisis, too, a narcissistically based crisis. The patient's hateful transferences are often . . . experienced as confirmation of the trainee's worst fears about himself or herself . . . The trainee who is in the midst of a transference/countertransference storm with a patient often . . . reenacts with the supervisor (through unconscious acts and behaviors) some of the very same things which the patient is doing to the trainee in the treatment sessions.

When field instructors' stress prevents them from using the parallel process as an opportunity for the intern's learning, the training director or field liaison can step in to put the supervisory relationship back on track. The following is an example of the kind of crisis intervention the field liaison might offer to interns and staff:

> An intern had been assigned a client at risk for suicide. The client indicated to the intern that he needed immediate answers from her in order to save him. The anxious intern then began to demand immediate answers from her field instructor, who became more and more frustrated. The situation was exacerbated by the recent reduction in psychiatric backup for the agency. The field liaison met frequently with the field instructor and intern, both individually and jointly, to offer support and some explanation of parallel process. She also emphasized the importance of establishing a clear chain of command in emergency situations, so that the intern and field instructor would not feel solely responsible for a potentially suicidal client.

GROUP PROCESS

Group process is indispensable in modifying interns' grandiose aspirations for themselves and idealized images of their field instructors. In teams, intern support groups, or seminars, the group protects interns from the narcissistic injuries of training and helps them explore their professional ideals. In addition, interns can observe the struggles and human failings of their mentors, and learn from exposure to several different perspectives (Weber, Costikyan, Fales, & Morgan, 1994). Unfortunately, exposure to dysfunctional group process can create too profound a disillusionment for interns. For example interns at the Jonah Clinic were dismayed at how interprofessional collaboration on teams was undermined by repeated agency crises.

> Since their hours had been drastically reduced during agency cutbacks, remaining psychiatrists were under pressure to concentrate their services on the most disturbed patients, and to put diagnostic consultations on hold. As a result, social workers and interns had to maintain fragile clients while awaiting psychiatric evaluation. The lack of medical and psychiatric backup occasionally led to deficiencies in client care which were extremely distressing.

Conversely, positive experiences in groups helped the interns survive the disillusionment of seeing the agency in disarray. Most teams dealt with the anxiety of change by an "interactive playfulness" that allowed adaptive contagion and amplification of affect (Weber et al., 1994).

> Although the treatment teams had been reinstated, all members knew that this would be the final year for teams. The training director's team found emotional survival by using "gallows humor": each crisis and disappointment was met with more and more outrageous jokes.

At the same time, the training director offered groups for interns and staff to reflect on the agency's crisis, to validate their feelings of confusion and anger, and to offer a positive role model for managing change. As another intern wrote in her final evaluation:

> One of the hardest experiences I have been through was being affected by what seemed to be a devaluing approach towards my profession. It was suggested that long-term psychotherapy is not helpful. Having my identity in the process of forming made it hard for me not to take some of that in. At one point I was asking myself: Am I in the wrong field and clearly in the wrong school? It was then very helpful to be able to process those feelings, and got some reassurances. The training director was always willing to explain to us what was going on. She especially helped us students to deal with the painful termination process we had to go through with our clients not knowing if they would be picked up in the future or not. I looked at her as a role model in terms of the way she handled the changes in the agency. She continued to care and protect us students in time when the message from the director was that students are not high priority. I was especially amazed how the training director was always able to deal with matters in a professional way. And always in good taste. I

feel that I am going to remember that next time I face such a situation with authority.

THE SOCIAL WORK CURRICULUM AND ORGANIZATIONAL CHANGE

The School of Social Work can offer another forum for interns to manage the anxiety of learning in a crisis-ridden agency environment. Group meetings with the field liaison permit interns to share their agency experiences and to learn new ways to deal with change and stress. However, the School of Social Work found that students needed to learn more formally about organizational change in order not to feel totally destabilized or disillusioned. Content on organizational analysis and change was introduced in several courses, but especially in the second year course — called "Clinical Work with Larger Systems: Transitions to Practice" — for which the field liaison for the Jonah Clinic taught one section. In contrast to the Jonah Clinic experience, this class offered suggestions for the optimal handling of organizational change, including motivating staff to overcome resistance, developing power centers to support change, and putting structures into place to manage the transition (Nadler, 1981). Students came to understand that the same conditions that allowed them as interns to master the narcissistic threats inherent in growth and learning could allow staff of organizations to adapt to rapid, discontinuous change; Schein (1993, p. 89) describes those conditions as:

> Opportunities for training and practice, support and encouragement to overcome the fear and shame of making errors, coaching and rewards for efforts in the right direction, norms that legitimize the making of errors, and norms that reward innovative thinking and experimentation.

INTERNS' REALISTIC PROFESSIONAL EGO IDEALS

Brightman (1984, p. 314) describes the more realistic and flexible professional ego ideal that evolves by the end of the training experience:

> As the conditions upon which their self-esteem depends becomes less idealized and restrictive, trainees will be able to contain an ever-increasing range of experience, in both the treatment and supervisory settings, without narcissistic threat. This process is often signaled by a shift in the trainee's manner of describing their (sic) patients in the direction of a more literary and multidimensional portrayal of the complexity of a human life.

This mature and flexible view is expressed by Nancy's self-evaluation at the end of the year. Remembering an instance in which she felt she had disappointed her client at the time of her vacation, Nancy wrote:

> I remember feeling crummy that I had fulfilled her transferential expectations of abandonment, crummy that by almost crying I appeared to be turning into a sniveling fool, crummy that I had further failed my weeping client by having only one Kleenex left which she, of course, carefully tore in half to share with me.

Nancy went on to understand the limits of her role with clients.

> It took a series of "failures" with my clients to look at my need not to fail them, and to free me to be less cautious, or perhaps more respectful of their resilience. And it feels a bit like stepping off the narcissistic roller coaster. After all, if I can respect my clients' capacity to tolerate doing the therapy with me, and if I can respect their capacity to do without me, it brings me more rightfully into the background and them into the foreground. I become less primary and more instrumental. I need to acknowledge that I am important to my clients, but I can't let that paralyze me. And I need to realize that I'm not as important as I think I am--or perhaps as I would like to be.

Brightman (1984, p. 314) goes on to describe the mature professional ego ideal within the supervisory relationship:

> As trainees develop a more stable and internal sense of being good enough, they will become less concerned with maintaining the supervisor's approval, and be able to relate to the supervisor as a hopefully useful but less formidable figure.

A student from another school of social work wrote:

> By the end of the year I am leaving behind the uncertainty whether I can be a therapist and I am feeling more and more like I am actually a successful therapist . . . In addition, feeling more self-assured about my professional identity made it easier for me to express my own opinions. It especially helped me to disagree with authority figures.

RESTORING THE PROFESSIONAL EGO IDEAL OF STAFF

The successful efforts to support training in a year of crisis had unexpected benefits. During the merger, staff of the mental health center had become embittered and demoralized. However, they had put their best efforts into training the "last class" of interns, and they felt that it was a special year. As one field instructor put it:

> For me, there was a poignant pressure in this last year of supervision. It was a "last hurrah" for the Jonah Clinic as I knew it and there was little time to make a good ending. While I felt that the clinic was hurtling towards death, I also felt the imperative to do what I could so that we could end whole and in adequate control. I knew this experience would never be replicated; what was different was the unrelenting wish to embody the clinic into the supervisory work. I was a product of Jonah training myself, connected to the life of the clinic and committed to its high standards of practice. As hard as times were, this was also the year to deliver the best of Jonah, even to try to make up for its imperfections. I wanted this year to end with pride and to be able to remember that I was a conduit for passing on the best of our history. After all, there would not be another chance.

The interns responded to this special effort with gratitude. The final goodbye party for the interns was particularly poignant, since most of the field instructors were leaving along with their interns. During this termination, the interns gave back to their field instructors the empathy and support that they had experienced. The interns presented the training director with a plaque that read:

> To A. W.,
> Jonah Training Institute,
> With appreciation for your faithful support and commitment
> From the Last Batch: the Interns of 1992.

The staff acknowledged that encouraging and mentoring social work interns had reaffirmed their own faith in their work, had restored their own bruised ego ideals, and had given them a feeling of hope and pride in producing a new generation of competent social workers.

REFERENCES

Bocage, M., Homonoff, E., & Riley, P. (1994). Measuring the impact of the current state and national fiscal crisis on human service agencies and social work training. Accepted for publication in *Social Work.*

Brightman, B. (1984). Narcissistic issues in the training experience of the psychotherapist. *International Journal of Psychoanalytic Psychotherapy, 10,* 393-417.

Frumkin, M. (1980). Social work education are the professional commitment fallacy: A practical guide to field-school relationships. *Journal of Education for Social Work, 16* (2), 91-99.

Gopelrud, E., Walfish, S., & Apsey, M. (1983). Surviving cutbacks in mental health: 77 action strategies. *Community Mental Health Journal, 19*(1), 62-76.

Lynch, V. (1987). Supervising the trainee what treats the chronically suicidal outpatient: Theoretical perspectives and practice approaches. *Clinical Supervisor, 5*(1), 99-110.

Miller, E., & Rice, A. K. (1975). Systems of organization: A conceptual framework. In A. Coleman & W. Bexton (Eds.), *Group relations reader*. Sausalito, CA: GREX.

Nadler, D. (1981). Managing organizational change: An integrative perspective. *Journal of Applied Behavioral Science, 17*(2), 191-211.

O'Brien, J., & Collier, P. (1991). Merger problems for human service agencies: A case study. *Administration in Social Work, 15*(3), 19-31.

Schein, E. (1993). How can organizations learn faster? The challenge of entry into the green room. *Sloan Management Review*, 85-92.

Weber, R., Costikyan, N., Fales, H., & Morgan, S. (1994). An observation and group dynamics model for teaching psychoanalytic psychotherapy. *Academic Psychiatry*, in press.

CHAPTER TWENTY-SEVEN

STUDENT EMPOWERMENT: MODELS FOR THE PRACTICUM PLACEMENT PROCESS

Joan Feyrer and Walene Whitaker

BACKGROUND

In 1984 the programs of the School of Social Work at the University of Victoria were expanding. More students were being admitted into the on-campus program, more students were choosing part-time studies, and more students were entering the distance education program. Adherence to an adult education model legitimized students' demands for more autonomy. All of these factors required more administrative resources in a time of recession. At the same time, computer technology was becoming more available.

With the increasing number of students, the field coordinator's ability to recall interest, availability, and characteristics of each student and agency reached a critical mass. The choices were to free the students to find their own placements, to designate the placements, or to move to some combination of the two. Several models were developed using a computer to provide information on the pool of agency placements available. This paper describes and discusses these models, and then looks at the advantages and disadvantages of each.

The first model is one in which the school matches the student with a placement (The-School-Matches-Model). This match may involve a veto from either student or agency. The second model is one in which the school makes several choices of agency interviews for each student (The-School-Chooses-Interviews-Model). Following interviews, both students and agencies rank their choice of placement, and a match takes place. In the third model, students choose several agencies from a pool of vetted placements (The-Students-Choose-Interviews-Model). Agencies and students interview each other, rank their choices, and a match is made. The fourth model is one in which students find their own placements with veto power from the school (The-Students-Choose-Placement-Model). The School of Social Work at the University of Victoria has used all four models in the placement process. Although this chapter emphasizes the field coordinator's and student's role in the placement process, agencies are also partners in the placement process.

OVERVIEW OF THE PLACEMENT PROCESS

Social work literature documents the struggles of field staff in its attempt to identify, standardize and prioritize the many variables involved in placement decisions (Brownstein, 1981). The field coordination staff must balance learning needs of individual students, agencies' expectations, and the university's administrative interest in an expedient process which satisfies everyone. Field coordination departments can get caught in an avalanche of paper as they attempt to remember every nuance of possibility and to satisfy multiple needs and to deal with the high volume of material which is involved in the placement process. The underlying assumption is if only field staff knew more or could identify the critical variables, they would make the right placement choices for students. All the models to be described have the following features which are common to most placement processes:

- Student completes needs assessment;
- Field education staff develops a pool of agency contracts;
- Student attends preplacement interviews;
- Student and agency matched on basis of choice.

Some considerations throughout this process are:

> How much control is exercised by the school, the student, and the agency? How is information about agencies shared with students and information about students shared with agencies? . . . What procedures characterize the exchange between the student, agency and school in making a placement (e.g., preplacement interviews, field fairs, the existence of student stipends, etc.)? (Grossman, 1991, p. 38)

Needs Assessment

The placement process generally begins with students completing a needs-and-interests-assessment form. Students may also submit a resume emphasizing volunteer and paid social service experience, as well as life experience. Students can be encouraged to be quite specific in their needs assessment, and to suggest new agency possibilities. Completion of a needs assessment is particularly important for students who have not previously been accustomed to articulating their learning needs.

Developing the Pool: Using a Computer

In order for a school to build a pool of agency placements, accurate and complete information is required from agencies. The use of a contract (in which agency supervisors spell out the tasks and responsibilities they would have a student undertake) facilitates consistent, comparable information. The ability to choose appropriate placements is governed by the reliability of the information available. This information can then be placed in a computerized data base. A computer program which can sort material by categories greatly enhances the placement process.

However, using a computer requires the time for someone to input a high volume of data often by a deadline. Additional changes required in the computer program may require a third party outside of a school of social work. This can cost a great deal, and may meed time and expertise from the field coordinator to articulate the changes required. Changes to software are slow and may be impossible. In most cases one must live with the original program and accept the idiosyncrasies that become built in.

Pre-placement Interviews

The conducting of one or more interview is usually an integral part of a placement process.

> The tradition of interviews is compatible with a market in which there are both
> many choices and many choosers; lots of supply and lots of demand.
> (Grossman, 1991, p. 44)

Pre-placement interviews are also compatible with a market in which there is a shortage of agencies. Agencies want choice, or at least veto power. Interviews provide opportunities for both students and agencies to find out about each other. Students' knowledge of agencies will depend on the accuracy of the information they are able to obtain. This information can come from the school, other students, and/or students' own experience. Examples are contract proposals, evaluations, field fairs, and volunteer or work experience. Pre-placement interviews may also provide students with information about future practicum placements, job possibilities or community resources.

If more than one student is interviewed for a single placement, competition enters the process. This may be similar to what students will experience when they go job-hunting. However, this similarity can be confusing both for agencies and for students, especially if students are encouraged to try a new field for their practicum. Students not only have to sell themselves, but also must interview agencies for a good fit with their learning needs. Although practicum is supposed to be an educational experience, agencies may be drawn to choosing students who can function like employees and be less attracted to students with little experience.

The Match

Whether or not students have any choice of pre-placement interviews, both students and agencies usually have veto power over the final match. If students have more than one agency to choose from, arranging choices in numerical order may be a method of deciding the final placement. Ranking choices can cause stress for students and agencies. Competition increases and learning needs are balanced against what seems easier, and which agencies seem likely to make choices similar to those of the student. After ranking is completed, some agencies and students may feel "bruised" if they were not successful in being matched with their choice.

DESCRIPTION OF MODELS

School-Matches-Model

Many schools ask students what they are interested in learning, and then, through the field coordinators' knowledge of what agencies have available, bring together, somewhat as a marriage broker would, the student and the agency. This method is supported by agency supervisors who request "a student just like last time. You know what works best for us." As one student said: "It's efficient, quick, less work for the student" (Student 1985, School Matches Model).

A student may be given the opportunity to interview the agency, and then both agency supervisor and student may have the options of veto power and "no-fault divorce." The information, knowledge and initial choice remains with the field education coordinator. The student and agency supervisor are the recipient of the good will and expertise of the university.

Matching is administratively dependent on the good memory of the field coordinator, often supplemented now by computer programs which list data for agencies, language requirements, location, population served, etc. (Mondros, 1989). Even with all these aides, matching is still reliant on the field coordination staff who may interview each student to supplement the needs assessment. The placement connection must still be made by the university; therefore the structural barrier to student autonomy is in the notion that "we know what is good for you and that we have the knowledge to make this important decision." The field coordination staff who control the information and make the decisions retains the power. The only power the agency and student have is veto power over the final decision. That kind of power is difficult to wield.

School-Chooses-Interviews-Model

In this model the field education coordinator still does the matching, but provides the student with several pre-placement interviews. Students and agencies rank each other, and a match is made. Limited control therefore shifts toward the student and agency. This model provides an illusion of choice, in that it is really identical to the School-Matches Model in terms of power. It still assumes that the field coordinator knows what is best for the student. Students' access to the practicum pool is only that which has been bestowed upon them. There is limited choice for agencies and students. The only difference between the School-Chooses-Interviews Model and the previous model (School-Matches Model) is that students and agencies have increased veto power, depending on the number of interviews.

Advantages of These Models

Both of these models have several advantages for some students. The field coordinator may have information about the community that students do not have; for instance, transportation requirements, safety issues, etc. (Mondros, 1989). These models may be more supportive of students who are unfamiliar with local agencies. Less-experienced students may achieve a placement more easily, as the field coordinator can choose agencies which are more appropriate for them. An advantage of these models for agencies is that agencies in fields which are sometimes less "popular" with students (e.g., services to the mentally handicapped, or work with seniors) are guaranteed students to interview. For the field coordinator, these models fit with the philosophy of the professional as expert. Some students discover a placement they would never have chosen.

> Some were in areas I had not thought of applying for and worked out very well.
> (Student 1991, School-Chooses-Interviews Model)

Disadvantages of These Models

In both these models the field education coordinator must interpret and clarify the written information from students. Personal interviews with students or long distance telephone calls may be required, which may or may not be possible, depending on the number of students and the school's resources. The information about students being used by the field education coordinator may change.

> My interests changed somewhat from the time I filled out the questionnaire and the time for placement. (Student 1990, School-Chooses-Interviews Model)

The field coordinator must also have current knowledge of agencies and agency supervisors. The process requires a lot of last minute tinkering which effects the quality of the matches possible.

> One of these two backed out at the last minute and I had to choose others for the coordinator to pick one more for me to interview with. (Student 1992, School-Chooses-Interviews Model)

And, if students are entitled to three interviews, the field education coordinator's matching tasks are tripled. The field education coordinator will likely make some inappropriate choices, and some agencies and students will be dissatisfied no matter how diligent the coordinator has been.

> Suggest you notify the student/supervisor that the process would not guarantee a matching of interests with placement (My placement was my least preferred area of interest on the needs assessment--worked out ok, though.). (Student 1985, School-Matches Model)
> I was matched with one agency I had shown no interest in. (Student 1990, School-Chooses-Interviews Model).

Student-Chooses-Interviews Model

In this model, students peruse the pool of placements that have been recruited and vetted by the field coordinator. Students then choose their own pre-placement interviews. If too many students apply for an interview an agency may be required to shortlist. Following interviews, students and agencies rank their choices for placement. The final placement decision is identical to the previous models, in that student and agency choose each other.

Student-Chooses-Placement Model

Some schools allow students, usually armed with specific criteria for the placement, to locate their own practicum. This model may be chosen when students are at a distance and are perceived to know more than the field coordinator about what is available. This may be chosen because there are high numbers of students and limited personnel resources and/or the school simply gives up control. Alternatively, in MSW programs, students may finally be perceived to be knowledgeable enough to be in charge of their own learning. This model usually includes veto power from the school (again difficult to wield), as students resent the suggestion that they have not made good choices.

Advantages of Both Models

An advantage of both these models to students is that students are "in the driver's seat." When students choose their placements they have the opportunity to match their learning needs to what the agencies have to offer. A benefit for field staff is that they don't have to presume to know everything about everybody. Agencies usually get students who are really interested in them. These models increase the commitment of both students and agencies because they have truly chosen each other and so the frequency of replacement may be reduced.

Disadvantages of Both Models

Students who have not been able to articulate their learning needs can be disadvantaged by these models. Students may choose placements for reasons other than learning needs (e.g., comfort, job prospects, or fear of the unknown). The possibility exists for agencies to be inundated or to be ignored by students, depending on numbers of students and popularity of certain agencies. Students may not expand their horizons or be unaware of existing agency placements. The potential for competition is present once students have more than one interview. When students find their own placements, sometimes neither they nor the agencies fully understand the school's requirements. This can demand delicate and time-consuming negotiations by the field coordinator.

WHICH MODEL TO CHOOSE?

The model chosen by a school often appears, on the surface, to be selected for pragmatic reasons. These reasons might include whether practicum begins when the student arrives, whether there is a delayed start, what resources are available, and what appears easier administratively. Student and agency satisfaction with the process also influences a school's choice. However, no matter which model is chosen, some will appreciate it, and some will look askance and ask for change.

> It is difficult if you come from out of town to know which agencies serve which clientele. I would rather have chosen a client group and had the school match it with the appropriate agencies. (Student 1993, Student-Chooses-Interviews Model)

The philosophical stance of the school, and the belief system of the faculty and administration underlie the choice of placement model.

> This method (School-Chooses-Interviews Model) would run in contradiction to the School's mission statement and objectives (self-determination, choice). (Student 1993, Student-Chooses-Interviews Model)

Philosophy of Empowerment

In the past, lack of student maturity has been a rationale for denying students access to the field education experience (Kilpatrick, 1991, p.168). This reasoning still underlies many of the placement processes used in schools of social work today. Challenges to this assumption have come from an increase in the proportion of older students entering schools of social work. In light of this challenge "schools of social work have had to re-examine some long cherished beliefs about how education should be structured" (McClelland, 1991, p. 179).

When adult education principles are valued, students are encouraged to be self-directed, faculty have a learner-centered focus and emphasize facilitation of learning and student autonomy. The student's experience is seen as a rich resource. This flows from a belief in these principles and in social work values (such as starting where the "client" is, and self-determination). A case can be made for students being in charge of matching their interests to that of agencies. This would necessitate choosing a model which builds on the belief that adults know their own learning needs best and are capable of getting these met. This may be seen as an empowerment approach to student placement, as it based on the belief that clients (or students) know themselves better than the worker (administration) does or can, either in terms of their individual experience, or in relation to their racial, ethnic or cultural experience (Rose, 1990).

Many schools still believe that they alone have the expertise and practice wisdom to choose what they believe to be best for students, even though the concept of empowerment is embedded in social work values.

> Often those who speak in favor of empowerment are themselves unwilling to share or relinquish the power or control they possess. (Sheafor, Horejsi, & Horejsi, 1994, p. 406)

A model which moves toward student choice, but which makes use of teaching, group process, coaching, role playing and a process of assisting students to realize their full potential (Sheafor, Horejsi, & Horejsi, 1994), not only assists students in finding placements which truly meet their learning needs, but also models good social work practice. Reflecting with students on how their role in the placement process is similar to and different from the role of client may assist them in preparing for practice.

> Empowerment places an emphasis on securing client access to and control over needed resources, on client involvement in decision making, and on helping the client acquire the knowledge and skills needed to function independently. (Sheafor, Horejsi, & Horejsi, 1994, p. 406)

CONCLUSION

If the model chosen is to be one of empowering students, empowerment must go beyond giving students choice. Choice can be disempowering when it is overwhelming. One must be careful not to translate empowerment into a "do it yourself" philosophy. One of the ways to support a process of empowerment is to develop horizontal types of social support, drawing on the students' strengths to further their own development.

> Uncover overlooked sources of power. Assist the client in making an inventory of his or her power sources such as knowledge derived from life experience, motivation, time, energy, knowledge of the community, understanding of particular problems, sense of humour, willingness to take risks, verbal ability. (Sheafor, Horejsi, & Horejsi, 1994, p. 407)

The school cannot bestow power, but the students can produce their own power from their own collective experience. As Evans (1992) has stated, "others can aid though, in this empowerment process by providing a climate, a relationship, resources and procedural means" (p. 143). This perspective gives new meaning to the role of the field coordinator.

This chapter has described four models for the practicum placement process. Although each of these models has a number of advantages and disadvantages, whatever model a school chooses should be congruent with the school's philosophy. Models which focus on the student as adult learner may more easily embrace an empowerment perspective.

REFERENCE

Brownstein, C. (1981). Practicum issues: A placement planning model. *Journal of Education for Social Work, 17*(3), 52-58.

Evans, E. (1992). Liberation theology, empowerment theory and social work practice with the oppressed. *International Social Work, 35*, 135-47.

Grossman, B. (1991). Themes and variations: The political economy of field instruction. In D. Schneck, B. Grossman & U. Glassman (Eds.), *Field education in social work: Contemporary issues and trends* (pp. 36-46). Iowa: Kendall/Hunt.

Kilpatrick, A. (1991). Differences and commonalities in BSW and MSW Field instruction: In search of continuity. In D. Schneck, B. Grossman & U. Glassman (Eds.), *Field education in social work: Contemporary issues and trends* (pp. 167-176). Iowa: Kendall/Hunt.

McClelland, R. (1991). Innovation in field education. In D. Schneck, B. Grossman & U. Glassman (Eds.), *Field education in social work: Contemporary issues and trends* (pp. 177-183). Iowa: Kendall/Hunt.

Mondros, J. (1989). *Prospects and pitfalls of computer software programs in field work*, Paper presented at CSWE, Chicago.

Rose, S. M. (1990). Advocacy/Empowerment: An approach to clinical practice for social work. *Journal of Sociology & Social Welfare, 17*(2), 41-51.

Sheafor, B. W., Horejsi, C. R., & Horejsi, G. A. (1994). *Techniques and guidelines for social work practice* (3rd ed.). Toronto: Allyn and Bacon.

CHAPTER TWENTY-EIGHT

REENGAGING SOCIAL WORK EDUCATION WITH THE PUBLIC SOCIAL SERVICES: THE CALIFORNIA EXPERIENCE AND ITS RELEVANCE TO CANADA

Bart Grossman and Robin Perry

INTRODUCTION

From the late 1970s almost to the present the profession of social work in the US has become disconnected from its classic focus on the needs of the poor and the institutions that address these needs, typically the publicly-supported social services. Training for social work has increasingly meant preparation for careers serving middle class clients in private practice. As social work participation in private practice increased, the profession's involvement in public and non-profit agencies declined, to the extent that many key public institutions became deprofessionalized. Deprofessionalization is associated with increased bureaucratization, decreased individualization of services, and increased focus on maintenance and protection rather than prevention and rehabilitation. Moreover, lack of professional assessment increases the frequency of bad choices that may result in harm to children and other vulnerable client populations. This chapter focuses on the following key questions:

1) How did this disengagement between social work and the publicly-supported agencies come about in US?

2) What has been the role of social work education in fostering disengagement?

3)   What can and has been done to refocus social work education in the US?
4)   What relevance does the experience have for Canada?

History of Disengagement

The erosion of the relationship between social work and the poor has many causes including: the decline of governmental and public commitment to social change, deteriorating working conditions in the public agencies, the popularity of psychotherapeutic and personal growth techniques in the profession and in the culture, and the lack of fit between content in social work education and current practice realities in publicly-supported agencies.

However, It is important to understand that the relationship between social work education and the public services in the US has never been particularly close. The profession arose at the end of the nineteenth century in the voluntary agencies at a time when government played little role in the social services. The development of social work education was linked to the search for a knowledge base to develop the early concepts of "scientific charity." At first the search focused in the social sciences; chiefly economics and sociology. But by the thirties teachings were integrated from psychiatry and Freudian psychoanalysis which tended to focus on intrapsychic problems and individualistic solutions. By the fifties the clinical perspective dominated and the focus of intervention became not the community or even the person in the environment, but rather the internal conflicts and psychological history of the "patient."

Graduate Social Work Education and the Public Social Services

Through the depression and two World Wars the social work profession maintained its primary commitment to the sponsorship of social services under nongovernmental auspices and to an individualistic practice. It was only with the 1962 amendments to the Social Security Act that the federal government began to provide financial supports to the states for social casework services.

These provisions were broadened year-by-year. In 1974, the addition of Title XX to the Social Security Act established the framework for the states to offer comprehensive programs of social services on a universal basis, and the states made considerable strides in that direction until the passage of the 1981 Omnibus Budget Reconciliation Act.

With the growth in public agency involvement in social services one would have expected a concomitant increase in social work education involvement with these settings. For a time this was the case. Title XX supported a number of innovative collaborative projects between schools and public agencies and agency-based field units were common. However, this connection was defeated by a powerful combination of blows.

The first, from the left, attacked the public agencies as tools of oppression designed to "regulate" the poor not alleviate poverty. This attack was often directed from the schools and transmitted in the most extreme form by students who went to the agencies with a mission not to help but to overthrow. The anti-poverty critique, while based in palpable realities, was exploited by the right. A string of Conservative Presidents and Governors undertook the dismantling of the American welfare state, and a conspicuous casualty was funding for profession education. Although enrolment in MSW increased 67% from 1969-1990, federal student support decreased by 69%, state and county support decreased by 51%. This left-right combination all but knocked out the relationship between social work education and public social services.

The disengagement between social work and the publicly-supported agencies can be glimpsed through many indicators. About 25-30% of social workers nationally are involved in private practice, primarily with middle class clients. Public child welfare, mental health, and other publicly-supported agencies charged with serving the poor and disadvantaged report enormous difficulty attracting and retaining MSW's. Nationally, less than 20% of child welfare workers currently hold a MSW. New recruits to the profession do not necessarily plan careers serving the poor. In Rubin and Johnson's (1984) study of entering MSW students more than 50% indicated that they were preparing for careers in private practice with middle class clients. We recently studied the entering class in the ten graduate schools of social work in California. We asked students to choose between two statements of mission:

1) Social Work should devote most of its attention and resources to the problems of the poor, or;
2) Social work should devote equal attention and equal resources to all social class groupings.

In 1991, 70% of the respondents choose the later.

Re-engagement

Yet in the late 80s a change began to occur in the US after a decade or so of keeping a guarded distance, public agencies and schools of social work began to tentatively explore new connections. The reasons for this exploration were many. Among these:

- increasing numbers of social workers were achieving top leadership positions in public agencies;
- the job market was growing in response to the growth of recognized social problems like child abuse, AIDS, drug-abuse, teenage pregnancy, and homelessness;
- many public agencies no longer had internal training divisions and many turned to the Universities for assistance in developing in-service education;

- in some states the availability of MSWs for public employment was not keeping pace with the demand (in California for example, MSW employment in public child welfare declined from 32% in '86 to 23% in 1991 while the number of child welfare positions substantially increased);
- highly publicized deaths in placement and other failures were creating pressure in the courts, Congress, and state legislatures for efforts to reprofessionalize services;
- key pieces of legislation like the Family Support Act changed the focus of intervention therefore created a need for new professional training;
- funders were increasingly interested in supporting school-agency coalitions rather than funding either sector independently, as a mechanism to enhance the quality of services;
- in some states changing demographics created a situation of marked ethnic disparity between clients and workers. In California children in foster care are 37.9% African American, 20.6% Hispanic, 2.4% Indian, less than 1% Asian (Harris, Kirk, & Besharov, 1993). In contrast, a CalSWEC study (1991) shows that the distribution of direct service workers in California is 19% African American, 16.4% Hispanic, .01% Indian, and 6.1% Asian.

Perhaps most significantly, schools and agencies faced a common enemy in the 80s strong enough to unite them, a political attack on the very idea of governmental support for the social services. But as schools and agencies began to explore partnerships and coalitions they encountered significant differences in approach and culture that created barriers to cooperation.

BARRIERS TO COLLABORATION

As Alicea (1978) points out, "Coalitions are characterized not only by unity but also by diversity of interests. . . . . The concept of coalition entails simultaneously both . . . centripetal and centrifugal forces." In the case of school-agency partnerships, barriers arise from differences in organizational culture, past experience with attempts to work on exchange relationships, and the divergent goals and perceptions of individuals involved in the process. It is important to understand the differences in values, norms, reward systems, and decision making and operational styles in the cultures of the institutions that constitute the membership of most university/agency coalitions.

Reward Systems

University reward systems highly emphasize individual professional and scholarly achievements. This value system contrasts with the organizational, problem solving orientation of the agency. It is extremely difficult for individuals to move between these frames of reference. Practitioners who take jobs in schools for example, are often perplexed by the lack of clarity about collective goals and performance standards and the lack of hierarchial supervision.

Knowledge and Theory

The most stereotyped version of these differences holds that university faculty rely on empirical and theoretical knowledge, whereas practitioners draw knowledge from precedent, experience, and intuition. Thus, faculty members may fail to appreciate that formal research alone cannot answer all questions. Practitioners may overvalue their own experience, assume it will be highly generalizable.

Constraints and Sanctions

Each cultural system has constraints and sanctions that are not familiar to the other. In addition, schools of social work operate under the constraint of the Council on Social Work Education and the Academic Senate, both of which make changes slowly through stately deliberative processes. Agencies, on the other hand, are pushed and pulled by political and economic forces at many levels. Upper level personnel often come and go quickly. Managers rarely last more than a few years. It is hard to maintain a partnership when the identity of one of the partners is constantly changing.

Decision-making

Authority in the university is diffuse and subtle. The nature and amount of authority delegated to the faculty vis-a-vis the Dean comes as a real shock to persons outside the system. Agency administrators take for granted that academic deans and directors can act on behalf of their institutions. They may be surprised at the degree to which some faculty seek to overrule or ignore the dean. In fact, agency directors have a much higher degree of administrative authority. The pace of change in academic settings can be frustrating. Coordinated efforts and team work are more the exception than the rule. This individualistic modus operandi, while it can promote some forms of scholarship, creates significant barriers to collaborative work between faculty and practitioners.

Inter-organizational Tensions

Who's to Blame?

As agencies and universities work together after a lapse, there can often be a beginning phase of assigning blame. Agency staff blame the universities for not training students to function in the current reality of the field. University faculty members blame difficulties in recruitment and retention entirely on deteriorating working conditions, ignoring the effects of inadequate training and negative bias in the University.

Can We Trust Each Other?

Basic trust is shaky. Agencies hesitate to escalate their support of field work opportunities and stipends unless there is solid evidence of commitment to curriculum reform. Universities know curriculum revisions will be far easier with the incentive of stipend support for students.

Who Goes First?

Distrust lingers from past failures at collaboration including research projects that either produced unreliable findings for faculty or, for the agency, outcomes that were presented in unusable form or were damaging to the agency.

THE CALIFORNIA SOCIAL WORK EDUCATION CENTRE (CALSWEC)

Given these barriers, how can schools and agencies develop a respect for each other's strengths and limitations and create new structures that fit organizational realities? The California Social Work Education Centre illustrates a successful new structure. It emerged from four years of local and regional collaborations on in-service training. The Deans prepared and succeeding in passing in each school, a common mission statement emphasizing preparation was practice in publicly-supported social services serving poor and disadvantaged clients. Fortunately, the Ford Foundation and the local foundation community in California were willing to provide start up funding.

The following elements were seen as crucial to the goals of change in professional education for the public social services:

1) A *new structure with shared governance* was created. While CalSWEC is linked to the University of California it is governed by a board of directors balanced among deans and public agency managers. State, nonprofit, and professional organizations also participate. All CalSWEC committees have co-chair teams of deans and agency managers.

2) A program was designed that *addresses the needs and limitations of both sectors and taps resources that neither could access independently.* It has three elements:

    a) the provision of financial aid to students linked to commitments to employment in public agencies (this helps the schools with their problems of supporting students and the agencies with recruitment). Furthermore, the schools agreed to give priority to returning employees (an agency need) and to under represented ethnocultural groups(a common concern). The source of funding for financial aid particularly illustrates the advantages of the agency-school partnership. The local match for this funding is achieved without cost to the agencies by using university, state funds and overhead.

b) the creation of a competency-based curriculum to meet the needs of public child welfare workers, and a second effort for public mental health. A collaborative process was employed to create a set of core competencies that each school would implement with the support of regional agencies.

c) the facilitation of collaborative research and development between schools and agencies. One resource for this effort is a five-year federal grant for interdisciplinary child welfare training and curriculum development. Receiving this grant gave the collaboration its first success and demonstrated the ability to attract new resources that could further the needs of the agencies for better trained staff and of faculty for new research and evaluation opportunities.

THE EFFECTS OF CALSWEC INITIATIVES — A THREE YEAR COMPARISON

As part of an ongoing effort to monitor the effects of CalSWEC initiatives, a demographic and attitudinal profile was collected from all entering MSW students throughout the State of California each year. The impact of IV-E entitlements, curriculum changes, and recruitment policies should be seen to have an affect on the type of student accepted into MSW programs. Although we have recently begun surveying the same students following the completion of their program (to examine the effect of their educational and placement experience on attitudes), this paper will focus on changes in the profile of entering MSW students from 1991 to 1993. Students sampled in 1991 provide a baseline for comparison to students sampled in 1992 and 1993 when various CalSWEC initiatives began to take shape and exert an influence on student funding, recruitment, and curriculums throughout the state. Every entering MSW student was sampled for the purposes of this study. This represents an overall response rate varying approximately between 80% and 86% for each year.

The questionnaire used for this study was developed by Dr. Bart Grossman and Dr. Tony Santangelo (then a research assistant with CalSWEC) and adapted from previous studies. Among these were the work of Reeser and Epstein (1990) and Golden, Pins, and Jones (1972) which suggested items on student demographics as well as students attitudes and beliefs about poverty and its causes. Questions from Abell and McDonnell's (1990) research were used to ascertain students' reasons for pursuing the MSW degree. Finally, the work of Rubin and Johnson (1984), Rubin, Johnson, and DeWeaver (1986) and Butler (1990) provided the framework for questions soliciting students' future career interests, and their preferences in working with future client groups and case situations. This questionnaire was extensively pretested with MSW and doctoral students prior to its' application to the entire population of entering graduate students throughout the state.

The proportion of African American and Hispanic students increased following the implementation of CalSWEC initiatives (see Table 1). Utilizing a 2-tailed test of significance for two independent proportions, the observed increase in African American students (p < .05) and Hispanic students (p < .012) proved significant. This change is accompanied by a significant decrease in Caucasian students between 1991 and 1993 (p = .0026).

Table 1 Ethnicity of Entering MSW Students in California by Year

Race/Ethnicity	(n=912) 1991	(n=946) 1992	(n=917) 1993
1. % African American/Black	09.7	08.6	12.6*
2. % American Indian	01.6	00.7	01.9
3. % Asian American	06.8	06.4	06.1
4. % Caucasian	65.4	64.0	58.6*
5. % Hispanic/Latino	11.5	12.1	15.5#
6. % Pacific Islander	00.2	00.8	00.4
7. % Filipino	02.0	01.0	02.1
8. % Other	02.8	06.5	02.9

*   Observed change between 1991 – 1993 significant p < .05
\#   Observed change between 1991 – 1993 significant p < .01

When examining attitudes regarding the appropriate goal for the profession, a significant increase is observed each year with respect to those students who believe that social work should devote most of its' attention to problems of the poor (see Table 2). In 1991 only 31.2% of entering students, when asked to decide between two statements that which best represents their attitude toward goals for the profession, believed the profession should devote most of its attention towards the poor. This figure increased to 38% (p = .022) in 1992, and 41% (p < .001 when compared to 1991) in 1993. In this regard, we have seen moderate and significant increases in ethnic diversity of graduate students coupled with an increase in perceived commitment or belief that the profession should focus or identify more profoundly with service to the poor.

Table 2   Perspective on Goals for the Profession of California MSW Students by Year

When asked to best describe their attitude toward goals for the profession of social work:

	1991	1992	1993
% said social work should devote equal attention to <u>all</u> social class groupings	68.8	62.0	59.0
% said social work should devote most of its attention to problems of the poor	31.2	38.0##	41.0#

\#   Observed change between 1991 and 1993 significant p < .01, 2-tailed test
\## Observed change between 1991 and 1992 significant p < .01, 2-tailed test

These changes appear to conceptually coincide with changes in the level of appeal attributed to various fields of practice. Table 3 outlines the rating of each field of practice by year according to the mean level of appeal attributed to 10 categories or listed fields of practice. A two-tailed significance test using a Wilcoxon Rank Sum test was utilized to determine if observed differences between year pairs by field of practice proved significant. Although ranked in the top five fields in 1993, there has been a consistent yearly and significant (when 1991–1993 comparisons are made) decrease in the level of appeal attributed to counselling (p = .0467), group work (p = .0250), and marital/family therapy (p = .0015). The drop in appeal for these fields of practice has coincided with a significant increase in level of appeal of protective service (p = .0331), although its ranking hasn't improved dramatically (from 8 to 7 in two years). The increase in appeal of protective services has also coincided with a consistent increase in the mean level of appeal for client advocacy and casework practice, although these increases have not shown to be significant. Regardless, these findings suggest a growing (although modest) interest in fields of practice more traditionally associated with public service as opposed to individualized approaches concurrent with private practice orientations.

Table 3   Rankings of Fields of Practice by Mean Level of Appeal for California MSW Students by Year of Admission

When asked to rate the <u>fields of practice</u> according to their <u>level of appeal</u> — on a scale from 1 to 7 where the top ranking reflects the highest level of appeal, student responses were:

		(n=912) 1991	(n=946) 1992	(n=917) 1993
1.	Counselling	1 (6.06)	1 (6.00)	1 (5.92)*
2.	Group work	2 (5.50)	2 (5.41)	3 (5.37)*
3.	Family/Marital therapy	3 (5.34)	4 (5.25)**	5 (5.06)#
4.	Client advocacy	4 (5.33)	3 (5.36)	2 (5.47)
5.	Casework	5 (4.96)	5 (5.02)	4 (5.12)
6.	Psychotherapy	6 (4.83)	6 (4.78)	6 (4.67)
7.	Program/Policy design	7 (4.58)	7 (4.59)	7 (4.64)
8.	Protective services	8 (4.50)	8 (4.47)	7 (4.64)*
9.	Community organizing	9 (4.34)	9 (4.46)	9 (4.48)
10.	Administration	10 (3.86)	10 (4.04)	10 (3.99)

*   Observed change between 1991 and 1993 significant $p < .05$, 2-tailed test using Wilcoxon Rank Sum Test

**   Observed change between 1991 and 1992 significant $p < .05$, 2-tailed test

Observed change between 1991 and 1993 significant $p < .01$, 2-tailed test

These findings hold true when one observes rankings of client groups or case situations by level of appeal detailed in Table 4. Of those groups or situations that show consistent increases or decreases in mean appeal ratings, where differences over 2 years prove significant (using the Wilcoxon Rank Sum Test); there is a significant increase in the appeal of working with abused and neglected children ($p = .0468$) and the poor ($p = .011$). These increases are contrasted with a consistent and significant decrease in appeal of working with people with marital and family problems ($p = .0468$). The level of importance attributed to such findings may be minimalized by the fact that all those groupings listed above were originally and consistently maintained an overall ranking in the top 5 of 21 client groups or case situations rated. Regardless, the significance levels observed suggest a trend, which when longitudinally evaluated may point to a reversal of tendencies for entering graduate students to aspire towards private practice at the expense of the poor.

Table 4 Rankings of Client Groups or Case Situations by Mean Level of Appeal for California MSW students by Year of Admission

When asked to rate the <u>client groups</u> or <u>case situations</u> according to their level of appeal on a scale from 1 to 7 where the top ranking reflects the highest level of appeal, student responses were:

		(n=912) 1991	(n=946) 1992	(n=917) 1993
1.	Teen mothers with limited resources	1 (5.28)	1 (5.30)	3 (5.28)
2.	Abused and neglected children	2 (5.25)	3 (5.27)**	1 (5.40)*
3.	People with marital/family problems	3 (5.22)	2 (5.29)	4 (5.11)*
4.	People in poverty needing resources	4 (5.09)	4 (5.21)	2 (5.28)*
5.	Teens experiencing turbulent adolescence	5 (4.96)	5 (5.15)**	5 (5.04)
6.	Alcohol/substance abusers	6 (4.77)	8 (4.69)	10 (4.63)
7.	People who are depressed	7 (4.74)	7 (4.70)	7 (4.70)
8.	Children with AIDS	8 (4.73)	6 (4.82)	6 (4.83)
9.	Homeless families	9 (4.68)	9 (4.68)	8 (4.68)
10.	Abusive parents	10 (4.54)	11 (4.58)	9 (4.67)
11.	People wanting to adopt a child	11 (4.44)	14 (4.42)	12 (4.45)
12.	Homeless adults	12 (4.41)	13 (4.42)	14 (4.40)
13.	Adults with AIDS	13 (4.40)	12 (4.54)	11 (4.49)
14.	College students in crisis	14 (4.35)	10 (4.63)##	13 (4.47)***
15.	Juvenile status offenders	15 (4.12)	15 (4.05)	15 (4.18)
16.	The Aged	16 (4.03)	17 (3.92)	17 (3.93)
17.	The Physically disabled	17 (4.02)	18 (3.81)	18 (3.90)
18.	Hospital discharge/care	18 (3.93)	16 (3.94)	16 (4.07)
19.	The Developmentally disabled	19 (3.74)	19 (3.59)	19 (3.58)
20.	The Chronically Mentally Ill	20 (3.45)	20 (3.51)	20 (3.43)
21.	Adult criminal offenders	21 (3.32)	21 (3.30)	21 (3.41)

*   Observed change between 1991 and 1993 significant $p < .05$, 2-tailed test using Wilcoxon Rank Sum Test

**   Observed change between 1991 and 1992 significant $p < .05$, 2-tailed test

***   Observed change between 1992 and 1993 significant $p < .05$, 2-tailed test

\#\#   Observed change between 1991 and 1992 significant $p < .01$, 2-tailed test

Indeed, this appears so. Students were asked to rate the degree of importance seven factors had in their decision to enter graduate school (see Table 5). The desire to serve the poor increased consistently and significantly from 1991 to 1992 ($p = .012$), and overall from 1991 to 1993 ($p = .0016$), while the desire to enter private practice significantly decreased from 1991 to 1993 (p=.0016). It is interesting to note that private practice has maintained a relatively low ranking in comparison to other motivating factors. This may lead one to suspect assumptions that private practice is a significant motivating factor for pursuing graduate studies. What this question does not ascertain is desirability or likelihood that students will enter private practice following completion of their graduate degree. Previous research has shown education and practice experiences can affect student motivations and practice aspirations (Rubin, Johnson, & DeWeaver, 1986).

Table 5   Rankings of Motivating Factors by Mean Importance for Entering Graduate School for California MSW Students by Year of Admission

Students were asked to rate a series of statements, according to how each best represents its degree of importance in their decision to enter graduate school in social work, where:

1=VERY UNIMPORTANT;   **2**=UNIMPORTANT;   **3**=NEITHER;   **4**=IMPORTANT; **5**=VERY IMPORTANT

		(n=912) 1991	(n=946) 1992	(n=917) 1993
1.	Contribute to society	1 (4.63)	1 (4.68)##	1 (4.69)#
2.	Versatility of the MSW	2 (4.53)	2 (4.57)	2 (4.53)
3.	Job promotion	3 (4.27)	3 (4.24)	4 (4.24)
4.	To serve the poor	4 (4.15)	3 (4.24)**	3 (4.26)#
5.	Personal growth	5 (4.05)	5 (4.07)	5 (4.12)
6.	Private practice	6 (3.69)	6 (3.66)	6 (3.52)#
7.	Extension of BSW	7 (2.88)	7 (3.08)##	7 (3.07)#

** Observed change between 1991 and 1992 significant p<.05, 2-tailed test using Wilcoxon Rank Sum Test

Observed change between 1991 and 1992 significant p<.01, 2-tailed test

Observed change between 1991 and 1993 significant p<.01, 2-tailed test

POVERTY IN CANADA

To judge the relevance and applicability of the CalSWEC initiative to Canadian schools of social work one must explore the similarities that exist between the two countries with respect to services for the poor; and the traditional barriers to the development of effective school-agency partnerships.

Poverty in Canada has become a more controversial issue given the increasing influence of conservative ideologies. Hendrickson and Axelson (1985) point out that conservatism represents ideological commitment to the work ethic and stigmatization of the poor. Canadian social work has its historical roots in poor relief but has been relatively silent on major social and economic issues confronting those most vulnerable and marginalized populations today (Riches, 1989). The poverty rate in the US is approximately 13% (US Bureau of the Census, 1990). Canada's poverty rate has been rising over the last 20 years (Statistics Canada, 1986) despite periodic declines (National Council on Welfare, 1992; Riches, 1989). Recent figures suggest the national rate to be similar to that in the US at 13.6% or 3.8 million people (National Council on Welfare, 1992). In Canada as in the US the poor are disproportionately women and children. For example, 60.6% of all families with children under 18 headed by a single female parent live below the poverty line in Canada. Over 1.1 million children under 18 (16.9% of all children) live in poverty for which the national poverty rate for two parent families is 12.1% (National Council on Welfare, 1992). The increasingly persistent and chronic nature of poverty issues, demands interventions that are becoming alien to a large percentage of professional social workers.

Social Work and the Public Social Services in Canada

Although the influence of private practice has received popular endorsement in some regions of Canada as a desired professional goal, its historical influence in shaping practice trends and graduate training has not been as pronounced as in the United States and particularly California. There is little doubt, however, that clinical social work practice has become the preferred focus of training by many graduate students throughout Canada. The appropriateness of clinical orientations in addressing needs of the poor or the effects of poverty in public agencies is a serious issue for the profession.

The public sector maintains an overwhelming dominance as a setting for field preparation and employment opportunities for graduating MSW students in Canada. Although international comparisons of welfare systems have classified both the United States and Canada as residual social welfare states, there are some distinct and unique differences between the two nations in the development, endorsement and role of the public sector in the provision of social services. Because the public social services are more universalized in Canada, training in these settings exposes students to a variety of clients across class boundaries.

Schools of Social Work have historically developed individualized field placement programs with regional differences associated with types of settings, type of placement, and qualifications of field instructors throughout Canada. Field instruction most often occurs however, in traditional public social welfare agencies, where agency staff as opposed to faculty have assumed responsibility for field instruction. As many students seek employment in these settings in which they are trained, field education can be of pivotal importance to MSW career choices (Watt & Kimberley, 1981). Effective working relationships have not always been an institutional characteristic of agency-school field relationships. Although some schools have successfully experimented with field placement models, conflicts do occur on a variety of issues including:

1) concerns regarding the quantity and quality of time and contact between field instructors and the School;

2) limited input of field instructors into curriculum content;

3) general concern that field instructors are not kept informed of current curriculum content; and

4) struggles between the academic demands of the School on students and the agency's requirements to deliver service (Thomlison & Watt, 1980).

With respect to this last point, historically field instructors in many programs throughout the US and Canada have expressed concern that the academic training received by students was irrelevant to direct practice situations. Only 50% of field instructors in one study (Watt & Kimberley, 1981) believed that students are ready to assume a professional role following graduation. There was a clear assumption that students need more field education or need to be taught skills and orientations that have direct practical applications to situations in public service agencies.

CANADIAN VERSUS AMERICAN STUDENTS

To understand the intended effects of any collaborative endeavor on students, it is important to have a descriptive profile of those students to be effected. In addition, it is important to ascertain characteristics of social workers and social work students predisposed to private practice as opposed to public service. More generally, attempts at understanding practice and professional trends have historically focused on demographics, attitudinal profiles, cultural dispositions, and political/ideological affiliations of social work students.

Given the noted differences in field education settings and subsequent employment in the public sector between US and Canadian graduates; one might expect to observe differences between student attitudes and ideological preoccupations regarding the profession and service for the poor. In an attempt to explore this question, data amassed from a small pilot study involving graduate students at the University of Calgary and the University of Windsor, was compared to responses obtained from graduate students in 10 Schools of Social Work throughout the state of California.

As part of an extensive evaluation project CalSWEC has solicited, via survey data, information regarding MSW students prior to and following their completion of their program in 10 Californian graduate social work schools. CalSWEC initiatives coincided with significant changes in attitudes and the ethnic makeup of students accepted and participating in MSW programs throughout the state. For the purposes of this paper data collected from students in 1991 were compared to data solicited from graduate students in two Canadian schools in 1994. Data collected in 1991 represents a student body (in California) unaffected by the introduction of IV-E stipends or a modified curriculum shaped by CalSWEC initiatives. Fifty students were sampled from the University of Calgary and twenty students were sampled from the University of Windsor. The response rates were 74% (37) and 35% (7) respectfully.

These comparisons were viewed as exploratory. The return rate severely limits the generalization of findings. None the less, these findings may be of assistance in raising questions about similarities and differences between graduate social work students educated in countries with very different views of public service. For reference purposes, the samples surveyed will be referred to as US and Canadian samples.

A review of the demographic profile demonstrates significant differences between US and Canadian samples with respect to ethnic composition but little else. In the Canadian sample no respondents (0.0%) identified themselves as black or hispanic compared to 9.7% and 11.5% (respectively) of students sampled in California (see Table 6). These significant ($p < .0316$; and $p < .0214$ respectively) differences may reflect differing proportion of ethnic minorities in the general population of each country or result from limitations associated with the representativeness of the Canadian sample. Regardless, in both situations there is clear concern regarding the ethnic profile of graduate students and the extent to which such a profile is proportionately representative of those populations most affected by welfare reform and poverty (Brosnan, 1994; Moore, 1991; Riches, 1989).

Students were similar on a number of demographic characteristics. The mean age for California students was 32 compared to 34.37 years for those Canadian students sampled. Both groups were predominantly female (84.6% – US, 85.4% – Canada), raised in a middle class home (62.9% – US, 70.7% – Canada), were full-time students (71% – US, 83.7% – Canada), and were similarly composed in terms of religious affiliations. Only 4.4% of California students compared to 14.6% of the Canadian sample currently lived in a domestic or "common-law" partnership. Further, 48.4% of California students compared to 29.3% of Canadian students were never married.

An overwhelming majority of both populations (85.7% of US and 95.5% of Canadian students) had some social work experience in the 5 years prior to their admittance to the MSW program. With respect to ideological identifications 64% of California students compared with 69.4% of Canadian students identify themselves as liberal or left-wing progressive.

Table 6 Comparison of Ethnicity of Entering MSW Students in California and Canada* by Year

Race/Ethnicity	US (n=912) 1991	Canada (n=44) 1994
1. % African American/Black	09.7	00.0**
2. % American Indian	01.6	02.4
3. % Asian American	06.8	00.0
4. % Caucasian	65.4	90.2**
5. % Hispanic/Latino	11.5	00.0**
6. % Pacific Islander	00.2	00.0
7. % Filipino	02.0	00.0
8. % Other	02.8	07.3

** Observed change significant p < .05
* Please note that the sample is not representative of a Canadian population of graduate students. Students from the University of Calgary and Windsor were samples as part of an exploratory study. *Canada* is used for reference purposes.

The observed similarities in attitudes and beliefs about the poor are striking. When asked to best describe their attitudes toward goals for the profession of social work, both populations responses were similar. 31.2% of California students compared with only 20.9% of Canadian students believed that social work should devote most of its attention to problems of the poor. The majority of both groups believed social work should devote equal attention to all social class groupings. Equality may have different meanings given the differing role of the public sector in these countries. However, the de-emphasis on poverty relief as a defining feature for the profession is clearly evident. It is, therefore, not surprising to observe similarities in attitudes and appeal of particular fields of practice and client groups. Students were asked to rate fields of practice according to their level of appeal on a scale from 1 to 7, where 1 represented low appeal and 7 represented high appeal. When the fields of practice are ranked according to their mean response (see Table 7), there are remarkable similarities between US and Canadian students.

Table 7   Rankings of Fields of Practice by Mean Level of Appeal for MSW Students in California and Canada* by Year of Admission

When asked to rate the <u>fields of practice</u> according to their <u>level of appeal</u> — on a scale from 1 to 7 where the top ranking reflects the highest level of appeal, student responses were:

		US (n=912) 1991	Canada (n=946) 1992
1.	Counselling	1 (6.06)	1 (6.37)
2.	Group work	2 (5.50)	3 (5.35)
3.	Family/Marital therapy	3 (5.34)	2 (5.67)
4.	Client advocacy	4 (5.33)	3 (5.35)
5.	Casework	5 (4.96)	5 (5.16)
6.	Psychotherapy	6 (4.83)	6 (4.77)
7.	Program/Policy design	7 (4.58)	7 (4.53)
8.	Protective services	8 (4.50)	10 (2.88)#
9.	Community organizing	9 (4.34)	8 (4.37)
10.	Administration	10 (3.86)	9 (3.47)

\#   Observed difference significant $p < .01$, 2-tailed test using Wilcoxon Rank Sum Test
*   Please note that the sample is not representative of a Canadian population of graduate students. Students from the University of Calgary and Windsor were samples as part of an explanatory study. *Canada* is used for reference purposes.

Counselling, group work and family/marital therapy are rated with the highest level of appeal for both populations. A Wilcoxon Rank Sum Test was utilized to determine if any of the observed rankings differed significantly. Only the rankings for protective services proved significant ($p < .0001$). In this case, protective services was ranked 10th (out of 10) in terms of its level of appeal ($X = 2.88$) by Canadian students. The de-emphasis on protective or child welfare services, as well as services to the poor by the Canadian sample is noteworthy. When respondents were asked to rate client groups according to their level of appeal, three groups that were rated in the top 10 (of 21) by California students were ranked significantly lower by Canadian students (see Table 8).

Table 8   Rankings of Client Groups or Case Situations by Mean Level of Appeal for MSW students in California and Canada* by Year of Admission

When asked to rate the <u>client groups</u> or <u>case situations</u> according to their level of appeal on a scale from 1 to 7 where the top ranking reflects the highest level of appeal, student responses were:

		US (n=912) 1991	Canada (n=44) 1994
1.	Teen mothers with limited resources	1 (5.28)	2 (4.86)
2.	Abused and neglected children	2 (5.25)	7 (4.40)#
3.	People with marital/family problems	3 (5.22)	1 (5.58)
4.	People in poverty needing resources	4 (5.09)	5 (4.63)**
5.	Teens experiencing turbulent adolescence	5 (4.96)	4 (4.65)
6.	Alcohol/substance abusers	6 (4.77)	10 (4.12)#
7.	People who are depressed	7 (4.74)	3 (4.72)
8.	Children with AIDS	8 (4.73)	10 (4.12)
9.	Homeless families	9 (4.68)	9 (4.14)**
10.	Abusive parents	10 (4.54)	6 (4.58)
11.	People wanting to adopt a child	11 (4.44)	14 (3.65)#
12.	Homeless adults	12 (4.41)	13 (3.79)**
13.	Adults with AIDS	13 (4.40)	8 (4.33)
14.	College students in crisis	14 (4.35)	12 (4.02)
15.	Juvenile status offenders	15 (4.12)	18 (3.33)#
16.	The Aged	16 (4.03)	14 (3.65)
17.	The Physically disabled	17 (4.02)	16 (3.56)
18.	Hospital discharge/care	18 (3.93)	19 (3.00)#
19.	The Developmentally disabled	19 (3.74)	17 (3.49)
20.	The Chronically Mentally Ill	20 (3.45)	21 (2.70)#
21.	Adult criminal offenders	21 (3.32)	20 (2.79)

**   Observed difference significant p < .05, 2-tailed test using Wilcoxon Rank Sum Test

\#   Observed difference significant p < .01, 2-tailed test

*   Please note that the sample is not representative of a Canadian population of graduate students. Students from the University of Calgary and Windsor were sampled as part of an exploratory study. *Canada* is used for reference purposes.

These groups are clearly characterized by issues of poverty. These included abused and neglected children (p=.0014), people in poverty needing resources (p=.0479), and homeless families (p=.0276). However, there is a relatively high level of appeal assigned to working with teen mothers by both populations. This group represents a significant proportion of the population that is affected by poverty and unemployment. Given the clear preference for counselling and therapeutic methods of practice, we can presume a lack of interest in structural interventions meant to address poverty. The desire to "contribute to society" is ranked the highest among seven choices of motivations for pursuing the MSW degree for both study populations (see Table 9). This may lead one to believe that students continue to maintain altruistic tendencies that may predispose them toward practice orientations or employment opportunities meant to offset social inequalities. For California students the desire to serve the poor is ranked above the desire to pursue private practice. However, the reverse holds true for the Canadian sample of students, where the desire to serve the poor is ranked significantly lower than their California counterparts and last in terms of other motivating factors for pursuing an MSW degree.

Table 9   Rankings of Motivating Factors by Mean Level of Importance for Entering Graduate School for MSW Students in California and Canada* by Year of Admission

Students were asked to rate a series of statements, according to how each best represents its degree of importance in their decision to enter graduate school in social work, where:

1=VERY UNIMPORTANT;   **2**=UNIMPORTANT;   **3**=NEITHER;   **4**=IMPORTANT;
5=VERY IMPORTANT

		US (n=912) 1991	Canada (n=44) 1994
1.	Contribute to society	1 (4.63)	1 (4.34)#
2.	Versatility of the MSW	2 (4.53)	3 (4.25)**
3.	Job promotion	3 (4.27)	2 (4.32)
4.	To serve the poor	4 (4.15)	7 (3.41)#
5.	Personal growth	5 (4.05)	6 (3.57)#
6.	Private practice	6 (3.69)	5 (3.66)
7.	Extension of BSW	7 (2.88)	4 (4.11)#

** Observed difference significant p<.05, 2-tailed test using Wilcoxon Rank Sum Test
\# Observed difference significant p<.01, 2-tailed test
* Please note that the sample is not representative of a Canadian population of graduate students. Students from the University of Calgary and Windsor were sampled as part of an explanatory study. *Canada* is used for reference purposes.

These findings seem to reinforce concerns regarding the level of commitment of graduate students toward serving the poor in Canada. A recently published study (Bogo, Raphael, & Roberts, 1993) suggests there is increasing support or desire to work with the disadvantaged among students sampled from the University of Toronto. However, child protection and community development tasks, activities typical of public sector social work were relatively low choices among their sample. Interest in private practice was higher. This was particularly true of nearly one third of their sample which self identified as therapist or clinical social worker.

Despite the historical reliance on public sector field placements for training in Canada, the trend toward individualized practice directed at servicing the middle class may be becoming a defining feature of Canadian social work. Canadian Schools ought to begin to respond to this trend, for while the public services address a broader population in Canada than in the US, class stratification in service may be growing and young social workers may be opting, like their US counterparts, to disengage from the poor and services upon which they rely. The development of CalSWEC, like school-agency partnerships may be an important element of an intervention in Canada to repair this rift at an earlier point than it was reached in the US.

REFERENCES

Abell, N., & McDonnell, J. R. (1990, Winter). Preparing for practice: Motivations, expectations, and aspirations of the MSW class of 1990. *Journal of Social Work Education, 1*, 57-64.

Alicea, V. G. (1978). *Community participation, planning and influence: Toward a conceptual model of coalition planning.* Doctoral Dissertation: Columbia University.

Bogo, M., Raphael, D., & Roberts, R. (1993). Interests, activities, and self-identification among social work students: Toward a definition of social work identity. *Journal of Social Work Education, 29*(3), 279-292.

Brosnan, J. W. (1994, June 12). Clinton's welfare proposals amount to a "culture reform." *San Francisco Examiner*, p. B-11

Butler, A. C. (1990, Winter). A reevaluation of social work student's career interests. *Journal of Social Work Education, 1*, 45-56.

Golden, D., Pins, A., & Jones, W. (1972). *Students in schools of social work: A study of characteristics and factors affecting career choice and practice concentration.* New York, NY: CSWE.

Grossman, B., Laughlin, S., & Specht, H. (1992). Building the commitment of social work education to publicly supported social services: The California model. In K. H. Briar, V. H. Hansen & N. Harris (Eds.), *New partnerships: Proceedings from the National Public Welfare Training Symposium 1991.* North Miami: Florida International University.

Harris, N., Kirk, R. S., & Besharov, D. (1993). *State Child Welfare Agency Staff Survey Report.* Washington, DC: National Child Welfare Leadership Center, Inc.

Hendrickson, R. M., & Axelson, L. J. (1985). Middle-class attitudes toward the poor: Are they changing? *Social Service Review, 59*(2), 295-304

Moore, D. E. (1991). Recruitment and admission of minority students to Schools of Social Work. *Canadian Social Work Review, 8*(2), 190-210.

National Council of Welfare. (1992). *Poverty profile, 1980-1990.* Ottawa: Minister of Supply and Services Canada.

Reeser, L. C., & Irwin, E. (1990). *Professionalization and activism in social work: The sixties, the eighties, and the future.* New York: Columbia University Press.

Riches, G. (1989). Unemployment and the state: Implications for Canadian social work education, practice, and research. *Canadian Social Work Review, 6*(1), 9-23.

Rubin, A., & Johnson, P. J. (1984). Direct practice interests of entering MSW students. *Journal of Education for Social Work, 20,* 5-16.

Rubin, A., Johnson, P. J., & DeWeaver, K. L. (1986). Direct practice interests of MSW students: Changes from entry to graduation. *Journal of Social Work Education, 22,* 98-108.

Statistics Canada. (1986, Fall). *Canadian Social Trends.* Ottawa: Minister of Supply and Services Canada.

Thomlison, B., & Watt, S. (1980). Trends and issues in the field preparation of social work manpower: A summary report. *Canadian Journal of Social Work Education, 6*(2&3), 137-158.

US Bureau of the Census. (1990). *Statistical abstract of the United States* (110th ed.). Washington, DC.

Watt, S., & Kimberley, D. (1981). Trends and issues in the field preparation of social work manpower: Part II, policies and recommendations. *Canadian Journal of Social Work Education, 7*(1), 99-108.

CHAPTER TWENTY-NINE

PRINCIPLES OF SOCIAL WORK
PRACTICUM EDUCATION

Luke J. Fusco

INTRODUCTION

The principles of field or practicum education in social work in this paper evolved from a combination of experience, observational research and a review of the literature. They are based on a qualitative study of social work field programs in five Australian universities in Sydney, Adelaide and Newcastle, and after more than 20 years of teaching in, administering and developing policy for social work practica. The objective was to compare Australian programs with the experience in Canada and to identify principles of practicum education in social work which transcend programs and their university contexts. The consistency of themes, which were repeated in various forms support some definite conclusions.

DISTINCTIONS BETWEEN BSW AND MSW DEGREES

The Canadian Association of Schools of Social Work (CASSW) describes BSW programs as professional studies within the context of university education. It is here that students gain a beginning general practice competence and basic social work knowledge, and a practicum is required (CASSW, 1993). MSW programs are graduate university education with a professional purpose shaped partly by the individual student's educational needs and interests. The CASSW defines the MSW as having the competence of the BSW plus "the ability to analyze, use, evaluate and develop theory in relation to complex practice situations" (CASSW, 1993).

MSW students with a BSW degree must have the "opportunity for a practicum." For MSW students with a bachelor's degree, other than in social work, a practicum is required. Some schools which admit only applicants with BSW degrees to their MSW programs sometimes allow non-BSW degree holders to complete a foundation year or make-up year prior to entry into the MSW program. That preliminary year may have a practicum requirement.

In the United States, BSW programs prepare students for beginning and generalist practice, while MSW programs are intended for advanced and specialized practice. In both cases a practicum is required (Kilpatrick, 1991). In Canada, the BSW degree requires 700 hours (100 days) in two or more practica. A one-year MSW must include 450 hours and a two-year MSW 1,000 hours of practicum (CASSW, 1993, 45). In Australia the BSW is the practice degree. Students spend between 140 and 176 days in two or three different practicum settings (AASWWE). The requirement in the Faculty of Social Work at Wilfrid Laurier University is for students to spend 145-150 days in two practicum placements during the two-year MSW program.

GENERAL METHODOLOGY AND PERSONAL OBSERVATIONS

The Australian study included the review of field manuals, papers and policy documents, and also personal observations and experiences. Increasingly the issues, relationships and dynamics in the area of practicum education in Australia reflected the Canadian experience. Faculty, professional staff, and/or support staff arranged student placements, made field visits, led practice seminar classes, and attended a series of seemingly endless meetings regarding the practicum. The experience of participating in all of those activities, and having discussions with numerous students, field instructors, faculty and staff, yielded valuable information and insights.

The result is a perspective on practicum education and administration, and the necessary roles for faculty and professional staff in the schools. The conclusions which follow were also influenced by a comprehensive review of the practicum carried out from 1989 to 1992 in the Faculty of Social Work at Wilfrid Laurier University (Task Force on Field Education, 1992). The similarities between the Australian study and the Laurier FSW report were startling; but sometimes a shoe fits more than one foot.

PRINCIPLES OF PRACTICUM EDUCATION

Community

Practicum education is a responsibility shared by a community consisting of the social work profession, universities and social service agencies. These groups have different purposes but are nevertheless compatible (Mulford, 1963, 10). Their mutual interest in professional social work education must be characterized by partnerships and collective cooperation.   Current members of the profession have a commitment to the next generation of social workers.   Each group contributes by meeting human needs, developing and maintaining ethical standards of practice, and by monitoring and adapting social work curricula.

Any review of a social work curriculum or of the practicum itself should include agency field instructors and administrators, recent graduates of the program, as well as faculty and students. The students, of course, participate first as students and then as professional social workers.   All committees, decision-making bodies and relevant administrative units should include representatives from the practicum. It might be useful to have agency field instructors serve three-year terms on any one body in order to maximize continuity and effectiveness.

Flinders, Sydney, Newcastle, New South Wales and Wilfrid Laurier University have practicum instructors on most or all of the relevant committees. Yet, while the agency people may have a substantial impact on a major curriculum or practicum review, they are seldom involved in the ongoing monitoring and administration of practicum education. They are not real partners in the process. This occurred in both Canada and Australia. Only in the last year has Wilfrid Laurier University's Faculty of Social Work created a Practicum Committee. One Australian university's Social Work Department has field teachers on its governing body but not on its field or special cases sub-committees. At another Australian university, field teachers are members of the field work advising committee but not the field work review committee.

Agency-based practicum instructors bring their practice expertise, including the current realities of service delivery to the somewhat insular process of curriculum review and development and to the administration of the practicum. Evaluation of specific schools of social work is not an aim of this paper. The point is to underline the fact that the principle of creating a community of social work educators drawn from all constituencies is incomplete in most university programs. Practicum instructors must participate in all decision-making processes which address field education. And there should be a continuity of service achieved through multiple year appointments.

The community of social work educators represented by heterogeneous governing councils and committees provides forums for exchanges of information and energy between the university's curriculum and the agencies' professional practice.

Practicum Education within the Social Work Curriculum

Practicum education is part of the curriculum of schools of social work. It does not exist separate and apart from other learning experiences. Too often the practicum is seen as "the doing" part of the program. Field teachers consistently report a sense that students are taught what to do in the classroom and the practicum placement is merely an opportunity to try out the students' newly learned skills. The literature of practicum education stresses the need for integration between theory and practice, the classroom and the field (Wilson, 1981; Bogo and Vayda, 1987; Sheafor and Jenkins, 1982). The ideal is a wholeness called professional social work. Koonin (1988) refers to the interdependence of school and placement as having integrity. That theme is repeated in the report of the Australian Association of Social Work and Welfare Education (1990).

Practicum curricula must include objectives that can be translated into criteria for the evaluation of student performance. Social work schools write mission statements which include what they want students to be, and what they should know and do as professionals. Those statements provide a context for curriculum development. Of necessity then, standards for student practicum evaluation are an inherent part of the conceptualization of the social work curriculum. Sydney University's social work program includes a wide range of practice, policy, research and other courses. Yet each course has at least one objective related directly to the student's field placements.

Another mechanism used by many social work departments to integrate the practicum and other learning is the field seminar which runs concurrently with the time spent in the agency placements (Walden & Brown, 1985). These courses create opportunities for students to discuss the applications of theory, bring forward questions regarding practice and ethics, examine and understand their personal reactions to clients, debate social policy issues, understand organizational structures and adminstration, appreciate the research possibilities in their professional work and to raise any other professional questions. Assignments may include journals, presentations, essays and small group discussions, with reports to the larger seminar.

At Sydney University the course which runs concurrently with the second field placement is organized around the field of service of the placements, with most of the students having the instructor as their faculty field advisor who sees them and their field teacher during the term. Participation in one such course as a self-described observer was not acceptable to the class. To be involved in any way meant becoming a member of the group with full rights and responsibilities. The collectivity of individual students became a closely knit group (with no "outside observers" permitted). Classes were a confidential and emotionally safe place to express frustration and doubts, to question theory and principles and to receive support and hear confrontation. The termination phase of this class was difficult. As the students looked ahead to their next placements they also wondered what their new concurrent field seminar would be like. There was a sense of loss about the current group and much discussion about whether its familiarity and intimacy were more valuable than the reorganization of the students according to the field of service of their next practicum.

There is no question that a concurrent integrative course is an essential aspect of the practicum. Schools structure such classes in a variety of ways. Whether it is planned around geography, field of service, faculty field advisor or in other ways, one basic objective should be met: the course outline must be flexible enough to invite students to freely bring to class any professional or personal issue which affects their practicum education. If one student raises a question it is likely that most if not all of the students in the group have the same question. Social work curricula must accommodate students' experiential agendas in their concurrent placement seminars. Ideally the instructor should be the person most familiar with each student's work. At the very least, the instructors of these courses should be active in the practicum either as advisors or administrators. Course structure must invite and accommodate all practicum issues brought by students and ensure confidentiality to all members of the class.

School, Agency and Practicum Instructor Contracts

The faculty or school of social work should contract with the social agency which is acting as a learning center and with the individual practicum instructor. These contracts can be based on the conceptualized curriculum. Specific educational principles may be part of such contracts. Two such principles are adult education models of teaching and learning, and knowledge of and respect for diverse learning styles.

There are tensions among faculty, field instructors and students regarding what should be done, taught and learned in the practicum placements. The process of resolving these tensions — through meetings, negotiations and generally finding consensus about the practicum — produces a practice curriculum. Ultimately a contract must be agreed to and perhaps signed by all parties.

The traditional view of field placements is that these students learn to integrate theory and practice. Bogo and Vayda (1987) add reflection or self-awareness to an articulated approach to field instruction. Linkage between theory and its direct application to specific practice interventions is the core of this approach. Practicum curriculum planning must include the teaching of these linkages. Bogo and Vadya (1987) found a strong trend toward using agency-based field instructors. If, as they suggest, over 90% of practicum teachers are agency-based then the need for agreement between schools and practica regarding an articulated model of field teaching should be abundantly clear. Students are helped to become "fully aware of what is involved in a practice act, know why that intervention is selected, and be prepared to determine how the necessary helping techniques should be performed" (Sheafor and Jenkins, 1982, p. 17).

The articulated model includes knowing and doing; academic and experiential learning. Tolson and Kopp (1988) stress that "the (articulated) model involves field-based and classroom instructors jointly designing curricula by delineating and sequencing content" (p. 124). If that collaboration does not occur then two curricula exist, creating a likely source of confusion or conflict between university-based and agency-based teaching. Tolson and Kopp (1988) go on to state that students' practica are "the most important influence on the development of practice." Their point is that efforts to develop and sustain a quality practicum, one which is congruent with what is taught in the university social work courses "are likely to pay large dividends" within the broad area of professional social work practice. With shrinking resources available to the university and social service sectors, the required investment of time by faculty and practicum instructors is unlikely to happen. However, the principle need not be abandoned. University faculty can bring practice experiences into the classroom in a variety of ways. Reluctance to do so may be a bigger obstacle than reduced funding.

The University is Responsible for Selection and Preparation of Practicum Instructors

In a recent survey of schools of social work in the United States, three times as many respondents described the training of field instructors as a weakness in their program as the respondents who saw it as a strength (Kilpatrick and Holland, 1993, pp. 131-132). The standard works on field education barely mention formal training of field instructors. Orientation sessions or annual meetings are commonly offered to practicum teachers. Bogo and Vayda (1991) found that few social work programs in Canada require any training or preparation before someone becomes a field teacher for the school (p. 60). Historically, the profession seems to have assumed that if someone is a competent practitioner then he/she will be a competent practicum instructor. In field instruction, the focus shifts from practice to education, from the client to the student. Teaching is a new role and as with any change, information, support and discussion can assist social work professionals in taking on this new responsibility.

Among the five Australian schools included in this study, all provided either periodic seminars or opportunities to discuss aspects of field teaching for their practicum instructors. An advanced course for experienced field instructors is described in the literature (Fishbein & Glassman, 1991, 226-232). A more basic course could include material on adult education models (Knowles, 1972, 1984) learning and teaching styles (Kolb, Rubin and McIntyre, 1974), student orientation to the agency, the curriculum, developing learning contracts and evaluations. Faculty field advisors could follow up with several meetings each term with new practicum instructors. The parallel process in the field teacher - student - client relationships is an obvious and useful learning tool.

Is the profession ready to require a formal credential for practicum instructors? The turnover rate for field teachers continues to plague schools of social work. Bogo and

Vayda (1991) found that 47% of field instructors were in their first or second year of teaching (p. 59). High turnover was certainly a problem at the Australian universities. To counter this some even suggest a return to the use of field education units (Conklin and Borecki, 1991). The responsibility for offering consistently good practicum instruction lies with the schools of social work. They must develop a core of practicum instructors through selection, training, support, involvement, recognition and reward. The field unit with four to eight students taught by one practicum instructor is a possible model. The instructor could have an academic title within the university and receive compensation from the school. Training resources would have to be invested in the practicum. Whether or not schools offer a formal diploma or certificate, they should require a course in field instruction and some form of one-to-one support during the first year of field teaching experience.

Recognition of Practicum Instructors is Essential

Lacerte and Ray (1991) found that professional commitment was the main motivation for field instructors first supervising and then continuing to supervise students. Their desire to teach and influence others' professional development caused them to continue to teach in spite of a perceived lack of recognition for their contributions. Universities should consider the following ways to recognize the importance of practicum instructors in professional social work education:

1. Demonstrate the value of field teachers through selection, training, periodic evaluation and opportunities for support and certification (Showers & Cuzzi, 1991).
2. Offer field teachers the title of adjunct practicum instructor after several years of successful field instruction, the completion of required courses and an evaluation period. Subsequent promotion in rank to assistant, associate or full professor could be part of such a scheme.
3. Consider joint appointments with social agencies similar to other professions.
4. Appoint practicum instructors to the appropriate committees and councils within the school.
5. Make university courses available to field teachers at no cost. Other faculty/staff privileges such as access to library, recreational facilities and parking should be given to field instructors.
6. Recognize practicum instructors in university calendars and other publications.

Within the agency practicum instruction is usually accorded a high status. The teacher is recognized for the expertise, skill and training inherent in the role of practicum instructor. Such recognition often parallels advancement within the agency, for example, to supervisory positions. The agency can also facilitate practicum learning by reducing the field instructors' caseloads (the student would take on those clients) to create time for teaching. In this way the agency establishes an environment which supports education and the teaching itself is under the auspices of the agency. The sense of community and common goals discussed earlier in the paper is exemplified by the agency-school collaboration in creating a practicum curriculum and how it manifests itself in the agency-based teaching center.

All Faculty must be Active in Practicum Curriculum

Field involvement is often marginalized within schools of social work and in the larger university. At one extreme, (there is an Australian example) non-faculty social workers do all the field administration and liaison functions. Faculty teach in the classroom and do scholarly work. The message is clear: the practicum is not worth the time of faculty. The practicum is a secondary service. But even when faculty perform the liaison role it is not considered as teaching for the purposes of workload credit or taken into account for merit, tenure and promotion. This is certainly the case at Wilfrid Laurier. Just as social work must continue to explain its purposes to the community, so must schools of social work explain professional education to the broader university community. No one else can.

In some schools in Australia and Canada, field advising is combined with teaching concurrent courses for students in their practica. At Sydney University all faculty who teach practice courses are involved in all aspects of field work, including its administration. At first the system seemed fragmented and inefficient, but it works well. In five months of observing it firsthand there were many instances of mutual support, teamwork and a general appreciation for all the dimensions of field work.

Finally, field work educators must write about what they do. Descriptive writing about field advising, concurrent seminars and the training and support of practicum instructors would assist all social work programs. Process and outcome research would be useful in evaluating practicum education, the field advising liaison function and integrative seminars. We are responsible for doing that. This is scholarship in the eyes of the university and will contribute to the knowledge base of social work education. Some of that work ought to be done in collaboration with practicum instructors.

CONCLUSIONS

The schools of social work are responsible for the conceptualization of the practicum and its adminstration. Within the departments practicum education must be no less valued than any other aspect of the program. Once these values are firmly established within the university, the other principles will follow. Practica require the involvement of agency practitioners and administrators. Their perspectives must be included in curriculum and program development and subsequent policy and administrative decision making. Representation on all bodies which discuss field matters is essential. Schools must have standards for field teachers and formal courses and one-to-one faculty consultation in order to train and assist beginning and advanced practicum instructors. Field advising must carry the status of teaching within universities. At the same time it is vital that faculty write about and do research in the area of practicum education. Social work must explain itself, including its range of teaching modalities, to the university community. Practicum instructors must be recognized in formal, tangible ways by the universities and the agencies. Finally, all faculty should be part of the practicum. With up to 50 percent of students' time spent in the field it is ludicrous that faculty members can opt out of half of their students' education.

REFERENCES

Australian Association for Social Work and Welfare Education National Working Party on Field Education. (1990). Field Education in the 1990's Policy and Curriculum. Sydney: Author.

Bogo, M., & Vayda, E. (1991). Developing a process model for field instruction. In D. Schneck, B. Grossman, & U. Glassman (Eds.), *Field education in social work contemporary issues and trends*, 59-66. Dubuque, Iowa: Kendall/Hunt Publishing Company.

Bogo, M., & Vayda, E. (1987). *The practice of field instruction in social work: Theory and process*. Toronto, ON: University of Toronto.

Canadian Association of Schools of Social Work (CASSW). (1993). Manual of standards and procedures for the accreditation of social work education. Ottawa: Author.

Conklin, J.J., & Borecki, M.C. (1991). Field education units revisited: A model for the 1990's. In D. Schneck, B. Grossman, & U. Glassman (Eds.), *Field education in social work contemporary issues and trends*, 122-130. Dubuque, Iowa: Kendall/Hunt Publishing Company.

Fishbein, H., & Glassman, U. (1991). The advanced seminar for field instructors: content and process. In D. Schneck, B. Grossman, & U. Glassman (Eds.), *Field education in social work contemporary issues and trends*, 226-232. Dubuque, Iowa: Kendall/Hunt Publishing Company.

Kilpatrick, A.C., & Holland, T.P. (1993). Management of the field instruction program in social work education. *Journal of Teaching in Social Work*, 7(1), 123-136.

Kilpatrick, A.C. (1991). Differences and commonalities in bsw and msw field instruction: In search of continuity. In D. Schneck, B. Grossman, & U. Glassman (Eds.), *Field education in social work contemporary issues and trends*, 167-176. Dubuque, Iowa: Kendall/Hunt Publishing Company.

Knowles, M. (1984). *The adult learner: A neglected species* (3rd ed.). Houston, Texas: Gulf Publishing Company.

Knowles, M. (1975). *The modern practice of adult education.* New York: Association Press.

Kolb, D.A., Rubin, I.M., & McIntyre, J.A. (1974). *Organizational psychology an experiential approach*, (2nd ed.), 23-31. Englewood Cliffs, New Jersey: Prentice-Hall Inc.

Koonin, R. (1988). Fieldwork: A Catalyst for educational change. In R. Berreen, O. Grace, O. James, & T. Vinson (Eds.), *Advances in Social Welfare Education*, 79-88. Sydney: The heads of schools of social work in Australia.

Lacerte, J., & Ray, J. (1991). Recognizing the educational contributions of field instructors. In D. Schneck, B. Grossman, & U. Glassman (Eds.), *Field education in social work contemporary issues and trends*, 217-225. Dubuque, Iowa: Kendall/Hunt Publishing Company.

Mulford, R.M. (1963). Untitled paper. In the future for field instruction: agency-school commitment and communication. New York: Council on Social Work Education.

Sheafor, B., & Jenkins, L. (Eds.). (1982). *Quality field instruction in social work: Program development and maintenance.* New York: Longman.

Showers, N., & Cuzzi, L. (1991). What field instructors of social work students need from hospital field work programs. *Social Work in Health Care*, *16*(1), 39-52.

Task Force on Field Education: Final Report. (1992). Faculty of Social Work, Wilfrid Laurier University, Waterloo, Ontario.

Tolson, E.R., & Kopp, J. (1988). The practicum: Clients, problems, interventions and influences on student practice. *Journal of Social Work Education*, *24*(2), 123-134.

Walden, T., & Brown, L.N. (1985). The integration seminar: A vehicle for joining theory and practice. *Journal of Social Work Education*, *21*(1), 13-19.

Wilson, S. (1991). *Field instruction techniques for supervisors.* New York: Free Press.

CHAPTER THIRTY

AN EMPIRICAL APPROACH TO DEFINING QUALITY COMPONENTS IN FIELD EDUCATION

Stephen Nixon, Steven Shardlow, Mark Doel,
Sheila McGrath and Rose Gordon

INTRODUCTION

Background to Social Work and Social Work Education

Before discussing how quality is might be identified in practice learning (field education) some contextual information about social work and social work education in the United Kingdom (UK) is provided. A glossary of terms used in this paper and throughout the UK is provided to assist the North American reader.

In the United Kingdom most social workers (a majority of whom are women) are employed in the state sector working either for local government or the probation service. However, there is a growing voluntary and private sector. This sector of the welfare services is expanding rapidly as there is considerable government pressure upon local authorities to divest themselves of much of the direct provision and to hand this over to the voluntary and private sectors. In the next few years it seems likely that welfare pluralism will become reality in the UK. The challenge for social work education is how to respond to this changed reality of practice.

There are 91 social work programs providing places for approximately 5,000 students each year on the Diploma in Social Work, (Dip SW) which is the first national, professional qualification for social work. Partnership between service agency and faculty has been institutionalized through a national requirement that all Dip SW courses are the joint responsibility of at least one university (or educational institution) and one agency working in partnership together. About half of each course is practice based, i.e., the student is on placement in a social work agency. The content of Dip SW courses is regulated and must conform to national regulations (CCETSW, 1991). These and other similar regulations are mandated by the Central Council for Education and Training in Social Work (CCETSW). This body is appointed by government and has a legal responsibility to promote education and training in social work; it is charged with regulating standards of social work education e.g., all Dip SW courses must be approved by CCETSW. In addition to the responsibility for basic professional training CCETSW also has responsibility for pre-professional and post qualifying training.

The Diploma in Social Work takes two years of full time study. In academic terms it must be at least equivalent to the standard required at the end of the second year of a three year undergraduate program. Confusingly it may be offered in concert with different levels of academic award, up to a Masters Degree or with no academic award at all. Hence, social work is not a full graduate profession in the UK. In recent years there has been a sustained effort to widen the recruitment base of the profession — with some success — to encourage non traditional entrants to higher education.

Why Quality is on the Agenda

Social work students in the UK undertake two practice placements, i.e., 50% of the two year social work training course. During this relatively short period of time students have to achieve a standard of professional competence through the development and integration of new skills, knowledge, understanding and values. Ensuring that these placements make an appropriate contribution to the students' development is therefore vital.

Over the last decade and a half, there have been a number of developments in approaches to the management and delivery of services which can be applied to the human services. One of the most significant features to emerge has been the focus upon quality. This has been seen in the work of Peters and Waterman (1982) and the seminal work of Donabedian (1980). This growth of interest in quality has influenced the sphere of education and training. Indeed in the university sector of the UK, the Higher Education Quality Council has been established to encourage and monitor the development of standards of teaching in particular. In the sphere of professional education and training, recent initiatives to improve the quality of field education in the UK have included the introduction of a new Award in Practice Teaching for agency-based practice teachers by CCETSW (1991). In addition, a requirement that agencies meet certain criteria before they can be registered as Approved Agencies for practice teaching has been introduced (CCETSW 1990).

The Requirements for the Award in Practice Teaching specify a limited 14-item list of knowledge, skills and values which neophyte practice teachers must be able to demonstrate in their practice. This is currently under review and while more complex requirements are expected to emerge, they are likely to be concise.

Agency approval requirements are more extensive, running to some 10 pages of guidance about placements and agency systems which must be in place before an agency can be approved. The guidance is produced by an accrediting body which seeks to lay down standards and encourage agencies to comply.

While the literature (e.g., Butler & Elliott, 1985; Danbury, 1993; Ford & Jones, 1987) describes the organization of placements and their requirements, little work has been undertaken which seeks to define the specific quality characteristics of a placement. The literature on quality has grown rapidly spanning differing approaches to its definition, with different models and means of implementation and of measurement and assessment (Cassum & Gupta, 1992; Kelly & Warr, 1992). The quality of a service depends in part on the organization and the workforce and any discussion of quality must be set in this broader context. However, the essence of quality is in the service delivered to the user or customer (Osborne, 1992). Quality must involve consideration of the inputs, processes and outcomes (Donabedian, 1980) and the achievement of satisfaction (Ackoff, 1974). Defining criteria for quality can be specified as objective or subjective (Osborne, 1992). Ackoff (1974, 1976) argues strongly for quality to be best evaluated not by external observers with surrogate measures but by the direct participation of consumers of the service.

In considering statements about quality, any criteria must be inspected and evaluated. The organizational position, experience and perspectives of those who drew up the criteria need to be considered. Several stakeholders can be identified in the network of field education: the practice teacher who is agency-based, the practice teacher's immediate line-manager or supervisor, the senior agency management, the agency's student placement manager, the social work student, the college-based tutor, the social work qualification validating body, the agency funding bodies and government department, and service users who have a significant stake in the process and outcome. Hence some nine stakeholders with potentially different sets of interest in the process of student training and its outcome can be identified. Each stakeholder brings their own experience of practice teaching, their particular role and any current responsibilities within or outside the agency. It is therefore possible that criteria derived from individuals with different perspectives may vary. How far these criteria have been influenced by the perspectives of individuals and their experiences should be considered.

The issue of whose perspectives and interests should be taken into account and whose should be paramount will also need to be considered.

Thus, for example, the perspectives of a student social worker or a practice teacher may be different. Equally, an agency manager, whose main task is to ensure delivery to service users within resource constraints may have a different perspective on the quality characteristics of student placements. Thus while the educational and training dimension must form the core focus of a placement, social work student training needs have to be managed within a broader focus of the agency's service delivery needs. Ultimately quality in field education is about the practice teaching and education delivered and the learning achieved by the student. This will also include enabling this to happen at the immediate agency level, senior management level and at validating body level. Such a view of quality is about the achievement of objectives.

While the aim of recent developments has been to raise standards and improve quality, there has been no comprehensive attempt to define just what quality in field education is. Indeed, any discussion of quality seems to be based on intuitive or a priori definitions rather than research. In the light of this, a research project was devised and the initial research hypothesis emerged from the assumption that the definition of quality will vary between the different stake holders in field education. The present project was undertaken to explore this.

METHOD

The Study: Introduction

The study was established as a joint venture of the universities of Birmingham and Sheffield in England. It was designed as a pilot study on a modest scale with limited financial resources. It was intended to explore views and develop hypotheses as the basis for constructing a more substantial study of quality in field education involving the different stakeholders. It focused on practice teachers and social work students as the two groups most actively and directly involved in the process. It was hypothesized that the definition of quality is likely to vary between these two main players in the process of practice teaching and learning. The aim of the study was therefore to explore practice teachers' and social work students' specifications of the components of quality, to compare such specifications and to draw conclusions from the findings.

The Sample

Two samples, one of social work students and another of practice teachers, were obtained. Social work students on the post-graduate Diploma/Masters degree in social work course at the University of Sheffield were invited to participate in the project. Eight students agreed to be interviewed about their perceptions and experiences of practice placements. All eight were in their first year of the two year course and had undertaken one placement. All the students were of European origin, four were female and four male.

Practice teachers who had completed the post-qualifying course in Practice teaching at the University of Birmingham and were holders of the CCETSW Award in Practice Teaching were invited to participate in the study. Eight agreed to be interviewed, five women and three men of whom four were black and four white. All had held the Award for at least one year and supervised at least five students on professional placements. Guided Interview schedules were used to ensure similar coverage of the experiences and thoughts of interviewees. Both practice teacher and student schedules covered the same areas but appropriately differentiated questions and prompts were devised to allow for their different roles. Interviews were tape-recorded and subsequently transcribed for analysis. Transcripts were analyzed in conjunction with the interviewer's notes taken at the time of the interviews. Topics were identified within transcripts and the ideas, thoughts and views expressed were summarized with key quotations.

Representativeness of the Sample

The means of obtaining the two samples were not random. While the students were a self-selected group, certain criteria were employed with respect to inviting the practice teachers to participate relating to gender, race and experience of field education in order to seek some balance. Although not a random sample, the respondents do represent a range of practice teachers and social work students. The aim of the pilot was to generate ideas and issues for a larger study. In this respect the samples have been effective in providing insight into some of the issues for further study.

PRELIMINARY FINDINGS

Introduction

Analysis was undertaken of the data derived from the student and practice teacher interviews. This provided an initial classification of responses into a series of criteria with some range specifications. These ranges were derived from respondents with varying attitudes and experiences which were both positive and less positive. A series of statements about placements were derived from practice teachers and from students.

At a relatively early stage analysis revealed that statements made by interviewees about their experience of placement were statements covering a range from:

- approval and satisfaction with specific aspects of a placement;
- adequacy or minimal acceptability;
- negative comments focusing on the inadequacy of a placement.

Subsequently an attempt has been made to classify the topics produced by the preliminary analysis into broader concepts about quality in field education. This has been done partly to explore the possibility of classifying and comparing student and practice teacher material and partly to see if a model of quality in practice teaching might be derived from the experience of the respondents.

The Social Work Students

The following issues were raised by students in relation to their experience of their first placement in year one of their course. It became clear that students, despite limited experience of placements, can have strongly held views, especially if the placement was particularly successful or unsuccessful. While some of these statements may be extremes, it is these which have prompted the preliminary analysis and classification attempted here.

1) *Criterion:* *Degree to which student has developed professionally*
   Range   (i)   placement experience enhances student's development
   to   (ii)   student's development is diminished through their experience of the placement.

In (i) the student benefits from the placement experience and acquires greater competence and professional development. In comparison in (ii) some experiences are so negative that the student loses confidence and competence. Examples of negative outcomes from placements were described by some of the students included poor experiences, and confused, haphazard, and unplanned placements with a practice teacher who generated dependency.

2) *Criterion:* *Degree of student's satisfaction with placement*
   Range   (i)   student expresses satisfaction with experience of the placement
   to   (ii)   student expresses dissatisfaction with the placement experience.

This is a very general criterion and is multifactorial in its origins. However it appears to provides a general overall impression of the students experience though is not specific in its nature. Factors which contributed to students' satisfaction included the planning of the placement, the attention paid to their individual needs, the nature of the relationship which developed and the positive approach to enabling learning to take place.

3) *Criterion:*   *Nature of the learning experience*
   Range: (i)   individually designed and focused placement
   to   (ii)   standard, routine placement is provided.

The placement in (i) takes into account the student's experience and specific learning needs whereas in (ii) a standard package is provided as used for several preceding students. This criterion exhibits several of the students' expectations and experiences about placements. Ideally students thought that a placement should be individually designed and some students experienced this. However, those students who arrived in placements which were designed for previous students or where the agency dictated a standard and routine approach found the placement a poor experience. Where student expectations had been low in the first place, such placements were seen as simply "just what they had expected."

4) *Criterion:*   *Degree of independence of student by the end of the placement*
   Range   (i)   student achieves independence in role as student social worker
   to   (ii)   student not assisted in achieving independence

In (i) the student is able to operate within the placement with an appropriate level of independence from the practice teacher, varying according to placement. In comparison, in (ii) the student is held in/or reduced to a dependent role in needing or seeking, for example, the regular approval of the practice teacher for even the smallest of actions. For the student to achieve independence, the practice teacher has to act to ensure the student is able to achieve and demonstrate independence in their work and placement interactions through, for example, induction and supervision. This criterion is related in part to knowing what is expected, and having a planned placement assists independence. However, personality factors and the level of previous experience were also important. In addition, some negotiation about independence took place with the student taking the initiative.

5) *Criterion:*   *Degree of knowledge of expected standard of performance*
   Range   (i)   student has knowledge of the expected standard of performance
   to   (ii)   student has limited knowledge of the expected standard of performance

In (i) the student knows with some clarity what s/he is expected to achieve compared with (ii) where the student is uncertain about the level of knowledge and skills expected to be achieved. Several students indicated that clarity is important in helping students to understand what they are expected to know and be able to do. Certainty in this area was a desirable characteristic. Any uncertainty created anxiety among the students. Some indicated the uncertainty and consequential level of anxiety had generated a fear of doing *anything* in the placement without seeking their practice teacher's view.

6) *Criterion:*   *Degree of planning of placement*
   Range   (i)   planned and purposeful placement
   to   (ii)   haphazard placement with little planning.

In (i) the careful selection of experiences with specific objectives to meet the students' learning needs occurs. This is in contrast to (ii) in which placement experiences lack any co-ordination and sequencing of learning. Some students had particularly strong views as to whether or not placements were well planned. Students seemed to be well aware when a placement had been haphazardly put together, and sometimes at the last minute with little systematic thought.

7) *Criterion:*   *Degree of freedom to question*
   Range   (i)   student able to freely question practice teacher
   to   (ii)   student experienced a restricted freedom to question

In (i) the student is able to raise questions over a whole series of issues including the placement, its aims and structure. Whereas in (ii) the student felt unable to question the practice teacher about the placement and often there was no one else available for discussion. The creation of an atmosphere which encourages questioning is related to both attitude of the practice teacher and the creation of conditions within a planned and purposeful placement. If the placement is not planned and there are uncertainties, the students indicated that they considered it is too risky to ask questions because of the practice teacher's powers in the assessment process. In addition, the location in the agency of other students assisted the formation of a network of mutual support which facilitated the students' freedom to question.

FINDINGS: PRACTICE TEACHERS

8) *Criterion:*   *Degree of personal satisfaction derived from the placement by the practice teacher*

| Range | (i) | practice teacher experiences personal satisfaction by seeing the student's professional learning and development during placement. |
| to | (ii) | practice teacher experiences little or no satisfaction or even experiences dissatisfaction over the placement. |

The practice teachers' satisfaction seemed to be related most closely to an involvement in, and observation of, the students' learning and development. Another component involved the practice teacher learning from the student. This covered a broad range of learning for example new knowledge being taught on the student's course or having evaluative comments about their own social work made by the student. Practice teachers did not report dissatisfaction over the whole of a placement. Dissatisfaction focused on one or two elements of the experience. In fact, this criterion of satisfaction with the parallel learning processes of practice teachers and students was perhaps the key dynamic in the work of the practice teacher. The placement involved a collaborative process in which practice teacher and student learnt together. The satisfaction generated enthusiasm and commitment to the activity as a whole.

9) *Criterion:*	*Nature of the relationship between practice teacher and student*	
Range:	(i)	the relationship between practice teacher and student is based on respect for and trust in each other.
to	(ii)	the relationship lacks trust and respect.

While this criterion is one of the more difficult to measure, this feature was identified as an important component for several practice teachers. They reported working at building the relationship through every aspect of the placement while students praised practice teachers who were sensitive to this.

10) *Criterion:*	*Degree of student's contribution to the work of the team*	
Range:	(i)	work is allocated to the student which enables him/her to make a contribution to the work of the team and which the team perceives as useful
to	(ii)	work is undertaken which is not seen as useful to the team/or the student is seen as a burden.

The practice teachers indicated the importance of the students' work being useful to the team and to avoid creating the impression that a student might be a burden to the team. From the students' perspective, making a contribution to the team was an important component in feeling at ease within a placement. There is also a further issue embedded within this of ensuring that a placement remains student- and learning-centered and does not become focused on service delivery using the student solely as an additional member of the work force.

11)	*Criterion:*		*Degree and quality of contacts between practice teacher and student's college tutor (liaison)*
	Range	(i)	the practice teacher has regular constructive contact with the student's college tutor.
	to	(ii)	the tutor rarely visits and shows little commitment or involvement.

This criterion concerns the level of support provided and discussion about the student's work during the placement by the student's college tutor. The kind of interaction described by practice teachers related to the tutor's lack of involvement and the sense of isolation to which this contributed. The positive element of this criterion recognized the importance of such support and interaction.

12)	*Criterion:*		*Degree of choice in selecting student social worker for placement*
	Range	(i)	practice teacher has a genuine choice when deciding whether to accept a social work student.
	to	(ii)	practice teacher is unable to exercise any choice in decision to accept the student onto the placement.

Lack of choice and being forced by the agency to accept any student was considered to be an important negative element. Practice teachers considered that they needed to be able to exercise professional judgement when considering the appropriateness of a student for a placement. Some reported filtering out students who would not have generated a satisfying placement.

13)	*Criterion:*		*Frequency and quality of meetings with other practice teachers*
	Range	(i)	the practice teacher has regular contact with other practice teachers who are readily accessible.
	to	(ii)	the practice teacher has limited contact with other practice teachers who are not readily accessible.

The opportunity to meet with other practice teachers diminishes the sense of isolation, enables practice teachers to discuss common concerns and keep up todate. The sense of relative isolation diminishes the potential vibrancy of a placement.

CRITICAL POINTS IN THE PLACEMENT

In addition to the quality components, analysis of the data revealed a series of statements about critical points in the placements which could, in the view of students, and practice teachers, determine the success of the placement. The statements concerning critical points were focused on three aspects. These were the preliminary informal meeting; the end of the induction period (some 2-3 weeks into the placement) and the conclusion of each regular weekly supervision session.

The Preliminary Informal Meeting

All students and practice teachers emphasized the critical importance of the preliminary meeting as an opportunity to establish the placement on a firm basis of shared knowledge. Without a satisfactory preliminary meeting, the students suggested that the placement could rapidly flounder or at least fail to deliver the quality of experience which might otherwise have been achieved. When the student and practice teacher meet together on this first occasion, it is likely to be after some exchange of preliminary information about themselves, the agency, the student's learning needs, and the practice teacher's approach to learning and teaching. The study emphasized how this meeting permits the relationship to develop between student and practice teacher. Discussion of the placement, its overall purpose; the initial negotiation of the way in which specific needs may be met; and other components of preliminary planning can be considered. This meeting can provide an opportunity for student or practice teacher to recognize that, for a variety of possible reasons, either may feel the placement would not be successful. The findings revealed the critical importance of this preliminary work in the experience of the students. It is in such meetings that placement requirements, including, for example, the quality criteria reported above, can be negotiated and agreed.

The study also indicated that there are other critical points which continue to provide opportunities to ensure that the placement is finely tuned to meet the student's learning needs. Such points were specified by respondents as including the end of the *induction period*, when the practice teacher will be in a position to ensure a more accurate analysis of student needs and how these can best be met. In addition, the *weekly supervision session* can be used to ensure that the placement continues to provide the optimum learning experience for students.

Each of these points provides a different stage as the placement continues of seeking to ensure that optimum learning is achieved. The development of a strategic plan for a placement is important to ensure the criteria are met at the critical points in the placement and that the student moves smoothly through the process.

DISCUSSION

A series of statements have been elicited from two sets of practice teachers and social work students which relate to their different experiences and perceptions of the agency-based components of social work training. While these initial statements were personal, none of the statements was raised by just one individual. Most statements were obtained from three, four or five respondents. In some cases, similar statements were made by most respondents in the set. From the preliminary analysis of the statements, several criteria have been identified. The dimensions of these criteria have emerged from the empirical evidence of these two (admittedly small) sets of stakeholders. This provides preliminary insight into the perceptions of quality of the members of the two sets. The statements give some indication of what is seen to be important to be assured of a quality experience in a practice placement.

While some of the statements presented are unlikely to be seen as new or revolutionary, what is important is that they are derived from the experience of those two groups of stakeholders directly involved. Many of the statements match intuitively derived statements from the literature which may provide some confirmation of the validity of the statements. The two sets yield different criteria and are based on variations in perspective. A different understanding of practice placements may be emerging from the statements as there are some indications that while there may be some shared common elements, others diverge between the two sets of stakeholders.

Added Value and Quality

Each criterion has a range along a continuum from desirable to less desirable characteristics. It is possible to suggest that the mid-point on the continuum represents an adequate though relatively limited aspect of a placement. The mid-point provides a base-line indicator and the range of positive statements indicate dimensions representing excellence. The interval between the base-line and the positive statement could be described as representing an added value dimension. This added value suggests, and may provide, a measure of what is required to transform an adequate placement into a quality placement. The concept differentiates an adequate placement from a quality one and provides the opportunity to compare characteristics of alternative placements.

Some further issues have emerged from the study. Implementation of the positive statements in some of the criteria would require only limited additional resources. Some are directly practice based and would be relatively simple and inexpensive to include as a key part of practice teaching and learning. While some dimensions would require additional resources, some extra time and careful planning would help to secure others. Several criteria demonstrate the importance of clarifying definitions and negotiating details very early in the placement.

The findings suggest that there are critical points when establishing and fine-tuning a placement in order to ensure the students educational and training needs are met to the best achievable level. It is not known how far implementation of these quality criteria would really advance quality in practice teaching as far as the respondents' statements suggest. This would need further investigation.

This study has sought to explore the notion of defining quality through an empirical approach. The findings suggest that participants' views in the process of practice teaching are at least as valid as those of an individual within an agency asked to generate quality criteria from a priori principles. Questions still remain concerning the definition of quality. Does quality rest in the minimum satisfactory level for a placement or is quality about excellence? The respondents statements in this study seem to suggest that satisfactory or adequate is not sufficient. Each criterion has been outlined as a continuum, but how should each criterion be defined and how should the dimensions of each criterion be decided upon. Several of the criteria specified are multi-faceted and each raises its own set of questions and issues for further exploration and elaboration.

It is not known whether a larger-scale project would generate similar criteria. This suggests an extended research and development project to explore these issues further. In fact further work is an hand to expand the number of stakeholders' perceptions. A key focus for this project will be to see if it is possible to identify a set of core criteria common to all stakeholders and a series of specific criteria generated from different stakeholders and their particular perspectives. It would appear that a single definition of quality and its criteria would be unlikely to emerge. Each group of stakeholders is likely to have their own set of criteria. There are at least another seven stakeholders who were identified in the first part of the paper whose views could help to elucidate the issues addressed.

SUMMARY OF ISSUES

Indicators

How might we develop indicators for each of the 13 criteria? For example, is "Degree to which student has developed professionally" self-explanatory or does it need a set of indicators? How might one develop these criteria? A hierarchy of indicators would enable us to discover, for example, what aspects of a placement were valued over others (Degree of student's satisfaction with placement.)

Universal Standards; Individual Discretion

Student's desire for an individually-tailored placement experience means we need to think carefully about how a practice curriculum designed for the program as a whole, with general standards and fairness in mind, can be adapted flexibly to individual students.

Time Frames

The significance of certain criteria may be much greater at certain points during the placement than others (this includes time before and after the placement). For example, concerning the increasingly autonomous activities of students (criterion 4), are there certain recognizable points during a quality placement when it can be expected that the student has achieved certain tasks independently?

Stakeholders

To what extent would stakeholders have the same list of priorities for the criteria? (For example, is the degree of freedom to question as important to practice teachers as it is to students?) In particular, how to involve the client stakeholders in the definition of quality? One notable difference amongst stakeholders might be the criterion concerning tutor-placement contact. To what extent is this based on a symbolic desire, important though symbols are? For example, is a tutor visit always the best way of providing support to practice teachers (would group workshops, etc. be more effective?) Choice of student might also open up differences between stakeholders' criteria. To what extent should practice teachers expect "choice" of students? College-based teachers have no choice about the students they work with; as part of the teaching team should this be true of practice teachers also? However, if choice is a mark of a quality placement, should we go with that whatever the "oughts" or "shoulds"?

Beyond the Practice Teacher-Student Dyad

The question, "What makes a quality agency backdrop for the quality placement?" was not asked. However, it is an area for further consideration, along with some understanding of whether isolated quality placements can exist in unfavorable agency contexts. This also relates to the tension between the student's differentness in the team (a student-learner not an employee-doer) and his/her desire not to be seen as ancillary or burdensome, is a difficult balance to achieve.

Some of the key questions emerging from the study:

- How can we harness knowledge of the critical significance of the pre-placement meeting to ensure that an adequate placement becomes a quality placement?
- Is there a hierarchy of criteria which helps to turn an adequate placement into a quality placement? To what extent would this hierarchy be applicable to all placements, and to what extent would it vary from one placement to another?
- How can we generate specific indicators for each of the criteria? Would these be transferable (and, therefore, very useful) or would they be too specific to each placement?
- How do the different stakeholders' views of quality vary, and what 'weight' should be given to the different stakeholders?

GLOSSARY (equivalent North American terms in brackets)

- Practice Placement (Field Practicum)
  — one of two periods of agency-based training under the supervision of a practice teacher. Students undertake and have responsibility for agency work. Integral to this is teaching on social work practice.

- Practice Teacher (Field Instructor)
  — agency-based social worker who supervises social work students on practice placement and whose role is to teach and enable students learning to take place.

- Tutor (Liaison)
  — college staff linked to the practice teacher and student.

REFERENCES

Ackoff, R. (1974). *Redesigning the future.* New York: Wiley.

Ackoff, R. (1976). Does quality of life have to be quantified? *Operational Research Quarterly, 27,* 289-303.

Alaszewski, A., & Manthorpe, J. (1993). Quality and the welfare services: A literature review. *British Journal of Social Work, 23,* 653-665.

Butler, B., & Elliott, D. (1985). *Teaching and learning for practice.* London: Gower Press.

Cassam, E., & Gupta, H. (1992). *Quality assurance for social care agencies.* Harlow: Longman.

CCETSW. (1983). *Research in practice teaching* (Study 6). Central Council for Education and Training in Social Work.

CCETSW. (1990). *Improving standards in practice learning* (Paper 26.3). London: Central Council for Education and Training in Social Work.

CCETSW. (1991). *Rules and requirements for the diploma in social work* (Paper 30) (2nd ed.). London: Central Council for Education and Training in Social Work.

Danbury, H. (1993). *Teaching practical social work.* London: Bedford Square Press.

Ford, K., & Jones, A. (1987). *Student supervision.* London: Macmillan.

Grant, G. (1992). Researching user and carer involvement. In M. Barnes & G. Wistow (Eds.), *Researching user involvement.* Leeds: Nuffield Institute for the Health Services Studies.

Harvey, L., Burrows, A., & Green, D. (1992). *Criteria of quality in higher education.* Birmingham: University of Central England.

Kelly, D., & Warr, B. (Eds.) (1992). *Quality counts: Achieving quality in social care.* London: Whiting and Birch/Social Care Association.

Osborne, S. (1992). The quality dimension. Evaluating quality of service and quality of life in human services. *British Journal of Social work, 22,* 437-453.

Peters, T. J., & Waterman, R. H. (1982). *In search of excellence.* New York: Harper Row.

Social Services Inspectorate. (1992). *Committed to quality: Quality assurance in social services departments.* London: Her Majesty's Stationary Office.

PART FIVE

FIELD EDUCATION AND
DIVERSITY:
ISSUES, TRENDS AND
PRACTICES

The seven chapters in this part of the book provide a significant offering and an up-to-date examination of current issues, trends and practices that address and promote cultural competence through field education.

The first of these by Narda Razack, Eli Teram and Myrta Rivera Sahas describes a project developed by a school of social work in collaboration with several social service agencies to enhance cross-cultural knowledge. The next chapter presents materials and guides to better prepare field instructors to help students practice with diverse ethnic, cultural and racial communities developed by Helena Summers and Roxanne Powers. A practicum experience designed to promote multiculturalism within a police service is described from the point of view of the student and host agency, written by David Este, Manuela Lacentra, Hal Wetherup and George Mayes. An often neglected area of concern but nonetheless an important consideration are students with disabilities which Martha Bial and Maxine Lynn discuss in relation to field education.

Building relationships with First Nations communities and agencies is the focus of the chapter by Helena Summers and Michael Yellow Bird. Mary Rodwell reflects on the history and development of Brazilian social work and suggests North American field educators can learn from their focus on participatory research and macro practice. The final paper in this section by M. Teresa Trainer presents a field practicum model from Mexico designed to promote community development projects which provide an alternative model for developing cultural competence.

Given the importance placed on graduating students who are ethnically sensitive, culturally competent and able to take action against discrimination and oppression, these chapters offer a range of valuable suggestions and useful strategies for field educators.

CHAPTER THIRTY-ONE

CULTURAL DIVERSITY IN FIELD WORK EDUCATION: A PRACTICE MODEL FOR ENHANCING CROSS CULTURAL KNOWLEDGE

Narda Razack, Eli Teram and Myrta Rivera Sahas

INTRODUCTION

Although many studies have concluded that social work curriculum must become more responsive to an ethnically diverse community, practical application and implementation of the recommendations continue to be lagging (CASSW Task Force, 1991; O'Neill & Yelaja, 1994; Yelaja, 1988). While social workers must face the challenge of working cross culturally, a mono-cultural approach to teaching seems to dominate most academic institutions. Considering cultural diversity in a context of anti-racist pedagogy in field work education can fill some of these gaps. In addition to heightening students' awareness and sensitivity to ethnicity and race, the initiative described in this chapter was designed to provide students with practical skills and to address some service gaps in the community.

Research studies conducted in the Waterloo Region confirm the existence of barriers to social and health services for a number of visible minority groups, recent immigrants and refugees (Multicultural Health Coalition, 1992; Ministry of Citizenship, 1991; Ministry of Health, 1991). Some potential clients do not seek help due to negative previous experiences, misperception of programs or lack of information about availability of services. Others have difficulty coping with the unfamiliar and formal culture of human service organizations (Teram & White, 1993).

In response to these community and educational needs, the Faculty of Social Work, Wilfrid Laurier University, the Kitchener-Waterloo Multicultural Centre and selected social service agencies collaborated to develop a model to enhance cross-cultural knowledge.[1] Initial funding for the project came from a number of sources;[2] Wilfrid Laurier University provides on-going support for professional development and training.

The account of our experience with this initiative focuses on the following:

a)   The evolution of the project;
b)   The educational and organizational objectives;
c)   Overall structure and procedures;
d)   Group process to support an integrated learning experience;
e)   Implications for social work education;
f)   Thoughts for the future.

THE EVOLUTION OF THE PROJECT

In the 1990 Winter term, two clinical students placed in generic counselling agencies — Kitchener-Waterloo Counselling Services and Interfaith (Kitchener) — spent one day a week (out of their four days in placement) at two multicultural agencies:[3] the Kitchener-Waterloo Multicultural Centre and Focus for Ethnic Women.[4] Although it was a valuable experience, the feedback received from the students and their supervisors indicated the need for: a) a clearer definition of roles; b) more effective coordination

---

1   The initial concept was developed by a committee which included: Eli Teram, Faculty of Social Work (Chair); Joan Leeson, Director of Field Work, Faculty of Social Work; Debbie King, Field Instructor; Myrta Rivera, Executive Director, Kitchener-Waterloo Multicultural Centre; and, Michael Alemu, Narda Razack & Prabha Vaidaynathan (MSW, Class of 1991).

2   The Ministry of Citizenship, the United Way, Wilfrid Laurier University's Academic Development Fund and the Faculty of Social Work.

3   This term refers to organizations, groups, and organizational units, with a mandate to serve immigrants and refugees, or to address multi- and inter-cultural issues.

4   The Multicultural Center offers programs to educate the community about multiculturalism as well as immigrant settlement and interpretation services; Focus for Ethnic Women is a work training program for visible minority women.

between the agencies; c) an orientation on multicultural issues; and, d) additional supervisory support for students.

Based on this feedback, we decided to develop a more centralized model with the Multicultural Centre providing the core link between the multicultural community and mainstream organizations.[5] In September 1990, the first group of clinical social work students were placed at the Kitchener-Waterloo Multicultural Centre as outreach workers for participating field placement agencies. Here, the students pursued their learning objectives in a multicultural context for one day a week (out of four days in placement). During this 15 weeks term the students maintained the primary agency as their base for supervisory support. The Multicultural Centre and Wilfrid Laurier University provided additional support and orientation for cross-cultural social work practice.

Building on this experience, and in response to requests to expand the project, it was decided to facilitate the development of a multi-agency model. Although the essence of this model is similar to the previous arrangement, a larger number of generic and multicultural agencies form dyads that provide an opportunity for work in a multicultural environment. Given the uniqueness of each agency, the evolving dyads devise working arrangements that take into consideration their realities.

GOALS AND OBJECTIVES

The main goal of this initiative is to enhance students sensitivity to cultural, racial and ethnic diversity and provide opportunities to develop knowledge and skills in cross-cultural practice. A secondary goal of the project is to build bridges for clients from immigrant settlement and ethno-specific agencies and mainstream social service organizations.

Accordingly, the objectives of this field practicum model are to:

- Sensitize students to the cultural and racial element in service provision;
- Provide conceptual knowledge and practical experiences to understand the barriers to service for immigrants and visible minority persons;
- Develop the students' ability to identify and meet the needs of clients in multicultural communities;
- Extend the service of generic organizations in order to include individuals who prefer the more informal environment of multicultural agencies;
- Provide links between ethnic and racial minority groups and social service agencies;

---

5   A mainstream, or generic, agency is one that serves the general population.

- Provide an opportunity for social service agencies, settlement agencies, specific ethnic groups, funding bodies and the Faculty of Social work to become partners in developing alternative models of service provision.

OVERALL STRUCTURE AND PROCEDURES

Voluntary Participation

Participation in this project is voluntary. Students are asked to express their interest in a one-day multicultural agency placement when indicating their field placement preferences. The Project Coordinator attends field orientation seminars and informs students about this opportunity. To assist students in making informed decisions, a list of participating agencies and learning opportunities is provided for each term. The assignment of students' primary field placement agency is not affected by interest or lack of interest to participate in this project. Initially it was difficult to recruit white students to this project. However, as the procedures have become more formalized, and as participating students shared their positive experiences with their colleagues and in the classroom, there is now more demand for this placement experience.

Primary Placement - Multicultural Agency Dyads

Students' interests and learning goals are the main consideration for matching students with multicultural agencies. At the beginning of placement, the students and their supervisors discuss the integration of learning goals and objectives in both agencies. This exploration allows the supervisors to become familiar with the culture of the multicultural agencies. Students are encouraged to try and build bridges between the primary placement and the multicultural agency; one example of these links is staff sensitivity training/workshops facilitated by the student with the support of the multicultural agency.

Supervision and Evaluation

To ensure an integrated field practice experience, the primary supervisor's responsibilities are extended to the work performed by the student at the multicultural agency. To assist supervisors with writing the evaluations, the multicultural agencies provide an account of the students' activities. The reports are prepared by the project facilitator in consultation with the liaison person from the multicultural organization. These reports provide an account of the student's activities and a general observation of performance and development at the multicultural agency and the group meetings. Both mid-term and end-of-term reports are discussed with the students prior to being forwarded to the supervisor.

Working with Clients

Mechanisms for referring clients to students may differ from one agency to another. For individual casework, an appropriate referral process is established at the outset of the placement in consultation with the primary agency supervisor and the multicultural agency liaison person. In some agencies students become involved in group work or community development projects. The primary placement agency may have certain documentation requirements with regard to clients seen at the multicultural agency. For the latter, it is very important to maintain client confidentiality. One way of satisfying both requirements is to provide to the primary placement agency statistical and categorical information. Reporting arrangements are usually established at the beginning of the placement in consultation with the supervisor and the multicultural agency liaison person.

The Multicultural Centre

In addition to providing a field placement opportunity for students, the Kitchener-Waterloo Multicultural Centre also plays a key role in providing a general orientation. The Multicultural Centre has a collection of relevant material and a network that may be contacted for specific purposes. Students are encouraged to use these resources and the expertise of the Centre's staff. The Multicultural Centre also organizes structured orientation workshops and conferences for students.

Communication Links and Professional Development

It is important that participants communicate regularly and provide on-going feedback about the project. To facilitate this communication there are three meetings of all participants each term: an orientation meeting early in the term; a mid-term meeting; and a final evaluation meeting. In addition, participants are encouraged to maintain on-going communication regarding new ideas, issues and concerns. Educational and professional development is an important component of the program. In addition to a major annual workshop, other professional development activities are available, including support for participation in occasional workshops and conferences. Supervisors and students are funded to attend training events while participating in the program. Former participants are also invited to attend the annual training event.

ROLES AND RESPONSIBILITIES

The Multicultural Agency Liaison Person

The purpose of having a liaison person is to establish effective communication channels between the multicultural agency, the students and their supervisors. This person is responsible for: hosting the students and facilitating a meaningful learning experience; administrative issues such as those related to work space, work schedule, supply of materials, etc.; orienting the students to the agency and its network; facilitating links with relevant individuals and organizations serving immigrants and refugees.

The Primary Supervisor

The supervisor's responsibilities regarding the multicultural agency placement are the same as those for the primary agency, including: the planning of learning goals and objectives; on-going supervision regarding individual clients, groups and projects; and, overall mid-term and final evaluations.

The Project Facilitator

The project facilitator is responsible for organizing and facilitating students biweekly group meetings; providing consultation to students and supervisors on an individual basis regarding specific clients, groups and other issues related to the practice at the multicultural agency; and, preparing mid-term and final reports about the student's experience at the multicultural placement.

The Project Coordinator

This person has the following responsibilities: provide overall coordination and evaluation of the project; facilitate the development and maintenance of organizational dyads; plan professional development activities and facilitate participation in relevant work-shops\conferences, in consultation with the project facilitator. The coordinator may be contacted regarding overall program issues that go beyond the responsibilities of the individuals directly involved with students (e.g., the program's philosophy and structure, roles and responsibilities, new ideas).

STUDENTS BI-WEEKLY GROUP PROCESS MEETINGS

Overview

This group process approach is discussed in detail since it is integral to the students ability to recognize and confront systemic inequalities. The goal of these group process meetings is to encourage students to examine biases and stereotypes while working in an ethno-specific or immigrant settlement agency. Students participate in a psycho-educational approach to learning with a strong emphasis on critical thinking and reflection of internal feelings and responses, as well as an analysis of socio-political factors which affect interventions, skills and approaches to working with a culturally diverse population. Fern (1990, p. 139) states that "social work education must face up to issues of social control, power and oppression in society." Education principles in social work with a culturally and ethnically diverse population have moved away from a cultural approach to a more integrated model of learning with opportunities for internal shifts in thinking around forms of oppression (Fern, 1990; Gonzales et al., 1991; Longres, 1991). Students are therefore challenged to examine their approaches and theoretical framework when working with people from different cultures.

Structure and Format

The group was established after the first term of the project in response to students' recommendation for some form of educational integration of their experiences at the primary placement and the multicultural agency. An integrative seminar/group process guided by a facilitator has proven to be very beneficial to the students. These bi-weekly two-hour seminars provide students with an opportunity to discuss the experience of being in a split placement at agencies with very different environment, philosophy and approach to work.

Since each group of students brings different experiences and realities, specific terms of reference are determined at the first meeting. However, the provision of mutual support and discussions of the applicability of traditional intervention theories in cross-cultural counselling were the commonly shared objectives of most groups. The majority of participants were white students whose experiences and knowledge of anti-racist education and cross cultural issues were, for the most part, at the very early stages of development.

The group is structured in a way that allows these students to question their beliefs, stereotypes and myths, and acknowledge their privileged status, while attempting to serve clients and plan projects. The assurance of confidentiality and mutual respect encourages open communication regarding these sensitive issues. During the first part of each meeting the students share their work experiences around projects being planned, clients, meetings and any matters which relate to their one day placement. The students share ideas regarding these experiences and exchange information regarding relevant resources. They are also encouraged to discuss client related issues with their primary supervisor. The students found the feedback from group members very valuable. The check in time was also very critical to allow students to process their feelings and challenge some of their deeply held myths and beliefs towards particular ethnic groups.

The Educational Component

The more formal educational component takes place in the second hour of the meeting, with a focus on different culturally sensitive models. Longres (1991) evaluates models of ethnic sensitive practice for different populations. He states that the cultural model is best suited to helping refugees and recent immigrants, and advocates a "status model of ethnic sensitive practice" where high and low status contexts of people's lives are duly considered. Rogers (1992) also explores different approaches to understanding and working with culturally diverse clients, and notes that the research has evolved to a combined approach of multicultural and anti-racist social work education. Students are encouraged to take time to read and view videotapes relating to cross cultural counselling. Role plays and case studies are also utilized for students to begin to understand the rage and powerlessness of minority clients who feel the effects of subtle and blatant racism on a daily basis. Reflecting on the group experience, one of the students stated:

> I appreciated the focus on experiential exercises which helped me to get a better focus on some of my own struggles. For me this awareness is a tool that I can use when working with people from different cultural and ethnic groups. I appreciated the alternative perspectives on therapy and agency work. I have been struck by the fact that these perspectives are not incorporated in my agency. There is still a lot of bridging that needs to occur. (Student, Winter 1994)

When new material is presented, it is important to analyze its content and consider its relevance for each participant. We discussed our respective position on the continuum of anti-racist social work education, and students were patient with each other's progress and learning needs. Being patient however, does not preclude the necessity for students to confront and challenge each other when they recognize injustice or inequalities.

The topics and material covered by the group included:

- the ethno-racial-cultural background of each student;[6]
- article on white privilege (McIntosh, 1990);
- Canadian demographics;
- planning and formation of different types of groups;
- traditional and non traditional approaches to counselling;
- generic and multicultural agencies: function, hierarchy, mandates, etc.;
- anti-racist feminist therapy;[7]
- terms of reference: racism, prejudice, discrimination, power, privilege, colonization, neo-colonization;
- understanding partner abuse and sexual abuse within specific ethnic and racial communities;
- bi-culturalism;
- the use of cultural interpreters.

Observations on the Role of the Facilitator

The facilitator's main role is to support the students in order to maximize learning opportunities and enrich the field practice experience. The facilitator's role is of primary importance. I speak here subjectively as the first author, after having been in this role since Winter, 1991, and being aware of limitations in the social work curriculum around race and ethnicity. I feel that my experiences as a racial minority immigrant woman, coupled with my education in social work, have equipped me with the expertise and skills to challenge the students around institutional and personal forms of racism, white privilege and myths, in a learning environment that is safe and leads to growth and change.

Mizio and Delaney (1981) state that students may be offered additional opportunities to confront their beliefs and challenge their thinking when the facilitator is from an immigrant or minority background. For a white facilitator to be effective he/she must have passed the stage where there is only acknowledgement of privilege and power. It is also important that the facilitator is especially informed of the treatment of different groups, aware of the factors of prejudice and power, has identified her/his own biases, and continues to challenge internal responses and external realities of the intersections of race, gender and class. To understand institutional forms of inequalities, there must be a deep conceptualization of colonization, neo-colonization, oppression, and internalized

---

6   It is important to have students identify themselves in an ethno-racial-cultural frame. The latest form being used is adapted from Christensen's model (1992).

7   Based on Narda Razack, "Anti-Racist Feminist Therapy," a workshop presented by at the Women and Therapy Conference, 1992, Guelph, Ontario. There have been several additions to this particular theme.

oppression. It would be insufficient to focus only on education of cultural patterns, norms and values.

Summary

This group process provides the space for students to share their experiences, challenge myths and stereotypes and become more deeply aware of values and beliefs when working within a culturally diverse context. Students often discussed how the group challenged their values and beliefs and spoke of the difficulty to confront their families and circle of friends when they exhibited racist and prejudicial behaviours. Their feelings of being labelled "radicals" were often compared with the backlash experienced by feminists. The group's support for challenging racist environments is essential; so is the sharing of the more encouraging experiences of bringing ideas to class and the positive feedback about the project from the faculty and other students.

IMPLICATIONS FOR SOCIAL WORK EDUCATION

This field practice model offers students the opportunity to enrich their experience and develop knowledge and skills for social work practice within a cross-cultural and anti-racist framework. Although the above account of the model can guide those interested in adopting it, a number of additional points must be taken into consideration. The two groups of organizations involved in this project are very different. The generic organizations are relatively larger, more formal and more professionalised than the agencies working with newcomers. While generic organizations are often staffed with social workers and other professionals, typical multicultural agencies do not employ social workers. In many ways, the lack of formalization and professionalization that makes these agencies more attractive to newcomers makes them less appealing to schools of social work.

Educators and students must be prepared to deal with the challenges associated with the shift between these two different working environments. The typical counselling assignments may not always be possible in multicultural agencies. Moreover, the type of counselling required by newcomers may often be instrumental and directive. Communication may sometimes be frustrating and preclude the ability to apply traditional models of social work techniques effectively employed in the mainstream agency. Conceptually, involvement in this project requires the participants to define social work in the broadest terms possible. Many of the people served by multicultural agencies are not familiar with the concept of "counselling" as practised in generic agencies. Some may come seeking instrumental assistance related to employment, income, housing and other basic needs some social workers prefer to ignore. Others may be looking for someone with whom to discuss their experiences as newcomers, to talk about the glory of their past and to share their dreams for the future. Since the nature of these interactions is different from formal client-professional relationships, students may not realize sometimes that they have a "client" or that they provide a "service."

On their part, multicultural agencies must be sensitive to these issues and facilitate the broadening of the definition of social work without devaluing the students' professional knowledge base. It is also important that these agencies have a clear understanding of the purpose of the field placement; learning opportunities should be planned in advance so that students are not left wandering or given inappropriate tasks. To make this project mutually beneficial for students and agencies, the work with individual clients can be supplemented with special projects. Such projects may entail, for example, group work, needs surveys and program development. In addition to their benefits for multicultural agencies and their clients, these initiatives demonstrate to students the artificial boundaries between casework, community organization and social planning.

To materialize the full potential of this field placement model, participants are expected to be flexible. For example, while students are required to spend one day a week in a designated multicultural agency, this day may be divided into two half days or in any way that best serves the needs of the agency and its clients. It is understandable that the working arrangements will vary based on the contingencies of each dyad of agencies.   Flexibility is also expected when it comes to initiatives that span traditional organizational boundaries.   The cooperation between mainstream and multicultural agencies for the purpose of enriching the field experience of students can lead to other collaborative projects. Students are encouraged to explore these opportunities and work as a group on projects that involve partnerships between their field placement agencies and other organizations. Flexibility is also important when it comes to students' learning needs. Students vary in terms of their knowledge of community resources and familiarity with the problems experienced by newcomers. In addition to the general orientation, some students may need time to gather information and learn about multicultural issues; others can proceed without this additional preparation. In line with the objectives of this model, the differential educational needs of students should be taken into consideration.

THOUGHTS FOR THE FUTURE

This project has evolved to suit the needs of a particular Faculty of Social Work within a small community. At present, the curriculum does not include specific courses around anti-racism or multiculturalism in Social Work. Therefore, this field education model supplements the learning needs of some students. Although it served less than 10% of our students, it continues to expand and may become an integral part of the field placement program of most, if not all, students.

In many ways, the evolution of this model demonstrates the ability to develop an inclusive framework for field practice independently of the academic curriculum. However, a number of things must be done to make this program an integral part of the curriculum. Most importantly, the program coordination must become the responsibility of the field practice department rather than remain that of a faculty member, namely the second author. In this sense, the program must be viewed as any demonstration project driven by the interest and energy of its initiators until it reaches a level of stability that makes it suitable for institutionalization. The full adoption of the program by the field placement department, which is currently being discussed, will entail its integration in the field education materials/manuals, field placement agencies fairs and workshops for students and instructors. Funding for the program will become permanent, which is crucial for operating all its essential elements.

This model takes into account a reality that makes other approaches to multicultural field education less feasible. Like other graduate social work programs, Wilfrid Laurier University requires that field instructors have an MSW degree. This requirement disqualifies the staff of most multicultural agencies and means that generic agencies' staff must provide the supervision. Although primary agency field instructors attend orientation sessions and relevant conferences, much more work must be done to educate them about the new reality encountered by their students. A comprehensive training program for these supervisors must be developed to address issues like anti-racism, supervision around cross cultural counselling, black student-white supervisor relationships and approaches to counselling ethnically diverse communities. Another area which requires further development is the education of multicultural agencies' staff about social work, field practice, students' learning needs and their role in educating these students. This training is crucial because these people may not always realize how much they can teach the, formally, more educated students.

CONCLUSION

This project developed in response to the need to serve members of racial and ethnic minority groups who are excluded from generic agencies because of many structural barriers. It was also a result of the recognition that students were not sufficiently trained to adequately serve the needs of a culturally diverse population. The formation of partnerships and commitment to collaboration are key elements for the success of this model. Although this chapter provides concrete ideas for making effective changes, it is important to revise the model based on variations in the student population, the nature of the community and the available resources.

Conceptually, the building of bridges between mainstream and multicultural agencies as a service delivery model has been undervalued and opposed for political reasons (Teram & White, 1993). Although some social work programs may prefer a uni-agency approach, the type of collaboration we initiated is an effective way of benefitting from the professional resources of mainstream agencies and the cultural richness of multicultural organizations. Without this cooperation, statements such as the following one could not have been made by our students:

> The placement has changed me by broadening my life experiences and perspectives to include the richness and diversity of so many cultures. It has furthermore increased my own cultural sensitivity, awareness level and passion for commitment to anti-racism work. I believe it should be a required part of the social work practice. (Student, Winter 1994)

REFERENCES

Canadian Association of Schools of Social Work. (1991). *Social work education at the crossroads: The challenge of diversity.* Report of the Task Force on Multicultural and Multiracial Issues in Social Work Education, Ottawa.

Christensen, C. P. (1992). Training for cross-cultural social work with immigrants, refugees, and minorities: A course model. *Journal of Multicultural Social Work, 2*(1), 79-97.

Ferns, P. (1990). Tracing the path of anti-racism - Race equality in social work education. *Issues in Social Work Education, 10*(1-2), 134-143.

Gonzales Del Valle, A., Merdinger, J., Wrenn, R., & Miller, D. (1991). The field practicum and transcultural practice: An integrated model. *Journal of Multicultural Social Work, 1*(3), 45-55.

Longres, J. (1991). Toward a status model of ethnic sensitive practice. *Journal of Multicultural Social Work, 1*(1), 41-56.

McIntosh, P. (1990, Winter). White privilege: Unpacking the invisible knapsack. *Independent School*, pp. 31-36.

Ministry of Citizenship, Government of Ontario. (1991, March). *Working with immigrant women victims of spousal assault.* Cambridge, ON: Wife Assault Prevention Initiative.

Ministry of Health, Government of Ontario. (1991, November). *Working together: Responding appropriately to the needs of immigrant and refugee women survivors of sexual abuse.* Toronto, Sexual Assault Prevention Initiative.

Mizio, E., & Delaney, A. (1981). *Training for service delivery to minority clients.* New York: Family Service Association of America.

Multicultural Health Coalition: Waterloo Region. (1992, September). *Working toward health: A needs assessment project with the Vietnamese, Hispanic, and Polish communities in Kitchener-Waterloo.*

O'Neill, B. J., & Yelaja, S. A. (1994). Multiculturalism in postsecondary education: 1970-91. In J. W. Berry & J.A. Laponce (Eds.), *Ethnicity and culture in Canada: The research landscape* (pp. 483-506). Toronto: University of Toronto Press.

Rogers, G. (1992). *Teaching and learning ethnically-sensitive, anti-discriminatory practice: Field placement principals for Canadian social work programmes.* A paper presented at CASSW Annual Conference, P.E.I.

Teram, E., & White, H. (1993). Strategies to address the bureaucratic disentitlement of clients from cultural minority groups. *Canadian Journal of Community Mental Health, 12*(2), 59-70.

Yelaja, S. (Ed.). (1988). *Proceedings of The Settlement and Integration of New Immigrants to Canada Conference.* Waterloo, ON: Wilfrid Laurier University, Centre for Social Welfare Studies.

CHAPTER THIRTY-TWO

ADDRESSING DIVERSITY IN THE PRACTICUM: WORKSHOP MATERIALS AND GUIDE

Helena Summers and Roxanne Powers

INTRODUCTION TO WORKSHOP MATERIALS

Preparing students for practice with diverse ethnic, cultural and racial communities is a mandated goal for accredited schools of social work in Canada. Additionally preparing for practice with the gay and lesbian, and disabled communities is equally important. The field practicum, particularly in larger cities, offers a great opportunity for teaching about diversity, since students are often assigned to agencies which serve populations from different ethnic, cultural, and racial communities than their own. Thus, field instructors are in an ideal position to assist students to successfully work with and understand people with different backgrounds, needs, and lifestyles.

One of the most effective ways of teaching about diversity is to call upon the participant's own life experiences and through the use of experiential exercises enhance the participant's own cultural sensitivity and self-awareness. The material presented on the following pages was designed for use in field education seminars to better prepare field instructors for the vital role of training students for practice in a rapidly changing society. The following exercises and vignettes were designed to assist field instructors to explore their own self-awareness, and to develop strategies for teaching diversity issues. Field instructors may also readily adapt some of this material for use in a dyad with the student, or use it in small groups of 4-5 students. We hope the workshop package is of value to field coordinators and field instructors in facilitating the educational process, so that students are well prepared to face the challenges of practice in the twenty first century.

WORKSHOP OUTLINE AND TIMELINE

15 mins.   1.   Introductions (facilitators and participants) and overview of workshop. Create climate, confidentiality. Introductions to include name, role (student/FI), whether agency serves diverse populations, location, and one factor that is important to you for effective group discussion.

25 mins.   2.   Large group: some brainstorming from personal, work, practicum experience to answer the question: "I know discrimination occurs when I see/think/feel . . ." Write the ideas down as they occur and divide into major recurrent themes (e.g. racism, sexual harassment, sexual orientation discrimination, discrimination re: disability/illness).

30 mins.   3.   Small group (exercises 1-6): have members break into small groups according to the theme area they wish to discuss (there may be more than one group in same theme area). Have each group appoint a recorder who will share the group's summary of discussion around how personal biased behaviors can be changed. Distribute the theme question list. The questions for group discussion include when were you first aware of (racial, gender, sexual orientation, cultural, ethnic background, or disability) this particular difference, what kinds of thoughts or feelings did you experience as a result of this first encounter, were there any conscious/unconscious biases formed and maintained as a result of this, how might these biases affect your present behavior in teaching and practice? How might these biased behaviors be recognized and changed in your own practice and organization? Have the group summaries pinned on wall. When exercise finishes, note the potency of this assignment and advise that facilitators will be available for debriefing during break.

15 mins.   BREAK

30 mins.   4.   Small group (vignettes 1-4): groups resume in the same composition and with a recorder. Present the group with a short vignette illustrating a field practice dilemma in the area they have chose to discuss. Note they may choose to role play. Have the group discuss the general issues involved and begin to FORMULATE INTERVENTION STRATEGIES TO ADDRESS THIS GENERAL AREA.

25 mins.   5.   Large group: share the group summaries of key strategies for change in personal and practice situations in each of the them areas. (facilitators synthesize recurrent themes)

25 mins.   6.   Large group: where do we go from here? How do we re-conceptualize or develop practicum learning opportunities to increase student skills in addressing diversity?
Identify: tasks, assignments, teaching materials, questions for supervision sessions.
Resource Registry: sign up if you have materials you are willing to exchange. Identify the materials.

2 mins.   7.   Brief summary and thanks.

WORKSHOP EXERCISES

Exploring Diversity

Exercise 1

Our most implicit and encompassing cultural learning takes place in childhood and adolescence. During these stages of development, many of us learned certain attitudes toward people who were different than ourselves. These differences may have been around race, culture, ethnicity, gender, sexual orientation or disability.
   Pick a recorder and a reporter. In the small group discuss the following:

•   What were some of the things you learned in childhood or adolescence about people who were from a different racial group?

Areas to Consider in Discussion

1.   How old were you when you first became aware of this difference?
2.   What feelings did you have?
3.   What thoughts did you have?
4.   What conscious or unconscious biases did you form?

After discussing the above, formulate interventions through exploring the following:

1.   How might biases learned in childhood or adolescence affect your present behavior in teaching and practice?
2.   What strategies might you use to identify when these biases are effecting your behavior?
3.   What general intervention strategies might be used to address issues of discrimination within your organization?

Exercise 2

Our most implicit and encompassing cultural learning takes place in childhood and adolescence. During these stages of development, many of us learned certain attitudes toward people who were different than ourselves. These differences may have been around race, culture, ethnicity, gender, sexual orientation or disability.
      Pick a recorder and a reporter. In the small group discuss the following:

•   What were some of the things you learned in childhood or adolescence about people of the other gender?

Areas to Consider in Discussion

1.   How old were you when you first became aware of this difference?
2.   What feelings did you have?
3.   What thoughts did you have?
4.   What conscious or unconscious biases did you form?

After discussing the above, formulate interventions through exploring the following:

1.   How might biases learned in childhood or adolescence affect your present behavior in teaching and practice?
2.   What strategies might you use to identify when these biases are effecting your behavior?

3.   What general intervention strategies might be used to address issues of discrimination within your organization?

Exercise 3

Our most implicit and encompassing cultural learning takes place in childhood and adolescence. During these stages of development, many of us learned certain attitudes toward people who were different than ourselves. These differences may have been around race, culture, ethnicity, gender, sexual orientation or disability.
    Pick a recorder and a reporter. In the small group discuss the following:

•   What were some of the things you learned in childhood or adolescence about people who had a different sexual orientation from yourself?

Areas to Consider in Discussion

1.   How old were you when you first became aware of this difference?
2.   What feelings did you have?
3.   What thoughts did you have?
4.   What conscious or unconscious biases did you form?

After discussing the above, formulate interventions through exploring the following:

1.   How might biases learned in childhood or adolescence affect your present behavior in teaching and practice?
2.   What strategies might you use to identify when these biases are effecting your behavior?
3.   What general intervention strategies might be used to address issues of discrimination within your organization?

Exercise 4

Our most implicit and encompassing cultural learning takes place in childhood and adolescence. During these stages of development, many of us learned certain attitudes toward people who were different than ourselves. These differences may have been around race, culture, ethnicity, gender, sexual orientation or disability.
    Pick a recorder and a reporter. In the small group discuss the following:

•   What were some of the things you learned in childhood or adolescence about people who were from a different culture?

Areas to Consider in Discussion

1.   How old were you when you first became aware of this difference?
2.   What feelings did you have?
3.   What thoughts did you have?
4.   What conscious or unconscious biases did you form?

After discussing the above, formulate interventions through exploring the following:

1.   How might biases learned in childhood or adolescence affect your present behavior in teaching and practice?
2.   What strategies might you use to identify when these biases are effecting your behavior?
3.   What general intervention strategies might be used to address issues of discrimination within your organization?

Exercise 5

Our most implicit and encompassing cultural learning takes place in childhood and adolescence. During these stages of development, many of us learned certain attitudes toward people who were different than ourselves. These differences may have been around race, culture, ethnicity, gender, sexual orientation or disability.
        Pick a recorder and a reporter. In the small group discuss the following:

•   What were some of the things you learned in childhood or adolescence about people who were from a different ethnic background?

Areas to Consider in Discussion

1.   How old were you when you first became aware of this difference?
2.   What feelings did you have?
3.   What thoughts did you have?
4.   What conscious or unconscious biases did you form?

After discussing the above, formulate interventions through exploring the following:

1.   How might biases learned in childhood or adolescence affect your present behavior in teaching and practice?
2.   What strategies might you use to identify when these biases are effecting your behavior?

3.   What general intervention strategies might be used to address issues of discrimination within your organization?

Exercise 6

Our most implicit and encompassing cultural learning takes place in childhood and adolescence. During these stages of development, many of us learned certain attitudes toward people who were different than ourselves. These differences may have been around race, culture, ethnicity, gender, sexual orientation or disability.

Pick a recorder and a reporter. In the small group discuss the following:

•   What were some of the things you learned in childhood or adolescence about people who had a disability?

Areas to Consider in Discussion

1.   How old were you when you first became aware of this difference?
2.   What feelings did you have?
3.   What thoughts did you have?
4.   What conscious or unconscious biases did you form?

After discussing the above, formulate interventions through exploring the following:

1.   How might biases learned in childhood or adolescence affect your present behavior in teaching and practice?
2.   What strategies might you use to identify when these biases are effecting your behavior?
3.   What general intervention strategies might be used to address issues of discrimination within your organization?

WORKSHOP VIGNETTES

Instructions for Vignettes

There are two choices for how to proceed with the vignettes. One way is to become involved with the scenarios and identify the emotional, as well as the cognitive issues through a role play. The other way is to use the vignette as a springboard to engage in a discussion piece within the small group. Please decide within your small group which way you wish to proceed.

Vignette #1 Practicum Issues Around Cross-Cultural Practice

Before you begin, select a recorder/reporter.

Practicum Setting: The setting offers individual and family counselling for clients, using a very intensive team approach. This particular team has worked successfully together for some time.

Practicum Issue: The student is involved in cross-cultural/racial counselling with a referred client who is engaged in delayed grieving for a lost relative. The student has voiced some reservations to the field instructor about the appropriateness of the usual agency practice intervention for this client. Through field instruction sessions and team observation of the student's work, it seems consistently apparent the student appears uncomfortable with the team's suggestions of ways to help the client explore this grief. The client does not appear to respond to the student's attempts to engage him in probing discussion of the emotional loss and when this happens, the student may lose eye contact, abruptly change topics, or unintentionally minimize the client's level of emotion. The team seems to be increasingly frustrated with this student who cannot seem to integrate their specific feedback into behavioral change as past students could. You suspect they are also becoming frustrated with you as the field instructor.

1.   What issues might this scenario and similar other cross-cultural/racial situations raise for the student and field instructor?
2.   What behavior strategies might be helpful to ensure discrimination will not occur and that diversity is respected?

Vignette #2 Practicum Issues Around Sexual Orientation

Before you begin, select a recorder/ reporter.

Practicum Setting: The agency offers individual and family counselling, and is highly regarded for its work by the community

Practicum Issue: The student is involved with counselling two lesbian women who are having problems with custody and access. The clients are very upset because they were assigned to a male worker. They fear he will side with the family court worker who, they believe, thinks that children should not live with lesbian parents. The clients are questioning the student as to why they were assigned to a male worker. The student comes to you and asks to be taken off the case.

1.   What issues might this and similar scenarios raise for the student and field instructor?
2.   What behavior strategies might be helpful to ensure that discrimination will not occur and that diversity is respected?

Vignette #3 Practicum Issues Around Disability

Before you begin, select a recorder/reporter.

Practicum Setting: The setting provides a variety of home care services to the frail, isolated elderly. Home visits by social workers are integral to service delivery.

Practicum Issue: After completing twelve practicum days, the student tells you s/he will be absent a day next week for medical testing. You had already noted the student appears more tired than other students at the end of a practicum day and s/he has declined to do occasional unanticipated (non-emergency) evening work, even though compensatory time would be given. As you begin to discuss the medical absence, the student seems upset and quickly discloses that s/he suffers from epilepsy. It had been under long-term control until this weekend when s/he had a seizure. Luckily someone was at home at the time.

1.   What issues might this scenario and similar other situations raise for the student and field instructor?
2.   What behavior strategies might be helpful to ensure discrimination will not occur and diversity is respected?

Vignette #4 Practicum Issues Around Sexual Harassment

Before you begin, select a recorder/reporter.

Practicum Setting: The practicum setting is the social work department of a small hospital. The department director and all of the members of the social work team have worked together for several years.

Practicum Issue: The field instructor, who is also the department director, has cartoons on his wall which the female student finds offensive. In addition, he tells sexually insulting jokes. The student voiced her discomfort with the cartoons and jokes to the field instructor. He acknowledged her concerns, but said humor was his way of blowing off steam in an emotionally demanding environment. The student later discovers that other social work staff are also upset with the director's behavior. No one has taken action to deal with the situation due to fear of reprisals.

1.   What issues might this scenario and similar sexual harassment situations raise for the student and field instructor?
2.   What behavior strategies might be useful to ensure discrimination will not occur and that the student gets appropriate support?

SELECTED BIBLIOGRAPHY

Cross Cultural

Carney, C., & Kahn, K. (1986). Building competencies for effective cross-cultural counselling: A developmental view. *The Counselling Psychologist, 12*(1), 111-119.

Chau, K. (1990). A Model for teaching cross-cultural practice in social work. *Journal of Social Work Education, 26*(2), 124-133.

Christensen, C. P. (1986). Cross-cultural social work: fallacies, fears, and failing. *Intervention, 74*, May 1986, 41-49.

Davenport, D., & Yurich, J. (1991). Multicultural gender issues. *Journal of Counselling and Development, 70*, 64-71.

Dhruev, N. (1992). Conflict and race in social work relations. *Journal of Social Work Practice, 6*(1), 77-86.

McMahon, A., & Allen-Mearle, P. (1992). Is social work racist? A content analysis of recent literature. *Social Work, 37*(6), 533-539.

McRoy, R., Freeman, E., Logan, S., & Blackmon, B. (1986). Cross-cultural field instruction: Implications for social work education. *Journal of Social Work Education, 22*(1), 50-56.

Nakanishi, M., & Rittner, B. (1992). The inclusionary cultural model. *Journal of Social Work Education, 28*(1), Winter 1992, 27-35.

Peterson, K. (1991). Issues of race and ethnicity in supervision: Emphasizing who you are, not what you know. *The Clinical Supervisor, 9*(1), 15-31.

Roberts, H. (1992). Contextual supervision. *The Supervision Bulletin, 5*(3).

Sue, D., Arredondo, P., & McDavis, R. (1992). Multicultural counselling competencies and standards: A call to the profession. *Journal of Multicultural Counselling and Development, 20*(2), 64-88.

Sexual Harassment

Employer liable for supervisor's sexual harassment, Supreme Court says. (1987). *Women's Employment Law, 3*(9), pp. 1-3.

England, M. (1984). Sexual harassment: Personal problem or power play? *Journal of American Women, 39*(4), 140-141.

Gray, S. Sexual harassment: A compensable injury. *Canadian Dimension, 19*(1), 23.

Hotelling, K. (1991). Sexual harassment: A problem shielded by silence. *Journal of Counselling and Development, 69,* 497-500.

Kaplan, S. J. (1991). Consequences of sexual harassment in the workplace. *Affilia, 6*(3), 50-65.

Legal, organization, and individual actions. *Journal of Social Issues, 38*(4), 5-22.

Livingston, J. A. (1982). Response to sexual harassment on the job: Legal, organization, and individual actions. *Journal of Social Issues, 38*(4), 5-22.

Maypole, D. (1986). Sexual harassment of social workers at work. *Social Work, 31*(1), 29-34.

Riger, S. (1991). Gender dilemmas in sexual harassment policies and procedures. *American Psychologist, 46*(5), 497-505.

Thacker, R. (1992). Preventing sexual harassment in the workplace. *Training and Development,* February 1992, 51-53.

Sexual Orientation

Buhrke, R., & Douce, L. (1991). Training issues for counselling psychologists in working with lesbian women and gay men. *The Counselling Psychologist, 19*(2), 216-234.

Gunter, P. Rural gay men and lesbians in need of services and understanding. *National Lesbian and Gay Health Foundation Inc.*, Special Populations, 49-53.

Jacobsen, E. (1988). Lesbian and gay adolescents: A social work approach. *The Social Worker, 56*(2), 65-67.

Sullivan, R. Moral decisions and public justice: Reconciling our human rights obligations to lesbian and gay youth. *Journal of Homosexuality*, (in press).

CHAPTER THIRTY-THREE

PROMOTING MULTICULTURALISM: SOCIAL WORK AND THE CULTURAL RESOURCES UNIT OF THE CALGARY POLICE SERVICE

Dave Este, Manuela Lacentra, Hal Wetherup and George Mayes

INTRODUCTION

The fall of 1993 marked the first time the Cultural Resources Unit provided a field placement for a fourth year BSW student from the Faculty of Social Work, The University of Calgary. This chapter describes the practicum experience from the perspective of the student and host unit and discusses the following: the organizing of the placement; the orientation of the student and the learning experience available at the Cultural Resources Unit; the activities engaged in by the student and in particular, the development of a needs assessment survey for use with Calgary's diverse communities; the challenges of the placement experience and the strategies used to deal with the challenges; and, the lessons gained from the experience.

Professional human services academic and training programs such as social work, nursing and policing are currently being challenged to address the needs of the nation's changing population. Some of this pressure stems from the perception that professions such as social work have not or are slowly responding to the ethnic and cultural population diversity. Commenting on this situation, Yelaja and O'Neill (1990) state that:

Despite social work's professed commitment to equal treatment of all persons, systemic barriers continue to impede racial and ethnic minorities access to mainstream services. Agencies need to form partnerships with ethnic organizations in order to effectively serve minority clients. Concepts regarding ethnicity have not been incorporated into social work theory, and minority differences are ignored in social work training. There is a consensus that social work education is not adequately preparing students to work with all members of the Canadian population. (p. 1)

Canada's immigration policy which during the period from 1990-1995, will allow approximately 1.25 million newcomers (cited in Managing immigration: A framework, 1990) to enter the country, represents another factor that will require human service professions to become more sensitive to the needs of divergent population groups. In 1990, 87% of all immigrants who came to Alberta settled in Edmonton and Calgary (cited in Immigration to Alberta, Decade in Review, 1992). With this established trend of immigrants venturing to the large urban centers, greater demands will be placed on human service professionals to develop and provide appropriate services.

In the late 1970's the Calgary Police Service (CPS) recognized the need for greater attention to the needs of the various ethnic groups residing in the city. As a result, in 1979, the Cultural Resources Unit, initially known as the "Race Relations Unit," was formed. During the next fifteen years the unit continued to evolve and today there is a staff complement of eight persons. The staff consists of six constables assigned to specific portfolio's such as Black/Hispanic, South Asia and Middle East. The unit is supervised by a sergeant.

In 1986, the unit was renamed the Multicultural Liaison Unit. This change reflected the unit's role as the Police Service recognized the need to adapt to and learn about the increasingly diverse cultures in Calgary. The unit's name changed again in 1994 and is now known as the Cultural Resources Unit. This change was prompted by the growing concern that the term "multiculturalism" was becoming limited to a few visible minority groups. The primary objective of the Cultural Resources Unit is to actively improve awareness, within the Calgary Police Service and the wider community, of the diverse cultures present in Canadian society, in an effort to enhance ethnic, cultural, racial, and religious harmony in Calgary. The three major goals of the unit include: to continuously increase the acceptance, communication and understanding between the Calgary Police Service and Calgary's Aboriginal and Multicultural Communities in an effort to reduce stereotypical negative images; to improve intergroup relations in Calgary through direct liaison and mediation with Calgary's diverse ethnic, cultural, racial and religious groups; and, to increase the representation of aboriginal and visible minorities as members of the Calgary Police Service to more accurately reflect the composition of Calgary's population.

In order to achieve the Unit's goals a variety of different strategies are utilized. Some of these include: providing culture specific training to other areas within the Police Service; serving as mediators in inter-cultural conflicts; liaison with Calgary's cultural, ethnic, racial and religious communities; and, provide training (lectures/workshops) and act as a resource/referral base for other Police agencies, educational institutions, health care and social service professionals as well as other professionals on cultural, ethnic, racial and religious issues/groups within Canadian society.

ORGANIZING OF THE PLACEMENT

The main catalyst in the development and organizing of the practicum was a social work student. Initial inquiries regarding the possibility of completing a practicum with the Unit occurred during the initial months of 1993. During this time period, a student made contact with the Unit's sergeant and explored the possibility of the Unit providing a field experience. Her request was well received by the incumbent sergeant. However, the student was informed by this individual that she would have to present her request to his successor, who took over the administrative responsibilities of the Unit within a short period of time.

In this interim period of time, in order to acquaint herself with the Police Service, the student actively sought out volunteer opportunities. She applied to the Victim Assistance Unit and was accepted as a volunteer. This proved to be a very strategic move on behalf of the student as she demonstrated her sincerity to make a contribution to the Police Service and secondly, working in a voluntary capacity provided the opportunity to gain some exposure to the culture of the organization. Following the advice provided by the departing Unit supervisor, the student approached this individual's successor with her request. Her idea was well received by the new unit supervisor although at this preliminary stage, the sergeant was not sure what would be involved in facilitating a placement experience.

One of the initial challenges faced by the student was to find a practicum supervisor who would meet the requirements of the Faculty of Social Work. Ideally, individuals who supervise students must have a social work degree. After spending some time consulting a number of individuals within the organization, an individual was identified in the Community and Youth Section who possessed a graduate degree in social work. The student approached the social worker who seemed quite receptive to the student's plan. At this stage in the process, the student was informed by the social worker and the supervisor of the Cultural Resources Unit that she would have to go through the formal procedures in order to have the practicum sanctioned by the Police Service. In a letter written to a senior police officer (Inspector) the student explained her plans for the practicum, her short and long term goals as well as the benefits the Police

Service would gain by having a social work student complete a placement with the Unit. The student subsequently received permission to proceed with her plans.

It must be noted that the student did not inform the Faculty of her organizing efforts. Her rationale for pursuing this particular strategy stemmed from her belief that if she approached the faculty after the placement had been arranged and organized, it would be extremely difficult for the Faculty to turn her down. Her strategy worked as the placement was approved by the faculty.

ORIENTATION

As mentioned in the previous section, in her volunteer role the student began to become familiar with the culture of the Police Service. In order to become acquainted with the Cultural Resources Unit, the student and the Unit's supervisor engaged in several discussions prior to and during the early stages of the placement experience. These discussions along with printed material assisted the student in becoming familiar with the Unit, the goals and objectives of the Unit within the context of the Service's mandate and the role of the Unit within the Community and Youth Section.

ACTIVITIES ENGAGED IN BY THE STUDENT

Throughout the practicum experience, the student engaged in a number of activities. She participated in the multicultural courses offered by the Calgary Police Service; attended "English as a Second Language" lectures that unit officers gave at various institutions throughout the city (eg. Alberta Vocational College, Columbia Institute); facilitated a multicultural awareness training seminar for the Victim Assistance Unit; and attended a one day workshop entitled "Cross Cultural Considerations in Crisis Situations" presented by a special agent of the Federal Bureau of Investigation (FBI).

The student's primary activity involved the development of a culturally sensitive survey questionnaire which would be utilized to perform a series of Community Needs Assessments within Calgary's diverse cultural, ethnic, religious, racial and linguistic communities. Three primary goals associated with the conducting of the assessments include:

- Determining the level of client awareness of the available services and programs of the Calgary Police Service;
- Establishing client based priorities for enhanced awareness and access programs developed;

• Identifying the most cost effective methods and languages in which such programs could be provided.

Rationale for Needs Assessment

As previously stated, the profession of policing is being pressured to adopt a law enforcement style that is consistent with the changing realities of a multicultural society (Fleras & Elliot, 1992). At a broad level, the objectives of the needs assessment are viewed by the Cultural Resources Unit as ways in which the Service could enhance its service provision to diverse communities within the city.

However, members of the Unit maintained the importance of actively involving the specific communities in not only determining what services should be delivered but, as well, how the services should be provided. Based on the experience of the Calgary Police Service, new Canadians from many parts of the world possess very negative, stereotypical perceptions of law enforcement agencies and their employees. Previous interactions with these officials in their own countries have resulted in attitudes ranging from distrust to outright hostility towards police officers. In describing this phenomena, Fleras and Elliot (1992, p.219) state:

> Police may be viewed as unwelcome intruders whose actions are motivated by self-interest and protection of the status quo. As defenders of vested interests, the police come under scrutiny for not safeguarding the rights of individuals or groups who have been victimized by society. In addition, new citizens from repressive or dictatorial regimes may possess negative attitudes about the police.

The existence of these attitudes by newcomers has made it difficult for police to gather information about the specific needs of the community and how they can assist communities in dealing with prevailing concerns and issues. The conventional police paradigm (See Table 1) also contributes to the reluctance of certain communities to form meaningful collaborative partnerships with the police.

However, the existence of a Cultural Resources Unit and the initiatives undertaken by this group represent a movement to what is known as community-based policing. In describing this model of police practice Fleras and Elliot (1992) state:

> Recent years have witnessed a reordering of police priorities. Police depart-ments have embarked on a variety of community-based policing programs in an attempt to reopen dialogue with disenchanted sectors. This reorientation has involved changes in both police organization and subculture, as well as in individual attitudes and behavior. Emphasis has been directed at replacing the confrontational model of policing and the isolation it engenders with a more

community-service oriented model sensitive to the needs of an increasingly heterogenous community. (p. 221)

Table 1   Police Paradigms

	CONVENTIONAL	COMMUNITY-BASED
FUNCTION	Professional Crime-Fighting	Community Service
STRUCTURE	Paramilitary Bureaucracy	Decentralized
PROCESS	Law Enforcement	Peace-Keeping
STYLE	Adversarial/Incident Based	Partnership Proactive Problem Solving Culturally Sensitive

In examining the attributes associated with the style of community-based policing, they appear to be quite congruent with some of the values and practices typically associated with the social work profession.

In the effort to develop and/or enhance partnerships with the different communities, members of the Cultural Resources Unit believed that a more efficient and non-threatening method of obtaining information on the needs of diverse groups was required. Because of the importance of the initiative, coupled with the arrival of the social work student, her learning interests as well linguistic skills (ability to speak Spanish), the decision was made to develop the survey for use with the Hispanic community.

Development of the Community Needs Assessment Survey

The following were the major activities undertaken in the development of the community needs assessment survey:

- Several meetings were held between the student and the supervisor of the Cultural Resources Unit to determine what types of information the Unit was seeking to obtain;
- Meetings were held between the student and the social work field instructor who provided feedback on question formulation and sequencing;

- Completing drafts of the instrument and reviewing the product with the Unit supervisor until both parties (student) were satisfied with the product.

A second related activity engaged in by the student involved the development and operationalizing of a plan designed to gain entry into the Hispanic community. The two objectives of this particular plan included: the gaining of support for the project; and, facilitating the involvement of community members in both the distribution of the survey and the data collection process. The plan consisted of two interrelated phases; activities described as preliminary preparations and the second, contact activities. The major steps of the preliminary preparation phase included:

- Obtaining a letter (the student) from the Inspector of the Community and Youth Section that introduced the student as a representative of the CPS and secondly, described the nature of the project engaged in by the student;
- The writing of a letter by the student describing potential survey participants, how they were chosen and how their cooperation could benefit their community and the police. The letter thanked individuals for their assistance.

The key steps in the contact phase involved the following:

- Development of a list of agencies or community associations who deal with and/or serve the Hispanic community;
- Development of a list of contact persons involved with the agencies or associations;
- Arrangement of meetings with the persons identified as key community contacts;
- Meeting with the community representatives to explain the project in detail and secondly, to explain how these representatives could assist in the project.

During this phase, the student utilized the knowledge of the member of the Cultural Resources Unit responsible for the Hispanic community.

The Value of the Community Needs Assessment Instrument

As a result of the student's efforts, a culturally sensitive needs assessment survey was developed for the Calgary Police Service. The survey will be adopted for use with several of Calgary's diverse communities in the effort to determine their service and information needs from a policing perspective. In the effort to implement the survey, community organizations, ethnic media sources and key community members were used to promote the survey, provide translation services (where required) and distribute the survey to ensure maximum community participation. Such a collaborative process epitomizes the ideal notion of partnership which is a central goal of community policing.

By working together, social work and the CPS possess the opportunity to facilitate the achievement of such a laudable goal.

Based on the student's interaction with the Hispanic community during the development of the survey, the initial impact of the project appeared to be quite positive. Members of the community appreciated the effort being made by the CPS to address the specific concerns of the community. Having a Spanish speaking individual facilitating the project and seeking input from the community enhanced the credibility of the CPS.

The challenge for the Cultural Resources Unit, especially in a time when economic resources are quite limited, will be to follow through with services that address the particular concerns of the diverse communities. If this can be carried out in a culturally sensitive manner, it is highly likely that positive relationships will develop. If this does transpire, the ideals of Canada's multicultural policy will be closer to being actualized.

CHALLENGES OF THE PLACEMENT

This practicum presented a number of challenges for the individuals participating in the experience. From the student's perspective, as previously discussed, the first major challenge involved organizing and selling the practicum to the Calgary Police Service. The student's ideas and plans for the practicum were fairly well established and clear. These attributes as well as the support she received from the supervisor of the Cultural Resources Unit and the social worker who became her field instructor enhanced the positive reception given to her proposal by senior management of the CPS and the Office of Field Education within the Faculty of Social Work.

Understanding and working within the constraints of a formal bureaucratic, and hierarchically structured organization while at the same time meeting the field requirements of the Faculty, proved to be another challenge. A number of strategies were utilized in dealing with this particular challenge. The presence of the student's MSW field instructor proved to be a critical key in operationalizing the practicum and its eventual success. The field instructor, through individual supervisory sessions, assisted the student's adjustment to the culture of the CPS. More specifically, the supervisor's three primary roles with the student included:

- Ensuring that the student's duties and tasks met the requirements of social work practice and fulfilled her learning contract;
- Acting as an advisor in regards to social work and other issues that arose;
- Discussing the integration of her practice experiences to social work theory.

The support provided to the student by her field instructor and the unit supervisor throughout the duration of the practicum contributed to the student's positive experience. A concern possessed by the field instructor and the student at the beginning of the placement centered on the Faculty's expectation that students complete and submit at least two taped interviews or process recordings for evaluation by the field instructor. Recognizing that the majority of the student's time would be spent on developing the needs assessment instrument, in consultation with her Faculty Field liaison (a representative from the Faculty who is responsible for monitoring the student's field experience) the student agreed to complete a document chronicling the activities undertaken in the development of the instrument. This flexibility regarding the Faculty's expectations alleviated the presenting concern and allowed the practicum to proceed as planned.

Difficulties in communication between the student and the supervisor of the Cultural Resources Unit proved to be the most contentious challenge that emerged during the practicum. The issues of concern involved the different terminology utilized by social workers and police officers and the interpretation of terms used. For example, terms such as "frontline conflict resolution" and "crisis intervention" used by the student were understood by the unit supervisor that the student was preparing to engage in activities beyond the scope of the planned project. The degree of mis-communication reached the point where the unit supervisor considered canceling the practicum. However, the field instructor's experience working within the CPS helped to alleviate the level of discomfort around the issue of communication. This individual served as an interdisciplinary translator who assured the student and the unit supervisor that both were working toward the same goal in relation to the needs assessment and that the difficulties in communicating were the result of each individual's discipline-specific training.

One of the reasons for the successful intervention of the field instructor stemmed from the fact that during the initial stages of the practicum, the student, unit supervisor and field instructor met on several occasions to discuss the roles and responsibilities of the field instructor in relation to the Cultural Resources Unit Supervisor. As well, the existence of ongoing communication between the unit supervisor and field instructor assisted in the resolution of communication difficulties. In the words of the field instructor, "If the latter [ongoing communication] did not occur, the practicum placement would have been less successful."

LESSONS LEARNED

For each of the individuals participating in this experience a number of lessons were learned. From the perspective of the student, major insights included:

- Recognizing the importance of familiarizing oneself with and respecting both the formal and informal structure of the agency.

- Being patient and flexible, realizing that despite how well one plans, the implementation process may not go as smoothly or in the order planned. For students it is important to remember that this does not constitute failure but a reflection of the reality of working in an organization, especially one that is a paramilitary bureaucracy.
- The need for a student placed with the CPS to be self-motivated, self-directed and whose work displays initiative.
- The recognition of the array of roles (advocate, mediator) that social workers can contribute to a police service and in particular a Cultural Resources Unit.

Major learnings from the view of the supervisor of the Cultural Resources Unit include:

- Realization of the contributions that social work can make.
- The importance of having a social worker available within the organization who can bridge the differences and point out similarities between social work and policing.

From the perspective of the MSW field instructor insights gleaned included:

- The necessity of maintaining open lines of dialogue with both the student and unit supervisor.
- The importance of working in a cooperative and collaborative manner with the unit supervisor.

For the Faculty Field liaison the following constituted major insights gained:

- The importance of being flexible regarding the Faculty of Social Work's field placement requirements. For example, allowing the student to change the nature of the process recording expected by the Faculty.
- Being enthusiastic about the placement opportunity and supporting the student and the individuals from the host organization. This is extremely important in a new placement like the Cultural Resources Unit.

It is important to note that at least two collective forms of learning occurred as a result of the practicum experience. First, a realization and recognition that the disciplines of social work and policing can work together in a collaborative and efficient manner. The goals of the Cultural Resources Unit seem to be congruent with basic social work values such as respecting the unique characteristics of diverse populations. Within both professions there seems to be a strong desire to improve service delivery to different groups residing in Calgary. The development and utilization of the community needs assessment is one mechanism by which human service professionals can increase their awareness and become more responsive to the concerns of Calgary's diverse population.

Just as important, the experience proved to be very educational for the social work and police representatives involved. Each group enhanced their knowledge of the range of activities performed by each profession as well as the goals the respective professions are attempting to achieve. Education of this nature will prove to be valuable as both professions, individually and in partnership, face increasing challenges as Canada's population continues to become more diversified.

REFERENCES

Elliot, J., & Fleras, A. (1991). *Unequal relations: An introduction to race and ethnic dynamics in Canada.* Scarborough, ON: Prentice-Hall.

Fleras, A., & Elliot, J. (1992). *Multiculturalism in Canada.* Scarborough, ON: Nelson

Immigration to Alberta - Decade in Review 1980 - 1990. (1992). Edmonton: Alberta Career Development and Employment, Immigration and Settlement.

Managing immigration: A framework for the 1990s. (1990). Ottawa, ON: Employment and Immigration Canada.

Naidoo, J., & Edwards, G. (1991). Combatting racism involving visible minorities: A review of relevant research and policy development. *Canadian Social Work Review, 8* (2), 211-236.

Osborne, D., & Gaebler, T. (1993). *Reinventing government: How the entrepreneurial spirit is transforming the public sector.* New York: Plume.

Yelaja, S., & O'Neill, B. (1990). *Multiculturalism and social work education: Resources for change.* Waterloo, ON: Wilfrid Laurier University.

CHAPTER THIRTY-FOUR

FIELD EDUCATION FOR STUDENTS WITH DISABILITIES: FRONT DOOR/BACK DOOR; NEGOTIATION/ ACCOMMODATION/MEDIATION

Martha C. Bial and Maxine Lynn

A lot of people think access means the ability to get into a building, no matter where or how you can get into it, whether you get into it through a back alley, or through an elevator that usually carries garbage or food. But shouldn't it mean that you can get into the building through the front door with everybody else? That for me is true access. Itzhak Perlman (Rothstein, 1993)

As social work field educators concerned about our profession's role in serving people with disabilities, we must pay increased attention to the needs of disabled students entering our own ranks. We must be sure that we are offering them "true access" to the full range of training opportunities in their field placements so that with MSW in hand, they can hopefully "get through the front door" of the profession to the jobs for which their interests and abilities qualify them.

The Americans with Disability Act defines the disabled individual as one with "a physical or mental impairment that substantially limits one or more of the major life activities, a record of such impairment or who is regarded as having such an impairment" (ADA, P.L.101-336, July 26, 1990). This definition appears in the social work literature as well (Reeser, 1992). It is interesting to note that the ADA definition includes the learning disabled and those with a history of mental illness or substance abuse, while earlier uses of the term referred mainly to those with physical disability. While accepting this newer definition, we shall be identifying disabled social work students as those who have acknowledged disabilities which require some adjustment by the placement agency. Our definition includes students with long standing, stable handicapping conditions as well as those recently disabled and those with chronic, intermittent or degenerative illness.

At the passage of the Americans with Disability Act in 1990, the number of Americans with physical or mental disabilities was 43 million and growing (US House of Representatives, May 15, 1990). At the same time, medical technology has provided the tools for people with a wide range of chronic conditions to live long lives and function independently enough to pursue a full career. While the disabled are entering all walks of life in record numbers, social work may hold a special attraction, especially for those who have had positive encounters with social workers in the course of treatment. Motivated by identification with those professional helpers or perhaps by a desire to "give back" help received, they are seeking training in our social work schools. Yet the path is often strewn with obstacles, both personal and organizational.

To fully understand the complexity of this issue one needs to look at disabled students in a social context. First, the disabled have been barred from full participation in a society which has treated them unequally and left them politically powerless. They face overwhelming discrimination and oppression which is often unnoticed (US House of Representatives, 1990; US Senate, 1989). As children they had few adult role models and most often none in their families. They have suffered social isolation and until recently exclusion or segregation in schools and the workplace. The wounds from such experiences run deep. As the Supreme Court ruled in Brown vs. Board of Education, "Segregation affects one's heart and mind in ways that may never be undone" (US Senate Report, August, 1989). Several experts testifying at Senate hearings on the proposed ADA noted that discrimination "destroys healthy self concepts" and leaves a "stigma that scars for life" (US Senate Report, August, 1989). These consequences often bear no relationship to the actual limitation imposed by the disability. However, they may seriously hamper the trainee in a field that relies on interpersonal relationship skills and requires conscious use of self in its practice.

Just as the disabled student carries the burdens of societal prejudice and discrimination, social work educators and agency personnel are a product of that same society. Until recently we have all too often either ignored the disabled or subtly practiced the same exclusion and discrimination we all consciously disavow.

A review of the literature reveals little attention to persons with disabilities (Reeser, 1992). In fact it was noted at a recent conference on social work and disabilities (Rimmerman, 1994) that the literature is scarce, especially in the field of physical disabilities. One of the authors had to help a student deal with having a client who was paraplegic and found few readings available on working with the disabled. The class members had limited experience — either personal or in fieldwork — to share with this struggling student. Because students shy away from placements with the visibly disabled, field directors anxious to please the student/consumer may underuse these placements with their valuable learning opportunities. Thus it would seem we are not adequately preparing our future practitioners and field instructors either through course content or field experiences to receive disabled students in the field.

As regards students specifically, the limited literature does confirm the presence of prejudice and discrimination towards disabled students in social work classes and practicum. Schools and placement agencies avoid "owning" such discrimination. Instead they blame building inaccessibility or inability to adjust schedules and task requirements. In the late 1970's, Hutchins (1978) recognized the need for affirmative action for the disabled in social work education; yet the need persists, despite laws such as the Americans with Disabilities Act.

While the literature has affirmed that social work educators must work harder to help these students achieve a successful practicum, it has given insufficient attention to the difficulties involved in doing so, especially after the placement is made. Weinberg (1978) touched on a key issue that is not always faced: disabled students have special learning needs that must be addressed by university field personnel and agency field instructors. Field directors must overcome personal prejudices and doubts in order to locate placements. They must then provide students with the necessary supports and skills to hurdle either physical or attitudinal barriers which may be encountered. Field instructors, in turn, must overcome their fears and biases in order to accept the students (along with the attendant challenges) while presenting to agency colleagues the positive contributions the interns will make to the service delivery system. Finally, field instructors must help the student workers relate professionally to clients with societal prejudices toward the disabled.

While field directors attempt to provide these students with placements equal in range and quality to those offered other students, professional responsibility and obligations to agency colleagues dictate that they not compromise educational standards or client service. Because agency and school have different constituencies and concerns, the disabled student may strain the university/field collaboration. Tension arises at three points: the securing of a placement and the agency's agreement to take a student; the student's entry into placement when necessary accommodations are worked out; and the emergence of performance problems apparently caused by the disability. We shall explore these points in depth with examples shared by field instructors, faculty/field liaisons and students.

It has been our observation that when placements of disabled students work well, the school, the agency and the student have each made some concession to the others' requirements. Indeed continuing negotiation, accommodation and mediation are the hallmark of these successful placements with a particular activity dominating in each phase.

TENSION POINTS

Securing the Placement — Time of Negotiation

Field department members seeking placements for their disabled students frequently experience a tension between their professional values, their prejudices and doubts about the student's capabilities, and the practical exigencies of making placements in a competitive environment under pressures of time. Professional values (to say nothing of law and student demand) press placement personnel to offer disabled students access to all kinds of placements on an equal footing with other students. As social workers trained to translate values into advocacy on behalf of oppressed groups, they feel compelled to educate, lobby, cajole or pressure agencies into accepting disabled students. They may bargain offering, for example, a presumably "trouble free" student in a package deal with the disabled student. However, they are loath to be too adversarial with agencies needed for other current and future students. Also, might they not win a pyrrhic victory for themselves and the student if they send him/her into a very reluctant field setting? The disabled student needs extra supports and good will to overcome real obstacles so the field department is wary of making a placement with a resentful field instructor or agency director.

Students are concerned about this as well with most saying they don't want to go where they won't be readily accepted. Yet, in a social environment where many agencies and field instructors share the same fears and stereotypes of the society at large, few agencies welcome the disabled student with open arms. They express a number of concerns, some realistic, some based on untested assumptions. Prospective field instructors anticipate an inordinate time commitment to supervision of the student with special needs. They worry that the student will not be able to perform key aspects of the job. They fear for the safety of the student or of the clients if the student cannot walk quickly or use all his/her senses. They voice concerns about negative reactions to the student from clients or from agency executives and colleagues whose support the field instructor needs to make the placement work. Reeser (1992) in her survey of field work directors reported these agency issues plus liability concerns, lack of space and limited accessibility. These concerns frequently lead agencies to turn down a student on the basis of the handicap alone without even meeting him or her and certainly without an opportunity to test their negative assumptions.

Students have realistic concerns that the school or the agencies will stereotype them with prejudgments about their abilities, inabilities and the kinds of clients they can work with. One student with cerebral palsy, interested in a second year placement in a family agency, tired easily because of her illness and asked for placement near her home. She felt misunderstood and unsupported when the placement coordinator suggested placement in a hospital far from her home where she could work with disabled veterans. To avoid this response students with disabilities not readily apparent may withhold this information from the field department and/or the agencies. Sometimes field placement personnel, knowing about the disability are reluctant to share its full extent with the agencies when negotiating for placement slots.

To Tell or Not to Tell

While field instructors almost unanimously say that advance information about a student's disability would not prejudice the student's acceptance into the agency, and could only help insure a better response to the student's need, the experience of field administrators in placement negotiation suggests the need for caution. One field instructor, supervising a student in a fast paced psychiatric emergency room and mobile crisis team, confessed:

> I am glad I didn't know my student had an artificial leg. I would have worried about her ability to move quickly and I might have refused her, but she's been terrific!

Withholding of information in a negotiation is an adversarial technique which placement makers want to avoid when trying to build trust and goodwill towards the school and the student (Fisher & Ury, 1986). Also, provided agencies do not run from the disclosure, field instructors can plan better for the student the more information they have.

While most students do inform the school and the agency about their disability in advance, it behooves field advisors to help students find an appropriate way to share their special placement needs with the agencies early on. Social work schools also need to address the agencies' concerns. They should offer the university's resources for help with adaptive equipment, readers, etc., assure them of the back up of a prepared faculty-field liaison, and provide an opportunity to talk with other agencies who have taken disabled students in the past. Most importantly, field department staff must believe in the benefits of this kind of placement to the agency as well as the student. Once convinced, they can encourage field instructors to see the placement as a challenge, even an opportunity, rather than primarily a burden or a threat.

In our survey of field instructors those most open to taking a disabled student commented on the positive contributions such a student could make to their clients. For example, a field instructor of a blind student placed in an inner city middle school said:

> Our kids, poor and of color, frequently see themselves as victims and respond with blame and hopelessness. My social work student is also a victim, but is not defeated by it. He's taking responsibility for building a life for himself. He's a wonderful role model.

It also helps to work with field instructors who have the authority to act on their convictions. In agencies which easily accept disabled students the field instructors were generally well established in their jobs, enjoyed the trust of superiors and co-workers and were confident about the rightness of taking the student. In such cases they were able to preempt or refute resistance that might arise. A field instructor with 33 years experience on the job, said "I didn't ask permission to take the student, I told my administrator what I planned to do." A newer but well respected field instructor in a traditional medical-dominated psychiatric hospital, said "as a social worker I always have to advocate for what I think is right. This is just one more thing I have to advocate for."

Entry into Placement — Initial Accommodation

When the student arrives at the agency, many of the fantasized obstacles fade away, only to be replaced by real ones which hadn't been anticipated — a bathroom door too narrow for a wheelchair to enter or agency forms which the learning disabled student finds confusing to use. Some of the obstacles may only become apparent over time as the student confronts the time and travel demands, the physical environment and the actual tasks of the field placement. As a result, contracting, the primary initial task of student and supervisor, may take longer than with other students as obstacles are discovered, accommodations tried out and terms of the work are negotiated.

The learning contract, whether written or oral, should include a plan for meeting the school's educational requirements, the agency's service need and the student's learning needs. It should outline the terms of the work and any special accommodations or supports which may be needed to accomplish them. Both field instructor and student have an obligation to be clear, thorough and honest with each other as they outline goals and expectations of each other. The supervisor must first determine the core duties of the job, distinguishing those which are essential from those which are traditional, but non essential and difficult for the disabled student to perform. In an after school teen program it had been traditional for the social workers to play basketball with the young clients. It took some creative thinking for a field instructor and blind student to think of an alternate activity for engaging these boys, such as playing rap music together.

Where possible the successful supervisor tries to redesign the job away from the student's deficits towards his strengths. In one agency where students took turns on telephone intake, a hearing impaired student with good lip reading skills was relieved of that responsibility but assigned additional in-person intakes so she could practice some of the same skills.

When the core activities are outlined in detail, students have an obligation to develop a work plan, including strategies for handling obstacles. They may need special equipment or extra time to complete some assignments and should be direct in explaining this to their supervisors. If the agency does not already have appropriate aids, they should make efforts through the university or government rehabilitation services to obtain adaptive equipment or helpers such as readers and transcribers. Students may need to pace themselves around their disabilities and prepare their supervisors for this. A student with cerebral palsy knew she was subject to unpredictable days of extreme fatigue so tried to get extra work done when feeling good so that the agency would relax its expectations of her work production on bad days. An accommodating field instructor will be on the lookout for how s/he can help the student do all parts of the job without taking over the job. A supervisor of a student with MS in a mental hospital wanted her student to have the experience of taking patients for assessment to a community program. Since she knew distant parking would strain the student's walking endurance, she drove the student and patient to the program and returned to pick them up.

As part of contracting, field instructor and student need to discuss how the student will handle problematic reactions of clients or other staff to the student's disability. The student needs to be prepared for extreme testing by some clients and sometimes total rejection (Weinberg, 1978). When student and field instructor are open, honest and realistic in their expectations of each other, the placements usually have a positive beginning. However, at times disabled students may feel a need either to minimize their incapacities in order to prove they can do it all, or to seek a reduced workload for fear they will not be able to measure up to full demand. Field instructors who fail to explore these messages fully and negotiate solutions may become angry at the students for not pulling their weight or may give the students less work to do, depriving them of their full training.

Another student with MS was having difficulty doing agency paperwork because of problems with vision and motor coordination. Her field instructor began doing her paperwork for her to cover agency requirements but then refused to give her more cases because he couldn't handle the extra paperwork of her caseload on top of his own. The faculty/field liaison was helpful here in making clear the school's expectation that the student have a full client load *and* find a way to complete required documentation. The faculty member's intervention brought out in the open this silent, dysfunctional accommodation which the field instructor had been making and was the stimulus for needed recontracting.

The Emergence of Performance Problems — the Role of Mediation

When any student falls short of performance expectations, both the student and the field instructor experience frustration, a sense of failure and shame (Frenkel, 1994). The situation also requires the supervisor to make an explicit demand for work and to exercise the authority aspect of the supervisory role from which many social workers shrink (Kadushin, 1992; Shulman, 1993). The field instructors we spoke with found it especially difficult to press demands of disabled students for several reasons. They feel the disabled student is already "struggling with so much." They are concerned that the disabled student may be especially sensitive to criticism or maybe that it is somehow rude on their part to criticize someone already oppressed. They are often unsure how much of the performance problem is caused by the disability and thereby deserving of compassion, and how much lack of skill or motivation for which the student can justly be held accountable. Finally, in a litigious environment, they may be reluctant to submit a very negative evaluation which may incur legal reprisals from a student who feels discriminated against because of his/her disability.

Yet when questioned about hypothetical situations, virtually all the field instructors attending a conference on working with the disabled student, felt that it was important to maintain standards (Bial, 1994). Competency, they said, is always the bottom line. They agreed that a wide discrepancy between expectations for disabled and non-disabled students leads to resentment by other staff and students who may feel the disabled student is getting an unfair advantage. It also deprives disabled students of their full learning and ultimate sense of achievement. Most important, it is a disservice to current clients and those the students will serve after receiving their degrees.

The tension, therefore, derives from the field instructors' commitment to high standards pulling against their compassion for the student and their reluctance to exert authority. The following areas of performance will serve to illustrate how this tension can come to a head, threatening the continuation of the placement: recording, handling client reactions and working with colleagues.

Recording: Process Recording and Agency Documentation

Process recording is central to the school's requirements of students in field work and documentation of client contacts and other work is critical to the agency's survival. The most compassionate field instructor cannot afford to overlook failure in this area. At the same time, most students (and workers) generally resist any kind of recording. It can be hard to distinguish whether a disabled student's recording is in arrears because of the disability or because of resistance to exposure, poor writing skills, inability to manage time or some other reason. Field instructors themselves not liking to record, may be sympathetic but at the same time angry if they feels students are using the disability as an excuse to "get away" with not doing it. Learning disabled students, as well as those with perceptual or motor difficulties, may find it difficult to write. If the field instructors set the quantitative demand for paper work too high, students are likely to become frustrated, guilty and defensive. If the demand is too low, they will not get sufficient practice in this important form of professional communication. Furthermore, if students do not submit enough process recording, they will not draw the best, most thoughtful teaching from their supervisors. Again when students are open about their limitations and show a desire to fulfil appropriate expectations, a reasonable compromise is often possible.

Several field instructors and students reported negotiating an agreement for the student to submit a combination of written and taped process recordings. In a couple of situations students were able to find volunteer or paid transcribers. When the spirit of compromise pervades the relationship, it can overcome doubts about why the student is resisting writing.

One field instructor suspected that some of her student's reluctance to write process was due to reluctance to disclose his feelings rather than his cerebral palsy. However, she saw the student as eager to comply in most ways and willing to write *some* process recordings so she decided to "take him at his word" and accepted most of the process recordings on tape. Conversely, another student with cerebral palsy seemed to her field instructor to be "using it as an excuse to avoid recording" and the matter became an unresolved bone of contention throughout the placement.

In cases where the student and field instructor have become too embroiled in conflict over this demand, the faculty advisor can mediate and perhaps provide a fresh solution. A learning disabled student was having trouble organizing his case histories and seemed unable to benefit from the outline provided him by his field instructor. The faculty advisor provided the student with a number of alternate outlines, helped him identify the one most understandable for him, then coached him on its use.

Handling the Reactions of Clients

This can create tension in the supervisory relationship because disabled students must possess a high degree of self-awareness and self-acceptance in order to be able to handle, and sometimes reach for, negative reactions from clients and staff towards their disabilities. They must be able to respond without anger, evasiveness or defensiveness. Less obviously, if they are not aware of their own feelings about being disabled, they may either overprotect their clients or expect too much from them.

The field instructor must explore the issue of disability with the student to evaluate how well the student has adjusted to the handicap and how it has contributed to his/her conception of self and ability to relate to both disabled and non-disabled people (weinberg, 1978). Problematic encounters with clients can be discussed or role played to help the student get in touch with his/her own feelings as well as the client's. He/she can then try out various responses. As with other areas of difference, such as race and ethnicity, field instructors must proceed sensitively. Otherwise they may contribute to the student's sense of oppression.

There is also tension between the student's right to have a full caseload of all kind of clients and a client's right to refuse service from a particular worker. Some of the field instructors we spoke to felt the client's refusal must prevail, while others said that reluctance to work with a disabled student/worker should be seen as similar to resistance to working with a worker of different race or gender — an issue to be explored and worked through. Still other supervisors said that agency intake workers and supervisors should express confidence in the student and encourage clients to "give the relationship a try."

A practitioner, after surveying a number of clients on their feelings about the hypothetical situation of having a disabled worker, concluded that most of the anxieties voiced reflected the client's own issues (Wilczynski, 1994). She noted a "parentified child" who worried about having to "take care of" a disabled student/ worker, and a client with low self-esteem who felt assignment to a disabled worker would be an indication of her own low worth. The supervisory challenge here is to help a student see this transferential reaction as an issue for the therapeutic work and not to personalize it.

One student in our survey may have wanted to avoid client rejection by volunteering to see primarily disabled clients in a family counselling agency. She presented this request as a desire to work with an underserved population for whom she had a special understanding. The agency was delighted to be able to offer extra service to a group of clients who had traditionally not stayed in treatment. Yet as the year wore on, the field instructor felt that this offer might have represented avoidance on the student's part. She was reluctant to push the student to an area in "which she might not be comfortable." The faculty/ field liaison supported the field instructor in her expectation that the student see more non-disabled students. At the same time, he expressed his confidence to the student in her ability to handle the new work. This act of mediation moved the student and field instructor past an impasse and advanced the student's learning.

Working with Colleagues

Students who fail to "fit in" to the professional team at the agency may engender impatience in staff, embarrassment in the field instructor and may risk having their work prematurely judged inadequate. Negotiating the new agency culture is a challenge for all students and some misread the cues or mishandle their own anxieties by becoming too familiar with other staff or too remote. They may expect considerations enjoyed in prior settings which are unacceptable in the field placement.

A number of field instructors felt that disabled students may make these gaffes more often than others because of social isolation and lack of work experience. Their prior treatment as disabled persons by their families or others, may have left them with limited social and workplace skills. This assumption while untested, has enough currency among teachers and field instructors that it should be addressed as a potential obstacle in placement.

Some disabled people have developed survival skills which have been adaptive for living in a hostile social environment but can be dysfunctional for getting along in an agency and relating to clients. Defenses such as denial and behaviors such as oversolicitous-ness, excessive dependence or unrealistic declarations of independence, rigidity and seeking exemptions from the usual rules, can all contribute to strained relationships on the job. When students are not liked by agency staff, it is an issue which field instructors must find a way to address in supervision and in dealings with staff. While this is never easy to discuss, it is particularly hard for sensitive supervisors to raise such issues with disabled students or their own staffs in a politically correct environment. One disabled student frequently took time off from placement for doctors' appointments and expected this to be included in her fieldwork hours. The supervisor had to make clear his expectation for make up of this time, a task made easier with backing from the school.

Sometimes field instructors feel responsible for making the staff accept the student and for making the student acceptable to the staff. The school can help by making clear to the field instructor and student that the student has a large part to play in making himself accepted. A field instructor whose student with Tourette's syndrome was socially awkward with the staff, found the staff ready to eject the student after a symptomatic outburst. The field instructor while sympathetic to her staff, felt obliged to plead on the student's behalf until the faculty advisor suggested asking the student to develop a plan for how *he* would address the staff's reaction.

Incompetent Practice

This is perhaps the hardest issue for all field instructors. It is especially difficult in today's political and legal environment to consider failing a student from an oppressed minority group, a category which surely includes the disabled. Since evaluation in social work is, and must be, largely subjective, field educators are even more reluctant to recommend failure when nagged by doubts about the accuracy of their judgments. For this reason, schools must have crystal clarity in their criteria for failure, be sure that reasonable efforts at remediation have been made and provide for more than one judge. In most schools of social work the protocol for failing students calls for these steps. With disabled students the failing evaluation must be carefully reviewed to be sure that the disability itself has not been introduced as proof of inability to do the work.

A student who was subject to unpredictable "sleeping episodes," probably petit mal seizures, was ejected from an agency after falling asleep in a staff conference. "What if she falls asleep with clients?" said the field instructor and agency director, as if the question needed no answer. This student was successfully replaced in another agency where the field instructor engaged the student in a joint problem solving effort to decide how to handle the sleeping episodes with clients and staff. The supervisor speculated that the student probably did occasionally fall asleep with clients, but added that her client retention was high and her process recording showed depth and sensitivity. This field instructor, in other words, saw performance problems as fodder for supervisory process, not a trigger for instant evaluation. Also she was willing to judge the student on the core of the work, and did not make a symptom the total measure of her performance.

Not every situation ends so happily. Sometimes a student, apart from the disability, fails to demonstrate the rudimentary knowledge and skills to be effective with clients, despite remedial efforts. Another student, also given to sleeping episodes because of sleep apnea, showed little self-awareness and poor engagement skills in a mental health clinic. His client retention record was poor and even after the field instructor redesigned his caseload to assign him only the most apparently motivated clients, almost all his clients failed to return, with a couple specifically asking for another worker. The student received a failing grade in field work. The student, whose first psychological defense against failure was to blame the agency and the school, engaged a lawyer, and seemed prepared to press a discrimination suit. A negotiated solution was reached in which the student agreed to get treatment for the sleep apnea and was allowed to repeat the field placement in a case management setting which allowed him to build on his strengths in assessment and in locating and following up with community resources. Despite extensive efforts by the faculty liaison and field department to show appreciation and support for the mental health clinic and its field instructor, they felt angry and understandably reluctant to take another student for a while.

Competence, at a minimum, must include self awareness, an ability to engage clients, to relate appropriately to professional colleagues, to incorporate professional values and to learn from supervision. Beyond this, a student must be able to demonstrate beginning mastery of technical skills, including contracting, data collection, assessment and intervention. Some will take longer than others to achieve this mastery. Some disabled students will need more time as well as more direction, task modification, adaptive equipment or advisor support. But when all efforts have been made to provide these, disabled students must still be held to the same standards of values, personal attributes and skills as their peers.

SUMMARY AND RECOMMENDATIONS

In the examples we cited and others too numerous to include, we noticed some common traits among disabled students and among field instructors in the placements that worked. *Students* were first and foremost accepting of their own disability and open and honest in communicating with the agency and clients about it. They were highly motivated, professional in manner, self-aware and open to supervision. They were realistic about their limitations but made efforts to comply with requirements and never seemed to be "cutting corners."

Field Instructors tended to be experienced workers in supportive settings or at least confident of their own position in their agencies. They carried few stereotypes about the disabled but were eager to learn details of the particular students' needs and abilities. They viewed the students positively either for their experience as disabled persons or for their skills apart from the disability. They saw deficits as problems to be solved rather than reasons for rejecting the student. They were patient, creative, solution focused and flexible in *how* assignments were done while holding to standards for quality of work. They were able to withhold judgments about the impact of the student's abilities until the results of the work were in. Interestingly, in our group, as in a group examined by Reeser (1992), a disproportionate number of successful field instructors were disabled themselves, had a disabled relative or worked with the disabled.

School personnel also had a part to play in successful placements. Students appreciated most the faculty advisors and field department representatives who listened to them, validated their efforts and concerns and appeared not to stereotype them. Field instructors appreciated school personnel who recognized their extra efforts on behalf of the disabled student, supported them in holding the student to standards and relieved them of the lonely sense of sole responsibility.

We have only begun to explore this topic. The unique nature of each student/agency match means that the "solutions" described here to the issues of securing placements, working out initial accommodations and mediating in cases of weak performance will not work for everyone. Still, some general recommendations seem in order. Field educators with good experiences need to "spread the word" about the feasibility and positive aspects of taking disabled students into placement. Educational programs by the university for groups of disabled students in agencies would be a start. Field departments should build a resource bank of experienced field instructors who can encourage, reassure, problem solve and share their "creative tips" with those first encountering a disabled student. Anticipatory guidance for groups of disabled students before placements start would help them plan better for obstacles and gain support from each other. Peer groups before and throughout placement would provide support, increase the sense of empowerment and give members a chance to share information about special services and strategies for handling issues of disability with the agency and with clients. Faculty field liaisons should be better informed about resources for the disabled student and be prepared to give extra time and support to student and agency. Since extra time is necessary for some disabled students to complete assignments and some are not able to work full schedules, consideration should be given to extended placements or extra hours if needed. Some of these recommendations would require change in school policy and others would require additional resources. The goal, however, is a worthy one and consistent with our professional values — to prepare disabled students to enter the "front door" of social work without apology and meet the highest standards of our profession.

REFERENCES

Americans with Disabilities Act, Public Law 101-336, July 26, 1990.

Bial, M. (Chair). (1994, March). *Students with special needs: Hindrance, handicap or opportunity.* Symposium for field instructors at Fordham University.

Fisher, R., & Ury, W. (1986). *Getting to yes.* Penguin.

Frenkel, B. (1994, March). Organizational and teaching concerns. In M. Bial (Chair), *Students with special needs: Hindrance, handicap or opportunity.* Symposium for field instructors at Fordham University.

Hutchins, T. (1978). Affirmative action for the physically disabled in social work education. *Journal of Education for Social Work, 14*(3), 64-70.

Kadushin, A. (1992). *Supervision in social work* (3rd ed.). New York: Columbia University Press.

Reeser, L. (1992). Students with disabilities in practicum: What is reasonable accommodation? *Journal of Social Work Education, 28*(1), 98-109.

Rimmerman, A. (1994, May). *Research in social work and disabilities: Current issues and future directions.* Keynote address at the joint conference on Social Work and Disabilities of the Young Adult Institute and National Association of Social Workers, New York.

Rothstein, M. (1993, October 24). For the disabled, some progress. *The New York Times*, section 10, pp. 1, 11.

Shulman, L. (1993). *Interactional supervision.* Washington, DC: NASW Press.

US House of Representatives, *H.R. 2273 Hearings*, Committee on the Judiciary, May 15, 1990. In M. Harrison & S. Gilbert (Eds.) (1992), *The Americans with Disabilities Act handbook*. Beverly Hills: Excellent Books.

US Senate, S. 933, Report No. 101-116, Committee on Labor and Human Resources, August 30, 1989. In M. Harrison & S. Gilbert (Eds.) (1992), *The Americans with Disabilities Act handbook*. Beverly Hills: Excellent Books.

Weinberg, L. (1978). Unique learning needs of physically handicapped social work students. *Journal of Education for Social Work, 14*(1), 110-117.

Wilczynski, B. (1994, March). What about the client? A view from the Field. In M. Bial (Chair), *Students with special needs: Hindrance, handicap or opportunity*. Symposium for field instructors at Fordham University.

CHAPTER THIRTY-FIVE

BUILDING RELATIONSHIPS WITH FIRST NATIONS COMMUNITIES AND AGENCIES: IMPLICATIONS FOR FIELD EDUCATION AND PRACTICE

Helena Summers and Michael Yellow Bird

INTRODUCTION

There is little information in the social work literature describing how to develop mutually beneficial relationships between First Nations communities and agencies[1] and schools of social work. Through these relationships social work faculty and students can become informed and sensitive to the issues that are important to First Nations peoples. Correspondingly, First Nations peoples can be empowered through understanding the dynamics of how schools of social work operate. The dialogue between the groups may also create possibilities for new methods of teaching, practice, and research.

Reciprocal partnerships are especially important for social work field education programs that are presently using or are planning to use First Nations agencies as student practica sites. A positive partnership essentially means three things: that social work

---

[1]   In this paper, the term "First Nations communities" refers to peoples of Aboriginal ancestry including status and non-status Indians, Metis, Inuit. First Nations agencies refer to social service organizations that are managed by Aboriginal peoples and serve predominately Aboriginal clientele.

students who choose these placements have experiences that sensitize them to issues important to the First Nations communities; that First Nations communities benefit from having these students at their agencies; and, that schools have increased opportunities to include the unique practices of First Nations agencies into their curricula.

The findings from a recent University of British Columbia School of Social Work survey of the use of First Nations agencies as student practica sites indicates a tremendous opportunity for learning in these placements.[2] New models for the practice of empowering and healing, that are, in fact, old practices to Aboriginal peoples, emerge in these settings. For example, the data from the UBC School of Social Work survey as well as a recent social work publication (Feehan & Hannis, 1993) show that First Nations organizations and academic institutions with First Nations faculty are using certain practices and policies that are guided by traditional native cosmology, communication, beliefs, and spirituality. In fact, many believe that returning to traditional Aboriginal empowering and healing practices is an appropriate way to achieve wellness and renewal for First Nations peoples (Absolon, 1993; George, 1992; LaFromboise, 1990; Morrisette et al., 1992; Napoleon, 1988; Jaine, 1992). Moreover, a recent Canadian Association of Social Work (CASW) "Policy on Indigenous People," submitted to the International Federation of Social Work (IFSW) states that, "Indigenous societies have a collective identity based on culture, tradition, and spirituality . . . therefore, Indigenous peoples must design and develop programs and services which will meet their collective needs . . ." (Allgaier, James, & Manuel, 1993, p. 162).

While First Nations models signal a new and exciting paradigm shift for social work, we do not advocate the appropriation or use of these models unless sincere partnerships have been achieved between a particular school and First Nations communities. Even then, some Aboriginal peoples have made it clear that they do not approve of non-First Nations people or organizations using traditional beliefs, practices, and spirituality (Smith, 1992).

This chapter has three objectives: describe the experiences of the school of social work and the field education program at the University of British Columbia in building relationships with First Nations communities and agencies; describe the experiences of the UBC School of Social Work in developing practica sites in First Nations agencies;

---

2   We are currently completing a "First Nations Field Education Placement Survey" of selected University and non-University social work programs across Canada. In this paper, we report only some of our preliminary findings. Five different University and two First Nations social work programs have responded. Almost all surveys were completed by Aboriginal social work faculty who are directly or indirectly involved with field education.

and, describe the innovative and creative teaching and practice principles that are used by various First Nations agencies to educate social work practica students.

HISTORICAL BACKGROUND

Building relationships with First Nations is a relatively new pursuit for schools of social work. The social work profession has had a dismal history of helping First Nations peoples to achieve self-determination and self-actualization. Indeed, social work practice reflecting such concepts as empowerment and self-determination, often regarded as hallmarks of the profession, have been the exception and not the rule in work with First Nations peoples.

Historically, social work practice with First Nations has been directed by various colonizing agents such as the federal and provincial governments, religious organizations and interested private sector organizations. These bureaucracies had little interest in building partnerships with First Nations since they had long before decided that Aboriginal beliefs, practices and spirituality were pagan and had nothing to offer to the more "advanced" and "civilized" Euro-canadian culture. More precisely, their main objective was to completely absorb and assimilate these groups into the Euro-canadian social fabric (Frideres, 1993; Joseph, 1992; Miller, 1992). Social workers, in executing this policy, unwittingly contributed to the cultural genocide of their clients.

In British Columbia, the destruction of the cultures of First Nations peoples has never been more ostensible than in the area of child protection (Liberating our children: Liberating our nations, 1992). For several generations, because of assimilation policies and the consequences of poverty, social workers removed Aboriginal children from their communities and placed them in settings where they were often abused by their custodians and, almost always, profoundly estranged from their families and culture. This "legalized abduction" of Aboriginal children by social workers greatly estranged First Nations peoples from the profession of social work (Liberating our children: Liberating our nations, 1992, p.63). As Ratner (1990, p.2) notes about this relationship, "there is something drastically wrong when professional social workers earn a reputation as interfering baby snatchers." The wounds from this relationship are still fresh in the minds of many Aboriginal communities. Until a 1992 moratorium was placed on the adoption of Aboriginal children by non-Aboriginal families (Adoption Legislative Review Panel, 1994), actions of the child protection social workers kept Aboriginal communities hypervigilant about what might happen to their children.

Indian residential schools and the adoptions of Aboriginal children into non-Aboriginal homes were two of the most effective ways to assimilate First Nations peoples into Euro-canadian society. The participation of social workers in placing Aboriginal children into these "assimilation camps" has left a troubled legacy between the social work profession and Aboriginal peoples. Building partnerships with First Nations communities is a good beginning to healing this legacy.

Despite efforts to extinguish the cultures of First Nations peoples, many have successfully resisted and held on to their traditional beliefs and practices. In the process of Aboriginal peoples taking control of social service organizations, some of these beliefs and practices have influenced agency policies and practices. These are contributing to the evolution of new models of social work practice. Patrick Kelly (1992) states, "one of the strongest gains to be realized by Canada and British Columbia in encouraging First Nations educational ideas to flourish is that the creative energy of the First Nations people, so long suppressed by social, economic, and political barriers would be made available for everyone's benefit" (p. 141).

TOWARD ABORIGINAL MODELS OF SOCIAL WORK PRACTICE

The distinct needs and cultural paradigms of Aboriginal peoples call for the creation of unique Aboriginal models of social work practice. These models must be translated into social work education that is culturally relevant and sensitive to Indigenous peoples (Allgaier, James, & Manuel, 1993).

Morrisette, McKenzie, and Morrisette (1993), advance a model of Aboriginal social work practice which was used successfully in Winnipeg, Manitoba at the Ma Mawi Wi Chi Itata Youth Support Program. This program provides comprehensive community based services for Aboriginal Youth. The framework of this model has four guiding principles:

1) recognition of a distinct Aboriginal world view;
2) the development of Aboriginal consciousness about the impact of colonialism;
3) cultural knowledge and traditions as an active component of retaining Aboriginal identity and collective consciousness;
4) empowerment as a method of practice.

Social work practice methods and knowledge relevant to the first three principles of this framework are not easily found in contemporary practice textbooks. Building relationships with First Nations communities will help schools of social work to begin to understand these principles and how to effectively apply them. The experiences of the British Columbia Alkali Lake Indian Reserve provide another example of social work practice using the Aboriginal cultural beliefs and practices. In the 1970s this community was affected by its members having a 100% rate of alcoholism. The model of practice used in this community was a holistic approach to treatment and life which involved the entire community creating body, mind, and spirit wellness for each member. Using this approach, this community achieved 100% sobriety in ten years.[3] The practice of group consensus and cooperation are cultural principles used by many First Nations peoples to resolve issues (Dubray, 1985, 1993; Lewis & Gringerich, 1980; Joe, 1989). The distinct needs and cultural paradigms of Aboriginal peoples have prompted Falcouer and Swift (1983) to suggest a social work model of practice in which child welfare workers:

- use and support Native-run support services whenever possible;
- recognize and become knowledgeable about the past history and current policy in your province regarding provision of child welfare services to Natives, both on and off reserves;
- educate themselves about Native culture and family structure;
- understand the norms and standards for child welfare are different in Native cultures;
- learn ways of communicating with Native people;
- support Native determination to be self-reliant.

Following the various principles described above helps social work students prepare for practice with Aboriginal peoples. Developing an extensive awareness of what each means further helps to provide effective services to these groups. First Nations field practica placements provide one way to develop this understanding and knowledge. Some of these principles discussed above, were identified as components of work in the First Nations agencies described in the UBC School of Social Work First Nations Field Education Placement Survey. Other elements of appropriate social work practice were:

- spirituality;
- connectedness and harmony with the earth;
- validation of aging;
- sharing and healing through increased use of group (i.e., talking circles and sweatlodge ceremonies);
- making practice more relevant through reconstructing practice boundaries, i.e., importance of working with extended families and less emphasis on the individual;
- reconstructing the supervision process so that it ensures a positive feeling at the end for social workers;
- empowerment; and

---

3   The members of the Alkali Lake community conceived the approach and implemented the actions that were necessary to attain sobriety for their membership. For a description of this approach see Maggie Hodgson (1987). *Indian Communities Develop Futuristic Addictions Treatment and Health Approach.* Nechi Institute of Alcohol and Drug Education, 1987.

- a holistic approach, including humanizing of social workers.

In the UBC "First Nations Field Education Practica Survey," First Nations cultural practices were reported to have played an important part in agency work and hence in student learning. Some of the traditional ways which influenced practice were use of the medicine wheel, smudging, talking circles, sweatlodge and pipe ceremonies, and use of elders as cultural resources. In addition, several respondents to the survey indicated that the students who have the best experiences in First Nations practica placements are those who accept and are respectful toward the beliefs and practices of Aboriginal peoples.

Links to Feminist Practice

The First Nations practice models and principles in the previous section share some commonalities with a feminist perspective. Gould (1987) described the feminist principles of empowerment, consciousness raising, establishing group identity, and translating personal analysis into political action as elements which are particularly compelling in informing social work practice with oppressed groups. Aboriginal, like feminist practice, offers students a unique learning situation. In Aboriginal and Women's agencies, students often develop the historical understanding and practice skills necessary to work with these groups. As Howse and Stalwick (1990) point out, students with this training can transform the common perception that social workers are concerned only with personal services within the confines of the agency to the exclusion of attention to broader social issues. We suggest that this training helps prepare students to begin addressing the issues that emanate from the troubled legacy between First Nations peoples and the social work profession.

Experiences in First Nations agencies, like experiences in Women's agencies, cannot help but develop a broader awareness in the student that clinical intervention goes beyond working with individuals, families, or groups. Factors such as poverty, unemployment, inadequate housing, and racism are viewed in a systemic context, where they become not only individual problems, but also public issues and social problems. This view point is consistently represented in both First Nations and feminist social work thinking where the personal becomes political and calls for social action.

DEVELOPING RELATIONSHIPS WITH ABORIGINAL COMMUNITIES

The experience of the UBC School of Social work suggests that establishing relationships between First Nations communities and schools of social work must be a process which involves the entire faculty as well as the field education office. The recent UBC First Nations Field Education Placement Survey also supports this approach.

Ideally, an important part of relationship building requires the hiring of First Nations Faculty and professional support staff to enhance the community outreach process, the admissions policy, the school curriculum, and the recruitment and development of practica. However, expecting only the field office and First Nations Faculty and professional staff to embark on this process independently is unrealistic since a considerable amount of effort is required to carry out the relationship building. Rather, several faculty are required to share the responsibility with their colleagues. Our experience in developing relationships with Aboriginal communities was a slow process. Occurring over the last decade, it can be divided into three stages (Summers & Seebaran, 1993).

1) Stage one was essentially an individualistic and ad-hoc approach. Efforts were initiated not as a result of system-wide school policy, but rather as a consequence of individual interest on the part of a faculty member, particular student or community member.

2) The second stage was characterized by a mixed re-active and pro-active approach. Here, the relationships were driven by interested faculty members and students but were also influenced by a number of external factors.

   a) The professional association in BC had passed resolutions calling on the School to train its graduates for multicultural practice.

   b) The First Nations House of Learning was established on campus in 1987 and began to work towards making the university's vast resources more accessible to BC's First People, and to improve the university's ability to meet the needs of First Nations. This included working towards expanding the range and depth of programs and course offerings related to the needs identified by First Nations people and communities in BC.[4] The First Nations House of Learning began questioning the low numbers of First Nations students at the School of Social Work, and expressed concerns about the School's perceived negative relationships with First Nations Communities.

   c) First Nations agencies began to negotiate field placements with the School.

3) The third stage involves an organizational policy approach. The school took a policy decision to deliver a curriculum and field experience which prepares its

---

4   For a more detailed description of these suggestions see The University of British Columbia, *First Nations Studies Calender* (1993-1994, p.6).

graduates for multicultural practice with special attention to First Nations issues. Implementation began by appointing a faculty member with outreach responsibilities to Aboriginal communities the establishment of a First Nations Faculty Committee, and hiring of a First Nations person to a tenure track position. Most recently the school decided to create a hospitable environment for First Nations students through decreasing admissions and designating one-half of the admissions for students with Aboriginal ancestry.

Within the field education area, the school took a decision to use degreed and non-degreed social service staff as field instructors in Aboriginal practica. Non-degreed instructors were provided with additional faculty liaison support. Active recruitment of Aboriginal practica sites was also initiated. This approach is supported by Marshack and Glassman (1991) who describe the importance of school efforts to serve as catalysts for bringing students to under-professionalised or emerging areas of practice and to stigmatized populations. Once a few First Nations practica sites were established the field coordinator began a partnership with a MSW Aboriginal field instructor to identify and implement strategies for reaching out to potential First Nations practica sites.

What was Learned from the UBC Experience

An openness to alternative knowledge needs to be an ongoing component of developing relationships with Aboriginal Peoples. Achieving this, however, may be problematic. Social work has had a long tradition of valuing the skills, experiences, and knowledge of mainstream Euro-canadians which often contrasts with those of Aboriginal peoples. The adult learner model used in many field education programs values the skills, knowledge, and experience that *all* students bring into social work programs. Using this model is a way to begin valuing the skills, experiences, and knowledge of Aboriginal peoples. Each of these areas need to be valued, and may be used to challenge current, yet outmoded, social work theories and practices. To not do so, may make it difficult for educators, especially those in an academy which grew out of a tradition of modernistic scientism and the separation of church and state, to accept the importance of spirituality in Aboriginal social work practice.

Letting go of some accepted notions of what constitutes social work practice in favor of learning about what will constitute appropriate social work practice for Aboriginal communities requires time and effort. This point was a reoccurring comment in the UBC First Nations Field Education Practica Survey. The recommendation was that the faculty liaisons be released from some teaching responsibilities to devote time to this effort. In the course of developing these relationships Faculty have become involved in community feasts, openings and circles activities. This involvement is essential to building trust relations. In addition it is especially important for schools to have an

Aboriginal faculty member who can make far greater strides in building relationships with First Nations communities than non-First Nations faculty.

Building partnerships between field coordinators and field instructors creates another important link with First Nations agencies, especially in schools without First Nations faculty members. Together they can co-facilitate information sharing meetings for Aboriginal agencies held in Aboriginal communities. On these occasions details about practica can be provided and other information distributed. The ambience of such meetings makes it more likely for new relationships to be established and further practicum recruitment and development. Having a wide variety of Aboriginal placements helps a school further diversify contacts with Aboriginal communities. It also communicates to potential First Nations students that a School is interested in Aboriginal peoples and values the learning provided by their agencies.

Agency Experience and Models

Agencies that have developed practice incorporating spiritual teachings and other traditional ways (something governments have previously tried to stamp out) are making important contributions to practice. In some of the First Nations agencies used as practica sites, students have been exposed to different social, cultural and historical principles that are important in social work practice with Aboriginal peoples. In one agency which works with Aboriginal street youth, social work students participated in smudging, talking circles and sweatlodge ceremonies with agency staff and clients. Agency staff thought that student participation in these activities would help to increase trust and understanding.

In another agency social work students were exposed to some cultural practices of Aboriginal peoples and, in addition, were given an extensive overview of historical events which had negative consequences for the Aboriginal group served by the agency. The Aboriginal field instructor shared this information to illustrate that the despairing state of some of the agency clients was not entirely of their own making and to prevent the student from "blaming the victim." In still another agency located on reserve land, understanding the operations of the band government became the most important learning objective for the student. Helping the student understand the importance of Aboriginal self-government was another goal of the placement.

The experience of the Hey-Way'-Noqu' Healing Circle provides a detailed example of the practice in one First Nations Agency. Hey-Way'-Noqu' has become a mini-training center for four to five UBC School of Social Work students each year. These students receive training in using the medicine wheel and talking circles as an important part of practice. The medicine wheel has been used in several different arenas for facilitating healing and teaching (Bopp, et al., 1985, 1988; Absolon, 1983; White, 1992). Hey-Way'-Noqu' utilizes the medicine wheel in its short term wellness/treatment plan to help clients achieve a balance in all four spheres of the wheel. The medicine wheel is divided into four spheres (see Figure 1) mental, emotional, physical, spiritual/ cultural. The center named the "will" is essential before healing can occur in all four areas of a person's life. For social work practice in Aboriginal agencies, the medicine wheel and talking circles are becoming widely used. Moreover, Aboriginal faculty suggest that "using the circle and medicine wheel to understand . . . to practice . . . [hold] powerful possibilities and promise." The client signs a contract to engage in the healing process, empowering him/her to become an important part in treatment. Every three months there is a "check in" to see how a client is developing in each sphere of the circle.

In the *mental* sphere, the client decides what s/he will do in an educational way which might involve activities such as attending groups or researching at the library. In the *emotional* sphere the client works on emotional wellness which might involve exploring past sexual abuse or discovering the origins of anger. Therapeutic modalities in this sphere might include individual counselling, art, dance or music therapy. The *physical* sphere sets out an exercise program which might include activities like jogging, walking, aerobics or racquetball. The final sphere incorporates *spiritual/cultural* aspects of the person's being and may include smudging ceremonies, sweats and pow wows. Counsellors at Hey-Way'-Noqu' provide services which incorporate healing and teaching activities of the four spheres and connect clients to other resources within Aboriginal Communities.

During the healing process at the agency three types of talking circles are used. The first type utilizes a short check in of how each person is doing. The second utilizes facilitators who can break in during a person's speaking to assist them to work through an area in which they are experiencing difficulty. The third is a traditional "sacred circle" wherein no one is allowed to interrupt when someone is talking and everyone remains in the room until all who wish to do so have the opportunity to speak.

This agency has been highly effective in several areas. A support group is provided to Aboriginal mental health patients who have traditionally fallen through the system. Art, dance and music therapy (recently "invented" by non-First Nations therapists) are well known traditional practices used by this agency. Overall, the agency's success may well be attributed to its use of helping, healing, and teaching models which incorporate native beliefs and practices.

DATE FROM : _____   DATE TO : _____

3 Months Period

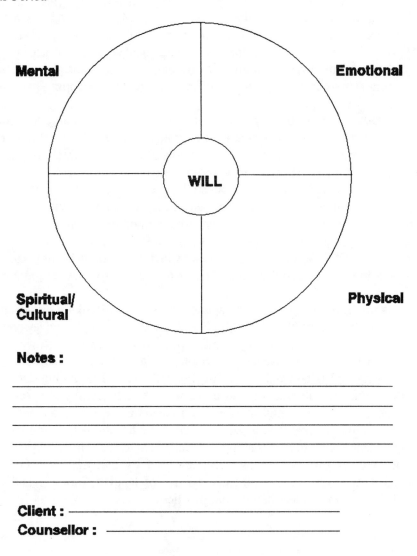

Notes :

_____

_____

_____

_____

_____

_____

Client : _____

Counsellor : _____

Figure 1   Hey-Way'-Noqu' Healing Circle
                  Short Term Wellness/Treatment Plan

IMPLICATIONS FOR SOCIAL WORK EDUCATION AND PRACTICE

Building relationships between schools of social work and First Nations agencies provides several opportunities to enhance social work education and practice. Students placed in Aboriginal agencies or instructed by Aboriginal faculty have increased opportunities to examine the negative effects that certain social work practices had on Aboriginal peoples. Indeed, making this information a part of social work education, enables students to critically analyze practice and creates opportunities to begin healing the troubled legacy between Aboriginal peoples and social workers. Relationship building also means that there is a sharing of Aboriginal models of social work practice and principles. This exchange can help schools of social work develop curriculum which is relevant to Aboriginal peoples. Aboriginal practice models, like feminist models, can contribute to the professional knowledge base and make social work practice more relevant to these groups.

The work at First Nations practica sites provides increased opportunity for sharing ideas between field instructors, students and faculty. This discourse may help facilitate the creation and development of new models of social work practice. Knowles (1972) described characteristics for an optimal learning climate which include informality, mutual respect, collaboration, openness, authenticity, trust and curiosity. The genuine application of these characteristics allows students to openly express beliefs about what works and does not work in practice. These characteristics also provide a good fit with the holistic Aboriginal world view which includes empowerment and permission for everyone to speak their truth. As a result more possibilities exist for field instructors, faculty liaisons and students to co-construct models of social work practice that include traditional Aboriginal beliefs and practices. Freire (1970) concurs, stating that teachers and students co-intent on reality are both subjects, not only in that they are joined in the task of unveiling that reality, and thereby coming to know it critically, but also are joined in the task of re-creating that knowledge. As they attain knowledge of reality through common reflection and action, they discover themselves as its permanent re-creators.

Upon graduation many students will find themselves working with First Nations peoples in non-Aboriginal or Aboriginal social services agencies. In either instance their learning from First Nations practica may influence their practice, particularly if they use the integration of theory and practice (ITP) loop articulated by Bogo and Vayda (1987). This method teaches students how to evaluate the effectiveness of their response and to construct an appropriate new one. Such work is achieved through reviewing the professional knowledge base and tying in appropriate theories to inform the next professional response. New workers trained at First Nations practica in using the ITP loop will search a professional knowledge base that includes First Nations thinking. The professional response may include elements of Aboriginal models of practice. Using

First Nations practice principles may also inspire workers to become change agents within traditional mainstream agencies.

Many Aboriginal communities are working toward self-government which will require increased understanding by all involved in the field education enterprise. Relationship building strengthens support for a Native-defined future in place of integration, assimilation or other programs conceived by whites (Howse & Stalwick, 1990). The UBC experience and the UBC School of Social Work First Nations Field Education Practica Survey have shown that there is much to gained through building relationships with First Nations communities and agencies. First Nations practica sites provide a tremendous opportunity for student learning and curricula enhancement. The new models of social work practice which are emerging through these partnerships assist social work education and practice to become more relevant to Aboriginal peoples.

REFERENCES

Absolon, K. (1993). *Healing as practice: Teachings from the medicine wheel.* Unpublished paper presented at WUNSKA meeting held in Saskatoon, Saskatchewan, February, 1993.

Adoption Legislative Review Panel. (1994). *A place to start.* Discussion paper prepared for Round Table Discussions in Vancouver, British Columbia, March 26, 1994.

Allgaier, L., James, M., & Manuel, S. (1993). Policy on indigenous people. *The Social Worker, 61*(4), Winter 1993.

Bogo, M., & Vayda, E. (1987). *The practice of field education in social work - Theory and practice.* University of Toronto Press.

Bopp, J., Boop, M., Brown, L., & Lane, P. Jr. (1984). *The sacred tree.* Lethbridge, AB: Four Worlds Development Press.

Dubray, W. H. (1986). American indian values: Critical factor in casework. *Social Casework: The Journal of Contemporary Social Work, 67*(3), March 1986.

Dubray, W. (1993). *Mental health interventions with people of color.* St. Paul: West Publishing Company.

Falcouer, N., & Swift, K. (1983). Canada's Native People. In N. Falcouer & K. Swift (Eds.), *Preparing for practice.*

Feehan, K., & Hannis, D. (1993). *From strength to strength: Social work education and aboriginal people.* Edmonton, AB: Grant MacEwan Community College.

First Nations Studies Calendar 1993-94. First Nations House of Learning, "Giving Voice to Our Ancestors." The University of British Columbia.

Freire, P. (1972). *Pedagogy of the oppressed.* New York: Continuum.

Frideres, J. (1993). *Native peoples in Canada: Contemporary.* Scarborough, ON: Prentice Hall Canada.

George, L. (1992). Native spirituality, past, present, and future. In D. Jensen & C. Brooks (Eds.), *In celebration of our survival: The first nations of British Columbia.* Vancouver, ON: University of British Columbia Press.

Gould, K. H. (1987). Feminist principles and minority concerns: Contributions, problems, and solution. *Journal of Women and Social Work, 2*(3), 6-19.

Hodgson, M. (1987). *Indian communities develop futuristic addictions treatment and health approach.* Nechi Institute on Alcohol and Drug Education, pp. 1-12.

Howse, Y., & Stalwich, H. (1990). Social work and the first nation movement: Our children, our culture. In Brian Wharf (Ed.), *Social work and social change in Canada.* Nelson Publishing, Canada.

Jaine, L. (1992). All my relations. In Linda Jaine & Drew Taylor (Eds.), *Voices: Being native in Canada.* University of Saskatchewan, Extension Division.

Joe, J. (1989). Values. In Edwin Gonzales-Santin (Ed.), *Collaboration: The key.* Tempe, AZ: Arizona State University.

Joseph, S. (1992). Assimilation tools: Then and now. In D. Jensen & C. Brooks (Eds.), *In celebration of our survival: The First Nations of British Columbia.* Vancouver, ON: University of British Columbia Press.

Kelly, P. (1992). The value of first nations languages. In D. Jensen & C. Brooks (Eds.), *In celebration of our survival: The First Nations of British Columbia.* Vancouver, ON: University of British Columbia Press.

Knowles, M. (1992). Innovations in teaching styles and approaches based on adult learning. *Journal of Education for Social Work, 8*, Spring 1992, 32-39.

LaFromboise, T. D., Trimble, J., & Mohatt, G. (1990). Counselling Intervention and American Indian Tradition: An integrative approach. *The Counselling Psychologist 18*, 628-654.

Lewis, R., & Gringerich, W. (1980). Leadership characteristics: Views of Indian and non-Indian students. *Social Casework,* October 1980.

Liberating our children: Liberating our nations. Report of the Aboriginal Committee Community Panel, Family and Children's Services Legislative Review in British Columbia. (October 1992).

Marshack, E., & Glassman, V. (1991). Innovative models for field instruction: Departing from traditional methods. In D. Schneck, B. Grossman, & V. Glassman (Eds.), *Field education in social work: Contemporary issues and trends* (84-93). Kendall/Hunt Publishing Co.

Morisette, V., McKenzie, B., & Morisette, L. (1993). Towards an aboriginal model of social work practice. *Canadian Social Work Review, 10*(1), 92-108.

Ratner, R. S. (1990). *Child welfare services for urban native Indians.* Report commissioned by the United Native Nations. (May 1990).

Summers, H., & Seebaran, R. (1993). *Addressing diversity: The practicum component.* Paper presented at the CASSW Learned Societies Conference at Carleton University, Ottawa. (June 1993).

White, L. O. (1992). *Nishnaabe Kinoomaadwin Naadmaadwin: Native human services.* Field Education Manual SW3605 EN / SWRK 4605 EN. Native Human Services Programme. Sudbury, ON: Laurentian University Press.

CHAPTER THIRTY-SIX

AFTER DEMOCRACY BREAKS OUT: CHALLENGES IN THE PREPARATION OF SOCIAL WORKERS FOR NEW ROLES IN BRAZILIAN SOCIETY

Mary K. Rodwell

INTRODUCTION

This chapter reflects on the history of the development of Brazilian social work including the current federal law that outlines expected social work practice. Detailed are the intellectual and practical challenges of moving the profession from a Marxist philosophical frame to a more functional interventionist frame. Implications for field education are explored for social work educators both in North America and Brazil.

Having been trained in the person-in-environment, person-in-situation, person-in-context tradition, I have long been puzzled about American social work educators' difficulties in creating field based macro and mezzo learning opportunities for our students. It is as if we in the United States have lost sight of a significant part of who we are and how we came to be a helping profession. Our field experiences seem to be rich with direct contact with clients and families. We sometimes are able to expose our students to the joys and complications of group work but we seem to be almost unable to provide meaningful institutional or community development change experiences for them.

My interest in the challenge of creating learning opportunities that involve individuals, families, groups as well as organizations and communities was further developed last year as a result of a six month Fulbright research and lectureship with sister and brother social workers in Brazil. Though Brazilian social workers see (as we do), Bertha Reynolds and Jane Addams as their intellectual foremothers, their development as a profession has taken a quite different direction than ours in the United States. Though I have had practice and consultation experiences in various parts of Brazil since 1966, it was only through this most recent time in consultation with several Schools and departments of Social Work that I came to realize the significance of our differences in direction.

It is hoped that this brief discussion of the history and current challenges to Brazilian social work education might give us some ideas of strategies and directions that we in North America might borrow as we attempt to create some semblance of parity regarding large and small system experiences in field placements. I suggest here that there may be much to learn because Brazilian social work education is facing exactly the opposite challenge in the field — how to offer individual and family direct practice experience to their students. Perhaps we can learn from each other.

SOCIAL WORK HISTORY IN BRAZIL

Since its development as a profession in the early 1940s, social work in Brazil has been built on the assumption of basic rights of the human being and the concomitant interactive responsibilities between the citizen and his or her society to assure the securing of those basic human rights. These assumptions of social work have remained constant over time. So, too, has the recognized role of social work: the articulation of the basic rights and responsibilities of the Brazilian government and its citizenry.

To understand the importance of this role of national conscience it would be well to understand the political context within which social work developed as a recognized Brazilian profession. Getùlio Vargas, a fascist leaning military strong man, lost the election of 1929, but came into power in a military coup in 1930 to serve as "interim" President. One way or another, through election or outright take-over, Vargas maintained control of the government (except from 1945 to 1950 when General Eunicio Gaspar Dutra succeeded in increasing the power of the central government) until 1954. After Dutra, Vargas even succeeded in throwing out the constitution, but committed suicide in 1954 when it became clear that he must resign or be overthrown. Vargas was replaced by his Vice President, Café Filho who served until the 1956 elections where Jucelino Kubitschek de Oliveira was elected and began a new era with a spirit of democracy. Unfortunately, Jucelino was the spendthrift who built Brasilia from scratch, leaving the country in disastrous financial straits.

The elections of 1961 saw the entry of the self-styled reformer, Jànio Quadros, who became an impatient, unpredictable autocrat who tried to ignore Congress. Jànio resigned, much to the relief of the populace, after only seven months in power. He was succeeded, after some struggle (the military were against him, but feared civil war) by his Vice President, João Goulart, on August 25, 1961. This occurred only after the military stepped in and significantly reduced the power of the President. Even with limited power, Goulart began efforts in land reform and responded to numerous strikes with concessions to the labor unions.

Between March 31 and April 2, 1964, a bloodless military coup placed Humberto de Alencar Castello Branco in the role of President. During the next 20 years, generals ran the government with various degrees of repression and cruelty. Marshal Costa e Silva became President in 1967 and promptly closed Congress. He died in 1969 and was replaced by General Emilio Garrastazu Médici who saw that newspapers were censored and political debate ceased. During this time, most federal and state universities with departments or schools of social work saw their education stopped or greatly curtailed due to their "communist" tendencies. The rule by intimidation continued through General Ernesto Geisel who became President in 1975. Only in 1979 did General João Figeiredo begin the return to democracy when censorship was ended and most political prisoners were released.

Elections for all offices except the President finally occurred in 1982. In 1985, Tancredo Neves was chosen by the electoral college, but he died mysteriously before taking office. He was replaced by his Vice President, the conservative friend of the military, José Sarney. When Sarney left office in 1989, the country was facing soaring inflation of 1,764% annually. For the first time in 29 years, on December 15, 1989, direct presidential elections occurred. The conservative, Fernando Collor de Mello, was elected over the socialist union leader Luis Ignacio "Lula" da Silva. Collor's term ended in disgrace in 1992 when he was impeached for corruption. Itemar Franco, his low profile Vice President, succeeded him and has kept the country on the road to democracy. There was an attempt to return to a monarchy in the Spring of 1993, but that effort was overruled by popular vote. Elections are again set for November, 1994. At this stage in the campaign, Lula, the socialist union leader, is the front runner (Moyer, 1985).

Whether during the time of strong central, but democratic, government from Vargas through Goulart or through the days of military dictatorship from 1964 to the presidential elections of 1989, the social work profession and the trained social workers served as the conscience of the country, calling for basic human rights. Prior to 1993, the idea that democracy could be sustained in a country fraught with such tremendous social and economic problems was kept alive by the profession's articulation of the basic principles of social work. Departments of social work (those that were allowed to remain open during the military dictatorship) focused on the philosophical underpinnings of a recognition of human rights. The focus was not on practice theories, but on philosophy, with Marxist thought having central importance in the shaping to the social work perspective.

Courses such as: Political Philosophy, Social Policy, Ethics and Economics, Anthropological Philosophy, Methods of Investigation of Social Practices, Social and Anthropological Determinants in the Relationship of the Individual and Family in Society, and Analysis of Legislation and Social Policy became the educational underpinnings of professional social work preparation. These mainly undergraduate courses (no more that four master's programs and two doctoral programs exist in a country geographically larger that the US) prepared students for field experiences that allowed them to understand the depth and scope of the problem with endangered human rights. Field experiences became opportunities for field-based, participative or action research aimed at community and/or organizational change in favor of human rights. Social, instead of individual, change was the goal of social work and social services.

BRAZILIAN PRINCIPLES OF SOCIAL SERVICE

Guided by such Marxist thinkers as Freire (1973), Almeida (1989), Belluzzo (1980), Chevalier (1978), Lehwing (1988) and many others and building on the assumptions of individual and societal aspects of human rights, the profession over the years, has developed five basic principles of social service. Now that democracy has broken out in Brazil, these principles have not changed. In fact, they have been clearly laid out in the 1993 federal law *Organic Law of Social Services*. To understand the current challenges to the profession, it would be well to examine in detail these five basic principles and how the profession has spoken to these principles during times of endangered human rights. Particular focus will be given to the role of student in field placement. These students did not act alone but were guided and supported by faculty and field supervisors who were as much involved in the activities described.

The Supremacy of Serving the Social Needs over the Economic Development Needs

Students in the field, as a result of field-based research, consistently acted on behalf of the disenfranchised. Organizing the homeless to take over public buildings in order to provide shelter for their families; stopping land development that would displace subsistence farmers; advocating for day care services as a part of the development of a new industry are some examples of student social work efforts since the early 1950s.

The Universality of Social Rights and the Responsibility of Public Policy to allow the Highest Possible Social Action

Field students consistently have been involved in the promotion of free speech and community education that are the building blocks of social action. From participation in consciousness raising processes in adult literacy using the Freire (1973) method to organizing students and unionists to go to the streets in protest, student field projects involved the analysis of public policy to underscore their intended and unintended consequences in such a way as to publically force policy change.

Respect for the Dignity and Autonomy of Citizens and Recognition of the Right to Benefits of Quality Social Services that assure Quality Family and Community Life

Field students in mayor's offices, students serving in community centers in the "bairros" used their experiences with individual clients to lobby for needed services for clients' families or neighborhoods. Marches on city hall for garbage removal, sitins at the mayor's office or home, fliers distributed throughout the city, vans with loudspeakers describing human or community needs travelling through targeted neighborhoods all are and were methods used by students during field placement experiences to garner services, if not respect, for their clients from the public powers.

Equal Rights to Access to Service without Discrimination of any Type and Guaranteeing Equivalence in Services to Urban and Rural Populations

Though few field placement sites are available in the interior far from departments of social work, students from the more rural areas during their field experiences have been known to take the knowledge and skills gained in the urban placement to their homes. Many students used their weekends at home to understand local social problems and organize for social change. This might be as simple as a conversation with the town mayor who lives down the street or as complicated as raising money to bring townspeople into the capitol to meet with the governor. This principle, like the one to follow, represents a grave challenge to the profession in such a vast country where financial and service resources appear to be concentrated in major metropolitan areas along the coast.

Dissemination of Available Benefits, Services, Programs and Assistance Projects including the Resources offered by the Public Powers and the Criteria for Eligibility

Even before the days of United States supplied "Food for Peace" in the 1960s and 70s, students were compelled to know what agency had what goods or services available. In the early days of the profession this might have meant understanding and disseminating

Catholic Church and foreign resources. More recently, this has included federal, state and local services and policies governing accessibility. Advocacy related to unmet needs, such as those of street children, or underserved areas, such as the Northeast, has always been apart of field assignment responsibilities.

These responsibilities from the 1950s to 1980s could have resulted in investigation by the secret police, imprisonment, disappearance/death, exile or being blackballed from university or employment opportunities. The professional responsibility and the potential negative consequences for students, the profession and the clients they served were very high. To maintain the level of commitment (and passion) necessary to complete the education and continue professional work, clarity about the reasons for the work was necessary. This was provided through thorough grounding in the philosophical structure of the profession. Ideology was heavily emphasized in the classroom.

In addition, as a result of the field placement and the anthropological or ethnographic research skills developed there, students could understand human service and structural issues that affect people in their neighborhoods, communities and at a national level. They learned to undertake needs assessments from the normative (standardized data-based norms), comparative (comparing to standards) and felt needs perspectives (Eng & Blanchard, 1991). They could provide demographic profiles of individuals and groups experiencing a particular social problem. They could identify organizations, association and institutions serving a geographical area or dealing with a particular problem. This included analyzing the characteristics of interaction, the referral network, coalition and conflict levels, etc. They could use field observation to make inferences about needs and resources in an area such that the community could be empowered to learn new skills to build communities and institutions within those communities. They could organize for social action.

But in the new democracy, the profession, by law, is being called on to guarantee services to address basic necessities. No longer is it enough to act as the conscience of the nation, calling for change in the status quo. Now social work and social services are responsible for the following:

1) The protection of the family across its life span;
2) Care for children and adolescents at risk;
3) Promotion of those in need into the work force;
4) The development and rehabilitation of people with special needs and the promotion of their integration into community life; and
5) The guarantee of one minimum salary (a minimum wage equivalent) for people with special needs and the elderly without means of self support or protection by their family. (Lei No. 4.100-D, de 1993, pp. 1-2)

On the whole, no professional Brazilian social worker would object to the current objectives of social service. Nor would they be willing to modify the basic principles under which the profession has been operating for more than fifty years. The challenge to the modern profession in Brazil is the movement from a philosophy of practice guided by Marxist principles that allowed the profession to have the courage to serve as the watch dog of the nation during times of oppression and intimidation to a more pragmatic, theory and knowledge guided micro and macro practice model involving real individual and community interventions. Brazilian social work must not lose its large system skills and passion, but it must immediately develop individual and small system skills, as well.

IMPLICATIONS FOR SOCIAL WORK IN THE NEW BRAZILIAN DEMOCRACY

The organization of social services in Brazil is now to be decentralized for the States, the Federal District and the counties with popular participation in policy-making via "representative organizations" and local, state and national "councils." Final responsibility, however, rests with each State in the development of social policy for each sphere of the government (federal, state, county) (Lei No. 4.100-D, de 1993, pp. 4-11). The infrastructure for such an undertaking does not exist currently in Brazil.

This means that social action to ensure the financing, the technical assistance, and the political will to confront the serious social problems of the nation will continue to be necessary. Social work students cannot forsake their large systems learning and skill development in favor of more individual and family practice. Social work educators must continue to engage the students in experiences that underscore the practical necessities of guaranteeing human rights and minimum social welfare benefits. But to respond to the mandates of the new democracy regarding meeting basic necessities, new knowledge and skills also must be addressed.

If the profession is to fulfil the current mandate of organizing services such that children and adolescents in "personal or social risk" are given priority in keeping with article 227 of the Federal Constitution, Law no. 8.069, July 13, 1990, then individual and family assessment, diagnosis, case planning and social casework knowledge and skills must also be introduced into the curriculum including the field experiences. Service delivery as well as social action must become a part of professional preparation. Aside from working with institution and popular groups, students must be given the opportunity and the challenge to work directly with individuals and families in need. Basic necessities must be redefined to include psychological as well as physical and social needs, so that students can work with benefits, services, programs and projects that go beyond what traditionally has been agitation for welfare assistance and basic freedoms.

This does not mean that Marxist philosophy must be replaced by Capitalist philosophy to undergird social work practice. This merely means that micro skills so much the focus of North American social work such as client engagement, client interviewing, assessment/diagnosis, service planning, theory-based interventions, practice and program evaluation must be integrated in some functional way. To do this the profession must determine the kinds of micro activities that must be undertaken to sustain the traditional Brazilian social service principles, while also attending to the new legal mandates of the profession. Most importantly, the passion and commitment provided by philosophical underpinnings must be allowed to remain or trained social workers will flee the chaos of the street level for the relative sanity of private practice, as we have seen in the States.

To expand the parameters of social work education and professional activities while protecting the values and traditions of the profession in Brazil, educators must determine or develop practice theories that are congruent with social work philosophy in Brazil. They must develop interventions guided by these theories that can be empirically tested in much the same ways that community-based action research has been undertaken in the past. Perhaps the transformation of field-based education can occur under this guise. Field education might not need to change its emphasis from research to direct practice, but rather include research on practice. In addition to large-scale research for action focus, a smaller scale research for practice focus could be introduced with the requirement for hands on practice experiences so that the research could be undertaken.

It would appear that the strong research focus of the field experience can be the fulcrum upon which both micro and macro practice skills can be developed by students and by the profession as a whole. It would also appear that to develop the level of expertise necessary, more advanced courses beyond those currently available such as "Specialization Course in Social Service in the Area of Family" or "Services to Children and Adolescent Victims of Domestic Violence" also should be considered and encouraged by the Federal Ministry of Education and the National Council of Social Service. Well distributed masters programs that allow for more class time and more field training will be a necessity if the profession can hope to serve its legal as well as its moral mandate.

CONCLUSIONS: WHAT CAN WE LEARN FROM BRAZILIAN SOCIAL WORK?

Perhaps we in North American do not have the same level of social problems as our brothers and sisters in South America, but then again, perhaps we do. Perhaps we have not been trained to see poverty as a national issue, only as one belonging to the individual welfare mother. Unlike Brazilian social workers, we may have the institutional infrastructure to serve individual need, but we may not have the political will or skill to recognize and mobilize responses to national needs. Perhaps we have never had the necessity until now that every 30 seconds a baby is born into poverty; every five minutes a child is arrested for a violent crime; every two hours a child is murdered; every four hours a child commits suicide; and every nine hours a child or young adult under 25 dies from HIV (Children's Defense Fund, 1994, p. xii). We in US social work may not need to serve as the conscience of society overcoming repression and torture as in Brazil. But we must begin to recognize that what is occurring in the privacy of violent families or in the distant inner city ghetto is a national problem affecting the very fabric of the nation and the profession's commitment to human rights.

From our Brazilian colleagues we should learn the role of philosophy in our practice and in our commitment to the goals of the profession. We should be challenged to recognize philosophical issues beyond the philosophy of science controversies embedded in paradigm dialogues or discussions about whether qualitative or quantitative research is more scientific or relevant for social work. Our professional discussions should go beyond what is "real" knowledge for professional practice to include what should be the philosophical underpinnings of the values and ethics of the profession. What does it mean for micro and macro practice to be Marxist, Capitalist, Existentialist, Constructivist, Deconstructivist, or other? From this effort perhaps we can develop the same sort of professional fire that exists in the profession in Brazil that for years allowed social workers to continue to work toward societal change while confronting terrible odds.

Those involved in field education can learn from the central role of research in the Brazilian field-based experience where research is at the core of action. It is the source of their knowledge guided macro experiences. It is central because it provides a necessary ingredient to action on a large scale. Research and macro activities are not "add ons" to be addressed only if possible, after the real work of direct practice. Research and large system practice are central to field education because the nation needed it and social workers wanted it because that is social work in Brazil.

Perhaps if we start with philosophy we will be able to honestly and completely embrace our weakest and their strongest dimensions of practice. At the same time, they may be able to transfer and modify our direct practice technologies while protecting the traditional social work role so important to Brazilian society. We truly must learn from each other, for both of our democracies are depending on it.

REFERENCES

Almeida, A.W.B. de (1987). Cidadania e conflitos no campo. *Revista Humanidades, 15.* Brasilia: UNB.

Belluzzo, L.G. de M. (1980). *Valor e capitalismo.* São Paulo: Brasiliense.

Chevalier, L. (1978). *Classes laborieuses et classes dangereuses.* Paris: Pruriel.
Children's Defense Fund. (1994). *The state of America's children: Yearbook 1994.* Washington, DC: CDF.

Eng, E., & Blanchard, L. (1991). Action-oriented community diagnosis: A health education tool. *International & Community Education, 11*(2), 93-110.

Freire, P. (1973). *Education for critical consciousness*. NY, NY: Seabury Press.

Lehwing, M. B. (1988). Distribruicão da renda e pobreza no periodo da crise. In J.P.Z. Chahad & R. Cervini (orgs.), *Crise e infância no Brasil: O impacto das politicas de ajustamento econômico*. São Paulo: IPE/Unicef.

Moyer, L. (Ed.). (1985). *Brazil primer*. Philadelphia: American Friends Service Committee.

CHAPTER THIRTY-SEVEN

A CREATIVE APPROACH TO REACHING OUT TO MARGINAL POPULATIONS

Maria Teresa Trainer

INTRODUCTION

The author visited the National School of Social Work at the National Autonomous University of Mexico (UNAM) in the summer of 1993 and the spring of 1994 and held interviews with members of the faculty and students. After becoming familiar with their educational program, participating in a field practicum project and reading their latest journals, great similarities came to light between the social problems of Canada and those of Mexico. Additionally, the growing involvement of the Mexican social work profession in the quest for social change to achieve social justice was also evident.

This chapter focuses upon their field practicum model which has been designed to initiate, promote and pursue community development projects in the belts of poverty surrounding Mexico City. The social problems in these areas are intensified not only by acute economic need but by intensive demographic growth exacerbated by migration from the rural areas. The value of the Mexican field practicum model is relevant to Canadian social work education in the context of supplying ideas and a creative approach to reaching out to marginal populations and empowering these populations to promote their own social change and improve their *modus vivendi*. Their projects are conducted by combining the efforts of the School of Social Work with other faculties in the university and by using the existing resources within each community. This model of collaboration is useful in times of economic hardship such as we are experiencing in Canada today.

Brief History

Columbus was followed by the Spanish conquerors who established New Spain in the territories that today we know as Latin America. In 1551 Charles I, King of Spain issued a decree establishing the University of Mexico and making it the first and oldest university of the newly discovered continent. On June 3, 1553, classes were opened with the announcement that Spaniards, Mestizos and Indians would be welcomed as students. Courses were firstly imparted in Spanish and soon after courses in the Indian languages of Otomi and Nahuatl were incorporated in the curriculum. The faculties of law, literature and theology were the first to open. The medical school, which included courses in surgery, was established in 1582, eighty-three years before Harvard University opened its doors (Shares, et al., 1961).

For almost 300 years the university functioned under the leadership and guidelines of the Roman Catholic Church. The concepts of liberty and equality of the 19th century, as well as the new scientific discoveries, led to an academic turmoil which caused the university to close down. It was reopened again in 1910 and at that time it was established that the university would not function under a pontifical rule but rather be based on scientific investigation "under the leadership of Mexican scholars who desired to cultivate the love of truth" (Shares, et al., 1961). During the Mexican Revolution between 1911 and 1920 the installations of the university were practically wrecked and everything had to be rebuilt. In 1929 under the newly elected government, the university was given the title of autonomous with the right to receive public funds and the right to elect its own faculty and its own council which functions with the full participation of student and faculty representation (Shares, et al., 1961). In 1945 over a million square meters were assigned to build the university in the Southern end of Mexico City where it stands today offering free tuition to over 250,000 students.

The School of Social Work is a young addition to this old university. The idea to establish a school of social work began to be studied in 1926, but it was not until 1937 when courses in social work began to be offered by the faculty of law to the employees of the young offenders' courts. During the 30's several Mexican doctors had the opportunity to study in the US and Europe and were impressed by the assistance that social workers gave in clinics and hospitals. The Faculty of Medicine suggested to expand the training of social workers by including subjects on medicine, in addition to the already offered subjects on law, psychology and social work theory, thus opening an opportunity for social workers to become judicial and medical social assistants (Bautista Lopez, 1990).

After World War II, in order to assist populations in isolated rural villages in the transition from agricultural activities to the industrialization and modernization of Mexico, the government established a multidisciplinary program called "Misiones Culturales Rurales" which included the participation of social workers (Bautista Lopez, 1990, p. 44). The objectives of these cultural missions were to fight against poverty, illiteracy and sickness; to reinforce the role of the family; to offer civic education programs; to promote national unity and love of country; to establish social services and recreational and artistic activities; to promote the idea that hard work is a source for wealth; to create an opportunity for training in other activities outside of agriculture; and to support community development by using the people's own local wisdom and natural helping networks. This movement promoted the idea of social work intervention in marginalized communities (Bautista Lopez, 1990).

In 1969, a four and a half year degree social work program based on the historical, political and socio-economic reality of Mexico was established within the Faculty of Law. In 1973, The National School of Social Work was given independent status and their new building was inaugurated. Today, they have an enrolment of 2,000 students and employ 180 full and part time professors. For the past 20 years the National School of Social Work has been qualifying professionals who serve approximately 20 million people in the judicial, health, familial and educational fields and emphasize the community development of marginalized populations living in the belts of poverty surrounding Mexico City.

THE MEXICAN PRACTICUM MODEL

We are on the threshold of a new millennium and the vision of the unification of the countries in North America has become a reality. The movement towards economic and social globalization and the North American Free Trade Agreement will enormously influence the fabric of Mexico. We are undergoing a period of transition and in order to keep abreast with the socio-economic, psychological and political changes that are in store, the Mexican National School of Social Work is committed to answer the social demands of marginalized communities by training students to organize and promote community resources and empower people to help themselves. During this learning process, under the leadership of their professors, the students are giving an enormous contribution to the nation. With scarce resources and without government funding, each year various projects are developed and delivered by the School of Social Work in 52 different marginalized communities in the Mexico City metropolitan area.

The practicum projects are an essential component of the Mexican degree program and provide an opportunity to combine theory, practice and research techniques. Teams of 25 students and one professor carry out each project which begins during the second year and lasts for 6 semesters. These teams carry out their field practice every Saturday and additionally hold 4-hour weekly workshops during class time. The objectives of the practicum are firstly to gain a thorough understanding of the social reality of each community and identify the needs of individuals, groups and families as well as the needs of the community as a whole. Other objectives are to analyze, interpret, plan and transform social processes by scientific means. The students are taught to influence the encountered reality by promoting actions which fit into the educational social work paradigms and to encourage the members of the community to use their local wisdom in solving their problems and conflicts.

Each professor and his/her team of students study the resources and the layout of a particular community by conducting a social and physical investigation. They identify the needs and deficiencies in the administration of the community resources, and the direction in which social policies have impacted upon the population. Each student identifies the areas in which social work theory and practice can best benefit the community. They report their findings to the team during their weekly workshops and come to an agreement regarding the critical areas they are going to target. Often the students work in multidisciplinary teams with other students from the faculties of medicine, nursing, law or education and although all the students work in the same community, each discipline identifies and targets the problems which can be addressed by their uniqueness and expertise.

The practicum design is divided into three spheres: social, professional and academic. In the social sphere the students weigh the schools' resources with the capability of each community to benefit from the students' intervention; they gain an understanding of concrete situations and propose feasible solutions; and they promote and participate in actions geared towards the achievement of solutions of the social problems. They seek out community leaders, analyze their role and promote the participation of volunteers. In the professional sphere students search for innovative intervention strategies in order to achieve a closer relationship between the professionals and clients. By linking academic knowledge to professional social work practice, the students discover how social policy affects marginalized people and they find tools for social change. The academic sphere encompasses research, planning, administration, direction and systematization of the social processes in which the student can apply the learned theory and develop and improve his/her skills and the attitudes that identify the social work profession. (See Appendix A)

Participant Observation of One Practicum Project

During the spring term in 1994, I was invited to participate in a practicum day in the community of Isidro Fabela, a poor neighborhood in the southern end of Mexico City. This project was designed as a collaborative program between the Faculty of Medicine, the Faculty of Education and the School of Social Work in order to address the role of elderly people in the community and create an arena for a multidisciplinary team experience. The growing numbers of elderly people among the Mexican population prompted the School of Social Work to target this population for research and social work practice. This project focused upon the health, familial and social support systems of senior citizens. The main goal of this project was to develop models which could be established in various communities in order to address and resolve the long and short term medical, educational and social needs of the elderly population.

The students followed a planned strategy which combined theory with their social work practice and participatory research skills. Firstly, they surveyed the physical aspects of the community and sensitized the residents to their study. They developed a questionnaire and teams comprised of one student social worker and one medical student interviewed 405 respondents and gathered information about the status of the people over 60 years of age living in the community. They gathered information about their health, living conditions, life satisfaction, ability to function independently and their role within the family (Barquin-Calderon & Nava-Aranda, 1993).

In the course of the survey the students found out that large numbers of elderly people were socially isolated, had treatable health problems and great numbers of them wanted to learn to read and write. Once the target needs of the group were identified as resulting from a lack of medical attention, a lack of social connectedness and illiteracy, the students made a physical survey of the community in order to find a suitable place to hold their weekly meetings. They approached community leaders and visited public buildings such as the parish, the schools, the Health Unit, etc. They found a good response at the local market place and found that it was accessible, centrally located and had no stairs to climb. The Vendors' Co-op was very supportive of the project and they allowed the students to establish their meeting place within the premises of the market. With the cooperation of the Faculty of Education, the students received training in the field of literacy and developed a plan which combined literacy classes with other social activities which gave twenty to thirty old people an opportunity to come out of their homes and attend organized weekly meetings every Saturday from 10 a.m. to 2 p.m. During these meetings, senior citizens had an opportunity to talk to the student social workers individually and voice their concerns; to gather with other people their age and talk about old times; to participate in workshops and other educational initiatives; to learn to read and write; and to participate in various arts and crafts projects. One Saturday a month the medical students approached the group and asked the participants questions about their health and general well-being, and took their blood pressure. With the assistance of the student social workers, the elderly people were encouraged to register in the Health Unit and go for regular check-ups. Within the Health Unit the medical students examined the patients, screened them for diabetes and updated their files. On certain Saturdays special programs were planned and educational workshops, videos and guest speakers were scheduled. This collaborative program between the School of Social Work and the Faculties of Medicine and Education and the resources of the community was established without government funding and was turned into a community project owned by the community. Community volunteers (some of whom are over 60) were recruited and trained during the course of the practicum and they will continue leading these weekly meetings after the students leave the community. The Health Unit and the Vendors' Co-op at the market place will continue supporting the project and, if needed, another team of students could come back to this community to continue this project or initiate a new one.

Using the Mexican Practicum Model for Teaching Cultural Sensitivity in Canada

The model developed by the National School of Social Work in the National Autonomous University of Mexico can be particularly useful in Canada when teaching students to become culturally competent and be able to deal with clients who come from cultures different than their own. Canadian Schools of Social Work often allow their students to participate in a practicum experience which concentrates on individuals and allows them to do casework and counselling without any exposure to the needs and conflicts of the community. This approach has a limited scope. In view of the growing numbers in the multicultural/multiracial population of Canada, social work students must be exposed to cultural patterns which differ from their own. They should be aware of the world view of other people and be taught to understand how the phenomena of culture interferes with traditional human service delivery systems. Cultural competence and tolerance for differences cannot be taught by theory and casework alone. A practicum model which includes training in participatory research techniques and community development skills would enable social work students to reach high levels of community awareness of the culturally different and understand how social policy impacts upon ethnic minorities. Students who are interested in becoming culturally competent practitioners should be exposed to community development projects in marginalized communities before undertaking the responsibilities of individual casework and counselling.

REFERENCES

Barquin-Calderon, M., & Nava-Aranda G., (1993). Modelo Asistencial, Docente y de Investigacion para la Atencion Integral del Anciano. *Revista de Trabajo Social, Vol. Ano 1*(3), 9-20. Universidad Nacional Autonoma de Mexico, Escuela Nacional de Trabajo Social.

Bautista Lopez, Elizabeth. (1990). Desarrollo Historico de la Profesion en Mexico. *Revista deTrabajo Social, 43*, 41-71. Universidad Nacional Autonoma de Mexico, Escuela Nacional de Trabajo Social.

Shares, L., et al, (1961). University of Mexico. *Collier's Encyclopedia, 11*. New York: Colliere Publishing Co.

Appendix A The Practicum Model Designed and Implemented by the National School of Social Work in the National Autonomous University of Mexico*

The process of the practicum focuses on community development to begin on the third semester of a nine semester degree program.

Third and Fourth Semesters

Objective: Apply the social research process to discover the social reality of the community.

Theme	Activities	Techniques	Workshop
Stage 1			
Location of practicum	Description of issues	Literature review Didactic techniques Annotated bibliography	Discussion of different theories and methods of the social sciences; Establish methodology Introduce practicum policies and procedures
Stage 2			
Selecting a community	Visit possible sites; Write a report on observations from each; Select practicum	Observation Interviews Review documents, field diaries, workshop recordings; Maps Photos References	Analysis of criteria for community selection; Compare data from all the communities visited
Stage 3			
Exploratory descriptive study	Survey area Collect information; Visit the institutions; Sensitize population to project;	Observation Interviews Selection of resources Maps, photos, plans Field diaries Outline of report	Prepare specific activities for semester; Analyze observations correlate with socio-economic theories;

| | Organize information by areas and themes; Select a target population; Prepare research proposal | | Set objectives for study; Place the community in its social context; Analyze information, prioritize by team's ability to design intervention; Interpret social reality using theory |

Stage 4

| Explanatory Study | Research design; Conceptual framework; Methodology Operationalization; Report writing | Observation Questionnaires Interviews Measuring instruments Statistical techniques Writing techniques Graphs | Prepare explanatory research proposal; Data Analysis |

Stage 5

| Systematization | Analyze and correlate theoretical and practical knowledge | Discuss written material | Analysis and synthesis of theory and methods developed |

Stage 6

| Evaluation | Valuation and measurement of teaching methods | Measurement instruments; Evaluation records | Analysis and synthesis of conclusions |

Fifth and Sixth Semesters

Objectives: Design group work with focus in social education, apply process to community needs.

Theme	Activities	Techniques	Workshop
Planing the intervention in community	Presentation of research results to community; Design overall plan of action; Define each program	Meetings with community; Displays Posters Slide shows, videos Community meeting summaries; Strategic planning Administrative techniques	Prepare material to be presented; Apply administrative process
Social planning by areas	Research policy and programs within the institutions; Program design Coordinate newly designed programs with institutions	Discuss documents; Programming techniques	Analysis of policies of institutional programs; Integration of practicum with institutional program
Project with groups	Sensitize students to organization of group work; Groups define project; Plan and control group activities	Communication, motivation, sensitization; Group techniques; Guidelines for monitoring groups; Educational group techniques	Prepare projects and support materials; Practice group and communication skills; Analyze group development
Systematization	Theoretical and practical correlation of knowledge base	Presentation of all learned material	Analysis and summary of developed theory and method

| Evaluation | Valuation using systems and specific criteria | Measuring instruments Final report | Analysis and summary of developed method |

Seventh and Eighth Semesters

Objective: Assessment and evaluation of the developed projects.

Theme	Activities	Techniques	Workshop
Integrate lead groups	Sensitize groups Formulate evaluation guidelines; Analyze programs; Implementation	Group techniques Minutes of meetings Registration and control of groups; Social education techniques	Analyze different social theories
Assessment of community project	Supervision of activities and orientation of groups	Administrative and supervision techniques	Analyze development of techniques
Evaluation of projects	Estimate of results	Measuring instruments	Evaluate and judge scope of projects
Systematization	Sequence and correlation of information	Discussion and presentations of finished projects	Evaluate and judge practicum process
Potential Outcome	Plan termination or continuity of working with community	Presentation of each team	Final document

* Information gathered by the author's participant observation, interviews and written material facilitated by the practicum director at the National School of Social Work of the National Autonomous University of Mexico (UNAM), April 1994.

PART SIX

FIELD EDUCATION: VIEWS FROM OTHER DISCIPLINES

This Part of the book provides a unique contribution in that it presents perspectives on field education from the disciplines of Clinical Psychology, Education, Nursing and Family Medicine all anchored around the issue of managing conflict related to field education. This multidisciplinary contribution emerged as a result of work done at The University of Calgary in collaboration with cognate professional faculties who deliver components of their curriculum through field education. Having been involved with the Faculty of Social Work for a number of years, I was curious how other disciplines within the university addressed field education issues and concerns and wondered if, through dialogue and collaboration, we might learn from each. One of the things that struck me when we first met and began describing our respective formats and structures, even language we use to talk about field education, was that we shared much common ground both pedagogically and administratively.

On the administrative side we all have policies and procedures to guide the delivery of the field education component of our programs. In one way or another we all deal with contracting with agencies or organizations providing placements. We found that we struggle in different ways and have evolved different responses and solutions to the issues of remuneration and recognition of the field instructor role and to preparing field instructors for that role. We each have structures in place to deal with failures and appeals. We are all bound by university policies on sexual harassment with which we struggle in their application to our respective field education courses. And, we are each challenged by evaluating and grading these courses in terms of criteria, objectives and the mechanisms to assign grades.

Pedagogically we concern ourselves with the quality of learning environments and the teaching capabilities of field instructors. We think about the roles, expectations and responsibilities of all the stakeholders, the relationships that develop amongst them and the complexities involved in combining professional standards and educational standards. We worry about the processes involved in field education such as matching students with placements and field instructors, orienting students and field instructors, establishing learning contracts, assigning work, monitoring progress, giving feedback, evaluating performance, and handling problems or conflicts. We all want to graduate students who are self-aware, adaptable, flexible, critically reflective, and intellectually and personally prepared to practice as professionals.

We have all of this in common and, unbeknownst to the other, we have each developed discipline-specific responses and solutions, drawing upon the knowledge base and the culture of our faculties and professions to guide us. What we have discovered through our work together is that we have much to learn from and contribute to each others' responses and solutions. That by lending to the other what we each do best, we believe we can co-create responses and solutions that are informed by other than our, all too often, narrow view of the universe.

Emerging from our work together we have discovered that each of us has found that problems expressed in the field, whether it is between student and field instructor, student and other student(s), field instructor and faculty are usually associated with, or are symptomatic of, larger problems in the system. We had no difficulty finding a common language to discuss and describe our understanding of the system-wide tensions and constraints that affect field education and the methods used to resolve or manage field related problems. We could all relate to problems in communication, in relationships and in attempts to resolve difficulties before they escalate into full blown conflicts. Conflicts in field education require many hours, invoke much stress and inevitably result in someone or several people being anywhere from dissatisfied or unhappy to more disastrous outcomes. We have all had similar experiences of losing a student, losing a community resource by way of a field instructor or placement, damaging collegial relationships within a department or faculty, and negatively affecting the learning environment, all due to our inability to understand and effectively deal with conflicts.

From our continued work together we hope to develop an increased understanding of the sources of conflict in field education; to identify processes undertaken in the management of conflict leading to both successful and failed outcomes; to develop strategies to predict and prevent conflict; and, to develop strategies to manage conflict at the interpersonal and organizational levels such that there are healthy outcomes for individuals and systems.

The chapters that follow in this section are an example of the type of contribution that can be gleaned from the perspective of four different disciplines. You will find that many of their issues ring true for social work. We begin with Candace Konnert's overview of the field practicum in clinical psychology and the systemic and individual sources of conflict in practicum training. From the perspective of education, Garth Benson provides a view of the "practical sciences" in relation to how a person becomes a professional, in his case, a teacher, and the ways in which that knowledge can inform the management of interpersonal dilemmas. The third chapter in this Part presents a view from family medicine by Russell Sawa who raises concerns about the medical education system and its role in residents' difficulties and faculty stress — a scenario which may parallel your own system. Finally, Arlene Johnston from Nursing describes her disciplines' recognition that conflict in placements is symptomatic of conflict at other levels and presents Nursing's attempt to manage conflict at the intersystems level. These four chapters in their own discipline-specific way each present issues and challenges with which you are likely quite familiar. It is hoped that you will find these perspectives informative and find benefit in seeing how issues and challenges are addressed in the context of field education in other disciplines.

CHAPTER THIRTY-EIGHT

THE NATURE AND RESOLUTION OF CONFLICT IN THE CONTEXT OF PRACTICUM TRAINING IN CLINICAL PSYCHOLOGY

Candace Konnert

An integral part of the scientist-practitioner model of training in clinical psychology is the practicum experience. Accreditation guidelines established by the Canadian Psychological Association encourage early exposure to clinical practice in community settings, and clearly specify that doctoral students must obtain a minimum of 600 clinical hours under the direct supervision of a chartered clinical psychologist. Most students obtain many additional hours in order to be competitive for the pre-doctoral internship which occurs during the fifth year of training. Thus, clinical psychology trainees spend considerable time working in community placements in addition to their course work and research responsibilities.

Traditionally university-based training programs have placed more emphasis on research accomplishments and have devoted less attention to practicum training. Often clinical faculty members view themselves as primarily responsible for the academic progress of their students but are less concerned about their development as practitioners. Thus, many critical issues related to practicum training are rarely dealt with at a programmatic level. One of the most important issues pertains to the identification, management, and resolution of conflict. The following discussion identifies potential sources of conflict and suggests ways in which conflict can be avoided or at least minimized in the context of practicum training in clinical psychology. Conflict can be due to both systemic and individual factors each of which are discussed in turn.

SOURCES OF CONFLICT

Systemic Sources of Conflict in Practicum Training

At the systemic level, students often report feeling "caught between two worlds," the academic and applied. Ideally, clinical psychology curricula should integrate course work with practice. That is, the practicum experience should complement course work and provide students with the opportunity to get hands-on experience with specific assessment and intervention techniques. All too often, however, students report a lack of integration and continuity across settings, and in fact students may be exposed to very disparate views and practices. A case in point is my own graduate course in psychological assessment, in which students are exposed to the poor psychometric properties of a very popular personality assessment measure. At the same time they are asked by practicum supervisors to use this measure for diagnostic purposes.

Compounding this problem are the expectations of supervisors in each setting, many of whom fail to appreciate the multiple demands placed on students. Research supervisors often cannot understand why students don't publish more; practicum supervisors tend to emphasize the need for the expedient completion of case notes and psychological reports. Given the demand characteristics of clinical work and students' general preferences for clinical versus research activities, it is often research that suffers much to the dismay of academic supervisors, who work within a system that values research above all. In addition, many of these academic supervisors have never worked as clinicians or at least have not done so for a very long time. Often they convey the message that clinical activities are somehow secondary in importance to research. Thus, their priorities contradict those of most trainees who are interested, first and foremost, in being clinicians.

Clinical supervisors and academic faculty involved in training may also have different perspectives on fundamental issues such as the role of clinical psychologists both now and in the future. Traditionally clinical psychologists employed in community settings have spent much of their time involved in direct service-delivery in the areas of assessment and intervention. Increasingly, however, due to economic constraints and the tremendous overlap in the duties and functions of mental health professionals, clinical psychologists are grappling with identity issues such as their unique contributions to the mental health system beyond the delivery of assessment and intervention services, and how best to prepare future generations of clinical psychologists (Fox, 1994). These issues were the focus of much debate at the recently held Mississauga Conference on

Professional Psychology (March, 1994).   Based on the recommendations of this conference, the newly-formed Program in Clinical Psychology at The University of Calgary developed the following statement of training philosophy, "The program subscribes to a vision that involves clinical psychologists as   clinical scientists, researchers, health care consultants, and program developers and evaluators, and is *not* intended to train clinical psychologists who wish solely to be therapists/practitioners." Those responsible for training predict that future clinical psychologists will be involved in a broader array of functions.

Moreover, future generations of psychologists will need to become entrepreneurs to ensure their economic survival (King, 1994).   Future-oriented training programmes need to include basic information about good business practices such as management skills, marketing, networking, selling, and cultivating business ethics.   Most training programmes to date have eschewed these topics and indeed many believe they have no place in an academic curriculum in spite of a high level of interest on the part of students, many of whom hope to pursue private practice.   Clearly, those involved in academic training, supervisors in the field, and students often hold different views with respect to how training is conceptualized and carried out, and these diverging views can lead to conflict in the practicum experience.

Another systemic factor which can precipitate conflict relates to the maintenance of quality control in practicum settings.   When training programmes rely on community agencies for practicum training, a loss of control is inevitable and, in contrast to classroom-based courses, standards become more difficult to monitor.   A variety of questions related to quality control need to be addressed. First, what are the necessary qualifications for practicum supervisors in terms of academic preparation and experience? For example, should Masters-level practitioners be permitted to supervise Doctoral candidates? This issue is particularly relevant in Alberta where Masters level training is currently sufficient to practice psychology. Second, what can be done in circumstances where practicum supervisors are performing poorly? What sanctions, if any, can a training program realistically impose and what is the best method to give negative feedback? This issue becomes particularly problematic when the information is obtained through anonymous evaluations provided by students. Third, what are the rights and responsibilities of practicum supervisors and how much power should they be given over training issues? For example, to what extent should practicum supervisors be involved in the evaluation of students? Should they be permitted to assign failing grades in a practicum or, at a programmatic level, be asked to serve on evaluation committees? How much input should they have into the training program itself (e.g. philosophy of training, theoretical orientation, policies and procedures)? Some would suggest that a high level of involvement is appropriate given that practicum supervisors are major stakeholders in the training enterprise, while others would resist this. Fourth, how can using students as cheap labor be avoided, particularly in a time when mental health resources are becoming increasingly scarce? This is less of an issue in settings where training is a mandate; it is likely, however, that in the future clinicians in other types of settings (e.g. private practices) will be called upon to provide supervision and it is here that quality control will be more difficult to monitor. These quality control issues can be very contentious causing conflict between training programmes and community settings, which will inevitably affect students.

Individual Sources of Conflict in Practicum Training

The potential for conflict is inherent in any human relationship and the supervisory relationship is no exception. A certain level of anxiety is expected for both supervisor and supervisee, however, it is more extreme for trainees. Their position is inferior within the power differential of the supervisory relationship and they face anxiety on two fronts, with the client *and* supervisor (Bernard & Goodyear, 1992). Rodolfa, Kraft, and Reilley (1988) surveyed clinical psychology trainees and found that receiving criticism from a supervisor was rated as highly stressful, second only to their perceived inability to help clients feel better. Although this anxiety can have negative consequences, at an optimal level it can facilitate growth as a therapist.

In general, conflict tends to arise around three types of situations (Moskowitz & Rupert, 1983). First, there are conflicts due to differences in theoretical orientation and beliefs about what interventions are effective. Second, conflicts are related to the supervisor's style of supervision. Common complaints include too little supervision, lack of positive reinforcement or conversely the absence of constructive criticism, and having little opportunity to watch one's supervisor actually doing clinical work. Third, personality differences exist which interfere with the supervisory relationship, or there are varying perceptions about the relationship, for example when one party views the relationship as collegial while the other favors a more traditional student-teacher relationship. Conflicts arising from personality differences are least likely to be resolved, while conflicts relating to supervisory style are often resolved to the satisfaction of both supervisee and supervisor. On a broader level, the following additional factors increase the probability that conflict will occur.

Definitional Problems

A core problem is the lack of consensus regarding what constitutes good supervision. Both research and anecdotal evidence suggests that dissatisfaction with supervision is a common experience for those in scientist-practitioner programmes (Marwit, 1983). Only a few studies, however, have investigated those variables that contribute to negative and positive supervisory experiences.

Negative supervisory experiences are characterized by supervisors who are unsupportive and aloof. Criticism without support is offered which leads to students feeling threatened and vulnerable. In response to this, students may begin to engage in anxiety-avoidant maneuvers such as censoring what is said to the supervisor, engaging in various forms of resistance, or game-playing (Hutt, Scott, & King, 1983; Kadushin, 1968). A particularly difficult situation arises when a supervisor attributes work deficiencies to defects in a student's personality (Rosenblatt & Mayer, 1975). If the student challenges the supervisor's attribution, this may be viewed as resistance. Allen, Szollos, and Williams (1986) report that authoritarian treatment and sexist behavior are particularly detrimental to the supervisory relationship.

In contrast, positive supervisory experiences are characterized by feedback that is simultaneously supportive and challenging, the supervisor is both mentor and evaluator. Students are allowed to function fairly autonomously and are permitted to make mistakes and to learn from their mistakes. Kennard, Stewart and Gluck (1987) suggest that positive supervisory experiences occur when the supervisor and supervisee share common behavioral styles and theoretical orientations, and when the supervisor perceives the trainee to be interested in feedback and suggestions regarding professional development. In their survey of Doctoral students' best and worst psychotherapy supervision experiences, Allen, Szollos, and Williams (1986) report that high-quality supervision is related to the perceived expertise and trustworthiness of the supervisor and to an emphasis on personal growth rather than the teaching of technical skills. Trainees prefer supervisors with psychodynamic as opposed to behavioral orientations and those who communicate their expectations and feedback in a clear and concise manner. The literature in this area, however, remains sparse and that which is available is rarely reviewed by those actually in training or providing supervision as documented below.

Lack of Education and Training

Although supervision is a common activity among clinical psychologists it is sadly neglected in terms of education and training (Leddick & Bernard, 1980). Less than 10 to 15% of supervisors have attended formal courses in supervision (Hess & Hess, 1983; McColley & Baker, 1982) and readings about supervision are rarely included in curricula at either the predoctoral or postdoctoral level. Fewer than 20% of supervisors routinely recommend readings about supervision (Hess & Hess, 1983). Although advanced students sometimes supervise junior colleagues, rarely do they receive instruction and feedback about their own supervisory skills. Professional and accreditation organizations have not adopted standard criteria for demonstrating expertise in supervision. As a result there is no consensus regarding the requisite skills necessary to assume supervisory responsibilities, and most supervisors begin the process blindly. Furthermore, the majority of supervisees (72%) do not know whether their supervisors have had training in supervision (McCarthy, Kulakowski, & Kenfield, 1994).

Ambiguous or Unmet Expectations

Rosenblatt and Mayer (1975) identified the "amorphous" supervisory style in which the supervisor fails to provide clear structure and is vague about his or her expectations and goals for the student. This ambiguity tends to increase anxiety. Research clearly indicates that trainees come to the supervisory relationship with a set of expectations about what will occur. These expectations vary somewhat as a function of training level, for example, novice students expect a highly structured experience with more negative feedback while advanced trainees are less concerned with didactic instruction and making mistakes. Nevertheless there are common and predictable student expectations which include the following: 1) supervision will be highly task-oriented and will provide large amounts of specific feedback based on observation and video and/or audiotape, 2) learning will occur in a variety of modalities (e.g. didactic, presentation, individual and group, observation of supervisor and peers), 3) criticism will be constructive, 4) supervisors will take initial responsibility for setting goals, conceptualizing cases, and planning therapeutic agendas but students will take more responsibility as their expertise increases, 5) supervisors will allay supervisee anxiety, 6) supervisors will demonstrate knowledge of and respect for gender and cultural differences, and 7) personal values and beliefs will not be punished or reinforced (see Leddick & Dye, 1987 for review).

Conflict occurs when trainees are unsure of their supervisors' expectations, when there is a mismatch between students' and supervisors' expectations, and when students receive conflicting messages about the expectations for supervision. Each of these are associated with greater work-related anxiety, general work dissatisfaction, and dissatisfaction with supervision (Olk & Friedlander, 1992).

Issues of Confidentiality

Although the boundaries of confidentiality are clearly specified in the therapeutic relationship, this is not the case in the supervisee-supervisor relationship. And unlike the therapeutic relationship, practicum supervisors, academic faculty, and trainees are likely (and often encouraged) to socialize. Supervision carries with it a degree of intimacy in which the student is not only being evaluated but may self-disclose important personal information. This extends not only to personal information but also to evaluation procedures. Who should be privy to the evaluation documents, the practicum supervisor, practicum coordinators and directors of training both in the setting and at the university, future supervisors considering working with the student, the departmental secretary who files the evaluation? Although some of these examples may seem extreme, experience suggests that much of the information disclosed in the context of the supervisor-supervisee relationship is not as private and confidential as one would hope, in spite of the fact that the Canadian Psychological Association Code of Ethics recognizes the rights of supervisees to reasonable personal privacy. McCarthy, Kulakowski, and Kenfield (1994) surveyed 229 supervisees and reported that 20% were not sure whether their supervisors maintained confidentiality, and 3% knew they did not.

Lack of Clarity Around Issues Related to Due Process

Students have rights and privileges which include the right to procedural and substantive due process in all aspects of academic training, including the practicum experience. Procedures for evaluation and remediation, as well as conditions for termination must be clearly specified at the onset of training. Feedback should be provided to the student at regular intervals and be continuous throughout training. Moreover, students should be given the opportunity to evaluate their practicum settings and supervisors, not as token gestures but in a meaningful way that has consequences for those who are found to be less than adequate. Recent research indicates that supervisors never (27%) or rarely (48%) solicit supervisee feedback (McCarthy, Kulakowski, & Kenfield, 1994).

Student deficiencies can be broadly grouped into academic and nonacademic categories, the latter of which includes personal factors such as lack of self-confidence or initiative, poor self-esteem, negativity, inflexibility, immaturity, or psychopathology (Benson, 1994). Policies and procedures around academic criteria are generally easier to establish and enforce because assessment is more objective. In contrast, expectations and standards about "necessary" personal attributes are more difficult to define and convey to students, although they often become most apparent in the practicum setting. Faculty members are often reluctant to take disciplinary action against students with personal deficiencies. Nevertheless the absence of clear criteria around these issues leads to conflict. Evaluations, sanctions, and the worst case scenario of termination, are perceived by students as arbitrary, capricious, and prejudicial.

Understanding Parallel Process and Countertransference

The concepts of parallel process and countertransference are discussed most often by psychoanalytic theorists. Conflict arises when supervisors are unfamiliar with the dynamics surrounding these processes and fail to identify them as such. Parallel process refers to the analogy between supervisor/therapist problems and therapist/patient problems (Ekstein & Wallerstein, 1958). When student therapists encounter a problem with a client, they may act like the client in a supervisory session. This is an unconscious process which occurs when trainees are unable to articulate a problem with which they need help.

Although literature on supervisor countertransference is virtually nonexistent, most clinicians recognize that the phenomenon is real and does influence the supervisory relationship. Supervisors countertransference is categorized into four areas (Bernard & Goodyear, 1992). First, characterological personality characteristics may affect how supervisors relate to trainees in a variety of ways. Supervisors may overidentify with the student, be personally possessive or, in a highly narcissistic way, view students as extensions of themselves. Second, interactions with supervisees may trigger supervisors' inner conflicts. Lower (1972), taking a psychoanalytic perspective, compares the supervisory relationship to a parental relationship and suggests that many of these conflicts may be Oedipal in nature. Third, characteristics of the supervisee may precipitate negative reactions, for example, when the supervisee is perceived to be brighter, or more knowledgeable, experienced, or socially adept. Finally, trainees may experience transference reactions to their supervisors who, in turn, respond with countertransference reactions. An awareness of supervision as a subjective process which is influenced by countertransference issues can help to minimize conflict in the supervisory relationship.

RECOMMENDATIONS FOR MINIMIZING CONFLICT IN PLACEMENTS

The consequences of conflict in practicum training are serious and can lead to anxiety, reduced confidence, and demoralization among students. Conflict can be minimized, however, by establishing guidelines, many of which follow from the preceding discussion.

First, a close liaison should be maintained between faculty in the academic program and clinical supervisors in the community. Ideally, this would entail reciprocal arrangements whereby academic faculty are involved in community activities (e.g. supervision, continuing education workshops, collaborative research), and those working in community settings are participating in university-based research and teaching endeavors. Greater interaction and communication across settings increases the probability that conflicts will be identified and resolved early on. Critical to this partnership is the appointment of a Practicum Coordinator in the training program, whose responsibilities include acting as a liaison to community agencies, disseminating information to students about practicum placements, monitoring student progress, and mediating conflict situations.

Second, the expectations and goals of practicum training should be clearly defined, including the parameters of confidentiality, the rights and responsibilities of supervisors and supervisees, and information about evaluation, remediation, and appeal procedures. Care should be taken to ensure that those responsible for evaluation are separate from those involved in hearing and adjudicating appeals. Given that clinical supervisors vary in terms of their expectations and goals for training, these should be reviewed and negotiated at the onset of each new placement.

Third, many of the problems and pitfalls associated with practicum training could be avoided by providing students with some preparation for practicum training. The stresses associated with beginning a practicum are predictable. Initially, many trainees report feeling like "impostors," or feel that they lack the requisite skills and knowledge to adequately help clients. In addition, there are stages of development in learning to be a clinician. As the trainee gains experience and moves through the developmental sequence, the supervisor-supervisee relationship changes as well (see Bernard & Goodyear, 1992, for a review of developmental models). These common experiences and developmental stages could be discussed in a forum which brings together students at various levels of training, with the idea that senior students would act as mentors assisting their junior colleagues in negotiating the hazards of training. Also included would be research-based discussions of the supervisory process such that the next generation of supervisors are better prepared to assume supervisory roles. Beginning students would also be well-advised to investigate placements before they commence training. They should determine service requirements, goals and expectations of the facility, and predominant theoretical orientations and styles of supervisors. This reduces the possibility of a poor match between what settings have to offer and students' needs.

In summary, the practicum experience has the potential to create conflict for students, practicum supervisors, and academic faculty alike. The responsibility for addressing the conflict is often diffuse and unrecognized. Identifying potential sources of conflict and establishing guidelines to avoid conflict are the first steps in creating a training environment in which all partners can work effectively and harmoniously.

REFERENCES

Allen, G. J., Szollos, S. J., & Williams, B. E. (1986). Doctoral students' comparative evaluations of best and worst psychotherapy supervision. *Professional Psychology: Research and Practice, 17,* 91-99.

Benson, G. (1994, June). *Managing dilemmas in field education.* Paper presented at the Conference on Field Education in Social Work, Calgary, AB.

Bernard, J. M., & Goodyear, R. K. (1992). *Fundamentals of clinical supervision.* Toronto: Allyn & Bacon.

Ekstein, R., & Wallerstein, R. S. (1958). *The teaching and learning of psychotherapy.* New York: Basic Books.

Fox, R. E. (1994). Training professional psychologists for the twenty-first century. *American Psychologist, 49*, 200-206.

Hess, A. K., & Hess, K. A. (1983). Psychotherapy supervision: A survey of internship training practices. *Professional Psychology, 14*, 504-513.

Hutt, C. H., Scott, J., & King, M. (1983). A phenomenological study of supervisees' positive and negative experiences in supervision. *Psychotherapy: Theory, Research, and Practice, 20*, 118-123.

Kadushin, A. (1968). Games people play in supervision. *Social Work, 13*, 23-32.

Kennard, B. D., Stewart, S. M., & Gluck, M. R. (1987). The supervision relationship: Variables contributing to positive versus negative experiences. *Professional Psychology: Research and Practice, 18*, 172-175.

King, M. C. (1994, Summer). Taking care of the business of Psychology. *Psynopsis*, p. 6.

Leddick, G. R., & Bernard, J. M. (1980). The history of supervision: A critical review. *Counselor Education and Supervision, 19*, 186-196.

Leddick, G. R., & Dye, H. A. (1987). Effective supervision as portrayed by trainee expectations and preferences. *Counselor Education and Supervision, 27*, 139-154.

Lower, R. B. (1972). Countertransference resistances in the supervisory relationship. *American Journal of Psychiatry, 129*, 156-160.

Marwit, S. J. (1983). Doctoral candidates' attitudes toward models of professional training. *Professional Psychology: Research and Practice, 14*, 105-111.

McCarthy, P., Kulakowski, D., & Kenfield, J. A. (1994). Clinical supervision practices of licensed psychologists. *Professional Psychology: Research and Practice, 25*, 177-181.

McColley, S. H., & Baker, E. L. (1982). Training activities and styles of beginning supervisors: A survey. *Professional Psychology, 13*, 283-292.

Moskowitz, S. A., & Rupert, P. A. (1983). Conflict resolution within the supervisory relationship. *Professional Psychology: Research and Practice, 14*, 632-641.

Olk, M. E., & Friedlander, M. L. (1992). Trainees' experiences of role conflict and role ambiguity in supervisory relationships. *Journal of Counseling Psychology, 39*, 389-397.

Rodolfa, E. R., Kraft, W. A., & Reilley, R. R. (1988). Stressors of professionals and trainees at APA-approved counseling and VA Medical Center internship sites. *Professional Psychology: Research and Practice, 19*, 43-49.

Rosenblatt, A., & Mayer, J. E. (1975). Objectionable supervisory styles: Students' views. *Social Work, 20*, 184-189.

CHAPTER THIRTY-NINE

MANAGING DILEMMAS IN FIELD
EDUCATION IN A FACULTY OF
EDUCATION

Garth D. Benson

The area of field education has a wide variety of interpretations and this is attested to by the individuals representing different disciplines in this collection of papers. Even though field education has a number of meanings there are commonalities from one discipline to another. My interest is in education and how a person becomes a professional in teaching, social work, nursing or medicine, etcetera. One commonality amongst these professions is that they represent the "practical sciences." As a consequence field education, regardless of the discipline, has a form of reasoning and a moral disposition which influences the nature of interpersonal relationships and how the actors become a teacher, social worker, nurse, or physician.

FORM OF REASONING AND MORAL DISPOSITION IN DISCIPLINES

Aristotle made a tripartite classification of disciplines as *theoretical*, *productive*, and *practical*. Each discipline has a purpose, a form of thinking and a temperament or a disposition in which its advocates act. The purpose of the theoretical disciplines is the acquisition of knowledge for its own sake and the form of thinking for theoreticians is contemplation. The temperament of its actors is one of speculation without concern for practical application. For the productive disciplines, the purpose is to make something in the form of a craft or a skill. The appropriate form of thinking for these disciplines is termed *poietike* which is translated as "making action" and this is seen in crafts such as stone masonry. The disposition of a craftsperson in the productive disciplines is termed *techne* and such a person acts in a true, fitting, reasoned way according to the craft's rules. The end product takes on significant importance and it dominates the reasoning involved in the craft. Thus, the productive disciplines are "means-end" oriented and very pragmatic.

The practical disciplines are the sciences that deal with practical wisdom and knowledge. These sciences are guided by a type of reasoning described as *praxis* which is a form of action where a wise, honorable, well informed, prudent individual acts in the best interest of the group, the situation or the self. Praxis is guided by *phronesis,* or the moral disposition to act truly and justly. Thus, the action and the moral disposition mutually influence and are influenced by each other. What makes the practical sciences different from the other two disciplines is the way in which the form of thinking and the action act on each other. Such action is informed because there is a reflexive aspect in the style of thought where the social setting is continuously reconstructed. This is termed dialectic thinking and in the words of Carr and Kemmis (1986):

> It is an open and questioning form of thinking which demands reflection back and forth between elements like *part* and *whole*, *knowledge* and *action*, *process* and *product*, *subject* and *object*, *being* and *becoming*, *rhetoric* and *reality*, or *structure* and *function*. In the process, *contradictions* may be discovered (as, for example, in a political structure which aspires to give decision-making power to all, but actually *functions* to deprive some access to the information with which they could influence critical decisions about their lives). As contradictions are revealed, new constructive thinking and new constructive action are required to transcend the contradictory state of affairs. The complementarity of the elements is dynamic: it is a kind of tension, not a static confrontation between two poles. In the dialectical approach, the elements are regarded as *mutually constitutive*, not separate and distinct. . . . In praxis, thought and action (or theory and practice), are dialectically related. They are to be understood as mutually constitutive, as in a process of interaction which is a continual reconstruction of thought and action in the living historical process which evidences itself in every real social situation. Neither thought nor action is pre-eminent. (pp. 33-34, italics in original)

When interpersonal relationships are considered against the background of these Aristotelian distinctions, field education becomes the implementation of practice and thus situations involving student teachers, co-operating teachers, faculty members, school based administrators and so on, are a matter of praxis.

Engaging in a Practical Science

To my mind there are three dynamics (Benson & de Leeuw, 1993) in any of the professions considered as practical sciences — the craft, the intellectual, and the moral/ethical. The craft dynamic is the skills an individual uses to engage in the profession; the intellectual dynamic is the knowledge of the theoretical and practical components of the discipline, (i.e., the subject matter, or disciplinary knowledge, the knowledge of practical theories, and the communicative competency used in expressing relationships amongst these forms of knowledge); the moral/ethical dynamic is the foundational assumptions or beliefs that form the individuals world-view about the profession and how one engages in it. When a person engages in the practice of any of these practical sciences there is an underlying set of foundational beliefs which guides that person's actions. Because the form of reasoning in the practical sciences is praxis, the person's set of beliefs must also be consistent with such reasoning or else incongruities develop between the stated position of the person and his or her actions. Such incongruities are referred to by Argyris and Schön (1974, 1978) and Schön (1987) as the differences between theories-in-use and theories-in-action. Schön (1987, p.255) states such theories of action "include the values, strategies, and underlying assumptions that inform individuals patterns of interpersonal behavior." Thus, interpersonal behavior is foundationally based and the underlying assumptions are revealed in personal theories-in-action. On the basis of this theory of interpersonal behavior Argyris and Schön describe two models of theories-in-use labelled Model I and Model II. Each model has a set of values which determine the actor's actions and the consequences for learning. The values of Model I are:

1) Achieve the objective as I (the actor) see it;
2) Strive to win and avoid losing;
3) Avoid negative feelings; and
4) Be rational.

These values lead to interpersonal situations which are "win/lose, closed, and defensive" (Schön, 1987, p. 256) and the type of learning that is encouraged is about how to achieve your objectives at the expense of others. Such learning is competitive and it places emphasis on the success of an individual as opposed to the group. This is "single loop" learning (Schön, 1987, p. 256) where methods and devices are developed to enhance one's own objectives. In contrast the values of Model II are:

1) Provide valid information for both parties in teaching/learning situations;
2) Provide free and informed choice for both parties; and
3) Have an internal commitment to the choice and constant monitoring of the implementation.

These values lead to interpersonal situations which are open, co-operative and collaborative. They are described as win/win situations. The type of learning which is encouraged is open, co-operative and one that benefits the larger group. Such learning is called "double-loop" because both parties learn something of the other party's perspective as well as some of the determining variables which underlie the situation and the behavioral strategies being used. For example, a co-operating teacher and student teacher might explore how the conjunction of the present field placement, attitudes, beliefs, and values have kept them from discussing opposing approaches to teaching and how they as individuals are now in "conflict."

CONFLICTS IN FIELD EDUCATION

In my role as Practicum Director for the Faculty of Education, I deal with conflicts that arise for student teachers. These conflicts are usually the result of interpersonal difficulties amongst student teachers, faculty members, university support staff, cooperating teachers, school based administrators and pupils. Any combination or permutation of these groups of people can be involved in the conflict situation. These situations are practical problems because a student teacher and at least one other individual are involved in a state of affairs and it is not what the two people expect it to be. For it to be a conflict, the foundational assumptions of the two people are in opposition and neither person is willing to alter, or overlook, a basic belief to resolve the disagreement. Thus, some of the problems in the practical sciences are unsolvable. The best that I can do is manage the dilemma. There is no "right" or correct answer to the disagreements I describe as conflicts. As a Director, when you consider a conflict there is more than one aspect which requires consideration. No matter what side of the issue you tend toward, the student teacher or other individuals are affected. There are many contradictory issues in any of these conflicts.

A Composite Sketch of a Conflict

Let me draw together a composite description of a typical conflict. John is a chemistry major who holds a BSc degree and currently is registered as a B.Ed. after degree student. During the professional year, when student teaching occurs, John is registered in a methods course which is prerequisite to the practicum experience. The intention of the methods course is to teach the theoretical background of science teaching plus give the student teachers initial practice in designing teaching situations and carrying through with the instruction. Although John was an excellent undergraduate student in chemistry he finds the theoretical component of the methods class difficult because it requires a broader epistemological framework with a shift from being a student to being a teacher.

What is required as a teacher is a broader conception of the essential relationships amongst chemistry concepts and an understanding of ways to transform teaching theories into practical, effective learning situations for pupils. John lacks confidence, lacks the ability to demonstrate reflective thinking, is reserved, and is concerned that he is not making necessary connections amongst chemistry concepts, theories of teaching and lessons for pupils. Once student teaching begins, John's inabilities become evident very quickly in errors in chemistry content, confused directions to pupils, poor classroom management and discipline. The cooperating teacher and the university advisor attempt to work with John on these difficulties but little progress is shown. John becomes defensive and attributes his lack of success to discrimination, the cooperating teacher's poor teaching ability, and that the pupils are "stupid." At this point the cooperating teacher contacts me and requests that John be removed from the teaching situation. Let me digress for a moment from this composite sketch of conflict to a construct that seems promising.

Individuals such as John are termed "high maintenance" students because of the time, energy, and commitment required on the part of field education personnel to make the practicum experience workable. "High maintenance" students experience extreme difficulty in satisfactorily completing the practicum experience and Benson and Larson (1993) have identified a set of student characteristics that profile such students. Benson and Larson list a series of characteristics in the areas of intellectual qualities, personality traits, and health conditions that "high maintenance" students bring with them to their practicum experiences and the resulting teaching behaviors and professional dispositions that the students demonstrated once the practicum starts. According to Benson and Larson some of the intellectual qualities are: below average basic skills, inadequate content knowledge, and low ability to express realistic self-analysis. For the personality traits they are: non-assertive behaviors and lack of initiative, apathy, unwillingness to take risks, negative attitude, and inflexible. Some of the health conditions these students present are: medical concerns, medication, illness, fatigue, emotional instability or depression, inability to deal with stress, and substance abuse. As a result of such personal characteristics some of the teaching behaviors manifested are: lack of organization, ineffective classroom management, difficulties in planning and evaluating pupils, failure to internalize complex demands of teaching — "not being able to see the big picture" and insensitive to pupils needs. Along with these inadequate teaching behaviors some of the characteristics of professional dispositions are: lack of perception of self in the teacher role, poor interpersonal relations with pupils and other professionals, inappropriate professional judgments, and inability to make connections between theory and practice. Obviously, the individual high maintenance student does not possess all of the identified characteristics nor does s/he exhibit all of the teaching behaviors and professional dispositions but many of these characteristics are exhibited by students in "conflict." Although John is a mythical student in conflict he exhibits many of the personal characteristics and teaching behaviors real students present when they reach the crisis stage in student teaching.

To return to the composite sketch, one might think the conflict is straightforward and the solution is to inform John that he lacks the abilities to teach. But dilemmas in the "practical sciences" are not so easily resolved. As Practicum Director, part of the role is being an advocate for the university student, but part of the role also, bears a responsibility to the field, and to the best educational interests of the pupils. Given this, no matter what action I take there are negative consequences for someone. If no action is taken and John is allowed to continue, the pupils are put at a further disadvantage and the cooperating teacher may see my lack of action as supporting John's charges of discrimination, poor teaching and that the pupils are "stupid." If I place John in a new teaching situation, once again the cooperating teacher may perceive my action as implicitly supporting John's charges and I may have placed a new group of pupils at an educational disadvantage. If I remove John from the situation and inform him that he is incapable of teaching then I have judged his incompetence and not given him an opportunity to learn.

I do not see solutions in situations that get to the conflict stage. What I see are tensions amongst individuals and the dynamics of teaching. Inevitably, my aims as director are in conflict with one or more of the individuals involved. There is an inherent contradiction in the role as a director of field education. The contradiction is a conceptual paradox and it grows out of the juxtaposition of responsibilities to the various parties involved in the conflict. In a conflict what is considered as a solution for one is considered as an absolute defeat for another person. Consequently, the very nature of the practical sciences is one where contradictions and conceptual paradoxes abound and as a result you cannot resolve conflict. You can merely manage the dilemmas that arise under the concepts of praxis and phronesis. This does not mean that the situation is hopeless and that you do not have a sense as to what is desirable. You construct a way to manage the situation such that learning takes place and there is minimum negative impact for the individuals involved.

At best, what individuals do in the practical sciences, when they deal with conflict, is manage the dilemma. There are no "right" answers to conflictual situations because each solution you generate leads to new problems. The implementation of every solution has negative consequences, yet some action must be taken. Therefore, given the concepts of praxis and phronesis, people in the helping professions act according to the best interests of those involved and we manage conflict, not resolve it because of the complex contextual, personal and relational variables involved. Also, as the Director of Practicum I am assured of being presented with a new conflict tomorrow!

REFERENCES

Argyris, C., & Schön, D. A. (1974). *Theory in practice: Increasing Professional effectiveness*. San Francisco: Jossey-Bass.

Benson, G. D. & de Leeuw, G. (1993). The deideation of teacher education. In C.J. Ball, L. Dupuy-Walker, O. Ricord, & D. H. Westgate (Eds.), *Advances in teacher education: readings from the Canadian Association for Teacher Education* (pp. 141-165). Ottawa: Canadian Association for Teacher Education.

Benson, S. A., & Larson, A. E. (1993). *Common characteristics of high maintenance students during early field experiences and student teaching*. Paper presented at the annual meeting of the A.T.E. National Conference.

Carr, W., & Kemmis, S. (1986). *Becoming critical*. London: Falmer Press.

Lampert, M. (1985). How do teachers manage to teach? Perspectives on problems in practice. *Harvard Educational Review, 55*(2), 178-194.

Schön, D. A. (1987). *Educating the reflective practitioner*. San Francisco: Jossey-Bass.

CHAPTER FORTY

TEACHING CARING IN CONFLICTED SYSTEMS:
FIELD PLACEMENT TEACHING IN
FAMILY MEDICINE

Russell J. Sawa

INTRODUCTION

Family medicine is a discipline which espouses to teach physicians to heal and provide care in an ongoing relationship with persons of all ages throughout their life span. Family medicine is intimately involved in a paradigm shift that is occurring between the biomedical model, which views disease as separate from persons, and a new paradigm in which the relationship between doctor and patient, as well as the context of the illness, has a profound effect on the illness and its course (McWhinney, 1989). Clinicians not adopting this paradigm shift still provide care, but primarily through the process of diagnosis and treatment.

In order to integrate this paradigm shift, it is my belief that the physician must care for him or herself, and the medical education system which teaches these values, must reflect caring and nurturing relationships among faculty. This can be difficult given the traditional models of organizations which are hierarchial, authoritarian, competitive and based on behaviorist punishment and reward principles which often accompany the teaching of the biomedical model. Thus, the department head and program director model to the faculty by how they treat them, the faculty to the student or resident, and the student to the patient. Since faculty and resident relate closely over a two year period, this relationship becomes an important learning experience. This relationship may be caring, or it may be based on control and manipulation rather than authenticity.

Both students and teachers are a part of a larger medical education/health care delivery system which often operates on a hierarchial/punitive model. Thus the teacher and student of family medicine may be caught in a conflict between the two models, because practitioners are also urged to adopt collaborative/empowering patient-centered behavior with their patients. Given a few cases of conflict, a dynamic tension may develop between administrators, teachers, and students whenever there is a perceived problem of performance by teacher or student. Effective practice is dependent on art as well as science, caring as well as astuteness, so that attitudes and values are extremely important along side the acquisition of knowledge and skill. Thus the goal is not merely to produce an outstanding technician, but to produce a competent, caring, conscientious, accountable, well-rounded clinician. To do this optimally, it is my opinion that the medical education system must itself be healthy. Otherwise there will be casualties among students and faculty.

Description of Students

Residents come into the family medicine learning situation after three or four years of medical school. Medical students themselves are recruited from a wide variety of disciplines, and may range from having two years of university to those with doctorates in any discipline. Thus the degree of intellectual and personal maturity varies widely, partly due to differences in age and life stage.

Residents, who are graduate medical students, vary widely in their skill level and their attitudes towards training and their perception of what the final product should look like. They also vary in their learning styles, maturity as self-motivated adult learners, their psychosocial adjustment and life stage, and their level of overall maturity and competence as a physician. By and large we attract very qualified and skilled students into our program. Their ability to adapt and do well in difficult circumstances may be one of the reasons that necessary changes get postponed.

Description of the Training Program

The training program is two years in duration. The degree to which program objectives are worked out and communicated to residents varies from university to university, as does the degree to which these objectives are learned and used varies with individual residents. In our program at Calgary, a great deal of effort has recently gone into defining objectives for the residents. This is not an easy task, since the field itself can be difficult to define. The discipline intersects with the content of many specialties, and individuals will reach differing levels of competence in any given clinical area.

In their first year, each resident spends four months in the academic family practice setting, where the full-time faculty have their practices, and four months in a community family practice setting in the second year. In addition, all residents spend one-half day in the academic practice setting where they follow a group of patients which they try to maintain as a small practice within the larger practice of their preceptor/teacher. When residents are not so engaged, they are rotating through a variety of learning situations which are by and large in the acute care hospital under the supervision of a teaching faculty in the specific discipline they are learning. Feedback/evaluation is sent back to the family medicine faculty about the accomplishment of the resident. These rotations include internal medicine, surgery, emergency, intensive care, psychiatry, obstetrics and gynecology, paediatrics and others.

Thus there is a significant possibility that the student is exposed to competing attitudes and values which are not consistent with those espoused by family medicine, where physical, logical, contextual, and spiritual values must all be taken into consideration in order to practice effectively. The doctor-patient relationship differs markedly among surgeons as compared with family doctors, for example. There are also differing attitudes and values among family medicine teachers themselves, some of whom may integrate to a greater degree than others, a collaborative patient-centered approach that takes family and wider systems into consideration. This wider view is officially promulgated, but there are difficulties in its diffusion into family practice (Becker, 1992).

Description of Learning Methods

The student learns primarily through direct contact with the patient and supervision/feedback from the preceptor. Responsibility for patients is gradually released to residents, depending on their level of competence at the time. In addition, formal knowledge dissemination takes place through discussion of cases, seminars and clinical rounds. Modelling by the clinical preceptor has enormous potential for influence on the attitudes and values of the student.

While residents are evaluated after each rotation, they also sit for a certifying exam at the end of their final year. Preceptors are also requested to give ongoing written and verbal evaluation of the resident performance in the clinical situation. When residents are having problems and this is not recognized and pointed out early in the rotation, a very difficult situation may develop. When recognition has occurred early in the residency, very successful remediation has taken place during the subsequent training through choice of electives and intensive work with the preceptor. This has created a win/win situation rather than potentially unresolvable conflict.

Teachers may use an apprenticeship model at times, by expecting the resident to learn by doing and following his or her example. Modelling behavior and demonstration of how to do things is especially relevant at the beginning of the residency. The preceptor also observes the resident through a one-way mirror or video camera. Most frequently the preceptor relies on the resident to recall what happened in the examining room and what they have said or done. This recollection may be very inaccurate, as is often recognized when the preceptor sits down and observes the interaction via videotape. The cases of a clinic are usually discussed briefly during the clinic or immediately afterwards. These discussions are supplemented by a series of seminars. The College of Family Physicians of Canada accredits the program and creates the certifying exam. Thus they ultimately control the content of what is to be accomplished by the learner.

DYSFUNCTION IN THE LEARNING SYSTEM

Over the past two years I have been running a seminar for all the residents which gives them the opportunity to discuss the difficulties they are having during the residency. Among the topics we discuss are resident/preceptor conflict, stress in the residency, women's issues, feelings about inadequacy, feeling abused during medical training, being a physician and a patient, isolation, difficult situations such as the dying patient, and others. The most recent group made it very clear that they all agreed that family medicine preceptors are compassionate compared to other rotations. To quote one resident, "I find that the preceptors recognize my needs, and cut some slack for me when I am overstretched." Another resident added, "The family medicine teachers are more caring and empathetic." They also disclosed how difficult it can be to give feedback to their preceptor when they fear that the preceptor may evaluate them poorly as a result of the feedback. They fear reprisal and they worry about hurting the feelings of preceptors who are trying hard to teach well. The difficulty they experience because of the balance of power between themselves and their preceptor can make it hard to have the kind of relationship they want, which is that of a colleague and, at times, a friend. As one resident stated:

> Some preceptors treat the resident as an equal, with others there is an imbalance of power. This makes it more difficult.

As another resident stated:

> There is a power differential, with the teacher pulling rank. It is not a discussion about management.

The feelings of inadequacy the residents have struggled with during medical training have echoed the same comments from a number of residents. As one put it, "I just feel like an idiot." This resident noted the sense of isolation he has had with these feelings, and what a sense of relief he felt when he finally got to discuss them among his colleagues. In one group all the residents acknowledged they had felt abused at some point during their training, with medical school being generally the worst. As one resident said:

> This is a situation of less power, where you are being asked to do things. Most of the class felt that there had been some form of abuse and dealt with it poorly. They felt put down and asked to do something they weren't ready for. In those situations I'd rather have someone with me to assist me.

Another stated that the system promotes "being grilled and feeling like an idiot."

> You can never meet those expectations. It's like being treated like a twelve year old again when I came back into medicine. I have no clout to fight back. I felt stupid in front of my patient on the second day because of my inability to distinguish his breath sounds.

One of the female residents disclosed her feelings by saying:

> Women residents, who took two weeks off to have babies, were scrutinized and harassed, as opposed to those who were off with the flu. Nurses treat women differently than men. The women are less respected by the nurse.

Residents also discussed how they perceive that preceptors can at times demonstrate unproductive behavior, such as dominating the resident or manipulating the resident to do work for them. One of the residents wasn't so sure about the excessive stress in residency and stated:

> Sometimes I think there is no other way to learn. It is in the nature of the work. Maybe it is eustress.

And about difficult situations, another stated:

> Dealing with death is difficult, you make mistakes, you make a fatal mistake. . . . Discussing and debriefing happens informally, in your social network.

And about the isolation, one indicated that:

> A main disappointment in medicine is how little contact we have with people outside of medicine. You lose contact. It is difficult to have a regular schedule.

Kate McKegney (1989), a family physician and teacher of family medicine in the United States, has written about her conviction that the medical education system may be compared to a family system that is often neglectful and abusive (McKegney, 1989). Unrealistic expectations, denial, indirect communication patterns, rigidity, and isolation are common to both. At the same time, the system implies that causes for this dysfunction lie entirely within individuals without regard to the system as a whole, thus leading to further dysfunction (McKegney, 1989). Adults who were abused as children may make excessive demands and have difficulties with boundaries and limits. They may become rigid, constricted, and isolated. When problems begun in an abusive childhood remain unresolved, they are more likely to be transmitted to the next generation. McKegney believes the same is true for the medical education system.

It is true that residency training can be painful because of neglect of physical and emotional needs of residents, both by themselves and their teachers. And some of these residents are vulnerable because of their own family backgrounds. It often fosters the attitude of unrealistic expectations and lack of skill at admitting human needs or admitting human mistakes (Dubovsky, 1986). Residents often deny feelings of pain, uncertainty, abandonment, and depression. This denial may be colluded with by the faculty. Further, the boundary between what is private for the resident and what is necessary to discuss in order to foster the resident's growth as a person and healer is not clearly demarcated or even discussed between faculty and residents. Residents may view these issues as private, perhaps fearing that they will be labelled as having an emotional problem, or out of fear of being labelled and judged. When any issue cannot be talked about, communication often becomes problematic as the number of things that can't be discussed seems to increase due to the avoidance of an important issue. Secrets lead to hidden alliances, splits, cut-offs, and mystify the communication process (Imber-Black, 1993). When problems cannot be addressed directly because of rules about mistakes and secrets, blaming and punishment replace nurturing feedback. Finding fault is confused with solving problems (McKegney, 1989). In such an environment trust is eroded and replaced by fear, which is the enemy of relationship. When those administering the program deal with conflict by punishing either resident or faculty rather than dealing with the underlying conflict, then an adversarial situation is set up where faculty and student protect themselves by complaining about the other party first so that the other will be labelled, not themselves. When residents have a representative in the administration and the faculty have no one, then power actually resides with the residents and it is the faculty who are at risk.

In this situation, students and faculty may become either conflicted or insensitive to each other. Both parties fail to receive the compassion and understanding which they are trying to exercise with patients. Students may become emotionally burned out. The environment may become rife with destructive gossip and negative judgement which then creates myths of both faculty and residents. When feedback focuses on the negative, or negative feedback is not specific enough, the student may become insecure about their competence (Rosenberg & Silver, 1984). When residents do not feel that their concerns can be heard, communication is rerouted when possible past faculty to review committees or senior administrators. In such a distrustful situation, faculty may not receive necessary feedback. Further, evaluation of faculty is often done in secret, thus shielding them from such important information as which resident is having a problem. Secrecy also removes accountability from the student, and this leads at times to inaccurate and destructive behavior by some residents. Secrets function in the system to mystify communication and reduce cohesion and trust. In family medicine, a close working relationship is necessary between the faculty and trainee, thus the impact of secrecy is not the same as it is in other disciplines at the university, where the relationship between student and teacher is limited to the classroom situation. A similar, close working relationship around patients/clients and families applies to all field placement situations.

In contrast to this need for closeness, medicine itself is often an isolated profession. Students may become isolated from their peers in their pre-medical years as they put in the time necessary to get into medical school. Once in medical school the demanding schedule may isolate students from socialization with students from other faculties. As residents they again have little time for fulfilling their social needs. Further, the profession as a whole is isolated from other disciplines, with medical faculties often being separate from the rest of the campus. It should be no surprise then, that residency may be associated with significant depression, as well as anger or emotional withdrawal among some of the residents. These internal states may then contaminate the student/teacher relationship. This is further compounded in the relationship between the faculty and student by transference issues which become evoked in the clinical and teaching situation (Stein, 1985). These phenomena are virtually never acknowledged, let alone discussed.

The structure and content of the learning situation are the responsibility of the program director, who is responsible to an associate dean of post graduate education, a physician who is not a family physician. The department head is ultimately responsible for the running of the department. There is a real possibility that each of the above have a distinct set of values which conflict with one another. Above these is the dean of medicine, who also likely has his or her own agenda. The view of how leadership should be exercised may differ among these people. Leadership can be exercised with mutual respect or with coercion. Coercion, broadly speaking, is violence, as forcing one person's wishes on another person. Violence is abusive and is disrespectful. Thus, if any of the key leaders is fundamentally authoritarian and hierarchial, this will have its influence on the system, and may create opposing values and confusion.

The relationship between the resident and his or her preceptor in family medicine is a very important one since it lasts for the entire two years on at least a weekly basis. There are usually about six residents with a preceptor at any given time. During this time, personality and learning style conflicts may arise and not be recognized as such, but rather defined as "something is wrong" with either the resident or the preceptor. These conflicts may lead to unrecognized stress for both preceptor and resident.

Conflict in the Learning Environment

The learning environment of the family practice unit also contains potential conflict with faculty colleagues, colleagues from different professions, and those who work to make the clinical setting function, such as secretaries, receptionists, clinical nurses, and clerical staff. Issues from the teaching environment may readily contaminate these areas, leading to breakdown of communication and unresolved conflict. Further, management issues and conflicts that do not get resolved in the clinical environment contaminate the teaching/learning environment. Residents find similar conflicts when they go to the different clinical rotations on the wards of the hospital or in other family physician offices. However, generally speaking, the offices in the community run in a much more efficient and smooth manner. This may be a reflection of how much the agenda of teaching residents within existing clinical practices of their clinical preceptors stresses those practices, as well as the fact that teaching practices are usually administered by the teaching hospitals which have strong union control of hiring and firing. Academic family physicians, with many competing jobs and focuses, may not be best suited to do administrative work, and when in authority may look to others (such as nursing unit managers) to handle the day to day problems. This further compounds the possibility of differing attitudes and values competing with one another and a resulting confusion amongst those working in the academic clinical environment. By contrast, in the community the family physician is focused solely on patient care, sets his own policy, and hires and fires whomever he wishes.

Family medicine interfaces with many disciplines. Thus interdisciplinary conflict can be an often unacknowledged issue for this discipline at many levels. This includes: working with other disciplines e.g., hierarchial and other issues; selecting what fits and what does not from the body of knowledge which is developing in the interfacing discipline; and, working with teachers who have conceptual models from their own discipline that they are trying to use with family practice learners i.e., nursing, social work, family therapy, psychology, etc.

Issues of power and conflicting culture, agendas, and horizons (Sawa, 1992a) lead to interdisciplinary conflict if they are not recognized and attended to. Allied professionals such as ward nurses may vent frustration about their roles in working with physicians or residents. ". . . nurses may use their power to both support and undercut the house staff, leaving trainees with ambivalent feelings about nurses and their importance in the medical education network" (McKegney, 1989). Conflict may also arise when nurses administer a family practice teaching unit and the nurse does not understand the culture and values of family medicine.

Psychosocial issues form a great part of what the physician does in his or her practice. Thus the discipline of family medicine interfaces with family therapy, psychiatry, psychology, nursing, and social work in important ways. The context of these disciplines differ from that of family medicine, and the conflict between differing assumptions about the nature of human beings, healing, epistemology, the roles of different health care providers are often not acknowledged or even in awareness. This leads at times to conflict of contexts (Glenn, 1987; Doherty & Burge, 1987). Different health-care fields also have different histories, traditions, values, and structures. These differences set the basis for conflict. In addition to the above, tensions over professional (hierarchial) and gender (male) dominance issues further cloud the situation (Glenn, 1987). The stresses felt by physicians in training are shared at least in part by the human service professions. The need for communication and conflict-resolution skills are common throughout the helping professions. Students are challenged not only to have knowledge, attitude and skills, but to become compassionate, ethical, caring and sensitive human beings.

> Stress in residency is not simply the result of long hours and fatigue. Becoming a physician requires major personal growth, and the development of attitudes that facilitate meeting the demands of the profession while retaining a sense of perspective as a person. Unfortunately, residency training is oriented to developing cognitive and technical skills and provides little time or support for personal development. These problems are not unique to physicians. The transition from student to worker is characteristically difficult for people who enter all human service careers. (Martin, 1986, p. 252)

THE JOURNEY TOWARDS HEALING

Cooperation rests on strongly shared values, deep affective ties, or mutual self-interest (Glenn, 1987). Since these will likely be lacking among at least some of those involved in medical education, there is need for an understanding of conflict and the positive role it also plays. Conflict, when it is directly and openly acknowledged and recognized, provides an opportunity for personal growth. But when conflict is hidden, destructive secrets, gossip, passive aggressive behavior, and interpersonal conflictual triangles may develop. Conflict pushes those involved to further define themselves, their ideas, and their values and goals. In order to move towards healing ourselves and our systems, we must look towards transforming models for change and growth.

The business world is leading the way in attempting to transform the work setting. New models which are affirmative rather than destructive are being devised and tested (Sawa, 1992b). At the heart of these models is the necessity of individual transformation. The extent to which those using these models recognize this requirement for individual change varies. Applying these models as new techniques without recognizing the need for individual change and transformation is an invitation to failure and frustration.

At the heart of these new models is the application of systems theory to social systems, along with existential and phenomenological thinking, and theology (Sawa, 1992b). The new models motivate through a shared vision which members of the organization strive to realize. Accomplishing the vision becomes the mission of the organization, and all involved are engaged in collaboration. In this model, systems thinking is incorporated in terms of the shared "meaning" of the enterprise as well as the application of systems theory to provide an understanding of the organization and to provide techniques for systemic change. Systems thinking is further utilized to build a shared vision, where goals, values and missions bind people together around a common identity. Life-long commitment to learning and a continual clarifying and deepening of a personal vision, including our highest aspirations is promoted in these "learning organizations." Team learning is proposed, which begins with dialogue, in which team members suspend assumptions and enter into a genuine "thinking together." These kinds of models require a shift to a systemic way of thinking and taking personal responsibility for how we influence the system.

Academic departments of Family Medicine are in conflict between the old ways of negative control and new methods of affirmative/positive control and collaboration. The old way is associated with high negative affect, stress, deficient cognition, learned helplessness, and the breakdown of social bonds. Positive affect on the other hand is associated with creative problem solving, more effective decision making and judgement, and increased learning activity (Cooperrider, 1990). Such models are difficult to implement, however, since they require that the leadership actually give up power to the collaborating parties, and the leader becomes one stakeholder (Gray, 1989). Self knowledge is important, since the more we know about ourselves, the more of reality we will perceive.

Healing the System

Our department, with credit to the leadership, has taken steps towards change and transformation. At the level of our family practice unit we have made a number of efforts at improving the situation. We went through two rounds of meetings which culminated in writing a mission statement, with goals and values for the department. This was a collaborative effort, and was viewed as a success. We also had a day's retreat, which was viewed as unsuccessful. In this case an expert was hired for a day and was briefed by the administrator as to what was to be accomplished. This approach requires that the client has made the right diagnosis and communicated it well to the consultant (Nevis, 1987). This experience was criticized highly by the department and the thrust to continue our growth was dropped from the agenda of the department for about a year. At that time a number of serious resident/preceptor conflicts once again brought the need for change back on the table and renewed the resolution to change.

The next step towards change was a faculty retreat which focused on the theme of conflict, which all full-time faculty attended. Sources of conflict were discussed. Scarcity of resources becomes especially onerous when we all want something different. At the interpersonal level, misuse of power and lack of mutual respect are important. The system generates conflict by allowing conflicting roles and tasks, while not providing adequate resources. Persons projecting on others their own disowned traits is another way that conflict may occur without the underlying dynamic ever being disclosed. Role ambiguity (if roles aren't defined — who makes what decision?), and institutional expectations vs. personal need are other sources of conflict. Personality conflicts can also be used as excuses for not addressing other issues, such as people just not doing their jobs. The most difficult conflicts to deal with are value conflicts, such as the hierarchy between biological or physical and logical or spiritual problems. Disagreement also occurs between the priorities of clinical activity and scholarly activity for faculty. At least half of the faculty indicated that they had been in painful conflict situations with residents and now had the opportunity to "tell their stories." Since the initial meeting the department voted to continue meeting to promote change.

The model of intervention which we have selected is Gestalt based. It is process consultation which focuses energy on the way the system approaches its problems, rather than making detailed analytical investigations and recommendations of preferred solutions. The basic activities of the consultant include (Nevis, 1987, p. 57): to observe, and selectively share observations; to attend to one's own experience i.e., feelings, sensations, thoughts and selectively share these; to focus on energy in the client system and the emergence or lack of themes or issues for which there is energy; to act to support mobilization of client energy so that something happens; to facilitate clear, meaningful, contacts between members of the system including the consultant: to help the group achieve heightened awareness of its overall process in completing units of work; and, to learn to complete units of work so as to achieve closure around problem areas of unfinished business.

> These fundamental activities of the consultant are exactly the skills that a Gestalt-oriented intervenor wishes to have the client system learn. Thus, while the consultant may design special learning "exercises" or serve as an observer of the ongoing activities of the client, a primary means of teaching is through the display of personal behavior, turning into or attending to what is going on in the system, and then moving from this into support of available energy and effective action. The endeavor is to give the client a sense of the nature of good process and a way of better understanding the characteristic interruptions and blockages to good process that develop in that system. Following from this, the

client then has the responsibility for making choices related to newly perceived awareness. This may or may not result in a decision to alter the structure and process through which the system carries out its tasks. (Nevis, 1987, p. 58)

CONCLUSION

Our system is beginning to change in that it has become aware of the need for change, and of the mutual desire of members to create change. In reflecting on what has happened to get us to this point, I see a number of important steps. An essential step occurred when the department head made a commitment to himself and the department to pursue change to a collaborative affirmative model to help the department become more healthy. Having identified conflict as a central problem, we are beginning to take steps to deal with it. It is hoped that workshops for faculty and residents will occur to help us learn new skills. We have the benefit of an inter-faculty working group at our university to help identify resources. A number of activities have occurred which invited the faculty to support the process of change at the interpersonal level, and they have done so to this point.

In our conflicts we will look to the ideal of justice, which insures that we are accountable to each other and to ourselves for our actions. It also insures that we do not ask each other to do the impossible when there are not enough personal and collective resources. And hopefully within our justice will be compassion and gentleness. Above all, we must be willing to continue to heal ourselves in order to be instruments of healing. We can then accept conflict as an instrument of growth, in spite of its painful nature. We will then be able to enter more fully into authentic personal relationships with one another, and become interdependent. In such an environment, we will not only continue to graduate good clinicians, but we will deal more effectively and compassionately with each other when problems arise for either faculty or resident. We will also, as a department, model to each other and all our students the caring we hope that our graduates will provide to their patients.

REFERENCES

Becker, L. (1992). Issues in the adoption of a family approach by practising physicians. In Russell J. Sawa (Ed.), *Family health care* (pp. 189-199). Newbury Park: Sage.

Cooperrider, D. L. (1990). *Appreciative management and leadership.* San Francisco: Jossey-Bass.

Doherty, W. J., & Burge, S. K. (1987). Attending to the context of family treatment: Pitfalls and prospects. *Journal of Marital and Family Therapy, 13*(1), 37-47.

Dubovsky, S. L. (1986). Coping with entitlement in medical education. *N. Engl. J Med., 315,* 1672-4.

Glenn, H. (1987). Structurally determined conflicts in health care. *Family Systems Medicine, 5*(4), 413-427.

Gray, B. (1989). *Collaborating: Finding common ground for multiparty problems.* San Francisco: Jossey-Bass.

Imber-Black, E. (1993). *Secrets in families and family therapy.* New York: W.H. Norton and Co.

McKegney, C. P. (1989). Medical education: A neglectful and abusive family system. *Family Medicine, 21*(6), 452-457.

McWhinney, I. R. (1989). Philosophical and scientific foundations of family medicine. *A textbook of family medicine* (pp. 43-71). New York: Oxford University Press.

Nevis, E. C. (1987). *Organization consulting: A gestalt approach.* New York: Gardner Press.

Rosenberg, D. A., & Silver, H. K. (1984). Medical student abuse. An unnecessary and preventable cause of stress. *JAMA, 251,* 739-42.

Sawa, R. J. (1992a). Three ways of thinking. In Russell J. Sawa (Ed.), *Family health care.* Newbury Park, CA: Sage.

Sawa, R. J. (1992b). Expanding our horizons: Visions of the future. In Russell J. Sawa (Ed.), *Family health care* (pp. 253-257). Newbury Park: Sage.

Stein, H. (1985). *The psycho-dynamics of medical practice.* Berkley, CA: The University of California Press.

CHAPTER FORTY-ONE

MANAGING DILEMMAS/ISSUES/CONFLICTS IN CLINICAL PLACEMENTS, FACULTY OF NURSING

Arlene Johnston

Nursing is a discipline founded in clinical practice and a profession guided by standards, a code of ethics, a caring philosophy, holistic theories and research based practice. In all of our nursing programs we strive to produce generic and graduate nurses who are safe, competent and ethical practitioners who can care for patients or clients in a diverse and complex health care system, in institutions, in agencies and in the urban and rural communities. My colleagues from the disciplines of social work, education, psychology and family medicine have each described issues and situations that are indeed similar and comparative to nursing. Early in our multidisciplinary meetings all of our disciplines soon realized that as a group we needed to find systems solutions to manage conflictual issues in clinical environments and not just resolve issues in our departments or units for a single student or point in time. The rapid changes within our environments make maintenance activity a step backward.

CONCERNS AT THE INTERSYSTEMS LEVEL

The issues, dilemmas and conflictual concerns in clinical placements that I wish to address in the nursing context are at the intersystems level. The issue of health care reform is multifaceted, multidimensional and multicomplex. The complexity involved in a rapidly changing health care system directly impacts the clinical environment for all of our nursing students regardless of level, regardless of program history. A further variable is that in 1993 after six years of planning, nursing mounted a collaborative undergraduate nursing program with a school of nursing and a college department; a program which promotes the attainment of baccalaureate preparation for all future nurses and which is part of a national professional mandate. We have a new curriculum for the "Calgary Conjoint Nursing Program" which is dramatically different in both cognitive and experiential approaches to teaching and learning.

These two occurrences affect the management of clinical or field placements, especially as one attempts to place some 600 students from four different programs in a chaotic, emotional, downsizing health care system. One understanding that assists nursing to effectively function in this dynamic unsettling environment is that of chaos or complexity theory.

Components for chaos theory are that order and disorder are essential elements for growth. Characteristics of this view involve complex systems interacting with environmental disturbances looking for systems balance in a way which permits stretching and folding, internal reorganization and continuing evolution. Chaos theory suggests the implications for professional education and its long term survival will depend upon its ability to adapt and grow relative to these interactions and changes. Planned change and social change theories have valuable principles that need to be considered in a multi-disciplinary approach to addressing current issues in health care reform. When one looks at the system as a living dynamic evolving entity, it permits conflict to be transformed into opportunity, and internal capabilities for flexibility, adaptation, and visionary change to be developed.

A MULTIDISCIPLINARY COLLABORATIVE APPROACH

One of the systems changes that has assisted flexibility and adaptation is a multidisciplinary collaboration to understand and plan practice experiences within educational and clinical programs. In the rapidly changing health care environment with cutbacks and shrinking resources, it is vital to have a collaborative partnership between educational institutions and clinical agencies in order to better use all resources in the most efficient way and effective way to promote student learning. Strong linkages between education and clinical practice are vital to ensure competent health care practitioners; levelled and sequenced clinical practicum courses are required to provide opportunities to apply and develop knowledge and skills that go beyond traditional learning.

Historically, clinical placements were negotiated individually on a first-come, first-serve basis, between each educational institution and clinical agency. The results of this practice produced a competitive, stressful and unhealthy environment for negotiations and an inefficient system for placement of students in clinical areas. The Calgary Clinical Resources Co-ordinating Committee (C.C.R.C.C.) was established in 1982, a unique committee with representatives from educational institutions, acute care, long term care and community agencies. The formation of this partnership allowed us to seek and coordinate in a collaborative way appropriate clinical placements for learners from diverse health care programs at various levels. Other outcomes resulting from the committee were significant, creative and innovative projects which strengthened the link between educational institutions and the clinical agencies. The process increased mutual trust and co-operation between the educational institutions and service agencies, and enhanced the learning environment for students. Now 12 years old with a broadened membership and a developing computer data base for Southern Alberta, the established trust and linkages are engendering creative strategies to deal with the chaotic environment now upon us.

The collaborative process was ahead of its time when it began over a decade ago, however, it is totally congruent with today's vision of health and education in the Province of Alberta. This is important today when practitioners are disillusioned with health care, are frightened for their patients/clients, are angry with their insecurity of employment and possibly even their profession. "Bumping" mechanisms to permit seniority choice of positions cause further insecurities, changing practices and further frustrations. This committee has provided an avenue for managing. As a model, it has become recognized locally, nationally and internationally from a group with singular concerns to a collegial, working partnership committed to improving and coordinating clinical placements on a continuing basis. The committee not only coordinates placements but raises issues, identifies real or potential conflicts and institutions measures for resolution. The intersystem structure permits conflict to be resolved rather than managed.

A NEW CURRICULUM IN NURSING

The introduction of a new curriculum in nursing which is dramatically different both cognitively and experientially from those or existing programs, has brought a new set of dilemmas with potential conflicts. These are not in any way mutually exclusive from issues and conflicts in health care reform, the consequences of downsizing health care institutions and nursing staff, and the need for more humanistic population focused health care.

A proactive strategy brought together the collaborative talents of clinical placement designates from each of the three members of Calgary Conjoint Nursing Program who work closely together throughout the year. In addition to planning for clinical placements for the new program, a vigorous public relations campaign was conducted to "sell" the new curriculum to all members of our Calgary Clinical Resources Co-ordinating Committee and through them, to the clinical agencies. This was an ominous task but a rewarding experience resulting in a relatively successful introductory year linking the new concepts and theories with matching learning clinical environments. Change in student learning and practice experiences has been effectively introduced as colleagues from practice prepare and educate themselves to the vision of a new kind of practitioner in a new kind of health care system.

CONCLUSION

I would like to conclude with what I see or envision for the future of the participants of our Multidisciplinary Professional Interest Group at The University of Calgary. Our future together provides an exciting learning environment for linking multidisciplinary faculty expertise into a multidisciplinary approach to managing conflict situations. As educators, I believe we can be the leaders in the research which will facilitate a more effective, less stressful, more caring and supportive clinical environment for students, faculty and the agencies and institutions that support our teaching. By taking a broad systems approach to the education of health practitioners in a structure that brings together varied professionals and stakeholders in a creative, mutually satisfying and effective manner, the outcome can be one of quality showing flexibility and adaptiveness. The environment can then become managed.

REFERENCES

Johnston, A., & Soltes, D. (1992). *A decade of partnership: A collaborative journey.*

Prigogine, Ilya, & Stengers, Isabel. (1984). *Order out of chaos.* New York: Bantam Books Inc.

Spradley, B. (1980). Managing change creatively. *Journal of Nursing Administration, May*, 32-37.

Thompson, B., & Kinne, S. (1990). Social change theory: Applications to community health. In N. Bracht (Ed.), *Health promotion at the community level* (pp. 45-65). Newbury Park: Sage.

PART SEVEN

IN PURSUIT OF QUALITY: FUTURE CONSIDERATIONS

CHAPTER FORTY-TWO

FIELD EDUCATION:
A PEDAGOGY OF ITS OWN

Gayla Rogers

Given all that has come before this final chapter, I am confident in arguing that field education has a distinct and distinguishable body of knowledge and skills which has been generated through research, built from experience and drawn from related disciplines. It can be articulated, transmitted and made accessible to faculty, field instructors and students through carefully designed and delivered programs and curricula. Central to the field education equation is a competent field instructor.

A PARADIGM SHIFT

Preparing field instructors for their role in the professional education of social workers requires a paradigm shift from a *training* to a *learning* emphasis. The training paradigm focuses on the acquisition of skills and techniques that lead to desired outcomes which will ultimately be demonstrated in practice. The learning paradigm focuses on the accumulation of a deeper understanding through critical thinking and reflection to enhance the quality of what occurs in the context of the field placement. Skills and techniques are a means to that end but the behaviors in and of themselves do not represent the gestalt of high quality, competent field education.

The learning paradigm instills the confidence to peel back the layers of practice and improve performance in light of this reflective and analytic process. It enables students to adjust to the demands of a rapidly and radically changing environment and equips them to deal with new, unspecified challenges. It is therefore incumbent on field instructors TO encourage students to become continuous learners, to extract meaning from their experiences and to disseminate the learning in collaborative contexts. Requiring students to simply engage in the experience of the practicum is not enough for quality learning to be realized. To transform *doing,* that is, the acts or skills of practice, into *learning*, that is, the understanding and critique of the accumulated experiences, requires a process of dialogue and reflection. This is the paradigm that quality field education encompasses.

The role of the field instructor needs careful consideration. Individual approaches to learning, affected by a whole range of human diversity variables, must be honored and respected while maintaining the integrity of expectations and course objectives. The field instructor must be a knowledge provider, a demonstrator, a model and a critic but, of equal importance, the field instructor must also be a learning partner, learning facilitator and a critical inquirer of his/her own practice. At one level, those learning to be social workers need to acquire specific information and skills by observing or listening to "expert" social workers who can model the expected role behaviors. The "neophyte" learner can begin by imitating or approximating the teacher. However, social workers-to-be come to training with a repertoire of experience and preconceived ideas about social work. Therefore, at another level, students need to begin by articulating and drawing upon what they know which is often embedded in their actions, by exposing to the scrutiny of co-learners and field instructors their underlying assumptions about practice (Brookfield, 1986). The field instructor then must help students process this material so that together they can decide what of this is accumulated wisdom, bad habits, misinformation, or valid theories-in use (Argyris & Schön, 1974), which can be discarded or expanded and applied in new or different ways.

Students come to the praticum with the resources and baggage derived from their personal histories. The role of experience and prior learning can be an asset if channelled and scrutinized for its relevance, appropriateness and applicability. It can be a hindrance if it is taken as a given and not subjected to a reflective process of its own. In that regard, the past may interfere with the present and entrench fixed ways of thinking and doing, that is, it reinforces practices that are not progressive or evolving. It can close the mind to new ideas rather than open it to different possibilities. Prior experience and knowledge is the place to begin but it must be seen as a departure point for new learning and making changes in thinking, doing, feeling and being.

When social work practitioners become field instructors, they must adopt a different perceptual stance from that which may have served them well with clients or consumers of their services. One such shift involves the assessment of a student's progress and performance which is based on acquisition and achievement, not on needs. This must be done despite the anxiety that grading may generate or its dissonance with egalitarian principles. Unlike the social worker concerned with client need, the field instructor must look beyond the felt needs of students to what the students must know and be able to do with and for clients (Wood & Middleman, 1991). Typical or traditional methods for assessing readiness for a given role (objective tests, standardized instruments, micro skills checklists) are not designed to assess the adaptation of students with unique characteristics and capabilities to particular environments, nor do they consider the accommodation of particular environments to the unique qualities of individual students (Jackson & Cafferella, 1994). Appraisal schemes that treat students as technicians presume that teaching and learning are processes that can be broken down into discrete and unconnected skills. The nature of social work involves a reliance on discretionary interpretation, decision-making based on insufficient or incomplete information, and working conditions that are often uncertain and unpredictable (Schön, 1987). Reports that attest to the student's abilities at the placement, videos of the student in-action with consumers/clients demonstrating specific behaviors, and reflective chronologies of the student's development and understanding, all serve to provide documentary evidence of an individual student's ability. In considering how well a student performs, it is also necessary to consider how well the system is designed to permit the achievement of intended outcomes (Smyth, 1991).

The Trouble with Outcomes: Whose Best Practice is it Anyway?

Competence and outcomes are two terms that have become inextricably bound with social work education in general and field education in particular. There is no objection to the application of these terms in principle but using them as the sole criteria for the design and evaluation of social work programs, begs the question, 'whose competences?' What counts as good practice in social work is at best debatable and at worst indecipherable. Whose voice is it that determines the criterion of best practice?

Is it the academics and researchers who ponder, pontificate and try to prove what constitutes best practice? Is it the practitioners and managers whose day to day practices are driven by factors of cost-effectiveness, efficiency and accountability which may or may not be related to 'best' practice? Should the service users or the general public have a voice in such matters? Could the profession (given this body is representative of the entity) agree on a list of competences? Or should the politicians decide? To complicate matters further, today's competences are not necessarily tomorrow's.

To orient curricula around competences, in the narrow sense of the term, means reducing best practice to a set of practical skills replete with behavioral indicators which is to reduce it to technical training. In arguing this very point in a different context Grundy (1987) suggests what we need is "less competence and more critical reflection."

In that regard professional education for social workers should equip students to form a view of their profession and its changing relationship with society, and society's evolving demands on and expectations of the profession. This requires contemplation about the competences themselves, to critique them, to embrace, discard or change them, to find new best practices and deepened understandings which in turn can be submitted to the rigors of critical thought. This type of professionalism, following Schön (1983, 1987), can be said to embody valid *knowledge-in-use* derived from *reflection-on-action* used to build *theories-in-use* for *reflection-in-action* that is grounded in a congruent set of personal and professional values. A genuine higher education for the professions, according to Barnett (1994, p. 89) "will not be content with reflecting the professionally defined competences but will insert alternative modes of reasoning, action and reflection into the curriculum." Barnett further suggests:

> To reduce human action to a constellation of terms such as 'performance', 'competence', 'doing', and 'skill' is not just to resort to a hopelessly crude language with which to describe serious human endeavors. In the end, it is to obliterate the humanness in human action. It is to deprive human beings of *human* being. (p. 178)

Questioning the Unquestionable

The assumptions and criteria governing what are considered to be appropriate curricula, methods, assessment procedures and research activities are reflective to some extent of the prevailing attitudes towards social work and the status accorded social work as a valued professional practice. There is a predominantly North American preoccupation with the ethos of "rugged individualism" which is played out in field instructor training and social work education through the popularity of concepts related to andragogy (Knowles, 1980) and self-directed learning (Brookfield, 1986). The application of principles that adults can and should be encouraged to design, conduct and evaluate their own learning in an independent manner as free from institutional control as possible means that any attempt to legislate or mandate a specific curriculum for field instructors would be soundly rejected. It is also a mechanism by which programs can argue against putting resources into field instructor training.

For example, if the resources cannot be located to provide field instructor training the response is to simply rely on the belief in adult and self-directed learning principles that would suggest that willing field instructors will find their own way to equip themselves to be competent field instructors. There is an underlying assumption that "training would be nice but after all experienced social workers know what to do with students and if they don't, they will develop themselves as any self-directing, life-long learning professional would do."

When training is provided for field instructors in Canada, it is primarily under the guise of providing salient information about the program, it's objectives and curriculum (Rogers, 1993). Any training over and above that is seen as a perk to field instructors designed to motivate them, entice them and thank them. A service-oriented rationale drives the criteria by which this training is determined. According to this rationale the responsibility for determining content and curricular direction rests largely with the field instructors who come to training as it is for their enrichment and enjoyment. The role of the teacher of field instructors becomes that of facilitating the acquisition of those skills or that knowledge which the learners themselves have specified.

One implication arising out of the adoption of this learner-led, service orientated rationale is that educational activities in which field instructors-to-be are challenged, in which their existing assumptions are called into question, and in which they are forced to confront aspects of their values and actions they would prefer not to examine, are likely to be avoided. In seeking to offer training which leaves participants feeling satisfied and pleased with the outcomes, the danger is that field instructors will never be provoked or confronted for fear of displeasing them. After all, this may cause them to change their mind about providing the essential service of taking students, which was the *raison d'être* of the training in the first place. Training field instructors under these conditions looks more like trying to slip in methods and techniques of good field education without demanding an undue amount of work, while at the same time flattering egos and fostering a commitment to the social work program.

EDUCATIVE AND EMPOWERING FORMS OF ACTION

A preoccupation with outcomes and behaviorally defined competences renders the learning process, as a valued entity unto itself, relatively unimportant. Yet, it is the *process*, the journey taken to find meaning and understanding in the practice of social work that transforms an eager student into an enabled practitioner. This new breed of practitioner is empowered to make an informed and personal commitment to the values and ethics of the profession. A field instructor who has insight and wisdom as well as knowledge and skills is an integral player in this transformation process.

Ultimately everyone loses when the quality of field instruction is poor. Employers become frustrated by the lack they see in graduates; consumers of social work services suffer from poor practice delivered by students and hasty practice delivered by overburdened field instructors; exposure to certain opportunities is often left to chance as students experience a huge variance and lack of consistency in the quality of learning; and, programs suffer a loss of reputation and poor relations with the practice community. A clear set of expectations and a reasonable and achievable pathway towards meeting the expectations will help all those involved.

Both from the point of view of field directors and field instructors, there is a clear consensus that field instructors require specific training (Rogers, 1995). It is believed that well developed programs for preparing field instructors will have an impact on the attitudes and outlook of practitioners who undertake this role and in turn socialize their students into the profession in a manner that epitomizes professional education rather than technical training. Education for field instructors is a form of individual professional development, if discerned as such by the individuals who partake in it. If sanctioned and valued by the organization, it can take its rightful place as staff development. And, it is a form of technical development if it is mandated by the social work program but not regarded as much in the way of professional or staff development by either the individual or the organization. The ideal form is a combination of all three perspectives where educating field instructors is a priority and is prized by the individual, the organization, the educational institution and the profession.

Each of these stakeholders must have a vested interest in the pursuit of the ideal form before it can be realized. To some extent this is determined by the image of the field instructor held by each stakeholder. There seems to be three current images that predominate. The traditional image is one where the field instructor is viewed as belonging to one domain, typically the organization, and for personal interest reasons may be peripherally connected to the other two, education and profession, as long as this does not interfere with the primary domain. The second image recognizes there are competing interests and views the field instructor as being in a precarious position pivoting on a point where work, school, occupation and home intersects, consequently pulling the individual in many directions. A third more collaborative image views the field instructor as being at the heartland, a vital and solid place, balanced at the nexus of practice, education, profession and personhood. It is the pursuit of this collaborative image, the image of choice, that will lead us to the confluence of quality and competence in field education and into the 21st century.

REFERENCES

Argyris, C., & Schön, D. (1974). *Theory in practice.* San Francisco, CA: Jossey-Bass.

Barnett, R. (1994). *The limits of competence: Knowledge, higher education and society.* Buckingham: The Society for Research into Higher Education & Open University Press.

Brookfield, S. (1986). *Understanding and facilitating adult learning.* San Francisco: Jossey-Bass.

Grundy, S. (1987). *Curriculum: Product or process.* Lewes: Falmer.

Jackson, L., & Caffarella, R. (Eds.) (1994). *Experiential learning: A new approach. New directions for adult and continuing education*, No. 62. San Francisco, CA: Jossey-Bass

Knowles, M. (1980). *The modern practice of adult education: From pedagogy to andragogy.* Chicago: Follett.

Rogers, G. (1993). *Field instructor training in Canada: What is, what could be.* Paper presented at the Annual Meeting and Conference of the Canadian Association of Social Work, Ottawa, ON.

Rogers, G. (1995). *In search of quality and competence: Practice teaching/field instruction in social work education. A study of training programs for practice teachers in the United Kingdom and field instructors in Canada.* Unpublished doctoral dissertation, University of Newcastle Upon Tyne, England.

Schön, D. (1983). *The reflective practitioner: How professional think in action.* New York: Basic Books.

Schön, D. (1987). *Educating the reflective practitioner: Toward a new design for teaching and learning in the professions.* San Francisco: Jossey-Bass.

Smyth, J. (1991). *Teachers as collaborative learners: Challenging dominant forms of supervision.* Milton Keynes: Open University Press.

Wood, G., & Middleman, R. (1991). Principles that guide teaching. In R. Middleman, & G. Wood (Eds.), *Teaching secrets: The technology in social work education* (p.111-118). Benghampton, NY: Haworth Press.

CONTRIBUTORS

Garth Benson, PhD, is the former Director of Practicum for the Faculty of Education, The University of Calgary, and he is interested in how novices become accomplished professionals. His research focuses on epistemology, philosophy of science, individuals' conceptions of science, and the process of knowing. Recent publications include *Process, Epistemology and Education*, which is a co-edited collection of papers on Whitehead's process philosophy.

Paula K. Bergman is both a social work educator and a direct practitioner. She has worked in both the public and the private sectors at the casework, supervisory and administrative/management levels. Ms Bergman currently is a field work trainer with the DSS/MSW Project at the School of Social Welfare, SUNY-Stony Brook, where she supervises first year graduate students placed at a number of field agencies. She is a member of NASW and the New York State Bar Association. She holds a MSW from SUNY-Stony Brook School of Social Welfare and a JD from Cardozo School of Law.

Martha Bial is Associate Director of Field Instruction, Fordham University Graduate School of Social Service. She chairs the committee which sets curriculum standards for the seminar for new field instructors required by the schools of the Greater New York Area Consortium. She has been a field instructor, a faculty field liaison and has spent many years in practice with clients who have physical and/or mental disabilities. She believes that field educators play an important role in enabling people with disabilities to enter the social work profession and in preparing the profession to receive them.

Marion Bogo, MSW, ADV DIP SW, is Acting Dean and Associate Professor, Faculty of Social Work, University of Toronto. Professor Bogo's academic, educational, practice and consultative activities focus on social work education and social work practice in national and international contexts, including practicum models, linkages to ethno-racial communities and the development of professional competence. She has been a consultant on field education programs to schools of social work in the US, Canada and Asia, particularly Japan and Sri Lanka.

Annette Bot, MSW, CSW, is Educational Coordinator, Department of Social Work, Mount Sinai Hospital, Toronto and Adjunct Social Work Practice Professor, Faculty of Social Work, University of Toronto, Canada.

Nick Coady is an Associate Professor, Faculty of Social Work, Wilfrid Laurier University, Waterloo, Ontario. His specific teaching interests include interviewing skills, group work, generalist direct social work practice, and faculty-field liaison functions. His practice experience includes group work with male batterers and counselling multi-problem adolescents and families. Nick's recent publications have included a critique of family systems therapy and an argument for a renewed emphasis on the worker-client relationship in social work practice.

Heather Coleman, PhD, is an Assistant Professor, Faculty of Social Work, The University of Calgary. She has been the field coordinator for the Lethbridge Division for a number of years. Prior to academia, she was the Clinical Director for Lethbridge Family Services. Heather has had over fifteen years clinical experience in a cross-section of social work settings.

Don Collins, PhD, is a Professor, Faculty of Social Work, The University of Calgary. Don has over 20 years of direct clinical social work practice. His teaching and research interests have primarily been in micro-skill training with continued interest and experience in field education, Native social work education and pro-feminist practice.

Nancy Costikyan, MSW, Simmons College School of Social Work and Clinical Fellow, Norman E. Zinberg Center for Addiction Studies, Harvard Medical School and Cambridge Hospital. Prior to social work, she worked as staff clinician, supervisor and program coordinator at the North Charles Institute for the Addictions. She completed internships at Trinity Mental Health Center and at the Sexual Abuse Treatment Team at Children's Hospital, Boston. She is currently on staff at the Federal Employee Assistance Program, and teaches at Harvard Medical School, Division on Addictions.

Mark Doel is Co-director of Practice Teaching Studies, University of Sheffield, England. He has worked as social worker, field instructor and has been a lecturer at Sheffield University for 10 years. He now specializes in developing teaching materials and distance learning programs. He is a freelance trainer in practice teaching, group work and task-centered practice. Major publications include *Task Centered Social Work* (Doel & Marsh, Ashgate, 1992) and *Social work practice: Exercises and activities for training and developing social workers* (Doel & Shardlow, Gower, 1993).

David Este is an Assistant Professor, Faculty of Social Work, The University of Calgary. He received his MSW from the University of Toronto and DSW from Wilfrid Laurier University. Teaching and research interests include management of nonprofit organizations, community mental health and social work practice with diverse populations.

Joan Feyrer is Field Education Coordinator, School of Social Work, University of Victoria, Canada. She was an auxiliary social worker for the Ministry of Social Services for many years before joining the School of Social Work in 1989. She is an advocate of adult education principles and sees many parallels with social work values. She presently teaches Introduction to Social Work Practice by distance education.

Diana Filiano, MSW, ACSW, is currently a field trainer for the DSS/MSW Project of the SUNY-Stony Brook School of Social Welfare in Long Island, where she supervises graduate students in direct practice, research, grant writing and policy formation. She has been an adjunct instructor in the BSW program and is involved with several research projects affiliated with the School. Special interest areas include social work education, domestic violence, feminist and international social work. She is presently completing doctoral work at Adelphi University and is a member of MASW.

Sheena Findlay has been a social work educator for over 25 years, first at Laurentian University, Sudbury and since 1973 at Memorial University, St. John's, Newfoundland. She has taught a variety of courses in both classroom and field as well as by distance education. At various points in her career she has coordinated field programs, been faculty field liaison and assisted in field instructor education. Sheena has a strong interest in the teaching of social work values and ethics. She is presently the Associate Director at Memorial University's School of Social Work.

Anne E. Fortune, PhD, ACSW, is Associate Professor and Associate Dean, University at Albany, State University of New York. Her writing on social work education includes student satisfaction, experiences in field and training of field instructors. She contributed a chapter, "Field Education," to Frederic Reamer's *The Foundations of Social Work Knowledge* (Columbia University Press, 1994). Her other research interests include short-term practice and termination of direct practice.

Ina-Ann Freeman is a front-line social worker whose practice focuses on issues regarding seniors and their families. She obtained a MSW in 1991 from The University of Windsor, a BSW in 1988 from The University of Calgary, and a BA in 1977 from The University of Alberta, Edmonton. One of her concerns is the quality of education of future social workers.

Judith Globerman, BSW, MHSC, MSC, PhD, is Associate Professor and Academic Coordinator of the Practicum, Faculty of Social Work, University of Toronto. Professor Globerman's research and practice focus on family care of the elderly, social work as a health profession and social work field education. Dr. Globerman is currently principal investigator on a longitudinal study funded by Health Canada examining families' experiences with a relative with Alzheimer's Disease.

Rose Gordon trained as a teacher and as a residential social worker in the United Kingdom. She combined and developed sets of knowledge and skills working with young people and their families before transferring her learning to the needs of students as a social work practice teacher. She is currently an assessor for practice teacher candidates and a research worker in higher education in the United Kingdom.

Bart Grossman, MSW, PhD is founding Executive Director of the California Social Work Education Center. He is Associate Adjunct Professor, The University of California at Berkeley, School of Social Welfare, and has been Field Director (currently on leave) for 12 years. Dr. Grossman was a founder of the Fieldwork Symposium and the North American Network of Field Directors, is a member of the CSWE Commission on Fieldwork and has published extensively on fieldwork including *Field Education in Social Work: Contemporary Issues and Trends*, with D. Schneck and U. Glassman.

Barry Hall, PhD, is an Associate Professor and Division Head, Faculty of Social Work, The University of Calgary, Lethbridge Division. The location of the Lethbridge Division is in a rural agrarian sector of southern Alberta. Many of the practica that are used to train the social work students occur in settings with small populations. His field education experience includes the teaching of integrative field practice seminars, faculty liaison and practicum coordinator.

Forrest C. "Bud" Hansen, PhD, is an Associate Professor, School of Social Work, University of Windsor, Canada. His main teaching areas are research methods, statistics, and computer applications for the human services. Formerly, he was the senior psychiatric social worker at the Alberta Child Guidance Clinic, Edmonton, Alberta. He obtained a PhD in social work from the Faculty of Social Work, University of Toronto in 1981, a MSW in 1963 and a BA from the University of Alberta in 1959.

Margot D. Herbert, MSW, RSW, has had extensive practice experience in both child welfare and health care, and has taught in the Edmonton Division, Faculty of Social Work, The University of Calgary, since 1981. Her research has been focused on the role of the social worker as advocate for clients in child welfare and health care settings.

Sherrill Hershberg, MSW, RSW, is a sessional lecturer at the University of Manitoba, Faculty of Social Work. She has been a faculty-based field instructor for several years, supervising students in a variety of practice settings including aging, clinical practice, child welfare, women's issues, and mental health. She practiced as a psychiatric social worker for several years at the Health Sciences Center, Winnipeg, and co-authored with Craig Posner "Social work practice in a psychiatric ambulatory care setting" in *Social work practice in health care settings* (1989), edited by M.J. Holosko and P.A. Taylor.

Emeline Homonoff, MSW, Simmons College School of Social Work and, PhD, Boston College School of Social Work, was a staff social worker and field instructor at the Judge Baker Guidance Center in Boston from 1967 to 1973. From 1973 to 1982 she was a staff social worker, supervisor and then co-director of the Jamaica Plain Outreach Program, a federally funded program jointly administered by the Judge Baker Guidance Center and the Massachusetts Mental Health Center. Since 1984, she has been an Assistant Professor in the field education sequence at the Simmons College School of Social Work.

Margarite Hutson, MSW, CSW is Educational Coordinator, Department of Social Work, Queen Street Mental Health Center, Toronto, Ontario. She is also a social worker in the Secure Observation and Treatment Unit, Queen Street Mental Health Center, and an Adjunct Social Work Practice Professor, Faculty of Social Work, University of Toronto.

Arlene Johnston, RN, BN, MEd, has spent a life's career in the nursing profession in four Canadian provinces and has extensive experience in nursing practice, administration, education and consultation. Arlene currently holds an administrative and teaching position in the Faculty of Nursing, The University of Calgary. She is responsible for the Learning Resource Center and is Clinical Placement Coordinator for 600 students in three Nursing programs. Arlene is an active member of the Alberta Association of Registered Nurses and she has received awards in teaching and community service.

Gail Kenyon, BA in Psychology, Trent University and MSW, Wilfrid Laurier University, has worked in the rehabilitation field with physically disabled adults in both education and health care settings. Gail has been the Field Education Coordinator at Ryerson Polytechnic University for 6 years and is active both nationally and provincially in field education activities. She has conducted a national survey on paid student placements and produced a student handbook on practicum safety. Further interests include field instructor training, practicum program evaluation, and international field education.

Candace Konnert, PhD, is an Associate Professor jointly appointed to the Department of Psychology and the Program in Clinical Psychology where she is Practicum and Internship Coordinator, The University of Calgary. Her teaching includes adult assessment, geropsychology, abnormal psychology and developmental-aging. Dr. Konnert's research focuses on social and clinical aspects of aging. A recent project, funded by Alberta Mental Health, investigates psychosocial predictors of depression in older adults relocating from their homes to nursing homes.

Jan Koopmans, MSW, RSW, has been a field instructor for the Faculty of Social Work, The University of Calgary for 10 years and has taught courses for the Faculty in the area of death and dying. Jan is a clinical social worker at the Tom Baker Cancer Center and counsels breast cancer patients and their families. She is an investigator on a Canadian clinical trial studying the impact of group support and emotional expression on survival in women with metastatic breast cancer. She presents at conferences and has published in several journals on adjustment to cancer.

Manuela Lacentra completed a BA in anthropology and sociology at The University of Calgary, 1987. She subsequently studied at the National University of Mexico and the University of Rome. In 1994, Manuela completed a BSW from The University of Calgary. She is a resident of Calgary and is employed as a counsellor with the Calgary Communities Against Sexual Abuse.

Jan Lackstrom, MSW, is Educational Coordinator, Toronto Hospital, Adjunct Social Work Practice Professor, Faculty of Social Work, University of Toronto and a sessional instructor, York University, School of Social Work. Jan's area of clinical expertise is eating disorders. She recently co-authored the book, *Eating disorders and marriage: The couple in focus.*

Ron Levin, MSW, RSW, has taught at the Faculty of Social Work, The University of Calgary since 1978 and is currently Division Head of the Edmonton Division. His research interests and focus is in the areas of health care, social work administration and independent social work practice.

Maxine Lynn is Director of Field Instruction, Fordham University Graduate School of Social Service. She is currently regional chairperson for the Greater New York Area Consortium of Directors of Field Instruction. Ms. Lynn's background includes many years in the psychiatric social work field, where she is a group specialist and has served a term as Vice Chair of the Association of Advancement of Social Work with Groups. She is interested in the complex issues involved with disabled social work students as more of these students are currently enrolling in graduate schools of social work.

Robert W. McClelland, MSW, MPH, PhD, has been both a university and agency-based field instructor over the past 20 years. He has presented on aspects of field education at a variety of professional conferences and authored "Innovation in field education" in *Field education in social work* (Schneck, Grossman & Glassman, 1991). Dr. McClelland has held teaching and administrative positions in several US universities. He is presently at the Faculty of Social Work, The University of Calgary where his field liaison responsibilities include a variety of graduate and undergraduate placements.

Kate McGoey-Smith, during the past 17 years has enjoyed the opportunity of working with consumers in a variety of service roles, initially as a registered nurse, then as a social worker and educator in eastern and western Canada, and parts of the US and UK. These consumer groups offered exposure to a rich cultural diversity as well as service needs ranging from direct practice to educating service providers with the following academic institutions: Catholic University of America, Wilfrid Laurier University, Algonquin College and currently, Mount Royal College and The University of Calgary.

Sheila McGrath is a lecturer in social services development and is qualified both as a teacher and social worker in the United Kingdom. Her practice experience is with children in a variety of settings, including day care and residential work. She works as a trainer, offering courses on new legislation and requirements and brings the perspective of the service user into all aspects of practice and training. She has been centrally involved in the major changes to social work education in the UK.

June McNamee, MSW, is Educational Coordinator and Director of Coordinated Client Services, Baycrest Center for Geriatric Care, Toronto. She is also an Adjunct Social Work Practice Professor, University of Toronto, Faculty of Social Work.

Sonia Michelson, MSW, Simmons College School of Social Work, MEd and Louis Lowey Certification in Gerontological Studies, Boston University. Ms Michelson has a special interest and experience in working with older adults and aging families. She is currently a social worker at B'nai B'rith Covenant House in Brighton, Mass. and maintains a private practice in geriatric social work and was a social worker for a multidisciplinary geriatric outreach program. She has been a social work consultant to nursing home staff, therapist to residents and provides supervision for social work interns.

Jaclyn Miller, PhD, Associate Professor and Director of Field Instruction, has been on the faculty of the Virginia Commonwealth University, School of Social Work for 15 years, where she has taught foundation and advanced clinical practice, mental health policy, and group work. Her publications appear in *Social Work,* the *American Journal of Orthopsychiatry*, and the *Journal of Social Work Education*. She is currently Treasurer of the National Federation of Societies for Clinical Social Work and President-Elect of the Virginia-NASW.

Joanne Moffatt, MSW, RSW, has been a sessional lecturer with the Faculty of Social Work, University of Manitoba since 1983. As a faculty-based field instructor, she has supervised students and been faculty liaison in a variety of gerontological agencies. Joanne has contributed to the manual for field instructors in the agency-based field instruction model. Classroom teaching includes social welfare policy and aging and social work practice with the elderly. Joanne is a part-time practitioner with a community-based seniors' agency.

Bertha Murphy is the Project Coordinator for a special training program in the School of Social Welfare, SUNY-Stony Brook. She has served as an Adjunct Professor in the School of Social Welfare. Ms Murphy is the Project Director of a Day Rehabilitation Treatment program for alcoholics and substance abusers. She has worked as a field work trainer and as a social worker in an alcoholism treatment clinic. She has a MSW with a specialization in substance abuse. She is a certified social worker with New York state.

Stephen Nixon is senior lecturer, Applied Social Studies, School of Continuing Studies, The University of Birmingham, England. He has been a social worker with children and families as well as a practice teacher. He is Director of the Practice Teaching Program at Birmingham, and has acted as a consultant to several agencies seeking to develop their provision of field education. In addition to on-going research on practice teaching, he is involved in a UK study of allegations of abuse in foster family care.

Richard W. "Butch" Nutter, PhD, is a Registered Social Worker and Chartered Psychologist in the Province of Alberta. He has taught in the Edmonton Division, Faculty of Social Work, The University of Calgary since 1973 and has been the Field Education Coordinator since 1992. In addition to hospitals and health settings, Dr. Nutter has conducted research and evaluations in child welfare, substance use and abuse, and community based programming for children and older adults.

Anthony Paré is the Director of McGill University's Center for the Study and Teaching of Writing. His doctoral research examined the psychosocial assessments and predisposition reports prepared by social workers of the Youth Court. His interest in social work writing continues; he is currently involved in a study of the transition from academic to professional social work writing.

Robin Perry is currently a doctoral student at the School of Social Welfare, University of California at Berkeley. Additionally, he serves as a research assistant with the California Social Work Education Center. Mr. Perry obtained his MSW from the University of Windsor and received practice training at the Center for the Child and the Family at the University of Michigan. He has several years of experience in the areas of public child welfare and family violence.

Narda Razack is a faculty member and Coordinator of Field Education, School of Social Work, York University. Her current research includes anti-oppression principles in field education and integration of multicultural field placements. She lectures on anti-racist feminist therapy and consults on sensitivity training, visioning and working relationships with boards, staff and community groups with an emphasis on diversity. Narda has extensive experience as a clinician and combines this with her knowledge of community in the classroom and in continuing education for field instructors.

William J. Reid is a Professor, School of Social Welfare, University at Albany, State University of New York, where he teaches research methods and clinical practice. His most recent books are *Generalist practice: A task-centered approach* and *Qualitative research in social work*, both published by Columbia University Press.

Mary K. Rodwell, PhD, is an Associate Professor, School of Social Work, Virginia Commonwealth University, Richmond. Her long-standing connection with Brazil began with 7 years in the Peace Corps and includes a Fulbright lecture/research grant in 1993. She has published articles and book chapters on child welfare practice and constructivist research in English and Portuguese. Other areas of publication include cross-cultural competence, family violence and child welfare policy. She also is the co-author, along with Donald Chambers and Kenneth Wedel, of *Social Program Evaluation*.

Gayla Rogers, MSW, RSW, is an Assistant Professor and Director of Field Education, Faculty of Social Work, The University of Calgary. Gayla has pursued her interest in field education through research, presentations and publications. She has developed and taught courses and workshops for field instructors, has been a Master Teacher and has provided consultation to social work programs in Canada, the US and UK. Gayla will complete a PhD this year from the University of Newcastle upon Tyne, where she has compared the training of field instructors in Canada and Britain.

Amy Frank Rosenblum, MSW, LCSW, is an Assistant Professor, Virginia Commonwealth University School of Social Work. She has taught in both the undergraduate and graduate programs. Her area of interest is the field practicum with particular focus on liaison activities. She has co-authored a number of articles and presented at various conferences on subjects related to the field practicum and the liaison role. Currently she serves as Assistant Director of Field Instruction.

Russell Sawa, MD, is an Associate Professor, Dept. of Family Medicine, The University of Calgary. Dr. Sawa is a clinical member of the American Association for Marriage and Family Therapy, a member of the American Academy of Family Therapy, a graduate of the Toronto Institute of Gestalt Therapy and has practiced and taught family medicine and family therapy for 17 years. He has published two books, *Family Dynamics for Physicians* (Edwin Mellen) and *Family Health Care* (Sage).

Myrta Rivera Sahas is the executive director of K-W Multicultural Center in Kitchener, Ontario. She has a graduate degree in Social Science and Cross Cultural Studies. Ms Sahas was project manager for Focus for Ethnic Women, a job development program for immigrants and visible minority women. She has also been the program coordinator at K-W Multicultural Center and a member of the Waterloo Region Police Services Commission. Ms Sahas has taught courses at Conestoga College, Waterloo, Ontario and for the Separate School Board of Waterloo County.

Dean Schneck, MSSW, ACSW, is Clinical Professor and Director of Field Education, The University of Wisconsin-Madison. He has 25 years of experience in field education as an agency field supervisor, a faculty field unit instructor, and field director. He is an editor of *Field Education in Social Work* (Kendall-Hunt, 1991) and currently serves as chair of the Commission on Field Education for CSWE. He was also instrumental in the formation of the North American Network of Field Educators and Directors and in the development of the annual Field Work Symposia for CSWE.

Steven Shardlow is Associate Director, MA in Applied Social Studies and Co-Director of Practice Teaching Studies, Department of Sociological Studies, University of Sheffield. He has worked as a field social worker, a residential social worker, a social work manager and now a social work lecturer. He is Chairperson of ATSWE (Association of Teachers in Social Work Education) and on the editorial board of Issues in Social Work Education. Publications include: *The values of change in social work* (Routledge, 1989) and *Enabling student learning* (Shardlow & Doel, Macmillan: currently in press).

Eric Shragge is an Associate Professor, School of Social Work, McGill University. He teaches in the areas of community organization and social policy. His most recent book is an edited collection, *Community economic development: In search of empowerment* (Black Rose Books, Montreal, 1993). Currently, he is working on a research project on the social exclusion of long-term unemployed older workers. He is active with several community organizations.

Carolyn Smith has international practice experience as a social worker in mental health and in family intervention with troubled youth. Educated as an undergraduate in England, she has an MSW from the University of Michigan, and a PhD in criminal justice from the State University of New York at Albany. She has served as an agency supervisor, a field instructor and a faculty field liaison. Her current interests include practice and research with involuntary clients, at-risk youth and social support mechanisms. She is an Assistant Professor, School of Social Welfare at Albany.

Helena Summers, MSW, is a faculty member and Coordinator of Field Instructor, The University of British Columbia School of Social Work. Previously, she was a field instructor and has practice experience in the areas of family and children's services, child welfare, women's health care, and staff training. She teaches a seminar series for field instructors and is researching approaches to field education for a multicultural society.

Helen Szewello Allen is the Field Coordinator, School of Social Work, McGill University. She completed a HBSW at Laurentian University and a MSW at McGill. She is currently a PhD candidate, doing research on effective field teaching. Other teaching and research interests include policy and practice in working with refugees.

Eli Teram, is Associate Professor, Faculty of Social Work, Wilfrid Laurier University, Waterloo, Ontario. Eli is interested in the interaction between organizations and clients and issues related to the organizational context of social work practice. With Prue Rains, he is the co-author of *Normal bad boys* (McGill-Queen's University Press, 1992). His current research and publications relate to interdisciplinary teams and to strategies for delivering services to immigrants and refugees. He has a BA in social work, a MSc in management from Tel Aviv University, and a PhD from McGill University.

Barbara Thomlison, PhD, is Associate Professor, Faculty of Social Work, The University of Calgary. She is an experienced field educator providing supervision and training for social workers and others in related disciplines. In addition to teaching at the undergraduate and graduate level in practice methods and child welfare, her research and evaluation interests include field education programs, teaching centers, and interdisciplinary team practice and learning. Barbara is co-author of *The social work practicum: A student guide* published by F.E. Peacock.

M. Teresa Trainer was born and raised in Mexico City and has lived and worked in five countries. She received a HBSW from Lakehead University and a MSW from the University of Toronto. Presently, she is working at the Department of Psychosocial Services at the Thunder Bay Regional Cancer Center and at Lakehead University where she teaches Cross Cultural Social Work Practice and is a field practicum instructor. M. Teresa has been a guest lecturer at both Canadian and Mexican universities and has presented papers nationally and internationally on culturally sensitive service delivery.

Sorele Urman, MSW, CSW is Educational Coordinator and Director of Coordinated Client Services, Baycrest Center for Geriatric Care. She is also an Adjunct Social Work Practice Professor, University of Toronto, Faculty of Social Work.

Arlene Weintraub, MSW, from the Simmons College School of Social Work. For many years she was a staff social worker, senior supervisor and director of training at Trinity Mental Health Center in Framingham, Mass. Currently she is a staff social worker and supervisor at Covenant House, an independent housing facility for the elderly in Brighton, Mass. and a field instructor for Simmons College.

Sergeant Hal Wetherup is the commander of the Cultural Resources Unit, Calgary Police Service which specializes in achieving peaceful resolutions to intercultural and intragroup conflicts. Sgt. Wetherup has instructed programs such as Cross Cultural Communication and Intercultural Conflict Resolution to numerous educational institutions, government and private organizations. An active community volunteer, he serves on the Board of Directors of Scouts Canada, the Alberta Association for Multicultural Education and co-chairs the federal Committee on Race Relations and Cross Cultural Understanding.

Walene Whitaker has been involved in the delivery of the field education program at the University of Victoria for the past 12 years, most recently as Coordinator of Field Education for both the on-campus BSW program and the distance education program. She holds BA, BSW and MSW degrees from the University of British Columbia. Her interests are in distance education for social workers, computer use and practicum and equity issues within the school of social work's community.

Michael Yellow Bird is a citizen of the Sahnish and Hidatsa First Nations and is from the Fort Berthold Indian reservation in North Dakota. He taught at the University of British Columbia, School of Social Work and is currently an Assistant Professor, University of Kansas. Teaching and research interests include social work practice and First Nations peoples, health care and health use, sustainable social and economic development and social justice. His most recent publication is, "American Indian Families", in R. Taylor's *Minority families in the United States: A multicultural perspective*, Prentice-Hall, 1994.